THE ARCHIVE OF ḤOR

EXCAVATIONS AT NORTH SAQQÂRA

DIRECTED BY W. B. EMERY

DOCUMENTARY SERIES

UNDER THE GENERAL DIRECTION OF H. S. SMITH

1. J. D. Ray, *The Archive of Ḥor*

NOTE. The excavations of the Egypt Exploration Society in the Sacred Animal Necropolis at North Saqqâra, initiated by the late Professor W. B. Emery in 1964, yielded a great many documents written in different scripts and languages. The various groups of documents, prepared for publication by many scholars, will appear in the order in which they are made ready in the series Texts from Excavations. Reports on the excavations and catalogues of special categories of objects, which will include discussions of the inscribed material in its archaeological context, will be published in the Excavation Memoirs of the Egypt Exploration Society.

PLATE I

FRONTISPIECE

The dromos of the Serapeum
(drawing by Barbot)

TEXTS FROM EXCAVATIONS

EDITED BY T. G. H. JAMES

SECOND MEMOIR

THE ARCHIVE OF ḤOR

BY J. D. RAY

EGYPT EXPLORATION SOCIETY
3 DOUGHTY MEWS, LONDON WC1N 2PG
1976

LONDON

SOLD AT

THE OFFICES OF THE EGYPT EXPLORATION SOCIETY

3 Doughty Mews, London WC1N 2PG

ISSN 0307-5125

ISBN 0 85698 061 7

Printed in Great Britain
at the University Press, Oxford
by Vivian Ridler
Printer to the University

TO
MY MOTHER
AND THE MEMORY OF
MY FATHER

PREFACE

IT is usual to open a preface with an apology for the book which follows. Οὐ φροντίς; not because these pages are free from errors and shortcomings, but because henceforth the work must speak for itself.

Yet one pleasant thing cannot be told by reading: the debt which the author owes to many of his teachers and colleagues. Some have acted as a source of constant encouragement to the present writer since he first became a student of Egyptology, and if names are to be singled out, they must surely include those of Professor J. W. B. Barns, Dr. I. E. S. Edwards, Mr. T. G. H. James, Professor J. R. Harris, Dr. G. T. Martin, Dr. E. A. E. Reymond, Mr. J. Ruffle and Dr. ʿA. el-Khouli. Their support underlies the pages which follow, even where it is unacknowledged.

Others in turn have had a direct influence on the arrangement of the present volume: Mr. T. C. Skeat and Professor E. G. Turner, who together reached an understanding of the Greek ostraca from the Ḥor archive; Professor R. H. Pierce, who read through transcriptions of several of the larger ostraca at Saqqâra and at Bergen, and whose remarks have influenced particularly Text **10** and the Appendix on the goddess Isis; Mr. A. F. Shore, who first suggested that a unity of purpose underlay these apparently contradictory texts, and who supplied many observations for improvement; and lastly, Professor H. S. Smith, who both entrusted to an untried student material which was his by right, and then added guidance to his generosity. Even the labour of these scholars would have come to little had it not been for the photographic work of Mrs. H. F. Smith, which alone made detailed study possible. I owe the frontispiece to the kindness of M. J-P. Lauer.

Two Universities, those of Cambridge and Birmingham, gave me leave from other duties to attend the excavations at Saqqâra, and I must here express my thanks to them; similar gratitude is due to the Committee and Members of the Egypt Exploration Society, whose support enabled these excavations to continue.

Miss Felicity Fildes typed a most difficult manuscript for a most difficult author; her speed and accuracy made the task enjoyable.

All these people made the qualities of this book; they are not responsible for its defects.

Birmingham
10 August, 1973

CONTENTS

LIST OF FIGURES

LIST OF PLATES

LIST OF PLATES

INTRODUCTION

'FOR the first time in history the sun was seen rising in the west. Towards the west ambassadors from Egypt went forth with silks and spices and precious stones. They returned, bringing with them an ivory chair, a coarse garment of purple, and a quantity of copper coin. These humble presents were received in a delirium of joy. The Roman Senate accorded its protection, and Alexandria was saved. But its independence was forfeited; its individuality became extinct. Here endeth the history of Egypt; let us travel to another shore.'

With this flourish Winwood Reade closed the account of Egypt given in his *Martyrdom of Man*. Reade's history is now a century old, and few still see in its dramatic pages a convincing likeness of ancient Egypt. Yet this passage has a claim to be included here, not merely because it reflects the Seleucid threat and the Roman intervention which forced it from Egyptian soil, relevant though these are to much of the material about to be presented. It stands here for another reason, for Reade was one of the first popular historians to appreciate truly the career of Alexander the Great. The force of Hellenism overran the ancient Orient, obliterating its old ways; and in the sequel it was itself spent and reformed, receiving where it gave. This great fusion is more than a talking-point of academic concern, for it is the hellenized Orient which underlies much of the practice, as well as the theory, of the Roman Empire, and which forms the pattern not only of Byzantium but of the entire western world.

Such a process, the absorption of one civilization by another, is by its nature largely a mental phenomenon, and such histories are bound to be hard to document; yet we are fortunate to be able to follow some of this evolution in the ostraca and papyri of Egypt. This is not to deny the role of the Seleucid Empire and its satellites in these events, but it is so far true that the Near East of the last three centuries before Christ has yielded little in comparison with the valley of the Nile. Such a situation is the reverse of that from earlier periods, whose clay tablets are all but imperishable, but the fact remains that it is to the Ptolemaic kingdom that we must look to trace the orientalizing of Alexander's heirs.

Within Egypt the balance lay between tradition, not all of it native, and innovation, not all of it Greek, and even by the end of the third century an equilibrium was forming. After Raphia a counterswing begins, and the key generation is that ruled over by the sixth Ptolemy, surnamed Philometor. Now it happens that one site in North Saqqâra, the Serapeum of Memphis, has acquainted us with five members of this generation, telling us through their papers not only the history of their lives, but also of their inner thoughts, by day in their letters, by night in their dreams. Four of these characters, Ptolemaios the recluse in the Serapeum, Apollonios his younger brother, and the twin sisters, Taous and Thavēs, are already known to us, and have received a worthy memorial in the pages of Wilcken. The purpose of the present work is to introduce a fifth: Ḥor of Sebennytos.

The importance of Ḥor of Sebennytos is not confined to his knowledge of political events, detailed though this is; nor is he valuable solely for his dreams, or for his accounts of the sanctuary in which he worked. His importance surely lies in the fact that to all these pieces of information he brings the picture of an individual personality, in whose light these disparate facts achieve their meaning. As such it is a pity to divide his sixty texts into categories and sub-categories, even though such a course was scarcely avoidable; but it is hoped that what was unavoidable will not be suffered to mislead.

A further point deserves remark: the papers of Ptolemaios and his associates were scattered almost a century and a half ago, and their early history is beyond recall. But the writings of Ḥor are provenanced by excavation. Some thirty of the ostraca here published were discovered by Emery in the winter of 1965/6 while clearing the sand from a rough stone-built chapel adjoining the ibis-galleries at Saqqâra; detailed references will appear in the text below. Three of these ostraca, notable for their size and immanent difficulty, were studied by Smith and the present author in the early months of 1969. These bear the numbers **1**, **3**, and **8** below. In the same season the discovery of Text **33** in a different part of the site encouraged the writer to take his leave of demotic studies; that he did not do so was due partly to the encouragement of Smith, partly to the peace of the Saqqâra garden. The remaining ostraca were copied and prepared for publication. A seminar held in London in June 1970 produced the support of Shore, and also of Skeat, who with Turner had already published the Greek ostraca from the same find. Few of the conclusions of this seminar were able to survive the final week of January 1972, when the Saqqâra excavations, now under the joint directorship of Smith and Martin, unearthed a further thirty ostraca, including some of the finest of the archive, in the space of nine days. Commitments in England had already claimed the writer at the end of these nine days, and the decipherment of the new texts, the recognition with mixed nostalgia and recoil of old problems of palaeography or translation, made these days days of *corvée* worthy of Text **8**. Excellent photographs by van Veen of the Rijksmuseum van Oudheden te Leiden later enabled the work to be revised at the necessary leisure.

After the writer's departure on 4 February 1972 excavation continued, but Ḥor closed his archive, producing only a number of small fragments and the completely erased Text **36**. Such are the texts which appear in this volume; the word 'archive', which implies a coherent collection of legal papers, is of course a misnomer for what seems to have been the waste-paper basket of a troubled man, notes discarded after their commission to papyrus. May the word be pardoned, and the pages which follow.

A NOTE ON SYMBOLS, TRANSLITERATION, AND NUMBERING

SYMBOLS

The following refer to observations of the ancient scribe:

⟨r⟩ word inserted in antiquity

[[r]] word erased in antiquity,

and the following to observations of the editor:

(r) word not written, but assumed in speech

[r] word in lacuna, or doubtfully read.

The last two do not count as evidence.

Possessive and subject suffixes are introduced by a dot, as *rn·f*; object suffixes are attached by a dash, as *gm·f-s*. In a few cases where ambiguity remains I have used both signs, as *ip-·f*, which may mean either 'assessing him' or 'he assessed'.

The method used for transcribing proper names is loosely based on the practice of Griffith in his *Catalogue of the Demotic Papyri in the John Rylands Library*.

TRANSLITERATION

The long debate between the 'phonetic' school of transcription and the 'historical' has now largely been resolved in favour of the latter, especially since the publication of W. Erichsen's *Demotisches Glossar*. It is the method of this dictionary which has been followed here: all words are transliterated historically except when clearly written out in phonetic characters. Thus the word for 'eat' is *wnm*, while the word for 'bitter' (historically *dḥr*) is transliterated *tḥ*, for so it is written. One resulting problem is the rendering of feminine plural nouns, for to write *ʿẖytw* conflicts with historicity, while to write *ʿẖywt* conflicts with the script. I have therefore written merely *ʿẖyt* in all contexts which demand a plural (e.g. following the article *nꜣ*). Apologies are therefore due for the hybrid *nꜣ mdt-nfrw*, which will offend some, although it reflects faithfully the habit of the scribe. For the generic pronoun I have used *pa-*, *ta-*, *na-* throughout.

NUMBERING

The texts in this volume are numbered consecutively from **1** to **65**, including those in the Addendum. Bold figures are used throughout to refer to them. Each text has in addition two other numbers, both of which are given in the preliminary descriptions of the pieces. The first is the excavator's number: those ostraca found by Emery are numbered by the grid square of the excavation, those found by Martin according to the season when they were excavated. The second number, that given in square brackets after the excavator's number, represents the entry of the object in the consecutive register of the excavation kept for the Egyptian Antiquities Service. Text **1** is thus numbered G7–25 [454], G7 being the grid square of discovery; Text **2** is 71/2–131 [5399], 71/2 indicating that the ostracon was found in the season 1971/1972.

A concordance of numbers is given on p. 191 below.

I. THE GREEK TEXTS

THE Greek texts which begin this volume were discovered by Emery in the last days of 1965, together with the first group of the demotic ostraca.[1] Immediately upon their discovery copies of all these texts were made by Smith and Martin, and the Greek ostraca were entrusted for publication to Skeat and Turner; this edition appeared in print some two years later.[2] A small fragment was found during clearance work in February 1972, and shown to supplement the published texts. This fragment was kindly entrusted to the present writer for inclusion in the main volume, and it appears below.

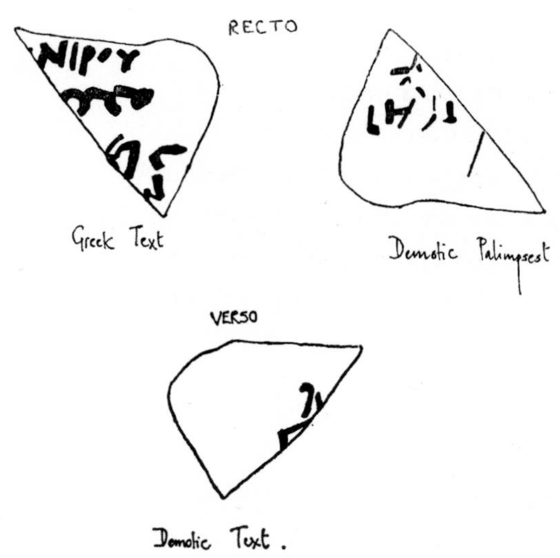

FIG. 1. Greek fragment

Greek Fragment

Height	3·8 cm.
Width	3·9 cm.
Thickness	0·85 cm.
Munsell[3]	5 YR 6/4
Photograph	Plate VI
Facsimile	Fig. 1
Excavator's no.	G7–45 [474]

This small piece of reddish-grey ware clearly forms the upper right-hand corner of the ostracon G7–42 already published by Skeat and Turner.[4] It does not join the published lines directly, and it is clear that a central portion is still missing; enough survives, however, to reconstruct the original on the lines proposed by the editors. The recto bears the endings of four lines of Greek with palimpsest traces of demotic, as in the main ostracon; on the verso are traces of two demotic lines, which are discussed below in the appropriate place.

Text

1.]ọνιρου
2.]ụπο
3.]εις
4.]ụ

Notes

Line 1: ọ minuscule, sc. [δι'|διὰ] ὀνείρου.
Line 2: only the link of υ remains.
Line 4: ụ supralinear, as if from ου.

Lines 2–4 fit neatly into the reconstruction proposed in *JEA* 54 (1968), 203, as 'Text B'; the first line, which must clearly have been inserted above the words τὰ ῥηθέντα μοι ὑπό, adds the information that the words had been spoken 'through (a) dream'. This addition to the text is incorporated below.

Apart from this small fragment, the present writer can have little to add to the remarks of

[1] Preliminary report in *JEA* 52 (1966), 3–5.
[2] *JEA* 54 (1968), 199 ff.
[3] All colour readings in this volume are given in accordance with the *Munsell Soil Color Chart* (Baltimore, 1970 edition).
[4] *JEA* 54 (1968), 200 ff.

Turner and Skeat, to whom he is greatly indebted for an understanding of these difficult texts. The various stages of the Greek texts are reprinted here for the sake of reference.

Text A

1. τὰ ῥηθέντα μοι
2. ὑπὸ μεγίστου καὶ
3. μεγίστου θεοῦ μεγάλου
4. Ἑρμοῦ χρήσιμον εἶναι τῶν πρα-
5. γμάτων ὅπως [[τραπήσεται]] τῶν [Αἰ-]
6. γυπτίων [[τάχεως]] τραπήσεται
7. τάχεως καὶ ʽεὐθέως δὲʼ ἐλθεῖν ἕως τῆς Θηβαΐ-
   δος
8. τὸν βασιλέα.

Text B

1. τὰ ῥηθ[έντα μοι ⟨διὰ] ὀνείρου⟩ ὑπὸ
2. μεγίστ[ου καὶ μεγ]ίσ-
3. του θεοῦ [μεγάλο]υ
4. Ἑρμοῦ περὶ χρ[ησίμων]
5. τοῖς βασιλεῦσι [βουλόμε-]
6. νος ἀπαγγεῖλαι [ὅπως]
7. τῶν Αἰγυπτίων [τρα-]
8. πήσεται τάχεως καὶ
9. ἐλθεῖν εἰς τὴν Θηβαΐδα
10. τὸν βασιλέα εὐθέως.

Note

Line 1: ⟨διὰ ὀνείρου⟩ supplied from fragment. For the demotic equivalent, namely *nꜣ i·ḏd-w pꜣ ntr ꜥꜣ Ḏḥwty ẖt rswt*, see Text **23,** V° 16.

Text C

1. [Ὧρο]ς παστοφόρος τῆς
2. [Ἶσιο]ς τοῦ ἐν Ἶσιος πόλει
3. ἱεροῦ τοῦ Σεβεννύτου.

Text D

1. ἐστὶ τ[
2. τῶν πρ[αγμά]των τὰ
3. ῥηθέντα μοι ὑπὸ μεγί-
4. στου καὶ μεγίστου [θεοῦ]
5. μεγάλου Ἑρμοῦ.

Note

Line 1: sc. τ[αῦτα] or the like, the whole corresponding to something like the **wn nꜣ mdt* ..... of several demotic introductions (Text **3,** V° 8; **4,** 1, etc.).

Text E

1. βασιλεῖ Πτολεμαίωι καὶ
2. βασιλεῖ Πτολεμαίωι τῶι
3. ἀδελφῶι καὶ βασιλίσσηι
4. Κλεοπάτραι τῆι ἀδελφῆ[ι]
5. χαίρειν Ὧρος παστοφόρος
6. τῆς Ἶσιος τοῦ ἐν Ἶσιος πόλ[ει]
7. ἱεροῦ τοῦ Σεβεννύτου β[ου-]
8. λόμενος περὶ τινων χρησ[ίμων]
9. τοῖς βασιλεῦσι ἀναγγεῖλαι ὅπω[ς]
10. τῶν Αἰγυπτίων τραπήσε-
11. ται ταχέως καὶ εὐθέως
12. δὲ ἐλθεῖν τὸν βασιλέα
13. ἕως τῆς Θηβαΐδος.

Note

Line 12: The change from βασιλεῦσι above to the singular βασιλέα is paralleled in the demotic texts (see notes to Demotic Text A, 3 and to Text **2,** R° 13 below). In such cases the writer regularly omits all reference to the second Ptolemy; he may therefore be acquitted of some of the lapses in syntax charged against him by the editors.

Such are the texts established by Skeat and Turner, with the sole addition of the new fragment above the opening line of Text B. From these reconstructions the editors draw the following conclusions:

(i) that the date falls within the joint reign of Ptolemy VI Philometor and his brother (November 170–May 163 B.C.), and more specifically between the years 168–164;
(ii) that the author is an Egyptian, a pastophoros of Isis in a 'city of Isis' (*Isios polis*) situated in the nome of Sebennytos;
(iii) that the writer's Greek was execrable; *and*
(iv) that the point of the texts is to communicate an oracle given on behalf of the two kings by 'the greatest and greatest god, the great Hermes',

in other words Hermes Trismegistos.[1] The new fragment adds the information that this oracle took the form of a dream.

Two emendations were proposed by the editors: (i) that the χρησίμων of Texts A, B, and E may be an approximation to χρησμῶν 'oracles', (ii) that τὸ τάγμα τῶν [Αἰγυπτίων] 'the battle-line of the Egyptians' may be intended for τῶν πραγμάτων. This would allow a neat correlation with the known revolt of Dionysios Petosorapis and other disturbances which seem to have taken place about the same time in the Thebaid (cf. A, 7; B, 9; E, 13).

On such questions the present writer is not qualified to give judgement, but it seems only fair to say that the demotic material which follows has failed to give support to either of these suggestions. Indeed, the very vagueness of such terms as χρήσιμα or πράγματα seems greatly at home among the *mdt-nfrt* and *ꜥš-sḥnw* of the writer's native idiom. The close correspondence between the opening of Text B, τὰ ῥηθέντα μοι διὰ ὀνείρου ὑπὸ μεγίστου . . . . . Ἑρμοῦ, and the *nꜣ ỉ·dd-w pꜣ ntr ꜥꜣ Ḏḥwty ḥt rswt* of Text **23,** V° 16 suggests that the writer of our Greek ostraca was thinking in Egyptian, and in such circumstances a little of the strangeness of the Greek may be explained.[2] The position of the Greek ostraca in the whole archive is discussed in the first section of the Commentary which accompanies this volume.

The associated demotic texts

In the edition of Skeat and Turner reference was made to a palimpsest demotic text lying beneath the exterior Greek lines of G7–42, and to the four preserved lines which occupy the upper portion of its interior. A preliminary translation of the latter was made by Smith and appears in *JEA* 54 (1968), 201; no translation of the palimpsest was given. The versions which follow were made with his cooperation.

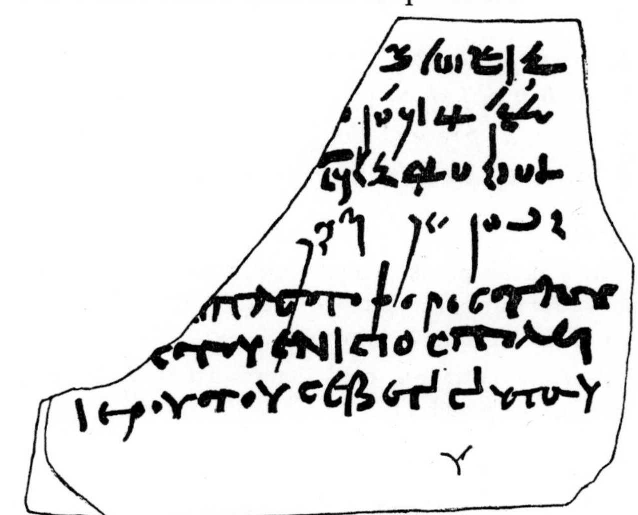

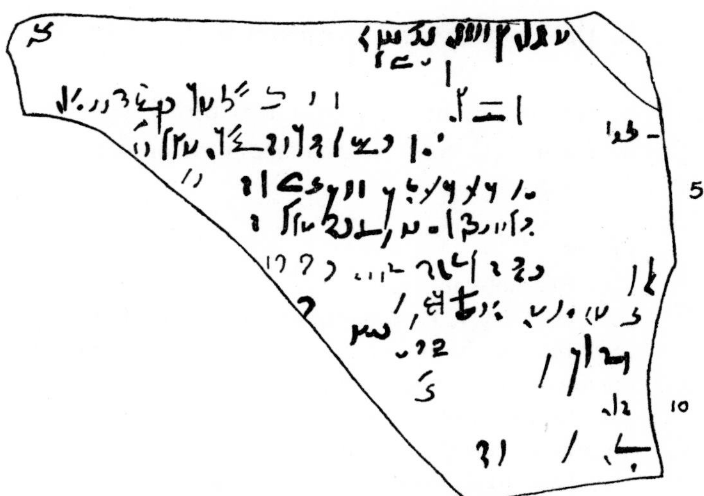

FIG. 2. *Above*: Demotic Text A. *Below*: Demotic Text B (palimpsest).

Demotic Text A

Munsell	5 YR 6/4
Photograph	*JEA* 54 (1968), pl. 32, 2.
Facsimile	this volume, Fig. 2
Excavator's no.	G7–42 (verso) [471]

[1] See Appendix 2 at the end of this volume.

[2] It may as well be admitted that this similarity of idiom is the strongest argument for the identity of Ὧρος of the Greek documents with the *Ḥr* of the demotic, an equivalence which is otherwise unproven. Other evidence may be summarized as: the similarity of the two names; the date and provenance; the apparent identity of hand between Greek and demotic texts on the ostracon G7–42; and the identification of *dmỉ-n-ꜣst* in the demotic with the *Isios polis* of the Greek. The mention of the Sebennytic nome in both Greek and demotic is another circumstantial argument. It is true that the writer of the demotic texts never calls himself a pastophoros, as does the writer of the Greek ostraca; possible reasons for this will be suggested in the Commentary below.

Other dimensions have appeared in *JEA* 54; small traces at the end of the first two lines are supplied by the new fragment published above.

Text

1. *ṯ3y·w gns*[a] *wn* [ ] *nb*(?)
2. *p3 b3k di·f sẖ p3* [ ] (trace)[b]
3. *nfr·s* (*n*) *p3y·k* *ꜥš-sḥn* [ ]
4. *n3*/*t3 nty sẖ n-im·f ẖt·f* (vacat).

Notes

a. For this phrase, and its connection with the Greek ἀδικοῦμαι ὑπό, see notes to Text **16,** R° 11 below, and § 1 of the ensuing Commentary.

b. Apparently an 'evil' determinative 𓅪, although *mn* is also a possibility.

Translation

1. Wrong has been done[a]: account [··········] every(?)
2. the document. He caused to be written the [·····]
3. it is beneficial (to) your fortune[b] [··········]
4. these[c] (things) which are written in it: its content.

Notes

a. See note above.

b. cf. Text **3,** R° for similar sentiments. For the use of *ꜥš-sḥn* see the index at the end of the volume. The person addressed in *p3y·k* may possibly be Philometor, and the whole phrase is reminiscent of the Greek περὶ χρησίμων τοῖς βασιλεῦσι.

c. Less likely 'she'. An active translation of *nty sẖ n-im·f* as 'who write(s) it' is scarcely possible; *sẖ* has therefore been taken as qualitative (ⲥⲏϩ). For *ẖt·f* as the copied contents of a document, cf. Text **12,** V° 8 *ẖt b3k ḥꜥ·f*.

Preliminary Remarks

The position of this text between the two Greek texts B and C is rather puzzling. Its purpose seems reasonably clear: the writer claims that wrong has been done, doubtless to himself, and prepares to introduce his account.[1] The words 'it is favourable (to) your fortune' may perhaps be addressed to the king, and refer to the Greek oracle on the other side of the ostracon. The similarity between the Greek hand and the demotic has already been observed by Skeat and Turner, and it seems perverse to claim that the two are not related in some way. One thing that is clear is that the entire ostracon is a preliminary draft, and it may even be that the small Greek text C was intended, with the usual disregard of syntax (!), to follow directly from the Greek lines of the recto. The demotic will then follow the whole, and mark the introduction to a long demotic narrative. This explanation will remove the awkward vacillation from Greek to demotic and back to Greek again, but it is a desperate recourse, and quite unconfirmed by other evidence.

Demotic Text B

This is the palimpsest beneath the recto of G7–42 [471].

Munsell	5 YR 6/4
Photograph	not given
Facsimile	Fig. 2

This palimpsest, which appears only on very close inspection, seems to consist of some twelve demotic lines, which lie upside down in relation to the Greek text written over them. The opening lines are clearer than the later, for on this edge of the sherd the erasure was less thorough, and the palimpsest lines lie between the lines of Greek; towards the end the demotic is completely overlaid by the later text. At the ends of lines 10–12 some groups have been supplied from the verso of the fragment G7–45 (Fig. 1).

Text

1. [a] *n-drt sẖ*[b]] (*n*) *p3 tš n Ṯb-nṯr*[c] *Ḥr nty ḥr* [*Mn-nfr*[b]
2. (traces)

[1] The suggestion of *JEA* 54 (1968), 201, that the demotic lines form part of the original (Egyptian) oracle is difficult to reconcile with the new translation.

3. (traces) *ḏd mdt rmt-(n)-Kmy*
4. *mdt* *Ḥp-nb·s (n) rn pꜣ ntr ꜥꜣ* [
5. *slsl-f*[d] *ỉw·f ỉr-rḫ-w*[e] [
6. *ḥwy n pꜣ ḥꜣty (n) pꜣ ntr* [
7. *nty nb* [
8. *pꜣy·f ḫrw ꜥḥꜥ·f* [
9. *m-sꜣ* [
10. *ỉp-f*[d] [ ] *ꜥrḏ*[f]
11. (traces) [ ] (trace)
12. (traces) [ ].

Notes

a. The upper part of many of the signs is missing, a fact which suggests that other lines may have preceded which are now lost; but the damage may equally be the result of wear, and the opening line is so natural that it is difficult to imagine what could have stood before it.

b. Restored, tentatively, from the very similar opening to Text **25**, *n-drt sḫ tš Ṯb-ntr Ḥr nty ḥr Mn-nfr*.

c. For the reading of this important group see notes to Text **2**, R° 2 below.

d. See the introduction for this method of attaching suffixes to the preceding word.

e. *-s* may also be possible.

f. This word, and the trace at the end of the following line, are restored from the fragment G7–45 published above.

Translation

1. [From the scribe] (of) the nome of Sebennytos,[a] Ḥor, who is in [Memphis(?)][b]
2. (*traces*)
3. [··············] speaking the words of the Egyptian(s)[c]
4. word(?)[d] [··········] Ḥepnēbes[e] (in) the name of the great god [[f]·····]
5. [··········] his adornment, he knowing ····· [·····]
6. [·······] cast to the heart(?) of the god[g] ··· [·····]
7. [············] every (thing) which
8. [··················] his voice. He stood [··········]
9. [·································] after [··········]
10. he assessed [························] earnest(?)
11. [(*traces*)] [(*trace*)
12. [(*traces*)].

Notes

a. See notes to Text **2**, R° 2 below.

b. See textual note above.

c. Perhaps a reference to the fact that the writer is now using demotic; a similar description occurs in the well-known 'promulgation' passage in *Rosettana*. An almost contemporary Serapeum text, Pap. Bologna 3173, has (V° 9–11) *ḏd ꜣplns mdt-Wynn, Pꜣ-dỉ-Ḥr-(n)-Py mdt rmt-(n)-Kmy* 'Apollonios speaks Greek, Petiḥarenpi Egyptian' (Botti, *Testi demotici*, 13 ff.).

d. Perhaps the original had *ḫt-mdt* 'utterance'; an approximation to the τὰ ῥηθέντα of the Greek texts.

e. This place-name, long known to be part of the Memphite necropolis, can now be located with greater precision as the area of the burial-places of the Mothers of Apis; see § 5 of the Commentary below.

f. The name of the god Thoth may have stood here; see Appendix 2 at the end of the volume.

g. This obscure phrase may possibly mean 'suggest to the god's mind', but the text is too faint even to guarantee the reading given here.

Preliminary Remarks

It is a pity that this text has so little to yield, for there is little doubt that in its complete state it would have told us much of the circumstances surrounding our archive. It is also difficult to understand why the text was erased; one possibility is that the writer, having written this introduction in demotic, decided to substitute a rubric in Greek which would be more likely to catch the eye of the authority for which it was intended. This Greek text would have been a mere summary of the demotic, particularly so if (as Skeat and Turner have suggested) the writer's knowledge of the language was minimal.

Little of the text can be reconstructed: the writer, who calls himself Ḥor 'of the nome of Sebennytos', has come to Ḥepnēbes in the Memphite necropolis. He seems to submit various matters to a god, possibly Thoth (the

Hermes of the Greek texts), although the name is lost. The sequel is unknown, but it may be that Demotic Text A, which occupies the other side of the sherd, is the continuation of the tale. Reasons have already been given for identifying the Ḥor of the demotic texts with the Ὧρος of the Greek,[1] and the remainder of the volume will proceed on this assumption.

[1] See p. 3 n. 2 above.

II. THE DEMOTIC TEXTS

§ 1 : Texts of direct historical significance

TEXT 1

Height	17·9 cm.
Width	21·9 cm.
Thickness	0·7 cm. (ave.)
Munsell[1]	2·5 YR 4/4
Photograph	Plate II
Facsimile	Plate IIA
Excavator's no.	G7–25 [454][2]

A reddish ostracon, taken from the side of a curved vessel, bearing on its exterior the traces of eighteen lines of demotic script. The interior is uninscribed. Nineteen fragments of the text were discovered by Emery in the winter of 1965/6, and pieced together by Martin; at least five other small pieces are missing. Preliminary study was carried out at Saqqâra by Smith, and a small photograph, described as 'Demotic Ostracon with Good Augury', was published in *JEA* 52 (1966), pl. I, 2.[3] Much of the writing had faded, and the sherd had clearly been broken in antiquity.[4] A small protrusion in the upper right-hand corner of the text (beginning of l. 3) has also disturbed part of the writing. The scribe wrote with a very fine reed, which lost ink rapidly, and in places (e.g. the word *Pr-ꜥꜣ* in the middle of l. 14) had clearly been overfilled. All of these circumstances, combined with the inherent difficulty of subject-matter, make interpretation of the ostracon difficult in the extreme.

Text

1. *wꜥ mḳmḳ ỉ·ḥr*[a] *nꜣ wꜥbw n-drt Ḥr pꜣ sẖ rmt Pr-Ḏḥwty*[b] *(n) pꜣ tš (n) [Ṯb-nṯr. ḫr ỉr·ỉ(?) pꜣ snt (n) ỉr]*[c] *nꜣ hrw*[d] *(n) tꜣ wꜥbt (n)*
2. *Wsỉr Mr-Wr*[e] *(n) 'Iwnw*[f] *pꜣy·s smt tꜣ wꜥbt (n) Wsỉr-Ḥp (n) Mn-nfr. ḫpr ḥꜣt-sp 21t tpy šmw*[g] *sw 2*[h] *tw·ỉ ḥr*[i] *'Iwnw ḏd*
3. ⟨(traces added below line)[j]⟩ *mšꜥ* [ ] *ḫꜣꜥ·ỉ*[k] *pꜣy·ỉ ḏmꜥ ỉrm pꜣy·ỉ gstỉ n-drt(·ỉ)*[l] *(n) Mn-nfr [r ṯꜣy-s]ꜣb*[m] [ ][n]
4. *pꜣ* [ ][o] *mnẖ wꜥb*[p] *pꜣ r-pr (n) 'Iy-m-ḥtp nty ỉw ḫn 'Iwnw r dỉt ḏd·w n·ỉ ḥꜥ·ỉ [ỉw·ỉ] ḏd n·ỉ n-ỉm·s ḏd*
5. *ỉw·ỉ ỉy (n) 'Iwnw ꜣbd-4 ꜣḫt*[q] *⟨ḫn⟩ [tꜣ] wꜥbt Wsỉr Mr-Wr ḏd·w n·ỉ (n) rswt (r) dỉt*[r] *nꜣy (n) sẖ i·ḥr nꜣ rmtw ꜥꜣy*
6. *[šm(·ỉ) ḫr tꜣ ḥꜣt* *[s]]tryn pꜣ ḥm-nṯr Ḫnsw*[t] *pꜣ sẖ Pr-ꜥꜣ (n) Mn-nfr ḥꜣt-sp 23t ꜣbd-3 ꜣḫt pꜣ nty mꜣꜥ*[u]
7. *pꜣ tr*[v] *wn-nꜣ 3tyks*[w] *ḥr pr-mḥ*[x] *(n) Pr-3wrys. Kmy*[y] *pnḳ n-ỉm·f.*
8. *ꜥḥꜥ·ỉ ỉrm Hryns (ỉ·)wn-nꜣ*[z] *ḫr tꜣ ḥꜣt tꜣ mtgt(y)* [ ][aa] *pꜣ rd (n) Pr-ꜥꜣ*
9. *Ptrwmys*[bb] *pꜣy·n ḥry. dỉ·ỉ gm·f nꜣ mdt*[ ] *i·ỉr ỉy [i·]ỉr·ḥr·ỉ*
10. *pꜣ ꜥš-sḥn (n) Pr-ꜥꜣ. tꜣ nbt tꜣwy*[cc] *3st tꜣ i·ỉr*[dd] *wꜣḥ-sḥn n-ỉm·w pꜣ nṯr ꜥꜣ Ḏḥwty pꜣ i·ỉr*
11. *ḏlꜥ-mdt*[ee] *ḫr·w ỉw·w ḏd*[ff] *n·ỉ rswt: tw-s(?)*[gg]
12. *3st tꜣ nṯrt ꜥꜣt n*[hh] *pꜣy*[ii] *Kmy pꜣ tꜣ Ḫr ỉw·s mšꜥ (n) rdwy·s ḥr ḥr*
13. *pꜣ mw (n) pꜣ ym (n) Ḫr. Ḏḥwty ꜥḥꜥ ḥꜣ·s šsp drt·s pḥ·s pꜣ ꜥwy-(n)-mr*[jj]
14. *(n) Rꜥ-ḳd ḏd·s Rꜥ-ḳd smn wbꜣ pꜣ*[kk] *ḫf. Pr-ꜥꜣ ḏlꜥ-mdt ḫn·f*[ll]
15. *ỉrm nꜣy·f snw pꜣ šr ꜥꜣ (n) Pr-ꜥꜣ grp. pꜣy·f šr grp m-sꜣ·f. pꜣ šr (n) pꜣy šr*

[1] See the note to the Greek texts above.

[2] On the numbering of the ostraca see p. xv above.

[3] The captions to numbers 1 and 2 on this plate should be reversed.

[4] Some fragments, for example, have faded much more than the others, and must have been exposed to different conditions in the ground.

16. *grp m-sꜣ·f. pꜣ šr (n) pꜣ šr (n) pꜣ šr (n) pꜣy šr grp m-sꜣ·f ssw*[mm]
17. *ky*[nn] *iw·f ꜥšꜣy m-šs*[oo]. *pꜣ ꜥḥꜥ-rd nꜣy*
18. *tꜣ Pr-ꜥꜣt ms šr ḥwty*[pp].

Notes

a. I have chosen this transcription to indicate the form without medial -*ir*- used by this scribe.

b. A place-name of great importance in our texts; for a discussion of its geographical setting and significance, see § 1 of the Commentary, p. 117 below. Here it is the reading which is of interest. The final element, with divine sign placed before the general determinative of a locality, would seem to be the name of the god Thoth (cf. ll. 10 and 13 of this text alone; clearer writings in the other texts seem to confirm this reading). The initial element, , would seem to begin with the sign for *pr*; the long horizontal line, though shown by examples in other phrases not to be the genitival particle (which is hardly ever written in these texts in any form) is not a major obstacle: such lines are common in place-names (cf. the writings of *Ṯb-ntr* and *Mn-nfr* in the palaeography, and the similar line over the *Pr* of *Pr-Pr-ꜥꜣ* in Demotic Chronicle 3/29 (Spiegelberg, *Demotische Chronik*, Orakelglossar, no. 89)). The problem lies more in the : in view of the reading of a very similar group as *pr-mḥ* 'north' (this text, l. 7; Text **2**, V° 11, and Text **23**, R° 5) it is tempting to translate the whole as **Pr-mḥ-Ḏḥwty*, but this, appropriate as it may be to a town of the northern Delta, lacks many of the virtues of grammar or syntax. The best clue is seen in Text **11**, V° 2 where *pꜣ tnꜥy* appears as ; here seems to be little more than a writing of the determinative , regardless of what the true meaning of *tnꜥy* might be. A further hint of this reading *pr* is suggested by the writing of *pry* 'grain' in *Insinger*, 32/8 as . Such is the evidence, slight though it is, which inclines me towards the reading *pr*-. A further point of interest is that both *Pr-Pr-ꜥꜣ* (περπερο) and *pry* (Boh. φιн) suggest from Coptic an unusual pronunciation of *pr*, though admittedly not a single one; may therefore represent a by-pronunciation (*περιθωογθ or φιнθωογθ or the like) current in the Sebennyte nome in the second century B.C.; cf. perhaps Redford, *JNES* 22, 119.

c. Largely restored from the faint traces with the aid of parallel texts. *Ṯb-ntr* is apparently given as the nome following *Pr-Ḏḥwty* in Text **28**, 3; *ḥr*, with its determinative, is perhaps clearer than most; *ir·i* is largely conjectural, *pꜣ* completely so, and *snt* bears some resemblance to the facsimile, but the whole is suggested with the utmost reserve.

d. The traces also suit *hꜣw* 'expenses' (ϩнγ) and the plural of *hꜣ* 'time' (ϩн), but these seem less appropriate here.

e. Faint, but confirmed by the connection with *Wsir-Ḥp* and the following place-name, both here and in Text **13**, 6–7.

f. The place-name written is also of importance in these texts, and occurs commonly; v. index for detailed references. From the present context, and from Text **13**, it emerges as a home of Osormnevis, and is said also to have a shrine (*r-pr*) of Imḥōtep in its midst. The semi-hieratic dream invocation, Text **18**, R° 4, 8 acquaints us with another of its gods, *Ḥr-ḥkꜣ* and mentions both its 'great mysteries' (*sštw ꜥꜣy*) and a 'soul' (*by*) of . One is therefore strongly moved to identify the group with Heliopolis,[1] the more so when we find in Text **13**, 7 that its necropolis lies in the *eastern* desert. The palaeography is not easy to explain however, although the writing () in Brugsch, *Thesaurus*, 897, 901 (where it is followed by *Šmꜥ*) and 902 (followed by the name of the god Montu) and the 'Faiyûmic' version given without reference in Erichsen, *Glossar*, 24, are somewhat similar.[2] The present writing may suggest a hieroglyphic * , a writing which presumably reflects the demotic traditions of Memphis and the Delta, rather than those of Upper Egypt which appear so largely in our dictionaries. For the political role of Heliopolis at this period, see note *d* to the translation below.

g. It seems to be characteristic of these hands that while *prt* normally contains a curved element at the end (or the like), *šmw*, which begins identically, is a series of straight lines (). Examples are common in our texts; but in such a faint context as this there is not much room for certainty.

[1] An identification originally suggested by Smith, on the basis of this text alone, and at first viewed with scepticism by the present author.

[2] Cf. the example in *JEA* 58 (1972), 248, note *b*.

h. Day-dates are a source of great uncertainty in these texts, cf. the note to Text **8**, R° 1, below. Most of the readings given in this volume are based upon an unpublished account papyrus found in 1971 by Dr. ʿA. el-Khouli near the site of Mariette's house at Saqqâra.[1] This papyrus contains a complete list of days in the hand of a Memphite scribe, which may be contemporary with, or slightly later than, the Ḥor documents. The marked tilt to the left of the sign for (*sw*)*2* is shown in about half of the examples given in Erichsen, *Glossar*, 707.

i. The choice is between *ḥr* and *wꜣḥ*: several of these texts seem to distinguish between the two as [demotic group] for *wꜣḥ*, [demotic group] for *ḥr*, but the majority does not, and the question becomes acute in statements of location (cf. Text **8**, R° 12–13). If we are to read *wꜣḥ*, it must be on the assumption that this is in the Qualitative, and means 'situated' or the like; it is then difficult to explain why the first-person example quoted above shows no sign of the ending *·k*. The reading *ḥr* is open to the objection that this preposition when used in expressions of locality is conventionally translated 'from' (Gardiner, *Grammar*, § 165, 2), whereas our context clearly demands the meaning 'at'; but on this point some elliptical but telling remarks by Goedicke (*MDAIK* 18 (1962), 17–18) should be called in evidence, and for this reason the reading *ḥr* has been preferred.

j. These traces, displaced by the fault in the surface of the pot, are extremely obscure. The first group bears a slight resemblance to *ḥꜣty*, but no satisfactory translation can be offered.

k. The sign preceding *šm* (?) suggests the reading for the entire group as *ḫꜣʿ* (Erichsen, *Glossar*, 345), but it is difficult to see why the scribe's palette and papyrus should be abandoned at this point; nevertheless, the reading has much to recommend it, v. note *f* to the translation below.

l. *·ỉ* is to be restored here, as with *šm*/*ḫꜣʿ* above, although clearly written out in *pꜣy·ỉ* and in *ʿḥʿ·ỉ* in l. 8.

m. Only]*ꜣb* remains, with a determinative which may be [demotic sign], sloping slightly to its left. *Ṯꜣy-sꜣb* (for *sbꜣ*), ϫⲓⲥⲃⲱ, is conjectured; it must be admitted that none of the examples in Erichsen, *Glossar*, 420–1 for *sbꜣ*(*t*) ⲥⲃⲱ show the metathesis of *b* and *ꜣ* which is common in the word *s*(*ꜣ*)*bỉ* 'enemy'. The reading adopted here is suggested by the determinative, by its general appropriateness, and by a similar writing of the word in Text **3**, R° 17.

n. A strange trace which I cannot interpret; possibly *n-drt* (?).

o. Again a crux: the traces at first suggested *nhs*, and with the following *mnḫ* were interpreted to refer to an act of incubation within the temple of Imḥōtep, but this palaeographically has little to commend it. The *mnḫ*, however, does seem clear, and with the following *wʿb* (if such be the true reading) suggests that we have here a proper name. The middle group has a slight resemblance to *ntrw*, but I cannot suggest a complete reading, and the first group, beginning with the article *pꜣ*, may be another title (*pꜣ ʿꜣ*) preceding this name. But all else is fabrication.

p. See note above; there is perhaps room for *pꜣ* between this word and the preceding.

q. A very faint passage, but the initial sign seems to resemble that of *ꜣḫt* at the end of the line below, rather than the opening sign of *prt*/*šmw*. The day, if any, is lost.

r. Here hesitation is in order whether *dỉt* is to be taken as Infinitive used for Imperative, opening a clause in direct speech, or whether (*r*) should be understood before it: if the first possibility is adopted, then the *šm* of the next line should perhaps also be taken as an imperative, but this raises difficulties, and the second possibility, suggested by Pierce, has been chosen here.

s. Terribly faint, and towards the end almost entirely lost. The version given here is suggested with every reservation.

t. There are slight traces of *w* before *tryn*, and the whole name perhaps read *Swtryn*. The following group (*pꜣ ḥm-nṯr Ḫns* seems preferable to *pꜣ ḥr-tb*) is either a title, or the name of the father; as a title it seems rather awkwardly placed before *pꜣ sḫ Pr-ʿꜣ* (*n*) *Mn-nfr*, but this may reflect the preferences of Ḥor. For a parallel, see note to the translation below.

u. *pꜣ nty* (*n*) *ḥt·w* is perhaps palaeographically better than the reading proposed here, but yields a rather awkward turn of phrase.

v. The writing of this word shows close links with the form adopted upon the Rosetta stone; another sign that we have here to deal with a Lower Egyptian tradition of writing.

w. Restored from Text **2**, V° 10–11, q.v.

x. Again confirmed by the parallel in Text **2**; the question of the reading of the group [demotic group] is,

[1] A brief reference to this interesting *sondage* by J. Leclant in *Orientalia*, 41 (1972), 255 § (b). The provisional number is 60 B. See now *JEA* 59 (1973), 153.

however, a complex one. The determinative shows us that we have to deal with the name of a locality of some kind, and this is confirmed by the information given in Text **23**, R° 5 where a temple of Osiris is said to lie *ḥr pꜣ ḏw* *Rꜣ-sṯꜣw* 'on the mountain of of Rostau'. These two examples strengthen the impression that we are dealing with a point of the compass, with the article *pꜣ* written, as so often in these expressions, as . This is confirmed again in Text **11**, V° 1 where *pꜣ tꜣ-rs* 'the south-land' is compared with a group written *pꜣ tꜣ-mḥ* 'the north-land'. The reading *pr-mḥ* is thus suggested for our group: *pr-rs* and *pr-ỉmnt* both appear unmistakably in Text **23**, and *pr-ỉꜣbt* would be very difficult to explain palaeographically.

y. Again restored, with the permission of the traces, from Text **2**, V° 9–10.

z. Taken as a relative with unwritten prosthetic *ỉ·*. The final vertical stroke seems to be merely part of the word, as in Text **2**, V° 9 (*wn-nꜣ Kmy*, etc.).

aa. Entirely lost: one may restore something like [*ỉw wn-nꜣ ỉr·f*] etc. *ad sensum*. An alternative possibility, that we have a change of subject to the first person, and that Ḥor is describing himself as the 'agent of Pharaoh', is *a priori* not so likely.

bb. The βασιλεὺς Πτολεμαῖος of the Greek texts. Reasons will be given below for thinking that this king is Philometor. The determinative, though faint, may well have been the 'foreigner' ; if so, there is a contrast, though not necessarily a serious one, with the practice of Text **2**.

cc. A common enough title of this goddess, cf. our Text **10**.

dd. The *tꜣ* is more of a straight line than one would wish, but seems permissible. This hand exhibits the strange characteristic of writing out the relative *ỉ·ỉr* in full, even after the definite article (cf. *pꜣ ỉ·ỉr/ḏlꜥ-mdt* at the end of this line). This is in strange contrast to the habitual omission of the relative stroke / before elements such as *wn-nꜣ* (cf. l. 8, and note *z* above).

ee. *ḏlꜥ-mdt* is a word of some significance in our texts. The basic meaning 'assemble words', thus 'record' is shown in Brugsch, *Thesaurus*, 986, Inschrift 50*b*, l. 7, *pꜣ nty ḏlꜥ-mdt* (*n*) *Pr-Wsỉr*, 'he who records in House-of-Osiris'. The compound noun, *gy-*(*n*)*-ḏlꜥ-mdt* (Text **19**, R° 17) seems to mean 'document, registration', and corresponds to χρηματισμός in *Canopus*, a, 24; b, 7. The toponym *mꜣꜥ/ꜥwy-n-ḏlꜥ-mdt* corresponds to the Greek χρηματιστήριον.[1] The meaning 'record' is thus relatively assured; in a context where dreams are mentioned, it is perhaps tempting to suggest the meaning 'interpret' (cf. also Text **17A**, 11–12), but there is no evidence to confirm this. Thoth's position as a recorder is well attested.[2]

ff. The standard introduction to accounts of dreams, cf. Text **8**, R° 1 and 12; also Bologna 3171, V° 1 and 8 (Botti, *Testi demotici*, 18, although the translation given there seems very dubious). The expression is presumably impersonal, and *ỉw·w ḏd n·ỉ* (*n*) *rswt* corresponds roughly to the English 'I had a dream'; hence the translation offered below.

gg. A strange phrase, not rendered easier by the break in the ostracon at this point. The entire group seems to recur in Text **4**, R° 4, and in both cases as the conclusion of an introductory explanation; there follows, after a gap, an account of the contents of something, in Text **4** of a letter, in this case of a dream. Its rough meaning might be expected to be *'as follows', but its exact reading is elusive. Its forms, in Text **4** and in the present document, suggest a form in *Normalschrift* *. Apart from a possibility that we are dealing with a writing of *tw-s* 'behold' (Erichsen, *Glossar*, 612; Spiegelberg, *Grammatik*, §§ 423–6) with a supralinear stroke, I can offer no explanation. The ink line which cuts across the group in this example is probably only a *lapsus calami* from a previous group, perhaps the *·f* of l. 9, which runs through to ll. 12 and 13.

hh. Slopes dramatically, and so more resembles *r*, but this yields little sense.

ii. A most strange turn of phrase, but alternatives such as **pꜣ tꜣ Kmy* seem quite excluded. The full writing for *pꜣy* is unlike the abbreviated forms in ll. 15–16 below, but exactly like the last occurrence of the word in l. 15.[3]

[1] Sethe-Partsch, *Bürgschaftsurkunden*, 7/7, 135–6 ('Ort der Protokollierung'); ibid. 111 for the meaning of the verb in general.

[2] e.g. Bonnet, *Reallexikon*, article 'Thot'.

[3] Perhaps it is not amiss here to point out that the principle upon which much palaeography, demotic and otherwise, is based (namely, that the same scribe will always write the same word in the same text in the same way) is groundless. (See, for example, the note to Text **3**, V° 4.)

jj. For such formatives in *ꜥt/ꜥwy-* cf. Spiegelberg, *Grammatik*, § 34. The present example seems unattested.

kk. A mere conjecture from the traces.

ll. The scribe seems to have altered *ḫn·s* to *ḫn·f*; the *·f* presumably referring to the city Alexandria.

mm. The stroke at the end of the line is probably a space-filler.

nn. This passage is largely restored from Text **2**, V° 2, where it recurs; the only clear elements here are *ssw*, *iw·f*, and the final word. Note the *-y* of the Qualitative of *ꜥšꜣ*, which does not tally with the Coptic evidence (Infinitive ⲁϣⲁⲓ, Qualitative ⲟϣ), and is presumably graphic.

oo. An interesting word, appearing as it does here in the form , in Text **3** as . The nature of the first sign, apparently *m*, and the position of the word as a qualifier of *ꜥšꜣy*, suggests the reading *m-šs*(*r*). The second sign may perhaps derive from hieroglyphic . Reasons will be given in the commentary below for the belief that while Text **2**, in common with many other documents in this series, represents a Memphite hand, the writings of Text **3** stem from the Delta, in fact from the Sebennyte nome. The example of *m-šs* here suggests that one of the greatest dangers of these texts will be the appearance of familiar words in entirely new disguises; none of the writings in Erichsen, *Glossar*, 521, except possibly the Rosetta hand, and none in the manuscript dictionary of Thompson[1] truly resemble the version seen here.

pp. The presence of two -signs, only the first of which is the determinative of *ms*, shows that we cannot be dealing with the abbreviated phrase *ms ḥwty* (Erichsen, *Glossar*, 178). Admittedly *šr ḥwty* is a tautology, but the alternative *šr ḥꜣty* 'eldest son' is difficult to reconcile with the traces, and it would seem that *ḥwty* has been chosen to add weight to the final pronouncement.

Translation

1. A memorandum[a] before the priests[b] from Ḥor, the scribe, a man of Pi(?)-Thoth in the nome of [Sebennytos. I observed the habit of spending] (my) days at the sanctuary[c] of
2. Osormnevis at Heliopolis(?), and likewise the sanctuary of Osorapis at Memphis.[d] It happened in Year 21, Pakhons,[e] day 2, (that) I was in Heliopolis. [My heart (?)] said,
3. 'Journey [··········]'. (I) abandoned my papyrus-roll and my palette from (my) hand[f] in Memphis [to receive instruction (?) from (?)]
4. [·······] *mnḫ*(?) (the) priest of the chapel[c] of Imhōtep which is within Heliopolis, to cause it to be told to me in person. (For)[g] I said this[h] to myself, namely,
5. 'When I came to Heliopolis in Khoiak [day . . .?],[i] ⟨within⟩ the sanctuary of Osormnevis I was told (in) a dream to put this (in) writing before the great men'.[j]
6. [I went before (?) *Sw*(?)]*tryn* the prophet of Khons,[k] the scribe of Pharaoh at Memphis,[l] (in) [Year] 23, Hathyr;[m] that which was verified
7. (at) the time (when) *ꜣtyks*[n] was to the north of *Pr-ꜣwrys*[o] (and) Egypt divorced itself.[p]
8. I stood with *Hryns*[q] who was at the head of the army [and who acted as (?)] the agent (of) Pharaoh
9. Ptolemy our Lord.[r] I caused him to discover the matters [·····] which had come before me,
10. the fortune of Pharaoh.[s] The lady of the two lands, Isis, was the one who ordained them, the great god Thoth the one who
11. recorded in connection with them.[t] I was told a dream [as follows]:
12. Isis, the great goddess of this Egypt and the land of Syria,[u] is walking upon the face (of)
13. the water of the Syrian sea.[v] Thoth stands before her (and) takes her hand,[w] (and) she reached[x] the harbour
14. (at) Alexandria. She said, 'Alexandria is secure [against (?) the] enemy. Pharaoh records within it

[1] In the possession of the Faculty of Oriental Studies, University of Cambridge. I am grateful to the Revd. Professor J. M. Plumley for granting facilities to consult these records.

15. together with his brethren.[y] The eldest son of Pharaoh wears the diadem.[z] His son wears the diadem after him. The son of this son
16. wears the diadem after him. The son of the son of the son of this son wears the diadem after him, for very
17. many lengthy days. The confirmation[aa] of this:
18. the Queen bears[bb] a male child.'

Notes

a. Coptic ⲙⲟⲕⲙⲉⲕ, Crum, 162a. The parent verb *mḳmḳ* 'consider' occurs in demotic in *Kufi*, 9/32, 21/7, also in Pap. Berlin 7059/24. The equation with the Greek ὑπόμνημα occurs in Pap. Elephantine 533 (Spiegelberg, *Demotische Denkmäler* (Cairo Catalogue), ii. 153). Pap. Loeb 53 (Spiegelberg, *Die demotischen Papyri Loeb*, 102 ff., also Zauzich in *Enchoria*, 2 (1972), 151) is an example of the characteristic opening formula: *wꜥ mḳmḳ n-ḏrt N sꜣ N*, etc.[1] Pap. Cairo 30966 (Spiegelberg, op. cit. ii. 205 and pl. LXXII), a Ptolemaic text from Gebelein, is a *mḳmḳ* concerning ibises, and even closer to the present text, Pap. Cairo 31221 (Spiegelberg, op. cit. i. 309) from Tebtynis contains a parallel to our opening phrase: *wꜥ mḳmḳ i·ir·ḥr nꜣ wꜥbw*. This text concerns a farmer (*wyꜥ*) of Pharaoh. The legal significance of the word as a written piece of evidence to support a petition is discussed by E. A. E. Reymond in *JEA* 58 (1972), 254 ff.

b. These priests remain anonymous, but they may be the staff of the ibis-shrine at North Saqqâra by which the ostraca themselves were found; if so, they will be the men whose council appears in Texts **19** and **21** below.

c. I have used this word as a conventional translation of the term *wꜥbt*, which ignores the connotation 'place of mummification' which the latter possessed, especially in the case of sacred animals (Preisigke and Spiegelberg, *Die Prinz-Joachim Ostraka*, 1–13, n. 1) and kings (Erichsen, *Eine neue Erzählung*, Column III). A similarly colourless 'chapel' is used for *r-pr*, and 'temple' for *ḥt-nṯr* whenever it occurs.

d. It is not surprising to find these two bull-cults so closely linked, and the same parallelism occurs elsewhere in these documents, notably in Text **13**, 4–7. Indeed, in the Ptolemaic period the cult of Mnevis and his deified counterpart had extremely close links with that of Apis, and became almost an extension of it (W. Otto, *Stierkulte*, 36 and for both cults combined under an ἀρχενταφιαστής cf. Wilcken, *UPZ* i. 48). Even the offices of High Priest of Ptaḥ at Memphis and *wr-mꜣw* at Heliopolis were combined already under Sheshonq I (Brugsch, *Thesaurus*, 950). Together with this combination went a decline in the importance of Heliopolis (Bergman, *Ich bin Isis*, 65), and the virtual dereliction of the place by the beginning of the Roman period is described by Strabo (xvii. 27).

e. Tybi is also possible, but less likely; the date given here, if the reasons to be given below for believing that the regnal year belongs to Philometor are sound, would correspond to the Julian 31 May 160 B.C.

f. This reading (v. note *k* above) 'I cast my papyrus-roll and palette from my hand in Memphis', implies that at this point Ḥor abandoned his scribal profession, in order to receive instruction in Heliopolis; the alternative reading, *šm·i*, pictures him on the journey, intending to make a record of the judgement he hoped to secure from the priest of Imḥōtep. It is difficult from the traces to decide between these two translations.

g. *iw·i* is circumstantial, 'I saying', tacked on to the main clause in a way characteristic of Ḥor's straggling style, but which is impossible to reproduce in English.

h. Literally 'it', in anticipation of the following *ḏd* clause. The order of pronouns (suffix before 'adverbial' phrase ***n-im·s***) is the standard for all phases of Egyptian, and the use of the preposition *n-im·* is explained by Parker's observation that the Coptic distinction between durative and limitative tenses is observed in demotic even back to the First Persian Period (*JNES* 20 (1953), 180).

i. In the January of 160 B.C.

j. The 'great men' (*rmtw ꜥꜣy*, also *rmtw ḏry*) appear on several occasions in our documents (cf. Text **7**, 14; Text **16**, R° 11–12; **17**, 5; **19**, R° 15; **27**, V° 8–9). In several of these references they are the subject of Ḥor's complaints (*ṯꜣy·w gns n-ḏrt nꜣ rmtw ꜥꜣy*), and it seems likely, though unproved, that in these latter cases they are his superiors among the staff of the ibis-shrine, against whom much of his energy seems to be directed; but the phrase is probably no more definite than the Greek οἱ ἐν τέλει, and in the present context seems to mean little more than 'those in authority at Memphis'.

[1] The view that the *wꜥ* in such phrases is any other than the indefinite article should now be abandoned, cf. the remarks of Hughes in *JNES* 17 (1958), 7.

k. Or possibly 'son of Pḥentkhons', a personal name. For the title, cf. BM. 10231, 18, *Tynsys pꜣ ḥm-ntr Ḫnsw* (also from the Serapeum).

l. 'Scribe of Pharaoh' is presumably a demotic translation of βασιλικὸς γραμματεύς. The name [..*w*]*tryn* may perhaps correspond to Σωτηρίων (Preisigke, *Namenbuch*, 401), but no person of this name appears in Peremans and van't-Dack, *Prosopographia Ptolemaica*, i. 49–54. The βασιλικὸς γραμματεύς had charge of the financial affairs of his nome (cf. the excellent discussion by A. Bernand, *Les Inscriptions grecques de Philae*, i. 187), and this general duty presumed the superintendence of the economic affairs of religious sanctuaries; it is for this reason that Ḥor addresses his statement to the *sẖ Pr-ꜥꜣ* (*n*) *Mn-nfr*. Dittenberger, *OGIS* ii (1905), no. 685 suggests that the Royal Scribe held a rank immediately below that of the στρατηγός of the nome.

m. December 159 B.C. It must be admitted that the proposed restoration of the beginning of this line leaves the final *pꜣ nty mꜣꜥ* (*n*) *pꜣ tr* hanging awkwardly: a restoration such as *tw·i ꜥn-smy i͗·ḥr* ..... *pꜣ sẖ Pr-ꜥꜣ* ..... *pꜣ nty mꜣꜥ* would yield much finer sense, but the traces would scarcely permit it.

n. Antiochus IV, Epiphanes; v. note on Text **3**, V° 10.

o. An unknown place-name; v. note ibid.

p. An enigmatic phrase, whose meaning is made a little clearer by the fuller writing in Text **3**, V° 9–10, *wn-nꜣ Kmy pnḳ n-i͗m·f* (*n*) *Rꜥ-ḳd*. The verb *pnḳ*/*prḳ* (Erichsen, *Glossar*, 136 with reference to *Mythus*, 2, 4; ⲡⲱⲣⲕ, Crum, 268b) is attested in the meaning 'pluck away, remove', and the reference is therefore to a time when Egypt had 'split away from Alexandria'. This was the state of affairs after November 170 B.C. (Skeat, *JEA* 47 (1961), 107 ff.; the statement on p. 109 recording the lack of dates for the thirteenth year can now partially be modified, v. note to Text **3**, V° 12). From this point until the eventual withdrawal of the Seleucid forces from Egypt there was a virtual state of στάσις within the country, with Egypt adhering to Philometor, while Alexandria supported the newly declared 'Ptolemy the Brother'.[1] This is the situation referred to here.

q. A transcription that may correspond to Greek Εἰρηναῖος (Preisigke, *Namenbuch*, 95–6 and variants), cf. the transcription *Hyrnꜣ* for Εἰρήνη, daughter of Ptolemaios, priestess of Arsinoe Philopator in the 170s (Glanville and Skeat, *JEA* 40 (1954), 51). The role of *Eirenaios as commander of the Egyptian cavalry forces against Antiochus is discussed more fully in the historical Commentary below.

r. A feature which will recur in both Text **2** and **3** is that in his retrospective narrative Ḥor constantly avoids all reference, except where inevitable, to Ptolemy 'the Brother', behaving as if Philometor had been sole ruler throughout the civil wars. The same phenomenon has already been observed in Demotic Text A above, and in the Commentary this reason will be given for believing that the bilingual ostraca may also be retrospective.

s. Cf. περὶ χρησίμων τοῖς βασιλεῦσι in Greek Text B; also the verso of Text **12** *nꜣ mdt nty nfr·w n pꜣ ꜥš-sḥn n Pr-ꜥꜣ*.

t. *ẖr* in the metaphor acquired from book-keeping 'under the heading of' (cf. Spiegelberg, *Grammatik*, § 296, 'Zur Bezeichnung der Absicht'); the same idiom in Text **17A**, 11–12.

u. For Isis as goddess of Syria, cf. Appendix 1 below. A similar, and not unexpected, linking of the two nations occurs in *Demotic Chronicle*, ii. 12: *wnmy Kmt pꜣy, i͗ꜣby pꜣ tꜣ Ḫr pꜣy*, 'the right hand is Egypt, the left hand the land of Syria (Khor)', Spiegelberg, op. cit. 10.

v. A strikingly Biblical turn of phrase, reminiscent of the עַל־פְּנֵי הַמָּיִם of Genesis 1: 2. Indeed such 'dramatic' phraseology, paralleled in Texts **14** and **27**, in the Demotic Chronicle, in Pap. Dodgson, and in the cryptic utterances ascribed to Amun in Pap. Rylands IX[2] seem to reflect the natural idiom of the Egyptian oracle.[3]

w. There may also be an underlying implication of the meaning 'guarantee' (ϣⲉⲛⲧⲱⲣⲉ) which this phrase can possess in legal language.

x. A change of tense less jarring in Egyptian, where the First Present is freely applied to any simultaneous action, irrespective of absolute time.

y. The 'brethren' (*snw*) may be an oblique reference to Ptolemy 'the Brother', and Cleopatra 'the Sister'; that at least the first of these was in Alexandria during the events referred to is confirmed by Text **3**.

[1] Cf. among others, Bevan, *Egypt under the Ptolemies*, 286 ff. The eventual date of the Roman ultimatum and the departure of Antiochus can now be determined, with the aid of our Texts **2** and **3**.

[2] Griffith, *Catalogue of Demotic Papyri in the John Rylands Library*, iii. 251–3.

[3] For an introduction to this subject, see Černý in Parker, *A Saite Oracle Papyrus*, 35–48.

z. The root *grp/glp* appears both as a verb (ϭⲱⲣⲡ, ϭⲱⲗⲡ) (Spiegelberg, *Orakelglossar*, no. 268 and *ZÄS* 50 (1913), 32; also *Raphia*, 9, 24), and a noun (*grpt*, ϭⲣⲏⲡⲉ). Spiegelberg (*Orakelglossar*) remarks that the same dual meaning of 'be manifest' and 'diadem' occurs with the root *ḫꜥỉ*; for the religious connotations of this, cf. Redford, *History and Chronology of the Eighteenth Dynasty*, 3–27. The existence of such symbolism, based presumably on solar imagery, would suggest that attempts, such as that of Erichsen, *Glossar*, 584 and 589, to distinguish semantically between *grp* and *glp* are probably misguided, the more so since the *-l-* forms that he shows may be derived from Faiyûmic Petubastis texts. For a writing of the *sḏm·f* of the verb as *krp·w*, v. Text **2**, R° 10 and note.

aa. Coptic ⲁϩⲉⲣⲁⲧ; cf. Sethe-Partsch, *Bürgschaftsurkunden*, 194.

bb. More likely to be First Present than the rare First Future with omitted *r*; it is therefore difficult to decide whether the action is to be regarded as taking place at the time of the utterance, or whether the mere truism is being expressed that the birth of the child, whenever it occurs, will be the confirmation of the oracle. This latter is perhaps the sounder conclusion.

Preliminary Remarks

The memorandum published here seems to have been drawn from the official records of the ibis-chapel. It deals with a dream experienced by Ḥor during the invasion of Antiochus Epiphanes, and his report before the βασιλικὸς γραμματεύς of the Memphite region, which took place some eight or nine years afterwards, in December 159 B.C. It will be seen that material from this memorandum, together with material from Text **2**, was reused in the writing of Text **3**; the hand, which is a fine Memphite one, may be that of a secretary. The same may well be true of the following document. In view of the discussion of the meaning of such memoranda in *JEA* 58 (1972), 254 ff., it would seem that the writer intended to incorporate this material into a petition of some sort. The reasons for this will, it is hoped, become clear as we proceed.

Text 2

Height[1]	17·8 cm.
Width	14·9 cm.
Thickness	1·0 cm.
Munsell	2·5 YR 6/6
Photograph	Plate III (R°, V°)
Facsimile	not given
Excavator's no.	71/2–131 [5399]

A finely preserved ostracon, in pink ware, bearing on the recto sixteen lines of demotic in a fine Memphite hand, and a similar fifteen lines on the verso. Although the surviving writing is remarkably clear, there are traces of considerable changes of mind on the part of its author, with two lines on the recto and one on the verso completely erased, and several phrases inserted into the text. The lines on the verso seem to be a paraphrase of the contents of the recto: they may perhaps represent a recension of some kind.

The document, one of the most remarkable discovered in Egypt, was part of the second batch unearthed by Martin on 3 February 1972.

Text: recto

1. *n-drt Ḥr pꜣ sẖ*
2. *rmt dmỉ-(n)-Ꜣst nbt tpḥ*[a]
3. *tꜣ ntrt ꜥꜣt n pꜣ tš Ṯb-ntr*[b]
4. *tꜣ rswt (ỉ·)ḏd·w*[c] *n·ỉ*[d] *(n) pꜣ wḏꜣ (n) Rꜥ-ḳd* (There follow two erased lines beginning *ỉrm rmt nb* which probably resembled ll. 9 and 10 of the verso).
5. *nꜣ mšꜥw (n) Ꜣtyks*[e] *ꜥws*[f] *ḏd ỉw·f šm n·f*[g]
6. *ḏd ỉw·f šm n·f*[h] *(n) sgr*[i] *r-bl Kmy šꜣꜥ*
7. *ḥꜣt-sp 2t ꜣbd-2 šmw ꜥlḳy. ỉr·ỉ*[j] *ꜥn-smy tꜣ mdt *ta*[k]
8. *(n) Hrynys (ỉ·)wn-nꜣ sꜣtrks*[l] *ḥꜣt-sp 2t ꜣbd-2 šmw sw 11*[m].
9. *bw-ỉr·tw*[n] *Grynꜣ pꜣ rd Ꜣtyks ꜥws*[f]
10. *šm n·f r-bl Mn-nfr. krp·w*[o] *tꜣ mdt *ta*[k] (erased space)

[1] On ostraca with two inscribed faces the measurements given here are read from the side of the recto. Choice of recto and verso is either decided by the text, or arbitrary.

11. *ḥr rdwy·s*[p]. *bn-pw·f mdt n-im·w ꜥn*[q] *hb·f* (*n*) *ḥty*[r]
12. *wꜥt šꜥt. di·i-s* ⟨(*n*) *nꜣ Pr-ꜥꜣw*⟩[s] (*n*) *Pr-Wsir-Ḥp pꜣ ꜥꜣ nty n Rꜥ-ḳd ḥꜣt-sp 2t ꜣbd-3 šmw ꜥlḳy*[t]
13. *n-drt ḫpr·f*[u] *mdt nbt nty ṯꜣy nꜣy swn*[v] *i·ir·ḥr·k*[w] (*n*) *pꜣ tr*
14. *rn·f tꜣ nty ṯꜣy r·ḥr·i ḫt*[x] *pꜣ ꜥw* (*n*) *tꜣ nty ḥr nꜣ ntrw*[y] (*n*) *ḥꜣty·k.*
15. *tw·i in n-im·s i·ir·ḥr·k ḏd tw·i in-iw*[z] (*r*) *Rꜥ-ḳd*
16. *ḥr Tytts pꜣ sꜣtrks ḫt* (rest erased).
17. (erased line)

Text: verso

1. *n-drt Ḥr pꜣ rmt dmi-*(*n*)*-Ꜣst*
2. *nbt tpḥ tꜣ ntrt ꜥꜣt* (*n*) *pꜣ tš Ṯb*[aa]
3. (erasures) *hb Hrynys* (*n*) *ḥty*
4. *wn wꜥt šꜥt*[bb]. *di·i-s* (*n*) *nꜣ Pr-ꜥꜣw*
5. (*n*) *Pr-Wsir-Ḥp pꜣ ꜥꜣ nty n Rꜥ-ḳd n*[cc]
6. *ḥꜣt-sp 2t ꜣbd-3 šmw ꜥlḳy. nꜣ mdt-nfrw* (*i·*)*ir·i ꜥn-smy*
7. *n-im·w n*[dd] *ḥꜣt-sp 2t ꜣbd-2 šmw sw 11 bw-ir·tw Gryꜣ*[ee]
8. *pꜣ rd Ꜣtyks*[ff] *šm n·f r-bl Mn-nfr.*
9. *iw·i ꜥš pꜣ wḏꜣ n Rꜥ-ḳd irm rmt nb nty ḫn·f*
10. *i·ir ḫpr ḫn pꜣ sḥn nfr* (*n*) *nꜣ Pr-ꜥꜣw. bn-pw·w pnꜥ*[gg]
11. *irm tꜣ nty ṯꜣy nꜣ mšꜥw Ꜣtyks ꜥws*[hh] *irm*
12. *pꜣy·f mšꜥ ḏd iw·f šm n·f r-bl Kmy* ⟨(*n*) *sgr*⟩ *šꜣꜥ ḥꜣt-sp 2t ꜣbd-2 šmw ꜥlḳy*
13. *n-drt ḫpr·f wn wꜥt mdt ꜥꜣt ḫꜥꜣ*[ii] *ḫn nꜣ mdt nty sẖ* (*n*) *tꜣ šꜥt*
14. *pꜣ tr* (*n*) *ir-nb ḫr*[jj] *tꜣ ḫt-mdt rn·s.* [[*pꜣ*]][kk] *ḫpr pꜣ sdny* (*n*) *Ꜣst tꜣ ntrt ꜥꜣt*[ll]
15. *irm Ḏḥwty pꜣ ꜥꜣ pꜣ ꜥꜣ pꜣ ꜥꜣ ḥr mdt nbt nty ṯꜣy nꜣy.*
(at the end of this line, and upon the one following, the phrase *ḏd n·i* [ ] *rswt* has been written, but erased).

[1] Cf. Montet, *Géographie*, i. 105 and n. 9.

[2] Revillout, *Corpus Papyrorum*, no. 5 (pl. IV); Spiegelberg, *Musées Royaux du Cinquantenaire*, 14.

[3] Note the hieroglyphic writing of this word as in the Bellagio statuette of Praꜥḥotpe (Brunner, *JEA* 54 (1968), 131 ff.). On the *tpḥt ḏꜣt*, a cult area at Memphis associated with the *štyt* v. Borghouts, *Magical Texts of Pap. Leiden I, 348*, 194–8.

Notes: recto

a. A cult title of Isis which occurs here and in the corresponding place on the verso. The reading *nbt* seems plausible; the following element is written here , on the verso . In the context of Isis and the Sebennyte nome, one thinks immediately of *Ḥbyt*, Behbeit el-Ḥagār, but this reading is palaeographically weak, and the group lacks any place determinative. In view of our reading of above as *pr-mḥ*, a transliteration **mḥy* suggests itself, and furthermore the goddess (*Ḥꜣt*)-*mḥyt*, known to have been worshipped in this part of the Delta,[1] but this has the disadvantage of being quite unattested. The reading *pt*, though prosaic, fails to conform with the writings of this word in Text **10.** However, there is a close resemblance to a group occurring in Pap. Louvre 2412, l. 4,[2] where among various endowments we read of the sixth part of a forecourt *nty ḥr thny ꜥnḫ-tꜣwy* (*n*) *pꜣ ꜥ-sbt thny ḥr pꜣ ꜥt-rs* *'Iy-m-ḥtp sꜣ Ptḥ pꜣ ntr ꜥꜣ*; the word, not transliterated in the publications, is perhaps to be read *tpḥ*, the older *tpḥt* (Erichsen, *Glossar*, 628 and *Wb*. v. 364, with the meaning '(sacred) cavern'),[3] and this identification is tentatively suggested in the present passage. A similar word appears in Text **23,** R° 4: see note *ad locum*.

b. The first full writing of the nome: see index for a complete list of the occurrences of this common name. The texts seem to yield two writings, neither resembling the published examples; the identification is proposed on *a priori* grounds, and on the identification of *Dmi-*(*n*)*-Ꜣst* with the Ἴσιος πόλις of Greek Text C, which is said to lie in the nome of Sebennytos:

(i) Texts which can reasonably lay claim to a Memphite palaeography (**1, 2, 7, 19, 24, 26, 31A**) show the writing (* with supralinear stroke)

(ii) The remaining texts, which show a large ungainly hand, generally write without the second sign. Reasons will later be given for believing that this hand is that of Ḥor himself, that it is Sebennytic, and that therefore represents the indigenous spelling of *Ṯb-nṯr* (cf. Text **8** below, and also Text **31A**, 4).

(iii) The reading is perhaps confirmed by the abbreviation found on the verso: v. note *aa* below.

c. Taken as relative with prefix omitted.

d. Note that all our texts, with the exception of Text **8**, consistently distinguish the group *n·i* from *-s*.

e. This name is written in a cartouche, and though the middle sign is very cursive, it would seem to be the rounded *k* seen, e.g., in writings of *ḳnḥt* 'shrine, vault' (Erichsen, *Glossar*, 541). The identification with Ἀντίοχος seems established from the occurrence in *Raphia*, 10, 15 (Gauthier–Sottas, *Décret trilingue*, 47 ff.).

f. Left in transliteration here, to show the variation in the spelling of Antiochus. Demotic writings such as for *nꜣ Pr-ꜥꜣw* suggest that the *ꜥws*-signs are little more than a determinative, and it is unlikely that they were of much significance in writings such as.

g. The 'ethic' (*sic*) dative which survives even in such Coptic phrases as ⲙⲁϣⲉ ⲛⲁⲕ, ⲛⲏⲧⲛ̄, etc.

h. Dittography.

i. The determinatives are presumably.

j. Use of *ir·f sḏm* with a compound verb; the same elongated writing for *ir·i* in V° 6 below and in Text **3**, V° 8.

k. A clearly written word, common in its recurrence; yet one of the greatest *cruces* of our texts. I have been able to collect the following examples:

(i) Text **2**, R° 7: *ir·i ꜥn-smy tꜣ mdt*
10–11: *krp·w tꜣ mdt ḥr rdwy·s*

(ii) Text **3**, V° 8: *wn nꜣ mdt pꜣ tr (i·) wn-nꜣ*

(iii) Ibid. V° 12–13: *bn-pw Hrynys nḥt nꜣ mdt*

(iv) Text **19**, V° 1–2: *šsp Ḥꜥ-Ḥp ... nꜣ mštw in·f-s n nꜣy·f ꜥwy*

(v) Text **31B**, x+6: *tꜣ mdt wpy Ḏḥwty irm tꜣ ḥt-mdt 2t ḥn·f-s n·i ḏd* (etc.)

(vi) Text **23**, R° 11: *smn pꜣ hp n tꜣ ḥt-mdt* (cf. ibid. V° 4)

(vii) Text **29**, 6: *mdt* (damaged context).

There is no doubt of the word's predilection for following *mdt*, but example (v), where a numeral intervenes, shows that it cannot be an integral part of it; example (iv) also demonstrates its ability to follow an animate noun. It may be a coincidence that in none of our examples is the preceding noun masculine singular, but it is surely significant that in every case the noun is itself preceded by the definite article. The word therefore behaves like a demonstrative of some sort, but one that follows its noun; its kinship with the ordinary demonstratives is shown by its similarity to *nꜣy* below. That it is not a writing of *rn·s*, *rn·w* (which would yield excellent sense) is shown by the writing *rn·f* in l. 14 below, and by Text **8**, R° 12, *irm tꜣ mdt-nfrt rn·s*.

The least exceptionable conclusion seems to be that we are dealing with a modified form of demonstrative pronoun (note, for example, the early writings of *na* 'those of' in Erichsen, *Glossar*, 203), possibly a dialect formation, which follows its noun. The only demonstrative which regularly does this, *nty n-im·w* (ⲉⲧⲙ̄ⲙⲁⲩ) has the advantage of being grammatically invariable; but though it is possible to imagine that may arise from or the like, it is very difficult to account for the disappearance of *nty* in such a phrase. The translation offered below ('the said') therefore represents a mere compromise.

l. A transcription, with metathesis, of στρατηγός; for other spellings, cf. Griffith, *Rylands*, iii. 429.

m. Restored from the clearer writing of V° 7.

n. The stroke at the beginning of this line is otiose, and presumably marks the abandonment of an original word.

o. Another spelling of *grp* (v. above, p. 14, note *z* to Text **1**, 15, translation). The syntax, however, is difficult: the context seems to demand a passive (an imperative would be very harsh) and it seems best to take the faint and smudged stroke following the word as a writing of the suffix *·w*.

p. A rare alternative with suffix to the common *ḥr-rdwy*.

q. is more likely to be a writing of *ꜥn* (ⲟⲛ), even though a very full one, than of the negative *in*, which does not normally follow *bn-pw*; the meaning is presumably 'he spoke no more of them'.

r. Another problem; the following examples occur:

(i) Text **2**, R° 11–12: *hb·f* … *wꜥt šꜥt*

(ii) Ibid. V° 3–4: *hb Hrynys* …: *wn wꜥt šꜥt*

(iii) Text **19**, R° 18: *hb·w* … *n Rꜥ-ḳd*

(iv) Text **22**, R° 3: *hb nꜣ Pr-ꜥꜣw* …

A striking feature of this group is the change in the final element: in the last example it is clearly written …. It is tempting to read this as *n-im·s*, letting the variant stand for *n-im·w*; the difficulty then lies with …. The obvious reading of this group would be *ḥꜥ·i* (ϩⲱⲱ) 'myself', but it is extremely doubtful whether this word could be used as the object of a *sḏm·f* in the way demanded by our examples; at the least, one would need to assume a complete suppression of the dependent pronoun *wi*. Furthermore, this reading, although yielding excellent sense in example (iv), strains the syntax of the others, particularly (iii), in a very abrupt way. One is therefore obliged to feel that the word is a unity; but the reading (*n*) *ḥty* and the translation offered here are conjectures.[1]

s. Inserted: see note to translation below.

t. The writing of *šmw* and *ꜥlḳy* much abbreviated; the present reading is confirmed by V° 6, and by Text **3**, V° 14. The scribe of the present text writes *šmw* in both examples as ….

u. A phrase which recurs in this text, V° 13, and alone on the V° of Text **10**. Its meaning is determined by the hieroglyphic translation … *r-ntt* in l. 9 of the Tanis Stela (Brugsch, *Thesaurus*, 1555) and the use of ἐπειδή in Greek versions (cf. Daumas, *Moyens d'expression*, 87 ff.). The following phrase is again a favoured idiom, cf. this text, V° 15, and Text **4**, R° *passim*, where *tꜣ nty ṯꜣy* is used constantly to introduce themes excerpted from an oracle. It seems clear from these examples that *ṯꜣy* in this phrase is used to mean 'refer to', and that, for example, **tꜣ nty ṯꜣy nꜣ ntrw* corresponds to the Greek τὰ τῶν θεῶν. Wherever the phrase appears, I have transliterated the article as the singular *tꜣ* (sc. *mdt*), but short of an unambiguous writing, the plural *nꜣ* is also quite possible.

v. Presumably Qualitative, the neuter meaning of *mdt nbt* encouraging the tendency to omit even the feminine ending of this form.

w. The *·k* is obscured by a striation running across the surface of the ostracon.

x. In its use, common in these texts, of paraphrasing a vague expression ('namely', 'that is'); this therefore differs slightly from the similar *ḏd*, which nearly always implies the reason for what precedes.

y. Yet another equivalent of τὰ τῶν θεῶν (v. note *u* above). In Tanis Stela, 12, *tꜣ nty ḥr Ḥp* corresponds to *ḥr ḫt* (pl.) *Ḥp* in the hieroglyphic version.

z. A common Memphite writing of the Qualitative ⲛⲏⲩ, cf. Erichsen, *Glossar*, 21.

aa. The scribe has written …, as in the writing of the place-name *Tb-tn*, as an abbreviation. The erasure following may have been **iw·f ḫn Mn-nfr*, or a similar phrase.

bb. The syntax of the sentences here is difficult: *di·i-s* cannot be linked to *šꜥt* as a relative form, because it is clearly followed by an object-suffix (Spiegelberg, *Grammatik*, § 549). *wn wꜥt šꜥt* is therefore left hanging, unless our interpretation of the preceding group (note *r* above) is at fault.

cc. It is difficult to decide whether the final horizontal line is a space-filler, or a writing of *n*; but the preposition is clearly written before the date in l. 7 below.

dd. The mark which appears above *n* here is probably part of the palimpsest, which again seems to have been **Hrynys*.

ee. A different spelling from that of the R°, but the same as in Text **3**, V° 11. The scribe may possibly have had difficulty with the final syllable. The determinative seems to be a highly cursive writing of ….

ff. For the reading see note *e* above. It is tempting here to attach significance to the use of the 'foreigner' determinative instead of the honorific ending of a cartouche, and perhaps even more tempting to read significance into the cartouche itself; but the presence of the cartouche around the name of Antiochus in the Raphia stela, where he is nothing if not a defeated enemy, suggests that it was standard practice among demotic

[1] The final sign of the group may perhaps be …, the determinative of *ḥtr* (ϩⲁⲧⲣⲉ) 'twin'; but this can occur with the related word for horse ('yoked animal'). Can this here be used metaphorically to describe a dispatch rider?

scribes to ascribe a cartouche to anyone who held the title of βασιλεύς, no matter where his kingdom. Even the use of the 'foreign' determinative implies little: common enough at the end of many Greek names, it even occurs frequently in the names of the early Ptolemies, as equally in that of (Augustus) Caesar.[1] Unless the hazardous assumption is made that these writings represent a conscious act of hostility towards the ruling powers, such determinatives should be treated more as indications that the spelling of such names is not yet fixed; in the case of our writings of Antiochus Epiphanes (whose sojourn in Egypt was brief), this conclusion is supported by Text **4**, R° 8, where the name appears as *ꜣtykys*, and by the curious example in Text **3**, V° 14, where the ending of the cartouche appears, but without the *ʿws*![2] In the historical discussion below (Commentary, § 2), the evidence for Antiochus' seizure of the Egyptian throne will be reviewed, and it would seem strong enough not to need the support of the demotic spellings.

gg. ⲡⲱⲱⲛⲉ, Crum, 264, though the use with *ỉrm* is unparalleled. Note the parallel phrase in Text **22**, R° 8–9.

hh. Here the 'foreigner' determinative seems to have been changed to *ʿws*. See note *ff* above.

ii. For *ẖrꜣ* as a writing of *ẖꜣ(i)* 'measure', cf. Erichsen, *Glossar*, 347; here perhaps a writing of the Qualitative ϣⲏⲟⲩ (Boh.) (Crum, 574b). For the metaphoric use with words, cf. perhaps the example on 548a (ⲁⲛⲓϣⲓ ⲛ̄ⲥⲁϫⲓ ϣⲱⲡⲓ).

jj. Offered with extreme reserve; the entire group may perhaps read *nʿw* (ⲛⲏⲩ), but this yields rather a weak translation. For *ỉr-nb*, cf. Erichsen, *Glossar*, 214 (= φροντίζειν).

kk. Difficult to reconcile with the syntax; perhaps the scribe changed his mind during the process of writing. The omission of this word enables the sense to be restored.

ll. Badly squashed into the margin, and tentative.

Translation: recto

1. From Ḥor the scribe
2. a man of the town of Isis,[a] lady of the cavern,
3. the great goddess, in the nome (of) Sebennytos
4. The dream which was told to me[b] of the safety of Alexandria
5. (and) the journeyings of *ꜣtyks*,[c] namely that he would go
6. [[that he would go]] by sail[d] from Egypt by[e]
7. Year 2, Paoni, final day.[f] I reported the said matter[g]
8. (to) *Hrynys*, who was *strategos*, (in) Year 2, Paoni, day 11[h].
9. *Grynꜣ*, the agent of *ꜣtyks*, had not yet
10. left Memphis.[i] (But) the said matters were revealed
11. immediately. He did not speak of them further, (but) he sent in the hour (?)
12. a letter. I gave it ⟨(to) the Pharaohs⟩[j] in the Great Serapeum which is in Alexandria,[k] in Year 2, Epeiph, final day.[l]
13. For every matter which refers to this was compensation for you[m] (at) the time
14. in question (for) that which concerns me, namely, the greatness towards that which concerns the gods (in) your heart.[n]
15. I brought it before you,[m] for I came to Alexandria
16. with[o] *Tytts* the *strategos*, namely [*the rest is erased*].

Translation: verso

1. From Ḥor the man (of) the town of Isis,
2. lady of the cavern, the great goddess, (in) the nome (of) Seb(ennytos).
3. (*erasures*) *Hrynys* sent within the hour (?).
4. Account of a letter: I gave it to the Pharaohs
5. (in) the Great Serapeum which is in Alexandria, in
6. Year 2, Epeiph, final day, (namely), the blessings which I reported
7. in Year 2, Paoni, day 11, (when) *Gryꜣ*,[p]
8. the agent of *ꜣtyks*, had not yet left Memphis.
9. I read out the salvation of Alexandria and every man who was within it,
10. which happened through the good disposition[q] (of) the Pharaohs. None could controvert

[1] Cf. Papyrus Carlsberg 67, dated to Year 25 of Augustus (from Tebtynis).

[2] See also note *hh* below.

11. that which referred to the journeyings of *ȝtyks* and
12. his army,[r] namely, that he would leave Egypt ⟨by sail⟩ by Year 2, Paoni, final day.
13. For there was a great matter measured within the words written (in) the letter,
14. (at) the time of paying heed to the utterance in question. There came about the counsel[s] of Isis, the great goddess,
15. and Thoth, the three times great,[t] in every matter which concerned these things [*more erasures*].

Notes

a. This 'town of Isis' (Temenēsi) clearly corresponds to the Ἴσιος πόλις of Greek Texts C and E, and is the alternative home of the narrator. An attempt to reconcile the two places of origin named in the texts will be given in the Commentary below. At present, the difficulty lies in trying to locate this name. Pliny the Elder, it is true, does mention an *Isidis oppidum* in the Sebennyte nome, and this is generally taken to refer to the great cult-centre of Isis at Eḥbō,[1] the modern Behbeit el-Ḥagār (see P. Oxyrhynchus 1380, 33, note, = *Oxyrhynchus Papyri*, xi. 208). There are, however, strong objections to equating this well-known site with our *dmỉ-(n)-ȝst*:

(i) Behbeit in late sources is regularly Ἴσειον, not Ἴσιος πόλις (Stephanus Byzantius, *Geography of Ravenna*, cf. Ball, *Egypt in Classical Geographers*, 172).

(ii) Behbeit already has an Egyptian name: *Ḥbyt* or *Pr-Ḥbyt* (Montet, *Géographie*, i. 107).

Against this it might be argued that *Ḥbyt* could well be the religious name of a town known commonly as (*pȝ*) *dmỉ-n-ȝst*, that there are unlikely to have been two cult-centres of Isis within the same nome, especially if Temenēsi is taken to be a place of some importance, and that the equation of *Isidis oppidum* with Behbeit el-Ḥagār may be wrong; but none of these objections is conclusive, and therefore we must reject the identification for lack of evidence.

b. For this idiom, see above, p. 10, note *ff* to Text **1** above.

c. For this phrase, which means in essence 'the retreat of Antiochus', cf. also Text **4**, R° 8.

d. Presumably from Pelusium to Antioch. This detail does not at first sight agree with the account in Polybius (xxix. 27, 8); see Commentary below for an attempt to reconcile this difference.

e. An idiomatic use of *šȝr*, cf. ϣⲁⲥⲟⲩⲁ ⲙ̄ⲡⲁⲟⲛⲉ, Crum, 542a.

f. 30 July 168 B.C. The use of 'Year 2' (a dating by the joint reign), suggests that this text is either a contemporary account, or closely based on one.

g. For this conventional translation see note *k* above.

h. 11 July 168 B.C.

i. The only thing which *Grynȝ* does of importance in these texts is to fail to leave Memphis; the implications of this negative are, however, of great interest (see Commentary, § 2 below).

j. i.e. Ptolemy VI Philometor, and his brother; the sister Cleopatra may perhaps also be intended in the expression.

k. The reading *pȝ nḥm* 'the saviour' is palaeographically less likely. The Great Serapeum with its adjoining libraries formed the major landmark of the south of the city, so much so that by the Roman period at Alexandria Sarapis was honoured with the epithet πολιοῦχος (H. Henne, *MIFAO* lxvii. 2 (1937) = *Mélanges Maspero*, ii. 297–307). The great temple had been the site of building projects under the first four Ptolemies[2] (A. Rowe, *Temple of Serapis at Alexandria*, *passim*; A. Rowe and B. R. Rees, 'A Contribution to the Archaeology of the Western Desert, IV: The Great Serapeum of Alexandria', in *Bull. J. Rylands Library*, 1956–7, 485–520), and the cult statue was probably installed by Ptolemy I (Stambaugh, *Sarapis under the Early Ptolemies* (Leiden, 1972), 25; 90–1). The early history of the Sarapis cult has been dealt with in two articles by P. M. Fraser ('Two Studies on the Cult of Sarapis' in *Opuscula Atheniensia*, 3 (1960), 1–54, and 'Current Problems', ibid. 7 (1965), 23–45. See now the same author's *Ptolemaic Alexandria* (Oxford, 1972), i. 268–70; ii. 84 ff.; iii. 71). Unfortunately our text does not make clear what the Pharaohs were doing in the Alexandrian Serapeum during this time of crisis: see Commentary below, § 1.

l. 29 August 168 B.C.

m. It seems clear that at this point Ḥor is addressing

[1] This vocalization of *Ḥbyt* is strongly suggested by the Manethonian version Νεκτανηβώς for *Nḫt-Ḥr-(n)-Ḥbyt* (*ⲛⲉϩⲧϩⲁⲣⲡ̄ⲛⲉϩⲃⲱ): the word has the same phonetic development as *Ḏbȝyt* 〉 ⲧⲃⲱ (Edfu), *mryt* 〉 ⲙ̄ⲣⲱ, *sbȝyt* 〉 ⲥⲃⲱ, *Wȝḏyt* 〉 -ουτώ, etc.

[2] Even, according to the Pseudo-Callisthenes, under Alexander!

Philometor directly, and that the singular pronoun represents the suppression, unconscious or (more likely) conscious, of 'the Brother': see note *a* to Demotic Text A above, and the information in Text **3** below, as well as Commentary § 1 below.

n. This characteristically awkward sentence may perhaps be paraphrased, 'For all of this was done at that time in recompense to you for that which concerns me, namely, your magnanimity towards the gods.'

o. For this concomitant meaning of *ḥr*, cf. Crum, 644b, ϩⲓⲛⲉϥⲉⲣⲏⲩ.

p. The change of spelling perhaps reflects difficulty with the final syllable -ων; the name corresponds either to Κρέων (Preisigke, 186), or, more likely, to the commoner Κλέων (ibid., 176). See note *i* above, also note *ee*, and the Commentary *ad locum*.

q. For *sḥn nfr*, v. Erichsen, *Glossar*, 446.

r. The word *mšʿ* in our texts seems generally to carry the meaning 'people'; cf. perhaps Text **3**, R° 9, *pꜣ sbty* (*n*) *pꜣy·k mšʿ*; Text **7**, 5; and almost certainly Text **19**, V° 10 *pꜣ mšʿ n Pr-Wsỉr-Ḥp*; and parallel texts.[1] The word *mtgt*(*y*), however, seems confined to a military sense: *Hrynys* in Text **1**, 8, is *ḥr tꜣ ḥꜣt tꜣ mtgt*, and subsequent references, notably Text **4**, R° 1, leave us in little doubt that his position was military. This is confirmed by the Greek translation in *Rosettana*, 7 as δύναμις. The mention of the word in Text **12**, V° 3 is therefore of some interest: see note *ad locum*.

s. For *stny*/*sḏny*, cf. Erichsen, *Glossar*, 480; the present spelling corresponds fairly closely to the Bohairic ⲥⲟϭⲛⲓ (Crum, 615b). For a recurrence of the word in our texts, v. Text 12, V° 4 (in the spelling *sgn*).

t. Clearly the demotic parallel to the Greek τρισμέγιστος. Early recurrences of this epithet have been discussed by Turner and Skeat in their publication of the Greek texts (*JEA* 54 (1968), 208), where it appears that the Saqqâra ostraca form the earliest unequivocal testimony to the title. One should add the comparative Egyptian material in Chassinat, *Dendera*, i. 30: *Ḏḥwty ʿꜣ ʿꜣ wr* (an interesting parallelism to μεγίστου.... μεγίστου... μεγάλου), and the ostracon from Tûna el-Gebel where Θωυθ Ѡ Ѡ Ѡ νοβ Ζμουν (= *Ḏḥwty ʿꜣ ʿꜣ ʿꜣ nb Ḫmnw*) occurs in a Greek text (V. Girgis in *MDAIK* 20 (1965), 121); the date is not certain, but it can hardly be earlier than 111 B.C. At present, it would perhaps be best to confine oneself to the observation that the title fits much more naturally into an Egyptian Text than into a classical Greek one.[2]

Preliminary Observations

This ostracon represents an attempt, with re-writing and erasures, to produce a coherent account of the events of the summer of 168 B.C., and of the author's contribution to them. The text looks very much like a preliminary draft, and even the final version lacks absolute clarity; but it is clearly either contemporary, or (more likely in view of the address to Philometor alone) a later account based on contemporary material, for it dates events by the joint reign of the two Ptolemies, and this system was abandoned after May 163 B.C.[3] This early account seems in turn to have been rewritten, and the result is our Text **3**, which follows.

TEXT 3

Height	23·6 cm.
Width	16·5 cm.
Thickness	0·8 cm. (ave.)
Munsell	2·5 YR 6/4
Photograph	Plate IV (R°, V°)
Facsimile	Plate IVA (R°, V°)
Excavator's no.	G7–26 [455]

A large reddish ostracon, taken from the side of a storage vessel, with characteristic curvature and grooved rim, and ribbed verso. The recto bears twenty-seven lines of demotic, tightly written, in a hand which is not that of the two preceding texts, and the verso bears a further twenty-five in the same hand. There are clear

[1] Note the interesting bilingual text in Brugsch, *Thesaurus*, 901, l. 3, where *pꜣ mšʿ* corresponds to hieroglyphic *rḫyt*.

[2] At this point the extremely important question arises of the extent of Egyptian influence on the Hermetic literature. Space does not permit discussion here, but v. B. H. Stricker in *Mnemosyne* (*Bibl. Class. Batava*), Fourth Series, vol. 2 (Leiden, 1949), 79, and in *Verhand. Koning. Ned. Akad. van Wetenschaap, Afd. Letterk.*, Decl. 62, no. 4 (Amsterdam, 1956); also Krause in *ZDMG*, Suppl. I (1969), part I, 48–57. The present writer, though hardly to be considered expert, is of the opinion that the Hermetica, far from being assigned to the limbo of the alchemist, should be treated extremely seriously as source-material for Egyptian religion (at least in its later forms).

[3] Pestman, *Chronologie*, 50 ff.

signs of erasures and changes of intention by the scribe, together with refillings of the pen. The text opens with a long encomium to Pharaoh.[1] A photograph of this ostracon has already appeared in *JEA* 52 (1966), pl. I, no. 1.

Text: recto

1. *Pr-ꜥꜣ Ptrwmys ꜥws pꜣy·n ḥry pꜣ nb (n) Kmy ỉrm*
2. *tꜣ Pr-ꜥꜣt ⟨Ḳrwptrꜣ⟩*[a] *nꜣ ntrw mr-mwt·w nty wꜣḥ-sḥn*[b] *n Rꜥ-ḳd: nꜣ-nfr n·k*[c]
3. *tꜣ rnpt. tꜣy·k rnpt nfrt rnpt nbt nty ỉw·w ỉy. nꜣ-nfr n·k*
4. *tꜣy*[d] *ỉrm·w. (nꜣ-)nfr·s*[e] *(n) pꜣy·k šꜣy nꜣ-nfr·s (n) tꜣy·k špšy*
5. *(nꜣ-)nfr·s*[e] *n*[f] *nꜣ rmtw*[g] *nty ršy ỉw·w nw r·k.*[h] *wpy-s*[i] *ꜣst*
6. *tꜣ nbt (n) tꜣ grpyt*[j] *nty (r) ḏꜣḏꜣ·k. bn-ỉw*[k] *gꜣ*[l] *ntr bl·s*
7. *ỉ·ỉr*[m]*-sẖy (n) tꜣy·k dnỉt ḥry*[n]*. nts (tꜣ)*[o] *nty ḥrḥ pꜣ ḳḥy*
8. *(n) Kmy. bn-ỉw·k snt mšꜥ, Ḏḥwty ỉrm·k ỉw·f ꜥš n·k sẖ (n) dỉt n·k*[p]
9. *pꜣ ḏry pꜣ sbty (n) pꜣy·k mšꜥ pꜣ wḏꜣ (n) tꜣy·k dnỉt ḥry. ỉ·ỉr*
10. *pꜣy·k ꜥš-sḥn nty ỉy ẖr hrw*[q] *[[n pꜣ]][mn sp-sn] mn sp-sn*[r]
11. *(n) ṯꜣy ꜣst*[s]*. bw-ỉr·s wy r·k wnwt nbt ḏd mr·k-s. ẖpr ntk*[t]
12. *pꜣ šr (n) pꜣy·s šr. dỉ·s ẖpr sẖny-nfr nb*[u] *n-ỉm·k. dỉ·s ms·k*[v]
13. *⟨tpy ꜣḫt sw 12*[w]*⟩ pꜣ ḥb*[x] *ꜥꜣ (n) Ḏḥwty pꜣy·s ỉt. ḥr nfr ḥꜣty·s*[y] *n-ỉm·f ḥr rnpt*
14. *r-dbꜣ nꜣ mdt-nfrw ỉ·ỉr ẖpr n-ỉm·k(?)*[z] *pꜣ hrw rn·f⟨st sẖ ẖn(?)⟩*[aa] *nty ỉw pꜣ ꜥḥꜥ-*
15. *rd smn ⟨pꜣ sẖ⟩ ḥr rꜣ ⟨tꜣ gꜣ ḥrt⟩*[bb] *(n) tꜣ ḥt-ntr (n) Pr-Ḏḥwty*[cc] *ỉ·ỉr·ḥr*
16. *rmt nb (n) pꜣ tꜣ [ỉ·dỉ·k (n) Ḏḥwty pꜣ rẖ(?) ỉꜥḥ pꜣ ꜥnḫ pꜣ wr-dỉw hb]*[dd]*. ỉ·ỉr*
17. *nꜣy·k*[ee] *nꜣ rmtw*[g] *⟨nty ỉw·w⟩ ṯꜣy-sꜣb*[ff] *n-ỉm·k. ẖr ỉr r·k ꜣst tym mḥy*[gg] *nb*
18. *ỉw·s ḏd mꜣꜥt(?)*[hh] *ḏd ỉr·k ẖn nꜣ ntrw bn-ỉ·ỉr·k ẖn*
19. *nꜣ rmtw*[g] *ỉn. ⟨ntk⟩ ꜥꜣ (n) ḥꜣty·k. nfr nꜣy·k sḏy. snt·k tꜣ nty*
20. *[[tꜣ nty]] ḥr*[ii] *nꜣ ntrw. mtw·k ḥꜣty mnẖ*
21. *wbꜣ nꜣ rmtw. dỉ·k*[jj] *mn(?) pꜣ spy (n) tꜣy·k ỉwš*[kk]
22. *[ ]*[ll] *ỉr·k ẖꜣꜥ (n) ḥꜣty·k*[mm] *n ꜣst ⟨mdt nbt⟩ ỉr·k (n) gy*
23. *(n) ꜣst n gyl*[nn] *nb. bn-ỉw·k ꜥš*[oo] *n*
24. *ntr m-sꜣ ꜣst ỉw·s rẖ[·k]*[pp] *wꜥt·s*[qq]
25. *tꜣ wꜥt wꜥt·s tꜣy ỉ·snt(?)*
26. *ḥḥ wꜥ*[rr] *ỉr·s sḥn·k ỉrm*
27. *nꜣy·k ỉryw dr·w*[ss]

Text: verso

1. *ꜣst ỉn nꜣ sḥn(w)*[a] *(n) pꜣy·k šr n ḥt-ntr Mn-nfr ỉrm*
2. *nꜣy·f ẖrdw m-sꜣ·f ssw ḳy ỉw·f ꜥšꜣy m-šs*[b] *ỉ·ỉr·k*
3. *r šm*[c] *(n) ꜥwy ꜣst ỉw·s*[d] *dỉt wḏꜣ pꜣy·k ꜥḥꜥ ỉw·s dỉt nꜣy·k*
4. *ḏdy*[e] *ḥr rdwy·k*[f] *ỉw·s dỉt*[g] *n·k (n) pꜣy·s rn(?)*[h] *nꜣ nty tkn*[i]
5. *nꜣ tšw ỉ·ỉr·k*[j] *wḥꜣ ỉw·w ỉr n·k škr ẖr [ ]*[k]
6. *tꜣ wpt ꜣst tꜣ Pr-ꜥꜣt (n) tm(?) nb nty wꜣḥ-sḥn*
7. *(n) pꜣ tꜣ dr·f.*[l] *dỉ·ỉ sẖ tꜣy·ỉ nḥy*[m] *ḥr·w ꜥn.*[n]
8. *wn nꜣ mdt (ỉ·)ỉr·ỉ*[o] *ꜥn-smy (n) Hrynys n-ỉm·w*
9. *r-dbꜣ ḏd*[p] *n·ỉ (n) rswt tꜣ mdt *ta*[q] *pꜣ tr (ỉ·)wn-nꜣ Kmy*
10. *pnḳ n-ỉm·f (n) Rꜥ-ḳd. ḥnn*[r] *ꜣtyks ꜥws n*
11. *pr-mḥ Pr-ꜣwrys. bw-ỉr·tw Gryꜣ pꜣy·f rd*
12. *wy Mn-nfr n ḥꜣt-sp 13 ꜣbd-2 šmw sw 1. bn-pw Hry-*
13. *nys nḥt nꜣ mdt *na*[q] *r-hn*[s] *(r) šm*
14. *bl Pr-ỉr-ỉmn (ỉ·)ỉr ꜣtyks*[t] *ḥꜣt-sp 13 ꜣbd-3 šmw ꜥlḳy.*
15. *ỉ·ỉr Hrynys py*[u] *nꜣy ḥꜣt-sp 13 ꜣbd-3 šmw ꜥlḳy ỉ·*
16. *ỉr*[v] *ꜣmnys nty ẖn tꜣ hyty*[w] *ỉrm ꜣrk-*
17. *hrts*[x] *nty ḥr Mn-nfr [[pꜣ]] sẖ*[y] *nꜣ mšꜥw mdt nbt.*

[1] This text occasions difficulty in spite of its excellent preservation. Palimpsest writings (ll. 5, 10, and large parts of 15, 16, and 21) and the general obscurity of the phraseology must cast doubt upon many of the readings offered here,

18. *wn-nꜣ·w sẖ tꜣ šꜥt iw·s pḥ. di·w šꜥt rn·s*[z] (*n*) *Pr-ꜥꜣ* ⟨(*tꜣ*) *Pr-ꜥꜣt*⟩[aa]
19. *Ptwrmys*[bb] *irm·f* (*n*) *Pr-Wsir-Ḥp pꜣ ꜥꜣ nty n*
20. *Rꜥ-ḳd* (*n*) *ḥꜣt-sp 13 ꜣbd-3 šmw ꜥlḳy. mšꜥ Pr-ꜥꜣ*
21. (*r*) *Mn-nfr ḥr rdwy. mšꜥ Nwmnys*
22. (*r*) *Hrmꜣ*[cc]. *mšꜥ Tynys*
23. (*r*) *Pr-ir-'Imn. dwn-s*[dd] *nꜣ sẖw*
24. *bn-pw rmt ḏlꜥ-mdt*
25. (*n*) *pꜣ tr rn·f.*

Notes: recto

a. Inserted as an afterthought, and obscured by the dynastic epithet below; the final signs (*ꜥws*?) are particularly open to doubt.

b. On very close inspection both Smith and the present writer became convinced that the scribe had written , with the last sign representing the plural suffix, and the penultimate altered from ; perhaps the scribe had written *ꜥꜣy*, as at the beginning of Text **7**. For the dynastic epithets of Philometor, see Pestman, *Chronologie*, 48, where *nꜣ ntrw mr mwt·w* is shown to follow the marriage of the King with his sister, although not commonly used in dating-formulae during the reign. The reading acquires some confirmation from the mention of *Nwmnys* on l. 21 of the verso (q.v.). For the snake determinative to *sḥn* cf. l. 26 below, and the note to verso, l. 6.

c. Again the singular pronoun, showing that the recipient is really Philometor alone.

d. here seems to be a writing of the demonstrative pronoun ⲑⲁⲓ (sc. *rnpt*).

e. The omission of *nꜣ-* here is more likely to be due to the cursiveness of the scribe than to any difference of phonology or syntax.

f. A long sloping stroke, resembling *r*, which, however, fits the sense badly.

g. The cursive also in ll. 17 and 19, and in Text **1**, 5 (*nꜣ rmtw ꜥꜣy*). Extreme abbreviation of this sort is characteristic of this hand, which is perhaps to be considered that of Ḥor himself.

h. A clear example of *nty* as a non-limiting relative, a sense frequently denied to it. The sense presumably is that all men look upon Pharaoh, not that only the section of the populace who choose to do so are happy.

i. The metaphor of 'opening' a year is clear enough from the early *wpt-rnpt* (*Wb.* i. 300) and in the 'new year formula', *wp* DN *rnpt nfrt n* NN. Its use suggests that we are here dealing with a greeting addressed upon an anniversary of some sort. For similar examples cf. Pap. Loeb 4, 2–3, and Erichsen, *Schulübung* (1947), 13 ('Schön sei dir das Jahr, dein Jahr sei schön').

j. See note *z* to the translation of Text **1** above, p. 14: the snake determinative appears here as in *wꜣḥ-sḥn* (note to verso, l. 6).

k. The palimpsest here has *Pr-ꜥꜣ*.

l. An alternative writing of *ky*, cf. Erichsen, *Glossar*, 570 and 558.

m. The preceding *bn-iw* suggests that, if we discount the possibility that the scribe has added a futuristic *r* into the construction, we are dealing with a writing of the infinitive alone. The answer, as often in these texts, perhaps lies in the later Bohairic dialect, when *ir-šhy* preserves an initial vowel (ⲉⲣϣⲓϣⲓ, Crum, 59b); Sahidic has lost this vowel from the construct infinitive ⲣ̄.

n. The phrase also in Text **4**, R° 6, where it clearly refers to the Ptolemaic kingdom. The metaphor of 'portion, inheritance' for *dni̓t* is clear enough, but the use of *ḥry* is less comprehensible; perhaps it carries the meaning 'derived from above (or from the forefathers)', or it may simply mean 'supreme', cf. Tanis Stela, 8, where *tꜣ iꜣwt ḥryt* in the demotic version corresponds to *iꜣt·f wrt* in the hieroglyphic, and in l. 15 (*nꜣ rmtw*) *nty ḥr tꜣy·f iꜣwt ḥry* corresponds to *m ndy n ḥm·f*, while in l. 21 the hieroglyphic translation reads *iꜣwt·sn n ḥkꜣ-tꜣwy*.

o. Presumably omitted by haplography.

p. Perhaps modelled on the idea of contracts such as the *sẖ n sꜥnḫ* (Lüddeckens, *Eheverträge*, 8), though hardly likely to be a technical term itself.

q. From this point much of the text is obscured by the palimpsest which here has *nꜣy*.

r. Very difficult. The first writing of *mn* (which often occurs in these texts preceded by) seems to have been a failure in the scribe's eyes, and he has written *mn sp-sn* again beyond the smudged area. The traces between *hrw* and *mn*, which may correspond to *n pꜣ* (?) make little sense (unless we attempt to read *pꜣ nty mn sp-sn*, which is very awkward), and should perhaps be disregarded, but without excessive confidence.

s. It is presumably this phrase which is emphasized by the Second Present of l. 9, end.

t. At this point the alternative *ḫpr mtw·k pꜣ šr* (*n*) *pꜣy·s šr*, 'there has been born in your possession (ⲛ̄ⲧⲁⲕ) the son of her son', i.e. a reference to the promised child of Text **1**, is full of interest, but extremely awkward syntactically, and has been rejected here. The genealogy here (Thoth–Isis–Horus–Pharaoh) is of great significance, see below, note *h* to the translation.

u. This position of *nb* shows that *sẖny-nfr* is to be regarded as a compound, such as *mdt-nfrt*, and perhaps *sḥn-nfr* above.

v. Here again it is tempting to take this as transitive, 'she has caused you to give birth' (to the promised son), but there are very grave grammatical objections to this meaning of *ⲙⲉⲥⲓⲟⲕ, and the general context suggests that we are celebrating the birthday of Philometor himself. See below, note to translation.

w. Inserted: the same date, also described as 'the festival of Thoth', occurs in Text **8**, R° 1, and in both instances doubt exists whether *sw 15* should not be read instead of *sw 12*, particularly so as the fifteenth day in the old lunar calendar, upon which religious ceremonies were still based, would be the day of the full moon, and thus ideal for a festival of Thoth.[1] But neither the writings in Erichsen, *Glossar*, 708–9, nor the unpublished Serapeum papyrus (see above, p. 9, note *h* to Text **1**) support the reading, and *sw 12* has been read here. The festival of Thoth, which I have been unable to trace in other sources, may of course have lasted from day 12 until, or even beyond, the fifteenth day of the month which bore his name.

x. See note to the writing in Text **8**, R° 1.

y. The small stroke immediately before this word seems to have no meaning.

z. The scribe may perhaps have written *ꜣst*, upon filling his pen, and then altered the word.

aa. An insertion, apparently abandoned and replaced by *pꜣ sẖ* in the line below.

bb. Extremely obscure, especially the signs at the end here taken as the feminine ending of *ḥrt*.

cc. Here, as in Text **23**, R° 2, clearly the cult-buildings associated with the ibis-galleries at Saqqâra. The writing here casts a certain doubt on our reading *Pr-Ḏḥwty* for a different group above (Text **1**, 1 and note *ad locum*, p. 8), a doubt which we can explain only by assuming a different pronunciation of *Pr* (*ⲫⲓⲏ for ⲡⲓ or the like), or a differing tradition of writing; the latter is perhaps more likely.

dd. Almost entirely obscured by erasures, and the palimpsest which here has *ỉ·ỉr pꜣy·k* (altered to *nꜣy·k*) *nꜣ rmtw* as in the text for the following line. The text is given with all reserve, and even the syntax is dubious.

ee. Presumably a writing of the possessive pronoun ⲛⲟⲩⲕ; but the syntax is again far from certain.

ff. See note to Text **1**, 3, above.

gg. Both *tym* (ⲧⲁⲉⲓⲙ) and *mḥy* (ⲙⲟⲉⲓϩⲉ, Crum, 211b) were suggested by Smith.

hh. Very dubious: *mdt* would be a better reading, were it not for the absurdity of **ỉw·s ḏd mdt ḏd*.

ii. The second phrase seems to be dittography; for the idiom, see Text **2**, R° 14 and note.

jj. The palimpsest, which again obscures the text, shows traces of a determinative .

kk. *rwš* has also been written, and it is an open question which is the palimpsest; *ỉwš* has the advantage of serving as a support for *tꜣy·k*.

ll. I regret that I cannot read these traces: *my* is hardly likely.

mm. *šm* is possible, but weak, but the sense of this clause is rather elusive. *ḥꜣꜥ* is perhaps best taken as Qualitative after *ỉr·k*; (*n*) must then be understood before *ḥꜣty·k*.

nn. ϭⲟⲉⲓⲗⲉ (Crum, 808a), in the meaning 'stranger'. A paronomasia may be intended with *gy* above.

oo. The group looks suspiciously like *ky*, which may have been written (it is difficult otherwise to account for *·k* at the top of the line); but this leaves no verb for the sentence, and we have already seen one instance of *ky* already in this text, written as *gꜣ*. The text as given, however, is far from being thought certain.

pp. This *·k* can hardly be the object pronoun, for the circumstantial would normally require **n-ỉm·k*; we are forced to conclude that this is the old first person ending of the Qualitative, perhaps no longer pronounced and misapplied to the third person feminine (Spiegelberg, *Grammatik*, § 98, end). A reading *kt*, involving the sign in the following line read *tꜣy*, is possible, but rather unconvincing: one would expect from Text **10** a feminine *t* to follow.

qq. Reading suggested by Smith.

rr. The initial group in the line presents difficulties: it occurs frequently in Text **18**, and in line 16 of the recto the name of the necropolis of Abydos, *ꜥlḳ-ḥḥ* (Ἀλχαί) contains the group as its second element. The reading *ḥḥ* is therefore proposed here, but it must be admitted that this will not suit all its appearances in our texts, and the identification is open to serious doubt.

[1] Cf. Parker, *Calendars*, 13 ff., and O. Neugebauer and A. Volten, *Quellen und Studien zur Geschichte der Mathematik*, Abt. B, Band 4 (Berlin, 1938), 383–406 (Pap. Carlsberg 9).

The juxtaposition of *ḥḥ* and *wʿ* is abrupt, but perhaps acceptable.

ss. A slight anacoluthon: *pꜣ sẖn n nꜣy·k ỉryw dr·w* would be the full version. *sẖn* from the determinative is more likely to be a noun in its own right than an infinitive used nominally.

Notes: verso

a. More likely plural of *sẖn* with unwritten plural ending, cf. Erichsen, *Glossar*, 446, than a feminine *tꜣ sẖn*(*t*).

b. A clear parallel to Text **1**, 16–17: q.v.

c. Presumably an example of the extremely rare Second Future, cf. Rylands IX, 6/1; 6/6; 13/19.

d. More likely a reading than *wꜣḥ·s*.

e. ϫⲁϫⲉ (Crum, 799b); for the notion, cf. Rosettana, 1, where *nty ḥr pꜣy·f ḏdy* corresponds to ἀντιπάλων ὑπέρτερος.

f. A parallel to this phrase below in Text **7**, 8–9.

g. Note two entirely different writings of *dỉt* within the same line.

h. Not palaeographically certain, and it must be admitted that *pꜣy·s rn* is a strange substitute for *rn·s*, but I can suggest no other reading.

i. *tg*[ ] is visible (perhaps corresponding to ⲧⲱϭⲛ?), but the restoration is merely conjecture.

j. A writing of the relative with *r*, though why the scribe should avoid *(*ỉ·*)*wẖꜣ·k* is unknown. For *škr* (ϣϭⲟⲣ) see Thompson, *JEA* 26 (1941), 71.

k. The final sign seems to resemble *pḥ*, but I cannot interpret the other traces. *rnpt* is a faint possibility after *ẖr*.

l. A parallel to this entire phrase in Text **10**, 16–17. The problem occurs in the group which is written after *Pr-ʿꜣt* in both these examples. The reading proposed here is tentative; see Appendix 1 for a list of the epithets conferred upon Isis in our documents.

m. This seems to be a rather garbled writing of a word which occurs clearly in Text **29**, 9, where it seems to correspond to the hieroglyphic *nḥt* 'plea, prayer', especially in the well-known divine epithet *sḏm nḥwt* ascribed to Ptaḥ and other gods from the New Kingdom onwards (*Wb*. ii. 289). The reading *tꜣy·ỉ* is conjectured: the scribe seems at one stage to have written *ḏd·ỉ*, or even *gꜣy* (?).

n. *nb* may also be possible here, though syntactically awkward, and the entire line is questionable in the extreme.

o. Cf. Text **2**, R° 7 and V° 6 above.

p. Presumably infinitive. The following *tꜣ mdt *ta* may have been connected to this in speech by a genitival particle *n*; if so *ḏd n rswt* is to be regarded as a complete phrase in itself.

q. See above, p. 16 for note on Text **2**, R° 10.

r. Difficult: *ẖnš*, 'stink' though excellent as a piece of propaganda, is not otherwise convincing; the suggestion of Smith, that we are dealing with a descendant of 'rage', is perhaps confirmed by the survival of Bohairic ϧⲉⲛⲓ = μάχεσθαι (Crum, 603b).

s. A better reading than *hrw*. The lack of article (not paralleled in Spiegelberg, *Grammatik*, §§ 46–8) could perhaps be explained by treating **hrw n šm* as an entire phrase, rather like *hrw nfr* and the like, but this is not convincing.

t. Concluded with the mere ending of a cartouche, see above, Text **2**, V° 8 and note *ff*, p. 17.

u. The group is to be taken either as a writing of the old verb *siꜣ* 'perceive' (*Wb*. iv. 30), which is not yet attested in demotic, or as an abbreviated spelling of *p*(*t*)*ry* 'behold' (cf. the group in Erichsen, *Glossar*, 136). Either fits the sense, but the latter is preferred here.

v. An astonishing piece of hyphen-work!

w. The same group occurs in a damaged context in Fragment **39**, 2. The reading therefore seems clear enough, but the interpretation is difficult, and the choice must be made between

(i) ϩⲁⲉⲓⲧ 'forecourt' (⟨*ḥꜣyt*[*y*], *Wb*. ii. 476)
(ii) ϩⲟⲩⲏⲧ 'sail' (⟨*ḥtꜣw*, *Wb*. iii. 182)
(iii) the reading *nꜣ ḥꜣw* (*pꜣ*) *dmỉ* 'the environs of the city'.

Possibility (iii) is difficult to maintain palaeographically, while (ii) is phonetically difficult and is hard to reconcile with the preposition *ẖn*. We are left with (i). Much the same problem, but with a different solution, is confronted by A. Volten in his *Ägypter und Amazonen* (Vienna, 1962), 77. It is possible that the title *nty ẖn tꜣ hyty* is the later counterpart of the older *smsw hꜣyt*; it is not easy to find a Greek counterpart for such an official, unless he is to be sought in the ἀρχεδέατρος, who was in charge of the reception of strangers at the Ptolemaic Court; but no equivalent for *ꜣmnys* is to be found in the *Prosopographia Ptolemaica*.

x. *ꜣrkmḳrts* is also possible, but less likely.

y. The preceding *ỉ·ỉr* requires a verb here, and the *pꜣ* before *sẖ* therefore becomes redundant.

z. This phrase conversely requires the insertion of *tꜣ*.

aa. Inserted, and very faint; *tꜣ* is entirely conjectural.

bb. The scribe seems to have begun the name *Hrynys*, which he altered. The result resembles the name *Hrmys*, but this is presumably accidental.

cc. Identified by the writing in Graffito Philae 416, l. 18 (Griffith, *Graffiti of Dodecaschoenus*, i. 114–15); cf. the title *Hrmꜣys Kysrs* = ʽΡωμαῖος Καίσαρ(ος) in the Ptolemaic chapel at Kalabsha (De Meulenaere and Dewachter, *Chapelle ptolemaïque de Kalabcha*, i, 2, and Spiegelberg, *ZÄS* 49 (1911), 86–7).

dd. With resumptive *-s* as in Spiegelberg, *Grammatik*, § 263. The reading *ḥn-s* (cf. Text **21**, R° 10) is also possible (ibid. § 262), but fits the determinative less convincingly.

Translation: recto

1. Pharaoh Ptolemy, our lord, the master of Egypt, and
2. Queen ⟨Cleopatra⟩, the gods who love their mother, who wear the diadem[a] in Alexandria: favourable to you[b]
3. is the year. Your favourable year is every year which comes, (and) favourable to you
4. is this among them. It is favourable for your fate, and favourable for your fortune,[c]
5. (and) it is favourable for men, who rejoice when they look upon you. It has been opened by Isis,[d]
6. the lady of the diadem which is (upon) your head. No other god but she shall
7. exercise authority (over) your supreme inheritance.[e] (For) she is (the one) who keeps watch over the territory
8. (of) Egypt. You shall not fear the multitude,[f] (for) Thoth is with you,[g] reading to you a document of giving to you
9. the might (and) the readiness of your army, (and) the salvation of your supreme inheritance.[e]
10. Your fortune which comes with every day is lasting, lasting, (?)
11. from Isis. She is not far from you (at) any hour, for you love her: it happens (that) you are
12. the son of her son.[h] She has caused all good fortune to befall you. She has caused you to be born
13. (on) ⟨Thoth, day 12,⟩[i] the great festival of Thoth, her father.[j] For her heart is continually favourable upon it[k] with every year,
14. because of the benefits which have befallen you (?) upon the day named ⟨they are written ·····⟩ whose confirmation
15. is established ⟨in writing⟩ upon the gateway ⟨(of) the upper chapel⟩ of the temple of the House-of-Thoth[l] before
16. every man on earth, (namely) that which you have given to Thoth [the wise, (the) moon, the living one (?), (the) Ibis].[m] (For)
17. yours are the men ⟨who⟩ receive instruction from you. Isis constantly makes for you all reverence and esteem (?)
18. saying, 'You are among the gods: you are not among
19. men.' ⟨You⟩ are great in your heart[n]: happy are your counsels: you revere that which concerns
20. [[that which concerns]] the gods.[n] You have a beneficent heart
21. towards men. You have caused to endure the remainder (of) your endowment[o]
22. [·······] You are abandoned (in) your heart to Isis ⟨in every matter⟩. You are of the like
23. (of) Isis to every stranger. You shall not call to
24. (any) god except Isis, (for) she is wise alone,
25. the one alone[p] is she, whom multitudes
26. revere (as) one (?).[q] She has made your diadem,[a] together with (that of)
27. all your companions.

Translation: verso

1. Isis has brought the diadem(s) to your son[a] in the temple of Memphis[b] together with
2. his children after him for very many lengthy days.[c] It is to the arms of Isis

3. that you shall go,[d] for she causes the salvation of your lifetime, and she places your
4. enemies beneath your feet,[e] and she gives to you of her own accord (?) those who encroach (?) (upon)
5. the frontiers, (those) whom you desire to pay you tribute[f] in the matter of [· · · · ·]
6. the business of Isis, the Queen of all entirety, who wears the diadem (in)
7. the entire land.
I have caused to be written my (?) plea in connection with them again.[g]
8. Account of the matters (which) I reported to *Hrynys*
9. because of the *said matters' being told to me (in) a dream,[h] at the time (when) Egypt
10. divorced itself (from) Alexandria. *ꜣtyks* fought to
11. the north of *Pr-ꜣwrys.*[i] *Gryꜣ*, his agent,
12. had not yet left Memphis in Year 13, Paoni, day 1.[j] *Hrynys* did not
13. believe the *said matters until the withdrawal
14. from Pelusium[k] (which) *ꜣtyks* made in Year 13, Paoni, final day.[l]
15. (But) on Year 13, Epeiph, final day, *Hrynys* perceived these things.
16. *ꜣmnys*[m] who is in the forecourt[n] and *ꜣrk-*
17. *hrts*[o] who is over Memphis[p] wrote the account of the journeyings[q] in every detail.
18. They wrote the letter which is pertinent.[r] They gave[s] (the) letter named to Pharaoh ⟨(and the) Queen⟩,
19. (and) Ptolemy with him[t] (in) the Great Serapeum which is in
20. Alexandria, (in) Year 13, Epeiph, final day. Pharaoh journeyed
21. (to) Memphis immediately. *Nwmnys* journeyed
22. (to) Rome.[u] *Tynys*[v] journeyed
23. (to) Pelusium. The scribes arose,
24. (but) no man recorded matters
25. (at) the time named.[w]

Notes: recto

a. Or 'exercise authority'; a similar metaphor occurs with *sḫn·k* in l. 26.

b. Masculine singular.

c. The *šꜣy* and the *špšy*, literally the personified destiny and the uraeus-goddess of the Pharaoh, are widely used as personifications of the ἀγαθὸς δαίμων of the King. For a possible bronze counterpart as two male and female serpents, cf. Kaiser, *Ägyptisches Museum Berlin* (Berlin, 1967), no. 997 and note. *Pꜣ šꜣy* as a deity is dealt with by Griffith, *Dodecaschoenus*, i. 12 (with *špšy*), and for *špšy* (ϣⲁⲡϣⲓ) as an epithet of Isis, cf. *Wb.* iv. 450. See further Appendix 1 below.

d. The use of this formula suggests an anniversary (see textual note *i* above), which would be either new year, the anniversary of the accession (cf. *Canopus*, l. 5), or Pharaoh's birthday, when his γενέθλια would be celebrated (cf. *Tanis Stela*, 7–8; 27). The reference in l. 13 below leaves us in little doubt that the latter is referred to here, the more so as in the Canopus Stela *wpt-rnpt* is used, via the connection with *mswt-Rʿ*, to refer to this event.

e. See above, note to Text *ad locum.*

f. Possibly in a military significance (note to Text **2**, V° 12, above) or simply in an imaginary one ('even a multitude').

g. One is immediately reminded of a temple scene in which the god stands before Pharaoh, declaring *di·n·i n·k nḫtw ḥr ḫꜣst nbt* or the like; a scene such as this may well have figured on the walls of Philometor's shrine at Saqqâra, where it would certainly have been familiar to the writer.

h. The notion is much more that Philometor is to be regarded as son and heir of Horus, than, presumably, that Epiphanes is to be hailed as this god; the reign of Philometor's predecessor can hardly have been a happy memory for those engaged in the ibis-cult, cf. Text **19**, R° 13–15.

i. For the possibility of 'day 15', see above, note *w* to the text. The date of Philometor's birthday was unknown before, but if we are right in assuming that he was aged three or four on his father's death (Otto, *Geschichte des 6. Ptolemäers*, 1–23; reviewed by Skeat and Bell, *JEA* 21 (1935), 263, n. 1, where Epiphanes' death is calculated by means of Ostracon Tait Bodleian 96 of 20 May 180), then his date of birth was probably 19 October 184 (or, less likely, 183). I know of little evidence to support Griffith's belief (*Rylands*, iii. 141) that he was born in 186, but if this is correct, the Julian date would fall one day later. This notion is presumably derived from a desire to increase Philometor's age on marriage, but as this seems to have been brought forward by the party planning the invasion of Coele-Syria, respectable age would probably have been sacrificed to efficiency. See below, note to Text **19**, R° 15, and Koenen, *Archiv Pap.* 17, i (1960), 13 n. 2.

j. The juxtaposition of two cult centres, one of Isis, one of Thoth, at North Saqqâra may have led to this belief, in which Thoth plays the role usually assigned to Geb. It may, however, have been prompted by a related idea, for the Aretalogy of Cyme, which is expressly said to be taken from a Memphite source, has in line 3b, καὶ ἐπαιδεύθην ὑπὸ Ἑρμοῦ (Bergman, *Ich bin Isis*, 301). The notion of Hermes (Thoth) as tutor of Isis may well have developed into the statement that he was her father,[1] a notion which persists into the Hermetic Corpus. It is therefore extremely interesting that Plutarch, writing almost three centuries after our present text, should have recognized this tradition, cf. *De Iside et Osiride*, 3, 352A (where it is said to be commonly, but not exclusively held), 12, 355F; see the note in the edition of J. Gwyn Griffiths (Cardiff, 1970), 263–4.

k. More likely than towards him (i.e. Thoth), although the syntax has become a little tortuous.

l. Philometor's benefits to the temples of Egypt, and particularly of Saqqâra, are a common theme of our texts (cf. Text **2** above, and Texts **7**, **19** below). This is a welcome confirmation of the character portrait given in Polybius XXXIX, 7, and both Ḥor's emphasis on the piety of Philometor, and the constant suppression of his brother, should be read in this light.[2] It is possible that *ḥr rꜣ* may mean simply 'at the entrance' of the shrine; the reference would then be to a donation stela, erected before the temple.

m. Extremely doubtful, see note to the Text *ad loc.*

n. cf. Text **2**, R° 14: *pꜣ ꜥw n tꜣ nty ḥr nꜣ ntrw n ḥꜣty·k*. The alternative reading *ỉrt*, though attractive, is palaeographically unlikely.

o. Possibly a reference to the donations, which we know to have been inscribed at the entrance to the ibis-shrine. But the context is not certain.

p. A common epithet of Isis, surviving in the Greek θιουῖν (Bergman, *Ich bin Isis*, 225, 281 ff.). See Appendix 1 below.

q. Syntax very difficult, and translation offered with hesitancy.

Notes: verso

a. The difficulty here is whether Ḥor is giving rein to his imagination, or whether he is describing a real event; in the latter case, it would seem that the reference is to an inauguration ceremony, possibly the ἀνακλητήρια, of Philometor's son and heir. This possibility must be taken seriously. The eldest known son of Philometor and Cleopatra, Ptolemy surnamed Eupator, who is probably the son listed in Greek Graffito Philae, no. 12 (A. Bernand, *Inscriptions Grecques de Philae*, i. 121–6, and extensive bibliography quoted there), is a shadowy figure, who predeceased his father (hence the confusion over the placing of his name in the dynastic lists, sometimes before, sometimes after Philometor). Pap. Rylands 16, of 28 March 152, gives the earliest known date at which the two appear together as sovereigns, but Eupator appears earlier, in 158/7 as an eponymous priest at Alexandria (Griffith, *Rylands*, iii. 141; IJsewijn, *De Sacerdotibus*, 49, no. 129; 108, no. 128). Now it would seem plausible that this honour was the initial step in the 'grooming' of Eupator for eventual kingship (cf. Glanville and Skeat, *JEA* 40 (1954), 52–3), and that the appointment would have been accompanied by a proclamation of some kind. This would perhaps have happened in 158, although the age of Eupator at the time is open to considerable doubt: Pap. Louvre 2329 (Wilcken, *UPZ*, no. 110) is dated to 21 September 164, and reports that the King, the Queen, Ptolemy 'the Brother', and the τέκνα are alive and flourishing. Whether the word τέκνα includes, or even implies, a son, is a question which reasserts itself in Greek Graffito Philae 35 (A. Bernand, op. cit. 252, and the observation quoted in connection with no. 48, p. 294); the conclusion seems to be that it is not implied. If so, the τέκνα are daughters, including Cleopatra Thea, and no son has yet been born.[3] A possible date

[1] One is reminded of the role of Nectanebus in the Alexander Romances, although here the idea of fatherhood is presumed to come before the tutorship; see Cary, *The Mediaeval Alexander* (Cambridge, 1956), and Merkelbach, 'Die Quellen des griechischen Alexanderromans', *Zetemata*, ix (Munich, 1954), where the possibility of an Egyptian popular tradition is seriously entertained. Fraser, *Ptolemaic Alexandria*, i. 4 and n. 10, supports a similar possibility, at least with regard to the tradition of the foundation of Alexandria.

[2] Such vindication of an ancient tradition may perhaps add strength to Bevan's remarks on the character of Ptolemy VIII Euergetes, cf. *Egypt under the Ptolemies*, 323–4.

[3] This would add an interesting touch to the last words of Text **1**, 'the confirmation of this is when the Queen bears a *male* child', but perhaps this sort of impatience is out of place in an oracle.

for Eupator's birth will be proposed below, in Text **5**, but whatever the truth of this (the epigram Palatine Anthology, vii. 241 is hardly conclusive), the date of 158 B.C. for our ostracon would be very appropriate. It is known that in October 158 Ptolemy Philometor visited the Memphite Serapeum, continuing his journey as far as Philae (Lepsius, *Denkmäler*, iv. 23); it is therefore very tempting to think that our present encomium was written for the king's birthday on 13 October 158.[1] This, however, should not be pressed too closely, for the writer is clearly paraphrasing the contents of the dream in Text **1**, even to the use of the same phrase beginning *ssw ḳy* ....., and he may therefore be indulging in wishful thinking; but it will be wishful thinking indulged in after December 159, when the final interpretation of the dream was reported to the great men, and this adds some weight to our chronology.

b. The traditional site of the crowning of Pharaoh, cf. Bergman, *Ich bin Isis*, 95 ff. The example of conforming to this Egyptian rite had already been set by Epiphanes, in 197/6 (Bevan, 260); a similar tradition concerning Alexander the Great is perhaps to be discounted (Skeat, *Reigns of the Ptolemies*, 27, n. 1).

c. Text **1**, R° 16–17; general considerations of context suggest that it is the present text which borrows the phrase.

d. Possibly on death, but perhaps merely as a metaphor of Isis as protecting deity, as often in her winged form on sarcophagus or shrine.

e. Again a motif common in Egyptian art, from the footstools of the New Kingdom onwards, cf. Rühlmann in *Wiss. Z. Martin-Luther Univ.* 20, 2 (1971), 61–84.

f. It is again difficult to see whether a specific event, such as the invasion of Coele-Syria, or the long dispute over the dowry of Cleopatra I, is intended here; probably not, as the memory of such happenings would hardly be suitable for recall, and the writer is determined to win the good will of the King.

g. Clearly the beginning of an entirely new section, which will narrate the historical circumstances of the writer's career, and the nature of his grievances, as in the opening sections of Pap. Rylands IX.

h. For the rather involved syntax see note *p* to the Text above.

i. See above, Text **1**, 7. This place-name is quite unknown, but clearly divides into the familiar *Pr-*, and a foreign name *ꜣwrys*. Skeat and Smith have made the very interesting suggestion that this latter element should be identified with Εὐλαῖος, the eunuch and tutor of the young Philometor.[2] This is plausible, as we know that Eulaeus and his accomplice Lenaeus succeeded in having coins struck in their own names, and from this dramatic act the naming of a city would be a small step. The main objection to this idea is that it is extremely unlikely that such a place-name (*Εὐλαίου πόλις?) would have survived the fiasco at Pelusium and the disgrace of Eulaeus; one would be driven to assume that Ḥor was relying on his memories of 168, and had since fallen out of touch. In this case he will have committed a *faux pas* of the first magnitude, an idea which does not commend itself.

No less easy to determine is the location of this place: Mount Kasion, near the scene of the Egyptian defeat in November, 170, is a candidate, but it is generally more likely that *Pr-ꜣwrys* lay near Alexandria, perhaps to the east of the city, for we known from Polybius that in June 168 Antiochus was encamped near Eleusis. This area is described to us by Strabo (XVII, 16 ff.). No *Pr-ꜣwrys* is mentioned, and this is not surprising, but in addition to Eleusis two smaller towns, Taposiris and Nicopolis, are described on a bar between the canal which led to the promontory of Zephyrium. Had Antiochus been to the north (*pr-mḥ*) of any of these, whether encamped or engaged in hostilities (*ḫnn*?), he would have been on the coast where he met the Roman envoys. The possibility that *Pr-ꜣwrys* was in some way an Egyptian name of Eleusis should equally be borne in mind.

j. Not 'day 11', as in the parallel account in Text **2**, which is likely to be the correct reading on the basis of *lectio difficilior*.

k. For the Egyptian name of Pelusium (ⲡⲉⲣⲉⲙⲟⲩⲛ), see Spiegelberg, *ZÄS* 57 (1922), 69; also Gardiner, *JEA* 5 (1918), 255–6, and Gauthier-Sottas, *Décret trilingue*, 26–7. Its importance as a frontier-station is well shown by its appearance, under its older name Si'nu, in the account of Asshurbanipal's invasion (Luckenbill, *Ancient Records of Assyria*, ii, § 876; see too P. M. Fraser, *Ptolemaic Alexandria*, ii. 196, n. 115). The most detailed discussion is still to be found in

[1] It must be admitted that a long and querulous complaint, for such the final document was almost certainly intended to be, is not a very suitable birthday-present, particularly if, like Apollonios, Ḥor chose to throw his petition through the window of the palace at the Anubieion. But such are the hazards of power.

[2] *Prosopographia Ptolemaica*, no. 14602. Contrary to general supposition, the man seems to have been a Macedonian, not an Oriental, cf. L. Robert in *Gnomon*, 35 (1963), 71–6 and P. M. Fraser, *Ptolemaic Alexandria*, ii. 211, n. 212.

Fontaine, 'Enquête sur Péluse', in *Bull. de la Soc. d'Études de l'Isthme de Suez*, 4 (1912), 17–80.

l. The date (30 July 168) is very close to Bevan's estimated June or July of the same year.

m. Apparently = Ἀμμώνιος; Preisigke, 26.

n. = ἀρχεδέατρος? See note to the text above.

o. Ἀρχιλαΐδας (Preisigke, 59) is possible, but not certain.

p. Presumably (unless the expression refers merely to his place of residence) as *strategos*; not given in *Prosopographica Ptolemaica*.

q. Probably more of a reference to the movements named below than to the retreat of Antiochus.

r. An idiomatic use of *pḥ* (cf. πετπηϩ, Crum, 282a) illustrated in *Rosettana*, 20, where *nꜣ mdt pḥ* (*n*) *nꜣ r-pyw* corresponds to τὰ τῶν ἱερῶν τιμιώτατα.

s. Probably passive, since the implication of Text **2** is that Ḥor himself gave the letter to the Pharaohs.

t. see note *bb* to the Text, above. The reference, without a cartouche or any other mark of distinction, is probably to 'the Brother'.

u. Polybius XXX, 16. This is the earliest reference to Rome known from an Egyptian text, and provides a confirmation of the dating of the events.

v. Possibly Δεινίας (Preisigke, 84), or conceivably Διονύσιος, a name which is known to have caused demotic scribes some trouble. A Dionysius τῶν φιλῶν is known from *Prosopographica Ptolemaica* (242 and 244) as *strategos* at Memphis in 163–161/0, but this may be coincidence.

w. A remarkably obscure statement. The writer may have in mind that no record of his own part in these events was made during this time, and he is therefore obliged to rely upon his memory.

Preliminary Remarks

This text divides into two parts: the first, covering the recto and the first lines of the verso, is perhaps to be interpreted as an encomium to Ptolemy VI, written for his birthday on 13 October 158, after the installation of the Crown Prince as priest of Alexander. The second part, the remaining lines of the verso, is the beginning of a plea or petition, showing the part played by the author in the events of Antiochus' invasion ten years earlier. This account is a rewriting of the similar lines in Text **2**, dating retrospectively to Philometor alone (thus introducing the fictitious 'Year 13'), and suppressing all reference to the other Ptolemy. The author is unnamed, but from internal evidence is very likely to be Ḥor, and the general similarity to the very abbreviated writings of the Rosetta Stone suggests that the hand is a Delta one, probably that of the narrator himself.

TEXT 4

Height	19·1 cm.
Width	15·4 cm.
Thickness	0·75 cm.
Munsell	5 YR 6/3
Photograph	Plate V (R°, V°)
Facsimile	Plate VA (R°, V°)
Excavator's no.	G7–37 [466]

A pinkish ostracon, taken from the side of a round vessel, inscribed on the exterior (recto) with twenty lines of demotic, excessively faded, especially in the central parts, and containing many erasures. All except the last seven lines bear diagonal ticks at their beginnings, perhaps made when the text was being copied on to papyrus. The verso bears faint traces only, written horizontally across the sherd, and 'ruled off' with a broad diagonal stroke. The fading exhibited by this ostracon has caused much difficulty.

Text: recto

1. *wn tꜣ šꜥt ỉ·ỉr-s*[a] *Hrynys* (*ỉ·*)*wn-nꜣ sꜣtrks*
2. *ḥtr n Pr-ꜥꜣ ỉrm tꜣ Pr-ꜥꜣt ỉw·f prty*[b] *r·ỉ r-dbꜣ nꜣ mdt*
3. (*ỉ·*)*ỉr·ỉ ꜥn-smy n·f n-ỉm·w*[c] *n ḥꜣt-sp 13 ꜣbd-3 šmw* [ ][d] [*pꜣ tr*(?)]
4. (*ỉ·*)*wn-nꜣ* [*Kmy pnḳ n-ỉm·f n*] *Rꜥ-ḳd*[e]: *tw-s*[f] *nꜣ mšꜥw mdt nbt*
5. *swn* [ ].[g] *tꜣ nty ṯꜣy*[h] *pꜣ šr ꜥꜣ* (*n*) *Pr-ꜥꜣ ḏd ỉw·w* (*r*) *ms-f*[i]

6. *iw·f (r) dìt wꜣḥ gꜣj tš n tꜣy·f dnìt ḥry.*[k] *tꜣ nty ṯꜣy*[l] *pꜣ wḏꜣ (n) Rꜥ-ḳd*
7. *ḏd ìw·f*[m] *smn ḥr pꜣy·f* [ ] *sḥn* [ ] *nb. tꜣ nty ṯꜣy*
8. *nꜣ mšꜥw ꜣtyks* [*ꜥws*][n] *ḏd ì·ìr·f šm r-bl*
9. *Kmy*[o] [ ] *tꜣ nty ṯꜣy*[p] *nꜣ skrw Pr-ꜥꜣ ḏd ìw·f (r) šm*
10. *(r) tꜣ mꜣy (n) pꜣ ym ìw·f ꜣrꜥ*[q] *(n) Rꜥ-ḳd ḥꜣty·f nfr.*
11. *tꜣ nty ṯꜣy pꜣ ꜣbd (n) gmꜥ(?)*[r] *ḏd bn-ìw pꜣ šr* [ ][s] *n-ḏrt* · · · · · *ꜥn*[t]
12. [ ] *wꜣḥ-sḥn* [ ] *tꜣ nty ṯꜣy*
13. *tꜣ dnìt ḥry* [ ][u]
14. *pꜣ tr mdt* [*wꜣḥ·s*][v] *n-ìm·f.*
15. *ꜥḥꜥ·ì ìrm ꜣrstn nty ẖn* · · · · ·[w]
16. *tꜣ nty ṯꜣy* [ ] *ḏd* [ ][x]
17. [ ]
18. [ ][y] *ḥꜣty·k* [ ]
19. *ìw·f šsp drt·ì* [ ]
20. [ ].

No connected sense is available from the traces on the verso.

Notes

a. The use of a resumptive pronoun seems strange here, and one wonders whether *ì·ìr n·ì* is not intended, but the writing seems clear, even to the small stroke (*r*) of *ì·ìr*.

b. An unknown word: *ḳrty* would be a possible reading, were it not for the fact that the word recurs clearly written in Text **17**, R° 6–7 *nꜣw ì·dì·f ꜥꜣy nꜣ ì·ìr gmꜥ r·f, nꜣw ì·ìr·f prty nꜣ ì·ìr ḫꜣꜥ tꜣ mìt*, 'those whom he made great are the ones who caused groaning against him, those whom he made *prty* are the ones who abandoned the path'. The parallelism makes clear the rough meaning of the word, which may share the root *prì*, 'forthcoming', cf. Latin *eximius*.

c. Parallel in Text **3**, V° 8.

d. The day is lost, but both Text **2** and Text **3** suggest that it may have been *ꜥlky*. The following traces indicate another date, Year 10 (+x), perhaps joined to the preceding by *šꜣꜥ*, to give the final limit of the events prophesied; the following phrase suggests that the whole period is to be contained within the joint reign, 'when Egypt and Alexandria were divorced', a period which lasted until May/June 163 B.C.

e. Restored from Text **3**, V° 10.

f. See note to Text **1**, 11, p. 10.

g. If the reading *swn* is accepted, one might expect something similar to Text **2**, R° 13–14; *swn ì·ìr·ḥr·k*. But *smꜣꜥ* is equally possible as a reading.

h. See note *u* to Text **2**, R° 13 above, p. 17.

i. The omission of the feminine *t* from the infinitive of 3ae inf. verbs is typical of the Later Bohairic dialect (ⲙⲁⲥϥ, ⲙⲉⲥϥ for ⲙⲁⲥⲧϥ). Doubt is permissible whether the tense here is Third Future or Circumstantial 'when he is born'; the former seems more suitable to an oracle.

j. For this writing of *ky* cf. Text **3**, R° 6.

k. See notes to Text **3**, R° 7.

l. The vertical line on the copy is part of the palimpsest (*ḥn·w*?).

m. Because of the loss of the following words doubt exists whether Alexandria is referred to here, or Pharaoh; perhaps the former. *pꜣy·f* here may well be *tꜣy·f* or *nꜣy·f* (?)

n. There is sufficient space for this restoration.

o. The traces are not easy to reconcile with this proposal; it may be that a palimpsest also exists at this point.

p. The scribe seems first to have written *pḥ* (?); the resultant attempt to alter this to *tꜣy* has produced this group, which at first sight resembles *dìt.*

q. A writing of *ꜥl* (ⲁⲗⲉ) 'ascend, climb', hence 'embark' (Erichsen, *Glossar*, 67). The form may be influenced by similar spellings of *ꜥlw* 'child' (ⲁⲗⲟⲩ), ibid. 68.

r. This entire phrase, especially the signs read *gmꜥ*, is subject to the utmost caution.

s. *šr* seems to have been inserted above the line, but the subsequent traces are very obscure. *wy* suggests itself as a possible reading, but without conviction.

t. As *ꜥn* usually falls at the end of its clause, it would seem that *n-ḏrt* was followed by a short suffix, perhaps *·f* or *·s*.

u. Only a determinative / can be seen in the middle of this faded line.

v. *wꜣḥ·s* (?) seems to have been followed by a word beginning with *y*, perhaps *ys* or the like.

w. May be followed by *·f*.

x. The traces here suit *ẖrt*, 'food', but the sense is obscure.

y. *ḥ3ty·f* may have stood here, but it is impossible to grasp the meaning of these final sentences.

Translation: recto

1. Account of the letter which was written by *Hrynys*, who was *strategos*
2. (of) horse[a] of Pharaoh and the Queen, when he was in command (?) over me,[b] because of the matters
3. (which) I reported to him in Year 13, Epeiph [·········· up to Year ··········[c] at the time]
4. when [Egypt divorced itself from] Alexandria: behold (?) the journeyings (in) every detail
5. [····················]. That which concerns the eldest son (of) Pharaoh means (that) he shall be born
6. (and) cause to endure another province of his supreme inheritance.[d] That which concerns the salvation of Alexandria
7. means (that) it[e] is secure upon its [··········] authority(?) [·······] every [·······]. That which concerns
8. the journeyings (of) *3tyks* means (that) it is from Egypt (?)
9. that he went [··········]. That which concerns the voyages (of) Pharaoh means (that) he shall go
10. (to) the isle (of) the sea, embarking at Alexandria, his heart being happy.[f]
11. That which concerns the month (?) of groaning (?) means (that) the son shall not [·······] from him (?) again.[g]
12. [···············] authority [··········]. That which concerns
13. the supreme inheritance [····················]
14. the time (when) [·······] spoke (?) [······· and she (?) ·······] him.
15. I stood with[h] *3rstn*[i] who was in it (?).
16. That which concerns [···············] means [·······].
17. [···]
18. [···············] your[j] heart [···············]
19. He guaranteed me[k] [····························]
20. [······························]

Translation: verso (traces only)

Notes

a. Reading plausible, but not quite certain, as the determinative is hard to trace; if accepted, it helps us to define further the role of *Hrynys* in the events of 168.

b. The implications of this expression, if its meaning has been guessed rightly, are of importance: we have seen from Texts **1–3** that Ḥor played an important part in the events described, but without knowing much of his function. It would appear now that he was either a soldier in the royal forces, or a member of the entourage of *Hrynys*, perhaps a soothsayer. See historical commentary below.

c. The period runs from July 168 (possibly day 30, cf. Texts **2** and **3**), until an unknown point in the joint reign. This ended in May 163 or thereabouts, which under the retrospective dating used here (and perhaps in official sources at the time) would fall in Year 18 of Philometor; as the traces clearly show Year 10 (+x) at this point, it is clear that the whole of the joint reign may be covered in the following narrative.

d. This 'other province', referred to in a rather cryptic manner, may well be the island of Cyprus. Already Griffith (*Rylands*, iii. 141–2) had noticed the large number of dedications from this place addressed to Ptolemy Eupator (Dittenberger, *OGIS*, nos. 121, 122, 123, 125, 126), and concluded that 'it seems probable that Cyprus was marked off in a special degree as Eupator's sphere of rule'. If this interpretation is correct, the events referred to here lie a long way beyond the joint reign, and we must assume that the retrospective account is a very belated one. The need to 'secure' Cyprus would be very appropriate after Ptolemy the Brother's attempt to seize the island in 154 (Bevan, 300–1), but such an explanation would lead us far into the reign.

e. Or possibly 'he', referring to Pharaoh.

f. It is difficult not to see in 'the isle of the sea' a description of Cyprus, always closely linked with the Ptolemaic kingdom. Late in October 164 Philometor sailed to Rome, in order to induce the Senate to support his claim to the throne against the scheming of his brother. On his return he lingered in Cyprus while the same brother exercised sole and unhappy authority at Alexandria. In May of 163 he finally returned, his claims vindicated, and the joint reign came to an end (Bevan, 291). 'His heart being happy' may therefore be a reference to the successful outcome of his travels, although it could hardly have been a just description of his mood when he left Alexandria, and forms a shabby contrast with the painter's garret of Diodorus. But this would have been of little concern to Ḥor, whose aim is clearly to win the goodwill of Pharaoh Ptolemy, by whatever means available.

g. The text as it stands suggests that misfortune, perhaps even death, has befallen the young prince. If so, the date of this passage must lie after 150. Griffith's conjecture that Eupator was in some way deprived of his position in Egypt and sent away to Cyprus (op. cit. 142) is unproven, but it may equally be an event of this sort which Ḥor has in mind; the writing, however, is too faded even to substantiate the readings chosen here, and no historical weight should be attached to this passage.

h. In Text **1**, 8, Ḥor 'stands with' *Hrynys*, and in Text **22**, R° 3, with the *ḥr-tb*; neither context suggests that the phrase means anything more than 'associated with' or even 'conversed with'.

i. Doubtless the Greek Ἀρίστων (Preisigke, 49); whether this is the Ariston of Text **26**, R° 1, who is described as a citizen of Daphnae, is an open question.

j. Probably addressed to Philometor.

k. Perhaps in a less literal meaning than Text **1**, 13. Whether Ariston is still active at this point it is not possible to say.

Preliminary Remarks

This difficult text seems to paraphrase a letter sent by *Hrynys*, possibly to the Pharaohs, at some point in the joint reign. Some of its points—the eldest son of Pharaoh, the safety of Alexandria, and the retreat of Antiochus—we have already met with; others are new to us, especially the voyage of Philometor to 'the isle of the sea'. These historical references are used to confirm and interpret cryptic utterances, possibly obtained from dreams or other experiences of Ḥor, who is now recalling these mantic episodes. If our interpretation of the references to Eupator is correct, and there is much evidence to the contrary, the text as we have it will have been written much later, perhaps even after 150; but whatever the truth, it is certain that our document was composed after May 163. It was perhaps intended to be sent to Philometor together with the other ostraca, and it is for this reason that the early lines have been scored off when the text was committed to papyrus.

TEXT 5

Height	8·3 cm.
Width	21·7 cm.
Thickness	1·1 cm.
Munsell	2·5 YR 6/6
Photograph	Plate VI
Facsimile	Plate VIA
Excavator's no.	G7–27 [456]

Ostracon, in three pieces, taken from the curved neck of a reddish-ware jar. The material of the sherd is porous and badly pitted, and the writing consequently extremely obscure. It is also clear that this text lay exposed for some time to the action of wind-driven sand.

Text **5A**, numbered by Emery G7–28 [457], is in two pieces (*height* 7·3; *width* 13·6; *thickness* 1·0 cm.), and clearly forms part of the same text, although it does not make a join with it. Text **5B** (*height* 12·4; *width* 10·9; *thickness* 1·0 cm., numbered G7–29 [458]) is a further fragment of the same text, bearing only a trace. The verso of all these ostraca is ribbed, and uninscribed. A faint buff wash seems to have been applied to the entire vessel.

Text **5**

1. (vacat) *ỉr·ỉ ꜥn-smy n ḥꜣt-sp 5t*[a] *ꜣbd-2 ꜣḫt ꜥlḳy*[b]

2. *ḫpr pꜣ ꜥḥꜥ-rd (n) pꜣ ꜥš-sḥn* [ ][c]
3. *Mn-nfr. wn tꜣ šꜥt (i·)di·i* [*n ḥt-ntr*] *'Iwnw*[d]. *bn-pw* [ ] *mdt n-im·w ꜥn.*[e] *bn-pw·w šn-i*
4. [ ]*s (i·)wn-nꜣ sꜣtrks ḥtr* [ ][f] *tꜣ nty tꜣy nꜣ mdt-nfrw* [*Hrynys*][g] [ ] *mdt-nfrt*
5. [ ] *tꜣy Ḏḥwty* (vacat) *h*[ ][h] *tw-s pꜣ wḏꜣ n tꜣ dnit ḥry*
6. *ḥt* [ ] (trace) *iw·i* [ ]

Text 5A

x+1.] *ꜥš* [
2.] *tꜣ iꜣwt* [ ] [
3.] *iw·s ḥbs pꜣy·s dmi nty ḥry* [
4.] *Ḥp-nb·s tꜣy rnpt 25*[i] [
5.] ··· *ḏd pꜣ tr wn-nꜣ·w smn* ··· [

Text 5B

(Trace only).

Notes

a. The trace supports this reading, rather than *1t*. Indeed, there is considerable doubt whether Year 1, Paoni of the joint reign ever existed (Skeat, *JEA* 47 (1961), 108). That the date is within the joint reign, rather than a year of Philometor alone, is suggested by the references to *Hrynys* below.

b. Very faint: the initial sign of the season suggests *ꜣḫt*, but the day date is not certain.

c. These final traces do not suit *Pr-ꜥꜣ*, or even *ḥt-ntr*, which is applied to *Mn-nfr* in the following line.

d. This writing differs slightly from that of Text **1**, 2, and the other examples. *ḥt-ntr* is a conjecture; perhaps **di·i sḫ·w* or the like also stood here.

e. See the similar phrase in Text **2**, 11. The lacuna after *bn-pw* is too long for a suffix, except perhaps *·i*. Possibly a name stood here.

f. *Hrynys* may perhaps have stood at the beginning. For his title, cf. Text **4**, R° 1–2. *Pr-ꜥꜣ* perhaps belonged in the lacuna following.

g. Restored, but with little confidence.

h. Doubtful, as the sign is broken by a cavity in the sherd. *m-sꜣ* or (less likely) *Wn-nfr* may also be considered.

i. *rnpt* is not certain, and 21 may also have been intended.

Translation

Text 5

1. I reported in Year 5, Paophi, final day.[a]
2. There happened the confirmation of the fortune [·······][b]
3. Memphis. Account of the letter which I gave [·······][c] Heliopolis [·······] did not speak of them further. They did not question me.
4. *Hryny*]*s*[d] who was *strategos* of horse [of Pharaoh?]. That which concerns the blessings of [*Hrynys*?] [·······]
5. from[e] Thoth. [························]. Behold the salvation of the supreme inheritance,
6. namely [····················]. I [··········
··········].

Text 5A

x+1.] call [
2.] the office ····· [
3.] she being in festival(?) (in) her town which is above[[f]
4.] Ḥepnēbes[g] for 25 years[h] [
5.] said (at) the time when there was established ····· [·

Notes

a. If correct, this date would correspond to 2 December 166. Alternative dates are much less convincing: see textual note above.

b. It is an open question what these words may mean. The same applies to 'the salvation of the supreme inheritance' in l. 5 below. It is a tempting possibility, but no more than this, to believe that Ḥor is describing the birth of Ptolemy Eupator at the beginning of December 166. There are, however, other events which occurred between the years 168–163 which may be dated at this point, and to which our text may refer. These questions are dealt with in the historical commentary below.

c. Or possibly 'caused to be written'.

d. Since only the very end of this name survives, and since the mention later in the line is far from certain, it is possible that we are dealing with another *strategos* of horse who has replaced Eirenaios since August 168. But Text **4** suggests strongly that Eirenaios survived for some time after the withdrawal of Antiochus, and our reconstruction may be correct in the end.

e. Or perhaps '[which] concerns Thoth'.

f. This line suggests that we had somewhere in the lost portion a reference to *dmỉ-n-Ꜣst*. What form the *ḥbs* took (if this is the correct reading) it is difficult to say. Perhaps it was similar to the one mentioned in Text **9**, which was written at about this time.

g. See Demotic Text B, 4, and topographical commentary below.

h. 21 is a possible reading; if Ḥor is referring to himself we may restore something like **iw·ỉ šms ẖn nꜣ wꜥbt Ḥp-nb·s ṯꜣy rnpt 25*, which would take his arrival in Memphis back to about 190. But we cannot be sure of this, and this part of the text may well be retrospective.

Preliminary Remarks

This frustratingly obscure text seems to have described a letter written by Ḥor at Heliopolis in early December 166, perhaps to Pharaoh, concerning certain benefits which have befallen the kingdom in general and the *strategos* of horse in particular, who is perhaps the *Eirenaios of the earlier texts. Everything else is lost.

TEXT 6

Height	11·3 cm.
Width	8·4 cm.
Thickness	0·9 cm.
Munsell	10 R5/4[1]
Photograph	Plate VII (V° only)
Facsimile	Plate VIIA (R° and V°)
Excavator's no.	H6–509 [4132]

A fragment of a red-ware ostracon; the surviving text suggests that a considerable portion may be missing. The 'recto', or convex surface, has been badly faded by sand, and mere traces remain of its inscription. The concave verso bears the final portions of eleven lines. The sherd was discovered in 1970 together with Texts **10** and **21** in clean sand above a mud-brick courtyard to the north of the ibis-shrine, where it had perhaps been discarded by looters.

Text: recto

No connected sense can be reconstructed.

Text: verso

x+1.] *ỉrm*
2.] *n-ỉm·s*
3.] *pꜣy·ỉ*
4. *sḏm*] *ẖrw·ỉ ẖr*
5.] *r snt wn-nꜣ·w*
6.] *tꜣ ḥꜣt ẖt pꜣ hp* (*n*) *Kmy*
7. *grpyt*][a] *nty* (*r*) *ḏꜣḏꜣ·k Pr-ꜥꜣ*
8.][b] *tꜣy·k dnỉt ḥry*
9. *Ꜣst tꜣ*] *Pr-ꜥꜣt n tm* [*nb*[c]
10.] *mtr*
11.] (traces).

Notes

a. Restored tentatively from Text **3**, R° 6.

b. The determinative [sign] is clearly visible. *wḏꜣ* is therefore unlikely, and *ḥrḥ* 'watch over' may be a possibility.

c. Restored from the parallels in Text **3**, V° 6, and Text **10**, R° 16–17. *iwꜥ nb* is also a possible reading; see notes to Text **10**.

Translation

x+1.] with (?)
2.] her[a]
3.] my
4.] (hear) my voice in the matter of
5.] according to the custom which they
6.] before, namely, the law (of) Egypt
7. the lady of the diadem] which is (upon) your head (as) Pharaoh[b]

[1] The ware is dark red on both surfaces, but the central core is a distinctly black layer.

8. who watches over] your supreme inheritance
9. Isis the] Queen of all entirety.[c]
10.] · · · · · · ·
11.] · · · · · · ·

Notes

a. 'It' is of course also possible; the translation is chosen because of the references to Isis below.

b. 'Pharaoh' may be the beginning of a new sentence, but this would be more difficult to reconcile with the following line.

c. See Appendix 1, and note to Text **10**, R° 16–17, pp. 48, 156.

Preliminary Remarks

This poor fragment contains part of an address to Pharaoh, and introduces epithets of the goddess Isis. The part surviving therefore resembles Text **3**, of which it may even represent a recession of some kind. The references to the law, and to former habits (ll. 5–6) recall the petitions to be described later. The phrase 'hear my voice' (l. 4) adds some weight to this comparison. Beyond this nothing is certain.

TEXT 7

Height	16·4 cm.
Width	15·6 cm.
Thickness	0·8 cm.
Munsell	5 YR 6/3
Photograph	Plate VII
Facsimile	not given
Excavator's no.	71/2–120 [5388]

A light red ostracon, pieced together from twelve fragments. A considerable proportion of the text is missing, and a thirteenth piece, catalogued by the excavators as 71/2–220 [5488], is almost certainly part of the lost portion. The recto, already badly damaged by salt at the time of discovery, bears remains of twenty-one lines. The verso, black and mottled, is uninscribed. The text was excavated by Martin at the beginning of February 1972.

Text

1. *Pr-ꜥꜣ [Ptr]wmys ỉrm [tꜣ Pr-]ꜥꜣt Ḳrwptrꜣ*
2. *nꜣ ntrw ꜥꜣy.*[a] *sm*[b]
3. *Ḥr pꜣ rmt Dmỉ-(n)-Ꜣst tꜣ ntrt ꜥꜣt nbt tpḥ*[c] *nty ỉw (n) pꜣ tš (n) Ṯb-ntr*[d]
4. *pꜣ hp wpyt tꜣ ẖrt nꜣ hbw (n) Kmy tꜣy*
5. *i·ỉr pꜣy·k ḏry pꜣ sbty (n) pꜣy·k mšꜥ pꜣ wḏꜣ (n) tꜣ dnỉt ḥry*[e]
6. *smn pꜣ htm*[f] *nty ỉw Tmpn*[g] *Tbny*[h] *ḥms ḥr*
7. *ꜣt·f Ꜣḳtryn*[i] *i·ỉr Tbny*[h] *smn*
8.] *ẖr wḏꜣ pꜣ [ꜥḥꜥ]*[j] *Pr-ꜥꜣ mtw·w dỉt n·f nꜣy·f sꜣbw*[k]
9. *ẖr rdwy·f].*[l] *my ỉr·w pꜣ [hp mdt] nbt h[p] tꜣ mdt-nfrt*[m] *⟨mtw⟩*[n]
10.][o] *Ḏḥwty ⟨· · · · · ꜣḫt sw 12⟩*[p] *ḏd* [ ] *i·ỉr·[ḥr·k · · ·] ꜥꜣt: dỉ·w n·ỉ šr ỉw·f*
11.][q] *i·ỉr·ḥr pꜣy·f ỉt. nꜣ nt[rw] nty ḫwy nꜣ ꜥḫyt n*
12. *K]my nꜣ ẖrdw (n) Ḏḥwty nꜣy*[r]*. st ṯꜣy tꜣy·f ẖrt. st mwt*
13. *(n) ḥḳꜣ mn sp-sn.*[s] *st ḫf nꜣ ꜥḫyt. st wrḥ*[t]
14. *n-ỉm·w grḥ mtry. nꜣ rmtw ḏryw*[u] *nty ỉw*
15. *gm]*[v] *lwḥ* [ ][w] *r·w. dỉ·w ỉr pꜣ ntr rn·f*
16.] *wḏꜣ* [ ][x] *tw·ỉ tbḥ*
17.][y] *Tmpn*
18.] *ẖr nꜣy mtw·f*
19.][z] *ḫpr n-ỉm·w*
20.] *ỉr tym*
21.] *ḳrs.*

Notes

a. This epithet seems also to have been written in Text **3**, R° 2. It is possible that this rather vague title antedates the official inclusion of Cleopatra into the royal protocol, an event which is known to have happened on Philometor's return to Egypt in 163 (Bevan, 292). This would suit the appearance of Ḥor as a citizen of Temenēsi, a location which he seems to have abandoned after his permanent settlement in Memphis (see Text **9** and biographical commentary below). The text is difficult to date: it may fall into the middle of the

160s, or it may equally reflect the abuses prevalent in the ibis-cult some ten years previously.

b. Probably an abbreviated writing of *smꜣꜥ* (ⲥⲙⲟⲩ), cf. Erichsen, *Glossar*, 431. The stroke following this word is probably a space-filler.

c. See the note to Text **2**, R° 2, p. 15 above; the present example is too faint to contribute to the discussion.

d. The writing with inserted element which probably represents the scribal tradition of Memphis, see note to Text **2**, R° 3, p. 15 above.

e. Perhaps the scribe intended *tꜣy·k*, as in most of the parallels. The whole sentence recalls Text **3**, R° 9.

f. The reading seems clear; the word probably corresponds to the earlier *ḥdmw* (*Wb.* ii. 505). It is the syntax of ll. 4–8 which presents difficulty. *tꜣy* in l. 4 is presumably introductory; *ỉ·ỉr* may be linked to it, but this leaves *smn* in l. 6 exposed, and it may be better to begin a new sentence with l. 5. The *ỉ·ỉr* which appears in l. 7 is also difficult to interpret; the translation offered below assumes that two parallel sentences of the form (*ỉ·ỉr* .... *smn* ....) are intended, but other interpretations are no doubt possible. It seems best, however, to let a new clause begin in l. 8 with *ḥr wḏꜣ pꜣ ꜥḥꜥ*. The name here transliterated *ꜣḳtryn* is also a problem. One solution may be to take both cases of *ỉ·ỉr* and *smn* as imperatives, but this reads very harshly indeed. The present writer is, however, far from certain that he has understood this passage.

g. The second writing below, and the writing of *ḳ* in the personal name in the next line, exclude the reading *Ḳmpn*.

h. Another difficulty: the group is clearly written [demotic], and differs from the very similar word in the following line only in the omission of the supralinear [demotic]. This may or may not be of great significance. Although the last element resembles *rnpt* or *ỉy*, it would seem more likely that here we have a place-name to supply. It is not *dmỉ-n-ꜣst*, which it resembles (l. 3, above); it may perhaps be an unusual writing of *Dpy* as *Tby*. But more than anything it recalls *Tbnt*, the Delta place-name associated by Erichsen (*Eine neue Erzählung*, 12–13) with Daphnae. This reading I have adopted here. Whether this is a true identification, and what relationship *Tbnt* bears to Taḥpanḥēs (Jeremiah 43: 7–9), or to a similar place-name *Nꜣ-ꜥꜣm-pꜣ-nḥs* (*ꜥOnkhsheshonqy*, iv. 6, 9, 18; Erichsen, op. cit. iii. 3), or to the Stratopeda of Herodotus (cf. M. Austin, *Greece and Egypt in the Archaic Age*, 56, n. 2), are not perhaps relevant here, where the very reading is in doubt. The group, clearly written, recurs in Text **26**, R° 1.

i. The initial *ꜣ* is very strange, but I cannot find a more convincing reading.

j. Restored; the determinative may have been ⲱⲩ.

k. Doubtless a writing of *sbỉw*.

l. Restored from the similar image in Text **3**, V° 3–4. The tail of the *·f* is visible in the following line.

m. Extremely faint and doubtful.

n. Some signs may have followed this insertion, but they are lost.

o. *mdt* is a possible reading for the traces.

p. Perhaps the date of the great festival of Text **3**, R° 13, but the *tpy* is not visible, and *ꜣbd-2* may even have been written.

q. A verb, whose determinative [demotic] is still visible, would have stood here.

r. Presumably the copula ⲡⲉ.

s. A recurrence of the idiom of Text **3**, R° 10.

t. *ḥrḥ* would fit the traces, but yields very bad sense.

u. For this writing of *nꜣ rmtw*, which is here obscured by a palimpsest, see note to Text **3**, R° 5, p. 22 above.

v. Only the final sign visible. For the idiom cf. Text **26**, R° 17.

w.]*tꜣb* or]*ḳꜣb* is visible; the whole is perhaps a curse or threat, like the *ꜣtyt r·f* of Texts **16**, V° 3 and **17**, 10.

x. A house-determinative is visible.

y. *Pr-ꜥꜣ* may perhaps have stood at the end of the missing section.

z. *nꜣy* is more likely from the traces than *Ḏḥwty*. *ḳrs* in the final line is far from certain.

Translation

1. Pharaoh Ptolemy and Queen Cleopatra
2. the great gods.[a] The greeting of
3. Ḥor the man of the town of Isis, the great goddess, lady of the cavern,[b] which is in the nome of Sebennytos.
4. This[c] is the law of the judgement of the food of the ibises of Egypt.
5. Your might, the readiness of your army,[d] (and) the salvation of the inheritance,
6. secure the throne upon which[e] *Tmpn* (of) *Tbny*[f]
7. sat, (and) *ꜣḳtryn*.[g] *Tbny* is secure

8. ·······]. Ever safeguarded is the lifetime of Pharaoh, and his enemies are placed
9. beneath his feet]. May they observe the law in every [matter], the [law of the blessing(?)] ⟨and may ·····⟩
10. Thoth [speaks] ⟨on [Thoth], day 12⟩,[h] saying in your presence a great [·······]: 'I have been given a son who
11. ·······] before his father'. The gods who protect the chapels[i] of
12. Egypt are the children of Thoth. They[j] steal his food. They[k] die
13. of hunger constantly, constantly. They destroy the chapels. They neglect(?)
14. them night and day. The mighty men[l] who
15. [find] fault ·····[m], [calamity] upon them! They have caused the god himself
16. ··········] salvation [····················] I beg
17. ·· ·] ··· *Tmpn*
18. ·· ·] in these matters, and he
19. ·· ·] happened to them.
20. ·· ·] make protection
21. ·· ·] burial(?)

Notes

a. The text may perhaps be dated to the middle of the 160s, see textual note above.

b. For this conventional rendering, cf. Text **2**.

c. The syntax until l. 8 is very doubtful.

d. See the note to the translation of Text **2**, V° 12.

e. Lit. 'upon whose back'.

f. *Tmpn* represents a foreign, perhaps Greek, name. Δημοφῶν (Preisigke, 86) is a possible equivalent, but an identification would be of little significance unless it could be determined what *Tmpn* was doing upon Pharaoh's throne. Some form of revolt or *coup d'état* seems to be implied, but it is certainly not one recorded in other sources, scanty though they are. Possibilities that *Tmpn* may have been a nickname of Antiochus, or that (*ꜣ*)*ḳtryn* was a Roman, though intensely entertaining, have little substance, and one is led to assume that Ḥor is describing one of the several revolts against Philometor which occupied the years from 168 to his voyage to Upper Egypt in 158/7. If the conclusion that after 166 Ḥor ceased to refer to himself as a citizen of Isiospolis were tenable (see notes to Text **9**), we would have to place the revolt of *Tmpn* early in these years, in the aftermath of the Seleucid retreat. Whether these events are connected with any of our Greek texts, or with the revolt of Dionysios Petosorapis (for which see Fraser, *Ptolemaic Alexandria*, ii. 212, nn. 218, 219) or with the ἄλλη κίνησις of Diodorus XXXI, fragment 17c, remains uncertain; the location of *Tbny* (?), if it is really Daphnae, would shed much light upon the question. To identify the revolt of *Tmpn*, if such it was, with the ἄλλη κίνησις, simply because its author is unknown, would be quite impermissible.[1] The evidence of Text **29**, however, in which Ḥor still calls himself a citizen of Temenēsi even in Year 30, shows that even this dating criterion is unsound, and the entire question must be left unanswered.

g. If correctly read, the first element may correspond to Ἀγαθο-, but both identification and syntax are highly doubtful.

h. Perhaps in an oracle given on his festal day, Philometor's birthday. A great difficulty lies in deciding where the god's speech ends; l. 15, with its reference to *pꜣ ntr rn·f*, is presumably part of the narrative. The complaints of ll. 12–15 are perhaps better placed in the mouth of Ḥor, and the version chosen here does have the advantage of making the sentence beginning *nꜣ ntrw nty ḫwy* act as a commentary upon the god's words. Other possibilities exist, however.

i. These gods are presumably Philometor and Cleopatra. Texts such as **16** and **17** suggest that the 'chapels' (*ʿḫyt*) are the centres of the ibis-cult dispersed throughout the land; see commentary.

j. Impersonal.

k. Sc. the ibises.

l. See Text **1**, 5, translation.

m. Text **26** suggests that *n·i* may be restored here.

[1] How literally should we take Ḥor's statement that *Tmpn* sat upon Philometor's throne? If seriously, then the revolt would have been much more than a provincial disturbance. It may be that the phrase is metaphorical, used to describe the mere intentions of the rebels; yet this seems a rather forced explanation. The entire incident is something of a mystery.

Ḥor is pleading for the downfall of his oppressors. See the biographical commentary below.

Fragment **7A**

See photograph on Plate VII. The traces show the words *ḳrs*(?) and *hb* 'send', but it is impossible to determine its place in our text.

Preliminary Remarks

This enigmatic text represents a plea from Ḥor to Philometor to rectify the neglect of the sacred ibises. Its date is quite uncertain; the mention of the ibises and their privations suggests that the text is a late composition, while other criteria point to an earlier date. The writer alludes to an attempt by a man named *Tmpn*, perhaps a Greek citizen of Daphnae, to seize the throne, and seems to rejoice at its lack of success. Everything else is obscure.

See further Additional Text **60** at the end of this volume (pp. 169–70).

§ 2: Dream-texts and oracles

TEXT 8

Height	20·1 cm.
Width	18·0 cm. (max.)
Thickness	0·7 cm. (ave.)
Munsell	2·5 YR 3/6
Photograph	Plates VIII (R°), IX (V°)
Facsimile	Plates VIIIA (R°), IXA (V°)
Excavator's no.	G7–31 [460]

A red-ware ostracon, taken from the shoulder of a rimmed conical vessel. The recto bears twenty-five lines of demotic, the verso a further eight; the lower half of the verso is blank. The text of the recto underwent considerable fading immediately upon discovery, and many of its readings are extremely doubtful. The verso, with its pitted surface, has fared no better, and the inherent obscurity of the subject matter has helped to make this text the most difficult of the entire collection. Indeed, were it not for the preliminary work of Smith, the present writer could have made little of this ostracon.

Text: recto

1. *sw 12[a] ḥb[b] Ḏḥwty. tꜣ mḥ-1t: ỉw·w ḏd[c] wꜣḥ wꜥ ṯs ẖl[d] ỉrm·ỉ ẖr bꜣk wꜣḥ·f wt[e] pꜣy dnỉ[f]*
2. *ỉw·w ḏd wš·ỉ bl[g] mšꜥ·w m-sꜣ·ỉ dỉ·w ꜥḥꜥ·ỉ (n) Ṯb-ntr[h] ỉn·w-y[i] (r) pꜣ mꜣꜥ wn-nꜣ pꜣy·ỉ*
3. *ṯs n-ỉm·f. ḫpr·f ỉw·ỉ snt m-šs[j]. ỉw·w ḏd pꜣy·ỉ ṯs gm tꜣ ḥt-ntr[k] ḏd·f n·ỉ Ḥr ỉr·k[l]*
4. *ḏnt ỉw·ỉ ḫꜣꜥ-rꜣ[m] mtw·k gm ꜥꜣ rꜣ·s[n]. ỉr·k (r) šm n·k bn-ỉw·k ꜥḥꜥ ỉ·ỉr·ḥr·ỉ[o]*
5. *ỉnk pꜣy·k ṯs Ḏḥwty[p] wꜣḥ·ỉ ḏd-s n·k (n) tꜣ ḥꜣt tm-ỉr[q] šms ntr ẖr-bl·ỉ[r]. ḏd·ỉ n·f*
6. *bn-ỉw·ỉ ỉr-s ꜥn. ḏd·f n·ỉ ḏd·i-s n·k ẖr ḥry Pr-[ ][s]. šm rmt ꜥꜣ n-drt*
7. *na Pr-Bnw[t] (r) dỉt n·f pꜣ ḏmꜥ ẖr pꜣ sẖny (n) tꜣ ḥt-ntr Pr-Bnw wḫꜣ·k ỉrm rꜣ·k[u]*
8. *ḏd ỉw·ỉ ḫpr ỉrm·f nꜣy·ỉ ssw (n) ꜥnḫ gmꜥ[v] ḫpr·f ỉrm pꜣ nty ỉw·w hb-s (r) wꜣḥ[w]*
9. *wꜥ rmt wꜥ ꜥš-sḥn. ỉn-nꜣ[x] bn-ỉw·f wꜣḥ pꜣ nty wḫꜣ·f ỉrm tꜣ mdt-nfrt nty ỉw·w ỉr-s n·f*
10. *šꜣꜥ tꜣ wnwt ỉw·ỉ ꜥḥꜥ wbꜣ·f[y]. ỉr·k gm ꜥꜣ pꜣ nty ỉw·w hb-k (r) wꜣḥ[w] tꜣ mdt pꜣy·s*
11. *smt ỉr·k[z] pꜣy·f mtry pꜣ nty ỉr·k[aa]. wn tꜣ mdt-nfrt nty ỉw·w ỉr-s n·k (n) ꜥwy-n-*
12. *ḥtp Mn-nfr ỉrm tꜣ mdt-nfrt rn·s. tꜣ mḥ-2t: ỉw·w ḏd tw·ỉ ḥr[bb]*
13. *tꜣ ẖny[cc] Mn-nfr. mḥ[dd] mwt ẖst wꜥ rmt sbḳ. dỉ·ỉ ꜥl·f[ee]*
14. *(r) ḏꜣḏꜣ·ỉ ỉn·i-s (r) ḥry Pr-Wsỉr-Ḥp pḥ·ỉ ḫftḥ[ff].*
15. *mdt wꜥ rmt ꜥꜣ wbꜣ·ỉ ḏd ỉm r·ḥr·ỉ gm·ỉ wꜥ ꜥwy*
16. *ỉw·f ḳd. ḏd·ỉ n·f ꜥn·f[gg] pꜣ ꜥwy pꜣ nty ḳd r ꜥwy*
17. *ỉw·f šn nꜣy·f sy[hh] ḥms·f ḥr tꜣ mtr ḫftḥ.*
18. *ḏd·f n·ỉ ỉn pꜣy·k ꜥtrm[ii] tꜣy ẖrt nꜣ hbw 60,000.[jj]*
19. *ḏd·ỉ n·f ỉw·f (n) Pr-Ḏḥwty[kk] ỉrm nꜣy·ỉ ꜥlꜣ[ll]*
20. *ḏd·f n·ỉ ỉn-s r-bw-nꜣy ỉrm nꜣy·k nkt*
21. *ḏd·f n·ỉ wn mtw·k by ꜥnḫ (n) ṯꜣy pꜣ hrw 35*
22. *ỉr·k mwt Mn-nfr ỉw·w ḳrs-k[mm] ḥr tꜣ ḳyt[nn]*
23. *Mn-nfr ỉw·w dỉt ḥtp·k n ꜥwy-(n)-ḥtp (n)*

24. *Pr-Wsỉr-Ḥp. sḏm nꜣ mdt*
25. *nty ỉw·ỉ ḏd n·k*

Text: verso

1. *m-šm m-bꜣḥ Ḏḥwty ỉ·ḏd-s*[a] *ỉm n·ỉ pꜣy·ỉ nb ꜥꜣ Ḏḥwty*
2. *ꜥn pꜣ ꜥḥꜥ ḳy (n) ḥb. m-šm m-bꜣḥ Ꜣst (ỉ·)ḏd-s ḏd*
3. *ỉm(t) n·ỉ*[b] *tꜣy·ỉ ḥnwt Ꜣst ꜥn tꜣ ḳrst ḥr*
4. *nꜣ sḥn(w)*[c] *(n) Mn-nfr. m-šm m-bꜣḥ Wsỉr ỉ·ḏd-s m-bꜣḥ*
5. *Wsỉr ḏd ỉm*[d] *n·ỉ pꜣy·ỉ (nb)*[e] *ꜥꜣ Wsỉr ꜥn pꜣy pr (n) nꜣ ḫꜣswt*[f]
6. *Mn-nfr, ꜥn pꜣ ꜥwy-(n)-ḥtp (n) Pr-Wsỉr-Ḥp. nꜣy dr·w*
7. *st sẖ (r)-ḏꜣḏꜣ·k*[g] *dr·w· tw-s ḥꜣty·k nḫt*[h] *(n) pꜣy·k*
8. *ꜥš-sḥn mdt nbt nty ỉw·w ḫpr n-ỉm·k dr·w.*

Notes: recto

a. Rather than *sw 15*, cf. notes to Text **3**, R° 13, p. 23 above.

b. The reading seems clear from the passage quoted immediately above. Smith has pointed out to me that the Memphite tradition of writing this word differs considerably from that of other localities, and he is of the opinion that some, if not all, of the writings listed under *gw* in Erichsen, *Glossar*, 574, represent such spellings of *ḥb*.

c. For this introduction to dream texts, cf. note to Text **1**, 11, p. 10 above. The present division into numbered paragraphs also occurs in Pap. Bologna 3171 and 3173, and in other such texts. Unusual, however, is its continued use in the body of a document, as in ll. 2 and 3 below.

d. The present reading, though not without its difficulties (particularly the position of *ḫl*) seems preferable to one involving ϣⲱⲗ, 'rob', which is hardly compatible with the remainder of the line.

e. *wbꜣ* is surely excluded.

f. Used in demotic for a wide range of taxes (cf. Mattha, *Demotic Ostraka*, 218), and to translate Gk. τέλος. Here the reference is perhaps to the fee paid for exemption from corvée (χωματικόν), but other interpretations may be possible.

g. A most interesting expression; the reading *w(r)š*, if correct here, seems to carry the meaning 'vacate, leave a space' (possibly from the ranks of the labour-gang). *Bl* gives direction to this rather vague idea.[1]

h. See the discussion in Text **2**, R° 3, p. 15 above.

i. Presumably to be understood as a writing of the dependent pronoun *-wỉ* following the semi-vocalic *·w* of the *sḏm·f*, for our texts regularly avoid the use of *-t-* before the object pronouns.

j. For this possible, but not certain, reading cf. Text **1**, 17, note *oo*, p. 11 above.

k. The original is too faint at this point to allow certainty; *ḥn·w* may perhaps replace *ḥt-nṯr*.

l. The use of the vocative here is abrupt, but not exorbitantly so, while the appearance of this proper name and that of *Pr-Ḏḥwty* in l. 19 below confirm that the present text is linked with the rest of our documents.

m. Careful examination convinced both Smith and myself that we are dealing with the predecessor of Coptic ⲕⲁⲣⲱ⸗ (Crum, 288b).

n. This form of *·s* without introductory stroke is paralleled in the *ḏd-s* of the following line; but both contexts are very faint.

o. Tentatively restored.

p. For some time it was doubtful whether this sentence should be taken as *ỉnk pꜣy·k ṯs (n) Ḏḥwty*, 'I am your officer of Thoth', i.e. employed by the temple of this god, or whether the divine name should be seen as in apposition to *ṯs*. The latter now seems more convincing.

q. It is typical of these texts that at the very point where the information is clearly at its most important, the writing should be the most faded. Here *tm* is (relatively) clear; the following group bears a certain resemblance to *stꜣ*, and this may be what the scribe originally wrote. The meaning would then be something like 'Do not draw (the image of any) god except me', and the god would be passing an injunction to remain within the priestly association of Thoth. But it seems clear that the last part of the group has been expanded into a large sign, and a determinative of movement added; hence our *šms*. This is the verb regularly used by Ḥor to describe his service at the shrines of various gods (cf. Texts **9**, R° 2; **13**, 12; **23**, R° 4, and **31A**, 5, 6, where the group bears an initial sign similar to the present example). For the vetitive

[1] One is reminded irresistibly of the colloquial English 'clear off'. The context, certainly, seems to demand such an idiom. Whether the Egyptian too is a vulgarism is difficult to decide.

tm-ỉr see Williams, *JEA* 38 (1952), 62.[1] The entire text is offered with great reserve.

r. The traces do not allow us to distinguish between *ḥr* and *ẖr* before *bl*, if either is the correct reading. For ϩⲁⲃⲟⲗ cf. Crum, 36a.

s. The traces suggest a place-name, but the obvious **Pr-ỉr·s-pꜣ-wꜥ* is not convincing; even *ḥry* itself is far from certain, and it may be that the whole is a gnomic utterance of some kind beginning with *ḥw*. If a place-name is still required, it may perhaps be the *Pr-pꜣy·f-ỉry* of Texts **12** and **25**, a locality which Ḥor is known to have visited while on the god's business.

t. Other readings, notably *Pr-Bḥt* and *Pr-Bt*, the latter possibly as a name of Mendes, are much less probable. The present version rests rather on the testimony of an unpublished papyrus from North Saqqâra,[2] where l. 4 makes mention of *pꜣ tš* (*n*) *Pr-*[demotic group], where there is said to be a *Pr-mḥ-wrt*, and l. 1 introduces us to a personage named *Ṯꜣy-Bnw*(?)*-n-ỉm·w*. See the geographical discussion below.

u. The sudden introduction of a second person pronoun is startling, and the reading may well be entirely wrong.

v. The syntax of the entire phrase beginning here and continuing to *ꜥš-sḥn* in the next line, and indeed the whole of the remaining section, is extremely difficult, and the translation offered below is by no means to be regarded as certain.

w. This idiom also below, l. 10, and in Text **12**, R° 1. The preposition *ḥr* seems excluded by the determinative, for one would expect the writing [demotic group]; see further, note *q* to Text **9**, V° 7, p. 45 below.

x. The scribe seems to have begun a different group, possibly *bn-ỉw* itself, before altering it to this, which is perhaps the conditional particle. The following words are very doubtful.

y. The palimpsest seems to have been *mtr* by anticipation.

z. This group has run over the determinative of *smt*, as if the writer had *ꜥḥꜥ* or the like in mind.

aa. *mtw·k* is hardly possible, but the whole sentence is very obscure.

bb. So perhaps, rather than *wꜣḥ*; see note *i* to Text **1**, 2, p. 9 above.

cc. A word otherwise unknown to me. A rather similar group appears in Cairo 31167, R° 4/5 (letter from Djeḥo to Petiēse concerning deliveries of oil). Spiegelberg equated it with the common word *ḥny* (ϩⲱⲛⲉ) 'canal', although the determinative is a little difficult to explain. The best hieroglyphic equivalent of our present word seems to be the [hieroglyphs] (various determinatives) of *Wb*. iii, 288, a word translated as 'Ruheplatz'. Its relationship with the root *ḥnr*(*i*) 'restrain' remains to be established.

dd. *Ḥr* is hardly possible here, but the entire sentence is far from clear. Smith has suggested for *ḥst* the reading *ꜥst* 'penalty' (cf. the writings from Insinger quoted in Erichsen, *Glossar*, 10).

ee. The traces suggest that *wꜥr* 'flee' may be possible, but the following *ḏꜣḏꜣ*, and the frequent use of ⲧⲁⲗⲟ in Coptic, may add some weight to the present reading.

ff. A word which commonly lacks the definite article, cf. Spiegelberg, *Grammatik*, § 46. One would expect this usage to be especially common among the inhabitants of the Memphite Serapeum.

gg. The absence of *nꜣ-* is strange, but a clear parallel occurs in verso, l. 2.

hh. Probably the Coptic ⲥⲟⲓ, cf. the common *mḥ n sy sbꜣ* of house-documents (Jelínková in *Bull. J. Ryl. Lib.* 49, no. 2 (1967), 473). The word is generally masculine, and it would seem that the text here is plural, with unwritten determinative. But in Coptic the word is occasionally feminine (Crum, 317b), and this may possibly be an early example of this. An alternative spelling of the same word seems to appear in Text **33**, 10.

ii. Presumably the Coptic (ⲉ)ⲧⲣⲓⲙ, Crum, 430b.

jj. The alternative reading, $\frac{1}{6}$ is possible, but perhaps awkward.

kk. For the reading, see note *b* to Text **1**, 1, p. 8 above.

ll. *ꜥlḥ* is also possible. The word may correspond to ⲁⲗⲓ 'fenugreek' (Crum, 4b), or less likely the ⲁⲣⲱ 'bean' of Crum, 489a. *ꜣrwy* 'reeds' is the least likely contender for the reading.

mm. For the omission of *-t* from the infinitive cf. *ms-f* of Text **4**, R° 5, and the other examples collected at the end of § 1 of the Commentary.

nn. The reading seems plausible, although the adjective *ḳy* appears in a very different form on the verso, cf. perhaps Text **18**, V° 15, *ḳyt* (?) *'Iy-m-ḥtp*.

[1] A less direct interpretation would be to regard *ỉr* as infinitive, (*r*) *tm ỉrt*; *šms* would then be used nominally, and depend upon the infinitive.

[2] Publication is vested in the hands of the Egypt Exploration Society, to whom I am grateful for permission to quote from the document. It bears the excavator's no. S.H5–106 [1704], R°.

Notes: verso

a. This and the following examples are writings of the imperative ⲁϫⲓⲥ.

b. Note the parallels in Text **10**, *passim.*

c. A recent discussion of this phrase, equating *sḥnw* with the Greek οἰκονόμοι, in Pierce, *Three Demotic Papyri*, 41. See also note *f* below.

d. The scribe seems first to have written *ỉ·ḏd-s*, which he may have intended in his final version.

e. An understandable omission by the writer.

f. It is possible that this word, whether to be read *ḫꜣst* or *smyt*, was also intended at the beginning of l. 4.

g. The ·*k* is extremely weak, below the determinative. The final lines suggest that the scribe's concentration was beginning to expire.

h. Far from certain.

Translation: recto

1. Day 12, Festival of Thoth. The first: I dreamt[a] (that) a young officer[b] was with me at work,[c] and had paid my tax.
2. I dreamt that I absented myself, (but that) they came after me and caused me to halt at Sebennytos.[d] They brought me to the place where my
3. officer was. It happened (that) I was very afraid. I dreamt that my officer discovered the temple(?).[e] He said to me, 'Ḥor, you are
4. on trial:[f] I shall keep silence, and you shall find that its mouth is great (?)[g] You shall go: you shall not stand before me (?).
5. I am your officer, Thoth.[h] I have told you before, "Do not worship any god except me." '[i] I said to him,
6. 'I shall not do it again.' He said to me, 'I told you it previously, in *Pr*-[··········]'.[j] There came a great man from among (?)
7. the men of Pi-boine[k] to give him the roll bearing the destiny of the temple of Pi-boine.[l] 'Your will (be) with your word (?),[m]
8. saying, "I shall remain with him (throughout) my days of life: should calamity occur with that which is ordained,[n]
9. one man one fate"(?)[o] If he will not pledge[p] that which he wishes together with the benefit which will be performed for him
10. immediately, I shall stand against him.[q] (But) you shall find (that) that which is ordained[n] for you is great, and the benefit
11. likewise. You are his witness, which you shall perform. (For) the benefit which shall be performed for you is in the house of
12. rest (of) Memphis, together with the benefit named.'[r] The second: I dreamt (that) I was upon
13. the necropolis(?) of Memphis. A foul death had seized a poor man.[s] I lifted him
14. upon myself (and) brought him up (to) the Serapeum. I reached the dromos.[t]
15. A great man[u] called out to me,[v] saying 'Come to me: I have found a house[w]
16. which is built'. I said to him, 'It is beautiful, the house which is built, more than a house which
17. lacks its roof-beams'. He sat down in the middle of the dromos.
18. He said to me, 'Bring your clover, this food (for) the 60,000 ibises'.[x]
19. I said to him, 'It is (in) Pi(?)-Thoth together with my fenugreek (?)'
20. He said to me 'Bring it here together with your property.'[y]
21. He said to me 'You (shall) have a living soul from the thirty-fifth day:[z]
22. you shall die (in) Memphis, (and) you shall be buried upon the high-ground[aa]
23. (of) Memphis. You shall be laid to rest in the house of rest
24. (of) the Serapeum.[bb] Hear the words
25. which I shall say to you.

Translation: verso

1. Go before Thoth (and) say, "Come to me my great lord Thoth:
2. beautiful is the lifetime long (in) festival". Go before Isis (and) say, saying,

3. "Come to me my lady Isis: beautiful is the burial within
4. the precincts of Memphis."[a] Go before Osiris (and) say before
5. Osiris, saying, "Come to me my great (lord) Osiris: beautiful is this house[b] (upon) the deserts
6. (of) Memphis, beautiful is the house of rest (of) the Serapeum." All these things
7. are written over you,[c] all of them. Behold, your heart is mighty in your
8. fate, (in) every matter which shall befall you in its entirety.'

Notes: recto

a. For this conventional translation, adopted here largely because of its occurrence in the body of the text, see note to Text **1**, 11, p. 10 above.

b. The word is the descendant of hieroglyphic *ṯ(ỉ)sw*, used of military commanders from the Middle Kingdom, and predecessor of the Coptic ϫⲟⲉⲓⲥ; but here it is used to denote the foreman of a labour-gang. The fact that this foreman is divine is probably coincidental to the use of the word, which seems to have had a wide range of meanings, like the modern Arabic *reîs*, and it is probably unwise to see this example as a precursor to the Coptic usage.

c. On a *corvée*; the tax is his exemption money.

d. It is not clear why he should be pursued if his tax had been paid, but in a dream it is not necessary to explain events in this way; the mention of Sebennytos too is probably irrelevant to the place where the dream was experienced. This was probably Memphis, where a festival of Thoth was held on day twelve of the first month.

e. Perhaps to extract an oath, cf. Kaplony-Heckel, *Tempeleide*, no. 217.

f. Crum, 775a–b.

g. Possibly, 'that this charge is serious'. But other translations are possible.

h. See note to the text above.

i. The implications of these words, if rightly read, are great. The notion of Egyptian cults' demanding exclusive service from their followers is contrary to the view that Egyptian religion was essentially vague and tolerant (e.g. among many, Morenz, *Ägyptische Religion*, Ch. VII), yet the idea of competition between cults over the interpretation of an oracle is implicit in Texts **16** and **17** below. The god, however, is not demanding that Ḥor deny the existence of other gods, as indeed he does not (witness the verso of the present text), but only that he consecrate himself to his service (*šms*). It is clear that the dream marks a change in Ḥor's life, for he has previously been a pastophoros of the goddess Isis. In Appendix 3 below, it will be discussed whether Ḥor falls into the category of persons known as κάτοχοι, people under a 'restraint' to serve a god. At present, one may observe that if the interpretation of these people given by Wilcken is correct, and if it is true that they adopted their status in response to a dream or oracle of some kind, then it is precisely the type of dream described here which would have prompted their behaviour.

j. Possibly the *Pr-pꜣy·f-ỉry* of Texts **12** and **25**.

k. A toponym which, like many in Ancient Egypt, may have been applied to more than one place. A Pi-Boine is known from the Seventh (Diospolite) nome of Upper Egypt (Gardiner, *Onomastica*, ii. 32*; this may be the [hieroglyphs] of the Naos of El-ʿArîsh, cf. Naville, *Onias*, pl. XXV, 36, where it is said to be between *Nšyt* (*Onomastica*, ii. 41* ff.) and *Ḥwt-dšrt* (ibid. 58*)). There may also have been a Lower Egyptian *Pr-Bnw*: a block of Nectanebo II from the temple of Onuris at Sebennytos (Naville, *Onias*, pl. VIA, 3) mentions a house of Horus 'in the midst of [.....] *Bnw*'. *Pr-* may have stood in the missing part. In this case Pi-Boine would not have been far from Sebennytos, and this suits our dream well. A falcon-headed god of *Pr-B(ỉ)nw*, whether Upper or Lower Egyptian, appears before Rameses III at Medînet Habu (Hölscher, *Medinet Habu*, vii, pl. 553).

l. Presumably a book of fate kept in the temple; whether such a thing existed at Pi-Boine is not perhaps the sort of question to address to a dream-text.

m. If this reading is correct, which it probably is not, since the change to direct speech is rather abrupt, the words may mean 'Say this with sincerity', but this is far from certain.

n. See textual note above; also Text **12**, R° 1.

o. The syntax of this entire sentence is puzzling, and Smith has suggested a version which is widely different. The phrase, if correct, may be a gnomic utterance expressing resignation in the face of destiny.

p. Crum, 506b supports this meaning in financial contexts, but other translations may be possible.

q. Perhaps in a legal sense?

r. The meaning of all these words is elusive. All are perhaps best placed in the mouth of the officer, Thoth, and are to be addressed to Ḥor. Ḥor is therefore instructed, after the book of fate is consulted, to stay with the great man of Pi-Boine for life, come what may. The great man is to agree to this solemnly, and Ḥor is adduced as witness; the great man will be rewarded for his co-operation, but will face the wrath of the god should he refuse. By this arrangement, Ḥor will receive two benefits, that of burial at Memphis, and 'the benefit named', which is probably the protection of the great man. Why this should be necessary is not clear. It may be that as a runaway he has lost his rights in law and must join the man's household as a servant, or even slave; but this may be to read too much into the words of a dream.

s. This is probably the significance of *sbk*, rather than 'young'. Ḥor is presumably intending to bury a man who could not have afforded his own tomb. If Smith's reading of *ꜥst* is adopted the sentence would read 'Death (as) a penalty had seized a poor man'.

t. Cf. the discussion by Reich in *Mizraim*, 1 (1933), 36–7, and the remarks of Guilmot, *CdE* 37 (1962), 359 ff.

u. In this eerie setting we should consider the possibility that this *rmt ꜥꜣ* is a ghost; this idea was already familiar to Spiegelberg (*ZÄS* 50 (1912), 32), where an ostracon with a dream-text from Strasbourg features a conversation between Pharaoh and a cantankerous *rmt ꜥꜣ* in the vault of the Apis. The equation is amplified by Volten[1] in his 'Studien zu den Moralischen Lehren des Papyrus Louvre 2414', in *Studi in memoria di I. Rosellini* (Pisa, 1955), 276, note to l. 6 and in *Archiv Orientální*, 19 (1951). An interesting intermediate use of the word appears in a demotic graffito from the tomb of Paḥeri at El-Kâb (Brugsch, *Thesaurus*, 1539), which prays that the good name of the writer may remain *m-bꜣḥ pꜣ rmt ꜥꜣ* 'before the great man (of the past)'. It would therefore seem that in essence a *rmt ꜥꜣ* is a tomb-owner, and by an extension, a ghost (*bꜣ*).

v. ⲙⲟⲩⲧⲉ ⲟⲩⲃⲉ, Crum 192a.

w. Perhaps a tomb, but since both meanings are present in the word, it may be that both are present in the dream; the roof-beams are otherwise difficult to explain.

x. Or possibly, 'this sixth part of the food of the ibises'. Whether the figure of 60,000 is to be taken as a serious description of the ibis-population of the Serapeum is discussed in § 4 of the Commentary below.

y. The mention of Ḥor's property suggests that he is being instructed to move his residence to Memphis, as the latter part of the dream suggests.

z. The point in the ceremony of embalmment when, the physical processes of extracting the internal organs and of desiccation being complete, the bandaging was begun and the body became capable of receiving its new life, cf. among others, Sauneron, *Le Rituel de l'embaumement* (Cairo, 1952), and Pap. dem. Berlin 3115 (Spiegelberg, *ZÄS* 54 (1918), 111–14); also A. Bataille, *Les Memnonia* (Cairo, 1952), 198–220.

aa. In spite of the common use of *ḳyt* (ⲕⲟⲓⲉ) to describe agricultural land requiring perennial irrigation (γῆ ἄβροχος), the reference here is probably to the desert plateau of the Memphite necropolis. In Text **18**, the 'high-land of Imḥōtep' is probably to be identified with the peak (*dhnt*) on which his temple was situated; however, the reading of this phrase is not certain, see note *ad locum*.

bb. Although this expression is the common description of the galleries of the mummified Apis or other sacred animals, the present context probably refers to the human necropolis in which the attendants of the animal-cults themselves were buried; see § 5 of the Commentary.

Notes: verso

a. The *sḥnw* are, of course, the human administrators of the Memphite area; this reference to the local bureaucracy is awkward to reproduce in translation.

b. Probably in a funerary sense.

c. i.e. 'as part of your fate'.

Preliminary Remarks

This text records two dreams experienced by Ḥor on the festival of Thoth in an unnamed year. Internal considerations suggest that this may have happened at Memphis, although the setting of the first dream lies in and around Sebennytos. In this first dream, the foreman of a labour-gang befriends the dreamer, disclosing

[1] Some doubt may perhaps be entertained whether the example discussed by Volten benefits from his interpretation, apt though his discovery may be to other texts.

that he is to spend the rest of his life in the company of a 'great man' from the town of Pi-boine. This foreman reveals himself to be none other than the god Thoth, to whose service Ḥor is ordered to devote himself. In the second dream Ḥor is in Memphis, helping a poor man to burial; he is confronted by another 'great man', perhaps a ghost, who addresses a series of questions to him, finally instructing him to go before various gods. The purport of both dreams is the same, namely that burial is guaranteed for the dreamer in the necropolis of the Memphite Serapeum.

(It is to be regretted that in a preliminary publication of this kind it is not possible to investigate in detail the psychology of such dreams; suffice it to say that there is a clear contrast between the first, where the subject is shown befriended by, and dependent upon, superior beings, and the second, where he is seen himself offering help to an inferior. It is perhaps not fanciful to see in the second an example of the well-known 'anxiety dream', in which a figure of authority elicits from the dreamer a confession of failure or inadequacy: the reply to the instruction to bring the clover is that Ḥor has left it behind in his home city (R° 19). Marked, too, is the dreamer's reliance upon authority, secular or divine, and this characteristic, which is of course not confined to this individual, will appear in many of the texts in this volume.)

TEXT 9

Height	10·9 cm.
Width	14·4 cm.
Thickness	0·9 cm.
Munsell	5 YR 6/6
Photograph	Plate X (R°, V°)
Facsimile	Plate XA (R°, V°)
Excavator's no.	71/2–130 [5398]

A buff ostracon, badly faded. The recto, which is almost entirely lost, bears traces of twelve lines, while the verso bears another ten in the same hand, of which the first two are lost, and the third extremely faint; this strange effect may have occurred through the sherd being buried vertically in the sand, and upside down, so that the first lines were exposed to a deeper and damper layer. The beauty of the hand, and the flourish of the final word, denotes that of a professional scribe.

Text: recto

1\. *ḥꜣt-sp 15*[a] *nꜣ wꜥbt*[b] [ ][c] *ms Ꜣst*
2\. *ỉw·ỉ šms* ⟨(*n*) *rd*⟩ *ỉ·ỉr·ḥr* [*pꜣ*] *r-pr*[d] *Pr-Ḏḥwty ỉw·w dḏ*
3\. *Ḥr-pꜣ-ẖrd pꜣ ntr ꜥꜣ* [ ] *ḏd mdt nbt nty ỉw·w ỉy*[e]
4\. *ỉ·ỉr·ḥr·k* [ ][f] *nꜣ wꜥbt tꜣ* [ ]
5\. *ỉw·ỉ ꜥḥꜥ ỉ·ỉr* [ ] *st ỉr wꜥ*[g] *ꜣpd* (*n*) *gll m-sꜣ ꜣgt*[h]
6\. *ẖt ỉ·ỉr ẖpr mꜣꜥt ḥr* [ ] *·f Pr-ꜥꜣ*
7\. *mdt ỉrm·ỉ ḏd ỉr·k nw* [ ]
8\. [ ][i] *ỉ·ỉr mdt ẖpr bn-ỉw·k ỉr-s* [ ]
9\. [ ][j] *ms ẖr rnpt* [ ]
10\. *dỉ·ỉ wꜣḥ*[k] *tꜣ pt ḏd·ỉ*
11\. [ ][l] *Ꜣst pꜣy·ỉ nb*
12\. *Wsỉr.*

Text: verso

1\. (traces)[m]
2\. *ḥꜣty·n nfr* [ ]
3\. [ ][n] *ỉw·ỉ ỉr wꜥ ꜣpd* (*n*) *gll* [ ][o]
4\. *ḥr tꜣ ẖwyt m-bꜣḥ Ꜣst ẖr rnpt nbt*
5\. (*n*) *nꜣ ssw nty ỉw·ỉ ỉr-w* (*n*) *Mn-nfr. ḏd·s n·ỉ*
6\. *ỉr·k smn Mn-nfr šꜣꜥ*[p] *ḏt. ḏd·ỉ-s*
7\. *ỉn wn rmt ḏt. ḏd·s pꜣy·s wꜣḥ*[q] *ḏd ỉr·k smn*
8\. *ẖn nꜣ nfrw*[r] *nꜣy·k ssw* (*n*) *ꜥnẖ. ỉr·k mwt ẖn*
9\. *nꜣ nfrw*[r] *ỉw·w ḳrs-k ỉw·w dỉt ḥtp·k* (*n*) *pꜣ ꜥwy-*(*n*)*-ḥtp* (*n*) *Pr-Ḥp*[s]
10\. *pꜣ ꜣyt*[t] *šꜣꜥ ḏt.*

Notes

a. The scribe apparently first wrote *ỉw·w ḏd*.

b. Reading based on the early writings listed for the related verb in Erichsen, *Glossar*, 82.

c. I cannot interpret the surviving traces; *ḥb* 'festival' is little more than a guess.

d. Only the very end of *r-pr* is preserved; *pꜣ* is completely restored.

e. The final stroke is clearly a space filler, as at the end of l. 6 of the verso.

f. *ḫr rnpt* is perhaps possible after *ỉ·ỉr·ḥr·k*; the rest is lost.

g. Largely restored from the almost equally faint verso, l. 3; *st* is debatable.

h. Perhaps a writing of ⲱϭⲧ 'throttle' (Crum, 540b), although the Bohairic forms of this verb are irregular.

i. *wḏꜣ* may suit the traces here.

j. The faint signs here may read *btw*, but there are other possibilities.

k. Note that in this text *wꜣḥ*, strangely, carries the flesh determinative 𓄹, while *ḥr*, to which it rightly belongs, is determined with two strokes. See note *i* to Text **1, 2**, p. 9 above.

l. *ḥnwt* is very possible before *ꜣst*.

m. These traces may perhaps suit *ḳrs*, but they are very faint. I can see no sign that a line preceded the present one, although there is clearly room for the same.

n. I cannot offer a reading for this group, clear though it is. The last elements resemble *sḥmt* 'woman', but this seems out of place.

o. Very faint traces follow *gll*, which I cannot interpret; *nty ỉw·f* is perhaps least exceptionable.

p. The stroke above *šꜣꜥ* is part of a palimpsest *ḏd*.

q. The old *wḥꜥ*, fused by demotic scribes into *wꜣḥ*. This identification may have been aided by the use of *wꜣḥ* itself in oracular contexts. A Ramesside example is quoted by Černý (*BIFAO* 35 (1936), 42) from Pap. BM. 10417, verso, where an absent person is 'placed' (i.e. reference to her is made) before Amenophis I in order to gain information from the oracle; a similar reference occurs in Pap. Turin 1975, 3–4, *wꜣḥ·ỉ nꜣ mdꜣt m-bꜣḥ pꜣ nṯr ꜥꜣ, wḏꜥ·f sn m wḏꜥ nfr* (Černý, *LRL* 37, 6–7). The use of *wꜣḥ* in the sense 'interpret' (*wḥꜥ*) is found in the unpublished Pap. BM 10237 *ỉw·f wꜣḥ wꜥt rswt*. The same survives in ⲣⲉϥⲟⲩⲉϩⲣⲁⲥⲟⲩ 'dream-interpreter' (Crum, 302b). See also Griffith, *ZÄS* 38, 87.

r. *nꜣ ḏyw* 'the walls', is a less likely reading.

s. Apparently so; it may, however, be an ellipsis for *Pr-Wsỉr-Ḥp*.

t. Possibly a writing of ⲉⲁⲧ 'furthermost part' (Crum, 61a), rather than some spelling involving *ỉꜣt* 'mound' or its derivatives; but this identification is far from sure.

Translation: recto

1. Year 15[a]: the sanctuaries [··········] birth of Isis,[b]
2. while I was serving ⟨as agent⟩ before the (?) chapel of Pi (?)-Thoth. I dreamt:[c]
3. 'Harpocrates the great god [·······] speaks every matter which shall come
4. before you [every year (?) ·······] the sanctuaries of [·····]
5. I was standing [before (?) ·····]. They were sacrificing a bird as a burnt offering after throttling (?) [it],
6. for truth[d] had happened upon [··········]. Pharaoh
7. spoke with me, saying, "You see [·········· ··········]
8. [is secure(?)]. A matter happens: you shall not do it [·····].
9. [······· evil (?)] is born with every year [·····]
10. I have established heaven".[e] I said,
11. [······· lady] Isis and my lord
12. Osiris'.

Translation: verso

1. '[·······]
2. our heart happy[f] [··········]
3. [·······] I shall offer a bird as a burnt offering [·····][g]
4. upon the altar before Isis every year
5. (during) the days which I shall spend (in) Memphis'. She said to me,
6. 'You are established (in) Memphis for ever'. (But) I replied,
7. 'Does a man exist for ever?' She told her meaning,[h] saying, 'You are established
8. in happiness (for) your days of life. You shall die in

9. happiness. They shall bury you (and) they shall cause you to rest in the house of rest of the House of Apis
10. (to) the furthest limit (?), for eternity'.

Notes

a. The year would be 167/6, within the joint reign. The text as we have it is therefore retrospective, cf. Texts **3** and **4**.

b. Perhaps the reference is to a *mammisi* attached to the temple of Pi(?)-Thoth. If a 'festival of Isis' is intended, this is more likely to be a calendar feast in the temple than a description of one of the five epagomenal days (Diodorus I, 13:4, and Plutarch, *De Iside et Osiride*, 12, 355F agree that the birth of the goddess took place on the fourth epagomenal day, cf. Schott, *Festdaten*, 112).

c. For this translation, cf. Text **8**, R° 1, p. 42 above.

d. *mꜣꜥt*, order or regularity, presumably in the ritual of the temple. The establishment of due orderliness (*mnt*) is a recurrent theme in our texts, notably those below which deal with the cult of the ibises.

e. This sounds very like a sentence from one of the Isis-aretalogies (see below, Appendix 1), corresponding to Greek *ἐγὼ τὸν οὐρανὸν ἔκτισα or the like; it may be that since Isis appears as the interlocutor of the verso, these sentences too should be put into her mouth.

f. Cf. Text **4**, R° 10, *ḥꜣty·f nfr*.

g. The traces are too small for 'throttling' again; [which is] may be admissible.

h. Or, 'interpretation'; see note to the text, and the final paragraphs of the Commentary, § 3.

Preliminary Remarks

This sadly faded text tells us something of the early life of Ḥor. In the year 167/6 he is serving in the sanctuary of his native Pi(?)-Thoth, when a long dream, perhaps involving Harpocrates and dreamt in the *mammisi* of Isis, but in which the goddess clearly has the paramount role, prophesies that he shall go to Memphis and remain there for ever, both in life and in death. The text, which was written after the end of the joint reign (May 163) has clear affinities both with Text **8** and with the following.

TEXT 10

Height	17·1 cm.
Width	16·2 cm. (max.)
Thickness	0·7 cm.
Munsell	2·5 YR 6/6
Photograph	Plate XI (R°, V°)
Facsimile	not given
Excavator's no.	H6–510 [4133]

A pinkish ostracon, in an excellent state of preservation, the recto bearing nineteen lines in a Memphite hand. The verso is blank save for two words in the upper right corner, which may represent scribal practice. The text was discovered by Emery in 1970 in the same location as Text **6**, but there can be little doubt of its relationship with the main archive.

Text: recto

1. *tꜣ mḥ-1t.*
2. *ỉmt n·ỉ Tꜣnꜣ*[a] *nbt knḥy*[b] *tꜣ nbt*
3. *ꜣrꜥy tꜣ nbt tꜣwy Ꜣst wry mwt-ntr tꜣ ntrt ꜥꜣt*
4. *pꜣ ḳꜣn*[c] *pꜣ šỉ nbt drt Ḥr [ỉ·dỉ n·f*[d] *Wsỉr]*
5. *(n) Sywt. sẖ Ḥr ḥꜣt-sp*[e] *12 ꜣbd-4 prt sw 17.*
6. *ỉmt n·ỉ tꜣy·ỉ Tꜣnꜣ Ꜣst n-drt·ỉ ỉrm pꜣy·t*[f]
7. *wy*[g] *Ꜣst wry mwt-ntr tꜣ ntrt ꜥꜣt (n) pꜣ tꜣ dr·f*
8. *ỉmt n·ỉ Ꜣst [[nbt]]*[h] *tꜣ ntrt ꜥꜣt nbt mrt*[i] *tꜣ špšy*
9. *pꜣ šꜣy. kt. sẖ Ḥr (n) Pr-Ḏḥwty.*
10. *ỉmt n·ỉ Ꜣst Tꜣnꜣ nbt pt ḥnꜥ tꜣ nbt bꜥy. kt.*
11. *tpyt nfrt*[j] *tꜣy. sẖ Ḥr (n) Pr-Wꜣḏyt.*[k]
12. *ỉmt n·ỉ Ꜣst tꜣy·t ḥst ỉwt nꜣ rmtw tꜣy·t šfyt*
13. *ỉwt nꜣ ntrw*[l] *ḏd ḫr dỉ·t tꜣ ẖrt*[m] *(n) rmt nꜣy·f ssw (n) ꜥnḫ*
14. *ỉw·f mwt ntt tꜣ nty ḳrs*[n] *ḏd n·ỉ Ꜣst st*[o] *r·k ḥꜥ·k tꜣ mdt-nfrt 2t:*
15. *tꜣy·k ẖrt smn wbꜣ·k nꜣy·k ssw (n) ꜥnḫ ỉr·k mwt ỉw·ỉ (r) dỉt*
16. *ḳrs·w-k. ỉmt n·ỉ tꜣy·ỉ Tꜣnꜣ Ꜣst tꜣ Pr-ꜥꜣt n tm nb*[p]
17. *nty wꜣḥ-sḥn n pꜣ tꜣ dr·f. sẖ Ḥr (n) Pr-Ḏḥwty.*
18. *ỉmt n·ỉ tꜣy·ỉ Tꜣnꜣ Ꜣst tꜣ nbt (n) pꜣ nwḥ nty snḥ*
19. *mtw·s dỉt wtn ꜥn. sẖ (n) dmỉ nty ḥry.*

Text: verso

n-drt ḫpr·f has been written in the upper right-hand corner, probably in the same hand as the recto. This may be the start of a narrative, 'Inasmuch as . . . . .', or it may be scribal practice of some kind.

Notes

a. *Tḥnꜣ* is an alternative, even perhaps *Ḥnꜣ*, and the meaning of this epithet remains unclear. It may possibly be a formation from the common Memphite cult-place *Ṯnnt* (*Wb*. v. 382, cf. Bergman, *Ich bin Isis*, 247–50); for this and other titles of the goddess in these ostraca, see Appendix 1. The small stroke above the *T* of the present example is probably accidental.

b. *pꜣ ỉnḥy* would be palaeographically possible, but one might expect a more suitable determinative, and *nbt knḥy* seems very appropriate for an ostracon found within a hundred metres of the burial-place of the Mothers of the Apis.[1]

c. The initial feeling was to adopt the reading *tꜣn*, and to connect this with *Tꜣnꜣ*; but *ḳꜣn* seems a truer version. Could this be the Coptic ϭⲟⲛ, 'ravine, *wady*' (Crum, 819b)?

d. Obscured by palimpsest.

e. The scribe seems to have begun *Pr-Ḏḥwty* (?), which he altered to *ḥꜣt-sp*.

f. Here, and in the examples of *tꜣy·t* in l. 12, the final *·t* is written almost as a vertical stroke.

g. This may be a writing of *wty* 'beget', or it may be that *hy* was intended by the scribe.

h. This large blot seems to represent *nbt mrt* altered into *wry mwt-ntr*; the *nbt mrt* then follows *ntrt ꜥꜣt*.

i. The scribe seems to have written [illegible], although the first group looks more like *ḏd*.

j. This feminine counterpart of *tp* occurs in *Demotic Chronicle*, 6, 14 as a designation of the source of the Nile. *Tp-nfr* (*Wb*. v. 286) is familiar even from the Eleventh Dynasty in the royal epithet *Nḫt nb tp-nfr*; also, from the following dynasty, *Ḥarwerreꜥ*, l. 14 *r tp nfr*, at the start of an expedition into Sinai. In Ptolemaic texts the meaning has developed, and in the Rosetta Stone τὸ δικαῖον is used to translate the phrase, cf. Bergman, *Ich bin Isis*, 191 ff.

k. Reading suggested by Smith.

l. I can make no sense of the line underneath this word.

m. The parallel with *ḳrst* suggests that *ẖrt* is the reading here, not a noun from the root *ḥrḥ*.

n. The *-t* here seems to be redundant, and the scribe probably had the noun (ⲕⲁⲓⲥⲉ) in mind rather than the verb (ⲕⲱⲱⲥ).

o. More plausible than an attempt to read *ḥnk* 'offer', although the writing is rather cramped.

p. See note to Text **3**, V° 6 (p. 24) and Appendix 1. *ỉwꜥ nb* is also possible, cf. *JEA* 55 (1969), pl. IX, 2 (*ỉꜥ nb ntry*) in an epithet of Osiris-Apis.

Translation: recto

1. The first:[a]
2. Come to me *Tꜣnꜣ*, lady of the vault, the lady (of the)
3. uraeus, the lady of the two lands, Isis the great one, divine mother, the great goddess
4. (of) the *wady* of the lake,[b] lady of the hand of Horus which [Osiris gave to him]
5. (in) Siut.[c] Written by Ḥor (in) Year 12, Pharmuthi, day 17.[d]
6. Come to me my *Tꜣnꜣ*, Isis, into my presence, together with thy
7. progenitor,[e] Isis the great one, divine mother, the great goddess (of) the entire land.
8. Come to me Isis [the great one], divine mother, the great goddess, lady of love, the uraeus-goddess,
9. the Fate.[f] An alternative.[a] Written by Ḥor (in) Pi(?)-Thoth.
10. Come to me Isis, *Tꜣnꜣ*, lady of heaven and earth, lady of the tomb.[g] An alternative:
11. this is an auspicious beginning. Written by Ḥor (in) Buto.
12. Come to me Isis: thy praise is among men, thy glory[h]
13. among the gods, for thou forever givest sustenance to a man (for) his days of life,
14. (and) when he dies, thou it is who performest burial. (For) Isis has said to me,

[1] The text was of course found in a sand deposit over a brick courtyard (see § 4 of the Commentary below), but this may be mere coincidence.

'They are for you yourself, the two benefits:

15. your sustenance is established concerning you (for) your days of life, (and) when you die, I shall cause
16. you to be buried'. Come to me my *Tꜣnꜣ*, Isis, the Queen of all entirety,
17. who wears the diadem in the entire land.[i] Written by Ḥor (in) Pi(?)-Thoth.
18. Come to me my *Tꜣnꜣ*, Isis the lady of the bundle which is bound,[j]
19. and she gives libations in her turn.[k] Written (in) the above town.

Notes

a. An introduction of this kind is familiar in dream texts, but the subject-matter here is clearly one of incantations, not dreams. The use of the feminine *kt* in ll. 9 and 10 below suggests that a feminine word for 'utterance', perhaps *ḫt-mdt*, is to be supplied throughout. Unfortunately it is not possible to say whether other such paragraphs were planned to follow the first. An even more mundane use of such numbering will be found in Text **33** below, where it introduces the resolutions of a committee-meeting.

b. An excellent description of the desert valley at North Saqqâra leading from the still traceable 'Pool of Abusîr' due south to the Serapeum, at the side of which the temples both of Thoth and Isis, Mother of the Apis, were found to stand (*JEA* 51 (1965), 8). This, and the mention of the *knḥt* in l. 2 suggests that Ḥor has the Memphite area in his mind while composing his addresses to the goddess. For further discussion, see § 5 of the Commentary below.

c. Apparently a reference to an unknown episode in the mythology of Horus, but the reading is open to doubt.

d. Corresponds to 18 May 169.

e. Presumably a reference to Thoth, father of Isis (Text **3**, R° 13). In the less likely event of the word 'husband' being intended, the god summoned would of course be Osiris.

f. See the notes to Text **3**, R° 4 (p. 26).

g. Probably a writing of the forerunner of Coptic ⲃⲏ (Crum, 28a), although no exact parallel is known to me.

h. *Šfyt*, cf. Bergman, *Ich bin Isis*, 182 and 190.

i. Note the parallel in Text **3**, V° 6–7 above.

j. An enigmatic phrase which either has a funerary significance, or is used as a metaphor for intractable destiny, see Appendix 1.

k. A very obscure turn of phrase: the sudden change from second to third person suggests that the words are in some way a comment upon the previous lines, but the significance is far from clear.

Preliminary Remarks

In this document we are presented with seven appeals to Isis, beginning with the common address *ỉmt n·ỉ*.[1] Although the general setting and phraseology appears to be Memphite, three of the appeals are said to be composed in Pi(?)-Thoth, and one in Buto, which probably lay near by. One of the appeals is dated to 18 May 169, a time when Antiochus was already in effective control of Egypt and the joint reign abrogated. The text therefore slightly antedates the events of Texts **1–3**, and it is even possible that the prayers of our ostracon were used to invoke the dream described in Text **1**. The possible mention of Thoth together with Isis in l. 7 may add some weight to this theory, but certainty is not possible. Isis is represented as pledging sustenance (*ḫrt*) and burial (*ḳrst*) to her worshipper, in exactly the same way as Thoth in Text **8** offers identical bounties, and Isis herself prophesies a similar fate in Text **9**. It would therefore appear that in 169 Ḥor still regarded himself as a devotee of Isis, but by Year 15 (*c.* 166) his loyalties had been commanded by Thoth.

[1] An early example appears in A. Roccati's publication of a Turin magical papyrus (*Il papiro ieratico N. 54003*, Turin, 1970) which dates from the early Middle Kingdom. L. 19 of the verso has *mỉ r·ṯ r·ỉ mwt·ỉ ꜣst snt·ỉ Nbt-ḥwt*; the demotic equivalent occurs also on the verso of Text 8 in the present work, and the Greek version in *UPZ* 78, 23 (the date of this document is 159). The phrase is standard in the later Greek magical papyri, cf. Wessely, *Griechische Zauberpapyrus* (1888), *passim*. A similar address to the dead Buchis occurs on the famous pebble (Mond–Myers, *Bucheum*, ii. 56): *ỉm n·ỉ Wsỉr-Bḫ pꜣy·ỉ nb ꜥꜣ*. One should compare also the plea of the Saite princess to Amenḥotpe son of Ḥapu, *my pꜣ swnw nfr* (H. Wild, *MDAIK* 16 (1958), 409 ff.).

TEXT 11

A	Height	7·9 cm.
	Width	9·8 cm.
	Thickness	0·6 cm.
	Munsell	5 YR 5/3
	Photograph	Plate XII (R°, V°)
	Facsimile	Plate XIIA (R°, V°)
	Excavator's no.	71/2–191 [5459]

An ostracon of brown ware, the recto being slightly darker than the verso. The recto bears portions of seven lines, and internal evidence shows that the sherd preserves almost all of the opening; the verso, which is obscured by a stain from a natron-like substance, bears a further seven lines in the same rather bold hand. General considerations, and the writing of *ỉrm* in R° 5, as υ/ (the Memphite hands normally write two initial strokes), suggest that this hand is the same as that of Text **3**, and belongs to Ḥor of Sebennytos.

B	Height	12·9 cm.
	Width	7·1 cm.
	Thickness	0·7 cm.
	Photograph	Plate XII (R°, V°)
	Facsimile	Plate XIIA (R°, V°)
	Excavator's no.	71/2–113 [5381]

This ostracon, which joins Text **11**A directly, was discovered previously in the same season. The verso is even more badly preserved than that of its companion piece, which in other respects it resembles.

Text: recto

1. *ỉw·w ḏd: dỉ·ỉ n·f*[a] *bꜣk 2*
2. *ꜥš·f-s*[b] *wꜥ n-ỉm·w dỉ·f nꜣy* (*n*) *tꜣ ḥꜣt*[c]
3. *ḏd·f n·ỉ pꜣy bꜣk pꜣy·k bꜣk pꜣy*[d]*: sḫ*
4. *nꜣy·k ỉtw*[e] *ỉn-s ỉ·ỉr·ḥr·ỉ* (*n*) *rsty* [ ]
5. *ỉw·ỉ smn tꜣy·k ẖrt ỉrm pꜣy·k* [ ]
6. *ỉw·w* [f] *n·k rtb sw 8*[g] [ ]
7. *mn sp-sn ẖr tꜣy·k* [ ]
8. *365 280*[h] *ẖr* [ ]
9. *201 ỉr·k ỉn* [ ]
10. *pꜣy·k mꜣꜥ ḫpr r pꜣy·n* [ ]
11. *sẖ mdt nbt ỉr·k šms* [ ]
12. *pꜣ hb*[i] *pꜣ bỉk* [ ]
13. *bn-ỉw·k* [ ]
14. *nty smy nḥḥ* [ ].

Text: verso

1. *m-bꜣḥ ꜣst ỉrm nꜣ ntrw* (*n*) *pꜣ tꜣ mḥ*[j]
2. *ỉ·ỉr swḥy ḥr pꜣ tnꜥy*[k] (*n*)
3. *pꜣ wn rs* (*n*) *Mn-nfr m-bꜣḥ ꜣst ỉrm*
4. *nꜣ ntrw n pꜣ tꜣ rs nꜣy* [ ][l]
5. [ ] *ỉw·w ꜥw*[m] (*n*) *ḥꜣty*[n] *ꜣst nty swḥy nḥḥ*
6. [ ] *nꜣ*[o] *ntrw* (*n*) *Kmy dr·w*
7. [ ] *ꜣst ḏd mꜣꜥt n nꜣ nty mꜣꜥ*
8. [ ] *ḏd·ỉ n·f* [ ] *gy*
9. [ ] *wꜣḥ·w hb* (*n*) *ḥty*[p]
10. [ ] *r-dbꜣ ḫpr ỉrm pꜣ ntr*
11. [ ] (traces) *nꜣ bꜣkw*
12. [ ] (traces) *dỉ·ỉ-s*
13. [ ] (traces)
14. [ ] (traces).

Notes

a. The *n* is very faint, but emerged on close examination.

b. A redundant *-s* of this sort is not usually attested for *ꜥš*, but this seems to be the best explanation here. Similar unusual examples (beside *dwn-s* of Text **3**, V° 23 and *ḥn·f-s* of Text **19**, V° 4 and **22**, R° 6) occur in Text **23**, R° 6, and **25**, 6 below.

c. The scribe seems first to have written *dy* 'here'.

d. Note the differing forms of the demonstrative ϥⲁⲓ and the copula ⲡⲉ within the same line.

e. The surviving traces are unclear, but it is difficult to suggest a satisfactory alternative.

f. The initial sign of this group resembles *ỉsw* (Erichsen, *Glossar*, 44; to be read *ỉw* in the light of Malinine, *JEA* 54 (1968), 190–1), and this would yield a fair sense, but the remaining signs are difficult to reconcile. The translation offered below is tentative.

g. *wꜥ* is perhaps also reconcilable with the traces.

h. The horizontal stroke, which gives the last sign a resemblance to the 'foreigner' determinative, is apparently part of an erased group which stood above the line.

i. Supplied almost entirely from the context.

j. See the notes on *pr-mḥ* in Text **1,** 1 and 7; the reading here is strongly supported by the contrasting *pꜣ tꜣ rs* below.

k. The determinative here is interesting: the reading of the final sign as *mḥ* 'northern' is possible, but rather unconvincing. An alternative may be to take it as a cursory writing of *ꜥꜣ* 'great' (cf. Text **24A,** 4 below), but it looks more as if the entire group ῦ/λ is intended for the determinative; see therefore note to the place-name *Pr-Ḏḥwty* in Text **1,** 1 above.

l. The vertical stroke at the beginning tends to exclude *dwꜣ*, and *Pr-ꜥꜣ* is scarcely likely.

m. A writing of the Qualitative ⲟⲓ, as often.

n. Almost entirely obscured by the stain which obliterates the centre of this side of the text.

o. Reduced to a single curving stroke, as generally in the writing of *nꜣ rmtw* (see note to Text **3,** R° 5, p. 22 above).

p. Note to Text **2,** R° 11.

Translation: recto

1. I dreamt: I gave to him[a] two documents.
2. He read out one of them, and placed these before (him).[b]
3. He said to me, 'This document is your document: write out
4. your corn (-rations) (and) bring it before me (in) the morning.
5. I shall establish your sustenance and your [[c]··········]
6. There are granted (?)[d] to you 8 (?) *artabas* of grain [··········][e]
7. lasting, lasting, for your [················]
8. 365: 280(?) for [························]
9. 201:[f] you shall bring(?) [·················]
10. your right (?) has happened according to our [··········]
11. write every matter: you shall serve[g] [·················]
12. the Ibis (?) (and) the Hawk [··························]
13. you shall not [·························]
14. which pleads for ever (?) [·····························]

Translation: verso

1. Before Isis and the gods (of) the north land,
2. who are assembled upon the dam[h]
3. (of) the southern dyke[i] (in) Memphis: before Isis and
4. the gods of the south land, these (being) worshipped (?)
5. [·····] (and) being great (of) heart: Isis who is assembled for ever (?)
6. [·····] the gods (of) Egypt, all of them.
7. [·····] Isis speaks truth to those (?) who are true
8. [·····] I said to him [ ] way(?)
9. [·····] they have sent in haste[j]
10. [·····] concerning dwelling with the god[k]
11. [·····] (traces) the documents
12. [··········] (traces) I gave them
13. [··········] (traces)
14. [··········] (traces).

Notes

a. The nature of this other party is not explained, and it may be that we have lost the beginning of our text on another ostracon; he is evidently a man of authority, however, who issues instructions in a similar manner to the overseer and ghost of Text **8.**

b. Cf. the use of ϩⲁⲑⲏ in Coptic = ἀπέναντι (Crum, 641b).

c. 'Burial' is not grammatically possible here; perhaps *ꜥḥꜥ* 'lifetime' should be restored?

d. Very doubtful; see textual note above.

e. *ḥr rnpt* would fit this lacuna well, but cannot be substantiated.

f. A doubtful reading; the balance of the other two numbers, 85, is, however, excluded.

g. Reminiscent of Text **8,** R° 5.

h. Possibly a writing of ⲧⲏⲡⲉ (Crum, 418b), although the inserted *ꜥayin* is puzzling. The feature is probably the same as the *tny ꜥꜣ* of Text **24B,** 5, and may be that of Text **15,** V° 4. It is discussed in the Commentary, §§ 4, 5.

i. Probably ⲟⲩⲁⲛ (Crum, 480a), a word similar in meaning to ⲧⲏⲡⲉ. The reason for the gods' assembly on the dyke is not over-evident.

j. Text **2,** R° 11.

k. Possibly in the sense of incumbent within the shrine of the god. See Appendix 3 below, p. 163.

Preliminary Remarks

The recto of this fragmentary text records a dream, in all probability recorded by Ḥor of Sebennytos, in which an unnamed official tells him to present his document and his ration of corn; his sustenance, a common promise in these texts, is confirmed, and a ration of eight (?) *artabas* of grain mentioned as his allotment. On the verso, Ḥor invokes Isis and the several gods of Egypt, continues his conversation with the mysterious being, and receives conditions for his 'dwelling with the god'.

TEXT 12

Height	16·5 cm.
Width	15·7 cm.
Thickness	0·9 cm.
Munsell	2·5 YR 5/4
Photograph	Plate XIII (R°, V°)
Facsimile	not given
Excavator's no.	71/2–129 [5397]

A sherd of reddish ware, smashed into sixteen fragments by a heavy blow which has desurfaced part of the recto. The eleven lines on this face are written in a Memphite hand, and a further four lines in the same hand follow on the verso. These are written upside down with respect to the recto, in the manner of a papyrus letter. The ware is coarse and has suffered considerably from the action of salt.

Text: recto

1. *n-drt Ḥr-Ḏḥwty*[a]*: ỉ·hb·ỉ r wꜣḥ*[b] *(n) Pꜣ-ḥm-ntr-ʾImn*[c] *ỉrm pꜣ bꜣk ḥꜥ·f*
2. *(n-)ṯꜣy ḥꜣt-sp 9t rnpt 5t r-bw-nꜣy Ḏḥwty hb n-ỉm·ỉ ẖr*[d] *Pr-pꜣy·f-ỉry*[e]
3. *(n) nꜣ mdt nty nfr·w*[f] *(n) pꜣ ꜥš-sḥn (n) pꜣ hb pꜣ bỉk. ꜥḥꜥ·ỉ ỉrm Pꜣ-šr-(n)-nꜣ-ỉsw*[g] *(n) Rꜥ-ḳd*
4. *ỉw·f n ḥr-tb*[h] *ẖn*[i] *nꜣ rmtw. wẖꜣ·ỉ*[j] *wbꜣ nꜣy*[k] *pꜣy·s smt ꜥn ḥꜣt-sp 1t ꜣbd-3 ꜣẖt sw 9*
5. *r-dbꜣ nꜣ mdt wn-ỉw·s*[l] *pḥ (r) ỉy*[m] *ỉ·wꜣḥ Pꜣ-ḥm-ntr-ʾImn n-ỉm·w ẖr tꜣ nty ṯꜣy*[n] *ḥt-ntr Pr-psḏt*[o] *(n) rswt.*[p]
6. *ꜥs*[q] *nꜣ mdt-nfrw ỉ·ỉr ỉy ỉ·ỉr·ḥr pꜣ ꜥš-sḥn (n) Pꜣ-ḥm-ntr-ʾImn sḏy·ỉ (n) ḥꜣt·w*[r] *ỉ·ỉr·ḥr*
7. *Bn-ỉw·w-sḏm pꜣ wꜥb*[s] *nty stp n pꜣ nty wꜥb.*[t]
8. *wn nꜣ mdt (ỉ·)ḏd·w n·ỉ r dỉt-s [ỉ·ỉr·ḥr Pꜣ-ḥm-ntr-]ʾImn: ẖt bꜣk ḥꜥ·f.*[u]
9. *Ḏḥwty*[v] *pꜣ ꜥꜣ pꜣ ꜥꜣ nty ꜥꜣ[y (n) ms nꜣ ntr]w nty n tꜣ ḥꜣt tꜣ Sktt*[w]
10. *snt n·f r-dbꜣ pꜣy·f*[x] *[ỉr] sẖ nfr. ꜥn sẖ r rmt ḳnḳn*[y] *pꜣy·s*
11. *ꜥḥꜥ-rd: pꜣ wyt*[z] *ḏry ꜥḥꜥ ẖn·f: ẖr sẖn nfr.*[aa]

Text: verso

1. *n-drt Ḥr:*
2. *wn nꜣ mdt nty nfr·w (n) pꜣ ꜥš-sḥn (n) Pr-ꜥꜣ*
3. *ỉrm pꜣ ḏry (n) tꜣy·f mtgtt. snt·ỉ n-ỉm·w: ỉn*
4. *ỉ·ỉr·ḥr·k pꜣ ḥm-ntr ꜣst*[bb] *sgn*[cc] *m-šs*[dd]*.*

Notes

a. More likely the common compound name than a name and patronymic; see note to the translation below.

b. Note the similar idiom in Text **8**, R° 8, 10. The reading *wꜣḥ* is confirmed by its use as a verb in l. 5 below; this text too exhibits the anomaly that the flesh-determinative, which rightly belongs to *ḥr*, is attached to *wꜣḥ*, while *ḥr* itself appears only in cursive forms; cf. note *k* to Text **9**, R° 10, p. 45 above.

c. Probably a proper name rather than a title, but see note *o* below. The reading *Wsỉr* for the final group is scarcely plausible.

d. This sign does not suggest itself as a writing of *pꜣ*, or of *ẖr*; this use of *ẖr* is similar to that listed in Spiegelberg, *Grammatik*, § 296, n.

e. *Pꜣy·f* here is abbreviated; the full spelling occurs in Text **25**, 9.

f. The plural ending of the Qualitative is regularly written out in this phrase.

g. The last element in this proper name is perhaps the word for 'rams' (ϵϲωογ), cf. the name Πεσῶϋ, Preisigke, 307.

h. A group common in our ostraca, where it is normally preceded by the definite article, and used as an epithet to proper names (Text **23**, R° 8; Fragment **45**, 5). In two cases the group is followed by the numeral 4 (Text **16**, R° 8; Text **17A**, 3). This last circumstance, and the horizontal stroke or diagonal tick written over the centre of the word (stroke in the present example, tick in all others) exclude the reading *Wꜣḥ-ib-Rʿ*, which would otherwise be very plausible. The reading *ḥr-tb* is suggested more by the sense than by resemblance to the writings of Erichsen, *Glossar*, 321.

i. The scribe seems first to have written *wn* 'pastophoros', which he erased in a desultory fashion.

j. There is a palimpsest beneath the suffix and the following *wbꜣ* which I cannot determine.

k. The short stroke before *nꜣy* appears to have no semantic purpose.

l. There seems to be bad grammar here, but the explanation is probably that the plural *nꜣ mdt* is regarded as a collective, and demands a singular verb, which retains the feminine gender. The spelling is presumably a writing of the relative imperfect ⲉⲛⲉⲥ—.

m. *iy* seems a more likely reading than *rnpt*. For the 'appropriate' use of *pḥ*, cf. note to Text **3**, V° 18 (translation), p. 29 above. The idiom *pḥ (r) iy*, which I cannot parallel, may mean 'to be about to happen', or 'to be appropriate to come', but either translation is to be treated with reserve.

n. The phrase as in Text **2**, R° 13; V° 15, and Text **4**, R° passim.

o. The middle sign bears beneath it a curving stroke thus: , and the reading *psḏt* is conjectural. If the lower sign is taken as accidental, or as an insertion from the line below, the reading *Pr-ʾImn* would be acceptable, and we should then have to inquire whether *pꜣ ḥm-ntr ʾImn* were not a title, instead of a proper name; but although this would yield good sense, it is very difficult to justify it from the text.

p. Although *R-sṯꜣw* is spelt elsewhere in these ostraca as *rswt*, the position of the determinative at the end of the previous group, and the general sense, weigh against this possibility here.

q. For this writing of ⲉⲓⲥ cf. Erichsen, *Glossar*, 70. The word *tw-s* (cf. Text **1**, 11; Text **4**, R° 4) seems not to be connected.

r. One might expect *ẖt* at this point, but the text seems clear, and the translation offered below is tentative.

s. The text is disturbed by a palimpsest *sẖ*.

t. *stp* is fairly clear, and it is the following group which occasions doubt. *Pr-wʿb* may also have been written. *Pr-iy-wʿb* is familiar from the First Cataract as a translation of the Greek ἄβατον (cf. Griffith, *Dodecaschoenus*, 898), and from *Tanis*, 6 *nꜣ wʿbw nty šm r pꜣ nty wʿb* we must assume that some equivalent lay in the Delta. Perhaps the feature was common to many temples. But the entire reading is far from certain.

u. Note the clear palaeographical difference between *ẖt* and *ḫʿ*.

v. Much of the text of these final lines is restored from the parallels in **12A**, and detailed references will not be given.

w. Erichsen, *Glossar*, 468; the final sign is perhaps the determinative of the divine, rather than of the plural.

x. The scribe wrote *ir* beneath *·f*.

y. This group occurs, also clearly written, in **12A**, 3. The natural reading *rsrs* 'wakeful' or the like, is not attested in demotic; the alternative *ḳnḳn*, though attested (notably in the phrase *rmt-ḳnḳn*) is hardly borne out by the determinative. The following reference to a 'mighty assemblage', and the encouragement given to Pharaoh's army on the verso, perhaps add some support to the latter reading.

z. The reading *wyt* 'stela' (ⲟⲩⲟⲉⲓⲧ) is excluded by the determinative in both passages; ⲁⲩⲏⲧ (Crum, 21b) is suggested tentatively. Some faint traces follow in the present example, which may suit *ʿḥꜣ* (*ꜣḥ*) 'fight', but it is impossible to be certain of this.

aa. Written over a palimpsest, and doubtful.

bb. Here probably a title of Ḥor, corresponding to παστοφόρος τῆς Ἴσιος of the Greek texts.

cc. Bohairic ⲥⲟϭⲛⲓ, cf. note to the translation of Text **2**, V° 14 above.

dd. See note to Text **1**, 17, p. 11 above.

Translation: recto

1. From Ḥarthoth.[a] What I ordained[b] for Pḥentamūn together with the document itself.
2. From Year 9 (for) five years until this time[c] Thoth sent me to Pi-peferē[d]
3. (concerning) the matters which are beneficial (to) the fortune (of) the Ibis (and) the Hawk.[e] I stood with Pshennesōw (in) Alexandria
4. while he was magician among the people.[f] I sought concerning these things likewise again (in) Year 1, Hathor, day 9,[g]

5. because of the matters which were appropriate to come,[h] which Pḥentamūn had laid down,[i] under (the heading of) that which concerned the temple of Pi-psīte,[j] (in) a dream.
6. Behold the blessings which befell the fortune (of) Pḥentamūn. I discussed them(?) with
7. Enneusōtem (?) the priest who is chosen[k] in the Abaton.
8. Account of the matters (which) I was told to place [before Pḥent]amūn: the content of the document itself:[l]
9. 'Thoth the great, the great, who is the [elder born: the gods] who are at the head of the *Sktt*-bark
10. revere him for his making a beneficial writing. The writing is beautiful for a fighting (?) man: its confirmation:[m] the mighty assemblage stands within it,[n] for (this is) lasting good fortune'.

Notes

a. The introduction of this character, unavoidable sooner or later, must cause considerable problems, for it now seems that there are two personages involved in our texts. Evidence will be given in full in the Commentary below (§ 1) to show that this second character, who was also named Ḥor, was the resident petition-writer at the ibis-shrine of North Saqqâra, who qualifies himself in our texts with such epithets as 'Ḥor who is over the petitions' (Texts **16, 17**), and, as here, 'Ḥarthoth' (possibly to be interpreted 'Ḥor of Thoth', cf. the fuller form *Ḥr Ḏḥwty nb ꜥnḫ* in Text **23,** V° 15). The fine Memphite hand which appears in many of our documents is his, as befits a professional scribe, and it is clear that he was used by Ḥor of Sebennytos as his secretary, while drafting his petition to Philometor; much of the material written in his hand is therefore narrated by Ḥor of Sebennytos, and is to be ascribed to him, but occasionally, as in Text **23** and in the present example, he has inserted experiences of his own, wherever judged relevant. His very close link with the other Ḥor is shown by the verso of the present document, which is to be attributed to Ḥor of Sebennytos. Occasionally (Text **23,** and perhaps **25**) the two appear together; but when an unqualified Ḥor is mentioned, it seems best to assume that the reference is to the Sebennytic one, whichever hand may have composed the text.

b. See Text **8,** R° 8, 10.

c. The temporal use of a spatial phrase, as frequently in Egyptian, where *dy* or *mꞽn* may mean both 'here' and 'now', 'today' and 'in this place', cf. James, *Ḥeḳanakhte*, 111–12.

d. An unidentified place-name, perhaps near Alexandria. The nature of 'his companion' is a subject for much speculation, none of it certain.

e. A phrase common to Texts **19–23,** the memoranda of § 3 (pp. 73 ff.).

f. i.e. the populace of Pi-peferē. The entire phrase may mean that, like a pastophoros, the office was exercised outside the confines of the temple proper, but it is unwise to read too much into such a statement.

g. 'Year 1' here follows Year 9, and therefore is best taken as the beginning of the joint reign (12 December 170, a date later than any of those given by Skeat in *JEA* 47 (1961), 108, but which may be retrospective). Year 9 of Philometor alone falls in 173/2, and yet we are informed in l. 2 that *five* years have elapsed since this time. Our best conclusion is therefore that the text was written in about 168, and that the events of 'Year 1' (= 170) were already in the past. The reference to the 'army of Pharaoh', for which the writer feared, would suit a date in 168, immediately after the retreat of Antiochus and the change in Pharaoh's fortunes.

h. See note to Text above.

i. i.e. to be interpreted by oracle, cf. note *q* to Text **9,** V° 7, p. 45 above.

j. Another obscure place-name. If rightly read, the reference may be either to the alternative name of Kherꜥaḥa south of Heliopolis (Gardiner, *AEO* ii. 137*, 140*), or to a locality in or near Mendes (ibid. ii. 150*), or to another unknown place. Pḥentamūn seems to be associated with this temple in some way, but it is not stated that he held any office there.

k. Compare the procedure outlined in Text **19,** V° 5 and parallels.

l. From this point the writer seems to be copying from Text **12A.**

m. Cf. the similar phrase at the conclusion of the dream in Text **1**; 'it' is feminine, and probably refers to an implied *rswt*.

n. 'It' is now masculine, and must refer to the *sẖ nfr*.

TEXT 12A

Height	8·0 cm.
Width	13·1 cm.
Thickness	0·6 cm.
Munsell	5 YR 6/3
Photograph	Plate XIV
Facsimile	not given
Excavator's no.	71/2–230 [5498]

Six faded fragments of a dull reddish-ware ostracon. The verso is blank. It would seem, from the text alone, that this ostracon preserves the 'document itself' which is copied out in Text **12**, and for this reason it is included here, and not among the fragments.

Text

(This is in large part restored from the writings of Text **12**, and detailed references are not given).

1. *ꜣbd-3 [ꜣẖt sw 9]*
2. *Ḏḥwty pꜣ ꜥꜣ pꜣ ꜥꜣ nty*[a] *ꜥꜣy (n) ms pꜣ ỉt [nꜣ ntrw nty n tꜣ ḥꜣt tꜣ]*
3. *Sktt [[ẖn·w]]*[b] *snt n·f r-dbꜣ pꜣy·f ỉr sẖ nfr*
4. *ꜥn sẖ r rmt ḳnḳn ⟨bn-ỉw·w ỉn ....)*[c] *pꜣy·s [ꜥḥꜥ-rd] pꜣ wyt*
5. *ḏry ꜥḥꜥ ẖn[·f ....]*[d] *Wsỉr nb R-stꜣw*[e]
6. *my [..........] rẖ [.......... ḥ]r ꜣtrm*[f]
7. *my ṯꜣy [....................................]*
8. *[..........]*[g] *nꜣ/tꜣ nty šms [...............]*
9. *[..........]* (traces)[h] *[...................]*[i]

Notes

a. Written over a horizontal stroke.

b. Apparently erased by the writer.

c. I cannot interpret the traces at the end of this inserted phrase.

d. There may just be room for the *ḥr sẖn nfr* of Text **12**, 11.

e. Written, as often in these texts, *rswt*.

f. Apparently the word for 'clover', with the 'speaker' determinative altered to .

g. The determinative is clearly visible, but I cannot identify the word.

h. *ṯꜣy* seems excluded by the traces.

i. Both *bn-pw* and *rn* are imaginable here.

Translation

1. [Hathor, day 9].[a]
2. Thoth the great, the great, who is the elder born, the father (?). [The gods who are at the head of the]
3. *Sktt*-bark revere him for his making a beneficial writing.
4. The writing is beautiful for a fighting (?) man. ⟨They shall not ....⟩. Its confirmation: the mighty
5. assemblage stands within it [..........]. Osiris, lord of Ro-stau,
6. may [..........] know [..........] with clover (?)
7. may (they) take [....................]
8. [..........] those (?)[b] who serve [..........]
9. [..........] (traces) [..........].

Notes

a. This restoration may seem perhaps overbold, as the initial sign may represent only a phrase added to the following line. The lack of a year-date is notable, although it may reflect the confused situation which prevailed in Egypt during the final months of 170, before the abrogation of the joint reign became generally recognized. The restoration is, however, offered with the utmost reserve.

b. The translation 'she who serves' is equally possible.

Preliminary Remarks

Text **12**, written in about 168 by the petition-writer of the ibis-shrine of North Saqqâra, records a five-year sojourn in a place named Pi-peferē near Alexandria; during this time, on 12 December 170, he consulted an oracle on behalf of a man named Pḥentamūn, perhaps a temple employee, or possibly a soldier involved in the hostilities against the invading Seleucid forces. In the resultant dream Thoth appeared, writing a document of encouragement, perhaps similar to the one envisaged in Text **3**, R° 8.

On the verso there appears a short message of encouragement to Pharaoh, perhaps addressed to him during the critical period when Antiochus was in control of Egypt. The author of this comforting text is described as 'the priest of Isis', and is doubtless Ḥor of Sebennytos. Ostracon **12A** seems to contain the original text of the dream, which, with a few omissions, was incorporated into the present document.

TEXT 13

Height	18·6 cm.
Width	15·8 cm.
Thickness	1·0 cm.
Munsell	5 Y 8/3
Photograph	Plate XV
Facsimile	not given
Excavator's no.	71/2–121 [5389]

A buff-ware ostracon, found in five large pieces, inscribed on the recto only. The lower right-hand corner is missing. The thirteen lines of text are clearly preserved, but have been attacked in places by salt, and the early lines are particularly affected by this. At the beginning, one whole line and a second partial one, perhaps an insertion, have been erased, and the second line of the preserved text is extremely faint. The condition of the sherd is otherwise good.

Text

1. *ḥꜣt-sp 26 ꜣbd-2 prt sw 11 pꜣ ꜥwy-(n)-ḥtp (n) pꜣ hb hrw m-sꜣ ỉr hrw 2*
2. *(n) ỉr sbr*[a] *ḏd* [b] [ ][c]
3. *ỉm n·ỉ pꜣy·ỉ nb Wsỉr-Ḥp ỉrm Wsỉr-Mr-wr*
4. ⟨*ỉm n·ỉ*⟩ *pꜣy·ỉ nb ꜥꜣ Wsỉr-Ḥp pꜣ ntr ꜥꜣ ỉrm nꜣ ntrw nty ḥtp (n) R-stꜣw*[d] *Pr-Wsỉr-Ḥp*
5. *ỉrm R-stꜣw*[d] *Ḥp-nb·s ỉrm nꜣ nty ḥtp ḥr tꜣ ꜣt (n) tꜣ štrt*[e] *Pr-Ḏḥwty*
6. *(n) Mn-nfr: sḏm ḫrw·ỉ pꜣy·ỉ nb Wsỉr Mr-wr*[f] *ỉrm nꜣ ntrw nty ḥtp n*[g]
7. *R-stꜣw Ḏdỉt*[h] *ỉrm nꜣ nty ḥtp (n) tꜣ ḫꜣst*[i] *ỉꜣbtt n ʾIwnw*[j]
8.] *ḏd·w ỉw·ỉ šms (n) Pr-Wsỉr-Ḥp ỉw·ỉ gm-s mtw·ỉ*
9.] *ỉw·f ꜥꜣy (n) ms wꜥ ṯꜣy-šs-nsw*[k] [ ][l] *ḥr ꜣt·f*
10. *sš*]*n*(?) *(n) ỉrt·f šl wt mstmy*
11. *r*]*dwy·f ỉw·f ḥms ḥr š*[·]*š*[m] *ḏwf*
12.]*šms n-ỉm·f Pr-Wsỉr-Ḥp*[n]
13. *l*]*wḥ dr·w*

    (further lines may be lost).

Notes

a. Close observation revealed the determinative ; the whole is a phonetic writing of *spr*, 'pray, petition', cf. Griffith, *Dodecaschoenus*, Glossary, 296.

b. A lotus-sign is visible, but little else.

c. *ỉ·ỉr·ḥr pꜣy·f* may be visible in the traces, but it is far from certain.

d. Spelt as the word for 'dream', cf. the example in Text **12A**, 5 above.

e. A semi-phonetic writing of *sḏrt* 'sleeping-place' (Erichsen, *Glossar*, 481).

f. The scribe seems to have written the word *mnḫ*, changing this to *mr-wr* as he proceeded.

g. This stroke is more strictly to be interpreted as a space-filler.

h. Doubtless to be seen as a writing of the necropolis of Heliopolis, but the writing, obscured by the break in the ostracon, is difficult to interpret. The entire group may recur in Text **18**, R° 1*, where it is clearly written and is coupled with the name of the necropolis of Memphis, *ꜥnḫ-tꜣwy*. One name of the Heliopolitan cemetery is preserved for us, namely *Ḏdỉt* (*Wb.* v. 630; Montet, *Géographie*, i. 137), and it is as a semi-hieratic version of this that one is tempted to read the group; note the determinative, and the forms of the hieroglyph given in Erichsen, *Glossar*, 616, under *twt*.

i. Cf. Text **8**, V° 5, where a plural word appears which may be another writing of the same group. I have chosen the reading *ḫꜣst* rather than *smyt*, whose very existence in demotic is rather doubtful. The following *ỉꜣbtt* overlies a palimpsest which I am unable to read.

j. The present context is the best evidence for the reading of this group, cf. note *f* to Text **1**, 2, above, p. 8.

k. The reading seems clear, if unparalleled; *ṯꜣy* in

such a phrase is presumably to be taken as *participium conjunctum*. The alternative, which is to take the verb as a First Present, seems weak, for *wrꜥ* on its own is hardly a convincing subject. For *ṯꜣy ḥr ꜣt* as an expression for donning a garment, cf. *Petubastis* (Spiegelberg), 7, 3.

l. A sign here seems to resemble *ỉr*, but it is very faint, and may even have been erased by the writer.

m. There is room for a middle radical, perhaps *r*, but the best solution seems to be to regard the word as a formation from *šš* 'scatter' (ϣⲱϣ); the translation 'thicket' is approximate only.

n. The scribe began another group after *Pr-*, which he altered as he went.

Translation

1. Year 26, Mekhir, day 11:[a] the house of rest (of) the Ibis,[b] the day after spending two days
2. (in) making supplication,[c] saying [.......] before [.......]
3. 'Come to me my lord Osorapis and Osormnevis:[d]
4. ⟨come to me⟩ my great lord Osorapis, the great god, and the gods who rest (in the) necropolis of the Serapeum
5. and (the) necropolis of Ḥepnēbes,[e] together with those who rest upon the sleeping-place (of) the House of Thoth
6. (in) Memphis:[f] hear my voice my lord Osormnevis (?) and the gods who rest in
7. the necropolis of Djedit, together with those who rest (in) the eastern desert of Heliopolis'.[g]
8. ....] they said:[h] I was serving (in) the Serapeum. I found [.....][i] and I
9. ....] who was great (in) age. A wearer of byssus upon his back[j]
10. .... lot]us (to) his eye: myrrh[k] fresh (?) (and) eyepaint[l]
11. ....] his feet, and he was sitting upon a thicket (?) of papyrus
12. ....] serve him[m] (in) the Serapeum
13. ....] fault (?), all of them ....

Notes

a. On the assumption that this year too falls within the reign of Philometor, the day would be 10 March 155; with the possible exception of Text **29** the latest date in our archive. See also p. 168 n. *b* below.

b. The ibis-galleries of North Saqqâra, where the writer, who is probably Ḥor, is petitioning the gods for an oracle.

c. The implication seems to be that on the third day of pleading, the writer was rewarded with an oracle, doubtless in the form of the dream which follows.

d. For the coupling of these two gods, cf. Text **1**, 2, and note, p. 12 above. It seems strange that these gods should be the ones addressed, when the location is given expressly as the ibis-gallery; perhaps a process of travelling from shrine to shrine has been compressed into the present text, or it may be that the prayer is intended for all the gods of the Memphite necropolis, and the ibis-gallery is incidental as a setting. A third possibility, less likely perhaps, is that the address to the god was delivered elsewhere, and that the ibis-gallery was only the place where the present text was drafted. The second explanation seems by far the most natural.

e. The area around the shrine of Isis, Mother of the Apis; see topographical commentary below. The 'gods' are presumably the sacred animals buried in their millions within the necropolis.

f. Presumably the dead, buried in the cemetery of the ibis-shrine, who might also instigate dreams if propitiated.

g. The cemeteries of Heliopolis would naturally lie to the east of the city, where several tombs of Mnevis bulls are known to exist (Daressy, *ASAE* 16 (1916), 195–219, and *ASAE* 18 (1918), 196–9, also in particular Gauthier, *ASAE* 27 (1927), 1–4; 15–18). The present text seems to imply that other sacred animals were also interred here, among which one can probably imagine the ichneumon of Atūm and the falcons of Raꜥ-Ḥorakhty. For the area in general, cf. Porter and Moss, *Bibliography*, iv. 59–65.

h. This phrase may mark the introduction of a dream-narrative, but the whole of these last five lines is very obscure.

i. Any third-person pronoun is permissible at this point.

j. Presumably a designation of a priest, for whom garments of byssus were a ritual necessity, cf. the description of Imḥōtep in Papyrus Oxy. 1381, and of the dream-figure *pꜣ nṯr iw·f n pꜣ smt n wꜥ wꜥb iw·f ṯꜣy ḥbs n šs-nsw ẖr ꜣt·f* of Lond./Leid., Col. 4.

k. Possibly the Coptic ϣⲁⲗ (Crum, 557b), though the dialect forms of this word (not to mention hieroglyphic writings) strongly suggest that the initial letter was *ḫ*; the other Coptic equivalent, ϣⲓⲗ, is too obscure to be of help, and a reading *ml* is not convincing.

l. For the older *msḏmt* and the Greek στίμμι, cf. Harris, *Lexicographical Studies in Ancient Egyptian Minerals*, 174 ff.

m. Possibly to be seen as an imperative, though the word could equally be part of an epithet **nty iw·w šms n-im·f* or the like.

Preliminary Remarks

In this ostracon, whose connection with the rest of the archive is suggested more by the handwriting than anything else, the writer records prayers addressed to the gods of the funerary regions of Memphis and Heliopolis. These are followed by a dream, or something very similar, representing a strange figure (the lotus and the papyrus-thicket suggest that the writer may have had the god Nefertēm in mind), and a 'wearer of byssus', who may be offering various precious substances before him. The resemblance between this figure and the apparitions of later magical texts is discussed in § 3 of the Commentary below. The rest is obscure.

TEXT 14

Height	11·4 cm.
Width	9·9 cm.
Thickness	0·6 cm.
Munsell	10 R 5/6
Photograph	Plate XIV (R°, V°)
Facsimile	Plate XIVA (R°, V°)
Excavator's no.	G7–32 [461]

This ostracon has the dubious distinction of being the most obscure document even in the present archive. It is a dark red sherd, broken into three pieces by a blow in the centre of the verso. Both sides of the text have been considerably altered, and contain several erasures and corrections, and both sides are badly faded. The verso is in large part covered by a blot of ink. These difficulties would not be so considerable if the content of the text, when deciphered, were clear, but the subject-matter is as obscure as the writing, and the following text is offered with all reserve. The sprawling hand may be that of Ḥor of Sebennytos, except for the lines at the top of the verso, which may be quite unrelated.

Text: recto

1. (lost)
2. (traces)
3. (traces)[a]
4. (traces)[b]
5. *in bn-pw·k*[c] *nw (r) pꜣ ḏmꜥ* [ ]
6. *kt: i·ḏd-s*[d] *nꜣ sḫsḫ* [ ]
7. *tꜣy·s*[e] *wpt*[f] *ḥy r tꜣ nḥbt*[g]
8. *(n) pꜣ ꜥꜣ. kt: n-drt bn-pw·k* ⟨*tn*⟩[h] *pꜣ ꜥꜣ*
9. *bn-pw·k dit ḳy nꜣy·k ḥb(w). kt:*[i]
10. *rswt*[j]

Text: verso

1. ⟨*r-dbꜣ ir ḥꜣty (n) sꜣb* [ ]
2. *wn-nꜣ ḏd mdt nb rḫ tꜣy* [ ]⟩[k]
3. *my n·i pꜣy·k wꜥ* [ ]
4. *tny n·k pꜣy·i ḥb.*
5. *kt: šms n·k* [ ]. *kt: pḥ*
6. *tꜣ ꜣtyt* [ ] *wn-nꜣ·i*
7. *n-im·w* [ ] *ḥꜣty·k* [ ][l]
8. *pꜣ ꜥꜣ. pꜣy·f*[m] *wꜣḥ ḏd*
9. *pꜣ hꜣ*[n] *ḳy (n) pꜣ tš* [[*pꜣ*]][o] *(i·)ir-rḫ·k*
10. *pꜣ wḏꜣ* [ ][p] *irm ẖrt iw·k iwt·w*[q]
11. [ ] *ẖr-ḥr·i.*

Notes

a. The writing of this line is small, and it may be an insertion.

b. This line probably began with *kt*, but I can make nothing of the later traces.

c. The group is written [demotic sign], and resembles *bn-pw·k*, more than *i·ir·k* or a strange writing of *ir·k*; in a text of this sort there is clearly little to be gained from a reading *ad sensum*.

d. For this writing of the imperative ⲁϫⲓⲥ, cf. Text **8**, V° 1, etc.

e. *tꜣy·t* is also a possible reading, but with it the syntax (if any) collapses.

f. The only certain features of this word are that it is a feminine noun, and a part of the human body; *wpt* 'forelock' is suggested here, but *ḥmt*, whether in the sense of 'palm' (*ḥnt*, cf. Fairman, *JEA* 54 (1968), 236) or 'vulva' (*Wb.* iii. 76) is also possible.

g. Very obscure, especially the *r tꜣ*, which resembles *pꜣ*, and it must be admitted that there is little room for the *b* of *nḥbt*.

h. This word is inserted over the line; its reading is suggested by the writing of the similar word for 'payment' (*tn*) in the ibis-memoranda.

i. *ḥb* seems to have been crossed out by the scribe, and it is therefore difficult to see what he intended. *kt* is written over a palimpsest which I cannot interpret.

j. *ꜣswt* (ⲁⲥⲟⲩⲓ) is also possible, but less likely.

k. These words are written in a smaller, neater, and different hand, which seems to recur at other points in the verso. It is perhaps the hand of the palimpsest. Why the writer should be so sparing of ostraca is difficult to see, although he seems to have done the same with Greek Text B, which was written over erased demotic lines.

l. I cannot interpret the traces following *ḥꜣty·k*.

m. The first sign of this group resembles *tꜣ*.

n. Cf. the early writings of the determinative in Erichsen, *Glossar*, 265.

o. The sign as it stands resembles *ḥḏ* 'silver', but this yields poor sense, and the sign is indeed so faint that it may have been partially erased. But this is far from certain.

p. The scribe may have written *nꜣy·k* here, omitting the noun in haste.

q. Extremely uncertain.

Translation: recto

1–3. (lost)
4. Another:[a] [lost]
5. Have you not seen the papyrus roll [·····]?
6. Another: tell the blows [··········]
7. her forehead (?): strike the neck (?)
8. (of) the donkey. Another: as you have not ⟨lifted⟩ the donkey,
9. you have not caused your festival(s) to be long.[b]
Another (?)
10. dream (?)

Translation: verso

1. ⟨*Because of making a heart (of) hostility [·······]
2. which said every matter [··········]*⟩[c]
3. Give to me your one [············]
4. Raise for yourself my festival (?)
5. Another: serve you [·····]. Another: attain (?)[d]
6. the vulva (?) [··········] *I was
7. in them*[c] [···················] your heart [·······]
8. the donkey. Its interpretation[e] says:
9. the long time in the land which (?) you know,
10. the salvation of your [·····] and sustenance (?), you being among them (?)
11. [ ] in my presence.[f]

Notes

a. This use of *kt* to introduce alternative phrases is reminiscent of Text **10**; here the phrases seem to be not encomia, but oracular utterances or excerpts from dreams. Donkeys, particularly in sexual acts, play a noticeable role both in Pap. Chester Beatty III, and in the demotic dream-books (cf. Pap. Carlsberg XIII, b, 2, 20; XIV, f, 3; see Volten, *Traumdeutung*, 86–7). These enigmatic phrases are followed (verso, l. 8) by an interpretation of a familiar type.

b. cf. Text **8**, V° 2 for a similar expression.

c. The excerpts enclosed in asterisks are perhaps from the palimpsest text (see note to the text above).

d. Possibly (if the reading is correct) in the obscene sense recorded for *pḥ ỉrm* (Erichsen, *Glossar*, 138).

e. Badly needed, one would have thought. For the translation, see note to Text **9**, V° 7, p. 45 above.

f. ϩⲁⲣⲟⲓ, cf. Spiegelberg, *Grammatik*, § 296, n.

Preliminary Remarks

Much of this strange and badly preserved text records motifs from dreams or similar oracular material, separated by the word *kt* 'alternative'. These are finally interpreted as a guarantee of the subject's life, perhaps put into the mouth of a god. The document thus fulfils a similar purpose to that of Texts **8, 9, 10,** and **11**.[1]

TEXT 15

Height — 11·0 cm.
Width — 14·3 cm.
Thickness — 0·5 cm.
Munsell — (R°) 10 R 5/3 (V°) 5YR 4/1
Photograph — Plate XVI (R°, V°)
Facsimile — Plate XVIA (R°, V°)
Excavator's no. — G7–(1+2) [432+433]

Two ostraca found by Emery in 1965/6 and subsequently joined. The recto, a fine red ware, bears some ten lines, the last having been lightly erased, while the verso, a dark grey ware with striations which make legibility difficult, contains a further nine lines in the same Memphite hand. The relationship of this ostracon with the Ḥor texts rests on external criteria only, but its general nature fits well with the other documents.

Text: recto

x+ 1. [*'I*]*bt*[a]
2. [ ] *r pꜣy·ỉ*
3. [ ] (trace) [ ]*·f ỉ·ỉr tym*
4. [ ] *nty ỉw·f wbꜣ·w sẖ* [ ]
5. [*pꜣ ḥm-*]*ntr*[b] *'Ibt pꜣ ẖr-ḥb*[c] *'Ibt šn-s*[d] *ỉrm snt 2t. Ta-Ḫrd*[e]
6. [*tꜣ ḥ*]*mt* (*n*) *Tysḵrts ỉrm tꜣy·s snt mdt·w ỉrm·ỉ ḏd nꜣy*
7. [*pꜣ ẖr-*]*ḥb 'Ibt 'Inp Ḥr-sꜣ-Ꜣst pꜣy tꜣ snt 2t Ꜣst ỉrm Nbt-ḥt tꜣy*
8. [ ] *nw·k r·w ỉrm·ỉ ꜥn nꜣy nꜣ nty ỉw·w ḏd n·k*
9. [[*ḥt*]*-ntr 'Ibt r ỉr ḥt·w*]]
10. [ ] (traces) [ ].

Text: verso

x+1. *nꜣ nḫt*[f] [ ]
2. *ỉn-nꜣ*[g] [ ] (trace)
3. *ẖrt* (*n*) *pꜣ hb* [*nty ẖn*] *Mn-nfr ỉrm* [ ]
4. *dỉt tꜣy·k ẖrt* (*n*) *pꜣ hb ḥr pꜣ tny*[h] *n-s*[i] [ ]
5. *wꜣḥ·k sẖr ẖr ꜥḥyt* (*n*) *šꜥt ỉw·ỉ dỉt wt·k* [ ]
6. *r tꜣ ꜥḥyt* (*n*) *ms mtw·k ỉr t*[*ym*[j]]
7. *swḥ*[k] *mn sp-sn*[l] [ ]
8. *Ꜣst pꜣ rmt Pr-*[[m]]
9. *tw·ỉ* [ ].

A tenth line has been inserted along the right-hand margin:

10. *ḏd bn-ỉw·k snt rmt ỉr·k ẖn* [ ].

Notes

a. Restored from the examples below.

b. Tentative: *'Ibt* has been altered from *Ꜣbt* here.

c. A writing not otherwise known to me, but palaeographically not impossible, and confirmed by the reference to Anubis in l. 7; the funerary connotation of the title is well brought out in the Greek translation ταριχευτής (Spiegelberg, *Demotica*, i. 4; Glanville, *Soter Archive*, xxiii. 1, and Gardiner, *AEO* i. 55*).

d. Suggested by the traces; the meaning 'seek (the interests of)' is aptly shown in *Demotic Chronicle*, iv. 10, where it is said of Hakoris that *ḥꜣꜥ·f pꜣ hp r tm šn r-dbꜣ nꜣy·f snw* 'he abandoned the law in order not to seek after his brothers'. The same text (ii. 4) uses the same word with *mdt*, *n-drt šn·f nꜣy·w mdt* (*n*) *Ḥt-nsw*, 'when he (Thoth) investigated their affairs in Heracleopolis'. The same idiom recurs in the next line (ii. 5), and confirmation of the meaning is given in *Rosettana*, 20, where *ỉw·f šn nꜣ mdt pḥ nꜣ r-pyw* corresponds to προσπυνθανόμενός τε τὰ τῶν ἱερῶν τιμιώτατα in the Greek text. See also the title in Text **19**, R° 17, and Text **22**, R° 6–7; also Texts **23**, R° 11, and **31A**, 3–4.

e. = Ταχράτις, Preisigke 423. *Ḫrd* as a divinity is rather elusive; he occurs in Pap. Dodgson V° 1 (Griffith, *PSBA* 31 (1909), 100), where he is likened to a local form of Horus in Elephantine, and also in Pap. Leiden I, 348, V° 2, 4 (Borghouts, *OMRO* 51 (1970), 181, who suggests either that he is Nefertēm, or, less likely, Ḥorḥeknu or Harsomtheus). The absence of any article is puzzling, and it would seem that one should follow

[1] Many questions arise about this text. The violent content of the recto makes one wonder whether the ostracon was smashed deliberately in a ceremony to secure the happy conclusion of V° 8–11, but even this is only the beginning of the mystery. See also p. 132 below.

Griffith and see in him an abbreviation of *Ḥr-pꜣ-ḫrd*, the child *par excellence*.

f. See perhaps the note to Text **3**, V° 7, p. 24 above.

g. I can think of no other reading for this strange sign. The following group may represent *ḥm-ntr*, or more likely a word beginning with *y*-.

h. Perhaps the same word as in Text **11**, V° 2 and Text **24B**, 5.

i. This word would be appropriate in religious contexts (cf. *wꜥ ḫꜥ n-s Ptḥ* of *Setne*, 3/10), but the reading is not unassailable.

j. Tentatively restored.

k. Cf. again Text **11**, V° 2.

l. Text **3**, R° 10 and Text **7**, 13.

m. Apparently not *Pr-Ḏḥwty*, as the supralinear stroke is missing, but nothing remains of the name itself.

Translation: recto

x+ 1. [························· Aby]dos
2. [·····························] to my
3. [···········] (trace) [·········] making protection
4. [···········] which is about them (in) writing [·······].
5. ['····· the pro]phet (of) Abydos and the lector-priest of Abydos investigate it,[a] together with two sisters'. Takhrati
6. [the wife] of *Tyskrts*[b] and her sister, they spoke with me, saying, 'These
7. [····· the lector-]priest (of) Abydos is Anubis (and) Harsiēsis: the two sisters are Isis and Nephthys.
8. [·······] you look upon them with me again: those are they who shall say to you
9. [····· (the) temple] (of) Abydos, according to their content (?)[c]
10. (traces)'

Translation: verso

x+ 1. the prayers (?) [··········]
2. Is it that (?) [··········] (trace)
3. food (of) the Ibis which is within Memphis together with (?) [··········]
4. place your food (of) the Ibis upon the dam[d] belonging to (?) [··········]
5. you have sworn (an oath) before the chapel-of-the-letter:[e] I shall (?) cause you to proceed (?) [·······]
6. to the chapel (of) birth,[e] and you shall make [protection (?) ·······]
7. assembled, lasting, lasting [·······]
8. Isis, the man of Pi-[[f] ·······]
9. I cause (?) [···············]
10. (*in margin*) for you shall not fear (a) man, while you are in [·······].[g]

Notes

a. See the note to the text at this point; 'it' may be vaguely impersonal, or refer to the temple of Abydos, cf. the common title *pꜣ nty šn ḥt-ntr*.

b. Perhaps *Δεισικράτης or *Τεισικράτης, neither of which is in Preisigke. Διοσκορίδης (ibid. 90) may also be possible.

c. This line may have been erased by the scribe.

d. Perhaps the same feature as the one in Text **11**, V° 2, where the 'gods of the north land' are said to be assembled upon it.

e. For these features of the cult of the Ibis, see § 4 of the Commentary below.

f. Probably a designation of Ḥor as author of this text.

g. One may restore either 'Memphis', or the like, or some phrase such as 'the favour of Thoth (?), the great god', depending upon the length of the missing portion.

TEXT 15A

Height	6·4 cm.
Width	5·1 cm.
Thickness	0·6 cm.
Munsell	as Text 15
Photograph	Plate XVI
Facsimile	not given
Excavator's no.	71/2–197 [5465]

This small ostracon, found in February 1972, seems to be part of Text **15**, although no join is observable, and is included here. The recto is completely faded, and little enough remains of the verso.

Text: verso

x+1. [ ] *Mn-nfr*
2. [ ] *ỉr rsrs*[a]

Note

a. Very uncertain: a sign appears before these words, but above the line, and does not seem part of a connected text at all.

This text bears two broad diagonal lines running from the end of *Mn-nfr* towards l. 2; these may be intended to cancel the writing.

Preliminary Remarks

The general meaning of this text is clearer than its details; a woman named Takhrati, wife of *Tysḳrts*, interprets for the writer, who is perhaps Ḥor, an oracle concerning the priests of Abydos. The personages named therein prove to be major gods of Egypt. The verso seems to contain instructions about the food of the sacred ibises. A final line adds that the subject need have no cause for fear.

TEXT 16

Height	11·2 cm.
Width	10·8 cm.
Thickness	0·9 cm.
Munsell	5 YR 7/1
Photograph	Plate XVII (R°, V°)
Facsimile	not given
Excavator's no.	71/2–114 [5382]

An ostracon written on the neck of a buff-ware amphora. The convex recto bears twelve lines in an extremely competent Memphite hand, that of the resident petition-writer of the ibis-shrine, and the first six have been ticked when copied off on to papyrus; the verso, upside down in relation to the recto, bears a further four lines in the same hand. Ll. 9, 11, and 12 of the recto bear considerable signs of revision, and l. 2 has been inserted into the completed text. This document, together with the two following, was found by Martin at the end of January 1972.

Text: recto

1. *n-drt Ḥr nty wbꜣ pꜣ smy n nꜣ ꜥẖyt n Kmy (n) pꜣ rn pꜣ ntr ꜥꜣ*
2. *⟨Ḏḥwty st ỉr-rẖ pꜣ*[a] *nẖt mdt nbt nty ṯꜣy*[b] *pꜣ hb (n) ḥꜣty·f⟩*
3. *r-dbꜣ dỉt ỉr·w*[c] *pꜣ nty nfr·f n pꜣ ꜥš-sḥn n pꜣ hb ẖt tm dỉt ꜣḳ mdt (n)*
4. *tꜣ nty ṯꜣy tꜣy·f ẖrt ỉrm tꜣy·f ḳrst. pꜣ nty mšꜥ ḥr tꜣ mỉt*
5. *rn·s nfr·s n pꜣy·f ꜥḥꜥ n wš ḳy ỉw·w ỉr mdt-nfrt*
6. *n pꜣ hb Yb r nꜣ wꜥbt*[d] *(n) Smꜣ-bḥdt.*[e] *wtwt*
7. *'Iy-m-ḥtp sꜣ Ptḥ ỉ·ỉr·w ꜥš n·f n nꜣ tꜣwy dr·w*[f] *r-dbꜣ pꜣy·f ỉr-spy*[g]
8. *smy·ỉ ḥr-tb*[h] *4. bn-pw wꜥ n-ỉm·w wpy*
9. *tꜣ nty ḥr nꜣ ꜥẖyt ꜥꜣy nty ỉw pꜣ hb ms n-ỉm·w*
10. *ẖn*[i] *nꜣ tšw ỉrm nꜣ ꜥẖyt tpyw*[j]
11. *nty ỉw nꜣy·w ꜣḥt ỉrm tꜣy·w ḥwt.*[k] *ṯꜣy·w gns n-drt*
12. *nꜣ rmtw ḏry. pꜣ wr-dỉw Ḏḥwty ỉrm pꜣy·f*

Text: verso

1. *nꜥš ỉr·w pꜣ smty (n) tꜣy·f*
2. *wtyt.*[l] *ꜥsy*[m] *ỉwt·w*
3. *ꜣtyw*[n] *r·f*[o] *bn-ỉw·w rẖ*
4. *ḥms*[p] *n-drt·f (n) pꜣy·f hrw (n) šnw.*

Notes

a. One might expect *pꜣy·f*, but the text seems clear.

b. For the phrase, see note to Text **2**, R° 13. The stroke which seems to run between *ṯꜣy* and *pꜣ* is perhaps not the preposition *n*, but part of the palimpsest.

c. The palimpsest has *ỉp*, which has not been erased.

d. A highly cursive writing, but other readings are less probable.

e. The second element is clear, and the meaning confirmed by the mention of *Yb* before, as an expression of the geographical limits of Egypt (cf. Gardiner, *JEA* 30 (1944), 40–1); but the form of the sign *smꜣ* is noteworthy. (See also the remarks of Spiegelberg, *Sagenkreis*, 84.)

f. A very clear example of an old dual treated syntactically as plural, cf. Spiegelberg, *Grammatik*, § 36, note.

g. A difficult group, which I am not convinced to have interpreted correctly; the parallel writing in

Text **17A**, 10 suggests that the first sign is a separate *ỉr*, and not to be read after the horizontal *s*; hence my *ỉr-spy*. The meaning of the second element is perhaps the same as in the *sp n ḥyk* of *II Khaꜥemwīse*, 6, 21, meaning 'magic spell', and the reference is presumably to Imḥōtep's powers of healing. The whole phrase resembles the description of Thoth in Text **12**, R° 10, where the gods are said to *snt n·f r-dbꜣ pꜣy·f ỉr sẖ nfr*.

h. For the reading of this title, see note to Text **12**, R° 4; the four 'magicians' mentioned here are presumably interpreters of oracles consulted by the writer.

i. The scribe seems first to have written *rꜣ*; the additional stroke is unlikely to be a copy-mark, which the scribe has ignored for the last three lines.

j. *dmỉw* 'towns' is a possible reading, but suffers from the lack of a suitable determinative.

k. *rꜣ* is an alternative reading, although the sense is far from satisfactory; see note to translation below.

l. The determinative seems to have been first , altered rather cursorily to , cf. the parallel in Text **17**, l. 9.

m. A writing of *ꜣsy* (ⲟⲥⲉ), according to Erichsen, *Glossar*, 10, but the confusion of *aleph* and *ꜥayin* at such an early date as the mid-second century B.C. is perhaps unlikely, and one therefore wonders whether the two words are not separate.

n. Apparently the plural of *ꜣt(w)*. A similar curse may perhaps be restored in Text **7**, 15; see note *ad locum*, p. 36 above.

o. A characteristic disregard for number in pronouns, with the scribe changing from singular to plural indiscriminately.

p. The sublinear stroke is perhaps the final *-s* of the root, rather than a redundant *·k* of a Qualitative used as Infinitive.

Translation: recto

1. From Ḥor who is concerned with the petition of the chapels of Egypt,[a] (in) the name of the great god
2. ⟨Thoth (whose) might is known (in) every matter which concerns the Ibis (in) his heart⟩
3. in order to cause to be performed that which is beneficial to the fortune of the Ibis, namely, not to detract from[b] (any) matter (of)
4. that which concerns his sustenance and his burial. He who walks upon the path
5. named,[c] it is favourable for his life for a long time, while benefit is performed
6. for the Ibis from Elephantine to the shrines (of) Sambeḥdet.[d] May there flourish[e]
7. Imḥōtep son of Ptaḥ, to whom they call throughout the entire two lands because of his magic-making (?).[f]
8. I petitioned four magicians, (but) not one of them gave judgement on
9. that which refers to the great chapels in which the Ibis is born
10. within the nomes, and the foremost (?) chapels
11. which are their fields and their shrine.[g] I have been wronged by[h]
12. the mighty men.[i] The Great of Five, Thoth, and his

Translation: verso

1. strength, may they perform the slaughtering of his[j]
2. progeny! Disaster in their midst!
3. Calamity upon him! None shall know how to
4. sit by him on his day (of) testing.[k]

Notes

a. The petition-writer, employed as secretary by Ḥor of Sebennytos in transcribing his own experiences, and author of the Memphite hand in our documents, see note to Text **12**, R° 1 above. The fact that this present text bears the secretary's name suggests that he is here recounting part of his own history, and that he too has been wronged by the 'mighty men' (ll. 11–12), but some, or even all, of the material may have been dictated to him by Ḥor of Sebennytos. The metaphor of the 'path', however (R° 4), does recur in other passages in his hand (cf. Text **23**, verso) and seems to be a characteristic of the Memphite Ḥor.

b. Lit. 'cause to perish' (ⲧⲁⲕⲟ, Crum, 405a).

c. A natural metaphor, but a remarkable one for that. The notion of 'walking on the way' of a superior, i.e. conforming to his edicts, is familiar from the *mḏd wꜣt nt smnḫ sw* of Middle Kingdom stelae (e.g. *Khusobk*, 1).

The phrase 'way of the living' (*wꜣt nt ꜥnḫ*) is familiar from Pap. Chester Beatty IV, V° 6/4; *Instructions of Amennakhte*, 1; *Urk.* iii. 19/4, stela of *Tꜣ-hbt*, 13. The phrase *mìt n ꜥnḫ* also occurs (e.g. *Amenemōpe* 1/7; 16/8), and these, together with Hebrew parallels, are discussed by Williams in *Legacy of Egypt* (2nd ed.), 267 ff. From this it is a natural step to describe a religious system as 'The Way (of God)' (Acts 24: 14; a similar metaphor seems to have been current in the earlier sect at Qumrân), and perhaps the best demotic parallel occurs in *Dem. Chron.* 4/7, where it is said of Psammuthis *bn-pw·f ḫpr ḏd bn-pw·f ḫpr ḥr tꜣ mìt (n) pꜣ ntr*, ' "he did not exist" means that he did not remain upon the path of the god'.[1] One is tempted to wonder, therefore, whether the frequent use of the metaphor by the secretary does not imply that he was an initiate into the mysteries of Thoth. (For the claim which an Egyptian deity could make on a man, cf. the words of Isis in Apuleius, *Metamorphoses*, xi. 6). Although the mere use of such phrases is hardly proof, the repeated use of *bn-pw·ì ḫꜣꜥ tꜣ mìt* (Text **23**, R° 7–8; V° 8, 17) surely does much to justify the assumption.

d. For Sambeḥdet, cf. Gardiner, *JEA* 30 (1944), 41 ff. The phrase is an expression of the northernmost and southernmost limits of Egypt.

e. ⲟⲩⲟⲧⲟⲩⲉⲧ in Coptic (Crum, 493b) seems to have lost any figurative meaning of this sort.

f. Cf. among others, Pap. Oxyrh. 1381, 49–57. But the reading is not certain.

g. Again rather obscure; see Commentary on the ibis-cult below. The alternative translation 'gateway' yields little sense.

h. ἀδικοῦμαι ὑπό, cf. Commentary, § 1 on the petition below.

i. Presumably the temple-authorities, against whom the petition was addressed; cf. Text **7**, 14 above.

j. An archetypal enemy.

k. A legal metaphor: none shall take his side when he is haled before the 'council that judges the deficient' (cf. *Merikarēꜥ*, 53–4).

Preliminary Remarks

This seemingly incoherent text is best understood by reference to Text **17**.

[1] There is of course a literal use of the words as 'divine road', rendered into Greek as δρόμος and ὁδὸς πλατεῖα τῶν θεῶν, which refers to the avenue, often sphinx-lined, leading to a temple, cf. B. Couroyer in *Orientalia*, 38 (1969), 118, and Pestman in *Revue biblique*, 68 (1961), 530–2, no. 76, note 197, but this use is less likely here. For further discussion, and parallels from the tomb of Petosiris, see Appendix 2 below.

TEXT 17

Height	25·1 cm.
Width	15·9 cm.
Thickness	0·7 cm.
Munsell	5 YR 5/3
Photograph	Plate XVIII
Facsimile	not given
Excavator's no.	71/2–115 [5383]

This brown-ware ostracon, with its adjunct **17A**, is an expanded version of the preceding text. The verso is dark and mottled, and uninscribed. The recto, which also bears a few stains, contains twenty-two lines in the same hand as Text **16**; all of these, with the exception of ll. 3 and 4, and the last three, have been ticked off for copying. A further twelve lines (one being erased) continue the text on a sherd broken from the lower left-hand side of Text **17**, but a consideration of the writing shows that the piece must have been broken away before the scribe began his work. This ostracon (Text **17A**) has the following features:

Height	16·4 cm.
Width	6·8 cm.
Thickness	0·7 cm.
Photograph	Plate XVIII

(Excavator's no. and Munsell reading are the same as for Text **17**).

Text **17**

1. *n-drt Ḥr nty wbꜣ pꜣ smy n nꜣ ꜥhyt (n) Kmy*
2. *(n) rn*[a] *pꜣ ntr ꜥꜣ Ḏḥwty st ìr-rḫ pꜣ nḫt mdt nbt nty ṯꜣy pꜣ hb*
3. *(n) ḥꜣty·f r-dbꜣ*[b] *dìt ìr·w pꜣ nty nfr·f (n) pꜣy·f ꜥš-sḫn ḥtꜥ tm*
4. *dìt ꜣḳ mdt (n) tꜣ nty ṯꜣy tꜣy·f ḫrt ìrm tꜣy·f ḳrst*
5. *ḏd ìw*[d] *ṯꜣy·w gns n-drt nꜣ rmtw ḏry n-drt ḫpr·f*

6. *nꜣw*[e] *(ỉ·)dỉ·f ꜥꜣy nꜣ ỉ·ỉr gmꜥ r·f nꜣw*[e] *(ỉ·)ỉr·f*
7. *prty nꜣ ỉ·ỉr ẖꜣꜥ pꜣ myt.*[f] *Ḏḥwty*
8. *nb* ⟨*ꜥḥꜥ*⟩[g] *ỉrm pꜣy·f nꜥš ỉr·w pꜣ smty*
9. *(n) tꜣy·f wty(t). ꜥsy ỉwt·w.*
10. *ꜣtyw r·f. bn-ỉw·w rẖ ḥms*
11. *n-drt·f pꜣy·f hrw (n) šn.*[h] *r*[i] *pꜣ Wr-dỉw*
12. *Ḏḥwty ỉr-rẖ r*[j] *pꜣ nty ỉr mdt-nfrt n*
13. *pꜣ hb Yb (r) nꜣ wꜥbt (n) Smꜣ-bḥdt*
14. *wtt*[k] *pꜣ nty mšꜥ ḥr tꜣ mỉt*
15. *rn·s nfr·s (n) pꜣy·f ꜥḥꜥ* ⟨*(n) wš ḳy*⟩. *pꜣ nty mdt*
16. *rmt-rẖ*[l] *r lẖ nw·f ssw r ssw.*
17. *nẖt (n) tkn mdt ỉw·s ỉn-ỉw*
18. *(n) pꜣ hp wꜥt wnwt bn-ỉw*
19. *sllꜥ·s.*[m] *nꜣ-ꜥšꜣ pꜣ nty ỉy*
20. *n-ỉm·s. wn myt nb*
21. *(n) ꜥwy-drt Ḏḥwty*
22. *pꜣ nb rẖ.*[n]

Text 17A

1. *bw-ỉr ꜣbẖ mdt ỉw·s ṯꜣy*
2. *pꜣ hb n gy n pꜣ tꜣ.*
3. *smy·ỉ ḥr-tb 4*
4. [[*r-hn ꜣbd-3 prt sw 16 (n) Mn-nfr*]]
5. *bn-pw wꜥ n-ỉm·w wpy tꜣ ẖt-*
6. *mdt*[o] *nty*[p] *ṯꜣy r*[q] *nꜣy r-hn*
7. *ꜣbd-3 prt sw 16 m-sꜣ·s*[r]
8. *pꜣ ḥr-tb ʾIy-m-ḥtp sꜣ Ptḥ*
9. *nty ỉw·w ꜥš n·f (n) nꜣ tꜣwy dr·w*
10. *r-dbꜣ pꜣy·f ỉr-spy.*[s]
11. *pꜣ ntr rn·f pꜣ nty ḏlꜥ-*[t]
12. *mdt ẖr nꜣy*
13. (traces erased).

Notes

a. The parallel text has *pꜣ rn*, perhaps wrongly.

b. The palimpsest has *ẖt*; another sentence runs beneath much of this line.

c. The palimpsest has *nty ỉr*.

d. The force of the *ỉw* is interesting. It is hardly likely to be circumstantial, and it would seem more like the affirmative use of *ỉw* before a *sḏm·f* familiar from Middle Egyptian, where it serves to emphasize the occurrence of the action ('The fact is that .....'). Its use in demotic is rare, but not unattested: a good example appears in Pap. Rylands IX, 18/8: *tw-s ỉw sḏm·ỉ-s*, 'See, the fact is that I have heard it'.

e. Probably a writing of ⲛⲏ 'those'; note the full writing of *ỉ·ỉr* after the article, familiar in these texts.

f. The masculine *mṯ(n)* (ⲙⲟⲉⲓⲧ, Crum, 188a), but doubtless with the same connotations as *tꜣ mỉt* (see note to Text **16,** R° 4–5 above).

g. For this title of Thoth as measurer of time, cf. Boylan, *Thoth*, Ch. 8 and p. 188.

h. The parallel in Text **16** writes the plural here.

i. This phonetic writing of *ỉw* (ⲉ) is not usual in our texts, and may be a flourish of the professional writer. The meaning is perhaps circumstantial.

j. An introduction to the direct object demanded by a 'durative' tense, cf. note *h* to the translation of Text **1,** 4, p. 12 above.

k. Either a secondary formation from *wt* 'flourish', or, less likely, a defective writing of *wtwt* (Text **16,** R° 6).

l. Presumably in the common meaning 'decent, wise' (Erichsen, *Glossar*, 247).

m. A similar word, spelt *srrꜥ*, occurs in Strasbourg Ostracon B (Spiegelberg, *ZÄS* 50 (1912), 35, l. 7). Its meaning in this case is hard to grasp, but here a translation 'fail, lapse', may be in order.[1]

n. Cf. *pꜣ rẖ* in Text **3,** R° 16.

o. The usual expression in our texts for an oracular utterance of some kind, cf. Text **23,** R° 8, where three *ẖt-mdt* are mentioned. Some of these 'utterances' seem to take the form of a dream or vision, and indeed a parallel can be found in Hebrew with the word מַשָּׂא, cf. Isaiah, 13: 1, where we are told of 'the oracle of (i.e. concerning) Babylon which Isaiah son of Amoz saw (חָזָה)'. Some other *ẖt-mdt*, however, are presumably the enigmatic utterances recorded in Texts **14** and **15,** which emanated from the god through his human servants. Such questions are discussed in § 3 of the Commentary below.

p. The palimpsest here has a word such as *bỉn* or the like (the determinative is clear), overlaid with *ẖt*, overlaid in its turn by the text.

q. Clearly written before *nꜣy*, and one wonders whether the complete reading of the phrase *tꜣ nty ṯꜣy* is not *tꜣ/nꜣ nty ṯꜣy r*; but none of the other examples writes the preposition.

r. The pronoun may possibly be redundant.

s. See note to Text **16,** R° 7.

t. The palimpsest seems to have *wbꜣ·ỉ*.

[1] The use of *bn-ỉw* before a *sḏm·f* is noteworthy, and may be deliberately formal.

Translation: Text **17**

1. From Ḥor who is concerned with the petition of the chapels of Egypt,
2. (in the) name (of) the great god Thoth (whose) might is known (in) every matter which concerns the Ibis
3. (in) his heart, in order to cause to be performed that which is beneficial (to) his fortune, namely not to
4. detract from (any) matter (of) that which concerns his sustenance and his burial:
5. for (the fact) is that I have been wronged by the mighty men, inasmuch as
6. those whom he[a] made great (are) the ones who brought grief upon him, (and) those whom he made
7. pre-eminent[b] (are) the ones who abandoned the path. Thoth,
8. the lord of ⟨lifetime⟩, and his strength, may they perform the slaughtering (of)
9. his progeny! Disaster in their midst!
10. Calamity upon him! None shall know how to sit
11. by him (on) his day (of) testing. For the Great of Five
12. Thoth knows him who performs benefit for
13. the Ibis from Elephantine (to) the shrines (of) Sambeḥdet.
14. He who walks upon the path named prospers.
15. It is favourable (for) his life ⟨(for) a long time⟩. He who speaks
16. wisdom rather than foolishness sees[c] days upon days.
17. The matter which comes to the law[d]
18. conquers swiftly, (in) a single hour: it shall not
19. fail (?). Numerous is he who comes
20. to it:[e] (for) every path is
21. (in) the hands of Thoth,
22. the knowing lord.

Translation: Text **17A**

1. No matter is ever forgotten[f] which concerns
2. the Ibis in (any) way on earth.
3. I petitioned four magicians
4. [[until Phamenoth, day 16, (in) Memphis]]:
5. (but) not one of them gave judgement on the utter-
6. ance which concerns these things[g] until
7. Phamenoth, day 16, except
8. the magician of Imḥōtep, son of Ptaḥ,
9. to whom they call (throughout) the entire two lands
10. because of his magic-making (?).[h]
11. The god himself was the one who
12. recorded[i] in connection[j] with this.
13. (*erasure*).

Notes

a. The god Thoth.

b. See note to Text **4**, R° 2, p. 30 above.

c. Strictly a *sḏm·f*, which has been taken in a gnomic sense.

d. See note to the translation of Text **25**, 8, p. 92 below; the imagery here seems to be that the man who walks in the way of Thoth is assured of victory before justice, and this is presumably connected with the idea of redress against the 'mighty men' who have wronged the servant of the god.

e. Or perhaps 'on behalf of it', the victorious cause.

f. There seems to be no grammatical subject to this sentence, unless the verb *ɜbḫ* be taken as passive, and the whole has been treated as an impersonal clause; perhaps a plural *·w* is to be understood after *bw-ỉr*.

g. Presumably an oracle concerning the fortunes of the Ibis, which Ḥor had communicated to several agencies, human and divine, in order to secure an interpretation.

h. See note to Text **16**, R° 7, p. 61 above.

i. For *ḏlꜥ-mdt*, see Text **1**, 11, and note, p. 10. In both these cases, it is significant that the word occurs when describing the outcome of a dream or oracle, and it is difficult to resist the idea that the word implies, not only mere recording of the material, but also its interpretation, for the point here is surely that the *ḥr-tb* of

Imḥōtep had succeeded in deciphering an enigma which had baffled all others.

j. Text **1**, 11 also has this preposition after *ḏlꜥ-mdt*.

Preliminary Remarks

This text, an expanded version of the preceding, is likewise the work of the Memphite Ḥor, resident petition-writer at the ibis-shrine. He has, he tells us, been wronged by 'the mighty men' (presumably the temple authorities), who have misused and perverted the responsibility entrusted to them by the god (ll. 5–7). A bitter curse is then directed against them. The text continues to describe the fortunes of the pious man, to whom Thoth offers support and victory over his enemies. In the adjunct (Text **17A**), an oracle, perhaps delivered by Thoth and possibly resembling the obscure passages of Texts **14** and **15**, is interpreted, after four unsuccessful attempts (ll. 3–6), by the magician (*ḥr-tb*) of Imḥōtep, whose cult lay near by. This event is dated to 16 Phamenoth of an unnamed year; if, as seems possible, this oracle is the one referred to also in Text **22** below, the year would be the fifth of the joint reign, and the corresponding date 16 April 165. But this is not entirely certain.

TEXT 18

Height	15·4 cm.
Width	21·6 cm.
Thickness	0·7 cm.
Munsell	5 YR 7/1
Photograph	Plates XIX (R°), XX (V°)
Facsimile	not given
Excavator's no.	71/2–112 [5380]

A large buff-ware ostracon, covered with writing on both sides. The main text of the recto (convex surface) comprises fifteen lines, with the occasional erasure or lacuna; in addition to these, two lines are added upside down at the bottom of the ostracon, and a similar three lines fitted into the small space at the top. The verso comprises twenty lines in the same hand, but the first three are short and may represent an afterthought on the part of the scribe. The hand seems to be Memphite, but the writer identifies himself merely as 'Ḥor', without qualification. The entire text, an invocation to various gods to appear in a dream, is naturally full of recondite mythology, a commentary upon which would be out of place in a preliminary publication; I have therefore confined comments to palaeography and other essential matters. The copy-ticks by the first five lines of the recto suggest that this text like others was copied on to papyrus. The language of this incantation is strongly coloured by archaisms, such as the frequent use of the preposition *m*, forms such as *ḥt-ntr·f* (R° 2*), and possibly the unusual negative *bn-ỉw tẖr·k/t* of R° 11, 14. Another feature is the common use of small space-fillers between words, often before the names and titles of divinities.

Text: recto

1. *wꜥb*[a] *wꜥb Rꜥ-Ḥr nb pt hy*[b] *Rꜥ-Ḥr ỉtn hy Rꜥ-Ḥr pr n mẖy hy Rꜥ ntr ꜥꜣ*[c] *hy Rꜥ-*
2. *Ḥr tpy ꜣẖt(?)·f*[d] *hy Rꜥ-Ḥr nẖt (n) 'Iwnw*[e] *hy Ḥr ḥḥ*[f] *hy Ḥr ḥrby*[g] *pt hy*
3. *Rꜥ-Ḥr n tꜣ hy Rꜥ n Mꜣꜥ-ẖrw*[h] *hy Rꜥ-Ḥr wbn hy Rꜥ-Ḥr sẖm hy Rꜥ-Ḥr sẖm n nꜣ ntrw*
4. *hy Rꜥ-Ḥr ḥḳ(ꜣ) n 'Iwnw hy Rꜥ-Ḥr pꜣ kꜣ*[i] *hy Rꜥ-Ḥr pꜣ kꜣ mꜣꜥ hy Rꜥ-Ḥr nty-ỉt·f*[j] *hy*
5. *Rꜥ-Ḥr mḥꜣ(?)*[k] *n ỉtn ỉrt·f n-drt·f m Dwꜣt*[l] *m ẖpry*[m] *mẖrr wꜥ ḥḥ*[f] *m st mẖy.*
6. *Mꜣꜥt tpy*[n] *wtn n Rꜥ Ꜣst tpy wtn n Rꜥ Ḥt-Ḥr tpy wtn n Rꜥ Ḏḥwty tpy wtn n Rꜥ*
7. *Ḫnsw tpy wtn nb Dwꜣt ⟨wtn⟩ tpy wtn n Rꜥ Skty*[o] *Mtꜣ(?)*[p] *pꜣ wtn n Rꜥ Ḥp(?)*[q] *wtn*
8. *nb Ḥp(?) sk nb nꜣ sštw ꜥꜣy*[r] *n 'Iwnw*[e] *by*[s] *'Iwnw by Mḥy(?)*[t] *by 'Iwnw By-ḥꜣ*[u]
9. *By-ḥꜣ Skr-Wsỉr n pt Skr-Wsỉr n tꜣ Skr-Wsỉr Skr-Wsỉr(?) Skr-Wsỉr n ẖt·f nbt*
10. *Skr-Wsỉr m ẖrb·f nb Skr-Wsỉr bẖn n·f ỉrt·f ẖy n·f ḥꜣty·f. lk nꜣ ꜥꜥtyw*

11. *nb tḥ nb r·f. spw·s.*[v]
bn-ỉw ṯḥr·k[w] *Wsỉr nb nỉwt nḥḥ kḥ nb* [ ]
nb[x] *st*
12. *n Mȝʿ-ḫrw ȝty n·k ḥty Ḥr-dšryt nsw-ntr*(?)[y]
nht [*st*][z] *ntr ʿȝ ḥty*(?)[aa] *n·k*
13. *ȝt·f* (*n*) *Wsỉr ḥms Ḥʿpy*[bb] *ʿnḫ mw ḥnš nb*
tḥ [*ȝḫr*][cc]
14. *bn-ỉw ṯḥr·t*[dd] *Ȝst wr*(*t*) *ḥk*(*ȝ*) *smn st Mȝʿt*
sy·s [*wḏȝ Dwȝt*]
15. *ḥty*(?)[aa] *Rʿ mn·s ỉ·ỉr šȝʿ*[ee] *ḏt. ḥms*
Ḥʿpy(?) *ʿnḫ* [(traces)].

(The five lines which appear upside down at top and bottom of the recto are probably the continuation of the verso, and will appear at the end of the latter).

Text: verso

1. *tw·ỉ ʿš n·k* [(*n*) *pt* (*n*) *ỉtn*(?)][a]
2. *ʾIy-m-ḥtp ḳmȝ*(?)[b] *rsnfy*[c]
3. *tȝ thn nb ʿnḫ-tȝwy*[d] [(*n*) *Mn-nfr*]
(The next line is added in the margin)
3a. *sḫ Ḥr ḥȝt-sp 10t ȝbd-2 šmw*[e] *sw 9*
4. *mdt ỉ·ỉr·ḥr·k Nfr-tm ssn nfr ʿḳ*(?)[f] *mdt ỉ·ỉr·ḥr·k Nfr-tm ḫkrw nfr ḫntt*(?)[g] *mdt ỉ·ỉr·ḥr·k*
5. *Nfr-tm ssn mdt ỉ·ỉr·ḥr·k nfr mdt ỉ·ỉr·ḥr·k tȝwy mdt ỉ·ỉr·ḥr·k ḥwy tȝwy ḥms Ḥʿpy*(?)[h] *ʿnḫ*
6. *mw ḥnš tḥ tn*[i] *ḥr·k nfr. mdt ỉ·ỉr·ḥr·k* ⟨*Rʿ-Šw m rn·f nb*⟩ [[*pȝ*]] *syf ỉ·ỉr pr pȝ ssn* [ ][j] *ỉ·ỉr*
7. *pr m ʿnḫ-tȝwy pȝ wny ỉ·ỉr wḏʿ pȝ kk ʿnḫ-tȝwy ḫnm*[k] *m ỉtn mḫrr ỉ·ỉr ḫpr*[l]
8. *Ḥr-bỉk snḳy*[m] *bn-ỉw nȝy·f ʿwyw ḥnš Ḥr-pȝ-ḫrd wr tp ʿȝ* (*n*) *Wsỉr ḥms Pr-ʿȝ mw ḥn*(*š*)[n] *tḥ rn*[o]
9. *mdt ỉ·ỉr·ḥr·k Ḏḥwty ḥḥ*[p] *ḏd wr ḥsf*(?)[p] *n nȝ ntrw Pr-nȝ-ỉḥy nȝ rdw nȝ ntrw nȝ ḥmw-ntr*[q] *nȝ ntrw*
10. *ỉḥy nb nfr dỉ·k Pr-ʿȝ tym*[r] *ḥkms*[s] *ȝpwt*[t] *ỉḥy nb nfr*[u] [*dwȝ-nsw ḏbʿ*(?)*·k*].[v]
11. *mdt ỉ·ỉr·ḥr·k Ḏḥwty ḥḥ nb Mȝʿt nb tȝ*(?)*-Mȝʿt*[w] *nty ỉw mȝʿ rn·f ỉw·f ỉr ḥḥ. mdt ỉ·ỉr·ḥr·k Ḏḥwty pȝ nb ỉr-rḫ*[x]
12. *nb spw.*[y] *ȝy rḫ rn·k m wtyt m pr m rȝ·k dỉ n·k* [ ][z] *n·k r-pr*
13. *sbty n·k wtḥ wpy snw*[aa] *ȝbwyw*[bb] *n tȝ nb Sḫmt ʿȝt sȝt n Rʿ*
14. *ḥr Ḥmkȝ*[cc] *ỉr·k*[dd] *smȝʿ Pr-ʿȝ šȝʿ ḏt. tn ḥr·k r*[ee] *nfr.*
15. *mdt ḥr·k ntr pr m Dwȝt*[ff] *ʾIy-m-ḥtp wr sȝ Ptḥ hȝy m-šs*[gg] *Wsỉr pr·k pr·k*[hh] *wsḫyt*
16. *m ʿt ỉr·k hs ʿrḳ-ḥḥ sḏm·k m ʿby tgg·k* (*r*) *šḳ·s*[ii] *šsp·k sy·s m ʿby*
17. *šsp ḫwy nḥḥ*(?) *snt*(?)[jj] *pȝ ỉ·ỉr m srȝ n·k šw* (*n*) *ḥbg*[kk] *m ʿw Ȝst ḥnʿ Nbt-ḥt ʿȝt*
18. *tw-s*(?)[ll] *ỉm r rswt n Ḥr-wr*(?)[mm] *pr by·k ḥry ḫt·k* (*n*) *tȝ Dwȝt sm n*
19. *Skr-Wsỉr m sḫ*(?)*·f Tyt*[nn] *sȝ wr n Ptḥ ỉ·ỉr-snfy mtw·k snt* (*n*) *pr*
20. *ršy* *ršy r mn·k*[oo]
(The text continues in the inverted lines of the recto)

1.* *ršy ršy hh nty ḫn ʿnḫ-tȝwy tȝy·k st nfrt Ḏdỉt*[pp] *ršy*
2.* *ms-rdwy nty ḫn ḥt-ntr·f*[qq] *bn-ỉw·ỉ ḫn ḫrw ʿȝ*
(The following lines appear in the space at the top of the recto)
3.* *m wsḫt*[rr] *ʿȝt. ỉm n·ỉ nb ỉ·ỉr šȝʿ ḏt*[ss] *mn·k ḥb*(?) *ỉtyw·k*
4.* *tn ḥr·k nfr nw ỉrt·k ḥty*(?) *mnḫ ỉr·k*(?) *m-sȝ·ỉ*(?)
5.* *ḥḥ*(?) *nfr nȝy*(?)

Notes: recto

a. Apparently preceded by a stroke, possibly a copy-tick, although only the first lines show this feature.

b. The scribe seems to have begun the *ȝy* of V° 12, and the result lacks the characteristic determinative ([hieroglyph]) of the other writings of *hy* which follow.

c. The palimpsest has *ḥs*.

d. An enigmatic title, clearly written though it is. For *tpy* cf. the similar writings in ll. 6–7 below. The final *·f*, which is unmistakable, suggests **tpy ḏw·f*, but this is normally confined to Anubis. The text as given is little more than a guess.

e. See notes to Text **1**, 2, p. 8 above.

f. See also notes to Text **3**, R° 26, p. 23 above. The present text contains many examples of this word, writings which seem to fall into two groups. The first, which appears as [demotic group], occurs in R° 5 and 5*; the reading *ḥḥ* is confirmed by the toponym *ʿrḳ-ḥḥ* in V° 16, while for the form of the hieroglyph [hieroglyph] in later hieratic, cf. Möller, *Paläographie*, iii. 37. The second writing (R° 2; V° 9, 11) appears as [demotic group]. Now the difference between these two writings may be quite illusory, but it is tempting to see in the second group a word such as *iꜣw* 'praise' (*Wb.* i. 28). Since this possibility is unproven, I have used the transliteration *ḥḥ* throughout. For a figurative use of what appears to be the same word, see Text **26,** R° 14 below.

g. Possibly the *ḥry-bꜣ* of *Wb.* iii. 146?

h. The reading *Mꜣʿt-špss* is excluded by the reappearance of the word in R° 12 below.

i. *Ḥr-dy* as a place-name (Ḥartai) is a possible reading, but the recurrence with *mꜣʿ* would be difficult to explain.

j. A semi-phonetic writing of *nḏ-it·f* (-ενδώτης). For similar spellings in the group used as a proper name see notes to Text **19,** R° 1, p. 75 below.

k. Tentatively identified with the *mḥ* 'offspring' of *Wb.* ii. 120; but the reading itself is not certain.

l. The palimpsest may have had *ʿnḫ-tꜣwy*, although some of the final signs are difficult to reconcile with this.

m. Unless *mḫpry* is to be taken as one word (of unknown meaning), it seems necessary to take *ḫpry* as some by-form of the root *ḫpr*, possibly as an approximation to *ḫprt* (ϣπηρε). The reading **m ir pry* is less convincing.

n. Unlikely to be a writing of *pꜣy* 'this', which appears in our documents only as [demotic group] or [demotic group]. See also note *d* above.

o. Cf. the similar writings in Text **12,** R° 9; **12A,** 3.

p. Possibly a semi-phonetic equivalent of (*m*)*ʿnḏt*; this tentative reading is suggested by the proximity of *Sktt*, and by the late variant [hieroglyphs] in *Wb.* ii. 48.

q. Similar abbreviated writings have been encountered in the stelae of the Mothers of the Apis, although usually only in the compound *Wsir-Ḥp*. The reading is therefore far from certain.

r. See notes to Text **3,** R° 17, p. 23 above.

s. In spite of the two different writings of this word in the same line, the identification is supported by V° 18, where it occurs in opposition to *ẖt* 'body'. See also the note to Text **19,** R° 5, p. 75 below.

t. This group [demotic group] is unknown to me. Its closest relative seems to be the *Šʿ-ḥy* of BM. 10591, V° 5, 7, where it may be an abbreviation of *Šꜣs-ḥtp* (Thompson, *Siut Archive*, 59); yet this is unlikely in the present context. *Bʿḥ*(*y*) 'Hermopolis' may be a possible reading. *Ḫꜣsy* 'Xois' is much less likely. The text is offered with reserve.

u. Possibly a variant of *Bꜣ-ḥr-ẖt* 'Buchis' (cf. Mond–Myers, *The Bucheum*, ii. 38), but not otherwise attested. Perhaps the name was prompted by the repetition of *by* earlier in the line. Other readings may be possible.

v. This group may represent *spy* (сєєпє) 'remainder', or the element known from *ir-spy* in Text **16,** R° 7; **17A,** 10. The latter seems to recur in V° 12 of the present text, but the writing is not identical, and I have chosen the former reading.

w. I have not been able to identify this word elsewhere. *tḫ*(*r*) (*dḫr*) 'to be bitter' occurs elsewhere in this text, but written quite distinctly. The determinative seems to be a phallus (?); hence the translation.

x. I cannot interpret the surviving traces, which resemble [demotic traces].

y. Not *ntr ʿꜣ*, which is written later in the same line.

z. The traces before *st* are too faint to read.

aa. The same group in l. 15 below. Reading tentative.

bb. The writings given in Erichsen, *Glossar*, 293, are widely different, but other readings (*Ḥp*? *'Iʿḥ*?) are even less convincing.

cc. I can make no sense of these traces, nor of *ꜣḥr* (?).

dd. *·k* was originally written below the line, then perhaps erased.

ee. The same extended use, which resembles *i·ir·ḥr*, in R° 3* below.

Notes: verso

a. Badly obscured by a lacuna. *itn* (єιτн̄) is suggested by Smith.

b. The flesh determinative is unusual; perhaps the word is to be understood in the sense of 'creature, offspring'.

c. For this semi-phonetic writing of *rs-inb·f* as a cult-epithet of Ptaḥ, cf. Brugsch, *Thesaurus*, 991, where it is confirmed by the hieroglyphic equivalents in bilingual texts. For an alternative spelling, *i·ir-snfy*, in which the first syllable probably corresponds to Coptic єр-, see l. 19 below.

d. Written in normal demotic characters, as opposed

to the hieraticized writings of V° 7 and R° 1* and of Text **23**, R° 6.

e. The same abbreviated writing as in Text **2**, R° 12 above.

f. The traces resemble *nkt* (ⲛ̄ⲕⲁ) more than the text, which is influenced by the following *ḫntt* (?), a word which shares a similar determinative. Unfortunately the latter is scarcely more than a guess, and the whole sentence is therefore far from understood.

g. See previous note; alternative readings may be possible, as *ḳntt*(?), but their meanings are no clearer.

h. See note *bb* to the recto above.

i. Further examples of the phrase in V° 14, and R° 4* support this reading rather than *ḥtp*.

j. This rather tangled group may represent an unsuccessful attempt to write *i͗·i͗r pr*, which the scribe abandoned and began again.

k. At first sight deceptively similar to *ḫḫ* as written above (see note *f* to the recto), but the determinative of the present group is different. For *ḫnm m i͗tn* see *Wb*. iii. 380 and especially *Sinuhe* R 7 = Blackman, *Middle Egyptian Stories*, 3, l. 7.

l. The final stroke seems to be part of the group itself, and not a following *·f*.

m. *snt*, which may be a possible reading, is, however, written differently in our texts (cf. Text **3**, R° 8, 25); it is also less appropriate to a description of the god Horus.

n. The final *-š* has been omitted by the scribe, but is confirmed by the parallels in the present line and in R° 13; V° 6 above.

o. The parallels have *rn·f*, which may have been intended here but fallen victim to the lack of space.

p. *ḫnm* or even *ḫnn* (Text **3**, V° 10) are also acceptable here. The whole is probably to be taken as some sort of divine epithet, like *ms-rdwy* or *rḫ-rn·k*.

q. A more convincing reading than *ḥtp-ntr*, cf. Tanis Stela (Canopus), 7, where *nꜣ ḥmw-ntr* appears as 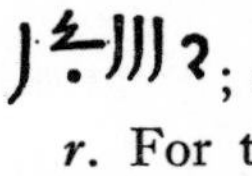 ; see Brugsch, *Thesaurus*, 1555, l. 4.

r. For this word, corresponding to Coptic ⲧⲁⲉⲓⲙ, see the notes to Text **3**, R° 17, p. 23 above.

s. Possibly the ϩⲟⲕⲙⲉⲥ of Crum, 664b; but the sense must be a figurative one.

t. Tentatively identified with *wpt* 'booty', cf. some of the semi-phonetic writings in Erichsen, *Glossar*, 85. The final signs seem to have been borrowed from the phonetically similar *ꜣpd*/*i͗pd* 'bird, goose', but the whole is far from certain.

u. *nfr* in the present example seems to have acquired a redundant final *-t*, which is absent from the writing at the beginning of the line.

v. The whole of this final group is obscure: *dwꜣ-nsw* is dubious, *ḏbꜥ·k* (?) so faint that it may even have been erased.

w. The initial group presents the difficulties. One would expect *drt-* to show an introductory sign, thus 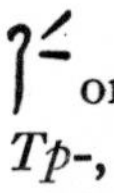 or the like. *Tꜣ-* in l. 13 below has a supralinear stroke. *Tp-*, which is palaeographically better, is unattested with *mꜣꜥt*. The translation is therefore conjecture.

x. So rather than *nb ꜥnḫ*; for these titles of the god Thoth see Appendix 2 below.

y. Taken in the sense of *i͗r-spy* in Text **16**, R° 7 and **17A**, 10; see also note *v* to the recto above.

z. I can make nothing of this group.

aa. Unfortunately not *mꜣꜥt*, combined as it often is with *wpy*; cf. Anthes, *JNES* 16 (1957), 176 ff. The expression must therefore be understood as a reference to Thoth's role as separator of the two combatants (*wp rḥwy*) in the myth of Horus and Seth, cf. Gwyn Griffiths, *Conflict of Horus and Seth*, 141 ff., although the historical reconstruction should be read in the light of Te Velde, *Seth God of Confusion*, 74 ff.

bb. Possibly the *ꜣbwt* of *Wb*. i. 8, with reference to the enemies of the sun god.

cc. I have taken this as a phonetic variant of *Ḥmꜣg*, 'the bandaged one', a late by-name of the god Osiris (*Wb*. iii. 94, cf. the spelling *ḥmꜣkꜣ* for the associated verb). But the reading is not assured.

dd. Not *mtw·k*, in spite of the strange initial sign.

ee. This preposition is not encountered in the parallels (V° 6; R° 4*); it may have been omitted in the parallels, or the scribe may have chosen to vary his formula. He does this considerably in V° 4–6 above, and is at liberty to do so now.

ff. The scribe seems first to have written *ḳyt*; see notes to Text **8**, R° 22, p. 43 above.

gg. This Memphite writing is quite different from those of Text **3**, V° 2, which is probably a Sebennytic hand, and Text **1**, 17, whose origin is unknown.

hh. These two writings of the same word differ, the first lacking the second element (cf. the season *prt* and the note on *Pr*(?)-*Ḏḥwty* in Text **1**, 1, p. 8 above). In l. 18 below the first element 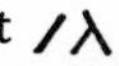 is missing. Some of this variation may be due to speed of dictation, but the rest stands as a reminder that the palaeography of Demotic is not static.

ii. Cf. Erichsen, *Glossar*, 524; the first sign is not *m-*,

jj. Neither reading is satisfactory.

kk. ϩωϐκ, Crum, 656b(?).

ll. It must be admitted that the other writings given in note *gg* to Text **1**, 11, p. 10 above, are more convincing; the present example is far from certain.

mm. This entire group is dubious: the first sign is not *ḫr* and unlikely to be *t-*, but the interpretation is a difficult problem.

nn. Taken tentatively as the name of the goddess of weaving (*Wb*. v. 231–2), perhaps used figuratively. For *sḥ*(?) = *sʿḥ*, cf. Möller, *Rhind*, Glossary, n. 353.

oo. The strange gaps in this final line are difficult to explain, but it is at least possible that the words represent an instruction or reminder to insert the additional lines from the recto (those numbered 1*–5* below); these lines can certainly be divided into two sections, one beginning with *ršy* (R° 1*), the other with *mn·k* (R° 3*). This would presumably have happened when the text was transferred to papyrus, and I have so reconstructed the translation below.

pp. See notes to Text **13**, 7, p. 55 above.

qq. A clear attempt at archaism, as with the repeated use of the preposition *m*, and possibly in *bn-iw tḥr·k* above. See the introduction to the text.

rr. Spelt elsewhere in these documents as *wsḫyt*; the strange sign after the determinative may have strayed in from the verb *pr*, a word which must have understandably obsessed the writer of this text.

ss. A rather cramped writing of the phrase in R° 15 above.

Translation: recto

1. Pure, pure,[a] Raʿ-Horus lord of heaven! Hail, Raʿ-Horus (the) disc, hail Raʿ-Horus, come forth from (the) balance,[b] hail Rēʿ, great god, hail Raʿ-
2. Horus at the head of his horizon (?), hail Raʿ-Horus, strong in Heliopolis, hail Horus (of) millions,[c] hail Horus, lofty soul (?) of heaven, hail
3. Raʿ-Horus of earth, hail Rēʿ of *mꜣʿ-ḫrw*,[d] hail Raʿ-Horus (the) shiner, hail Raʿ-Horus (the) power, hail Raʿ-Horus (the) power of the gods,
4. hail Raʿ-Horus ruler of Heliopolis, hail Raʿ-Horus the bull, hail Raʿ-Horus the true bull, hail Raʿ-Horus avenger of his father, hail
5. Raʿ-Horus offspring (?) of the disk, his eye in his hand,[e] in the Netherworld, in the form (?) of scarab, a millionfold in the place of weighing![f]
6. Maʿat, at the head of the bark[g] of Rēʿ, Isis at the head of the bark of Rēʿ, Hathor at the head of the bark of Rēʿ, Thoth at the head of the bark of Rēʿ,
7. Khons at the head of the bark, lord of the Netherworld, ⟨bark⟩[h] at the head of the bark of Rēʿ, (*M*)*sktt*, *Mʿnḏt*(?), the bark of Rēʿ, Apis(?), every
8. bark, Apis(?), every destruction(?),[i] the great mysteries of Heliopolis, soul (of) Heliopolis, soul (of) Lower Egypt(?), soul (of) Heliopolis, Buchis(?)
9. Buchis(?), Seker-Osiris of Heaven, Seker-Osiris of earth, Seker-Osiris, Seker-Osiris(?), Seker-Osiris in all his embodiments,[j]
10. Seker-Osiris in all his transformations,[k] Seker-Osiris, whose eye is effulgent[l] for him, whose heart is elated for him! Cease the limbs!
11. Lord of all bitterness against him![m] Its remainder: Thou shalt not copulate (?), Osiris, Lord of the city of eternity, of every land, of every [·····], of the place
12. of *mꜣʿ-ḫrw*! Calamity to thee, shining one, Horus the red,[n] king of god(s), strong [·····] place, great god! Terror(?) to thee,
13. back of Osiris![o] Subside, living Nile! Foul water, lord of bitterness [······················]
14. Thou shalt not copulate(?), Isis, great of magic! Establish the seat of Truth, its beam [secure in the Netherworld]!
15. Terror(?) (to thee), Rēʿ! It[p] abides for eternity. Subside, living Nile(?) [·····················]

Translation: verso

1. I call upon thee [in heaven, in earth(?)],
2. Imḥōtep, creation of south-of-his-wall,[q]

3. (in) the peak, lord of ʿAnkhtawy [(in) Memphis].

3a. (*in margin*) Written by Ḥor in Year 10, Paoni, day 9.[r]

4. There speaks before thee Nefertēm, the beautiful lotus *ʿḳ*-offerings(?), there speaks before thee Nefertēm, the beautiful adornment *ḫntt*-offerings(?), there speaks before thee

5. Nefertēm the lotus, there speaks before thee the beautiful, there speaks before thee the two lands, there speaks before thee the protector of the two lands![s] Subside, living Nile(?),

6. foul water, bitterness! Raise thy beautiful face! There speaks before thee ⟨Raʿ-Shu in all his names⟩, child[t] who came forth, the lotus who

7. came forth from ʿAnkhtawy, the light which dispelled the darkness (of) ʿAnkhtawy, imbued with the disc, scarab who came into being![u]

8. Horus the falcon, suckling, his houses shall not stink![v] Horus the child, the great, great first(-born of) Osiris! Subside, Pharaoh, foul water, bitterness (by) name!

9. There speaks before thee Thoth a millionfold(?). Great-of-retribution says to the gods of House-of-the-spirits,[w] the agents (of) the gods, the prophets of the gods,

10. (and) every good spirit, 'Mayest thou give Pharaoh reverence, esteem(?) and booty(?), every good spirit, [may thy finger (?) adore the king]'.

11. There speaks before thee Thoth a millionfold(?), lord of Truth, lord of the land(?) of Truth, whose name is true, when he performs millionfold(?). There speaks before thee Thoth the knowing lord,

12. lord of spells,[x] 'O knower-of-thy-name in begetting, in coming forth from thy mouth, there gives to thee [· · · · ·] to thee (a) chapel(?)

13. preparation to thee the pourer(?), the separator of the brothers, the dissidents of every land, Sakhmis the great, daughter of Rēʿ,

14. from[y] the bandaged one:[z] thou shalt greet Pharaoh for ever. Raise thy face to the good!'

15. There speaks before thee the god who comes forth from the Netherworld, Imḥōtep the great, son of Ptaḥ. 'Hail in truth, Osiris, comest thou forth, forth (to? the) forecourt

16. from the chest![aa] Thou art praised in ʿAleḳḥaḥ,[bb] mayest thou hear amid offerings, mayest thou hasten (to) its vault(?), mayest thou seize its beam(?) amid offerings!'[cc]

17. Radiance which protects eternity(?) [· · · · ·] who performs for thee in prediction, free from goading, with the might of Isis and Nephthys the great,

18. [behold]!—come for a dream of *Ḥrwr*(?),[dd] come forth, thy soul upon high, thy body (in) the Netherworld, *setem*-priest of

19. Seker-Osiris in his woven shroud(?),[ee] eldest son of Ptaḥ south-of-his-wall, (for) thine is the custom of coming forth (20),[ff]

(R°) 1* rejoice, rejoice, flame which is within ʿAnkhtawy (and) thy place of beauty Djedit,[gg] rejoice

2* fashioner-of-feet who is within his temple[hh]—I shall not be in great voice—[ii]

3* in the great forecourt! Come to me, lord for eternity: mayest thou abide the festival(?) of thy fathers!

4* Raise thy beautiful face! May thine eye see the goodly moment(?), thou being behind me![jj]

5* This is good, a millionfold.[kk]

Notes

a. This opening is similar to the commencement of an 'Opening of the Mouth' ceremony (cf. Lefebvre, *Tombeau de Pétosiris*, ii. 131, Inscription 82), but the resemblance may be a coincidence; other translations are possible.

b. Taken, as in l. 5 below, as a writing of *mḫꜣt*; *mḫy* (ⲙⲓϣⲉ) 'fight' would require a different determinative.

c. See note *f* to the text above.

d. Used by extended metaphor to describe the Netherworld, third element, after heaven and earth, in the Egyptian universe.

e. Presumably a reference to the mutilation of the young god by Seth, cf. Gwyn Griffiths, *Conflict*, 28 ff.

f. See note *b* above.

g. The reading seems secure in spite of the redundant -*t* which decorates certain examples of the word; see textual notes above.

h. This insertion seems tautologous, and may be mistaken, but it may well mark the beginning of the 'fragmentation' of the spell, a process used again in V° 4–5, in which strict sense is sacrificed to repetition and verbal effect.

i. The writing seems clear enough, but one might expect a further reference to sacred barks in this context; I can think of no suitable equivalent.

j. The phrase reminds one greatly of *Wsỉr m rn·f nb* as a possible title for the 'Book of Hours' (BM. 10569), cf. Faulkner, *An Ancient Egyptian Book of Hours*, and the remarks of Gwyn Griffiths, *JEA* 46 (1960), 123; the latter rejects the idea that the multifarious gods and epithets of the 'Book of Hours' are to be seen syncretistically as aspects of one and the same deity (Osiris). Such an interpretation should probably be rejected here too, for the role of protagonist on the recto is played by Raʿ-Horus and other solar divinities, while on the verso this function must be ceded to Imḥōtep, who is asked to appear from the Underworld. The question is, however, a complex one.

k. ϩⲣⲃ, Crum, 701b.

l. The meaning of *bḫn*/*bḫn* is unknown, and this translation a mere guess.

m. This sudden change from the transports of praise to a bitter curse is striking. At first reading the context resembles the imprecation of Text **16**, V° 2–3 (= **17**, 9–10), which is addressed to a living agency, but the text as a whole suggests that this curse is being directed at the gods, in order to secure their co-operation. From the simple evocation of the opening lines, the petitioner turns to threats. These cover the remainder of the recto. On the verso, he resorts to persuasion, representing several gods speaking to the deity, offering inducements to him to come forth. Such changes of approach are not rare in Egyptian magic.

n. For this title as a name of the planet Mars, cf. Brugsch, *Thesaurus*, 65–79; a similar astronomical term may be hidden in *Rʿ-Ḥr pꜣ kꜣ* of l. 4 above, for *Ḥr kꜣ* (*pt*) (ϩⲁⲣⲕⲟ) is a regular name of the planet Saturn. Whether these connotations are uppermost in the writer's mind is less easy to decide; they are not supported by the rest of the text.

o. Lit. 'his back (of) Osiris'; perhaps the construction outlined in Spiegelberg, *Grammatik*, § 61, although none of the examples given antedates the Roman period.

p. Feminine, and refers to the *st mꜣʿt* above.

q. Doubtless an elevated variant of the usual *sꜣ Ptḥ* 'son of Ptaḥ' which follows the name of Imḥōtep. For a discussion of the Peak (*thn*) and of ʿAnkhtawy, see the Commentary, § 5 below.

r. The date corresponds to 10 July 171. It is possible that these three lines together with the date are to be understood at the end of the entire text.

s. A further example of 'fragmentation'; see note *h* above.

t. For *s*(*y*)*f* cf. *Wb*. iv. 114 under *sfj*.

u. These lines seem to evoke a belief that the sun-god was born in ʿAnkhtawy, the necropolis of Memphis; this would certainly explain the lotus image. An identical belief seems to have been attached to the necropolis at Hermopolis Magna (Ḥesrō, the modern Tûna el-Gebel), cf. Lefebvre, *Tombeau de Pétosiris*, ii. 193, Inscription 126, 5, and one may suspect that the same held true for the other great religious sites of Egypt.

v. The 'houses' (*ʿwyw*) of Horus are perhaps the galleries of the Hawk which adjoin the temple-site at North Saqqâra; see further Texts **19–23** below and the Commentary, § 4. As for the prediction that the hawk-galleries would not stink, a modern visitor might be forgiven for wishing that it had been more effective.

w. Pi-nīkhi, presumably a mythical locality.

x. For this and other titles of the god Thoth, see Appendix 2.

y. Possibly in the sense of the preposition *ḥr* used after verbs such as *ḫsf* 'protect' (*Wb*. iii. 336, 16).

z. For *ḥmꜣg* as a late name of Osiris cf. among others Brugsch, *Thesaurus*, 642; Posener, *Première domination perse*, 4, n. *a*.

aa. Presumably a funerary object; the theme of the burial of Osiris is developed in the remainder of the line.

bb. For this locality (Greek Ἀλχαί) as a name of the

necropolis at Abydos cf. Pap. Dem. Berlin 8027, Col. 5, 5 in a litany from the late Book of the Dead.[1]

cc. Apart from the general theme of the burial of Osiris which pervades the line, many of the details remain obscure, and the text is offered with reserve.

dd. A doubtful group; if the initial *Ḥr* is correct, one is reminded of the division of dreams into 'dreams of Horus' and 'dreams of Seth' encountered in Pap. Chester Beatty III (Gardiner, *Hieratic Papyri in the British Museum, Third Series*, 10 ff.). This division clearly lasted beyond the Middle Kingdom, as the notion of Horus as a god embodying truth in prediction reappears in a Ramesside oracular question (Černý, *BIFAO* 35 (1935), 48, to be seen in the light of Volten, *Demotische Traumdeutung*, 13, n. 1). The request may therefore be for a truthful dream to visit the petitioner; unfortunately the reading is not certain enough for this interesting idea to be accepted without question. The possibility of a proper name should also be sustained, in which case the preposition ***n*** must be translated 'to'.

ee. Lit. 'in his shroud of (the goddess) Tayit'; see textual notes above.

ff. This reconstruction has the effect of ignoring the final line, which seems to consist of a reminder to insert the remaining material from the recto; see textual notes above.

gg. The name of the necropolis of Heliopolis; cf. Text **13**, 7 above.

hh. Presumably the name of a divinity or demon, as with *rḫ-rn·k* in V° 12 above.

ii. It is difficult to see what Ḥor means by this interjection. It may imply that he is about to cut short an incantation which is already overlong, or that his voice is now lowered in the presence of the arcane. Such a possibility recurs in the later magical papyri, where the worshipper is instructed to lie down without speaking after finishing his prayer; such an idea may well underlie the present text.

jj. Possibly in the sense of 'close by, hard upon', but I cannot parallel this, and the reading is open to doubt.

kk. Apparently a comment on the efficacy of the spell; a similar afterthought occurs in Text **10**, R° 11, *tpyt nfrt tꜣy*. For what seems to be an adverbial use of *ḥḥ*, cf. Text **26**, R° 14 *gm·i-s ḥḥ hꜣ*(?).

Preliminary Remarks

Although so many of its details remain unsolved, the position of this text in the main archive is fairly clear; it records an incantation, addressed to various gods, sometimes solar, sometimes chthonic, to appear in a dream. The would-be dreamer is Ḥor, probably Ḥor of Sebennytos, and the date is 10 July 171, before the onset of the Sixth Syrian War. It is unfortunately impossible to identify the dream, if any, which this text provoked; such points are discussed in § 3 of the Commentary below. An unexplained feature is the Memphite colouring, especially with the references to Ptaḥ, Imḥōtep, Seker-Osiris, and Nefertēm, for the ostracon would seem to antedate the permanent arrival of Ḥor in the region of Saqqâra. One answer to this problem is to ascribe the entire text to Ḥor of Memphis, in whose hand it was written; but this too is difficult, for we know from Text **12** above that during the years before 168 the secretary was absent in Pi-peferē on the business of the god. An alternative is to attribute the text to Ḥor of Sebennytos while on an earlier visit to the area. It is of course possible that the ostracon is a later rewriting of a much simpler text, to which many Memphite allusions were added. In this latter case the original incantation could well have been produced elsewhere.

§ 3: Texts dealing with the cult of the Ibis

TEXT 19

Height	21·1 cm.
Width	15·6 cm.
Thickness	1·1 cm.
Munsell	5 YR 7/2
Photograph	Plate XXI (R°, V°)
Facsimile	not given
Excavator's no.	71/2–116 [5384]

A large and well-preserved buff-ware ostracon, the recto (convex) bearing twenty-five lines of script, together with the usual insertions and

[1] The name occurs also in the well-known Abydos inscription of Peftuꜥaneith (reign of Amasis), where it seems to be applied to a sanctuary building, cf. Jelínková-Reymond, *ASAE* 54 (1957), 284 n. 26, where the reading is slightly different.

erasures, and the verso, which exhibits slight traces of salt, a further nineteen lines in continuation written, as is not uncommon, upside-down to the recto. The verso shows light ribbing. The rather squat hand may possibly be that of Ḥor of Sebennytos.

Text: recto

1. *n-drt sẖ tš Ṯb-nṯr Ḥr (sꜣ) Ḥr-n-drt·f*[a]
2. *bn-ỉw rḫ rmt šm (r-)bl ḥr*[b] *mdt ỉw·s ṯꜣy Ḏḥwty*
3. *pꜣ nṯr rn·f ỉ·ỉr-sẖy n ḥt-nṯr Mn-nfr*
4. *m-ḳdy Ḥr-Ḏḥwty*[c] *ḥn·f. tꜣ mdt-nfrt nty ỉw·w ỉr-s n*
5. *pꜣ hb pꜣ by*[d] *(n) Ḏḥwty pꜣ ꜥꜣ pꜣ ꜥꜣ pꜣ ꜥꜣ st ỉr n-ỉm·s*
6. *(n) pꜣ bỉk ꜥn pꜣ by (n) Ptḥ pꜣ by (n) Ḥp*[e] *pꜣ by (n) pꜣ Rꜥ*
7. *pꜣ by (n) Šw ⟨pꜣ*[f] *by (n) Tfn⟩ pꜣ by (n) Gb*[g] *pꜣ by (n) Wsỉr pꜣ by (n)*
8. *Ḥr pꜣ by (n) ꜣst pꜣ by (n) Nbt-ḥt ⟨nꜣ nṯrw ꜥꜣy (n) Kmt⟩ pꜣ hb pꜣ bỉk*
9. *pꜣ nty ỉw·w ḏd-s*[h] *(n) nꜣ byw ꜥꜣy n*[i] *Ḥp-nb·s ⟨n r-pr Ḏḥwty⟩ [[bn-ỉ·ỉr ḫpr ỉn]]*[j]
10. *dỉ Ḏḥwty ḫpr·f n·w snt (n) dỉt mnt ⟨bn-ỉw·f wš⟩ ḥr pꜣ hb pꜣ bỉk*[k]
11. *ḥn·f ḥr ỉr·s smt (n) šty*[l] *pꜣ ỉnḥy*[m] *ḥr·f ḥn nꜣy·f ꜥwyw-(n)-*
12. *ḥtp ⟨mtw·w dỉt ꜥrḏ nb ḥr nꜣ mštw*[n]*⟩ tm nḥt nꜣ sdm-ꜥš (n) nꜣ hbw ỉrm nꜣ sdm-ꜥš (n) pꜣ bỉk*
13. *pꜣ nṯr rn·f ỉw·w ỉr*[o] *ḳrs·f. ḫpr·f nꜣy smn r-hn ḥꜣt-sp 16 (n) pꜣ ỉt*
14. *(n) pꜣ ỉt. ỉr tꜣ ḥt-mdt rn·s hwš rnpt 32 r-hn ḥꜣt-sp 9t*[p] *ꜣbd-4 prt sw 29*[q]
15. *(n) nꜣ Pr-ꜥꜣw šꜣꜥ*[r] *ḏt. ḥms nꜣ rmtw ꜥꜣy (n) ms ḥn nꜣ wꜥbw (n) Ptḥ (ỉ·)wn-nꜣ·w*
16. *ḏlꜥ-mdt ḥn pꜣ r-pr (n) tꜣ wsḫyt ỉrm ʾIꜥḥ-ms (sꜣ) Pꜣ-dỉ-Nfr-tm*[s]
17. *pꜣ rd (n) Pr-ꜥꜣ (ỉ·)wn-nꜣ šn n ḥt-nṯr. ꜥš nꜣ sḫw (n) Ptḥ nꜣ gy-(n)-ḏlꜥ-mdt.*
18. *hb·w (n) ḥty*[t] *r Rꜥ-ḳd r-dbꜣ smn pꜣ hp (n) mdt nty ṯꜣy nꜣy pꜣ snt*
19. *wn-nꜣ smn nḥꜣt.*[u] *ỉn·w nꜣ sdm-ꜥš (n) nꜣ hbw (r) Mn-nfr [[ꜣbd-4 prt ꜥlḳy]]*
20. *ỉrm nꜣ sdm-ꜥš (n) pꜣ bỉk (r) tꜣ wsḫyt. štf*[v] [ ] *nḥm·w*[w]
21. *Wn-nfr*[x] *(sꜣ) Ḥp-ỉ·ỉr-dỉ-s ⟨pꜣ ỉ·ỉr pꜣ mšt⟩*[y] *ỉrm Ḥr-gmy*[z] *ỉrm Nfr-tm-ỉ·ỉr-dỉ-s ỉrm Ḏ-ḥr-*
22. *pꜣ-trš*[aa] *ỉrm Ḥr (sꜣ) Ḫns-Ḏḥwty ỉrm Ḥr (sꜣ) Ḥp-ỉ·ỉr-dỉ-s r s 6.*[bb] *ṯꜣy·w-s*
23. *(r) pꜣ dtḥ ꜥḏ·w-s (n) pꜣ ꜣmr.*[cc] *dỉ·w ỉn·w nꜣ mštw*
24. *(n) nꜣ ꜥwyw-(n)-ḥtp (n) pꜣ hb nꜣ ꜥwyw-(n)-ḥtp*
25. *(n) pꜣ bỉk (n) tꜣ mtrt ỉ·ỉr·ḥr nꜣ wꜥbw.*

Text: verso

1. *šsp Ḥꜥ-Ḥp pꜣ ḥm-nṯr ḥms (n) ꜥn*[a]
2. *nꜣ mštw *na*[b] *ỉn·f-s (r) nꜣy·f ꜥwyw*
3. *ỉr pꜣ 25 wꜥb ḳd·f (n) ḳdy nty ỉw ḥt·f*[c] *sẖ (r) ḥry*
4. *sḫ·w-s r pꜣ šwry*[d] *n ḥꜣt-sp 10t. ḥn·w-s ỉ·ỉr·ḥr n*[e] *nꜣ wꜥbw*
5. *stp wꜥb rnpt s 3 ỉw·w nḥty mtw·w šn tꜣ ḫrt ỉrm*
6. *pꜣ ꜥš-sḫn (n) pꜣ hb mtw·w ỉy (r) Ḥp-nb·s tn nb mtw(·w) ỉr*
7. *pꜣ šn (n) nꜣ nṯrw (n) pꜣ ꜥwy-(n)-ḥrry (n) pꜣ nṯr nty ỉw·w gm-f ḥr pꜣ tr*
8. *mtw·w*[f] *dỉ·w mnt*[g] *ḥr·f wꜥ nṯr (n) wꜥt mgt.*[h] *ḫpr sp (n)*
9. *dỉt ḥtp pꜣ hb pꜣ nty ỉw·w ỉr-f*[i] *(n) wꜥt rnpt ỉw·s krp*[j] *ꜣs*[k]
10. *mtw·w thm pꜣ mšꜥ*[l] *(n) Pr-Wsỉr-Ḥp (r)*[m] *Ḥp-nb·s mtw·w*
11. *ṯꜣy-ꜥḳ pꜣ hb pꜣ bỉk (r) pꜣy·f ꜥwy-(n)-ḥtp pꜣ wꜥb*[n]
12. *(n) ḫrt·f*[o] *m-sꜣ·s mtw·w*[p] *nꜣ mštw (n) nꜣ ꜥwyw-(n)-ḥtp (n) pꜣ hb*
13. *nꜣ ꜥwyw (n) pꜣ bỉk (n) wꜥt ḏnyt*[q] *mtw·s tbꜥ tꜣ ḥny*[r] *(n)*
14. *pꜣ wꜥb s 3 mtw·w dỉt-s n-drt nꜣ wnw*[s] *(n) tꜣ wsḫyt (n)*
15. *Pr-Wsỉr-Ḥp mtw nꜣ wꜥbw ỉp ḥr*[t] *pꜣ swt*[u] *⟨tn 2 n nṯr⟩ ḥḏ 1*[v]
16. *wš pꜣ swt tꜣ mnt ḥn·f*[w] *tn 1¼*
17. *pꜣy·s gns*[x] *tn ¾*[y] *r ḥḏ 1 ḥḏ ½*
18. *ỉr pꜣy·f ỉwꜣ*[z] *ḥḏ ½ mtw·f ḫpr*
19. *pꜣ dmḏ n nꜣ rmtw nty dỉt ḥtp.*

Notes: recto

a. Another phonetic writing of *Ḥr-nḏ-it·f*, cf. Text **18,** R° 4.

b. Presumably an idiomatic phrase meaning 'lapse from, ignore'.

c. This group is unclear, and its reading far from certain.

d. The palimpsest seems to have been *pꜣ bik*; although the text word *by* is common in the meaning 'soul' (ⲃⲁⲓ), a similar word is also found in the Memphite necropolis to designate the priestly masons employed in the excavation of galleries; as such it is common in the stelae of the Serapeum (cf. the published examples in Bresciani, *Nuovi testi demotici dal Serapeo di Menfi*, in *Studi in honore di G. Botti*, Rome, 1967) and corresponds to hieroglyphic [hieroglyph] (ⲃⲟⲓ) (Brugsch, *Thesaurus*, 970). The divine determinative tends towards the first reading, but this is not certain. It is unlikely, however, that all the divinities mentioned possessed masons and galleries at Saqqâra.

e. Not the same writing as in ll. 21 and 22 below; if the initial stroke be assigned to *by* (cf. the writing before *Nbt-ḥt* below), *'Imn* would be a possible reading.

f. *tꜣ* is probably to be rejected, as none of the other goddesses has a feminine *by*.

g. The final sign is presumably the goose commonly found as ideogram in this name.

h. Although this phrase commonly introduces accounts of dreams, the present context seems to exclude any notion of this kind.

i. *tꜣ* seems to have been supraposed here, although its purpose escapes me.

j. These words may have been considered erased by the scribe; certainly they seem very awkward as they stand.

k. The scribe seems to have added the group *Ḥr* at the end of this word.

l. Reading offered with the greatest reserve; the reading *šty* is based on Text **23,** R° 14; an alternative *fty* (in spite of similar writings in the stelae of the Mothers of the Apis) is more doubtful. The two words seem to overlap rather uncomfortably, and it may be that one is in fact a palimpsest. The whole is therefore extremely obscure.

m. Context, and the parallel texts, suggest this reading rather than *knḥy*, cf. *contra*, Text **10,** R° 2.

n. The reading *ššt* (for which see Text **23,** V° 22) is excluded by the sense.

o. This writing of the infinitive occurs commonly in these ibis-texts. For other remarkable forms of this verb, cf. note *j* to Text **2,** R° 7, p. 16 above.

p. A rather individual writing: the numeral is written vertically instead of at its usual slope, and the following *t* has a supralinear stroke, perhaps borrowed inadvertently from the 6 in the line above. The whole therefore seems very dubious, but it is difficult to suggest another reading. A parallel is to be seen in Text **25,** 7 below.

q. The season has been rather cramped, but the final curved sign, which distinguishes *prt* from *šmw* (Text **1,** 2, note *g*, p. 8) is fairly clear. The reading is confirmed by the admittedly faint writing at the end of l. 19.

r. Abbreviated almost to resemble *nty iw*.

s. Were it not for the lotus determinative, *Pꜣ-ḥm-ntr-'Itm* would be a very admissible reading; so much so, that one wonders whether it is not the true one.

t. See note *r* to Text **2,** R° 11, p. 17 above.

u. See the example in Text **23,** V° 17.

v. I have taken this as a metathesis, perhaps dialectical, of the common *šft* (ϣⲱϥⲧ, Crum, 611a).

w. It is yet again remarkable that the most important passage should be the most obscured; the missing traces suggest *šm* or the like, but without conviction. *nḥm·w* is slightly clearer.

x. The scribe seems first to have written *Ḫnsw*, but altered this. If this person is the same as the Onnophris τῶν ἐκ τοῦ Σαραπιείου ἰβιοβοσκό[ς] of *UPZ* 119, 17 (August 156 B.C.), he will have survived his ordeal, but there is no proof of this identification.

y. *mšt* is inserted in a bold hand, but the preceding signs are faint, and may not have been intended as read.

z. Obscure: possibly the Ἀρχῆμις of Preisigke, 58, but the final signs are difficult to understand.

aa. The final element is perhaps a metathesis from *dšr* (Erichsen, *Glossar*, 658), and may refer to the flamingo (note in Crum, 432b, cf. the hieroglyph [hieroglyph] G27). Indeed, in many of the compound names with *Ḏ-ḥr*, the second element is the name of an animal, presumably sacred, or the name of a divinity (*Ḏ-ḥr-pꜣ-hb*, *Ḏ-ḥr-pꜣ-bik*, *Ḏ-ḥr-pꜣ-ʿʿn*, *Ḏ-ḥr-pꜣ-imi*, *Ḏ-ḥr-bs*; Preisigke adds, among others, Τεεβαάμφι, Τεενεφθῖμις, and Τεεφραῖος). The first element may mean 'carefree' or the like (Crum, 648a); the transliteration *ḏd-ḥr* is therefore misleading, and the fact that hieroglyphic texts show [hieroglyph] as often as [hieroglyph] suggests that the writing *ḏd* is a phonetic one (Coptic ϫⲉ-). See also notes to Text **23,** R° 10 and Text **33,** 9, pp. 107, below.

bb. This fortunate total gives the clue to the distribution of the patronymics: the initial name is so qualified, as being an important personage, and father's names are allotted to the common name Ḥor. Whether the two men *Ḥp-ỉ·ỉr-dỉ·s* are identical is impossible to say.

cc. An unknown word, clearly an instrument of confining, and possibly connected with the verb *mr* (ⲙⲟⲩⲣ) 'bind'.

Notes: verso

a. A very dispiriting end to an opening line: *ḥm-nṯr* seems more plausible than *ỉ·ỉr*, and *ḥms* in its meaning 'be in session' is familiar from the rules of the priestly guilds (cf. de Cenival, *Associations religieuses*, i. 21). *ꜥn* is more problematic, although the reading seems clear enough, and it is difficult to decide whether it is being used to qualify *ḥms*, or adverbially to *šsp*; the former is perhaps the less tortuous alternative.

b. See note *k* to Text **2**, R° 7, p. 16 above.

c. A remarkably difficult group of words; the first phrase recurs in Text **22**, R° 7–8 in a similar context, and the phrase *ỉr-ḳdy* 'go round, review' is attested (cf. *Demotic Chronicle*, 2, 11, where Spiegelberg compares the Coptic ⲣ̄ⲡⲕⲟⲧ; for a similar use of *ḳdy* alone cf. the same author in *ZÄS* 51 (1913), 137, on *ZÄS* 50 (1912), 32). The following word appears to be a cognate, perhaps to strengthen the meaning; the whole phrase might therefore be translated 'pass in review, revolve (in deliberation)' or the like.[1] The following signs are more obscure; the reading chosen here seems to demand an ellipsed object, and the reading *ḥt·f* is open to some doubt, although other readings (e.g. *sn·f*) do not inspire confidence. It is perhaps better, therefore, to treat the whole as unread.

d. *mwry* is perhaps also possible; I cannot identify the word, and the translation offered below is a mere guess.

e. A rare example in our texts of this preposition followed by the genitival particle (ⲉϩⲣⲛ̄-).

f. The same strange syntax in Text **21**, R° 16; short of assuming a 'conjunctive *sḏm·f*', which seems very unlikely, it would seem necessary to take the group as a writing of the infinitive *dỉt*; the alternative, to regard *mtw·w* (ⲛ̄ⲧⲁⲩ) as a possessive qualifying *tr*, is scarcely convincing. For the syntax cf. Nims, *JEA* 24 (1938), 77.

g. Presumably the abstract noun from *mn* (not in Crum). The natural meaning would be 'permanence', etc., but its use in our texts seems to approach the modern 'efficiency'; hence the translation 'regularity' offered below.

h. This word, which closely resembles *mnt* except for the tick applied to the second sign, is clearly of importance. If read correctly, it would seem to be the forerunner of Coptic ⲙⲟⲕⲓ (Crum, 161b) with reference to the pottery jars which contained the mummies of the birds (*JEA* 52 (1966), pl. II, 4). One may suspect a connection with the *mgwtt* 'Sänfte, Bähre' of Erichsen, *Glossar*, 183.

i. Another anomalous writing of this verb; see note to *ỉr* in R° 13 above.

j. See Text **2**, R° 10; the entire phrase corresponds to (*n*) *wꜥ sp* in Text **21**, but the use of *ỉw·s* shows that the phrase refers to *rnpt*. The translation below is tentative.

k. Possibly a writing of *ys* 'hasten', but uncertain.

l. Here clearly in the meaning 'people'; see note to Text **2**, V° 12, p. 20 above. For the use of *thm* in the regulations for a priestly guild, cf. Pap. Dem. Lille 29, 9 (Spiegelberg, *Papyrus démotiques de Lille*, 63; de Cenival, *Associations*, i. 5).

m. Restored from Text **21**, V° 12.

n. The plural stroke seems to be redundant.

o. This group resembles the following *m-sꜣ* quite disconcertingly even in the parallel texts, but the present reading seems more plausible.

p. Text **21**, V° 15 inserts *dỉt* at this point, and its omission here is presumably accidental.

q. An unknown word, perhaps corresponding to Coptic ϫⲁⲛⲉ = κιβωτός (Crum, 773*b*); see note to the translation below.

r. Reminiscent of the word in Text **8**, R° 13, and the underlying root *ḫn*(*r*) may be the same for both. The translation is again approximate.

s. Distinguished in this hand from *ḥmt* 'wife' (Text **15**, R° 6) by the curved -*n*- before the determinative.

t. The parallel texts confirm this reading, although the present example resembles the *ḥnꜥ* of Text **10**, R° 10.

u. Confirmed by the determinative, cf. Erichsen, *Glossar*, 418; the meaning here is presumably that of the bandaging of the mummified birds, with associated ideas, and the word is the causative of the older *wt* (*Wb.* i. 378) 'embalm'.

[1] It is very tempting to wonder whether the significance is not 'appoint in rotation'; this would fit the passage in Text **22** well, but more evidence is surely needed before assuming such an interesting procedure for our ibis-cult.

v. This group may equally stand for *mtw*, or may even have been erased.

w. The scribe seems also to have begun *ḫn* above the line, but decided to write the word over the palimpsest.

x. This word also in Text **21**, V° 7, but I am unable to identify it. The context in both cases suggests that the word represents a reduced payment or deduction imposed upon inefficient burial. The word *ḳns* (or *gns*, as regularly spelt in these texts) is familiar from the rules of the cult-guilds in its meaning 'fine', but this identification is offered with all reserve.

y. The fraction is slightly different from the numeral 2 above; the reading, which is tentative, is based on the need to provide a balance to the 1¼ immediately beforehand, but it is offered with great reserve.[1]

z. This looks like another financial term; the common *iwyt* 'pledge' is excluded by its gender. Another possibility, which I have tentatively followed below, is to see the word as the ancestor of ⲉⲓⲁⲁⲩ (Crum, 88a), as the word *ꜥꜣt* quoted in *Wb*. i. 166 (cf. Erichsen, *Glossar*, 55) is of the wrong gender, and philologically rather remote.

Translation: recto

1. From the scribe of the nome of Sebennytos, Ḥor son of Ḥarendjiōtef.[a]
2. No man shall be able to lapse from a matter which concerns Thoth,
3. the god in person who holds sway in the temple of Memphis,[b]
4. and likewise Ḥarthoth(?) within it.[c] The benefit which is performed for
5. the Ibis, the soul[d] of Thoth, the three times great,[e] is made
6. (for) the Hawk also, the soul of Ptaḥ, the soul of Apis(?),[f] the soul of Prēꜥ,
7. the soul of Shu, ⟨the soul of Tefnut⟩, the soul of Geb, the soul of Osiris, the soul of
8. Horus, the soul of Isis, the soul of Nephthys, ⟨the great gods (of) Egypt⟩, the Ibis (and) the Hawk.
9. That which was spoken to the great souls of Ḥepnēbes[g] ⟨in the chapel of Thoth⟩:[h]
10. 'Thoth has caused the habit to occur to them of imparting regularity ⟨and it shall not fail⟩ into the Ibis (and) the Hawk
11. within it:[i] for it affects(?) likewise the excavation(?) of the courtyard which contains him[j] within his houses of
12. rest: ⟨and all earnestness is to be imparted into the inspectors[k]⟩ not to trust the servants (of) the ibises and the servants (of) the Hawk
13. the god in person, when they perform his burial'.
    It happened that this lasted until Year 16 of the father
14. (of) the father.[l] (But) the said utterance was abused (for) 32 years, up to Year 9, Pharmuthi, day 29
15. (of) the Pharaohs for ever.[m] The elders among the priests (of) Ptaḥ who
16. recorded within the chapel held session (in) the forecourt[n] together with[o] ꜥAḥmosi (son of) Petineftēm,[p]
17. the agent (of) Pharaoh, who was controller of the temple.[q] The scribes (of) Ptaḥ read out the documents.
18. They sent in haste to Alexandria to determine the law (of) the matter which concerned these things habitually
19. (and) which was established for ever. They brought the servants (of) the ibises (to) Memphis [in Pharmuthi, day 30][r]
20. together with the servants (of) the Hawk (to) the forecourt. Guilty [· · · · ·]. They seized(?)
21. Onnofri (son of) Ḥapertais ⟨who made the inspection⟩, and Ḥarkhēmi and Neftēmertais and Djeḥe-
22. petrōsh and Ḥor (son of) Khensthoth and

[1] During the season of 1971/2 at Saqqâra, the author was allowed, through the goodness of Professor E. Edel and of the Inspector of Antiquities, Dr. ꜥA. el-Khouli, to read through several ostraca discovered by the former at North Saqqâra; in one of these, an accounts list, a fraction occurs, similar to the present, which by dead reckoning should correspond to ¾. I am grateful to have been given this opportunity.

Ḥor (son of) Ḥapertais, making six men. They took them (to)

23. the prison (and) secured them (in) the stocks(?).[s] They caused the inspectors to be brought
24. (of) the houses of rest (of) the Ibis (and) the houses of rest
25. (of) the Hawk openly before[t] the priests.

Translation: verso

1. Khaʿḥapi, the priest in session (in) splendour(?)
2. received *the said[a] inspectors (and) took them to his house.
3. The 25 priests[b] passed in review the matter whose content[c] is written below,[d]
4. (and) they wrote it into the regulation(?) for Year 10.[e] They commanded in the presence of the priests
5. to choose three priests (of the) year, who are reliable, and who shall direct the sustenance and
6. the fortune (of) the Ibis. They are to come (to) Ḥepnēbes (at) every counting,[f] and shall perform
7. the investigation (of) the gods[g] (in) the house of waiting[h] (of) the god which they shall find at the time,
8. and they are to impart regularity into it,[i] one god (in) one vessel. (When) the occasion occurs
9. (of) the burial of the Ibis which is performed in one completed[j] year swiftly (?),
10. they shall assemble the people of the Serapeum (at) Ḥepnēbes, and they shall
11. lead in procession[k] the Ibis (and) the Hawk to his house of rest, the appropriate
12. priest in attendance. They are to (place) the inspectors (of) the houses of rest (of) the Ibis
13. (and) the houses (of) the Hawk (in) one chest,[l] which[m] is sealed (in) the storeroom (?) (of)
14. the three priests and they shall give it into the hand of the pastophoroi (of) the forecourt (of)
15. the Serapeum. The priests are also to assess for the bandaging ⟨two payments of the god⟩ one *ḥḏ*[n]
16. apart from the bandaging: regularity in this, $1\frac{1}{4}$ payments:
17. its[o] fine(?), $\frac{3}{4}$ payment, making $1\frac{1}{2}$ *ḥḏ*:
18. its[p] linen(?) makes $\frac{1}{2}$ *ḥḏ*: and this becomes
19. the total for the men who perform the burial.

Notes: recto

a. The Sebennyte Ḥor, apparently now resident in Memphis.

b. This is probably no more than a metaphoric statement of the power of the god, rather than a distinct reference to a cult-chapel in the main temple of Ptaḥ, where Thoth would be a σύνναος θεός; but the latter is possible, as we know nothing of the temple of Ptaḥ at this period.

c. This may be a reference to the Memphite Ḥor, the petition-writer, 'who is within it (Memphis)'. But the context is not at all certain.

d. See note to the text at this point.

e. See notes to Text **2**, V° 15, p. 20 above.

f. Amūn may perhaps be read.

g. See topographical commentary below, p. 147.

h. I have omitted the words at the end of the line: see text note.

i. Presumably the chapel.

j. See topographical commentary, and the introduction to Text **6**.

k. These officers are familiar from the Prinz-Joachim Ostraca (Preisigke–Spiegelberg, op. cit. 14, n. 5); see § 4 of the Commentary below.

l. The context here leaves little doubt that we are dealing with a royal name, and it would be quite natural to assume that this is the grandfather of the reigning king. This assumption is strengthened when we read in Pap. Tebtunis 62, ll. 29, 36, and 315, of the πάππος τοῦ βασιλέως (Grenfell, Hunt, Smyly, *Tebtunis Papyri*, i. 234–51 and 237 ff.). The date seems to be 119/118 B.C., and the king therefore Euergetes II; the πάππος is thence Philopator, who is also the πρόπαππος of the following papyrus (ibid. 252), written under Soter II. A similar use under Philometor is therefore quite possible; less clear is the reason for its use, unless this lies in an attempt, both by Philometor and later by his brother, to stress their origins in the legitimate line.[1] For the plural, *nꜣ ỉtyw (n) Pr-ʿꜣ*, cf. Text **26**, R° 6.

Year 16 of Philopator corresponds to 207/6.

m. The ninth year of Philometor fell in 173/2, and the date on this assumption would be 31 May 172. Ḥor's statement that thirty-two years had elapsed between the two dates must therefore be taken, as often in Egyptian calculations, as an *exclusive* estimate; thirty-two whole years intervene between the two dates (204–173).[2] Historically this is most interesting, for within these thirty-two years of abuse falls the entire reign of Epiphanes, with the adulations of the Rosetta Stone, and the evidence is clear that by the ninth year of Philometor the officials of the ibis-cult were obliged to send to Alexandria to ascertain what the law itself required.

The nature of 'the Pharaohs' is also interesting. The epithet *šꜣʿ ḏt* implies that they were still on the throne when the text was drafted. The early years of Philometor were largely dependent upon his mother, Cleopatra I, whose death occurred shortly before the marriage of the young king (Wilcken, *Archiv für Pap.* 3 (1906), 366). This latter event may have been brought forward, before the king's maturity, because of the impending Seleucid threat (A. Bernand, *Les Inscriptions grecques de Philae*, 118). The death of Cleopatra I, fixed by Skeat between *8 April and 14 October 176 (*JEA* 21 (1935), 263; also Hintze, *Archiv Orientální*, 20 (1952), 102–4) can be dated yet more closely: on 8 April 176 both Philometor and his mother are still named (Pap. BM. 10518), but a Cairo papyrus of 17 May (Samuel, *Ptolemaic Chronology* (Munich, 1962), 140), and Pap. BM. 10726 of 14 September 176 name Philometor alone. The marriage of Philometor to his sister, Cleopatra II, took place before 15 April 175 (Pap. BM. 10589: Shore and Smith, *JEA* 45 (1959), 55, note *b*). Pap. Berlin 3112 of 22 February of the same year mentions the king alone, and the marriage, if already celebrated, would have been a very recent event; cf. also Oates in *Études de papyrologie*, 9 (1964), 71–2; the official cult-titles of the earlier Ptolemies were reorganized at this period, in the optimism engendered by the oncoming trial of strength with the Seleucids. The 'Pharaohs' are therefore Philometor and his sister-wife.[3]

n. L. 19 implies that this court was held in Memphis; the 'forecourt' is therefore probably that of the temple of Ptaḥ. Note the similar writing in Brugsch, *Thesaurus*, 895, l. 1 (biography of ʿAnemḥo) and the fine metaphor in Menkerēʿ (ibid. 898) *šm r tꜣ wsḫyt n tꜣ Dwꜣt*, with its connotations of judgement.

o. An idiom reminiscent of Greek ἄλλως τε καί, introducing what is in fact the most important element; the implication is presumably that ʿAḥmosi was president at the session.

p. 'Pḥentatūm' is perhaps possible.

q. This title (for the connotations of *šn* see note *d* to Text **15**, R° 5, p. 59 above) probably corresponds to the Royal ἐπιστάτης of Bevan, 181, who surveyed the affairs of the temple on behalf of the king (Oertel's doubts quoted by Bevan, loc. cit., that the office was a royal appointment seem answered here by the additional epithet *pꜣ rd n Pr-ʿꜣ* applied to the holder). The title is to be carefully distinguished from that of λεσῶνις, *mr-šn*, which was a religious function as head of the body of priests, even if, as in Pap. Rylands IX and in the period discussed here, he received a government stipend. In Text **22**, R° 7 both officers appear together. These questions are discussed in § 4 of the Commentary below.

r. Perhaps erased; the date is 1 June 172.

s. See note to the text.

t. In the legal sense of ⲧⲁϩⲛⲉ (Crum, 191a).

Notes: verso

a. Text **2**, R° 7, note, p. 16 above.

b. In Text **21**, R° 11 these are distinguished as *pꜣ 25 wʿb nty mnḳ mdt*, the βουλευταὶ ἱερεῖς and *wʿbw*

[1] A similar expression, *pꜣ ỉt n Pr-ʿꜣ*, occurs in the inscriptions from the baboon-galleries at Saqqâra. It would hardly be relevant here to express curiosity about the lack of kinship terms in all stages of the Egyptian language, when one's knowledge of Egyptian practice, especially litigious, leads one to place great emphasis on family relationships. The fact remains, however, that in the Inscription of Mose kinship terms are very loosely employed (Gardiner, *Mes*, 12, n. 6). The occasional agnate term (Smith in *JEA* 44 (1958), 122) indicates that there may have been many such terms hidden in the spoken language; not of course that the lack of a word must mean the lack of its subject.

[2] With this proviso, these figures provide independent confirmation of our dating to Philometor, for there is no other king in the Ptolemaic dynasty whose ninth year falls thirty-two years after the sixteenth of his grandfather.

[3] The dating of Greek graffito Philae, no. 11 (Bernand, op. cit. 118 ff.), written in the short interval between the death of Cleopatra I and the marriage, should be revised from the 172 of Bernand to the winter of 176/5.

nḏ-ḥt of the Tanis and Canopus Stelae. In the Ptolemaic period, and in all probability earlier, five priests were chosen from each phyle of the priesthood; after the introduction of a fifth phyle in 237, the executive council numbered 25 in place of the previous 20 (cf. Tanis Stela, 31). The present texts show this system still in use early in the reign of Philometor (cf. Bevan, 179–80). See further Commentary § 4 below.

c. See textual note above.

d. An alternative reading of *sẖ* (*n*) *ḥry* as 'public scribe' (cf. ἐν ἀγυιᾷ of Greek contracts such as Pap. Oxyrh. 261 and 266) is perhaps less likely in the present text.

e. Doubtless a book of minutes and resolutions kept by the year.

f. Perhaps a yearly census of the sacred ibises and hawks: see Commentary below.

g. The mummified birds, 'whose salvation has occurred' (*Mizraim*, I (1933), 57).

h. Familiar from ʿOnkhsheshonqy (IV, 6 = Glanville, n. 49) as the title of a prison, but this is hardly appropriate in the present context. From the fact that dead birds are clearly to be stored there, and that provision is made for different 'houses' to be in use at different times, it is tempting (if rash) to see in the place the name given to the side galleries, opening from the communicating corridor, in which the birds, bandaged and stored in their jars, were stacked. When full a gallery would be sealed, and a new one occupied (cf. Plan in *JEA* 52 (1966), 4). The similar group in Brugsch, *Thesaurus*, 888 is to be read *st wry*, and is not relevant to our discussion.

i. Presumably the gallery.

j. Literally 'revealed'; see textual note above.

k. The idiom, *ṯꜣy-ʿḳ*, is used in both the Serapeum and the Mother of the Apis stelae to denote the funeral cortège and the accompanying ceremonies.

l. This rather ludicrous picture may imply that a papyrus, inscribed with the names of those authorized to conduct the funeral rites (we may even conjecture that it began **wn nꜣ rmtw nty ṯꜣy-ʿḳ pꜣ hb pꜣ bik*+date, or the like) was enclosed in the chest, which was sealed to prevent forgery.

m. Possibly *mtw·s* is a phonetic writing for *nty iw·s*; *tbʿ* is Qualitative.

n. For the financial arrangements of this and the parallel text, see Commentary below.

o. The regularity.

p. The bandaging.

Preliminary Remarks

This text in essence records the minutes of a session of the Council of the ibis-cult held in the temple of Ptaḥ at Memphis on 1 June 172 B.C. At this meeting Ḥor of Sebennytos may have been present as scribe. The history of the cult is related: efficiency and order had prevailed until about the year 205 B.C., whereupon, for a reason not stated, abuses had set in.[1] As a result of the hearing, six persons are condemned and imprisoned, and a series of regulations drawn up to restore order into the burial of the sacred birds, and to lessen the risk of corruption and fraud. A scale of payments for the men employed in the cult is instituted.

TEXT 20

Height	12·6 cm.
Width	14·8 cm.
Thickness	0·7 cm. (ave.)
Munsell	5 YR 7/4
Photograph	Plate XXII
Facsimile	Plate XXIIA
Excavator's no.	G7–40 [469]

This buff-ware ostracon was part of the original group discovered by Emery. The recto, the only face inscribed, is faded and in parts desurfaced. The verso is ribbed.

Text

x+ 1. [ ] *Pr-Wsir-Ḥp*[a]
2. [ ] (traces)
3. [ ] *iw·f ḏd n·i mdt* [
4.] *di mnt ẖr pꜣ hb pꜣ bik* [
5.] *pꜣ* [ ] *pꜣ by* (*n*) *Wsir pꜣ nṯr ʿꜣ pꜣ by* (*n*) *Ḥr pꜣ ẖrd* (*n*) *ꜣst*[b]

[1] It does appear, however, that considerable native revolts occurred, at least in Upper Egypt, after the sixteenth year of Philopator (Bevan, 239; Skeat, *JEA* 59, 169); if the administration of the ibis-cult had suffered from restlessness among the local population, it is natural that Ḥor would not mention this. Further details are discussed in § 4 of the Commentary below.

6. *pꜣ by* (*n*) *Nbt-ḥt tꜣ snt* (*n*) *ꜣst* ⟨*mtw·s ḥr*⟩ *nꜣ twtw*[c] (*n*) *Wsỉr* [
7.] *rswt*[d] *by ḥr·s pꜣ wꜣḥ* (*n*) *ꜣst* [
8.] *Mḥy dỉ·ỉ-s* ⟨*r-dbꜣ*⟩ [
9.] *ḥt-nṯr pꜣ hb nb ḥtp nꜣ twtw* [
10.][e] *Mn-nfr ẖn pꜣy·f ẖr* [
11.] *Wsỉr-Ḥp pꜣ ꜥꜣ pꜣ ꜥꜣ* [ ] *st* [*f*
12.] (traces and insertion)
13.] *ỉ·ỉr·ḥr* [ ] *nꜣ hbw* [.

(other lines may be lost)

Notes

a. The determinative enables the restoration of the first sign.

b. The syntax is doubtful here. The word *bik* seems to have been inserted above the middle of the line.

c. Cf. l. 9.

d. Possibly a writing of *R-stꜣw*, as in Text **13**.

e. A house-determinative is visible before this word.

f. These final signs may represent the name *Ḏ-ḥr*.

Translation

x+ 1. ························] Serapeum
2. ························] (traces)
3. ···········] he said to me a matter [·······
4. ·····] impart regularity into the Ibis (and) the Hawk [·····
5. ·····] ······· the soul (of) Osiris the great god, the soul (of) Horus the child (of) Isis,
6. the soul (of) Nephthys the sister (of) Isis ⟨and who is over (?)⟩ the statues[a] (of) Osiris [·······
7. ·····] dream (?)[b] ······· the interpretation[c] (of) Isis [·····
8. ·····] Lower Egypt(?). I gave it ⟨because of⟩ ·····
9. ·····] temple of the Ibis, lord of contentment, the statues(?) [··········
10. ······· Memphis within its plundering[d] [···············
11. ······· Osorapis the twice great ····· ····· [·············
12. ······· (traces) [······················ ················
13. ······· before ·········· the ibises [··················

Notes

a. Or possibly '*ḏd*-pillars (?)', Erichsen, *Glossar*, 617.

b. Or possibly 'necropolis'.

c. Text **9**, V° 7.

d. One is tempted to connect this reference with the invasion of Antiochus, but there is no ground for this, and most of the ibis-texts in the present section seem to antedate the Syrian War.

Preliminary Remarks

This fragmentary text bears such close similarities to the preceding that it would appear to be some form of recension of the same.

TEXT 21

Height	18·2 cm.
Width	11·6 cm.
Thickness	1·1 cm.
Munsell	5 YR 6/4
Photograph	Plate XXIII
Facsimile	Plate XXIIIA
Excavator's no.	H6–511 [4134]

This buff-ware ostracon was found together with Texts **6** and **10** in the sand above the mud-brick courtyard (Emery, January 1970). The effects of fading and sand erosion, particularly on the convex recto, and the porosity of the sherd made decipherment almost impossible until the discovery of Text **19.** The recto bears eighteen lines, probably in the same hand as that of **19,** while a further twenty-one lines complete the verso. Central parts of some lines on the recto are lost. Much of the notes to Text **19** may also serve as commentary for the present document.

Text: recto

1. *wꜥ mḳmḳ ỉ·ỉr·ḥr*[a] *nꜣ wꜥbw* (*n*) *Ḏḥwty* [ ][b] *ỉrm*
2. *nꜣ ntrw nty ḥtp ỉrm·f n-drt sẖ tš Ṯb-ntr Ḥr* (*sꜣ*) [*Ḥr-nḏ-ỉt·f*][c]
3. *tw·ỉ ẖn ḥt-ntr*[d] [ ] *ỉw·ỉ ẖr ẖt*[*-mdt*
4. *Ḏḥwty tꜣ nty ỉw·f ḏd·s* [ ] *ẖr nfr pꜣy·s*
5. *sbty ỉ·ỉr·ḥr·ỉ ḏd smn pꜣ nty nfr n-ỉm·s ẖt*
6. *tꜣ mdt pḥ pꜣ hb* (*n*) *ḥꜣty·f*[e] *dỉt mnt*
7. *ẖr·f n Pr-wꜥb-nb·s ỉw·w ḳrs-f* (*n*) *nꜣ ꜥwyw-*(*n*)*-*
8. *ḥtp nty ḥr pꜣ ḏw. smn-s Ḏḥwty* ⟨*Mn-nfr*⟩ *bn-ỉw·s*
9. *wš. dỉ nꜣ rmtw ḫpr sḏy ỉrm tꜣ ḳnbt*[f]
10. (*n*) *ḥt-ntr Mn-nfr ḥꜣt-sp 8t tpy ꜣḫt sw* [ ] *r-hn* ⟨*ḥꜣt-sp 8t tpy ꜣḫt sw 17*⟩.[g] *ḥn-s*
11. *pꜣ 25 wꜥb nty mnḳ mdt* [ ][h] *stp*
12. *wꜥb s 3 r šn pꜣ ꜥš-sḥn* (*n*) *pꜣ hb pꜣ bỉk wꜥ*
13. *tn šꜣꜥ-mtw·f*[i] *ỉy* (*r*) *Pr-wꜥb-nb·s*[j]
14. *tn 3t*[k] *mtw·f mšt*[l] *tꜣ wꜥbt* (*n*) *pꜣ hb*
15. *tꜣ wꜥbt* (*n*) *pꜣ bỉk pꜣ ntr rn·f* ⟨*nty ỉw·f gm-f*⟩[m]
16. *ḥr pꜣ tr mtw·f dỉ*[n]
17. *mnt ẖr pꜣ hb*
18. *wꜥ ntr* (*n*) *wꜥt mgt.*

Text: verso

1. *mtw·f ỉp ỉrm nꜣ sdm-ꜥš* (*n*) *nꜣ hbw*
2. *nꜣ sdm-ꜥš* (*n*) *pꜣ bỉk ẖr ỉr swt*
3. *nty ỉw·w dỉt-s tn 2 n pꜣ ntr. ḫpr·f*
4. *bn-ỉw rmt gm ẖsy* (*n*) *dỉt ḳrs*
5. *pꜣ hb pꜣ bỉk mtw pꜣ swt*
6. *mnt r·s*[o] *tꜣy·s pẖt*(*t*)[p]
7. *tn 1* ⟨*wš ẖn tꜣ mnt*⟩ *pꜣy·s gns*[q] *tn ½*
8. *r ḥḏ 1 ḥḏ ½ mtw pꜣ sp ḫpr wbꜣ rꜣ*
9. *pꜣ ỉnḥy ẖr pꜣ hb pꜣ bỉk*
10. *ḫpr sp* (*n*) *dỉt ḥtp pꜣ hb nty ỉw·w ỉr-f*
11. (*n*) *wꜥt rnpt* (*n*) *wꜥ sp. tn šꜣꜥ-mtw·w*[r]
12. *thm pꜣ mšꜥ* (*n*) *Pr-Wsỉr-Ḥp r*
13. *Pr-wꜥb-nb·s mtw·w ṯꜣy-ꜥḳ pꜣ hb*
14. *pꜣ bỉk* (*r*) *nꜣy·f ꜥwyw-*(*n*)*-ḥtp* (*n*) *mtr*
15. *pꜣ wꜥb* (*n*) *ẖrt·f m-sꜣ·s mtw·w dỉt*
16. *pꜣ mšt* (*n*) *wꜥt ḏnyt mtw·w*
17. *tbꜥ-s*[s] (*n*) *tꜣ ḫny* (*n*) *pꜣ wꜥb*
18. *mtw·w dỉt-s* (*n*) *nꜣ wnw*
19. (*n*) *Pr-Wsỉr-Ḥp*
20. *mtw·w smn-*
21. *s.*

Notes

a. Restored from the writing in l. 5 below; the writing *ỉ·ḥr* seems to be confined to Text **1**.

b. Presumably a title of the god stood here.

c. It must be admitted that it is difficult to reconcile this restoration with the traces, which may equally suit **nty ḥr Mn-nfr*.

d. The usual absence of article in such expressions: Spiegelberg, *Grammatik*, § 46.

e. Cf. Text **16**, R° 2; **17**, 2–3.

f. Rather a bold restoration, although it would suit the context well.

g. Much of the eye of faith has been required to determine these dates, by dampening the ostracon, and they do not appear in the photograph.

h. One may perhaps restore **n r-pr Ḏḥwty* or the like.

i. The singular refers grammatically to (*pꜣ*) *wꜥb s 3*, although the sense is plural.

j. Largely restored from V° 13.

k. The word is nowhere else feminine; the *-t* may therefore be redundant here. A similar example will be seen in Text **33**, 6 below.

l. Very faint in the original, and restored from Text **19**, R° 21; *šn*, which is used in the parallel text, does not seem to fit the traces.

m. The scribe seems first to have written *mtry*.

n. See note to Text **19**, V° 8, p. 76 above.

o. *n-ỉm·s* is perhaps possible.

p. I am unable to identify this word: a connection with ⲡⲱϩⲧ (Crum, 283a) seems tenuous. The context suggests a translation 'reward, bonus', or the like.

q. See Text **19**, V° 17.

r. At this distance from the grammatical subject the natural number seems to have emerged; see note *i* above.

s. The traces resemble **ḫy-s*; *tbꜥ* is obtained from Text **19**, V° 13.

Translation: recto

1. A memorandum[a] before the priests (of) Thoth [··········] and

2. the gods who rest with him,[b] from the scribe of the nome of Sebennytos, Ḥor (son of) Ḥarendjiōtef(?).
3. 'I approached the temple [·········], I being charged with the utterance
4. (of) Thoth, which he spoke [·········], for excellent was its
5. preparation in my sight, namely, to establish that which is beneficial to him, namely,
6. the matter which concerns the Ibis (in) his heart: to impart regularity
7. into him in Pi-waʿb-nēbes[c] when they bury him (in) the houses of
8. rest which are upon the mountain.[d] It was established by Thoth ⟨(in) Memphis⟩, it shall not
9. fail. The men caused a debate(?) to take place with the council[e]
10. (of) the temple of Memphis in Year 8, Thoth, day [·····] through to ⟨Year 8, Thoth, day 17⟩.[f] It was commanded by
11. the 25 priests who conclude affairs [······ ····][g] to choose
12. three priests to investigate the fortune (of) the Ibis (and) the Hawk: one
13. payment until they[h] come (to) Pi-waʿb-nēbes,
14. three payments when they inspect(?) the sanctuary[i] (of) the Ibis
15. (and) the sanctuary (of) the Hawk, the god in person, ⟨which[j] they shall find⟩
16. at the time, and impart
17. regularity into the Ibis,
18. one god (in) one vessel.

Translation: verso

1. They shall (also) assess with the servants (of) the ibises
2. (and) the servants (of) the Hawk concerning the performance of the bandaging,
3. what they shall pay, (namely) two payments of the god. (If) it happens (that)
4. no man experiences slackness (in) performing the burial
5. of the Ibis (and) the Hawk, and the bandaging:
6. regularity within it, its *pẖt(t)*[k] is
7. one payment: ⟨failure in the regularity⟩, its fine (?) is $\frac{1}{2}$ payment,
8. making $1\frac{1}{2}$ *ḥḏ*: and the rest occurs before the gate (?) of
9. the courtyard containing the Ibis (and) the Hawk,
10. (when) the occasion (of) the burial of the Ibis happens which they shall perform
11. (in) one year (at) one time; a payment until they
12. assemble the people (of) the Serapeum at
13. Pi-waʿb-nēbes and lead in procession the Ibis
14. (and) the Hawk to his houses of rest (in) contentment,
15. the appropriate priest in attendance,[l] and they are to place
16. the inspection[m] (in) one chest, and
17. seal it (in) the storeroom (of) the priest,[n]
18. and give it (to) the pastophoroi
19. (of) the Serapeum,
20. and establish 21. it'.

Notes

a. Cf. the opening of Text **1**.

b. The other sacred animal cults of the necropolis: the hawk, the baboon, and Isis, Mother of the Apis, who share the temple terrace by the galleries (*JEA* 57 (1971), 3 ff., pl. 14).

c. 'Abaton-of-her-lord': a place-name not elsewhere mentioned in our texts, but apparently the site of the ibis- and hawk-galleries, and thus immediately to the south of Ḥepnēbes. See Commentary § 4 below.

d. i.e. which are cut into the limestone cliffs (*gebel*) behind the temple buildings (*JEA* 56 (1970), pl. 18).

e. The standard deliberative and executive council, whose roots extend far back into Pharaonic times, even to the Old Kingdom (Pirenne, *Histoire des Institutions*, ii. 293 f.). Bruyère, *Rapport sur les fouilles de Deir el-Médineh (1934–1935)*, iii (Cairo, 1939), 36–9, gives archaeological evidence for meetings. Černý, *BIFAO* 27 (1927), 159–203, offers the information of written sources for the same locality, and Gardiner, *The Inscription of Mes* (Leipzig, 1905), 32–8 discusses the nature and function of the great *ḳnbwt* of a slightly earlier period. See Commentary below.

f. On the assumption that the year date is that of Philometor, the period would cover October 174, through to the 23rd of the month. This would rather conflict with the evidence of Text **19**, which implies that abuses had gone unchecked before 1 June of the following year. One solution would be to regard Year 8 as a date in the joint reign (October 163); no such date is known for the joint reign, however, and we should have to assume either confusion or uncertainty in the mind of the scribe. This is not entirely out of the question (note the reappearance of 'Year 9' of the joint reign in Pestman, *Chronologie*, 51), but it is not an attractive notion, and it would clearly be better to assume that the present text describes a preliminary attempt at reform, before the great investigation of Year 9 of Philometor.

g. Restore 'in the chapel of Thoth', or similar.

h. See textual note *ad locum*.

i. The embalming-place: see translation note *c* to Text **1**, 1, p. 12 above.

j. Grammatically the reference should be to the god.

k. 'Reward, bonus' (?); see textual note.

l. A more literal translation might be 'in his proper place behind it (the procession)'.

m. Hardly 'the inspector': see note *l* to the translation of Text **19**, V° 13, p. 80 above.

n. Presumably the three appointed above.

Preliminary Remarks

Like Text **1**, the present document is the draft of a memorandum prepared by Ḥor of Sebennytos. Its purpose was to establish the part played by the author in various reforms proposed for the administration of the ibis-galleries. In its details, the ostracon resembles Text **19**.

TEXT 22

Height	18·0 cm.
Width	21·4 cm.
Thickness	0·85 cm.
Munsell	7·5 YR 6/4 (interior 2·5 YR 6/6)
Photograph	Plates XXIV (R°), XXV (V°)
Facsimile	not given
Excavator's no.	71/2–122 [5390]

A large ostracon, roughly triangular, of fine red ware with horizontal striations to which a buff wash has been applied. The recto bears fourteen lines, faded in parts, with insertions, in a hand which is recognizably that of the Memphite Ḥor. Upon the verso are traces of seven lines completely erased, which are followed by a further six, the continuation of the recto. The sherd is slightly curved. The entire ostracon is a palimpsest, with traces appearing beneath the writing of both faces; on the verso, these traces are upside down.

Text: recto

1. *n-drt Ḥr. dỉ·w mnt ẖr pꜣ hb ỉwty šb*[a] *tꜣ mdt smn m-sꜣ·ỉ*
2. *ẖt snt ḏt.*[b] *tꜣ mdt pḥ Kmy tꜣy tꜣ ẖt-mdt (ỉ·)wꜣḥ pꜣ ntr ꜥꜣ Ḏḥwty r·ỉ ⟨tꜣ nty ṯꜣy nꜣ ꜥẖyt nty ỉw (n) nꜣ tšw⟩.*[c]
3. *ỉr·ỉ pꜣy·s smy ⟨ḥꜣt-sp 5t tpy šmw sw 14⟩*[d] *hb nꜣ Pr-ꜥꜣ (n) ḥty*[e] *n-ỉm·s. ꜥḥꜥ·ỉ ỉrm pꜣ ḥr-tb*[f]
4. *ḥr rꜣ tꜣ wmtt (n) Ḥp-nb·s ḏd·ỉ n·f tꜣ nty ỉw·ỉ ỉr-rẖ-s r-dbꜣ*
5. *dỉt ỉr·w pꜣ nty nfr·f (n) pꜣ ꜥš-sḥn (n) pꜣ hb pꜣ bỉk ẖt tm dỉt ꜣḳ mdt*[g]
6. *(n) tꜣ nty ṯꜣy tꜣy·f ẖrt ỉrm tꜣy·f ḳrst. ḥn·f-s (n) Pꜣ-šr-(n)-tꜣ-ỉḥt (sꜣ) Pꜣ-ym*
7. *nty šn ḥt-ntr ỉrm Pꜣ-dỉ-Mntw*[h] *pꜣ mr-šn (r) dỉt ỉr nꜣ wꜥbw (n) Ptḥ*
8. *ḳd·f (n) ḳdy*[i] *rmt s 5 (ỉ·)snt·w ỉw·w nḥty bn-ỉw·w*
9. *pnꜥ*[j] *mtw wꜥb 2 n-ỉm·w šn tꜣ ẖrt mtw 3 ẖn·w*
10. *šn*[k] *pꜣ ꜥš-sḥn [[nfr]] (n) pꜣ hb ⟨pꜣ bỉk⟩ tꜣ wꜥbt (n)*
11. *Ḥp-nb·s tn*[l] *nb n pꜣ ntr nty ỉw·w gm-f*
12. *ḥr pꜣ tr mtw·w dỉt mnt*[m] *n-ỉm·s*
13. *ỉw·f ḳrs swt*
14. *wꜥ ntr (n) wꜥt mgt.*

Text: verso

(For the erased traces, see below).

The following lines have been partially desurfaced, but not erased.

1. *nꜣ ḥḏw nty ỉw·w twt m-sꜣ nꜣy mtw·w dỉt-s wbꜣ rꜣ Ḥp-nb·s*[n]
2. *mtw·w dỉt nꜣ mštw*[o] ⟨(*n*) *nꜣ ꜥwyw*⟩ (*n*) *wꜥt ḏnyt mtw·w tbꜥ tꜣ ḫny*[p] (*n*)
3. *nꜣ wꜥbw nty šn mtw·w dỉt-s* (*n*) *tꜣ wsḫyt n-drt nꜣ wnw*[p]
4. *nty ỉw·w wḏꜣ ỉw·f wpy tm nḥt nꜣ sdm-ꜥš*
5. (*n*) *nꜣ hbw ỉrm nꜣ sdm-ꜥš* (*n*) *pꜣ bỉk nꜣ ntrw* [ ][q]
6. *ỉw·w ỉr ḳrs·f.*

(At the bottom of the sherd, upside down and therefore part of the palimpsest, the words *mtw·k Wsỉr-Ḥp* have been erased).

The remaining lines were vigorously erased by the scribe:

1.* *bꜣk*
2.* *Ḏḥwty pꜣ ꜥꜣ* *bꜣk*
3.*
4.*
5.* *ꜥš-sḥn*
6.* *Kmt* *mtw·w* *nꜣ ntrw ỉp·i*
7.* *dr·w tꜣ ḫt-mdt wꜥt·s.*

No connected translation is possible.

Notes

a. The same group occurs in Text **26**, 5, in a similar context. The group here read *ỉwty* resembles *nḥḥ*, and is open to some doubt.

b. The *s* of *snt* looks rather like a *b*, but this yields little sense.

c. Although inserted below the line, these words seem most naturally placed here.

d. This date has been added below, but before any of the following line was written, as this line is displaced downwards to allow for the insertion. With *ꜥḥꜥ·i* the scribe filled his pen, and this supply of ink lasted throughout the next line. It would therefore seem that the additional date was written before *ꜥḥꜥ·i*, and that it belongs here.

e. See note to Text **2**, R° 11, p. 17 above.

f. See note to Text **12**, R° 4, p. 51 above.

g. The lotus (?) at the end of this word is part of the palimpsest.

h. A doubtful reading, and **mỉ-nn* (*sꜣ*) *Mn-Rꜥ* would be equally possible, though the latter name (an abbreviation of *Mn-k*(*ꜣ*)*-Rꜥ*?) is difficult to maintain.

i. See Text **19**, V° 3.

j. Cf. the similar phrase in Text **2**, V° 10.

k. The scribe has made an erasure which partially obscures this word.

l. Partly restored from Text **19**, V° 6.

m. The effect of the palimpsest has been to make this word resemble *mgt* below.

n. Restored from Text **21**, V° 8–9.

o. The scribe has clearly written *šštw*, but this makes little sense.

p. Rather hazardous, and suggested by the parallels.

q. *ꜥꜣy* will not suit the traces, though (*n*) *rn·w* may.

Translation: recto

1. From Ḥor.[a] Regularity has been imparted into the Ibis without change: may (?) the matter be secure after me,
2. namely, founded for eternity. The matter which affects[b] Egypt is the utterance which the great god Thoth laid upon me ⟨that which concerns the chapels which are in the provinces⟩.[c]
3. I made its petition ⟨in Year 5, Pakhons, day 14⟩.[d] The Pharaohs sent in haste(?) upon it. I stood with the magician
4. at the gate of the tower[e] (of) Ḥepnēbes, and I told him what I knew concerning
5. causing to be performed that which is beneficial (for) the fortune (of) the Ibis (and) the Hawk, namely, not to detract from (any) matter
6. (of) that which concerns his sustenance and his burial.[f] He ordered Pshenteḥe (son of) Payom
7. who investigates the temple,[g] and Petimonth (?) the *lesōnis*, (to) cause the priests (of) Ptaḥ
8. to pass in review(?)[h] five men (whom) they respect (and) who are trustworthy without
9. gainsay, and two priests of their number

shall investigate the sustenance, and three among them
10. investigate the fortune (of) the Ibis ⟨(and) the Hawk⟩ in the sanctuary (of)
11. Ḥepnēbes, (at) every count of the god which they shall find
12. at the time. They are to impart regularity into it[i]
13. when he is buried (and) bandaged,
14. one god (in) one vessel.

Translation: verso

1. The moneys which are collected after this, they are to give them[j] before the gate(?) (of) Ḥepnēbes
2. and they are to place the inspectors ⟨of the houses⟩[k] (in) one chest and seal the storeroom (of)
3. the priests who investigate, and place it (in) the forecourt into the hand of the pastophoroi(?)
4. who are secure, it being judged(?) not to trust the servants
5. (of) the ibises and the servants (of) the Hawk, the gods in person(?)
6. when they perform his burial.

Notes

a. As unqualified, perhaps Ḥor of Sebennytos, cf. translation note to Text **12**, R° 1, p. 53 above.

b. Text **3**, V° 18.

c. A clear reference to Text **16**, R° 9–10, and one which makes very likely the identification of the *ḥt-mdt* named in either text. The motif of consulting a *ḥr-tb* also appears in both texts, and the words of ll. 5–6 of the present document are also present in the earlier. This identification may allow us to date the events of Texts **16** and **17** above; see preliminary remarks to the latter.

d. The low year-date, and mention of plural Pharaohs, suggests the joint reign of Philometor and his brother. The date would then be 13 June 165. This would add weight to the statement in l. 1 that order had now been installed into the affairs of the Ibis, whereas we have seen in Text **19** that such a state of affairs did not occur before 172. To identify our Year 5 with that of Philometor and his mother (177/6), while not impossible, would make nonsense of much of Text **19**, and would antedate most of the events of our ostraca.

e. ⲟⲩⲟⲙⲧⲉ, Crum, 480a; not an uncommon feature for temples (cf. Rylands IX, 2/14, 17, and the example quoted in Crum, loc. cit.), and denoting either a tower, or a monumental entrance such as a pylon. See Commentary below.

f. These words are identical to those of Text **16**, R° 3–4 and **17**, 3–4.

g. See note to Text **19**, R° 17, p. 79 above.

h. Text **19**, V° 3.

i. The sanctuary.

j. The syntax at this point is rather difficult, and suggests that a clause may have been lost in the erased lines above.

k. i.e. the galleries of the Ibis and the Hawk.

Preliminary Remarks

This ostracon seems to act as a continuation of the preceding in outlining the activities of Ḥor in securing reforms at the ibis-galleries: an oracle (*ḥt-mdt*), which may be that referred to in Texts **16** and **17** above, has been interpreted[1] and its contents communicated to the administrators of the temple. This seems to have taken place in 165, when the reforms instituted in Text **19** were already advanced, and the additional measures seem designed to reinforce them.

TEXT 23

Height	21·6 cm.
Width	15·5 cm.
Thickness	0·95 cm.
Munsell	2·5 YR 5/6
Photograph	Plate XXVI (R°, V°)
Facsimile	Plate XXVIA (R°, V°)
Excavator's no.	71/2–128 [5396]

[1] We learn from the other texts that the interpretation was secured by the oracle of Imḥōtep, and that this had happened on the previous 16 April.

An ostracon of thick reddish ware and considerable difficulty. Smashed in antiquity into thirteen pieces by a blow to the middle of the recto, the ostracon has suffered badly from the action of salt. A fourteenth piece is missing. The writing, apparently composed in haste, with its numerous erasures and insertions, is that of Ḥor of Sebennytos. Twenty-four lines in this hand appear on the recto, a further fourteen on the verso. At the foot of the verso the Memphite Ḥor has added a further twelve lines in his own very neat script. The initial lines of the recto in particular present many difficulties.

Text: recto

1. *n-ḏrt Ḥr nty ḥr tš*[a] *pꜣ mtry*[b] *(n)*
2. *nꜣ stb(ḥw)*[c] *(n) Ḏḥwty ꜥꜣ nb Pr-Ḏḥwty nty ḥr*
3. *pꜣ ḏw rs (n) Pr-Wsỉr-Ḥp pꜣ nty (n) Mn-nfr*
4. *ỉw·f šms nꜣ hrw*[d] *(n) Ḥp-nb·s (n) tꜣ ḥꜣst*[e]
5. *Pr-Wsỉr [[ḏw]]*[f] *ḥr pꜣ ḏw pr-mḥ*[g] *(n) R-stꜣw*
6. *ꜥnḫ-tꜣwy.*[h] *ỉw·ỉ wš-s*[i] *nꜣ ssw (n) Pr-Ḏḥwty*[j]
7. *ỉw·]ỉ smy ḥr nꜣ (ỉ·)ḏd-w pꜣ nṯr ꜥꜣ Ḏḥwty. bn-pw·ỉ*
8. *ḥꜣꜥ tꜣy·f mỉt.*[k] *tꜣ 3t ḥt-mdt dỉ·ỉ hb*
9. *Ḥtp-'In-ḥrt*[l] *pꜣ ḥr-tb n-ỉm·w ḥꜣt-sp 3t ꜣbd-4 šmw*[m] *sw 20 ỉw·w dỉt*
10. *pꜣ*[n] *gy-(n)-ḏlꜥ-mdt (n) Ḏ-ḥr-pꜣ-ỉmỉ*[o] *pꜣ rd (n)*
11. *Pr-ꜥꜣ nty šn n*[p] *nꜣ r-prw ꜥnḫ-tꜣwy mdt nbt*[q] *smn*
12. *pꜣ hp n tꜣ mdt *ta* [ ] *ḫt pꜣ snt (ỉ·)wn-nꜣ*
13. *ḫpr (n) tꜣ ḥꜣt*[r] *ḫt [dỉt] mnt ẖr pꜣ hb pꜣ bỉk (n) Ḥp-nb·(s)*
14. *šty pꜣ ỉnḥy*[s] *nꜣy·f ꜥwyw-(n)-ḥtp n*
15. *pr-ỉmnt*[g] [ ].[t] *pꜣ rmt nty ỉr (n) pꜣ hb ỉrm*
16. *nꜣy·f swtw dỉt ḫpr mdt nbt (n) tꜣ nty ṯꜣy*
17. *nꜣ mštw (n) nꜣ ꜥwyw mtw·f*[u] *dỉt-s (n) wꜥt ḏny*
18. *ỉw·s tbꜥ mtw·w dỉt [tꜣ ḏ]ny rn·s n-ḏrt*
19. *nꜣ wnw [(n) tꜣ wsḫ]yt ⟨ḥt-nṯr⟩ Pr-Ptḥ*
20. [ ][v] [*ḥꜣt-sp 3]t ꜣbd-4 šmw sw 20 nꜣ rmtw*
21. *⟨nꜣ sdm⟩*[w] *ỉp r tm dỉt ỉr rmt [nb] sẖy (n) pꜣ nṯr rn·f ⟨pꜣ hb ỉrm nꜣ sdm-ꜥš⟩*[w]
22. *pꜣ bỉk [[ỉw·w ỉr ḳrs·f]]*
23. *ỉw·w ỉr ḳrs·f ỉrm (pꜣ)*[x] *nty ḫpr ꜥn*
24. (erasure).

Text: verso

1. [ ][a] *rn·s ỉ·ỉr·ḥr nꜣ wꜥbw*
2. [ ] *r·w tꜣ nty ṯꜣy pꜣ mšt*
3. [*nꜣ*] *mštw*
4. **na* [ ] *mn sp-sn*
5. *pꜣ ꜥwy-(n)-ḥtp* [ ][b] *ḫt pꜣ snt (ỉ·)wn-nꜣ*
6. *smn nḥḥ r-ḥ[n] tꜣ wnwt*
7. *tw·ỉ tbḥ n-ỉm·s.*
   (there follows a space)
8. *[n-ḏrt Ḥr] nty smy n wš*[c] *ḥr nꜣ (ỉ·)ḏd-w pꜣ nṯr ꜥꜣ*
9. *[Ḏḥwty bn-pw·ỉ ḥꜣꜥ tꜣy·]f mỉt* (erasures)
10. [*pꜣ*] *hb pꜣ bỉk pꜣ nṯr*
11. [ ] *šty pꜣ ỉnḥy*[d]
12. [ ] [e] [ ] *ḫt gy-(n)-ḏlꜥ-mdt (n)*
13. *Ḏ-ḥr-pꜣ-ỉmỉ*[f] *pꜣ rd (n) Pr-ꜥꜣ [nty šn] nꜣ r-prw*
14. *ḥꜣt-sp 3t ꜣbd-4 šmw sw [20]*[f]
    (There follow twelve lines in the hand of the Memphite Ḥor)
15. *n-ḏrt Ḥr Ḏḥwty nb ꜥnḫ*
16. *nty smy ḥr nꜣ (ỉ·)ḏd-w pꜣ nṯr ꜥꜣ Ḏḥwty ḫt rswt*
17. *bn-pw·ỉ ḥꜣꜥ tꜣy·f mỉt r-nḥḥ.*
18. *tw·ỉ tbḥ n-ỉm·s ỉw·s ḥs ỉw·w ỉr nꜣ ỉpw*
19. *tm dỉt ꜣsk*[g] *pꜣ ḥr-tb ḥr tꜣ mdt*
20. *smn pꜣ hp (n) pꜣ hb*[h] *pꜣ bỉk (n) Ḥp-nb·s*
21. *tꜣ nty ṯꜣy tꜣ mnt ỉrm pꜣ šty (n) pꜣ ỉnḥy nꜣ rmtw ⟨nꜣ wnw⟩*
22. *ỉrm nꜣ nty ḥr nꜣ šštw ḥr tꜣ wsḫyt*
23. *n ḥt-nṯr tꜣ thnyt*[i]
24. *r-dbꜣ dỉt wḏꜣ pꜣ hb*
25. *pꜣ bỉk (n) pꜣ ꜥwy-(n)-*
26. *ḥtp.*

Notes: recto

a. *ꜥš* is scarcely possible; the following signs, which resemble *nfr*, are perhaps to be taken as a rather clumsy writing of the determinative.

b. This seems to fit syntactically with the following word rather than with *tš*. This leaves the latter hanging, and we must assume either that the scribe intended to add **Mn-nfr* here, or that he relied upon *tš* on its own to convey this meaning. Neither is completely satisfactory, but the other options are even less so. A similar abbreviation, in which *tš* seems to stand for *Ṯb-nṯr*, will be found in fragment **48,** 1 below.

c. In spite of the abbreviation, the word seems close to the writings in Erichsen, *Glossar*, 477.

d. See note to Text **2,** R° 2; the resemblance to the word *tpḥ*, even in its meaning 'roof', is fortuitious, however, as is its similarity to the plural of *pt*, both of which yield very stilted translations. The reading offered with caution here assumes that the supralinear line is redundant.

e. Or *smyt*, see note to Text **8,** V° 5, p. 41 above. The palimpsest here has *Pr-Wsỉr*.

f. The presence of the determinative before this group tends to exclude the reading *Ḥp*; if the present reading is correct, it may be that the scribe was anticipating the idea expressed more fully in the subsequent words.

g. See note to Text **1,** 7, pp. 9–10 above, and to Text **3,** V° 11, p. 28.

h. The same hieraticized writing as found in Text **18.**

i. Unless the following pronoun is an example of the pleonastic use after *ḫn-s*, *tw-s*, etc., I can suggest no explanation for it.

j. The diagonal stroke is probably the usual complement to *pr*; cf. *Pr-Ptḥ* in l. 19 below, and note on *Pr-Ḏḥwty* in Text **1,** 1, p. 8.

k. Restored from the traces, and from parallels on the verso. The strange sign at the end of the word is probably the 'legs-determinative' as it appears in Ḥor's handwriting.

l. Reading very doubtful, though less so than **Ns-'In-ḥrt*.

m. The traces also resemble *ꜣḫt*, but *šmw* appears more clearly in l. 20, and V° l. 14.

n. The beginning of this word is obscured by a palimpsest, *šm* or the like.

o. The final group, which recurs in V° 13, is difficult to interpret, and the present reading is not certain: one may also read **Ḏ-ḥr* (*sꜣ*) *Pꜣ-dỉ-'Itm*, or more likely a compound of the type *Ḏ-ḥr-pꜣ-trš* in Text **19,** R° 21–2. *Ḏ-ḥr-Nfr-tm* (Τεενεφθῖμις) is unfortunately excluded by the absence of a determinative. **Ḏ-ḥr-pꜣ-ỉpd*, which fits the traces, is not attested elsewhere.

p. No other example of this phrase shows the *n*, which may be a space-filler.

q. Extremely uncertain, especially the group *mdt*, as the ostracon has suffered badly from salt at this point.

r. Likewise conjectural.

s. The traces may also suit *nb ꜥnḫ*; the text is based on V° 11, and Text **19,** R° 11.

t. **Mn-nfr* may have stood in the lacuna.

u. Faint traces only survive, far from conclusive.

v. Just possibly the *wmtt* of Text **22,** but otherwise uncertain.

w. These words seem to have been inserted in a most awkward fashion; the translation is based on the most plausible syntax, and the parallel in Text **21,** V° 1–2.

x. Perhaps omitted by haplography.

Notes: verso

a. Is *tꜣ ḫt-mdt* to be restored here?

b. The final traces may suit (*pꜣ*) *bỉk*, but it is then difficult to see what has become of *pꜣ hb*.

c. The palimpsest has *nꜣ ḏd-w*.

d. Cf. R° 14, and Text **19,** R° 11.

e. One would expect *mtw·w dỉt* to have stood somewhere here, but the traces hardly support this.

f. Restored from recto.

g. A variant of *ỉsḳ* 'delay' (Erichsen, *Glossar*, 44); *ꜣhy* (ibid. 8) seems less convincing.

h. The palimpsest has *tꜣ 3t ḫt* (*-mdt*).

i. The present spelling, not elsewhere attested, seems to correspond to the Bohairic ⲧⲉϩⲛⲓ (Crum, 460b).

Translation: recto

1. From Ḥor who is upon the nome,[a] the witness[b] (of)
2. the equipment (of) Thoth the great, lord of the House of Thoth, which is upon
3. the southern mountain (of) the Serapeum which is (in) Memphis,
4. who serves (his) days (in) Ḥepnēbes (in) the desert
5. (of) the House of Osiris which is upon the mountain (of) the north (of) the necropolis
6. (of) ꜥAnkhtawy.[c] 'I spend (my) days (in) the House-of-Thoth,
7. petitioning upon the (things) which the great god Thoth has said. I have not

8. abandoned his path.[d] The three utterances:[e] I caused
9. Ḥetpanḥūri(?)[f] the magician to send concerning them in Year 3, Mesorē, day 20. They gave
10. the document (to) Djeḥepemou,[g] the agent (of)
11. Pharaoh who investigates the chapels of ⸢Ankhtawy(?) in every detail(?), (to) ascertain
12. the law of the *said matter [·······], namely, the custom which
13. prevailed beforehand(?), namely, to impart regularity into the Ibis (and) the Hawk (in) Ḥepnēbes,
14. to excavate(?) the courtyard (of) his houses of rest to
15. the west [of Memphis]. The man who serves[h] the Ibis and
16. his bandagings shall cause to happen every matter (of) that which concerns
17. the inspectors (of) the houses, and he shall place them (in) one chest
18. which is sealed, and they are to give the chest itself into the hand of
19. the pastophoroi [of the fore]court of the ⟨temple of⟩ the House of Ptaḥ
20. [··········][i] (in) Year 3, Mesorē, day 20. The men
21. ⟨the servants (of) the Ibis and the servants (of) the Hawk⟩[j] shall assess to prevent any man having control over the god himself (22)
23. when they perform his burial and (that) which shall further come about.

Translation: verso

1. [·········· the utterance] itself before the priests
2. [·························] to them (in) that which concerns the inspection
3. [································· the] inspectors
4. *said [·······························] lasting, lasting
5. the house of rest [····················] namely, the custom which was
6. established for ever until this hour.
7. I beg this.
8. [From Ḥor] who petitions in spending (his) time[k] concerning the (things) which the great god
9. [Thoth has said. I have not abandoned his] path.
10. [·········· the] Ibis (and) the Hawk, the god
11. [in person? ·······] to excavate the courtyard of
12. [the Ibis ················] namely, (a) document (to)
13. Djeḥepemou(?),[g] the agent (of) Pharaoh [who investigates] the chapels
14. in Year 3, Mesorē, day 20.'

(*The following lines are added by the Memphite Ḥor*)

15. From Ḥor (of) Thoth, lord of life,[l]
16. who petitions concerning the (things) which the great god Thoth has said through a dream.[m]
17. I have not abandoned his path for ever[n]
18. I beg this, if it is favoured,[o] that when they make the assessments,
19. not to allow the magician to slacken in the matter,
20. (but) to establish the law (of) the Ibis (and) the Hawk (in) Ḥepnēbes,
21. (in) that which concerns the regularity and the excavation (of) the courtyard, the men, ⟨the pastophoroi⟩,
22. and those who are over the windows[p] upon the forecourt
23. of the temple of the Peak,[q]
24. concerning the salvation of the Ibis (and)
25. the Hawk in his house of
26. rest.

Notes

a. *Mn-nfr* is presumably to be supplied, either explicitly or by implication. The handwriting makes it very likely that this is a reference to Ḥor of Sebennytos, possibly while on an early visit to the Memphite shrine.

b. Possibly to an inventory of the vessels, statues, and cult-objects kept within the chapel of Thoth. This practice is known even from the Abusîr Papyri under the Old Kingdom (Posener-Kriéger and de Cenival, *Hieratic Papyri in the British Museum, Fifth Series*, 8–13).

c. For the details of this important topographical survey, see Commentary below.

d. An extension of the metaphor in Text **16**, R° 4–5; cf. the observations there listed. The phrase is repeated in Text **17**, 14–15.

e. It is not stated what form these utterances (oracles) took, although they may well have resembled the contents of Text **14**. We have seen from Text **22** that such oracles, interpreted if need be, could provide the stimulus to reforms in the administration of the cult. The appearance of the magician (*ḥr-tb*), both here and in the previous text, suggests that the question was one of oracular material, and that in such questions the authority of the magician carried weight. See Commentary below.

f. *Esanḥūri is perhaps also possible.

g. Possibly also 'son of Petatūm' (?); see textual note.

h. For *iri n*, cf. *Wb*. i. 109.

i. See textual note for this lacuna.

j. The effect of reconstructing these lines (see textual note above) has been to remove l. 22 altogether from the translation, consisting as it does merely of an insertion and an erasure.

k. Apparently an alternative to the more frequent construction with this verb, for which see R° 6.

l. The Memphite Ḥor. This appellation, not previously attested, sheds light on his habit of naming himself *Ḥr-(n)-Ḏḥwty*. See note to Text **12**, R° 1, p. 53 above.

m. Very reminiscent of τὰ ῥηθέντα δι' ὀνείρου of Greek Text B above; see note *ad locum*.

n. An interesting use of preterite and prospective in combination.

o. Cf. the use of *ḥs·ti* in Middle Egyptian with the connotation 'please' (*Westcar*, 9, 2–3; *Eg. Gr*. § 313).

p. If this is not a miswriting of *mštw* 'inspectors' (which we have already seen in Text **22**, V° 2), the reference must be to 'windows of appearance' (*šštw n ḫʿ*). The inscription of ʿAnemḥo (Brugsch, *Thesaurus*, 904, ll. 9–10) introduces us to the title *ḥm-ntr n ššt n ḫʿ*, and the deity, Horus, who presides over the window (ibid. and 914, l. 5). See further Commentary, § 5 below.

q. For this important feature of the Memphite necropolis, which included, among others, the temple of Imḥōtep-Asclepius, see Commentary, § 5.

Preliminary Remarks

The importance of this text lies in direct proportion to its difficulty. The recto bears a communication from Ḥor of Sebennytos, who is apparently in Memphis at this time (September 167) to an unknown person, perhaps Pharaoh, in which he describes his role in bringing about reforms at the ibis-galleries of Saqqâra. The verso contains two petitions from the same man, that these reforms should be rigorously followed, and a postscript, added by the secretary, Ḥor of Memphis, to the same effect. The ostracon is topographically of great importance.

TEXT 24

A	Height	7·1 cm.
	Width	9·4 cm.
	Thickness	0·75 cm.
	Munsell	(Ware) 5 YR 5/4 (Slip) 10 YR 6/3
	Photograph	Plate XXII
	Facsimile	Plate XXIIA
	Excavator's no.	G7–41 [470]

An ostracon, joined from two fragments, of red ware with a thin buff slip, defaced in parts. The recto, which is slightly convex, bears traces of five lines, possibly in the hand of the Memphite scribe, while the verso, which shows a blackish incrustation, is uninscribed.

B	Height	9·7 cm.
	Width	7·4 cm.
	Thickness	0·7 cm.
	Photograph	Plate XXII
	Facsimile	Plate XXIIA
	Excavator's no.	G7–38 [467]

This ostracon is clearly part of the same original sherd, although it does not join it.

Text 24A

1. *n-drt Ḥr nty ḥrḥ* [[a]]
2. *gm*[b] *wḏꜣ pꜣ hb* [ ]
3. *Ḏḥwty r ḥtp*[c] *r-ḫn* [*tꜣ mỉt*[d]]
4. *m-ḳdy Mn-nfr ỉrm nꜣy·f* [[e]]
5. *nb tꜣ wryt*[f] *šꜣꜥ pꜣ tny ꜥꜣ* ⟨insertion⟩[g] [ ]

Text 24B

x+1.] *ꜥš*[h] *Pr-Wsỉr*[-**Ḥp*]
2.] *tꜣ ḫt-mdt ỉw·s*[i] [ ]
3.][j] *ḏd dỉ·ỉ ỉr·w* [**pꜣ nty nfr·f n pꜣ ꜥš-sḥn n*]
4. *pꜣ hb ḫt tm dỉt ꜣḳ* [**mdt n tꜣ nty ṯꜣy tꜣ ḫrt ỉrm*]
5. *tꜣ ḳrst* (*n*) *pꜣ hb pꜣ* [**bỉk*]
6. *pꜣ by* (*n*) *Wsỉr pꜣ b*[*y*]
7. *nꜣ ntrw ꜥꜣy* [**n Kmt*].

Notes

a. The traces faintly suit *pꜣ ntr ꜥꜣ*.

b. Cf. the early example quoted in Erichsen, *Glossar*, 580.

c. ϩⲧⲟⲡ, Crum, 725b.

d. Far from certain.

e. The traces may suit *ntrw*; otherwise *tꜣy·f* may be read.

f. For the determinative, cf. Erichsen, *Glossar*, 93, final example.

g. The initial sign seems to resemble *ỉr*.

h. So, rather than *tš* (?); *sdm-ꜥš* may have been intended.

i. I cannot interpret the final trace.

i. *ḥb* is but one of many possibilities.

Translation: Text 24A

1. From Ḥor who watches over [·························]^a
2. power. The Ibis is secure [·························]
3. Thoth will fall into [·························][b]
4. likewise Memphis and its [gods(?) ·························]
5. all, the great one[c] up to the great dam[d] [········].

Translation: Text 24B

x+1.] servants (?) (of) the Serapeum (?) [···········]
2.] the utterance which [·························]
3.] namely, I caused to be performed [that which is beneficial for the fortune of]
4. the Ibis, namely, not detract from [a matter which concerns the sustenance and]
5. the burial (of) the Ibis [(and) the Hawk[e] ··········]
6. The soul (of) Osiris, the [soul ················]
7. the great gods [of Egypt(?)[f] ··············].

Notes

a. Possibly 'the great god (Thoth)' is to be supplied. This may be another epithet, like that of the preceding text, acquired by Ḥor of Sebennytos during his duties at the ibis-shrine.

b. Possibly 'the way (of destruction)', or a similar phrase.

c. An epithet of Isis; see Appendix 1.

d. Perhaps the feature mentioned in Text **11**, V° 2 above.

e. Largely supplied from Texts **16** and **17**.

f. Supplied from Texts **19** and **20**.

Preliminary Remarks

These two fragments seem to represent the opening of an appeal by Ḥor of Sebennytos similar to Text **19**; the destruction of Memphis and all its gods seems to be envisaged (whether as a result of the mistreatment of the ibises is uncertain) and Ḥor's part in securing reforms is again described.

§ 4 : Biographical Texts

TEXT 25

Height	12·4 cm.
Width	9·3 cm.
Thickness	0·6 cm.
Munsell	5 Y 7/3 (interior 2·5 YR 5/4)
Photograph	Plate XXVII
Facsimile	not given
Excavator's no.	71/2–124 [5392]

A small buff-ware ostracon, bearing eleven lines in the hand of the Memphite Ḥor. Although the script is clearly preserved, erasures, changes of mind and of syntax make the sense difficult to grasp. The verso is blank. This text formed part of the corpus unearthed by Martin in January 1972.

Text

1. *n-drt sẖ tš Ṯb-ntr Ḥr nty ḥr Mn-nfr.*
2. [[*ssw ḳy r-bw-nꜣy*]][a] *r-dbꜣ dỉt ỉr·w pꜣ nty nfr·f*
3. (*n*) *pꜣ ꜥš-sḥn n pꜣ bỉk pꜣ by* (*n*) *Wsỉr Ḥr Ꜣst*[b]
4. *ẖt-mdt pḥ n pꜣ hb pꜣ by* (*n*) *Ḏḥwty ꜥꜣ ꜥꜣ*[c]
5. *dỉ·ỉ*[d] *ỉr·w smn-s ỉwty šb*[e] ⟨*pꜣ hp* (*n*) *tꜣ ẖt-mdt*⟩ ⟨*ẖt pꜣ snt* (*ỉ·*)*wn-nꜣ ẖpr*⟩[f]
6. *ẖt wd-s*[g] *n nꜣ wꜥbw nty ꜥḳ m-bꜣḥ Ptḥ n*
7. *tꜣ wsẖyt n ḥꜣt-sp 9t*[h] *ꜣbd-4 ꜣẖt sw 29*
8. *r-hn pꜣ hrw ỉw·ỉ* (*n*) *hp n mdt n hb*
9. *ẖr*[i] *Pr-pꜣy·f-ỉry r-dbꜣ ỉr*[j]
10. *nꜣ mšꜥw nꜣ nty ỉw·w ḏd n·ỉ* (*n*) *wꜣḥ n-ỉm·s*[k]
11. (*r*) *ỉr-s wꜣḥ nꜣ* (*ỉ·*)*ḏd-w pꜣ ntr ꜥꜣ Ḏḥwty.*

Notes

a. For a parallel to this erased line cf. Text **12**, R° 2.

b. The palimpsest has *pꜣ ntr ꜥꜣ*.

c. The first *ꜥꜣ* is far from certain.

d. The scribe seems to have written *pꜣ by* again, erased it, written *dỉ·ỉ* over this, and then again below for the sake of clarity.

e. See note to Text **22**, R° 1, p. 85 above.

f. Although this phrase stands below the line, it seems to fit more aptly here than into the following clauses.

g. A similar pleonastic object to those discussed in note *b* to Text **11**, R° 2, p. 49 above.

h. See Text **19**, R° 14, and note *p*, p. 75.

i. Text **12**, R° 2.

j. The final stroke is apparently a space-filler.

k. Syntactically this sentence is complex, and one might expect **n-ỉm·w* and *ỉr-w*. The singular pronoun has perhaps been influenced by the collective idea inherent in *nꜣ nty*.

Translation

1. From the scribe of the nome of Sebennytos, Ḥor who is in Memphis,[a]
2. concerning the performance of that which is beneficial
3. (to) the fortune of the Hawk, the soul[b] (of) Osiris, Isis, (and) Horus.
4. The utterance (which) appertains to the Ibis, the soul[b] (of) Thoth, the twice great:
5. I caused it to be established without change (?), ⟨the law (of) the utterance, namely the custom which used to prevail⟩,[c]
6. namely, to decree to the priests who enter before Ptaḥ in
7. the forecourt in Year 9, Khoiak, day 29,[d]
8. until this day (that) I was (in) the right[e] in (the) matter of sending
9. to Pi-peferē[f] because of performing
10. the journey[g] which was told to me (in) an oracle
11. to perform, (the) oracle which was spoken by the great god Thoth.[h]

Notes

a. A general title for Ḥor of Sebennytos in his self-imposed (or better god-imposed) exile; an alternative, to supply 'and' between *Ṯb-ntr* and the proper name, and take the whole as a description of both characters named Ḥor, is less happy.

b. Perhaps to be taken in apposition rather than conjunction.

c. See textual note above.

d. The date probably corresponds to 31 January 172; see note to Text **19**, R° 14, p. 79 above.

e. The word *hp* (cf. *Wb*. ii. 488) is of considerable interest in our documents. Much light has been shed on the word in general by Nims, *JNES* 7 (1948), 243 ff.; for the plural *nꜣ hpw* used to indicate the general body of law, cf. Hughes, *Saite demotic land leases* (Chicago, 1952), 70, § q. That the word transcends the meaning 'law' is shown by the epithet *tꜣ mr-hp* used as a translation of δικαιοσύνη in titles of Cleopatra III (Pierce, *Three Papyri in Brooklyn*, 31, § 16); whether the epithet was deserved is another point. The same extension of meaning is brought out in *Canopus* 14/52, where *nꜣ nty n hp n ỉr-w ḥr pꜣy·s ỉr-ntr* corresponds to τὰ πρὸς τὴν ἐκθέωσιν αὐτῆς νόμιμα. The opposite of *ỉw·f n pꜣ hp*, namely *ỉw·f ẖꜣꜥ pꜣ hp*, is seen in *Demotic Chronicle*, ii. 16, with a similar phrase in criticism of Pharaoh Hakoris, ibid. iv. 10.

f. See note to Text **12**, R° 2, p. 53 for this locality.

g. The translation as a collective singular is chosen to aid the syntax, but that it is justified is suggested by Text **2**, R° 5, and **4**, R° 8.

h. A very similar phrase in Text **23**, V° 16.

Preliminary Remarks

The main purpose of this rather incoherent text seems to be to place on record the fact that Ḥor's journey to Pi-peferē, which we know to have taken place between 172 and 168 (Text **12**), was justified by an oracle of Thoth, decreed to the priests of Ptaḥ at Memphis.

TEXT 26

Height	19·8 cm.
Width	13·6 cm.
Thickness	0·8 cm.
Munsell	(R°) 5 YR 5/4 (V°) 5 YR 3/1
Photograph	Plate XXVIII (R°, V°)
Facsimile	Plate XXVIIIA (R°, V°)
Excavator's no.	G7–24 [453]

An ostracon of dark grey ware overlaid on the recto with a red slip. Six fragments were recovered by Emery and joined, but there are still missing portions at the beginning of the recto and at the ends of ll. 5–11. The hand is that of the Memphite Ḥor, although clearly dictated by Ḥor of Sebennytos; twenty-one lines fill the recto, and a further seventeen the verso. The latter have been written in a slightly enlarged hand to allow for the greater curvature of the surface. Much of the middle portion is faded beyond recall.

Text: recto

1. [*wꜥ mḳmḳ*][a] *(n) ꜣrstn (n) Tbny*[b]
2. [*n-drt Ḥr rmt*] *dmỉ-(n)-ꜣst (n) pꜣ tš (n) Ṯb-ntr*
3. [ ][c] *ms (n) dmỉ nty ḥry. wn mtw·s nꜣy·s*[d]
4. [ ] *sꜥnḫ ỉrm nꜣy·s nkt* [ ]
5. [ ][e] *ỉw·w smn* [ ]
6. [ ] *nꜣ ỉtyw (n) Pr-ꜥꜣ*[f] [ ]
7. [ ] *ḏd tꜣ ḫrt (n) nꜣ* [*hbw*]
8. [ ] *ḫrt (n) nꜣ hbw ỉw* [ ]
9. [ ] [[*tꜣ ḫrt nty ỉw·w ỉr-s*]] [ ]
10. *mtw·w ỉn-s (r) tꜣ ꜥḥyt* [*m*]*n sp-sn*
11. *tꜣ nty ỉw pꜣ hb* [ ] *r·s. ỉp·ỉ n*
12. *Pꜣ-dỉ-Ḥr-pꜣ-*[ ][g] *pꜣ ḥm-ntr ꜣst pꜣ wꜥb nty ỉr mnḫ (n) ꜣst*
13. *tꜣ ḫrt rn·s r dỉt wḏꜣ·s šꜣꜥ-tw·w*[h] *hb*
14. *pꜣ nty (r) ḫt·w. gm·ỉ-s ḥḥ*[i] *hꜣ. tꜣ nty ḫpr ỉp·ỉ (r)*
15. *dỉt wḏꜣ·ỉ dỉ·ỉ wy n-drt·ỉ pꜣ ꜥḳ (ỉ·)ỉr·w smn-f*
16. *ḥr·ỉ ḥn pꜣ r-pr. dỉ·ỉ wꜣḥ·f nꜣ ꜥḳw*
17. *(n) rn·f tꜣ ḫrt (n) nꜣ hbw. gm n·ỉ Ḏḥwty lwḥ. ỉr·f šn*
18. ⟨ *swg·ỉ*⟩[j] *r-dbꜣ·s. dỉ·f ỉr·s ḥtr r·ỉ*
19. *(n) smy*[k] *n·k ḏd wn nꜣ gmꜥw*
20. *ỉrm nꜣ tm-hp*[l] *nty ỉw·w ỉr n-ỉm·w*[m]
21. *(n) tꜣ ꜥḥyt rn·s.*

Text: verso

1. *ỉw·s ṯꜣy r·k (r) dỉt lk* [[n]]
2. [ ] *ḥn-s* [ ]
3. [ ] *sḏm ḫrw·ỉ* [ ]
4. [ ] (traces)[o] [ ]
5. [ ] *nꜣy wš r·w* [ ]
6. (trace) [ ][p] *ỉp tꜣ ḫrt (n)*
7. *nꜣ hbw* [ ][q] *ỉ·ỉr·f dỉt wpy*[r]
8. ⟨inserted line⟩[s] *nꜣ wꜥbw (n) ꜣst ỉr pꜣ šn (n) nꜣy (n) ꜥrḏ*

9. *mtw·w hb n·k n-ỉm·w ḥr-rdwy·s*[t]
10. *⟨r-ẖt⟩ ẖt-mdt Ḏḥwty pꜣ ꜥꜣ pꜣ ꜥꜣ pꜣ ꜥꜣ pꜣ ḥry pꜣ nb*
11. *(n) pꜣ ḥꜣty ỉw·f dỉt n·k ꜥḥꜥ ḳy (n) ḥb*
12. *ỉr·k pꜣ rdwy*[u] *(n) nꜣy·k ẖrdw m-sꜣ·k ẖn*
13. *nꜣ ḥst (n) Pr-ꜥꜣ šꜣꜥ ḏt ỉrm*
14. *nꜣy·k ẖrdw šꜣꜥ ḏt.*[v]

Notes

a. The determinative is clearly visible.

b. See note to Text **7**, 6, p. 36 above.

c. An ambiguity arises here from the feminine pronouns which follow; we may restore either **wn wꜥt sḥmt ỉw·s ms*, taking the following pronouns as personal, or equally **r-dbꜣ tꜣ ꜥẖyt n ms*, with pronouns impersonal. The context seems to indicate the latter.

d. *tꜣy·s* is equally possible.

e. The surviving signs may represent *n-ỉm·w*.

f. The curved sign following *Pr-ꜥꜣ* may mark the opening of a cartouche.

g. The final element resembles greatly the group following *Ḏ-ḥr* in Text **23**, R° 10 and V° 13, but this may be coincidental; *ỉry* 'companion' would require different determinatives. I have therefore suggested no reading. The epithet *ỉr mnḫ* (possibly as the equivalent of στολιστής) is, however, paralleled from Tanis Stela (Canopus), 6 *nꜣ wꜥbw nty šm r pꜣ nty wꜥb r ỉr mnḫ n nꜣ ntrw*; see Brugsch, *Thesaurus*, 1555, 4–6.

h. The intervening sign resembles *dỉt*, and I can suggest no explanation for its presence, except by the perhaps wishful assumption that it was deleted by the scribe; certainly it seems much fainter than the surrounding characters. Much doubt surrounds all of this latter part of l. 13.

i. See notes to Text **3**, R° 26 and to Text **18**, R° 2, pp. 23, 67–8 above. Both reading and translation are offered with reserve.

j. *swg* is doubtful, and the group preceding it unidentified.

k. It seems more plausible to take this as infinitive dependent upon *ḥtr* than as *sḏm·f* with first person suffix omitted.

l. The reading *šꜥt (n) hp*, though plausible, is hard to reconcile with the writings in Text **3**, V° 18, and Text **4**, R° 1. I can find no parallel for the reading offered, and do so with reserve.

m. *gm-w* is less convincing.

n. The traces seem to show the top of *ḥḥ*; see note *i* above.

o. The obscurity of these middle lines may be due as much to erasure as to natural fading, and I can suggest few readings.

p. These traces may suit *(ꜥš-)sḥn*.

q. The remaining group escapes me.

r. This reading, which is Smith's, is more plausible than my own *ẖsy*.

s. Smith, in his earlier copy, read *(tꜣ) nty ẖpr n-ỉm·f*.

t. For this expanded form cf. Text **2**, R° 11.

u. Doubtless an alternative writing for *rd* (ⲣⲓⲧⲉ).

v. These last three lines are obscured by the palimpsest, which, apart from *pꜣy·k ḥry* in the centre of l. 13, is illegible.

Translation: recto

1. [A memorandum[a]] (to) Ariston[b] (of) Daphnae(?)[c]
2. [from Ḥor, man of] the town of Isis (in) the nome (of) Sebennytos
3. [concerning the chapel of][d] birth (in) the above town. It possesses its
4. [··········] maintenance and its property(?) [··········]
5. [··········] them, they being secure [··················]
6. [··········] the fathers (of) Pharaoh [[e]·················]
7. [·······] ······· namely, the food (of) the [ibises ······]
8. [······] food (of) the ibises, being [··················]
9. [·····] [[the food which is offered]] [·················]
10. and they shall bring it to the chapel [·······] lasting, lasting,
11. upon which the Ibis [·······].[f] I assessed to
12. Petiḥarp[ ], the prophet of Isis, the priest who performs service (for) Isis,
13. the food named to keep it safe until they sent
14. that which was appropriate (?)[g] I found it utterly(?) ruined(?). That which happened: I reckoned (to)

15. save myself. I rid myself[h] of the bread[i] (which) was established
16. for[j] me within the chapel. I caused him to deposit the loaves
17. (in) his (own) name, the food of the ibises. Thoth found fault with me. He made an investigation
18. ⟨····· of my wrongdoing⟩ concerning it. He caused it[k] to lay upon me (the) compulsion
19. (of) appealing to you: for the calamities
20. and illegalities(?)[l] which are being committed
21. are (in) the chapel named.

Translation: verso

1. It behoves you to cause [·················] to cease.
2. [·······] command it [·······························]
3. [·········] hear my voice [··························]
4. [···········] (traces) [·····························]
5. [···············] these fail(?) them [················]
6. (trace) [············] assess the food (of)
7. the ibises [··········]. He caused to judge(?)
8. ⟨that which had happened(?)⟩. The priests (of) Isis made the investigation (of) these things (in) earnest,
9. and they sent to you concerning them[m] immediately
10. ⟨according to⟩ the utterance of Thoth, the three times great,[n] the master, the lord (of)
11. the heart, who gives to you a life long (in) festival.[o]
12. You are the agent (of) your children after you, within
13. the favours (of) Pharaoh for ever, together with
14. your children for ever.[p]

Notes

a. For other memoranda see Text **1** (with note to l. 1, p. 12), and Text **21** above.

b. Ἀρίστων, Preisigke, 49. Whether the present character, who is clearly from V° 12–14 a personage of importance, is the same as that of Text **4**, R° 15, is impossible to decide; but he may well have been familiar to Pharaoh, and therefore, like *Hrynys*, used to add credibility to the complaints of Ḥor.

c. See textual note above, and note to Text **7**, 6, p. 36.

d. See textual note.

e. The name 'Ptolemy' may have followed.

f. Some such word as *ḥtp* may be supplied.

g. Literally 'according to their nature'; see also note *u* to Text **1**, 6, p. 9 above.

h. The characteristic formula of a cession-document; whether such a document was in fact made, or whether the phrase is used more loosely, is not easy to decide.

i. Although this word would be natural in the sense of 'income', the following lines seem to imply that it is the actual substance of the food of the ibises, and I have left the literal translation. It is not easy to see where Ḥor's transgression lay. The prophet of Isis seems to have held food in trust for him pending the issue of new rations; this appears to have perished. Ḥor, who would be held responsible for this loss, colludes with the prophet, and the bread is ascribed to the latter. The god, however, finds this reprehensible, and Ḥor is obliged to appeal to Ariston for redress against the temple authorities.

j. See note *t* to Text **1**, 11, p. 13 above.

k. Presumably 'the matter in question'.

l. See textual note.

m. ***n-ỉm·w*** could not stand as the object of the conjunctive; hence the reading ***nty ỉw·w***.

n. Cf. Text **2**, V° 15.

o. The same phrase as in Text **8**, V° 2, although it is there offered to Ḥor, whereas here Ḥor wishes the same for Ariston.

p. It is possible that these final lines would have been revised in transcription on to papyrus.

Preliminary Remarks

In this sadly incomplete text Ḥor, who describes himself as a citizen of Temenēsi (Isiospolis), relates the history of a dispute in the birth-chapel of the Ibis which stood in this town. Its revenues had apparently been established traditionally, and food for the ibises was customarily transported thither. A proportion of the food was the responsibility of Ḥor, and while this was entrusted to a colleague, a prophet of Isis (Ḥor in Greek text C describes himself as a pastophoros of this goddess), the food suffers a mishap. Ḥor's attempt to conceal this misfortune invokes the censure of the god, and he is forced to appeal to higher authority. It may have been this scandal which prompted his departure to Memphis, although we may suspect that his reputation was vindicated for him to have mentioned the incident at all.

TEXT 27

Height	12·6 cm.
Width	10·3 cm.
Thickness	0·7 cm.
Munsell	5 YR 4/3
Photograph	Plate XXVII (R°, V°)
Facsimile	Plate XXVIIA (R°, V°)
Excavator's no.	G7–35 [464]

A small brown-ware ostracon. The recto, upon which traces of some ten lines can be seen, is greatly faded and crossed with vertical lines which may have been intended to cancel the text. The verso, which is written upside down to the recto, is more satisfactorily preserved, and bears eleven more lines, in the hand of Ḥor of Sebennytos.

Text: recto

1. *Pr-ꜥꜣ Ptrwmys ꜥws.*
2. *sm*[a] *Ḥr* (*sꜣ*) *Ḥr-*[*nḏ-ỉt·f*][b] *pꜣ sẖ rmt dmỉ-*(*n*)-
3. [ ][c] [ ][d] *tꜣ Pr-ꜥꜣt*
4. *ḫpr* [ ] *nty ẖn* [ ]
5. *ꜣst pꜣ ḥm-ntr* [ ] *mdt-nfrt*
6. [ ] *pꜣ ntr ꜥꜣ* [ ] *ḥr ꜣt*
7. [ ] *pꜣy·k ḥḏ*
8. [ ] *ꜥḥꜥ* [ ]
9. [ ] *Wsỉr*
10. *st* [ ] *ẖn·w.*

Text: verso

1. *wn kt wꜥbt. ẖn*
2. [[*r-dbꜣ dỉt ỉr·w*]] *nḥḥ*[e]
3. *r-dbꜣ dỉt ỉr·w nꜣ mdt* (*n*)
4. *Wsỉr ẖn·f ỉw·w wꜥb*
5. *ḥr pꜣ rd.*
6. *nꜣ ꜥḫyt* (*n*) *Kmy ỉrm nꜣ mww*
7. *m-sꜣ·w ỉrm nꜣ*[f] *trw nty ḫpr pꜣ hrw sẖ*
8. *Ḏḥwty ỉw·f ỉn sgny*[g] *n-drt nꜣ rmtw*
9. *ḏryw* (*n*) *wꜥ sp.*[h] *st ṯꜣy tꜣ ẖrt* (*n*) *pꜣ hb*
10. *st mwt*[i] (*n*) *ḥḳ*(*r*) *ỉ·ỉr·ḥr·f bw-ỉr·w*
11. *dbꜣ pꜣ ntr ꜥn.*

Notes

a. Cf. Text **7**, 2, note *b*, p. 36.

b. Restored from Text **18**, R° 1.

c. The traces do not suit *ꜣst*, which one would expect, and it may be that a palimpsest has obscured the line.

d. *Ḏḥwty* may be visible, but the context is too obscure: there is no trace of *Ṯb-ntr*.

e. The group resembles *ỉwty* of Text **22**, R° 1, and is far from certain.

f. Disfigured by an accidental stroke of the pen.

g. For this spelling, cf. Text **12**, V° 6.

h. Concealed beneath the following word.

i. Traces resemble *dỉt*, which may be correct. The text is drawn from Text **7**, 12–13.

Translation: recto

1. Pharaoh Ptolemy.[a]
2. The greeting of Ḥor (son of) Ḥarendjiōtef, the scribe, a man of the town (of)
3. [Isis? ································] the Queen.
4. There happened [··········] who is within [··········]
5. Isis the prophet [··········] blessing
6. [·······] the great god [·······] upon [·······]
7. [·····························] your silver(?)
8. [··········] stand [··········]
9. [································] Osiris
10. they [····················] within them.

Translation: verso

1. There is another sanctuary: approach
2. [·······················]
3. in order to perform the words (of)
4. Osiris within it,[b] they being pure
5. upon the foot(?)[c]
6. The chapels (of) Egypt and the waters
7. behind them and the times which are to come this day(?);[d] the writing of
8. Thoth when he brought consolation to the mighty
9. men together. They steal the food (of) the Ibis.
10. They die(?) (of) hunger before him: no longer
11. do they requite the god.

Notes

a. Ptolemy VI Philometor.

b. A masculine noun is referred to, which must lie in the missing portion of the recto.

c. This may be nothing more than an elevated version of *ḥr rdwy*, but it is more likely to refer to a ritual requirement, cf. Herodotus, II, 37.

d. The text greatly resembles *ʿḳ* 'loaf', but this yields insufficient sense even for an oracle. At the time of the discovery, Smith suggested *nꜣ ꜣḥt nty ḫpr pꜣ ʿḳ*, which still has much to recommend it. A similar utterance to the present may perhaps be seen in *Demotic Chronicle*, iv. 22, *nꜣy·n šỉ(w) nꜣy·n mꜣy(w)*.

Preliminary Remarks

The meagre traces of the recto show that this text is the draft of a message of greeting to Pharaoh; upon the verso an enigmatic text, an oracle of Thoth, lays down requirements for the ritual. The text concludes with an accusation: the mighty men, to whom this oracle was vouchsafed, abuse the trust of the god and neglect the care of the ibises.

TEXT 28

Height	17·2 cm.
Width	13·3 cm.
Thickness	0·6 cm. (*top*)–1·1 cm. (*bottom*)
Munsell	10 YR 7/4
Photograph	Plate XXIX
Facsimile	Plate XXIXA
Excavator's no.	G7–36 [465]

A buff-ware ostracon, in two roughly equal parts, taken from the shoulder of a storage jar. Part of the curvature of the neck is visible at the bottom of the text. The verso shows a brownish incrustation, and is uninscribed, and the recto has been painstakingly erased with a moistened finger: a clear print is visible in the upper right-hand corner. The contents are thus largely obliterated.

Text

1. *⟨Pr-ʿꜣ⟩*[a] *Ptrwmys ỉrm Pr-ʿꜣ*
2. *Ptlwmys*[b] *pꜣy·f sn ỉrm tꜣ Pr-ʿꜣt*
3. *⟨Ḳlwp[trꜣ]⟩ n-drt Ḥr* (*sꜣ*) *Ḥr-[nḏ-ỉt·f]*[c] *rmt Pr-Ḏḥwty* (*n*) *pꜣ tš* (*n*) *Ṯb-ntr.*[d]
4. *tw[·i] ỉy [r pꜣ ʿwy-(n)-ḥtp]* [(traces)]
5. *ḏd* [ ] *mdt* [ ] *hp* [ ]
6. [(traces)]
7. [(traces)]
8. [(traces)]
9. *ꜣst* [(traces)]
10. *smn* [(traces)]
11. *ḏd* [ ] *mn ḥt-ntr wbꜣ·k* [ ]
12. *Ḏḥwty ʿꜣ ʿꜣ nb Ḫmnw* [ ] *⟨ḥt ꜣst⟩ htp ỉrm·w*
13. [(traces)] *tꜣ Pr-ʿꜣt*
14. [(traces)] *ỉn·w-s*
15. *ḥꜣʿ·w-s smy·w nꜣ ʿš-sḥnw. ỉr tꜣy·s*[e] *ḥnwt ꜣst*
16. *wʿt pḫrt* (*n*) *tꜣ Pr-ʿꜣt* [ ][f] *Pr-ʿꜣt bn-pw·w*
17. *ỉr tꜣy pḫrt* [(traces)]
18. *Pr-ʿꜣt* (traces) [ ]
19. *tꜣy·w gns n-ỉm·w. ḏd·f ḥt-mdt ḏd* [ ]
20. *Pr-ʿꜣt wn* [(traces)]
21. *ỉw wḫꜣ·k ḫr nꜣy.*

Notes

a. It is difficult to see why this word should be inserted thus, particularly as the following *ꜥws.* is on the line; possibly the original writing of *Pr-ꜥꜣ* had been defective.

b. The scribe seems clearly to have written *-l-*, as in the name of the Queen below.

c. Restored from Text **19,** R° 1.

d. Meagre traces only, but clear; see therefore note *b* to Text **2,** R° 3, p. 15 above.

e. *tꜣy·n* is perhaps possible.

f. This section of the text appeared on close examination to be quite blank, yet the context clearly demands a continuation.

Translation

1. ⟨Pharaoh⟩ Ptolemy and Pharaoh
2. Ptolemy his brother[a] and Queen
3. ⟨Cleopatra⟩ from Ḥor son of Ḥarendjiōtef, a man of Pi(?)-Thoth (in) the nome (of) Sebennytos.
4. I came [to the house of rest ·························]
5. saying [··········] word [··········] law [··············]
6. [(traces)]
7. [(traces)]
8. [(traces)]
9. Isis [(traces)]
10. secure [(traces)]
11. saying [···············] the temple endures before you [·····]
12. Thoth the twice great, lord of Hermopolis(?) [···············] ⟨according to(?) Isis⟩ rest(s) among them
13. [(traces)] the Queen
14. [(traces)] they brought it[b]
15. they abandoned it.[b] They pleaded (for) the fortunes. Her(?)[c] mistress Isis made
16. a remedy for the Queen [···············] Queen. They did not
17. make this remedy [(traces)]
18. Queen ·········· [(traces)].
19. They have wronged them.[d] He[e] said an utterance, saying [··········]
20. Queen: there is [(traces)]
21. you wish in this matter.

Notes

a. Ptolemy VIII Euergetes II, ὁ ἀδελφός. The present text was written during the joint reign (170–163), but the precise date, if ever written, is now lost to us.

b. Or 'her' (?).

c. Or possibly 'our' (?).

d. See Text **16,** R° 11, and Demotic Text A, 1 above, for the meaning of the term.

e. Possibly the god Thoth, who appears in l. 12.

Preliminary Remarks

Deliberate erasure in antiquity has destroyed much of the value of this ostracon. It was written at an unknown point in the joint reign, and addressed to both Ptolemies together with the Queen; indeed, it may have been the mention of 'the Brother' which prompted the erasure. The Queen is apparently ill,[1] and Isis proposes a healing remedy. This is not the end of the matter, as another oracle is mentioned, given perhaps by Thoth. Ḥor's part in these events will have appeared in the missing portion; all we know is that he now describes his home town as Pi(?)-Thoth in the Sebennyte nome.

TEXT 29

Height	18·0 cm.
Width	28·3 cm.
Thickness	1·00 cm. (av.)
Munsell	(Ware) 2·5 YR 6/4 (Wash) 10 YR 8/4
Photograph	Plate XXX
Facsimile	Plate XXXA
Excavator's no.	G7–39 [468]

A long ostracon from the side of a storage jar, whose pink ware has been coated with a thin buff wash. The verso bears a brownish incrustation, and is uninscribed. The recto, which

[1] The restless mind of the historian will suggest that childbirth is at cause, but it will find no peace among the evidence.

originally bore some thirteen or more lines of script, has, like the preceding text, been deliberately erased, and even the bare traces shown here have been recovered with the severest difficulty. The ostracon was discovered by Emery, together with the preceding, in the find of 1965/66.

Text

1. *Pr-ꜥꜣ Ptrwm[y]s ⟨ỉrm tꜣ Pr-ꜥꜣt Ḳr[wptrꜣ]⟩*
2. *[n-drt] Ḥr [(sꜣ) Ḥr-nḏ-ỉt·f] pꜣ sẖ rmt dmỉ-(n)-ꜣst [(n) pꜣ tš Ṯb-]ntr. [ḥꜣt-sp 2 ỉ·ỉr ḥꜣt-sp 30*[a]*] ḫpr [ỉw tꜣ] ḥrt [(n) nꜣ] h[bw] [*]
3. [(traces)]
4. [ ] *ḏd* [ ] *Kmy ḥr·w. ḫpr ỉw nꜣ mdt*
   [(traces)]
5. *pꜣ sḥn* [ ] *ḫpr ḳrst bỉnt r ḥry mdt nbt ỉr-rḫ-s bn-ỉw·k ḫr mwt mtw·ỉ gm*
   [(traces)]
6. *mdt *ta*[b] *ỉn-s mtw·ỉ mdt* [ ]
   mwt ḥn [ ] *ỉr-rḫ·ỉ*
   [ ] *ḫpr wn-nꜣ·w*
7. [ ] *tꜣ nty tꜣy* [ ]
   m-sꜣ ḫpr ḥtḥt [ ][c] *ḥr·w* [
   ] *mdt nbt ḫr*
8. [(traces)]
   ḥb ỉ·ỉr ḫpr tꜣ ḥꜣt.
9. *Pr-ꜥꜣ Ptrwmys ỉrm [tꜣ] Pr-ꜥꜣt Ḳrwptrꜣ nꜣ ntrw ꜥꜣy nḥy*[d] *Ḥr (sꜣ) Ḥr-nḏ-ỉt·f*[e] *pꜣ sẖ rmt dmỉ-(n)-ꜣst (n) pꜣ tš Ṯb-ntr.*
10. *Rꜥ-ḳd* [(traces)]
    ḥt-mdt [(traces)]
    Pr-ꜥꜣ
11. *Pr-ꜥꜣ* [[f] (traces)]
    ḏd ḥr pꜣ [ ] *ḫpr ḥtḥt* [ ][c]
    [ ]
12. *[r]-hn pꜣ tr* [ ] *ḫf·f r-dbꜣ*
    tꜣy tꜣ ḥrt n nꜣ ntrw [ ]
13. *nꜣy·f ꜥḥyt* [(traces)]
    bn-ỉw[·w] šm n·w ỉrm·f ꜥn ⟨mdt . . .⟩ bw-ỉr·w ỉr pꜣ wḏꜣ [ ].
    (no traces of other lines are visible).

Notes

a. The first group before *ḥꜣt-sp 30* is extremely doubtful. In the space above the scribe seems to have inserted *tꜣ ḥꜣt* (or perhaps *nḥḥ*) *ḫpr ꜣḳ*, but it is difficult to see where these words belong.

b. For this transliteration, see note to Text **2**, R° 7, p. 16.

c. This word, which in both l. 7 and l. 11 follows *ḥtḥt*, is obscure; it most resembles *ḫr-ḥb*, which yields poor sense, but both examples are faint and no reading may command belief.

d. See Text **3**, V° 7 and note *m*, p. 24 above.

e. Restored from the parallels; the surviving traces, though explicable as a writing of **n-drt·f* (see Text **19**, R° 1), are capable of other interpretations.

f. The meagre traces may suggest that the name *Ptrwmys* followed here.

Translation

1. Pharaoh Ptolemy ⟨and Queen Cleopatra⟩ [the great gods · · · · ·]
2. from Ḥor [(son of) Ḥarendjiōtef] the scribe, a man of the town (of) Isis (in) the nome of [Sebennytos]. Year 2(?) which makes year 30:[a] it happened (that) the food [of the ibises ·]
3. [(traces)]
4. [· · · · · · · · · ·] saying [· · · · · · · · · ·] Egypt under them. It happened (that) the words [· ·]
5. the command(?) [· · · · · · · · · ·]. There happened a bad burial above (?) in every matter (which) it knows (?). You shall not be subject to death:[b] and I found(?) [· · · · · · · · · ·]
6. the *said matter: bring it:[b] and I spoke [· · · · · · · · · ·] die(?) within [· · · · · · · · · ·] · · · · · · · · · · I know [· · · · · · · · · ·] it happened (that) there were
7. [· · · · · · · · · ·] that which concerns [· · · · · · · · · · · · · · ·] after there happened the inventory[c] [ ] concerning them [· · · · · · · · · ·] every matter: for
8. [(traces)] festival(?) which happened formerly.

9. Pharaoh Ptolemy and Queen Cleopatra, the great gods: (the) plea of Ḥor (son of) Ḥarendjiōtef(?) the scribe, a man of the town (of) Isis (in) the nome of Sebennytos.[d]
10. Alexandria(?) [(traces)] utterance [(traces)] Pharaoh
11. Pharaoh [Ptolemy(?) ····· (traces)] saying in connection with the [··········] ····· there happened the inventory [ ] [···························]
12. up to the time [·······················] his destruction, concerning stealing the food of the gods[e] [···············]
13. his chapels [(traces)] they shall not walk with him again ⟨[in any] matter (?)⟩: they do not make the salvation [··································].

Notes

a. The thirtieth year of Philometor corresponds to 152/1; the 'Year 2', if correctly read, will be that of the short-lived Eupator, whom we first encounter associated in the kingdom on 28 March 152 (Pap. Rylands XVI: Griffith, *Rylands*, iii. 141). This is the latest date given in our archive. It is therefore difficult to see why Ḥor should refer to himself as a citizen of Temenēsi, although an explanation may perhaps appear in the repetition in l. 9 below, for he may be quoting a document written years before. Nevertheless it would still seem that he regarded Temenēsi as his home town, even after some fifteen or more years' residence in Memphis. The whole subject is difficult in the extreme.

b. The following conjunctives suggest that a quotation may perhaps have ended at this spot, but it is not possible to be certain.

c. ϩⲟⲧϩⲧ, Crum, 728a, although the verb may have been intended.

d. This repetition will either be due to the author revising his text (and the traces do show much repetition of the preceding lines), or represent a text quoted by him from an earlier date; the latter is plausible, but the traces are too meagre to admit certainty.

e. An alternative term for the birds (cf. *wꜥt ntr n wꜥt mgt* of the ibis texts **19–23**).

Preliminary Remarks

This document, apparently the latest in our series, is largely obscure. The text begins with an address to the Philometores, and mentions their thirtieth year (152/1), and the food of the ibises. It is interesting to note that Ḥor still describes himself as a man of Temenēsi. The burial of the sacred birds may also have gone awry, and an inventory or search is mentioned. A second address, described as a 'plea' (*nḥt*) follows: the food of the gods has apparently been stolen, and the birds neglected. The offender is finally cursed. The deliberate erasure of the text may suggest that the writer regarded the contents as incriminating himself.

TEXT 30

Height	10·6 cm.
Width	9·5 cm.
Thickness	0·6 cm.
Munsell	5 YR 6/3
Photograph	Plate XXIX
Facsimile	not given
Excavator's no.	71/2–231 [5499]

An ostracon in a dull brownish ware, in seven pieces, but not complete. The recto bears portions of twelve lines in the hand of the Memphite Ḥor. The verso is blank. It is possible that some of the unassigned fragments published later in this volume (nos. **51–5**) may belong to this document, which generally resembles Text **12A** above.

Text

1. *n-drt Ḥr-Ḏḥwty.*
2. *nꜣ sḏyw (n) Ḏḥwty ḥr* [ ]
3. *nꜣ sẖw (n) Pr-ꜥꜣ ẖt nꜣ gyw-(n)-ḏlꜥ-[mdt* (trace)]
4. *r dỉt n·ỉ pꜣ rꜣ kḥy*[a] *nꜣ trw nty wbꜣ tꜣ ẖrt* [*ỉrm*]
5. *tꜣ ḳrst n pꜣ hb r-dbꜣ ỉr pꜣ šn(n) pꜣ*[b] *nty tꜣy* [*nꜣy*].
6. *rnpt 5t r-bw-nꜣy Ḏḥwty hb n-ỉm·ỉ* [*ẖr Pr-pꜣy·f-ỉry*][c]

7. *ḫt* [(traces)] *tꜣ nty ṯꜣy tꜣy·f* [
8. [(traces)]·*i ḫrw·i* (*n*) *Rꜥ-ḳd* [
9. [ ] *di·i pḥ·s r Mn-nfr* (*r*) *dit mn*[*t*]
10. [*Ḥp*-]*nb·s iwty šb*[d] *ḫt* [ ]
11. [*ḥꜣt-sp*] *16* (*n*) *pꜣ it* [[e]]
12. [ ] *m-bꜣḥ Wsir*[f] [ ]

(other lines may have followed).

Notes

a. The determinative favours the masculine *kꜥh* (ⲕⲟⲟϩ) rather than the feminine *kꜥht* (ⲕⲁϩ), but this is not certain, and the latter word often shows the extraneous *-y* present here. I have chosen the translation which seems less exceptionable.

b. Unless *pꜣ nty* is to be taken as in apposition to *šn* (which is feasible), it must be judged a variant of the more usual *tꜣ* (or *nꜣ*?) *nty ṯꜣy*; see note *u* to Text **2**, R° 13, p. 17 above.

c. Restored, perhaps boldly, from Text **12**, R° 2.

d. cf. Text **22**, R° 1.

e. Tentatively reconstructed from Text **19**, R° 13.

f. *Ḏḥwty* is a dubious alternative.

Translation

1. From Ḥarthoth.[a]
2. The discourses(?) (of) Thoth upon [·······
·············]
3. the scribes[b] (of) Pharaoh, namely, the docu[ments(?) ····· ····· (trace) ·····]
4. to give to me at the corner gate[c] (at) the times which concern the food [and]
5. the burial of the Ibis, in order to make the investigation which (?) concerns [these things].
6. Five years up to now Thoth sent me [to Pi-peferē[d]]
7. namely, [·········· (traces) ··········] that which concerns his [···············]
8. [······· (traces) ·······] I [·····] my voice (in) Alexandria ····· [················]
9. [·····················] I caused(?) it to reach to Memphis, to impart regularity(?) [·················]
10. [············ Ḥep-]nēbes without change, namely ·········· [··············]
11. [·········· Year] 16 of the father(?)[e] [·················]
12. [················] before Osiris(?) [·······
················]

Notes

a. See note to Text **12**, R° 1, p. 53.

b. For this title, cf. note *l* to Text **1**, 6, p. 13; 'the writings of Pharaoh' is an alternative translation.

c. 'District gate' is also possible; the mention of Ḥepnēbes in line 10 below suggests that this feature may have been located in the area, but no parallel suggests itself.

d. Cf. Text **12**, R° 2 above, where a date is suggested for this interlude.

e. Text **19**, R° 13 suggests that the reference is to Philopator, the date 207/6, and that this period marked the beginning of negligence in the cult of the Ibis.

Preliminary Remarks

This text seems to incorporate material from Texts **12** and **19**, and perhaps represents a recension of some kind. The reference to the interlude in Pi-peferē, and the phrase 'five years till now', may indicate a date in 168 or thereabouts. The document seems to have sketched the part played by Ḥor in the reforms of the ibis-cult, and in an incident at Alexandria, of which one may imagine a considerable number in the year 168. The missing portion of the text may have outlined the history of the ibis-sanctuary at Memphis.

§ 5 : Associated Texts

These texts, with one exception, share the provenance of the others, but their relationship to the main archive is not certain.

TEXT 31

A	Height	8·5 cm.
	Width	14·5 cm.
	Thickness	0·7 cm.
	Munsell	5 YR 5/2
	Photograph	Plate XXXI
	Facsimile	Plate XXXIA
	Excavator's no.	G7–4 [435]

A reddish ostracon, roughly triangular, bearing upon the recto some six lines in an unidentified hand. The ware is crossed with horizontal striations; the verso, stained black, is uninscribed.

B	Height	12·1 cm.
	Width	11·1 cm.
	Thickness	0·7 cm.
	Photograph	Plate XXXI
	Facsimile	Plate XXXIA
	Excavator's no.	G7–3 [434]

This ostracon provides a further eight lines in continuation of A, which it does not join. Both texts were discovered by Emery.

Text **31A**

1. *wꜥ mḵmḵ* (*n*) *Srpyn pꜣ ḥm-ntr Ḥr*[a]
2. *pꜣ wꜥb ꜥꜣ* (*n*) *Pr-ꜥꜣ ꜣrgsntrs*[b]
3. *n-drt Ḥr-nb-ꜥnḫ Ḥr-pꜣ-sn Ḥr-ẖb ḥm-ntr ꜣst* [*nty*]
4. *šn pꜣ tš Ṯb-ntr. rnpt* ⟨*25*⟩ *r-hn ḥꜣt-sp 16 pꜣ* [[c]]
5. [ ] *ir·i šms tꜣ nbt tꜣwy* [ ]
6. [ ][d] *šms* [ ].

Text **31B**

x+1.] (trace)
2.] *bn-iw rmt gm n-im·w*
3.] *ꜣmyt*[e] *in·f pꜣ ꜥt*[f]
4.] *tꜣ nbt* (*n*) *tꜣ mdt nfrt ir·w*[g] *pꜣy·f*
5.] (trace)[h] *tꜣ mdt wpy Ḏḥwty irm tꜣ ẖt-mdt*
6.] *2t *ta. ḥn·f-s n·i ḏd šn*
7. *m-sꜣ tꜣ ḥmt* (*n*) *Srpyn*
8. *in-s i·ir·ḥr·i*[i]

Notes

a. This stroke is a space-filler.

b. The *n* is very rudimentary.

c. The traces do not suit the *it* of Texts **19** or **30**.

d. A second *ir·i* may well have stood here.

e. Perhaps the word of Erichsen, *Glossar*, 5.

f. I am not confident of the meaning of this word, or even of its reading. The resemblance to some writings of *ꜥt* 'limb' is clear, but the gender prevents the identification. I can find no evidence for its being an alternative writing of *ꜥwy* 'house', although the determinative indicates a word of this sort. I have therefore identified it with the *ꜥt* (*ꜥd*) of Erichsen, *Glossar*, 74.

g. This pronoun seems to have been altered.

h. The word must clearly have been a short one; *wš* suggests itself to the mind.

i. The pronoun has been altered from *·n*.

Translation: Text **31A**

1. A memorandum (to) Sarapion,[a] the prophet of Horus,
2. the great priest of Pharaoh Alexander,[b]
3. from Ḥarnebōnkh, Ḥarpason, (and) Ḥarkhēbi,[c] prophet of Isis, [who]
4. investigates the nome of Sebennytos. ⟨25⟩ years until year 16,[d] the [··············]
5. [·········] I served the lady of the two lands[e] [······]
6. [·········] I(?) served [································]

Translation: Text **31B**

x+1. [·········] (trace)
2. [·········] no man will find them
3. [·········] soul(?). He brought (to) the bank(?)[f]
4. [·········] the lady(?) (of) the benefit. They made his
5. [····] the word (of) judgment (of) Thoth and the two
6. utterances *said. He commanded me saying, 'Enquire
7. after the wife (of) Sarapion:
8. bring her before me'.

Notes

a. The Σαραπίων of Preisigke, 363. This holder of the 'great priesthood of Pharaoh Alexander', i.e. the eponymous priesthood of Alexander the Great, was clearly a personage of importance; we note too that as in the case of]*tryn*, prophet of Khons and *basilikos grammateus* (Text **1**, 6) the preference of the writer has been to let the native Egyptian title (in the present case *pꜣ ḥm-ntr Ḥr*, which is hardly likely to be a patronymic) take precedence over the administrative function; this seems to reflect the priorities of our archive.

No Sarapion is recorded in Glanville and Skeat, *JEA* 40 (1954), 50 ff., and this entire period in the middle of Philometor's reign is scantily represented; in *Prosopographia Ptolemaica* the most likely candidate may be 914, attested at Memphis as τῶν διαδόχων about this time; 328, a personage of considerable importance prominent in the archive of Ptolemaios the *katochos*, is equally to be considered. For the spread of the name itself, see Stambaugh, *Sarapis under the Early Ptolemies* (Leiden, 1972), 99–100.

b. For this priesthood, cf. IJsewijn, *De sacerdotibus*, 134 ff.

c. This cluster of names may conceal a patronymic, but the general lack of titles suggests that the words may have been in the form of a list. The final epithets may apply to all three men; the following singular pronoun is hardly a reliable guide.

d. If correctly taken as Philometor's, the date would be 166/5. The ostracon would then be retrospective, written after the end of the joint reign.

e. An epithet of Isis, cf. Text **1**, 10.

f. See textual note above; the reading is not certain.

Preliminary Remarks

This text, a memorandum to Sarapion, eponymous priest of Alexander in the late 160s(?), is written by three men, connected with the cult of Isis in the Sebennyte nome; the coincidence of these facts with the career of Ḥor make it likely that these men are connected with the characters of the main archive. The text refers to the period from about 180 to 165, and to the cult of Isis, a span of time which we may surmise to have corresponded with the early career of Ḥor of Sebennytos. An oracle of Thoth is mentioned, but the rest is obscure. It is tempting to believe that the text is in some way a substantiation of the activities of Ḥor at Temenēsi, but no proof can be offered for this.

TEXT 32

Height	11·1 cm.
Width	7·1 cm.
Thickness	0·8 cm.
Munsell	10 R 5/6
Photograph	Plate XXXI (R°, V°)
Facsimile	not given
Excavator's no.	G7–5 [436]

A sherd of fine reddish ware, the recto very slightly convex. On this side stand the endings of ten lines in a Memphite hand, possibly that of the secretary Ḥor. The verso bears a further six lines in the same hand. The ostracon is perhaps half complete. The text was found by Emery together with the preceding.

Text: recto

1. [a]] *m-bꜣḥ Ḏḥwty ꜥꜣ wpyt nꜣ ḥtrw*[b]
2.] *n-ỉm·f grḥ mtry hrw nb*
3.] *sḥwr·f nꜣ pẖrt*
4.][c] *n-ỉm·w pꜣ gy (n) ỉr-w nty ỉw·w*
5.] *rn·f kt 2t mtw·w dỉt-s*
6.] *wpy-s pꜣ ntr ꜥꜣ Ḏḥwty*
7. *ḥt-*]*ntr 'Iwnw ḥt-ntr*
8.] *ỉ·ỉr·ḥr 'Imn-pꜣ-ym*
9.] *mtw·w smn*
10. *ḥt-*]*ntr.*

Text: verso

1. *ỉw·ỉ gm-s*[d] *mtw·ỉ* [
2. *šn·f-n ḏd wꜣḥ·tn dỉt* [
3. *m-ỉr sbḳ (n) ḥꜣty tꜣ* [
4. *st ḥr pꜣ ꜥš ỉw·w dỉt* [
5. *dỉt ḏd·f n·ỉ tkr·k sẖ* [
6. *nꜣy r nty ḥry.*

Notes

a. The text may have been one of the type *ḫrw bꜣk* NN *m-bꜣḥ* DN (cf. Hughes, *JNES* 17 (1958), 6; *JEA* 54 (1968), 179).

b. The position of the vertical sign, whose base is lost in the following line, precludes the reading *tꜣ ḥtr*. The use of plural pronouns (*·n*, *·tn*) on the verso supports the suggestion given here, but it is impossible to be certain.

c. Traces of a 'violent' determinative are visible.

d. Evidence of a northern dialect, as in the main archive.

Translation: recto

1.] before Thoth, great of judgment: the twins(?)[a]
2.] upon him night and noontime[b] every day(?)
3.] he despised the remedies
4.] them the way (of) making them which they [undertake]
5.] himself another two and they gave(?) them
6.] the great god Thoth judged it
7.] temple of Heliopolis (and) the temple[c]
8.] before Amenpayom[d]
9.] and they secured
10.] temple.

Translation: verso

1. I found it[e] and I ····· [
2. He asked us saying 'Have you given [
3. do not be faint (of) heart: the [
4. they are upon the summons,[f] giving [
5. cause(?) him to say to me 'make haste: write [
6. these things according to (what) is above.'

Notes

a. For the reading see textual notes above; the temptation is strong indeed to see in these twins the two sisters of the Serapeum, Thavēs and Taous, whose affairs are so richly documented in the papers of Ptolemaios and Apollonios. Both date and locality support the identification, but other evidence is quite lacking.

b. A common metaphor in appeals to gods, cf. the Buchis pebble, lines 4–6 ff. (Mond–Myers, *Bucheum*, ii. 56). The unpublished Pap. Carlsberg 67, a healing-prayer to Soknebtynis, has as its concluding phrase *grḥ m-ḳdy mtry*. A complaint to Thoth in the Michaelidis Collection (Hughes, *Studies J. A. Wilson*, 48[1]) produces a much fuller variant *hblꜣ grḥ ꜣyt mtry* (l. 5) 'misery by night, misfortune by day', cf. also Pap. Cairo 50110, 6–7 (cf. *JEA* 54 (1968), 178, note to l. 1). The purpose is clearly to attract the attention of the god at all hours ('has he his hour of dying, when he does not hear?'); in the vicinity of the sacred hawks and ibises, with their respective solar and lunar connotations, such words become especially apt.

c. Possibly of Memphis, cf. Text **1**, 2 and Text **13**.

d. An unknown personage, possibly the one for whom the remedies were intended; for the name (Ἀμφιῶμις, Presigke, 28), cf. Fecht in *MDAIK* 16 (1958), 113.

e. Or any other third person pronoun.

f. A doubtful phrase, although any connection with *ʿ(y)š n Pr-ʿꜣ* 'public auction' (cf. *Enchoria* 1 (1971), 79 ff.) is probably to be discounted.

Preliminary Remarks

This fragment records part of an appeal by Thoth from two twins, concerning the remedies to be offered to a sick man; the writers are urged to put their case into writing. All else is obscure, and even the relation of this text to the main archive is debatable.

TEXT 33

Height	13·8 cm.
Width	16·8 cm.
Thickness	0·8 cm.
Munsell	2·5 YR 5/2
Photograph	Plate XXXII
Facsimile	not given
Excavator's no.	H5–778 [2525]

The present text is in many ways the stranger

[1] The provenance of this remarkable text is a matter of interest. The editor, judging by the prominence given to Thoth in his text and in its companion of *JNES* 17 (1958), 1 ff., naturally supposed this to be Hermopolis/Tûna el-Gebel. In the later article the mention of Ibis, Hawk, and Baboon prompted the suggestion that the origin of these appeals may rather be sought at Saqqâra. It should certainly be noted that the writer of the 'Cruel Father' writes *wꜣḥ·s ms-n* instead of *mst-n*, a dialect form prevalent in Memphis.

to this volume. It was found late in 1968 by Emery near the surface of the southern end of the great temple platform, at a point opposite the entrance to the hawk-galleries discovered two seasons later (*JEA* 56 (1970), 11). Hence a hundred yards separated the ostracon from the courtyard where the other texts lay. It may have reached this location by looting, for it was further along the route leading from the courtyard, find-spot of Texts **6, 10,** and **21.** It must be admitted that no internal evidence can be found to link the text with Ḥor of Sebennytos. Nevertheless, the information here, and its closeness to Texts **19–23,** plead for its inclusion.[1]

The sherd is of brownish ware, slightly curved, and complete save for the lower right-hand corner. The recto bears fifteen lines, with traces of a sixteenth. The verso is blank. The unidentified hand resembles that of the Sebennytic Ḥor rather than his Memphite namesake.

Text

1. *ḥꜣt-sp 25 tpy ꜣḫt sw 19.*[a] *smy·i ḥt-ntr Wsir-Ḥp (r) smn*[b] *hp r-dbꜣ nꜣ mdt*
2. *nty iw pꜣ hb lwḥ* ⟨*n-im·w*⟩ *(n) tꜣ ꜥḫyt (n) ms nty iw ḫn pꜣ ši (n) Pr-ꜥꜣ. tw-s*
3. *nꜣy(i·)wpy·f ḥr 3t ḥt-mdt ḫn·w. tꜣ ḫrt (n) Pr-ꜥꜣ* [ ]*[c]* *wꜥ ꜥḳ (n) ḫrt*
4. *prḫ-s ḥr pꜣ sḫn*[d] *i·ir·ḥr pꜣ hb. bn-iw pꜣ* [*ḫn 20*]*[e]* *pꜣ i·ir-sḫy*
5. *ḥwy drt·f*[f] *ḥr·s ir nhy*[g] *n-im·s m-sꜣ pꜣy·s swḫy ꜥḳ iw·f* [ ]*[h]*
6. *ꜥꜣ ꜥḳ 3t*[i] *mtw nꜣ rmtw nty ir bꜣk wnm sm*[j] *ḥr pꜣ sḫn i·ir·ḥr pꜣ hb.*
7. *tꜣ mḥ-2t:*[k] *smn* [*mn-niwt*][l] *rmt-rḫ wbꜣ pꜣ hb tꜣ mst n-s*[m] *pꜣ hb*
8. *šꜣꜥ-mtw pꜣ Rꜥ ḥtp iw·f ḥrḥ pꜣ hb dit wdꜣ·f*[n]
9. *tꜣ mḥ-3t: i·ir Ḏ-ḥr-pꜣ-hb pꜣ sdm-ꜥš (n) nꜣ hbw ꜥnḫ (n) Pr-ꜥꜣ tm dit*
10. *ṯꜣy·w sꜥy*[o] *n-im·s r tꜣ ꜥḫyt rn·s iw·s šm*[p] *ꜥn. di Ḏ-ḥr-pꜣ-hb*
11. *pꜣ ꜥn-smy (n) tꜣ s(n)tgsy*[q] *nty iw·w dit n·f n-im·s ḥr rnpt (n) rn Pr-ꜥꜣ*
12. *wbꜣ pꜣ ꜥš-sḫn (n) pꜣ hb mtw·f ir ꜥnḫ (n) Pr-ꜥꜣ ꜥnḫ (n) pꜣ ntr r sk*[r]
13. *n*]*hy nty iw·f gm-f n-im·w. n-drt ḫpr·f wꜣḥ*[s] *pꜣ mw ṯꜣy pꜣ* $\frac{2}{3}$ *(n) tꜣ gyr*[t] *iw·s*
14.][u] *pꜣ spy nty wd n-im·w wꜥt sꜥnḫt*[v] *ḫr pꜣ hb ḥr pꜣ tr*[w]
15. *n*]*-drt ḫpr smy nꜣ*[x] *nty wꜣḥ ḥry dit ḳd·w ꜥḫyt*
16.] (trace).

Notes

a. The 9 is short, but other readings are unconvincing.

b. I can do no more with this group than to read *smn*(?) overlying some cult-title of the god.

c. The divine determinative suggests *Ḏḥwty*, but this is hardly acceptable. Other divine names are even less likely, and one is led to see here an awkward writing of the group *(i·)wn-nꜣ*, joyless as this may seem.

d. For the writing cf. Thompson, *PSBA* 35 (1913), *passim*; Mattha, *Ostraka*, *passim* (v. index). The translation 'table' offered below is conjectured from the word's use to indicate the Greek τράπεζα in the financial sense, and from the meanings of the earlier *sḫnt* 'support' (*Wb.* iii. 471).

e. A very debatable group: the whole resembles *ḳnbt* or *ḫn* more than any of the writings of *snt* listed in *MDAIK* 16 (1958), 150. I know of no masculine word from the root *ḳnb(t)*, and have therefore chosen *ḫn*. The word is shown by the context to be an administrative notion, for which *ḫn* (ϩⲓⲛⲉ) might be appropriate. The following numeral is very doubtful.

f. For ϩⲓ-ⲧⲟⲟⲧϥ; cf. Crum, 734b.

g. This same group recurs in l. 13 below. Its reading and meaning are not clear, although it bears a resemblance to the *nhy* (older *nhw*) of Erichsen, *Glossar*, 221.

h. The traces perhaps suit *ḥs* (in the sense of 'consecrated'?), but are too faint for certainty.

i. I can see no reason for the feminine numeral, although a similar miswriting occurs in Text **21,** R° 14.

j. For such a writing of *s(y)m* cf. Erichsen, *Glossar*, 430; a very tempting reading, *wnm m-sꜣ* (in the sense of Coptic ⲟⲩⲱⲙ ⲛ̄ⲥⲁ) is rendered difficult by the joining of the *m-sꜣ*-like group to the previous sign.

[1] See also the introduction to Additional Text **61** below, p. 170.

For clarification here, and in much of this text, I am very grateful to Professor J. W. B. Barns.

k. See the translation note to Text **10**, R° 1.

l. This group, though clear, defeats me. It is not convincing as a writing of *gl-šr*. The second element resembles most *ỉpt* 'assessment' (ⲏⲡⲉ); the first is more difficult. If it is a writing of *ỉn* as *participium conjunctum*, one must assume that the vertical stroke which follows is a rewriting of the opening of *ỉpt*, which had been obscured by the group above; it is unlikely as a form of *s-n* (ⲥⲁⲛ). I suggest *mn-niwt*, the second element being the word for 'city'; the whole is a semi-phonetic writing for *mnt* (ⲙ̅ⲛⲟⲩⲧ) 'door-keeper, *bawwâb*'.

m. This word, if correctly read, seems to have been written twice, the first attempt having met with failure.

n. The pronoun is rudimentary, but none other seems possible.

o. Cf. Text **8**, R° 17; the medial *ʿayin* may be an attempt to express the pronunciation ⲥⲟⲓ.

p. This short group is strikingly obscure, and its reading offered *faute de mieux.*

q. A transliteration of σύνταξις, interestingly preserving the gender. For the omission of *-n-* before *-t-* cf. *ꜣtyks*. A note on the word is contained in Mattha, *Ostraka*, 59–60; the present example seems to have abandoned any attempt to reproduce a Greek inflection.

r. These traces are too faint to inspire confidence; the reading given assumes that the initial *s-* has been rather awkwardly misshapen.

s. Although the writings of *ḥr* and *wꜣḥ* seem to be confused in this text (compare *ḥr·s* in l. 5; *ḥr pꜣ sḫn*, l. 6; *nꜣ nty wꜣḥ*, l. 15), the latter seems a more likely reading before *pꜣ mw*; cf. in contrast, note *i* to Text **1**, 2, p. 9 above.

t. Reading made difficult by the faintness of the initial sign. For *gyr/glw* (ϭⲟⲉⲓⲗⲉ) cf. Erichsen, *Glossar*, 589.

u. A mere determinative is visible, possibly a plural stroke.

v. The reading seems clear, although a feminine formation from this well-attested verb does not seem to occur elsewhere in demotic, or to have survived into Coptic.

w. This group is partly obscured by the signs extended down from l. 13, and by its position at the left edge of the sherd.

x. *tꜣ* is also a permissible reading. The same problem arises with the phrase *tꜣ/nꜣ nty ṯꜣy*, cf. note *u* to Text **2**, R° 13, p. 17 above.

Translation

1. Year 25, Thoth, day 19:[a] I petitioned (in) the temple of Osorapis to ascertain(?) (the) law concerning the matters
2. in which the Ibis was deficient (in) the chapel (of) birth which is within the lake (of) Pharaoh.[b] Behold
3. these things in (which) he[c] gave judgement, comprising three utterances: the food (of) Pharaoh,[d] namely(?) one loaf of food,
4. scatter it upon the table before the Ibis. The twenty(?) administrators(?)[e] who possess authority will not
5. lay hands upon it (or) detract from it after its collection: a loaf which is consecrated(?)
6. (is) great(?) (as) three loaves:[f] and the men who labour[g] shall eat rations upon the table before the Ibis.
7. The second: Appoint a decent[h] watchman(?)[i] over the Ibis (and) the offspring of the Ibis,
8. until the sun sets he shall guard the Ibis (and) keep him safe.
9. The third: Djeḥephibi[j] the servant (of) the ibises made[k] an oath (of) Pharaoh not to allow
10. a beam to be taken from it for the chapel named while it proceeds(?). Djeḥephibi gave
11. the report (of) the *syntaxis*[l] which is given to him yearly (in) the name of Pharaoh
12. for the fortune (of) the Ibis, and made an oath (of) Pharaoh (and) an oath (of) the god to suppress
13. (any) loss which he discovers therein.[m] When it happens (that) the water subsides,[n] take the 2/3 (of) the deposit which
14. [forms?] the remainder which is paid to them (as) one maintenance[o] for the Ibis at the time.
15. [······] when the petition occurs (of) the things laid down above, cause (the) chapel to be built
16. [···········].

Notes

a. On the assumption that the unnamed sovereign is Philometor, this date corresponds to 19 October 157.

b. For the topography of the area, see Commentary below; this lake may well be that of Text **10**, R° 4, over which Isis was said to preside.

c. The construction is somewhat elliptical, although Osorapis is presumably the subject.

d. Doubtless a royal ration, perhaps financed from the subsidy mentioned in l. 11 below.

e. For these hypothetical characters see textual note above.

f. The syntax and significance of this clause have largely escaped me.

g. ⲉⲣⲃⲱⲕ, Crum, 30a; the reference is presumably to the ἰβιοβοσκοί or to the masons (*by mnḫ*) of the galleries.

h. This sense of *rmt-rḫ* was communicated by Professor J. W. B. Barns.

i. See textual note.

j. Τεεφῖβις, Preisigke, 426; see note *aa* to Text **19**, R° 22, p. 75.

k. The use of the Second Present to emphasize the clause beginning with *tm dỉt* makes it difficult to be sure of the absolute tense; I have taken this as preterite because of the following *sḏm·f* and the end of l. 10.

l. For a brief description of this subsidy paid by the Ptolemies to the temples cf. Bevan, 187–8; the point that the σύνταξις which was paid was personal, even if issued in the first instance to the temple *en bloc*, is well brought out by the present lines.

m. Or possibly 'among them': the 'servants of the Ibis' who came under his control.

n. One might have expected this already to have happened at Memphis by 19 October, but an interval may have been allowed for reconstruction after the flooding; it may even be that the operation was deferred until Khoiak, when the calendrical season of inundation came to an end.

o. For the form of the word see textual note; the concept is of course familiar from the marriage-documents (Lüddeckens, *Eheverträge*, 317; Pestman, *Marriage and Matrimonial Property* (Leiden, 1961), 104–8). Further discussion will be found in Thompson, *Siut*, 12, n. 8, cf. *JEA* 58 (1972), 263.

Preliminary Remarks

This text records a request submitted to Osorapis, as presiding god of the necropolis, by an unnamed person; criticism has been applied to the Ibis (presumably by means of an oracle, unless the phrase is a euphemism for a censorius meeting of the council), and in particular to the 'chapel of birth', where the young birds were incubated and reared. Three immediate reforms are suggested, and the supervisor, Djeḥephibi, sworn to observe them; when these are carried through, the building of the chapel may be resumed. The connection of this document with the main archive, though likely, is quite unproven.

TEXT 34

Height	10·0 cm.
Width	23·7 cm.
Thickness	0·8 cm.
Munsell	2·5 YR 4/4
Photograph	Plate XXXII
Facsimile	not given
Excavator's no.	71/2–123 [5391]

Two fragments of the rim and shoulder of a pink-ware bowl, inscribed with the date *ḥꜣt-sp 34t ꜣbd-4 prt* (or *šmw*) [*sw*·····]. If the reigning king is Philometor, these dates would fall either in about May or about September of the year 147. It is pleasant to imagine that we have here the remains of the jar in which the ostraca were kept, and that the date in 147 marks in some way the completion of the Ḥor archive; but there is no proof for this, or even for our assumption that the king is Philometor. Philadelphus (251) is a remote candidate; Ptolemy VIII Euergetes (136), or less likely Soter II (83), may also be borne in mind.

TEXT 35

Height	15·2 cm.
Width	10·3 cm.
Thickness	1·0 cm.
Munsell	5 YR 5/3

Photograph	Plate XXXIII
Facsimile	not given
Excavator's no.	G7–46 [475]

This brownish-ware sherd seems to consist of a drawing of a human head, perhaps a warrior, several curving lines vaguely resembling the calyx of a lotus, and illegible traces of a line of demotic. Its significance is not immediately grasped.

§ 6 : Fragments

(Some of these fragments may have noble pedigrees, and belong to the texts already published; others are certainly recensions of material already seen; several may perhaps have been relegated unfairly, being larger than some whole texts. Such possibilities are indicated where they occur.)

36

Height	21·8 cm.
Width	20·3 cm.
Thickness	0·9 cm.
Munsell	10 R 5/3 (interior 5 YR 5/1)
Photograph	Plate XXXIII
Excavator's no.	71/2–160 [5428]

A large brownish ostracon, deliberately erased in antiquity; traces survive on the recto of some twenty-one lines, perhaps more. The fourth line seems to have begun with *n-drt Ḥr nty ḥr Mn-nfr*(?), and the lines above this may perhaps have been continuations of the bottom line. *Pr-ꜥꜣ* is clearly visible at the end of l. 16(?), and the previous line begins with *wn-nꜣ·w sẖ tꜣ šꜥt*, a phrase reminiscent of Text **3**, V° 18. The remains of the hand and the reed show a distinct resemblance to Text **4**, and we may conclude by attributing the present text to this group. The verso is blank.

37 and 38

(These may have belonged to the same text, but no join is observable.)

37

Height	5·6 cm.
Width	8·7 cm.
Thickness	0·8 cm.
Munsell	5 YR 5/3
Photograph	Plate XXXIV
Excavator's no.	71/2–185 [5453]

A small sherd of fine brown ware. The verso is blank.

Text

x+1.] (trace)[a] *ỉw·ỉ šms Pr-Wsỉr-Ḥp tꜣ nty ṯꜣy* [
2.] (traces) *Pr-ꜥꜣ P*[
3.] (traces) *tꜣ Pr-ꜥꜣt* [
4.] (traces) *Pr-ỉr*[[b]
5.] (traces) [.

Notes

a. Trace suits *mn*.
b. Perhaps *r-bl Pr-ỉr-'Imn*.

Translation

x+1.] ····· I served the Serapeum: that which concerns [
2.] ································· Pharaoh P[tolemy]
3.] ····························· (the) Queen [
4.] ································· Pelusium [
5.] ··[.

38

Height	5·4 cm.
Width	5·6 cm.
Thickness	0·8 cm.
Munsell	5 YR 5/3
Photograph	Plate XXXIV
Excavator's no.	71/2–186 [5454]

Text

x+1.] *nfr ḥꜣty*[a] [
2.] *ỉw·f ḫpr* [
3.] *ỉy (r) K[my*
4.] *ꜥw (n) ms m-šs*[b] [
5.] *pꜣ hp* [
6.] *mdt* [.

Notes

a. No suffix pronoun is visible.
b. See note to Text **1**, 17.

Translation

x+1.] gracious (of) heart [
2.] ········· it happened [
3.] ········· came (to) E[gypt
4.] exceedingly great (in) age [
5.] the law [
6.] matter(?) [.

The hand of both ostraca seems to be that of the Memphite Ḥor.

39–44

(These six ostraca also seem to belong together, but do not join. They are listed in the order of their excavator's numbers.)

39

Height	6·1 cm.
Width	7·4 cm.
Thickness	0·7 cm.
Munsell	5 YR 5/3
Photograph	Plate XXXIV
Excavator's no.	71/2–183 [5451]

An ostracon of brownish ware. The verso is blank. A space precedes the first line, which suggests that we may have here a portion of the beginning of the text.

Text

1.] [a] *nty ỉw·f ḫpr wꜥt mdt*[b] [
2.] *tꜣ hyty*[c] [
3.] *mdt nbt* [.

Notes

a. A lotus(?) determinative is visible: perhaps *ḥb*(?)
b. A long horizontal line follows.
c. Cf. Text **3**, V° 16, and note, p. 24.

Translation

1.] ········ which shall happen: one matter ····· [
2.] the portal (?) [
3.] every matter [.

40

Height	9·8 cm.
Width	10·6 cm.
Thickness	0·8 cm.
Munsell	5 YR 5/3
Photograph	Plate XXXIV
Excavator's no.	71/2–184 [5452]

At this point of the text the scribe's pen was clearly failing; it has been refilled at the end of l. 5.

Text

x+1.] (trace) [
2.] *šm·f r-bl Kmy* [
3.] (*n*) *ḥty*[a] *ỉw ꜣt·f* [
4.] *ḫpr n-ỉm·f ỉrm pꜣy·f sn ḫr* [
5.] *ỉw·f* [ ][b] *ḫt-mdt st* [ ][c]
pꜣy·w ꜥḥꜥ [
6.] (traces) *nꜣ-ꜥꜣ* (traces) [
7.] (traces) [.
(other lines probably followed)

Notes

a. See note to Text **2**, R° 11; the phrase *hb·w* is presupposed.
b. Too faint for certain reading.
c. Entirely lost.

Translation

x+1.] ······· [
2.] he left Egypt[a] [
3.] in haste:[b] his back(?) [
4.] happened to him and his brother:[c] for [
5.] he ················utterance: they ···· ···· their life(?) [
6.] ················ great ················ · [
7.] (traces) [.

Notes

a. Probably a reference to Antiochus (Text **2**, **3**, **4**).
b. The context suggests a letter, perhaps to the Pharaohs (Text **2**).
c. Philometor and Ptolemy the Brother (Text **2**, **3**).

41

Height	3·3 cm.
Width	5·2 cm.
Thickness	0·7 cm.
Munsell	5 YR 5/3
Photograph	Plate XXXIV
Excavator's no.	71/2–187 [5455]

A sherd excerpted from the middle of a text.

Text

x+1.] (traces)[a] *hb* [
2.] *Rʿ-ḳd ḏd ỉw* [
3.] [b] *ẖr rnpt* [
4.] *snt* [.

Notes

a. These may suit *sy/py tꜣ mdt *ta* (Text **3**, V° 15), but are very indistinct.
b. Traces may suit *ẖn*, but no suffix is visible.

Translation

x+1.] ·········· sent [
2.] ····· Alexandria, saying ····· [
3.] among(?) ····· yearly [
4.] custom [.

42

Height	3·7 cm.
Width	5·4 cm.
Thickness	0·8 cm.
Munsell	5 YR 5/3
Photograph	Plate XXXIV
Excavator's no.	71/2–188 [5456]

Sherd largely defaced.

Text

x+1.] *pꜣ sn* [
2.] [
3.] [
4.] (traces) [
5.] *ỉw·f ḫf* [.

No reliable translation is possible.

43

Height	5.6 cm.
Width	3·7 cm.
Thickness	0·8 cm.
Munsell	5 YR 5/3
Photograph	Plate XXXIV
Excavator's no.	71/2–189 [5457]

This sherd, like **39** above, seems to belong to the upper line of a text.

Text

1.] *Mn-nfr ỉrm* [a] [
2.] [b] *nꜣ ntrw wn-nꜣ·w* [
3.] *r-dbꜣ* [
4.] *nb* [.

Notes

a. *pꜣy·f* or *nꜣy·f*(?); cf. Text **24A**, 4.
b. Determinative visible.

Translation

1.] Memphis and its(?) [
2.] the gods (who) were [
3.] concerning [
4.] all(?) [

44

Height	3·6 cm.
Width	2·1 cm.
Thickness	0·7 cm.
Munsell	5 YR 5/3
Photograph	Plate XXXV
Excavator's no.	71/2–190 [5458]

Text

x+1.] (trace)
2.] *s*[a] [
3.] *bn-ỉw* [.

Note

a. End of a foreign, doubtless Greek name.
(No connected translation possible.)

The original text probably dealt with the events of 168.

45

Height	12·3 cm.
Width	9·6 cm.
Thickness	0·8 cm.
Munsell	5 YR 6/4
Photograph	Plate XXXV
Excavator's no.	71/2–192 [5460]

A fine sherd of red ware, with the final sections of nine lines, clearly written in the hand of the Memphite secretary. The fifth line shows signs of erasure. The verso is blank.

Text

x+1.] *r-dbꜣ dỉt*
2.] *dỉt ỉr·w pꜣ nty nfr·f (n) pꜣ ꜥš-sḫn (n) pꜣ hb*
3.] ⟨insertion⟩[a] *pꜣ myt r dỉt wḏꜣ pꜣy·f ꜥḥꜥ*.
4.] *ꜣst n-drt·f r-dbꜣ·s tꜣ ḫt-mdt rn·s*
5.] *ỉrm na*[b] *pꜣ ḥr-tb ʼIrt·w-r·w (sꜣ) sp-sn*[c]
6. *P*]*r-Ḏḥwty r-hn pꜣ tr ỉw·w wbꜣ*[d]
7.] *ḫt tꜣy (ỉ·)wpy·s ḥr*
8.] *ꜥꜣ ỉw·f ỉwt·k*[e] *ỉrm*
9.] (trace).

Notes

a. The main sign may represent *ỉr·w* or, more likely, *rmt*, followed by what seems to be a space-filler; but I cannot claim to have understood its purpose.

b. A reading made difficult by the preceding stroke.

c. Written over an erasure, and consequently uncertain.

d. The reading is confused by the palimpsest.

e. A somewhat eccentric and archaic writing, if correctly interpreted.

Translation

x+1.] in order to give
2.] cause to be performed that which is beneficial (to) the fortune (of) the Ibis
3.] ⟨*insertion*⟩ the path[a] to cause his life to prosper.
4.] Isis with him concerning it: the utterance named
5.] with those(?) of the magician Iturōw (son of) the same
6. P]i(?)-Thoth until this hour, they being concerned with
7.] namely, this (which) she judged: for
8.] great, he being between(?) you and
9.] (trace).

Note

a. The same metaphor as in Text **16**, R° 4–5; **17**, 14–15.

The relation of this fragment to the main archive is clear from the language, and the mention of Pi(?)-Thoth in l. 6; a judgement of Isis seems also to be described.

46

Height	7·6 cm.
Width	11·1 cm.
Thickness	1·0 cm.
Munsell	7·5 YR 6/4
Photograph	Plate XXXV
Excavator's no.	71/2–193 [5461]

An ostracon of fine light-brown ware of considerable thickness. The convex recto is entirely blank, though whether because uninscribed or as the result of natural elements is not clear; the verso is in parts desurfaced. The hand resembles that of Ḥor of Sebennytos.

Text

x+1.] (trace) [
2.] *nꜣy rḫ* [
3.] *nꜣy Mtpr*[a] [
4.] *ms* [ ] *nty ḥry st* [
5.] *di-i-s n·f (n) sḫ rmt (n) Kmy* [
6.] *r·w ꜥn pꜣ sḫ* [b] [
7.] (traces) *gyr* [
8.] (traces) [
9.] (traces) [.

Notes

a. Apparently a foreign name.

b. The last signs resemble a sum of money, but are too indistinct for certainty.

Translation

x+1.] (trace) [
2.] these know [
3.] these (?) *Mtpr* [
4.] birth ············ which is above:[a] they [
5.] I gave it to him (in) writing of the Egyptian(s)[b] [
6.] ······ to them again(?): the writing ······ [
7.] (traces) deposit(?) [
8.] (traces) [
9.] (traces) [.

Notes

a. Very reminiscent of Text **26**, R° 3.

b. See note to Demotic Text B, 3, p. 5 above.

The fragment seems to record financial transactions, and an unidentified *Mtpr*; a 'chapel of birth' may have been under consideration (see note *a* above), but the sherd also bears certain resemblances to Text **11**. It seems difficult to offer a clearer interpretation.

47

Height	8·3 cm.
Width	4·9 cm.
Thickness	1·0 cm.
Munsell	10 YR 7/4
Photograph	Plate XXXV
Excavator's no.	71/2–194 [5462]

The recto of this reddish-ware sherd has suffered from the action of salt; the verso is entirely illegible, although it was clearly once inscribed.

Text

x+1.] *ꜥꜣt ꜣst irm·w*[a]
2.] *iw·s mšꜥ ḥr*
3.] *pꜣ mw (n) pꜣ ym*
4.] [b] *nw nꜣy*
5.] *bn-iw·f*
6.] [c] *pꜣ ꜥꜣ*
7.] *ḫr tꜣ ḫt[-mdt*.
(other lines followed).

Notes

a. Altered from *irm·s*.

b. The final *-r* of *Ḫr* may be visible.

c. A divine determinative remains: *Ḏḥwty* possible, but not certain.

Translation

x+1.] the great [goddess] Isis among them
2.] walking upon [the face (of)]
3.] the water (of) the sea (of)
4.] Syria (?). There sees this
5.] ······ he shall not
6.] Thoth (?) the great
7.] in the utterance [.

The upper lines are clearly almost complete, and the text related the dream of Isis recorded in Text **1**.

48

Height	4·3 cm.
Width	4·8 cm.
Thickness	0·6 cm.
Munsell	5 YR 6/3
Photograph	Plate XXXV
Excavator's no.	71/2–195 [5463]

A small sherd of red-slipped ware, with recto blank; the verso bears the openings of three lines and a trace of a fourth, written across the grain of the sherd. The hand seems to be that of the Memphite Ḥor.

Text

1. *n-drt sẖ tš Ḥr nty ḥr* [*Mn-nfr* ····· *r-dbꜣ dỉt ỉr·w*
2. *pꜣ nty nfr·f* (*n*) *pꜣ ʿš-sḫn* [*pꜣ hb* ····· *ẖt tm dỉt ꜣḳ*
3. *mdt* (*n*) *tꜣ nty ṯꜣy* [
4.] (trace)[a] [

Note

a. Slightly resembles *m-bꜣḥ*.

Translation

1. From the scribe of the nome,[a] Ḥor who is in [Memphis ····· concerning causing to be performed]
2. that which is beneficial (to) the fortune [of the Ibis ····· namely, not to detract from a]
3. matter (in) that which concerns [*etc.*[b]
4.] (trace) [.

Notes

a. For a similar abbreviation see perhaps Text **23**, R° 1.

b. Restored from similar phrases in the ibis-memoranda; the lacunas represent other phrases (*pꜣ bik*, etc.), according to the length of the ostracon.

The relation of this fragment to the ibis-texts is evident.

49 and 50

(Two small fragments of an extensive text, written on the verso with a new reed).

49

Height	7·1 cm.
Width	3.9 cm.
Thickness	0·9 cm.
Munsell	(V°) 5 YR 4/2
	(R°) 2·5 YR 6/4
Photograph	Plate XXXV
Excavator's no.	G7–30 [459]

Four lines of text are visible; the space beneath the fourth suggests that the end of the ostracon had been reached.

Text

x+1.]*w nty ỉw* (*n*) *nꜣ* [ ]*w*[a] [
2.] *nty ỉw ḫf·w*[b]
3. *mdt*] (*n*) *tꜣ nty ṯꜣy tꜣ ḥrt* [
4.] [c] *n-ỉm·w bn-pw·k* (trace) [
(A space follows).

Notes

a. The word is difficult to identify, but cf. perhaps Text **16**, R° 10–11.

b. This line cancelled with a bold stroke.

c. The determinative suits *nw*, among others.

Translation

x+1.]s which are (in) the ······· [
2.] [[which(?) they have plundered]]
3. matter] (in) that which concerns the food [
4.] them: you have not ······· [.

The text seems to have described the neglect of the ibis-sanctuary.

50

Height	5·6 cm.
Width	1·8 cm.
Thickness	0·6 cm.
Munsell	5 YR 6/3
Photograph	Plate XXXVI
Excavator's no.	71/2–196 [5464]

The endings of five lines from the same(?) text as the preceding.

Text

x+1.] *nfr·f*
2.] *ỉrm*
3. *rn*]*pt 35*
4.] (trace)[a]
5.] *nty ʿḳ*
6.] (trace?).

Note

a. *Pr-ʿꜣt* is a possibility, followed by a space-filler.

Translation

x+1.] is beneficial(?)
2.] with(?)
3.] 35 years
4.] (trace)
5.] who enter[a]
6.] (trace?)

Note

a. Cf. perhaps Text **25**, 6.

The mention of years in line x+3 suggests that Ḥor is describing his loyal service.

51–5

Five small fragments of reddish-brown ware, perhaps all from the same text. The versos are blank, and the hand is probably that of the Memphite Ḥor.

51

Height	4·0 cm.
Width	4·8 cm.
Thickness	0·6 cm.
Munsell	5 YR 6/3
Photograph	Plate XXXVI
Excavator's no.	71/2–221 [5489]

Text

x+1.] *ỉw·s šm* [
2.]*my*[a] *ḥr* [
3.]*t* (vacat) [

Note

a. Possibly *Kmy*.

Translation is far from certain.

52

Height	3·4 cm.
Width	1·9 cm.
Thickness	0·6 cm.
Munsell	5 YR 6/3
Photograph	Plate XXXVI
Excavator's no.	71/2–222 [5490]

Text

x+1.] *tꜣy·w ḳr*[*st*
2.] *n-ỉm·w ỉy* [
3.] *n-ỉm·w* [.

Translation

x+1.] their buri[al
2.] them: came [
3.] them [.

53

Height	3·5 cm.
Width	2·8 cm.
Thickness	0·6 cm.
Munsell	5 YR 6/3
Photograph	Plate XXXVI
Excavator's no.	71/2–223 [5491]

Text

x+1.] *ꜣḳ tꜣ*/*nꜣ* [
2. [(ink smudged) [
3.] *smn* [.

Translation uncertain.

54

Height	7·2 cm.
Width	4·9 cm.
Thickness	0·6 cm.
Munsell	5 YR 6/3
Photograph	Plate XXXVI
Excavator's no.	71/2–224 [5492]

(In two pieces, joined).

Text

x+1.] *n-ỉm·s ḏd ỉw·s* [
2.] *ḏd n·ỉ whr* [
3.] *r·w* (vacat) [
4.] *tꜣy n pꜣ tꜣ* [
5.] *bn-pw·f mdt* [
6.] *pꜣ ỉ·ỉr hb n-ỉm·*[*ỉ*
7.] *st* [
8.] (trace) [.

Translation

x+1.] her,[a] saying, she[a] is [
2.] said to me ······· [
3.] to them. [
4.] this on earth(?) ····· [
5.] ······· he(?) did not speak [
6.] he who sent me(?) [
7.] they(?) [
8.] (trace) [.

Note

a. Alternatively 'it', antecedent uncertain.

55

Height	3·5 cm.
Width	5·0 cm.
Thickness	0·5 cm.
Munsell	5 YR 6/3
Photograph	Plate XXXVI
Excavator's no.	71/2–225 [5493]

Text

x+1.] *my* [.
2.] *nꜣ nty šn ḥt snt* [
3.] *ḏd n·ỉ pꜣ wꜥb ḥn* [
4.] *tꜣ mdt ỉ·ỉr* [
5.] (traces) [.

Translation

x+1.] may [
2.] those who investigate, namely the custom [
3.] said to me the priest within ····· [
4.] the matter which ····· [
5.] (traces) [.

These fragments, which seem to conform to the type of the ibis-memoranda, bear a close resemblance to Text **30**, of which they may even be part. Fragment **54** seems to refer to *Hrynys*, and his dispatching Ḥor to Alexandria (Text **2**, **3**).

56

Height	17·5 cm.
Width	18·3 cm.
Thickness	0·6 cm.
Munsell	5 YR 5/3
Photograph	Plate XXXVI
Excavator's no.	G7–33 [462]

A large ostracon of fine brown ware, bearing on the recto traces of some twenty-five(?) lines, all erased in antiquity. The verso is blank. The text may have begun with the words **n-drt Ḥr nty ḥn* [ ]; l. 4 commences with *ỉw·f ḥꜣꜥ*, and the clear ending of a later line in *bn-ỉw·k* shows that the original was addressed to a second person. The rest is conjecture.

57

Height	3·6 cm.
Width	3·6 cm.
Thickness	1·25 cm.
Munsell	7·5 YR 7/4
Photograph	Plate XXXVI
Excavator's no.	G7–34 [463]

A small buff-ware sherd of surprising thickness. The slightly convex recto bears faint traces, *ỉw·f*(?) being the least so; the verso carries three lines, the middle reading *pꜣy·s wꜣḥ* 'her interpretation'. The evidence of Text **9**, V° 7 suggests that the original may have treated the goddess Isis.

58

Height	15·0 cm.
Width	11·0 cm.
Thickness	1·0 cm.
Munsell	5 YR 5/3
Photograph	Plate XXXVII
Excavator's no.	H6–62 [1388]

So much doubt attaches itself to this ostracon that it has been left until the end. Of reddish-brown ware, the sherd seems to have borne some thirteen lines on the recto; the verso is quite blank. These lines have been so erased that scarcely anything remains to be read. At the beginning of l. 2, *rmt dmỉ-(n)-ȝst* seems tolerably clear, and the name *Ḥr* may have stood before this. The link with the main archive, in spite of the separate provenance by the main temple, would then be clear, and the traces suggest that the text began with the second line, the first being only the conclusion and continuation of l. 13. The contents of the ostracon are of course far from clear: *tw·ỉ* in the centre of l. 10 reveals a first person narrative, and *nȝy* (possibly *r-bw-nȝy*) in l. 11, and *pȝ tš (n) Pr-Wsỉr* (apparently not *Wsỉr-Ḥp*) in the twelfth are still legible. Line 3 may have begun with **ỉw·ỉ wš nȝ ssw*, and the faint traces of **ḳrs* in l. 7 may suggest a link with the ibis-texts translated above. All else is beyond recall.

III. THE COMMENTARIES

§ 1 : The career of Ḥor

THE arrangement of the texts in the previous part of this volume is quite arbitrary, and the broad classes into which the ostraca are divided are very crude, the more so as many obviously refer to the whole experience of their author. In this rough pattern it is clear that the reader will lose much; to clarify the picture, and above all to construct a plausible chronology, is the only purpose of these Commentaries. To say that they are incomplete, preliminary, and unadorned is unnecessary, except to save them from being credited with an authority to which they do not lay claim.

Very little can be seen of the early life of the central character, Ḥor of Sebennytos. The name of his father, Ḥarendjiōtef, is given clearly in one passage,[1] and in another five which are too obscure to be given in evidence. Of this man's life we are told nothing. The date of Ḥor's birth is similarly missing; from the sequence of years given to us in the main archive, it may be conjectured that he was born about 200 B.C. If the statement of Text **5A,** 4, that in 165 he had already served in Ḥepnēbes for twenty-five years is correctly understood,[2] he may have been older, for his career was already advanced when he came to Memphis.

In Text **1,** 1 Ḥor describes himself as a man of *Pr-Ḏḥwty*, Pi(?)-Thoth, a locality which Text **28,** 3 seems to situate in the Sebennytic nome. This designation is not his commonest, and this distinction must be awarded instead to the *Dmi-n-ꜣst* with which in Texts **2, 7, 26, 27,** and **29** he is associated. This 'town of Isis' would, however, seem to be the Ἴσιος πόλις of the Greek Texts,[3] where Ḥor is said to have been employed as a pastophoros, and this fact, together with the more intimate associations given to Pi(?)-Thoth in Text **8,** R° 19 and in Texts **9** and **10,** lead one to the belief that the latter was his birthplace. I cannot find the locality named elsewhere, but an uneasy suspicion that Pi(?)-Thoth would pass into Greek as Ἑρμοῦ πόλις propels us unwillingly into the meshy problems of the Egyptian Hermopolis. Stephanus of Byzantium (quoted in Ball, *Egypt in the Classical Geographers*, 171) follows Herodian in ascribing no less than five towns of the name to the area of Egypt: one 'the great', which a consensus of opinion would place in the great site of Ashmunein, with its necropolis Tûna-el-Gebel in Middle Egypt (cf. Text **28,** 12), 'the small', or Hermopolis Parva, a third surprisingly described as 'near Egypt', a fourth near Thmuis, and a fifth 'in the river'. If we discount the third, perhaps an oasis site,[4] we are left with three other towns of this name, and may pass to the account of Strabo, who locates the same number in the Delta. One is said to be on an island near Butus (XVII, 18, end), a second is unqualified, but mentioned after Xois and in conjunction with Lycopolis and Mendes (ibid. 19) while a third (ibid. 22) is situated on the riverine route from Schedia to Memphis, where it is said to precede Gynaecopolis and Momemphis. The last has frequently been compared with Damanhûr (Ball, loc. cit., although Gardiner, *AEO*, ii. 196* seems to prefer the charms of the island near Buto). This identification is followed by A. Bernand (*Le Delta égyptien d'après les textes grecs*,

[1] Text **19,** R° 1, in the spelling *Ḥr-n-drt·f*.

[2] See note *ad locum*.

[3] Greek Texts **C,** 2; **E,** 6.

[4] A site in Baḥrîya oasis is a possibility, for extensive ibis-cemeteries are known there, cf. Fakhry, *Baḥria Oasis*, ii, Ch. 4 and pls. XII–XXIII; the site itself is given as Ḳaret el-Farargi.

i, third part, 515–50), who finally follows Gardiner and Wilcken in seeing in Hermopolis and *Dmỉ-n-Ḥr* (cf. *JEA* 30 (1944), 35–6) two adjoining towns, or suburbs, which eventually coalesced and were named after the latter. There we may with some relief leave them. The 'small' Hermopolis of Stephanus of Byzantium may well be identical with this conurbation.

The second Hermopolis seems located in the central Delta, and its counterpart might plausibly be seen in the ancient *Bʿḥ*, modern Tell Baqlîya. This city, well attested, might seem a good candidate for our Pi(?)-Thoth (the dual name need not be a serious problem), were it not for the clear fact that Hermopolis–Baqlîya in the Ptolemaic period formed an entirely separate nome from Sebennytos.[1] Even if some political union were recognized, it is surely unlikely that a native of Baqlîya would consistently refer to himself as 'scribe of the nome of Sebennytos'. Much interest therefore centres upon the final candidate, the island near Buto (Būtus). The location of Buto at the modern Tell el-Faraʿîn was already proposed by Hogarth ('Three North Delta nomes', in *JHS* 24 (1904), 2 ff.). A canal, under the name of the Θερμουθιακὸς ποταμός, marked in Roman (post-Hadrianic) times the boundary between the Boutite (Phthenetic) and Lower Sebennytic nomes; that the latter corresponded to what in the Ptolemaic period was called more simply *pꜣ tš n Ṯb-nṯr* is shown by the Satrap Stela, 14–15 (*AEO* ii. 195*). A town upon an island, or on the east bank of this canal might well have been included in the Sebennytic nome. Several mounds in this area are mentioned by Hogarth, notably Khawâlid (Phragonis?) and Haddâdi, but there are no grounds for identifying any of these with our *Pr-Ḏḥwty*.[2] It is upon such a site, nevertheless, that we are tempted to place Ḥor at the beginning of his career; the proximity of Buto (*Pr-Wꜣḏyt*) to his home town is clearly suggested in Text **10.** In this connection it should be remembered that the great Litany of Oxyrhynchus mentions a Ἑρμοῦ πόλει which lay near Iseum and Sebennytos, but the reading is not too certain (*Oxyrhynchus Papyri*, xi. 208, note); this is unfortunate, as the context is very apt.[3]

We next encounter Ḥor employed at *Dmỉ-n-ꜣst*, 'the town-of-Isis', another locality in the nome of Sebennytos.[4] The Greek Texts **C** and **E** describe him as a pastophoros of Isis in the temple there, and Text **26,** which also seems to refer to events at Temenēsi, shows him involved in the affairs of an *ʿḥyt n ms* attached to an ibis-cult in the town. Other priests of Isis (Text **26,** R° 12 and Text **31A,** 3–4) seem also to have been concerned with these affairs, and it is possible that the three writers of Text **31** were his early colleagues; if this idea is correct, the purpose of the text may well have been to supply testimony of his good conduct. It is doubtless during this time that the training took place which gave Ḥor some of his knowledge of

[1] The bibliography on Hermopolis–Baqlîya is extensive: Naville, *Ahnas-el-Medineh*, 22–6; Daressy in *ASAE* 13 (1913), 179–85 and *ASAE* 30 (1930), 69 ff.; Habachi, *ASAE* 53 (1953), 441–80; Montet, *Géographie*, i. 137 ff., and Gardiner, *AEO* ii. 195*. The most recent discussion seems to be A-P. Zivie, 'Hermopolis–El-Baqlieh et le nome de l'ibis', *Annuaire de l'École Pratique des Hautes Études, Sci. Relig.* 79 (1971–2), 491–4.

[2] It is true that a place-name ⲑⲟⲓⲧⲉ/ⲧⲑⲟⲓϯ is mentioned in the trilingual list of Bishoprics as lying somewhere in this area, but even on the assumption that such a pagan name as *Pr-Ḏḥwty* had been allowed to survive into Coptic, there are serious philological obstacles to the identification.

[3] The following identifications are therefore proposed for the five Hermopolis of Stephanus of Byzantium:

a. Hermopolis 'the great' (*Magna*), at Ashmunein (*Ḫmnw*) in Middle Egypt.

b. 'The small' (*Parva*), perhaps at or near Damanhûr.

c. 'Hermopolis near Egypt', in Baḥrîya Oasis(?).

d. 'Hermopolis near Thmuis', at Baqlîya (*Bʿḥ*, *Wnw mḥty*).

e. 'Hermopolis on the river', *Pr-Ḏḥwty* in the nome of Sebennytos.

b is probably the third Hermopolis of Strabo, on the riverine route from Schedia to Memphis; *d* is his second, near Xois and Mendes, while his first site, the island near Buto, will be our *e*, and the *Pr-Ḏḥwty* of Ḥor. For more information about *Pr-Ḏḥwty* see Add. Text **59** below (pp. 167–9).

[4] For detailed references see Index, and the note to Text **2,** R° 2, p. 19, where the possibility of an equation with Iseum (Behbeit el-Ḥagār) is discussed, and left open.

Middle Egyptian idiom (Text **18,** *passim*); how he acquired his somewhat dubious Greek (*JEA* 54 (1968), 204) is less certain.

Great obscurity now begins to surround his career. The only certain fact, indeed, is that he later appears at Memphis and attaches himself to the sanctuary of the Ibis at Saqqâra. His links with Temenēsi, however, are never completely broken, and even Text **29,** written in the thirtieth year of Philometor (152/1), describes him still as a citizen of the town. It is likely, however, that when he left Temenēsi he would have abandoned his role of pastophoros, and this may well be the reason that none of the demotic texts repeats his Greek title. Some reasons will be given in the Appendix below for a suspicion that Ḥor's position at Saqqâra was that of a κάτοχος. If this belief is correct, he may well have regarded his residence in Memphis as incidental; indeed, it is possible that Temenēsi (Isiospolis) remained his legal place of registration (τόπος). Whatever the truth, it is evident from his signatures that he never ceased to regard himself as a man of Sebennytos.

Text **26** shows that while serving at Isiospolis he became involved in a dispute concerning the food of the ibises, and incurred the censure of the god Thoth. Quarrelsomeness seems to have been marked in his disposition, but we are not told whether this incident prompted his departure; indeed the tenor of several other texts makes it clear that he was already being assailed by divine visitations, and he seems to be at pains to demonstrate that it was the will of the gods which for ever directed his steps.

In the later 170s the great reforms were instituted in the ibis-shrine of North Saqqâra, which we find recorded in Texts **19–22.** In their surviving form, these ostraca are clearly dictated by Ḥor, and the impression given is that he was present (in some capacity) at the deliberations; there is no compelling reason, however, to believe that he was in Memphis permanently at such an early period, and the texts may well be retrospective drafts, designed to add the background information for a history of the ibis-cult. Clearer information comes from Text **18,** which shows him on 10 July 171 invoking a dream; the setting, with its references to Imḥōtep (V° 2–3, 15) and ʿAnkhtawy (V° 3, 7; R° 1) is that of the Memphite necropolis. The gods summoned are legion, and it is not easy to determine the particular shrine in which the dream was elicited, but the desire to seek the prognostications of the gods is a characteristic of Ḥor throughout these years.

Political events were already on the turn: the policies of Eulaeus and Lenaeus had prevailed, and in October/November 170 the joint reign was proclaimed in Alexandria (Skeat, *JEA* 47 (1961), 108). Within a month the Egyptian army was defeated, and Philometor in the hands of Antiochus Epiphanes. The history of the Sixth Syrian War, and of Ḥor's part therein, will be discussed in the next section; here only a few personal events will be noted. By 18 May 169, the date given in Text **10,** we find that he has taken himself, or been taken by the course of the war, to the Delta, where at Buto and back in his native Pi(?)-Thoth, he writes short *proskynemata* to Isis; the final lines, emphasizing the protection afforded by the goddess to those who turn to her, seem appropriate to such an unsettled time. One purpose of these, and perhaps similar unrecorded, addresses may well have been to obtain dreams of encouragement while the Seleucid occupation of Egypt continued. One such sign of encouragement, in all probability addressed to Philometor, occurs on the verso of Text **12,** which by internal consideration may possibly have been written early in 168, perhaps even in the short interlude before Antiochus' second invasion, when the joint reign seems to have been reinstituted. The 'prophet of Isis' referred to in this brief text as having quelled apprehension may possibly be Ḥor, but as he nowhere else bears this title, it is equally likely to represent an official of the goddess to whom he had turned for oracular advice. The direct address to Pharaoh, however, suggests strongly that Ḥor of Sebennytos had already acquired a considerable reputation as a seer, and had begun his habit of communicating with Philometor. This communication reached its peak with the audience in the Alexandrian Serapeum which took place on 29 August 168 (Text **2,** R° 12; V° 4–12), when Ḥor read out before his sovereigns his prophecy of the salvation of Alexandria and all its people.

The fortunes of Ḥor in the years immediately following are unclear; unclear too is the reaction of Pharaoh to his ministrations. By 2 December 166, Ḥor seems to be at Heliopolis, again commenting upon political events (Text **5,** 1–2), and in the year preceding this (167/6) we must date the important Text **9.** Here (R° 2) he describes himself as 'agent' in the chapel of Pi(?)-Thoth, a town to which he may well have returned after the cessation of hostilities. A dream is interpreted by the goddess Isis: he will go permanently to Memphis, and shall die there. It seems characteristic of Ḥor of Sebennytos that such a profound change in his life should be augured by a divine revelation, and equally typical that he should record the information for later reference. The episode in Heliopolis described in Text **5** may possibly have been a stage on his inspired journey.

The prophecy of Isis makes mention only of the Serapeum, and we are ignorant of the process by which Ḥor came to settle amid the temples of the ibis-cult. His previous experiences would doubtless have helped determine the matter, as well might his reputation, but it is clear that from 166 the centre of his attentions is no longer Isis, but the god Thoth. The testimony of Text **31,** if rightly understood, similarly suggests that his service to Isis came to an end in about 165. It is appropriate, therefore, to date here Text **8,** which records dreams experienced on the great festival of the moon-god (12 Thoth 166/5?). The significance of the first dream is that he is to devote himself exclusively to the worship of Thoth, and the conclusion of both dreams that his sustenance in life, and eventual burial, boons once guaranteed to him by Isis, are now in the bestowal of the ibis-deity.

Whether or not by this dream Ḥor undertook the strict vows of a κάτοχος,[1] the latter part of his life lacks much of the earlier incident. At some point in the continuing joint reign, in short before May 163, he reports to the Pharaohs another augury in which Isis offers a healing remedy for the Queen. It is to be regretted that so much of this ostracon (Text **28**) is obscured beyond recall, but it is notable that he continues to call himself a man of Pi(?)-Thoth (ibid. 3). Also during this period must be placed the interpretation of an oracle covering the sanctuaries of the Ibis (Text **16**), an interpretation obtained from the magician of Imḥōtep (Text **17A,** 3–10); the following 13 June seems to have witnessed the communication of this interpretation to the competent authority (Text **22,** R° 2–3), but the details of this oracle need not detain us here.[2]

The critical events which marked the end of the joint reign seem to have left little impression upon our texts. After the re-establishment of Philometor as sole ruler and his great φιλάνθρωπα of 17 August 163 (Louvre 63; cf. Bevan, 291) the king visited the Serapeum (October 163; Bevan, 292), and in all probability Ḥor of Sebennytos may have witnessed the festivities; but none of our documents sees fit to refer to the occasion. Indeed, a second period of obscurity now falls upon the career of Ḥor, unbroken until the events referred to at the beginning of Text **1.** During much of this time we may picture him as acting as scribe or secretary for the affairs of

[1] See Appendix 3 below.

[2] They are discussed in § 4 below.

the ibis-cult. We are at least told (Text **1**, 1–2) that he had become accustomed to dividing his time between the sanctuary of Osorapis at Memphis and that of his counterpart Osormnevis at Heliopolis; what is not disclosed, however, is the length of time that this habit had continued. Nevertheless, on 31 May 159 he is in Heliopolis, and informs us that he had arrived in the city at some time in the previous January (ibid., l. 5); he had left the instruments of his scribal profession in Memphis, and was seeking instruction from the priest of Imḥōtep, for a dream experienced upon his arrival had told him to lay his experiences in writing 'before the great men' (ibid., l. 5). We may only guess at the reasons for his curiosity; the eventual birth of an heir to Philometor, foreshadowed in his dream of 168, may have given a fillip to his mantic powers,[1] or it may be that difference of opinion between Ḥor and the 'great men' (the temple authorities) had impelled him to seek divine encouragement. Whatever the truth, we find that in the December of 159 he obtained an audience with [So]terion(?) the *basilikos grammateus* at Memphis. To this highest authority for temple affairs he explains in detail his dream of 168 (ibid., l. 6); the fact that this information is contained in a memorandum (*mkmk*) suggests strongly that it was recorded to provide evidence for a legal dispute. It is of course difficult to determine the exact date of this dispute, or its terms and outcome, and the entire text may be greatly retrospective. Ignorance of such matters need not prevent us from consulting Text **4**, which seems to provide confirmatory evidence of Ḥor's divinatory powers, written, we are told, by the important general *Hrynys*, who had supported his activities during the war of 168 (Text **4**, 1–2); we may suspect that this document too would have been cited in evidence at some stage in his disputing.

The summer of 158 was an important one for Egypt, and for the Serapeum in particular. Apollonios, brother of the κάτοχος Ptolemaios, himself joined his brother in the House of Osorapis, and his quarrel with the sons of Djeḥebēs must have provided much gossip among its population.[2] Stirring, too, would have been the news of the public proclamation of Ptolemy Eupator, and his appointment as eponymous priest of Alexander, and, as autumn approached, the preparation for the second visit of Philometor, on the tour of state which was to extend to distant Philae. It is indeed in the culmination of such excitement that one is tempted to place Text **3**, a birthday greeting to Philometor (whose γενέθλια fell so auspiciously on the feast day of Thoth), and a confirmation of the survival of his line (R° 8–9; V° 1–2). Yet this text is no mere encomium, for it incorporates in the verso a tactfully re-edited account of Text **2**, recalling Ḥor's role in the war with Antiochus, but suppressing all reference to the joint reign and to the embarrassing Ptolemy 'the Brother'. Doubtless this was done in the hope of securing the goodwill of Pharaoh to the cause.

Once again it becomes difficult to follow Ḥor's activities. The strange dream of Text **13** is recorded for 10 March 155, after two days of supplication to the Ibis, but it is not an easy matter to explain; the entire text is perhaps best taken merely as evidence that Ḥor continued upon his path of incubation.

It is not until the later 150s that the significance of the majority of our texts becomes clearer. We have already seen that several of the ostraca appear to have been written in a Memphite hand, and its author now makes himself known to us. In Texts **16**, R° 1 and **17**, 1, he describes himself fully as 'Ḥor who is concerned with the petition of the chapels of Egypt', and elsewhere he appears briefly as Ḥarthoth (probably 'Horus (of the god) Thoth') (Texts **12**, R° 1; **19**, R° 4(?); **30**, 1) while in Text **23**, V° 15

[1] This possibility is elaborated in § 2 below.

[2] As indeed for Reich, *Mizraim*, i (1933), 147 ff.

he is 'Ḥor (of) Thoth, lord of life'. The general nature of the texts in his hand, notably **12, 16, 17, 25,** and the verso of **23,** together with the obvious competence of his script, suggest that he is the resident secretary or petition-writer of the ibis-cult. Most of the texts in his hand seem to have been dictated by Ḥor of Sebennytos, and we therefore know little about his Memphite namesake. Nevertheless the five short texts mentioned above give a small amount of information. Texts **12, 25,** and possibly **30,** acquaint us with a journey undertaken by him at the request of the god to *Pr-pꜣy·f-iry*, an obscure locality which seems to have lain near Alexandria. This journey, which seems to have lasted some five years (*c.* 172–168) is described in fullest detail in Text **12,** where the oracular nature of much of his business is made clear. Text **25** appears to contain the draft of a decree justifying this prolonged departure from Saqqâra, an absence for which he may have been blamed at home, but this like much else in our documents is a matter of inference. Inference too is the only support for the belief that the Memphite Ḥor was an initiate into the mysteries of his god.[1] Whatever the truth of this, the clear Memphite hand of this professional writer is seen in Texts **2, 4, 6, 10, 12** and **12A, 13, 16, 17, 18, 22, 24A**(?) and **B**(?), **25, 26, 30, 36–44**(?), **45, 48, 49, 50, 51–5,** and at its best in the graceful lines of Text **9.** Text **16,** with its verso upside down, reflects clearly the habit of a letter-writer. The method of dictation is shown by many of the erasures, and the numerous insertions, which were presumably added during a second reading, demonstrate the polishing of texts into final versions. Several texts seem not to have been dictated, but are written directly on to the sherd in the large ungainly hand which is probably that of Ḥor of Sebennytos. Texts **3, 7, 11, 14**(?), **19**(?), **20**(?), **21**(?), **23, 27, 28**(?), **29**(?), **46, 47,** and possibly **33,** together with the Greek ostraca, are apparently the work of the latter; the remainder are best left unassigned. Both Greek Text **B** and Demotic Text **14** are written over palimpsests, and Text **14** shows the clear signs of haste. That some of our ostraca were intended to be second drafts is shown by the occasional dittography, as in Text **2,** R° 5–6, or Text **3,** R° 19–20, where the writer's attention was momentarily diverted from the rough text before him. The final step, which naturally we cannot trace, would have been the transfer of the entire corpus to a papyrus, doubtless in the hand of the Memphite secretary; that this step was ever accomplished we cannot be sure, but the copy-ticks against several lines, notably in Text **4** (R°), and Texts **16, 17,** and **18** (R°), suggest that this was done. That Pharaoh was the intended recipient of this entire document is indicated by the addresses to Texts **2, 7, 28,** and **29,** and by the general tone and purpose of the whole archive. More difficult to reconcile with this interpretation are the five Greek Texts which begin the present volume; an obvious assumption is that they were intended as an eye-catching protocol, but the clear reference which they contain to the joint reign, and to Ptolemy 'the Brother' makes it more likely that they would have been incorporated into the appropriate section of the historical narrative.

The question has so far been begged concerning the purpose of such a petition. The fact that four of our documents are legal memoranda[2] (Texts **1** and **21,** *i·ir·ḥr nꜣ wꜥbw*; Text **26,** to Ariston of Daphnae(?), Text **31** to Sarapion), and the technical significance of the word *smi* 'petition for a hearing' (Gardiner, *Mes*, 14, n. 18), demonstrate that some form of litigation had taken, or was taking, place. Some pale light is shed on the nature of this litigation. The phrase *ṯꜣy·w gns*, first appearing in Demotic

[1] The evidence is discussed in the notes to Text **16,** R° 4–5; **17,** 6–7, and 14–15; **23,** R° 7–8.

[2] See *JEA* 58 (1972), 254 ff. and the notes to Text **1,** 1, p. 12 above.

Text A, 1, is repeated in Text **16,** R° 11 and **17,** 5, with the additional phrase *n-drt nꜣ rmtw ḏry*. *Tꜣy-gns* as a legal term is discussed by Barns, *JEA* 58 (1972), 165–6, and one suspects that the phrase used by Ḥor is the demotic equivalent of the Greek ἀδικοῦμαι ὑπό, the regular opening of complaints and petitions (cf. *UPZ* 18, 2, and the revised text, p. 648, l. 6). These 'mighty men', doubtless the high temple authorities, are described in Text **7,** 14 as having 'found fault' with the writer (*gm lwḥ*, the phrase used of Thoth in Text **26,** R° 17). In Text **27,** V° 8–9 Thoth is shown bringing advice to these same authorities, advice which they doubtless were supposed to have ignored. Further details are scarce; Text **7,** end and **27,** V° 9 make accusations that the food of the ibises is being stolen, and poignantly describe the birds in the extremity of hunger; Texts **16** and **17,** and apparently the end of **29,** direct curses against an enemy, doubtless the perpetrator of these crimes. It is not a great step to identifying this enemy with the 'mighty men'. The last-named text also mentions an inventory (*ḫtḫt*), which may also have been used to establish guilt, but this text is deliberately erased; a tempting explanation is that this was because of the incriminating nature of its contents. Further speculation is hard to resist, but it is out of place here.

The grouping of all our ostraca into a connected petition raises questions about their reliability as sources. The oracular material and the dream-texts were clearly worked into a preamble designed to prove the author's reliability as a seer and true exponent of the divine. The historical material is introduced only inasmuch as it serves to reinforce this impression, and must be read in this light. In a similar way the ostraca concerned with the reforms of the ibis-cult are present only to point the contrast between the ideal cult and the irresponsibility and maladministration of the present authorities. All references, therefore, to the piety of Philometor, or the war against Antiochus, or even the accounts of dreams or trivial experiences, are to be regarded as tendentious. Appeals to the monarch are common enough in the Ptolemaic period, and a very fine note on the Greek examples is to be found in A. Bernand, *Les Inscriptions grecques de Philae*, i (Paris, 1969), 188–91. The tactics employed in such petitions are twofold: either constant appeal is made to the pathetic, as consistently in later Roman advocacy, or, more subtly, to the insinuated notion that the goodwill of the gods towards the ruling sovereign is dependent upon the proper upkeep and administration of their cults. This second approach is that preferred by Ḥor. Such a compendium of historical narrative, oracles, and expressions of loyalty is familiar already from Pap. Rylands IX, a text which has much in common with the archive of Ḥor. Indeed, it may not be too fanciful to suspect that such was the standard form of an Egyptian petition to the highest authorities. It is even possible that other such petitions may have gone unrecognized, and one is led to wonder whether such a text as the Turin Strike Papyrus is not part of a similar document addressed to Ramesses III or his successor.[1]

The possible date of this petition is difficult to determine. The reference to 'Year 30' in Text **29,** and the very vague possibility that Text **4,** R° 11 refers to the death of Eupator brings us to the very end of the 150s; the dating of Text **34** to the May or September of 147 may be taken merely as a symbol of the end of our archive.[2]

The results of this petition are of course

[1] Such an idea can be readily obtained from the remarks of Edgerton, *JNES* 10 (1951), 144–5.

[2] It is unfortunate that the idea that this text, the rim of a jar, represents the remains of the container for our ostraca cannot be proved; see note *ad locum*.

unknown, and we have no way of telling whether Ḥor survived his sovereign, and if so, what became of him in the disturbances of the following years. We are forced, therefore, to return to the texts themselves, written in the dialects of Sebennytos and Memphis (the frequent loss of *-t* from the infinitives of *tertiae infirmae* verbs, as in *ms-f*, Text **4,** R° 5; *ḳrs-k*, **8,** R° 22; *ỉr-s*, **25,** 11; *ỉn-s*, **26,** R° 10; *gm-s*, **32,** V° 1, *r-dbꜣ·s*, **45,** 4; the spellings of *ỉ·ỉr-sḫy* and *thnyt* in **3,** R° 7 and **23,** V° 23, the writing *sgny* for *sḏny* in **12,** V° 4; **26,** V° 8, and the pronominal form *ỉn·w-y* in **8,** R° 2).

Such is the evidence for this remarkable figure. In some ways he resembles the priest Manetho, also a native of Sebennytos, who moved south, γένει Σεβεννύτης ὑπάρχων Ἡλιοπολίτης,[1] while in others he is reminiscent of the prophet who says 'I have dreamed, I have dreamed'.[2] In all ways he is uniquely worthy of our attention.

§ 2 : Historical information

The preceding section dealing with the career of Ḥor, and his petition to Pharaoh, has laid emphasis on the fact that his writing is not objectively detached from questions of his own interest, and his historical material is no less subject to this reservation than the rest of his petition. Nevertheless, if a man feels that the facts justify his cause, he will go to a certain length to get them right, and it is clear that Ḥor, Egyptian though he was, had a surprising grasp of the political events of his time. Whatever the truth, it is undeniable that his importance as a contemporary source for events known otherwise largely or even solely from the fragments of Polybius is too great to be ignored, and that consequently the burden of proof falls upon those who suspect his reliability to find support for their suspicion.

Ḥor's most important contributions to the history of his times lie in the dynastic information he gives, and in his observations on the sixth Syrian War. Philometor's birthday is said in Text **3,** R° 12–13 to have fallen on 12 Thoth in the Egyptian calendar;[3] in order to convert this into a Julian date one must identify the year. Arguments, though possibly not conclusive ones, have been given above for attributing Text **3** to the year 158, in accordance with the proclamation of Eupator (in summer) and the visit of Philometor to the Serapeum (October). The Julian date for the king's birthday would then be 19 October 184. Reasons have been given above for preferring this year for the king's birth, rather than 186. As the Egyptian calendar slides with respect to the Julian, the king's birthday would by the year 158 have been celebrated on 13 October, and it is here that our Text **3** must be dated.

Philometor's accession to the throne after May 180 (Skeat, *Reigns of the Ptolemies*, 32) finds no reflection in our documents, and the whole period between his coronation and the death of his mother (before September 176)[4] is badly represented. Text **19,** R° 14–15 which is dated to 31 May 172 names 'the Pharaohs' (*nꜣ Pr-ꜥꜣw*), who can scarcely be other than the king and his young wife, Cleopatra II; the text may therefore be quoted as confirmatory evidence for the belief that Philometor's marriage, together with his ἀνακλητήρια, is best dated to the spring of 175.[5]

By far the most perplexing piece of dynastic information is offered to us in Text **5.** Ḥor, writing on 30 Paophi of Year 5, informs us that 'the confirmation of the fortune (*pꜣ ꜥḥꜥ-rd (n) pꜣ ꜥš-sḥn*) [··········] has occurred in Memphis'; unfortunately the context is too obscure to define what he means, and all we can ascertain is that some sort of benefit (*mdt-nfrt*) has been granted

[1] Waddell, *Manetho*, x. 208.
[2] Jeremiah 23: 25.
[3] See note *ad locum*; the reading 15 is less plausible.
[4] Pestman, *Chronologie*, 46.
[5] See note *m ad locum* p. 79 above.

by Thoth. If the fifth year is in fact that of Philometor alone, the date would correspond to 4 December 177, and explanations of the auspicious occasion would be difficult to find. The assumption that we are dealing with a year of the joint reign is made more likely by the reference to the general *Hrynys* in the following lines (Text **5**, 4); the date would then come down to 2 December 166. Guesses are out of place in a preliminary publication, and the author may only note in passing his suspicion that the event which has so excited Ḥor is the birth of Ptolemy Eupator. This at least would be the confirmation of the Isis-dream of 168 (cf. Text **1**, 17–18). The birth of this ill-fated prince has generally been placed during these years (Otto, *Geschichte*, 9; L. Pareti, *Ricerchi sui Tolomei Eupatore e Neo Filopatore* (*Reale Accademia Scienze*, Torino 1907–8), 506, n. 2); note that children (τέκνα) are ascribed to the royal couple already on 21 September 164.[1] Of even greater interest here is our Text **28**, which was written at a point within the joint reign, and which clearly shows a remedy (*pẖrt*) being fashioned for the Queen. Unfortunately there is no proof that childbirth was the cause for this, or if childbirth, that the child was Eupator, and here our speculation must reluctantly give way.

Of greater value is Ḥor's treatment of the sixth Syrian War. The primary sources for the campaigns of Antiochus IV Epiphanes into Egypt are numerous (Polybius XXVIII–XXXI; Diodorus XXX; Livy XLIV; and, written with a very different purpose, Daniel 11; the commentary of St. Jerome on the latter is also of great value). The present account is based on these in conjunction with the findings of Skeat (*JEA* 47 (1961), 107 ff.); the last-named is of particular importance for its revision of the chronology of the two Seleucid invasions.[2] This chronology is followed in the present commentary.

In the latter part of 170, the policy of Eulaeus and Lenaeus prevailed in Egypt: after 5 October of the same year the joint reign of Philometor and his brother had been proclaimed in Alexandria.[3] This joint reign is reflected in the prooemia to two of our documents,[4] and the two Pharaohs in several more. By the end of November, however, the Egyptian army had been utterly defeated in the neighbourhood of Mount Kasion, Eulaeus and Lenaeus disgraced, Philometor captured and in the hands of Antiochus, and the joint reign formally repealed. At this point we should note that our Text **12**, written on 12 December 170, continues to use the discredited form of dating, and is later than any quoted by Skeat;[5] this may either be a lapse of memory, or a mere reflection of the uncertainty in Egypt at the end of the year, but it need not seriously affect his proposed reconstruction.

The victorious Antiochus seems to have remained in Egypt throughout 169, acting nominally as champion of the powerless Philometor.[6] His withdrawal to Syria (probably as a result of negotiations) seems only to have taken place at the end of the year, a period to which it is possible to ascribe the encouraging words of Text **12**, V°. It is, however, more than likely that Antiochus maintained his garrison at Pelusium, and probably in other Egyptian cities as well. From the Egyptian defeat of 170, the country was in a condition of *stasis*, with Egypt supporting the claims of Philometor, Alexandria

[1] Pap. Louvre 2329 (= Wilcken, No. 110); see note *a* to Text **3**, V° 1, p. 27, and the discussion following.

[2] The account in Bevan, *House of Seleucus*, ii. 136 ff. is now in need of supplementing.

[3] Skeat, op. cit., 108. P. M. Fraser (*Ptolemaic Alexandria*, ii. 211, n. 212) rejects the view that the establishment of joint rule was overtly a political gesture, preferring to stress the economic aspect, especially the near bankruptcy of the Ptolemaic state at this time.

[4] Greek Text E and Text **28**; and by implication of date in several others. Ptolemy 'the Brother' appears also in Text **3**, V° 19.

[5] Op. cit. 108: see note *g* to the translation of Text **12**, p. 53 above.

[6] Pap. Lond. Inv. 1974 shows him still in Egypt on 23 April 169: Skeat, 110.

upholding those of 'the Brother', and it is this condition which Ḥor refers to as 'the time when Egypt divorced itself (from Alexandria)', *pꜣ tr (i·)wn-nꜣ Kmy pnḳ n-im·f (n) Rꜥ-ḳd.*[1] This state of affairs persisted, according to Texts **3** and **4**, into the year 168, although a reconciliation between the two kings seems to have taken place upon Antiochus' withdrawal, whereupon the joint reign, with its connotations of an aggressive foreign policy, was declared for a second time. This reconciliation is in fact confirmed by Ḥor himself, when he states in Text **2**, R° 12; V° 4–6, and **3**, 18–20, that both kings were together in the Alexandrian Serapeum on 29 August 168. The phrase describing the separation of Egypt from Alexandria must therefore be taken as a general description of the period when hostilities continued against Antiochus, and little more.

During the summer of 168 Ḥor 'stood with' a personage named *Hrynys* (Text **1**, 8); this phrase, used elsewhere in our documents,[2] seems to mean little more than 'had an interview with', and the contents of this interview are made clearer to us in Text **2**, R° 7–8. Antiochus had reinvaded in the spring (Skeat, 112). Cyprus was also seized, and there is considerable evidence that during this second invasion, far from acting as protector of the rightful king as he had previously done, the Seleucid set aside the entire government of Egypt. Antiochus was advancing towards Alexandria, the home of the Queen and the two Ptolemies (Text **3**, V° 18–19; cf. the account in Polybius, XXIX, 27). Antiochus is situated[3] to the north of *Pr-ꜣwrys*, a locality, possibly bearing the name of the discredited Eulaeus, which may have lain by the coast to the east of the capital.[4] At this time of peril for the city, Ḥor has had a dream prophesying both the salvation of Alexandria, and the birth of an heir to Cleopatra; this dream is communicated to *Hrynys* on 11 July 168, and we may therefore suppose it to have happened recently before.[5] *Hrynys* must now be introduced: he is described in Text **2**, R° 8 as general (στρατηγός), in Text **4**, R° 1–2 and **5**, 4 as 'general of horse of Pharaoh and the Queen', and in Text **1**, 8–9 his duties are paraphrased as '*Hryns* who was at the head of the army [and who acted as] the agent of Pharaoh Ptolemy our Lord'. There can therefore be little doubt that he was a commander, perhaps even the supreme commander, of the Egyptian army in its defence of the homeland. The name may perhaps correspond to *Eirenaios (*Helenos being far less convincing), but no plausible identification can be suggested from the *Prosopographia*.[6] He may well, like many Ptolemaic generals, have been a soldier of fortune from abroad. The relation of this important personage to Ḥor is also difficult to grasp: in Text **4**, R° 2, he seems to act as his superior, and it may be that during the national crisis Ḥor of Sebennytos had been serving in the army in some capacity. That *Eirenaios survived the war seems to be shown by his reappearance in Text **5**, 4, at the end of 166. *Eirenaios clearly did not believe in the dream told to him by his mantic associate; the reason for this, apart possibly from the professional soldier's natural lack of sympathy, is said to be that *Gryꜣ* was still in Memphis.[7] This name, alternatively spelt *Grynꜣ*, will correspond to the Greek Creon, or perhaps more likely Cleon. The fact that on

[1] Texts **1**, 7; **3**, V° 10; **4**, R° 4.

[2] Cf. among others Text **4**, R° 15 and Texts **12**, R° 3; **22**, R° 3.

[3] The word used in Text **3**, V° 10 may mean 'campaigning', but this is not certain.

[4] See note *i* to the translation of Text **3**, V° 11, p. 28 above.

[5] In Text **3**, this date has been altered to 1 July; this may be a lapse of memory, for Text **3** is known to be retrospective, or it may perhaps reflect the date of the dream itself. The former alternative is perhaps sounder.

[6] See further, note *q* to Text **1**, 8, p. 13 above. The Eirenaios of Pap. Tebtunis 64b, 18 is probably also that of Pap. Tebtunis 7 (Grenfell, Hunt, Smyly, *Tebtunis Papyri*, i. 65, 267), but the date, at 116/115, is far too late for the present character.

[7] Text **2**, R° 9; V° 7–8; Text **3**, V° 11.

11 July this personage had 'not yet left Memphis' implies that he did at a later date leave, and his constant epithet 'agent of Antiochus' leads us to the conclusion that *Cleon was the acting governor installed at Memphis by the Seleucid forces. The presence of such a governor implies in its turn that Antiochus now looked upon Egypt as conquered territory, and it raises yet again the old question of Antiochus' claim to the Egyptian throne. For a Seleucid monarch to lay claim to the throne of his Ptolemaic neighbour is a bold act, and the scepticism of Bevan[1] seems at first sight justified; even the presence of coins, struck in Egypt in the name of the invader,[2] and the clear statements of Jerome (*In Daniel*, xi. 21 ff.) and of Porphyry (*F.Gr.H.* 260, Fr. 49a) that he was crowned at Memphis *ex more Aegypti regnum accipiens* may possibly be accounted for by the compromise that Antiochus' assumption of royal titles was a piece of theatre, a trait in the character of the Seleucid which was to reappear in his later career. Now it is true that Ḥor consistently writes the name of Antiochus in a cartouche, although he suffers from an embarrassment over the exact spelling; but no two writings of the name and its determinatives are alike,[3] and the evidence of the Raphia Stela shows that no weight may be attached to the use of the cartouche.

Much more telling, however, and unknown when Bevan wrote, is the testimony of Pap. Tebtunis 698, which preserves the heading of an edict addressed by the king to the cleruchs of the Faiyûm (*Tebtunis Papyri*, iii; Lenger, *Corpus*, 32).[4] In this heading the entire province has been renamed the Crocodilopolite nome, doubtless, as van Groningen saw, because of the nationalistic tones of the name Arsinoite. When we add to this evidence the appearance of *Cleon as governor of Memphis, the argument becomes very strong: a regime which installs military governors, and renames whole provinces while striking coins, is surely not indulging in the histrionic. We may also think it likely that the Romans took an extremely serious view of this 'performance', for on the 22 June 168, immediately after the battle of Pydna, the envoy G. Popillius Laenas was already on his way southwards. The declaration of Seleucid overlordship in Egypt meant the unification of the Hellenistic East, and the overthrow of Rome's consistent policy. The action of Antiochus was thus intolerable to the eyes of the Senate.

On 30 July 168 *Eirenaios became convinced of Ḥor's reliability (Text **3**, V° 15), for this is the day given in our texts for the Seleucid evacuation of Pelusium.[5] Ḥor indeed manages to give the impression that this exact day had been prophesied in his dream; this is possible, but it is extremely difficult for a casual observer to extract this from the account in Text **1**, and it may perhaps be that Ḥor is 'reading back' the day into his narrative in order to enhance his own reputation. The details of the Roman ultimatum are familiar from Polybius XXIX, 27, and Ḥor adds the information that Antiochus and his army withdrew from Egypt by sea (*n sgr*, Text **2**, R° 6; V° 12), presumably along the coast to Antioch. Cyprus at the same time reverted to the Ptolemaic kingdom. It is not perhaps a coincidence that the Seleucid withdrawal took place on the final day of an Egyptian month, for Polybius (XXIX, 27, 8) expressly states that a time-limit was set upon the king's actions; advanced knowledge of the Seleucid retreat may well have stimulated Ḥor's interview with *Eirenaios.

[1] *History of Egypt*, 284–5.

[2] Cf. ibid., *House of Seleucus*, ii. 138; Mahaffy, 336; Bouché-Leclerq, ii. 14–15, shares the scepticism.

[3] See note *ff* to Text **2**, V° 8, p. 17 above.

[4] See the review by H. Henne in *Revue des études anciennes* 37 (1935), 29–33, and van Groningen, 'Petite note sur Pap. Tebt. 698', in *Aegyptus* 14 (1934), 120. The importance of the text is well brought out by Préaux, *CdÉ* 11 (1936), 537. The matter is rediscussed by P. M. Fraser, *Ptolemaic Alexandria*, ii, 211, no. 213 where the discrepancy between the proposed reconstruction and the date given by Porphyry is again emphasized.

[5] Text **2**, R° 5–7; V° 11–12; Text **3**, V° 13–14.

*Eirenaios' action was suitably prompt: Ḥor was dispatched to Alexandria to announce his news to the kings (Text **2**, R° 11; V° 3–4). His audience was granted on 29 August; unfortunately the intervening month may as well have been occupied in gaining the audience as in travelling, and we cannot use these figures to estimate the position of the Egyptian forces. Text **2** describes his arrival in the capital with an unknown general named *Tytts* (*Diodotos), and continues with a vivid account of Ḥor's recital of 'the salvation of Alexandria and every man within it' before the Pharaohs in the Alexandrian Serapeum. The retrospective version (Text **3**, V° 18) mentions also that the Queen was present on this occasion. The reason for this great assemblage may well have been one of public thanksgiving for the delivery of Egypt from its peril, a mood confirmed by the later dispatching of Noumenios' embassy to Rome. It is possible here to interpret the syntax of Text **2**, V° 7–9 with its circumstantial *iw·i ꜥš* to mean that when the interview took place at Alexandria, the governor *Cleon was still in Memphis, but this seems unlikely (he probably withdrew with Antiochus), and the other texts lend little support to this view. It is of interest to see, however, that Ḥor's optimism was not shared by all his countrymen: two Serapeum letters (*UPZ* 59 and 60), written on this very day (29 August), refer desperately to 'such times as these'. Presumably economic conditions within Egypt were still stringent, and may long have remained so.

Text **3** introduces at this point two obscure characters, *ꜣmnys* (Ammonius) and *ꜣrkhrts* (*Archelaidas?), who are described respectively as 'within the portal' (*ẖn tꜣ hyty*, perhaps a title used at court), and situated at Memphis. They seem to have made a detailed chronicle of the retreat of Antiochus, but little more can be said of them, and they do not reappear.[1]

The scene in the Alexandrian Serapeum is followed immediately by three journeys (Text **3**, V° 20–3):

Pharaoh (by whom Philometor is almost certainly meant) went to Memphis, doubtless to restore order and loyalty after the withdrawal of *Cleon and the Seleucid forces from the city. The visit to Memphis, home of Egyptian kingship, would have been politically expedient, but it was temporary, as Philometor, the Queen, and the Brother continued to reside in Alexandria.

Nwmnys (Noumenios) went to Rome. This reference, the earliest to Rome in an Egyptian text, confirms the account of the embassy recorded by Polybius (XXX, 16) and Livy (XLV, 13). The kings, in their mood of gratitude after the Seleucid expulsion, sent this ambassador to Rome to offer formal thanks to the Senate, and the envoy chosen had already achieved distinction.[2] Son of Herakleodoros, and prominent in Alexandrian court circles, he had been nominated πρόξενος at Gortyn in the most exalted company,[3] and in such capacity his diplomatic talents must have been developed. Between 171 and 169 he seems to have been *strategos* of the Thebaid (Bengtson, *Strategie*, iii (1952), 226, no. 118) and to have received the rank of ἀρχισωματοφύλαξ (Pap. Grenfell I, 38), while in the spring of 169 he was appointed eponymous priest of the royal cult in Ptolemais, a title which he retained at least until the end of 165. By this time two of his daughters were already devotees of the deified Arsinoe Philopator and Berenice Euergetis at Alexandria. He was by the mid 160s presumably advanced in years, and may soon have died. His son and grandson likewise

[1] See the notes to Text **3**, V° 16–18, p. 29 above. There is a possibility that the account of the retreat was incorporated by Ḥor into the material which he read out before the Pharaohs on 29 August.

[2] For Noumenios in general see Paully–Wissowa, 17 (1937), 1296, no. 6, and A. Bernand, *Inscriptions Grecques de Philae*, i (1969), 194 ff.

[3] Bernand, ibid., and Peremans–van't Dack in *Historia, Zeitschrift für alte Geschichte*, 3 (1954–5), 338–45.

attained considerable rank. The significance of this personage in our present texts is that Ḥor, as often, shows himself to be very well informed. Some of this knowledge may have been common, but it is not difficult to conjecture that a good part of his information came from *Eirenaios.

Tynys (Deinias?)[1] went to Pelusium. Whatever the doubt over the name of this personage, there can be little over the nature of his mission, which would have been to supervise the evacuation of the Seleucid garrison, and to reclaim the vital frontier in the name of the Ptolemies.[2]

Ḥor's importance as a contemporary source extends beyond the events of the sixth Syrian War. Text **4**, although lamentably faded, gives the content of a letter written by *Eirenaios. This letter is said to cover events reported to him by Ḥor of Sebennytos from August 168, through to year 10 (+x), i.e. not later than 163/2. It thus provides a chronicle of much of the joint reign, although there is no doubt that some of its prophecies are long retrospective. The 'eldest son of Pharaoh' is now said to be born,[3] and his dominion over Cyprus, which took place in the late 150s, forecast. The retreat of Antiochus is recalled, and a voyage by Pharaoh to 'the isle of the sea', again probably Cyprus, is described. This voyage may be that of Philometor's appeal to Rome against his brother, which took place during the winter of 164/3 (Bevan, 291), and which was instrumental in putting an end to the joint reign. A final, very obscure, statement may mean that a disaster had befallen the auspicious son; if death is meant, this overtook Eupator early in 150, and we would have clear proof that our text was written long after the events it seems to foretell, but the text is not such as to encourage certainty.

Equally mysterious is the event recorded in Text **7**. The purpose of this text was to describe the abuses of the ibis-cult, and to alert the attention of Philometor and his Queen to the neglect of the shrines. The date may therefore fall in the late 150s, during the drafting of Ḥor's great petition, but there is no certain proof of this. He adds in the introduction (Text **7**, 5) that the might of Pharaoh and the readiness of his army have saved the royal throne, upon which *Tmpn* in *Tbny* sat. The possibilities that *Tmpn* may represent the name *Demophon, and that *Tbny* may be Daphnae, are discussed *ad locum*; whatever the likelihood of these identifications, it would seem that Ḥor is triumphantly relating the suppression of an otherwise unknown attempt on the king's throne. The role of another person, *ꜣḳtryn*, is quite obscure. The latter years of Philometor's rule, though much less stormy than the joint reign, were not without their troubles (cf. the intrigue of Archias in Cyprus, Polybius XXXIII, 3, and the attempt by Euergetes to seize the island in 154, the following year). Above all, the growing involvement of the king in Syrian affairs may have given many opportunities to dissidents, among them perhaps *Tmpn*, but it is unwise to speculate further.

In one more respect does Ḥor help to confirm our knowledge. The character of Philometor is sketched for us in Polybius XXXIX, 7. Ḥor adds to this picture. Although we must remember that he is for ever anxious to secure the goodwill of the supreme authority, he places emphasis, both in Text **3**, where Philometor's concessions to the ibis-shrine at Saqqâra are described, and in Text **2**, R° 13–14 upon the piety and magnanimity of his sovereign.[4] This emphasis is surely

[1] See note to translation, Text **3**, V° 22.

[2] For the importance of the city see note *k* to Text **3**, V° 14, p. 28 above.

[3] Text **4**, R° 5; note that the original dream, as described in Text **1**, prophesies that *five* generations of Philometor's heirs shall ascend the throne, and five is precisely the number of Philometor's predecessors. The dynastic excitement of Philometor's earlier years is shown by his reorganization of the earlier cults upon his marriage (Oates, *Études de Papyrologie*, 9 (1964), 71–2).

[4] Cf. also the decree of the Cretans in honour of the same quality, *OGIS* 116; in corroboration P. M. Fraser, *Ptolemaic Alexandria*, ii. 212, n. 217. That the reign of Philometor in other respects provided great stimulus to the production of

genuine, even if it is expedient, and it helps us to enrich our picture of Philometor, most admirable of the Ptolemies.

§ 3 : Dreams and oracles

We have until this point been following Ḥor of Sebennytos along rational and well-ordered paths, but we must now turn away into a dimmer region. To distinguish between rational and irrational, between the world of the prosaic and that of the gods, is not the ancient manner, and in nearly all our texts personal narrative, historical allusions, and the most recondite dreams and visions mingle without comment or distinction.

Vocatus atque invocatus deus aderit; but the difference between sought and unsought is a fundamental one. The unsought omen, that sudden admonition of the divine, plays an apparently lesser part in Egyptian texts than in those of other cultures, but there are still clear signs of it in our sources; even Prince Osorkon, by affirming the absence of an eclipse before catastrophe, reveals an implicit belief in such phenomena,[1] and several royal dreams, such as the Sphinx Stela of Tuthmosis IV, or the vision of Merneptaḥ, show the same belief in action.[2]

Of more interest to the present study is the solicited omen, a deliberate inquiry after divine will. This form of omen is in essence nothing more than a question, addressed to a god rather than a human agency, and inasmuch as it is a question, we may apply to it the distinction made by Gardiner[3] between questions for *corroboration*, and those for *specification*. The first type, which requires for answer either 'yes' or 'no', is the form of the New Kingdom oracle, for the mechanism involved allows the god only to agree (*hnn*) or to decline (*nˁi n-ḥꜣ*).[4] The common category of 'oracular questions' are always inquiries of this sort;[5] in other words, they presuppose that the questioner knows the nature of the problem before him. The second type of question makes no such assumption, for it requires from the god more information, both about the nature of the difficulty, and about its possible solution. The clearest example of this is incubation, the habit of consulting the god in moments of crisis to obtain his advice through a dream. The belief that dreams are the agents of divine premonition is of some antiquity in Egypt,[6] but there is no reason to suppose that such dreams were deliberately provoked; the sought dream appears in fact only in the later periods of Egyptian history. This may partly be due to the inadequacy of early material, but it is difficult to resist the suspicion that the appearance of incubation and of dream-invocation does correspond to a clear change in Egyptian thought, one in which the human mind becomes increasingly conscious of fate, of its own shortcomings, of hostile forces beyond its control, and begins to reach towards the magic and other means necessary to circumvent them.[7]

oracular works with an Egyptian flavour is shown by the fact that it was probably at this time that the astrological manual of Nechepso and Petosiris was compiled (Fraser, op. cit. i. 437). Several of the events of Texts **1–4,** such as the hostility of Egypt and Syria, and the journey of Pharaoh to Cyprus, seem to be reflected in this work, a typical product of the generation of Ḥor and of Ptolemy the κάτοχος.

[1] Caminos, *Chronicle of Prince Osorkon* (Rome, 1958), 88–9. A fuller treatment is found in Parker, *A Vienna Demotic Papyrus on Eclipse- and Lunar-Omina* (Providence, 1959). Although this text is undoubtedly transcribed from a Near-Eastern original, it would surely not have been transcribed had it not corresponded in some degree to Egyptian thinking.

[2] A convenient collection of such dream-texts (by Sauneron) will be found in *Les songes et leur interprétation* (*Sources Orientales*, ii, Paris, 1959), 19 ff.

[3] Cf. *Eg. Gr.* § 490.

[4] Černý in Parker, *A Saite Oracle Papyrus*, 44–5. On the public appearances of gods in shrines at festival times, see W. Barta, *MDAIK* 23 (1968), 75 ff.

[5] Černý, op. cit., 46 ff.

[6] e.g. Merikarēˁ (Pap. Petersburg 116A), R° 136–7; Volten, *Traumdeutung*, 40–1.

[7] One is very conscious, to quote but a single example, of the difference in mentality between the *sbꜣyt* of the Old Kingdom, as Ptaḥḥotep and Kagemni, and the later Amenemōpe and Papyrus Insinger.

The sacred animal, with its clear resemblances to man, yet essentially divorced from his experiences, was the natural medium for the solicited omen, at least in Egypt with its tradition of animal manifestations of the divine. It is hardly surprising, therefore, that a man such as Ḥor of Sebennytos, trained as a priest in the cult of that most polymorphous deity, Isis, and employed in the sanctuary of that most teeming of sacred birds, should be acutely conscious of the visitations of gods. In his case, too, we can hardly doubt that personal traits disposed him towards an interest in such matters,[1] matters which he is at pains to record.

That Ḥor practised incubation is clear from Text **13**, where he describes himself as making supplications before the house of rest of the Ibis; for two days he appeals to Osorapis and to Osormnevis, and to the gods of their respective resting-places, and on the third (10 March 155), he receives a dream. Neither the reason for his request nor the interpretation of his dream is given, but it is clear that the incident was deliberately provoked. It is possible that the short addresses to Isis of Text **10** are intended to conjure dreams, and a similar, but longer dream-invocation is seen in Text **18**, written some fifteen years before Text **13**, where a whole range of divinities and demons, notably creatures of the Underworld (*Dwꜣt*) and forms of Raʿ-Horus, are conjured to 'appear in a dream'. That this text too is set in Memphis seems extremely likely, judging from the names of gods and of localities which it contains. Similar dream-invocations from a much later date are known from the London/Leiden Magical Papyrus, and the similarities, both in phraseology and in the proposed result, are striking.[2] From a similar date there survives a bilingual text with additional Coptic glosses, Pap. BM. 10588, with a similar appeal to the god Ḥarthoth.[3] Even the Greek magical texts of the same period contain similar material.[4] It is all the more interesting, therefore, that the dream-apparition recorded in Text **13**, 8–12 should bear a certain similarity to the figure to be conjured by the formula in London/Leiden IV, 7. That such a tradition should last for more than four centuries is in itself remarkable, and it raises difficult questions. Is one to assume that Ḥor himself was so influenced by a convention that he found himself dreaming according to a fixed pattern, or is it better to explain the resemblance in our two accounts as a coincidence, shaped only by the vague assemblage of myths, iconographies, and symbols which were shared by all Egyptians? A preliminary account such as this can do little but point out such problems as they arise, and leave their resolution to later works; the present writer can admit only to an inclination in favour of the second answer, while confessing his inability to prove it.

The other dream texts of Ḥor tell us little about their circumstances: Text **8**, we are told, is dated to a festival of Thoth, in all probability that of the twelfth day of the month which bears his name.[5] The great dream of Text **9**, with its remarkable interlocution between dreamer and goddess, is apparently ascribed to a festival of Isis. This clear attempt

[1] That personal reactions to dreams and omens could vary considerably is *a priori* likely, and is shown by the behaviour of Ptolemaios, in contrast to the angry scepticism of his brother, cf. *UPZ* 12 and 13, although the attitude of Apollonios was perhaps still unformed. Similar 'dreamers' seem to include Zoïlos in the Zeno papyri, the writer of Pap. Oxy. 1381, and, in all probability, Nectanebo II and the Meroitic Ḥarsiōtef.

[2] R° V and V° XVII contain clear references to the conjuring of dreams, V° XXIV possibly so. The editors, Griffith and Thompson, dated the papyrus by its hand to the third century A.D. The origins of such texts are uncertain, but they may lie far back in Egypt's past; cf. the similar invocation of a ghost in *Khensemḥab* (Gardiner, *Late-Egn. Stories*, 89 ff.).

[3] Bell, Nock, Thompson, *Magical Texts from a Bilingual Papyrus in the British Museum* (London, 1933), 7–8, R°, V.

[4] Cf. Nock, *JEA* 15 (1929), 219 ff. Note especially Greek Pap. Leiden I, 384 (Lexa, *La Magie dans l'Égypte antique*, i. 111 ff.).

[5] Cf. Text **3**, R° 13.

to associate both texts with auspicious occasions should alert us to the possibility that here too we are dealing with cases of incubation, although the texts at no point make this explicit. One thing which seems clear, however, is that both ostraca have undergone considerable recension (conscious or unconscious): the elaborate syntax, the confident description, and the parallelisms of the closing sections of both texts, show us material which has already matured in the thoughts of the writer. The events precipitated by these dreams, namely Ḥor's journey to Memphis and devotion to the ibis-cult, were of such importance in his life that it is scarcely surprising that these clear signs of divine guidance should have been constantly elaborated, either mentally or in the form of numerous written versions. Whatever this previous history (and in the case of the dream narrated in Text **1** this may well have been considerable), such dream accounts differ from the sort of abbreviated and unmethodical writings shown in Pap. Bologna 3171 and 3173, or in several of the more unsystematic demotic texts from the same archive published by Wilcken.[1] The latter type represents jottings, often elliptical and generally unformed, in several cases obviously written in haste. A plausible explanation of these balder dream accounts is that they represent attempts to preserve the memory of dreams to be presented to a dream-interpreter,[2] or at least to record them until they can be accommodated into a fuller narrative. It is of course impossible to be certain from such scanty records whether the original dreams were spontaneous, or whether they were the result of incubation, but the absence of a clear reference to the latter may suggest that some at least are the records of chance experience. In our present archive two documents, Texts **11** and **14**, resemble these casual jottings, and the latter text in particular seems stark and unformed; nevertheless we cannot be sure of the reasons for this, and our explanation—that the text represents an attempt to record a fresh dream, with preliminary interpretations of some of its details—remains a conjecture.

Further evidence for the practice of incubation seems to be contained in Text **12**. Reasons have been given above for assigning the events of this ostracon to the second Ḥor, the Memphite petition-writer, but this makes little difference to the present question. The secretary, while on duty at a locality in the Delta, made certain inquiries on behalf of a man named Pḥentamūn. On 12 December 170, while trying to ascertain the fortune of this man and of a temple with which he seems to have been associated, the writer is rewarded with a dream (Text **12**, R° 4–5); although not stated as an act of incubation, the event is difficult to explain as a coincidence, and it is entirely consistent with the drift of our ostraca that such a method should be employed on behalf of a third person. In all probability both Ḥor of Sebennytos and his Memphite namesake had by 170 acquired considerable reputations as interpreters of the future, and it is not difficult to believe that 'commissions' would be entrusted to them. One is reminded of the communications of dreams sent to Ptolemaios by his friend Nekthonbes (*UPZ*, no. 79), although there is no evidence that the latter was a professional divine, or that he had used incubation to obtain his visions.[3]

Whether the dreams recorded by Ḥor were spontaneous or provoked, we can gain much information from their contents. Several deities appear in our dream-accounts; with the exception of the abstruse catalogue of Text **18**, these are in general familiar to us. Thoth, the god of Ḥor's adopted home, figures prominently in

[1] Note, for example, those translated in *UPZ* i. 350–1, and compare the associated Greek texts (nos. 78, 79) where similar material has been 'worked up' into epistolary form.

[2] For this category of persons, cf. Wilcken, *UPZ*, 13 and n. 4.

[3] Op. cit., p. 364.

Texts **1** and **12**, and notably in the dreams recorded in Text **8**. Isis, goddess of his earlier devotion, occupies a leading place in **1**, **9**, the verso of **11**, and the appeals of **10**. Harpocrates, a rarer divinity in our texts, occurs in the recto of **9**, while Text **13** gives a prayer to the deified bulls, Osorapis and Osormnevis. At the end of Text **8**, Ḥor is told to go before three gods of the Memphite necropolis, Osiris, Isis, and Thoth. In most of these cases Ḥor is addressing himself consistently to the major powers of the Serapeum where he lives and writes.

More interesting is the information to be gained upon the emotions and mentality of the author. Some account of this has already been given in the Preliminary Remarks to Text **8**, where we have seen the insecurity which underlies the first dream of this ostracon. A similar sense of undergoing interrogation appears in the recto of Text **11**, where another unnamed figure of authority orders him to bring a document. A more confident note is heard in the remarkable verso of Text **9**, where Ḥor is seen questioning the judgement of Isis. The goddess tells him that he is to be established in Memphis for ever, and to this he replies (Text **9**, V° 7), 'Does a man exist for ever?' However, this sounds like a proverb, or an observation rather than a retort, and it remains true that the general tone of our dreams is one of restlessness and anxiety. It is this which perhaps explains their insistence upon the proper maintenance of Ḥor. Reference is made in Text **8**, R° 14 to 'benefits' (*mdt-nfrt*) which are divinely granted to him. These benefits are explained obliquely in the prayers of thanksgiving which occupy the verso, and explicitly in the promise of Text **10**, R° 14, where two are said to be offered: maintenance (*ẖrt*) throughout life, and burial (*ḳrst*) after death. The first is specified in Texts **10**, **11**, and **14**; the second, more fully, in **8**, **9**, **10**, and possibly in **14**, under the euphemism *wḏꜣ* 'salvation'.[1] These essential supports are guaranteed first by Isis (Text **10**), and later by Thoth (Text **8**), as Ḥor's allegiance moves from the one to the other. An interesting observation is that food and burial, ταφὴ καὶ τροφή, are the usual services performed for a sacred animal by his human attendants, and the expression seems to be a usual one for the maintenance of any agent, animal or human, of the divine.

The preternatural activities of the gods are not confined to dreams. Frequent reference is made to the 'utterances' (*mdt* or *ẖt-mdt*) of various divinities, utterances which seem to be binding upon their devotees. Some of these statements do seem to have been administered through dreams, as in Text **23**, V° 16, where reference is made to *nꜣ (i͗·)ḏd-w pꜣ ntr ꜥꜣ Ḏḥwty ẖt rswt*, 'the matters which the great god Thoth spoke through a dream', a phrase which corresponds to τὰ ῥηθέντα [μοι διὰ] ὀνείρου of Greek Text **B**.[2] Other statements, however, equally clearly have nothing to do with dreaming. In Text **33**, three 'utterances' (*ẖt-mdt*) are mentioned which look very much like the resolutions of a committee-meeting. We are told (l. 2) that the three matters referred to were ones in which the Ibis had been found deficient, and although the subsequent resolutions are introduced as judgements of Osorapis, or at least of one of his officers, the following paragraphs look very much like the deliberations of a human agency. Such 'utterances' are therefore unlikely to be truly oracular. Other examples of such administrative precepts (which were perhaps ascribed to divine will, without regard to their origin) occur throughout the texts devoted to the management of the ibis-cult (**19**, **21–9**, and **33**).

More important for the present chapter are

[1] Cf. the metaphor in Pap. NYHS 373a, 2; Reich, *Mizraim* 1 (1933), 57–8.

[2] A slightly similar use of a general word specifically to refer to a dream occurs perhaps in Isaiah, 13:1: 'the oracle (*massâ'*) of Babylon which Isaiah son of Amoz saw'. The word used seems literally to mean 'elevation of the voice', and thus bears a resemblance to the Egyptian term.

the cases of a divine instruction being addressed to an individual. Texts **16** and **17** refer to an oracle, delivered apparently by Thoth, which dealt with 'the great chapels in which the Ibis is born among the nomes and the foremost(?) chapels which are their fields and their shrine' (Text **16,** R° 9–11). This utterance of the god seems to be mentioned again in Text **22,** R° 2, where its meaning is communicated to the temple authorities. Texts **16** and **17** (with **17A**) tell us more about the history of this oracle. It was apparently enigmatic, and the writer, the Memphite Ḥor, was reduced to placing the matter before four 'magicians' (*ḥr-tb*) to obtain its interpretation (Texts **16,** R° 8–9; **17A,** 3–7). Not one of the four was able to do this, until the magician of Imḥōtep, whose shrine lay elsewhere in the necropolis,[1] proffered an explanation (Text **17A,** 7–8). It is unfortunate that neither text gives details of the oracle or its interpretation, but the fact that interpretation was necessary suggests strongly that the utterance was one from the god (through dream or ecstatic or some other medium unknown to us) and was not the mere resolution of his human servants.

In another text (**31A** and **B**) the intentions of the god are made much clearer. Thoth commands, 'Enquire after the wife of Sarapion; bring her before me'. The reasons for this request are not stated, nor is the medium of its delivery. The clarity of the statement suggests that perhaps a straightforward utterance was given through a priest of the god, but the principal intention of the writer is to inform Sarapion of these events, and he has either omitted details irrelevant to this purpose, or recorded them in the portion now lost to us. It must be emphasized that the interest of our texts, in spite of the clear predilection of their authors for such happenings, is not directed to dreams and oracles *per se*, but only to those which add support to their petitions; all else is subordinated to this end.

An extended use of divine visitations, well attested from the Ptolemaic period (at least in Greek sources), is that found in the healing of the sick. Our present documents give very welcome confirmation in demotic that such practices were observed at North Saqqâra. In Text **28,** 15–16 we are told that 'her(?) mistress Isis made a remedy (*pẖrt*) for the Queen'. The text is unfortunately too faint for the details of this remedy to be known, but it seems undeniable that we are dealing with a case either of instructions given through a dream or similar medium, or of the composition of a medical recipe under divine auspices.[2] A further indication of the use of the Saqqâra cults for medical purposes occurs in Text **32,** 2 ff. Although the relation of this interesting text (above all, of the group read as *nꜣ ḥtrw*, 'the twins') to the main archive is debatable, the content of the ostracon is still relevant to the present theme. We are told that an unknown man 'despised the remedies' (*sḥwr·f nꜣ pẖrt*). A judgement of Thoth follows. It is possible to interpret this text to mean that a sick man, distrustful of medical recipes offered to him, turned instead to the ministrations of the god. Unfortunately the sherd is incomplete, and other explanations are also acceptable, but it seems reasonable to conclude that the context is a medical one, and that the intervention of the god is relevant in some way. It remains to note that the question of healing through incubation falls between the two notions, specification and corroboration, discussed above. It is clear that the petitioner knows the nature of the problem to be solved, yet he requires further steps to be taken, steps which he may not be able to take himself. The truth seems to be that the sufferer from disease is not posing a question to the god, but placing himself into the god's hands, believ-

[1] See topographical commentary below.

[2] Recipes were composed in the same way in the Greek world, under the direction of Aesculapius, cf. Edelstein, *Asclepius*, ii (1945), 152–4 ff.

ing that the answer to his distress lies beyond his own capacities.

Much has already been made of the question of interpretation. The archive of Ptolemy the *katochos*, in its edition by Wilcken, has already told us something of the ways in which meaning could be extracted from the oracles of the gods. We know that there existed at the Serapeum professional interpreters of dreams (ἐνυπνιοκριταί), who offered this service to all comers. Some of these experts seem to have been attached to the personnel of the main temples (at least that of Osorapis), others to have acted in a freelance capacity.[1] It is likely that the functionaries who appear in Texts **16** and **17A** as *ḥr-tbw* 'magicians' are the demotic equivalents of Wilcken's ἐνυπνιοκριταί. Four of them are mentioned, although it is not stated whether they were temple employees or private practitioners, but a fifth is clearly said to be 'the magician of Imḥōtep, son of Ptaḥ, to whom appeal is made throughout the two lands because of his magic(?)-making' (Text **17A,** 8–10). The latter is presumably the official dream- or oracle-interpreter of the Asclepieion, and it is therefore possible that the other magicians named stood in the same capacity at other shrines. It looks at first sight as if there was competition between cults for the interpretation of oracles, and for the prestige associated with success, but this seems unlikely as a regular feature of the Serapeum. Texts **16** and **17A** are tendentious documents, designed to shed bad light upon those 'who have abandoned the path', and the writer is more concerned to point out the censure of the god than merely to provide an advertisement for the magician of Imḥōtep. It is noticeable that he does not try to enhance the prestige of the latter by naming the unsuccessful competitors, and his intention seems to be to show the importance of the oracle, rather than to belittle its would-be interpreters.

It is not only magicians who take it upon themselves to elucidate the wishes of the gods. In Text **9** the goddess Isis herself makes clear her own words (V° 7 ff.), while in Text **15** explanations of an enigmatic utterance are given by 'Takhrati, the wife of *Tysḳrts*, and her sister' (R° 5–6). There is no reason to suppose that these two women were any other than private persons offering their own opinions on a matter of concern, and the same feature is seen readily in the letters of Ptolemy, who at least on one occasion sees fit to give interpretations of his own dreams.[2] It is hardly surprising, therefore, that Ḥor, with his undoubted knowledge of such matters (indeed his reputation would probably have been enough to make him widely consulted as a dream-interpreter), should attempt such explanations by himself. The interest here is that he hardly ever does so; in Text **1,** 3–4, we see him deliberately journeying to Heliopolis to gain instruction from a priest, again of the god Imḥōtep. Indeed, with the exception of the small fragment **57,** which is open to considerable doubt, there is only one text in which an interpretation is offered without comment. This occurs in Text **14,** V° 8, after words of such utter obscurity that an interpretation is unavoidable. Even here, there is no certainty that the interpretation is that of Ḥor himself, although such a possibility is very likely. We are left with a distinct impression of reticence in these matters; Ḥor is more concerned to demonstrate his veracity than to indulge in displays of his own expertise.

[1] *UPZ* i. 48–9. The stela of the Cretan dream-interpreter, probably a freelance agent, has been republished in Roeder, *Kulte und Orakel im alten Ägypten* (1959), 192–4 and pl. 14. The position of the *ḥr-tb* is so natural in Egyptian texts that considerable doubt applies to Wilcken's judgement (ibid. 49) that dream-interpretation is a creation of the Hellenistic world. One suspects that behind Ḥor and the *ḥr-tb* of Imḥōtep lies a very long native tradition, a tradition of which the Greek 'dream-interpreter' is merely a translation. For a *ḥr-tb* attached to the ibis-cult, cf. Text **23,** R° 9.

[2] *UPZ* 78, 39 ff.

There remains one question. In the Greek texts at the beginning of this volume, Ḥor describes himself as a παστοφόρος of Isis (**C**, 1; **E**, 5). This title does not appear in the demotic documents, and pastophoroi (*wnw*) play only a minor part in our archive, in Texts **19–23** where they are the recipients of a financial stipulation. The reasons for this reticence are unclear, and will probably remain so as long as our ignorance of the nature of this title persists. A good treatment of the problem is to be found in Bataille, *Les Memnonia* (Cairo, 1952), 144 ff. The functions of these priests are specified in the Gnomon of the Idios Logos: they may not practise officially (χρηματίζειν) as priests (§ 82), nor appear as such in processions, nor lay claim to their functions (§ 94), but they are free to accept private commissions (ἰδιωτικαὶ τάξεις). This last privilege is barred to regular priests, and some of the commissions take the form of choachyte-duties (op. cit. 147). The conclusion seems to be that pastophoroi are an inferior grade of priest, whose activities seem directed, not to the care and worship of the god, but to the public at large. A rather similar conclusion is reached by Reymond (*Cd'É* 28 (1953), 53 ff.) as well as by Dunand (*Cd'É* 44 (1969), 306 ff.); their duties are here said to be the supervision of the lay members of the temple staff. An unpublished demotic text, Pap. BM. 10237,[1] features a lector-priest 'laying down a dream (*iw·f wꜣḥ wꜥt rswt*) before a pastophoros'. It may be possible to see in the pastophoros a priest whose duties lay among the general population (note that at every point where they occur in our present texts, they are said to belong to the 'forecourt', the most public part, of the temple of Ptaḥ). Among these duties would be included the interpretation of dreams. If this is correct, then the early training of Ḥor may well have included the study of dreams and oracles, possibly even the learning of dream-books such as Pap. Carlsberg XIII and XIV, verso.[2] Such duties, together with the title of pastophoros, may have been abandoned after his migration to Saqqâra. This may explain the reluctance of our texts to interpret dreams directly, but the explanation is one offered with great reserve. We should like to know more; but of how much in Egyptology can this be said! The present study can be no more than an outline, and it is clear that whoever wishes to investigate further the complexities of the Egyptian oracle must now take into account not only the utterances of Pap. Rylands IX, the Demotic Chronicle, Pap. Dodgson, or the Oracle of the Potter, but also the writings of Ḥor of Sebennytos.

§ 4: The administration of the Ibis-cult

Of all the many sacred animals of Egypt, none was worshipped in greater profusion than the ibis. Temples to maintain the cult of this bird, land to provide its sustenance, and subterranean galleries to house its mummified remains were common in the provinces of Egypt. Text **16** (R° 9–11) reminds us of the many chapels dedicated to the Ibis, and to his patron god Thoth, which were scattered throughout the nomes of the Two Lands. Anyone surveying the remains of known ibis-cults at Hermopolis (Tûna el-Gebel), Thebes, Abydos, Baḥrîya Oasis, and the Delta Hermopolis (Baqlîya) will understand ruefully why the sacred ibis, with its characteristic black head and tail-feathers and shining white body, is now extinct in Egypt.[3] To this considerable, and by no means complete list, our texts add the information that an ibis-chapel stood at Temenēsi in the Sebennytic nome (Text **26**,

[1] To be edited, it is hoped, by the present writer.

[2] Volten, *Demotische Traumdeutung* (Copenhagen, 1942), *passim*.

[3] This list is of course not exhaustive, and it is quite likely that any town known to the Greeks as Hermopolis possessed such institutions. For Thebes, cf. PM ii. 609; for Abydos, inside the Shûnet el-Zebîb, op. cit. v. 53; for Baḥrîya, Fakhry, *Baḥria Oasis*, ii, Ch. 4; for Baqlîya, PM iv. 39–40, although no such cemeteries are mentioned, and Tûna el-Gebel, op. cit. iv. 169 ff.

R° *passim*).[1] The existence of such a cult even in an obscure place must increase the probability of other similar institutions coming to light elsewhere in the future; the references to the secretary's visit to *Pr-pꜣy·f-ỉry*, a locality perhaps near Alexandria (Text **12**, R° 2 is the fullest statement) may imply that a similar cult flourished in this place as well.

It is natural, however, that the main part of our texts should concentrate on the area of North Saqqâra where Ḥor eventually made his home. It is clear from many passages that at Saqqâra lay an extensive complex of buildings devoted to the worship and maintenance of the Ibis, and its associate, the Hawk.[2] The reasons for this combination, paralleled at Thebes and in other centres of ibis worship, are clear in their outline; the Ibis, sacred bird of the moon and of night, finds its natural counterpart in the Hawk, with its associations of sun and daylight, and this link is so close that from the Roman period, if not earlier, we even encounter the composite deity Ḥar-thoth. The discoveries of the Egypt Exploration Society have confirmed the evidence of our texts, and cleared both hawk- and ibis-galleries within its concession.[3] For clues to the theological status of these birds, and of the other animal cults of the neighbourhood, we must naturally turn to the inscriptions and graffiti of the galleries themselves. The writings of Ḥor, largely secular in intent, are generally silent on such matters. The fullest statements occur at the beginnings of two administrative texts. Text **19**, R° 5 names 'the Ibis, the soul (*by*) of Thoth, the three times great', and (l. 6) 'the Hawk, the soul of Ptaḥ, the soul of Apis, the soul of Prēʿ(?), the soul of Shu, the soul of Tefnut, the soul of Geb, the soul of Osiris, the soul of Isis, the soul of Nephthys, the great gods of Egypt'. Here the Ibis is clearly described as an extension or emanation of Thoth, while the Hawk is the essence not only of the principal gods of Memphis, but of most of the Heliopolitan ennead as well. A similar picture comes from Text **25**, 3, where we find 'the Hawk, the soul of Osiris, Horus, and Isis; the Ibis, the soul of Thoth, twice great'. Such is the opinion of Ḥor of Sebennytos upon the nature of these sacred birds.

We are understandably told more about the organization of the shrine. Ḥor in general confines his remarks to the cult of the Ibis, but passages such as the two quoted above, and phrases such as 'the servants of the Ibis and the servants of the Hawk' (Text **19**, R° 12, 19–20; Text **21**, V° 1–2, Text **22**, V° 4–5) make it clear that both cults were administered jointly, and that a remark concerning the cult of the Ibis will serve, *mutatis mutandis*, for that of his solar companion.

The cult of these birds lay in the area of the necropolis known as Pi-waʿb-nēbes[4] 'Abaton of her Lord', a place discussed in the topographical section below. Here all that needs to be said is that *a priori* one would expect this area to lie near the complex of galleries explored and cleared during the recent excavations. The cult buildings of Thoth, known collectively as *Pr-Ḏḥwty*, 'House of Thoth', lay in the same area, and consisted, according to Text **3**, R° 15, of a temple (*ḥt-ntr*) and an 'upper chapel' (*gꜣt ḥrt*), in which the donations made by Philometor to the shrine were 'established in writing before every man on earth', or at least those who had access to the sacred area. It is tempting, though unproven, to identify this 'upper chapel' with the rough stone shrine situated at the mouth of the southern ibis-galleries, excavated by Emery in the season of 1965/6.[5] There are nevertheless other buildings, mainly of mud brick, in the same area which may also merit this description,

[1] It is true that the precise words are lost; but the reference to a chapel, to the food of the ibises, and the clear evidence of a complex administration leave little doubt upon this point.

[2] See the index under *pꜣ hb*, *pꜣ bik* for detailed references.

[3] Preliminary Reports in *JEA* from 51 (1965) onwards.

[4] See index for references.

[5] *JEA* 52 (1966), 3 ff.

and the question is better left open. The same is also true of the other cult-buildings named in our texts. The commonest mention is of a building termed *ꜥḥyt n ms* 'birth-chapel' (Text **15**, V° 6), which is clearly a focal point of the cult. Text **33** is concerned entirely with its upkeep, and l. 2 of this ostracon adds the information that it lay 'within the lake of Pharaoh'. The preposition is probably not to be taken literally, unless in the sense that the chapel stood on an island in the lake, but whatever the exact meaning, it is clear that we should locate the building somewhere in the area of a lake. The 'pool of Abusîr', now dry, but which contained water into living memory, would be an obvious candidate for the 'lake of Pharaoh', the more so now as a northern group of ibis-galleries, excavated in Emery's final season (1970/71), faces this lake directly, and a path was traced running from these galleries towards the lake-bed.[1] At first sight, it would seem that an *ꜥḥyt n ms* resembled the *mammisi* of a Ptolemaic temple, but this theory has little to commend it. It is much more likely that it was a building, or group of buildings, intended for the incubation of eggs and the rearing of young birds. Quantities of eggs were found in the excavation of the cult-buildings, and it seems likely that the breeding of ibises (and possibly hawks, if in smaller numbers) was a necessary part of the cult. Unfortunately it is difficult to estimate the number of ibises maintained at Saqqâra at any one time; Text **8**, R° 18 seems to give the number sixty thousand, but this is a dream-text, and caution must be exercised. Nevertheless, it is difficult to estimate the number of ibises alone buried at North Saqqâra at under four million, and if four centuries are allotted for their accumulation, we are still forced to admit a burial rate of ten thousand birds a year. The number in Text **8** may therefore be reliable, or even conservative; and the point remains that it is the only number that we have.

Another chapel is mentioned, although without embellishment, in Text **15**, V° 5, where an unknown person, possibly Ḥor, is addressed as follows: 'You have sworn (an oath) before the chapel of the letter. I shall cause you to proceed(?) [·····] to the chapel of birth.' This 'chapel of the letter' (*ꜥḥyt n šꜥt*) may have been a record office, where the documents of the ibis-cult were housed, but it does not appear elsewhere in our texts, and we know nothing more about it.

A further feature of the cult is revealed to us in Text **33**, 3–4, where a resolution is passed. 'The food (-ration) of Pharaoh, [namely] one loaf of provisions, scatter it upon the *sḫn* before the Ibis'. The word *sḫn* is familiar from its use as a financial term for 'banking-house', but it is probable here that an original meaning 'table' (as in the Greek τράπεζα) has been preserved to us. This table, or bench, would seem to be an eating-place; l. 6 of the same text lays down that 'the men who perform labour shall eat rations upon the table before the Ibis'. In the latter case, and possibly the former too, 'the Ibis' may have been a cult-image, in which case we should locate the 'table' in a chapel or similar building devoted to the worship of the divine bird.

A more puzzling feature occurs in several texts. Text **15**, V° 4 mentions 'the dam belonging to ·····' (*pꜣ tny n-s* [ ]), in a context concerned with buildings of the ibis-cult. Another dam or dyke appears in Text **11**, V° 2 as the scene for an assembly of the gods of the north land. Here it is qualified as the 'southern dyke', and a similar name, the 'great dyke' (*pꜣ tny ꜥꜣ*) is seen in Text **24A**, 5. All these contexts refer to Memphis, but it is only the first which suggests that the dyke may be linked with the

[1] Preliminary report for this season, *JEA* 57 (1971). For the position of the Pool of Abusîr, and a discussion of the canal Φχῆτ, see Reich, *Mizraim*, 1 (1933), 24 ff. and pl. I. See further, Commentary § 5, p. 150 below.

cult of the Ibis.[1] The feature may therefore be a geographical one, unconnected with any specific deity, and chosen simply for its prominence.

Surer ground is reached with 'the courtyard of the Ibis and the Hawk' (*pꜣ inḥy ḥr pꜣ hb pꜣ bik*), which is described most fully in Text **21,** V° 9. The excavation of this courtyard is mentioned briefly in Texts **19,** R° 11 and **23,** V° 11, and a courtyard with walls of mud brick, apparently sunk below the surface of the surrounding sand, was cleared by Emery during the season of 1969/70.[2] The debris which filled this courtyard contained considerable quantities of bird's eggs, some loose, others stored in large jars. Here for once an identification between excavations and texts seems likely. It is a pity that our ostraca tell us so little of the relative positions of these cult-buildings, but this information is not the chief concern of our writer, and we must rest content.

We are told something of the maintenance of the sacred hawks and ibises. The phrase *tꜣ ẖrt* (*n nꜣ hbw*) is familiar from many documents, and is generally translated 'feeding-place (a term corresponding to the Greek τροφή) of the ibises'.[3] The reference is clearly to plots of land set aside for the upkeep of the birds, and administered by the sanctuaries although frequently leased to cultivators. However, the use of the expression in our own texts is evidently a wider one; the agent of Text **15,** V° 4 is told to 'place his *ẖrt* of the Ibis upon the dyke [· · · · ·]'. The common use of the word *ẖrt* alone as the complement to *ḳrst* 'burial' (both with reference to the birds, and to a human being), and finally the sentence in Text **8,** R° 18 'bring your clover, this *ẖrt* of the 60,000 ibises' leave little doubt that the word refers simply to the food required to nourish the birds. That this fodder consisted partly of clover is suggested by Text **8,** even though this is a dream-account, and it is very likely that vegetable produce of this sort was the main crop of the feeding-places, many of which seem to have been border plots of arable land.[4]

Text **33,** 3 introduces us to a second kind of *ẖrt*, 'the food of Pharaoh'. This is said to consist of one loaf (*ʿḳ*), which is at first spread upon the table before the Ibis, or his cult-image. In the following lines we find the labourers also eating before the Ibis, and it may be that the 'food of Pharaoh' was a ration, nominally offered to the god, which was destined for consumption by his servants: the common Egyptian practice of reversion (*wḏb*) of offerings. Whether this *ẖrt* was intended for the birds, or for their human keepers, the epithet 'of Pharaoh' indicates that, like the *syntaxis* to be described below, it was a royal subvention, intended as financial aid for the cult.

At the end of the life of a sacred ibis came mummification and burial. Many questions raise themselves at this point. Was each bird allowed to die naturally, or was it put to death in some way? Was this done at the request of one of the many pilgrims who we know were attracted to the site, or did the visitor merely pay for an embalmment which had already taken place? Our ostraca do not help much with these questions, and the answers must await a full review of the evidence. On the burial itself, however, they have more to say. Frequent reference is made to the 'houses of rest' (*ʿwyw-n-ḥtp*) of both Ibis and Hawk. The same expression is used for the burial of a human being in Text **8,** R° 23 and V° 6, and Text **9,** V° 9, and the use of the word to describe the galleries of the Apis bulls and their divine mothers is well documented. In such circumstances it seems clear that the

[1] The mention of the dyke of course brings to mind the 'lake of Pharaoh' above, where the birth-chapel of the Ibis lay. But excavation has so far failed to shed light upon this. The description 'southern dyke' is also difficult to reconcile with a locality so far to the north of ancient Memphis.

[2] It was from the sand overlying this court that Texts **6, 10,** and **21** were recovered; see introductory notes *ad loca*.

[3] Cf. most recently, Reymond in *JEA* 58 (1972), 254–5 and 257, and literature cited; also the same author's *Djed-her-le-sauveur*, 113–17.

[4] Reymond, *JEA* 58 (1972), 255.

'houses of rest' are the galleries themselves where the mummified birds were stacked. Less certain is another building clearly connected with the burial. In Text **19,** V° 7 three trustworthy commissioners are to carry out a yearly investigation of 'the house of waiting (*ʿwy-n-ḥrry*) of the god which they will find at the time'. This seems to mean that the 'house of waiting' varied from year to year, and for this reason I have suggested that this is the demotic name for the side galleries in which the mummies were stored.[1]

The texts describing reforms in the ibis-cult (Texts **19–23**) give us a picture of the ideal burial. A mass burial was performed once yearly (**19,** V° 8–9 and parallels), for which the birds had presumably been mummified in advance.[2] The population of the Serapeum, doubtless a loose name for the whole area of North Saqqâra, was to be assembled, and a procession (*ṯꜣy-ʿḳ*), attended by appropriate priests and ceremonies, to be led to the galleries where the burial would take place. The galleries would probably be opened for this occasion only, and then resealed, although this is not stated in our texts. The processes of mummification (if such is the true description of the rudimentary treatment of some of the specimens examined) and bandaging (*swt*) are also mentioned in the reform texts (**19,** V° 16; **21,** V° 2; R° 13; **23,** R° 15–16), but details are not given.

The greatest value of our ibis-ostraca lies in the picture which they give of the administration of the cult, a picture which far surpasses the disjointed information of the Prinz-Joachim ostraca.[3] Over-all responsibility for the many cults of Memphis was probably entrusted to the royal scribe (βασιλικὸς γραμματεύς, *sẖ-Pr-ʿꜣ*), and it was to this official that Ḥor went to communicate his dream of 168 (Text **1,** 6). During the period covered by our ostraca (*c.* 172–162) this office seems to have been held by [ ]*tryn* (Soterion?), prophet of Khons, but apart from his appearance in Text **1,** he plays no further part in our archive.

Below this level, it would seem that in practice authority over the ibis-cult was vested in the priests of the temple of Ptaḥ in Memphis (Text **19,** R° 15–16).[4] It was before this body that the investigation of the shrine took place on 1 June 172. This council seems to have had considerable power, for it ordered the imprisonment of six men and a complete review of the arrangements for burying the sacred birds. It seems to have been free to make its own decisions, its only limitation being the need to act within the law; indeed at one point the council clearly felt obliged to send to Alexandria in order to clarify the legal position (Text **19,** R° 18). The freedom of this deliberative body is a useful counterpart to the common vision of ancient Egypt as an authoritarian state; it is clear that Pharaoh possessed controls, a financial one (through the Royal Scribe) and a legal one, but within these checks some considerable autonomy was allowed.

Another body which clearly had the right to inspect the cult was the temple of Osiris-Apis (Text **33,** 1). This is natural, as the god Osorapis (Osiris-Apis) was the presiding deity of the entire necropolis. The relations between this body and the temple of Ptaḥ are unknown. As the latter was by far the principal shrine in the whole of Memphis, one would expect the priesthood of Ptaḥ to take precedence over that of Osorapis, but there is no evidence from our texts to support this; indeed, there is no evidence

[1] See note *ad locum*, p. 80. The embalming-place itself (*wʿbt*) is known from Text **22,** R° 10, and seems to have been different.

[2] This contrasts with the irregular methods in use at Kôm Ombo in the following century, cf. Preisigke and Spiegelberg, *Die Prinz-Joachim-Ostraka*, 28 ff.

[3] Preisigke and Spiegelberg, *Die Prinz-Joachim-Ostraka* (Strassburg, 1914).

[4] This institution seems to have had authority over the temple of the Mother of the Apis as well (written communication from Professor H. S. Smith), and perhaps over the entire Serapeum.

from any source that the interests of the two temples ever came into conflict.

At Saqqâra itself, the corporation of the ibis-shrine was headed by a *lesōnis* (*mr-šn*). This official, well known from other sources, seems to have acted as the administrative head of the cult.[1] He appears rarely in our texts, and only one man is mentioned as holding the office throughout the period of the reforms. This is the Petimonth(?) of Text **22**, R° 7.

More is heard of another important official, the controller of the temple (*pꜣ nty šn ḥt-ntr*).[2] This title differs from that of the *lesōnis*; the latter was a priestly appointment, or at least one created internally by the priestly staff, whereas the controller (Greek ἐπιστάτης) was an agent of the king, and was directly responsible to him. It is for this reason that he carries the secondary title 'agent of Pharaoh' (*pꜣ rd n Pr-ꜥꜣ*).[3] It is interesting to observe that the council meeting of 1 June 172 was presided over by a royal controller (Text **19**, R° 16–17), in what was clearly a third form of control (in addition to fiscal and legal) exercised by the Crown over the affairs of its temples. In contrast to the single *lesōnis*, the holders of the controllership seem to change with marked frequency. The following are known, with the dates at which they are attested:

(*a*) ꜥAḥmosi son of Petineftēm (June 172): Text **19**.

(*b*) Djeḥepemou(?) (September 167): Text **23**.

(*c*) Pshenteḥe son of Payom (June 165): Text **22**.

The reasons for this rapid change, whether royal dissatisfaction with temple or officials, or promotion to higher office, or even a form of appointment by rotation, are quite unknown. It is also impossible to say whether the authority of the controller extended to other cults in the region of the Serapeum; Text **23**, R° 11 would seem to imply that it did, but the line is not certainly read. All that we can say is that such an official, which may have been a Ptolemaic innovation, was the burden which the ibis-shrine was to bear in return for the *syntaxis*, the donations of Philometor, and the 'ration of Pharaoh'. In mitigation, it may be said that all three appointees seem to be native Egyptians, and that nowhere in our texts is any criticism applied to them, or the impression given that their authority was an irksome affair.

Beneath these senior officials would have ranked a professional priesthood of Thoth and the Ibis, and Horus the Falcon, but these do not appear in our texts. We do hear of the *wꜥbw*, the ordinary priests organized into their phyles (Text **19**, *passim*; Text **21**, R° 1, *nꜣ wꜥbw n Ḏḥwty*, and others), and we are shown the deliberative council of the ibis-cult. This consisted of 'twenty-five priests who conclude affairs' (Text **21**, R° 11).[4] The 'twenty-five priests' recur in Text **19**, V° 3, without the qualifying phrase.[5] The system is familiar to us from the Canopus decree.[6] Before the passing of this decree (6 March 237) the deliberative priests (βουλευταὶ ἱερεῖς) numbered twenty, five being nominated by each of the four phyles. After the creation of the fifth phyle in honour of Berenice Euergetis, the number was raised to twenty-five. That this system was still in operation in 172 is shown by our texts, and it is likely that the 'great men' so often criticized by Ḥor

[1] See notes to Text **22**, R° 7, pp. 84 ff. The title is also discussed by F. de Cenival, *Les Associations religieuses en Égypte* (Cairo, 1972), i. 154–9. The possibility of the appointment being an annual occurrence is discussed op. cit. 167 ff. This is neither confirmed nor denied by our present texts.

[2] See notes to Text **19**, R° 17, p. 79. This official is mentioned in passing by de Cenival, op. cit. i. 155, 166.

[3] Ibid., and Texts **22**, R° 6–7; **23**, R° 11. For the term *rd* (*rwḏ*) in general, cf. de Cenival, op. cit. i. 164–6.

[4] See note to Text **19**, V° 3, pp. 79–80.

[5] A possible reference to the 'twenty administrators' in Text **33**, 4 is too conjectural to serve as evidence here. Another obscure figure, the 'priest in session in splendour(?)' of Text **19**, V° 1, is also unparalleled; for the use of *ḥms* for sessions, cf. de Cenival, op. cit. i. 21, note on 3, 5.

[6] Bevan, 179–80.

are the temple authorities in general, and the council in particular. General deliberation and administration seem to have been in the hands of this council of twenty-five, and it is this body which seems to have initiated the reforms of 174 (Text **21**). These reforms seem not to have had the desired effect, as some two years later we find the entire question of the administration of the ibis-cult referred to the council of the priesthood of Ptaḥ (Text **19**); but the significant fact is that the initial attempt to correct abuses was an internal one, a resolution of the council of twenty-five. Such resolutions are shown by Text **19**, V° 3–4 to have been inscribed in a minute-book (or similar) for future reference. Whether a separate priesthood or council existed for the cult of the Hawk is unknown, though perhaps unlikely.

Alongside the priesthood, and those responsible for the ritual of the temple, were the men concerned with the handling of the birds themselves. Whether this distinction was one readily made by the Egyptians themselves we do not know; indeed it is likely that all personnel of the Ibis were regarded as priestly and as subject to the usual rules of purity and abstention. Nevertheless, the difference is a convenient one for our purpose. Text **33**, 7 introduces us to an officer, whose name is unknown to the present writer. If the reading *mn-niwt* is anything like correct,[1] a translation 'door-keeper' may be admitted; but if there is doubt about his name, there is little about his function. He must, the text says, be a reliable man, supervising the ibises and their young 'who until the sun sets will guard the Ibis and keep it safe'. He is clearly a watchman or guardian, responsible for protecting the birds from harm. The reference to 'offspring of the Ibis' suggests that it is the living bird which he is to guard, not the mummies in their sepulchres.

The attendants of the Ibis are referred to generally as 'the servants of the ibises' (*nꜣ sdm-ꜥš n nꜣ hbw*).[2] These occur entirely in the ibis reform texts, and in passages which leave little doubt that their duties were the routine ones of maintaining (perhaps feeding), and burying the ibises. They may have had a priestly function, although this is not stated, and it is more likely that, as with the workmen of Deir el-Medîna, the title *sdm-ꜥš* implies a menial status.[3] It is also interesting to see that the *sdm-ꜥš* are always said to be 'of the ibises' (in the concrete and plural), not 'of the Ibis', which latter would suggest that they dealt with the religious abstraction which lay beyond the birds themselves. Whatever the truth of this, it is clear that at the level of the *sdm-ꜥš*, both ibises and hawks each had a separate corps of servants. Whether this was true of the higher orders is unknown.

In Text **33**, 9, a man named Djeḥephibi is called 'the servant of the ibises'. Unless this individual is named as being particularly open to blame, we must assume that the singular term 'servant' means that he was the senior *sdm-ꜥš*, an official or unofficial overseer, or a spokesman for his colleagues. From Greek texts we hear quite frequently of people called ἰβιοβοσκοί, feeders of ibises.[4] No such demotic equivalent has appeared from our texts, and one wonders whether the Greek word is not simply the equivalent of *nꜣ sdm-ꜥš n nꜣ hbw*. It is at any rate likely that the feeding of the birds, which plays such a large role in our texts, would have been among the duties of the 'servants', even if this was not the limit of their functions.

The activities of these servants were supervised by 'inspectors' (*mštw*). These officers were already known from the Prinz-Joachim ostraca.[5] Their power over the servants is evident, but it

[1] See note *ad locum*, p. 106. [2] See index for references.

[3] Note the composition of the priesthood of Amenophis I described on a column-base from the village (Černý, *BIFAO* 27 (1927), 194–5 ff.). Here the *sdm-ꜥš* is distinguished from the six *wꜥbw*.

[4] *Prinz-Joachim-Ostraka*, 25 and literature cited. We also hear of feeders of hawks (ἱερακοβοσκοί), who may perhaps correspond to the *sdm-ꜥš n pꜣ bik*.

[5] Op. cit. 14, n. 5.

is also clear that by 174 the familiar problem of guarding the guardians had raised itself. A former inspector, Onnofri son of Ḥapertais, was among the six men arraigned before the tribunal in Text **19,** R° 20 ff. (where he seems to be listed among the 'servants'), and distrust of the inspectorate seems to have been one of the reasons for the appointment of a select body to supervise both the 'servants of the ibises' and the inspectors originally set over them; indeed, the problem resembled that of the Ramesside tomb-robber, who was easily controlled except when the police who controlled him were themselves corrupt.[1]

In addition to these officials, there are occasional references to workers *en masse*. Text **19,** V° 19 introduces us to 'the men who perform the burial' (*nꜣ rmtw nty dỉt ḥtp*), and Text **23,** R° 15 to 'the man who performs service for the Ibis and his bandagings' (*pꜣ rmt nty ỉr n pꜣ hb ỉrm nꜣy·f swtw*), probably an embalmer. Whether these anonymous workers were part of the corps of 'servants' (*sdm-ʿš*) is not stated, although it is likely that they were. Text **33,** 6 mentions also 'the men who labour' (*nꜣ rmtw nty ỉr-bꜣk*). A further category, familiar to us from the stelae of the Serapeum and of the Mothers of the Apis, is that of the masons who excavated the galleries, the 'efficient carvers' (*by mnḫ*). These are not mentioned in our documents, although this need imply nothing about their existence.

Such was the administration of the ibis-cult at Saqqâra. Text **19** tells us something of its history. Affairs had been conducted well until the sixteenth year of Philopator (207/6); after this, for some untold reason, abuses had set in. The nature of these abuses is never described, but an outline may be deduced from the reforms which are most emphasized. Whenever the burial of the ibises and hawks is mentioned, the phrase is added 'one god in one vessel' (*wʿ ntr n wʿt mgt*).[2] Both birds were regularly bandaged and placed in earthenware jars, and Emery, when opening several jars, had already noticed that some were empty, or contained mere bones. He concluded that the empty jars represented an attempt by priests of the shrine to swindle the pilgrims, and it is very likely that such an irregularity lies behind this rather strange phrase in our texts. Text **21,** 4–8 also gives details of payment for more efficient and careful bird-potting, doubtless in an attempt to correct this scandalous abuse.

It may also be that the funeral procession of the Ibis and the Hawk had become lax and disorganized, for the relevant passage in the texts always adds the phrase 'the appropriate priest in attendance' (*pꜣ wʿb n ḫrt·f m-sꜣ·s*);[3] this gives an impression that absenteeism or impersonation had occurred. That peculation, fraud, or embezzlement had also been encountered is suggested very strongly by the elaborate precautions taken to secure the inspectors.[4] They (i.e. probably their names inscribed on papyrus) are to be placed in a sealed box; this box is to be stored in the *ẖny* (storeroom?) of the special commissioners, or to be entrusted to the pastophoroi of the forecourt of the temple of Ptaḥ, for 'it has been decided not to trust the servants of the ibises and the servants of the Hawk when they perform its burial' (Text **22,** V° 4–6).

Such deleterious practices continued throughout the reign of Epiphanes (205/4–180), in spite of this king's dedication of a chapel for the Apis at Memphis, and it was not until the eighth year of his successor, so Ḥor tells us, that attempts were made to suppress them.[5] In October 174,

[1] Pap. Leopold-Amherst, 3, 1–5; *JEA* 22 (1936), 188 ff.

[2] Text **19,** V° 8; **21,** R° 18; **22,** R° 14.

[3] Text **19,** V° 11–12; **21,** V° 15.

[4] Text **19,** V° 12–14; **21,** V° 15–21; **22,** V° 1–6; **23,** R° 17–19.

[5] Some uncertainty surrounds the date of the relevant text; for discussion see notes to Text **21,** R° 10, p. 84. For Epiphanes' Apis-shrine, cf. *Rosettana*, 33. A similar picture of neglect and dilapidation in the ibis-cult of Memphis is contained in Papyrus Louvre 3334, a petition dated to

according to our Text **21**, a meeting took place of the council (*ḳnbt*) of the temple of Memphis. The meeting had been summoned following an oracle of Thoth, and various resolutions were passed by the twenty-five deliberative priests who formed the governing body.[1] Three commissioners were to be appointed from among the priests to supervise the burial of the birds, and a scale of payments instituted. If our dating of the ostracon is correct, this proposed reform can have had no effect, for a second meeting took place in Memphis on 31 May 172 (Text **19**). The elders of the temple of Ptaḥ, whose authority extended to the ibis-shrine of the Serapeum, met under the presidency of the royal ἐπιστάτης or controller (R° 16–17). On the following day, 1 June 172, six men, including a former inspector, were found guilty of irregularities, and imprisoned (R° 20–3). The council of twenty-five then passed another reform, to take effect with the next regnal year (i.e. from 5 October 172). This second reform was substantially that of the previous text, and we are not told why it was necessary to re-enact it.

The events of the sixth Syrian War now occupy our attention, and we gain no new information about the ibis-cult until the end of these hostilities. Text **23** preserves for us the date 18 September 167, over a year from the withdrawal of Antiochus from Egyptian territory. On this day Ḥetpanḥūri, a magician attached to the cult of the Ibis, sent a document, apparently on the instigation of Ḥor of Sebennytos, to the royal controller. This document seems to have contained an interpretation of three oracles given by the god, and the sense of the interpretation was clearly to introduce more reforms. Here the excavation of the 'courtyard of the Ibis and the Hawk' is urged, and more measures are recommended, very similar to the ones explained above, whose aim shall be 'to prevent any man having control over the god himself, when they perform his burial' (Text **23**, R° 21–3). A further plea is added on the verso of the same text from Ḥor the secretary, that the magician should not fail to follow up these measures, and the evidence of the following text suggests that the plea was effective.

Some eighteen months elapse. On 16 April 165 the oracle of Thoth concerning the chapels of Egypt is interpreted (Texts **16** and **17**), and Ḥor of Sebennytos acts again. Text **22** is dated to 13 June of the same year. In this the reforms have apparently taken effect, and regularity has at last been restored into the burial arrangements of the Ibis. The result of Ḥor's interview with the magician is to produce further reforms (R° 3–7). Five commissioners are now to be appointed, instead of the original three, and their functions are to be divided. Three are to continue their supervision of the burial itself, while the remaining two shall occupy themselves with the food of the ibises (R° 8–14). Payment is similarly reviewed (verso). After this, we hear little more of the cause of reform, and it would seem that the ibis-cult returned to its former well-being. By the summer of 158, the list of Philometor's donations stood in its chapel (Text **3**, R° 15), and its population witnessed the arrival of Pharaoh and his Queen. Prosperity may have continued beyond the dark years of Ptolemy VIII, for this latter in 118 undertook to meet the burial expenses of Apis, Mnevis, and other sacred animals.[2] Ḥor of Sebennytos probably did not live to hear this announcement, and after his time the history of the ibis-shrine is known only as part of the larger history of the Memphite Serapeum. Yet none can doubt that, while Ḥor lived, he was a priceless witness.

Year 7 of an unnamed king (Revillout, *Rev. Ég.* 2 (1882), 75–8). This text, which is badly in need of republication, may date to this unsettled period.

[1] It is not stated whether this was the council of the ibis-shrine, or of the temple of Ptaḥ, but the former is perhaps more likely.

[2] Pap. Tebt. I, 5, ll. 77–82.

Postscript

Some notice should perhaps be taken of the financial measures in the reform texts. The present writer can claim no special competence in this field, and is far from having read the relevant lines with any certainty; the following section is therefore tentative.

In Text **22,** V° 1 reference is made to 'the moneys which are collected after this' (*nꜣ ḥḏw nty ỉw·w twt m-sꜣ nꜣy*). This money was presumably drawn by the commissioners from the funds of the ibis-shrine. We know something of the income of our shrine. Much will have been derived from the land held in various parts of Memphis, even of the whole of Egypt (Text **16,** R° 11); a further amount will have been represented by the government subsidy, the *syntaxis* received annually as a contribution towards the salaries of priests (Text **33,** 11), and a final proportion from the donations of pilgrims, either as contributions to the mummification of the birds, or in the form of bronzes or other temple furniture.[1] From this wealth the commissioners are instructed to make payments to the men employed in the funeral arrangements. The two fullest accounts are found in Text **19,** V° 15–19, and Text **21,** R° 12–18; V° 1–9, and it is comforting to find that they are in substantial agreement. The figures are expressed in 'payments' (*tn*), in full 'payments of the god' (*tn n nṯr*),[2] and these figures are sometimes followed by amounts in 'silver' (*ḥḏ*, the demotic equivalent of the drachma). Many of the details are obscure, and the notes *ad loca* should be consulted.

Text 19

(*a*) Sum assessed for bandaging (etc.), 2 *tn*: *ḥḏ* 1
(*b*) efficiency payment, $1\frac{1}{4}$ *tn*
(*c*) 'its *gns*(?)' $\frac{3}{4}$ *tn*[3]: *ḥḏ* $1\frac{1}{2}$
(*d*) 'its *ỉwꜣ*', *ḥḏ* $\frac{1}{2}$.

(Note that in (*c*) the word 'its' seems to refer to the efficiency; this is not grammatically possible for the entry in (*d*), which must refer to a masculine word, whether *tn* or the preceding *gns*.)

Text 21

(*a*) until the three priests come to *Pr-wʿb-nb·s*, 1 *tn*
(*b*) when they inspect the sanctuary and restore efficiency, 3 *tn*
(*c*) sum assessed for bandaging (etc.), 2 *tn*
(*d*) payment for untiring efficiency: its *pẖt*, 1 *tn*
(*e*) 'its[4] *gns*(?)', $\frac{1}{2}$ *tn*: *ḥḏ* $1\frac{1}{2}$ (here it is noted that the remainder shall be paid at the gate of the courtyard)
(*f*) until they assemble the people for the procession, 1 *tn*.

A few points seem clear. In each text, the sum assessed for bandaging and mummification is 2 *tn*. The list of Text **21** is fuller, including payment to be made before the burial proceedings. The payments proposed for efficiency (19 (*b*); 21 (*d*)) are probably optional, and the sum described as *gns*, if the interpretation of this word as 'fine' is correct, will have been deducted from the total (19 (*c*); 21 (*e*)). The use of the expression 'until' in 21 (*a*), (*f*) is interesting; the word is probably used in its limiting sense ('by' a certain date, as in Text **2,** R° 6–7, where the date of Antiochus' withdrawal is forecast). If this is correct, payment will be in arrears, and will not occur before the duty has been carried out.

[1] See in general the remarks of Kemp in Ucko, Tringham and Dimbleby (eds.), *Man, Settlement and Urbanism* (London, 1972), 657 ff.

[2] Text **19,** V° 15; **21,** V° 3.

[3] See textual note to Text **19,** V° 17.

[4] i.e. the efficiency.

The unknown quantity is the value of the *tn*. It is true that at several points sums are added in silver, but there seems no obvious rule for comparison between the two currencies. The silver sums are therefore not equivalents for the *tn*-payments, and seem to be additions to them. If this is correct, a *tn* may have been a large amount, for in 19 (*c*) a sum of $\frac{3}{4}$ *tn* is supplemented by 1$\frac{1}{2}$ *ḥḏ*. It would therefore seem that 1$\frac{1}{2}$ *ḥḏ* was worth less than $\frac{1}{4}$ *tn*, for otherwise the scribe would have written a unit (1+x) *tn*. By this reckoning, a *tn* would be worth more than 6 *ḥḏ*. If this solution is unpalatable, it may be possible to avoid it by assuming that a *tn* was not a money-payment at all, but one in corn or the like, and that the *ḥḏ*-figures are supplementary payments in coin. This second explanation has much to recommend it; but a clearer explanation may be gained only by a detailed study of economic sources, a study which lies outside the scope of the present work and beyond the competence of its author.[1]

§ 5: The topography of Memphis

It remains for us, after discussing the contents of Ḥor's writings, to place their author in his setting. We have seen that much of his life was spent in travel, from his home town of Pi(?)-Thoth to the 'town of Isis', from Sebennytos to the shrines of Buto and Heliopolis, during the war against Antiochus to Alexandria and its temple of Sarapis, even into the presence of his sovereign. But it is his eventual home, Memphis, and more particularly the northern part of its necropolis, which occupies the greatest part of our attention. Ḥor was not a geographer, and his descriptions of towns and temples are merely incidental to his theme; but there is no reason to suppose that he invented buildings which did not exist, or that confused descriptions would have passed the notice either of himself or of his secretary, and we may therefore place some confidence in his directions. Our findings are embodied in the maps given as Figs. 3 and 4 at the end of this commentary.

It is not surprising that Memphis, and the name of its necropolis, *ʿnḫ-tꜣwy*, should appear so commonly in our documents.[2] In Text **8**, R° 12–13, at the beginning of a dream-account, Ḥor describes himself as 'in the *ḫny* of Memphis', and if this term has been righly identified, it too will be a name for this necropolis.[3] Yet the drift of our texts is not entirely towards the funereal; Text **19**, R° 15 ff. shows us the forecourt of the great temple of Ptaḥ, used as the setting for a council of priests.[4] Six men are condemned by this tribunal, and are conveyed to a prison (ibid. 23). This presumably also lay in Memphis. Another and more elusive feature of the capital is seen in three texts.[5] The 'dam of the southern dyke in Memphis' seems to be the assembly place of the gods of Lower Egypt (Text **11**); in Text **24B** it is qualified as 'the great dam'. No

[1] I have left out of consideration, for example, the inflation of coinage which is known to have taken place in Egypt after 217. The sharp changes in the value of money during this period may well have been critical in producing our reforms; they may even have been a major cause of the abuses described above. Such a situation would almost certainly have provoked the regulations specifying the amounts to be paid. Modern parallels for this 'wage-fixing' are of course not hard to find. For the inflation in copper during this period, cf. Reekmans, *Studia Hellenica*, 5 (1948), 15 ff., and *Cd'É* 24 (1949), 324 ff.

[2] See index for detailed references. For *ʿnḫ-tꜣwy* see Sandman–Holmberg, *The God Ptaḥ*, 214–15; also Westendorf, *ZÄS* (1966), 153 ff., and Bergman, *Ich bin Isis*, 44–5, where the idea is proposed that the name signified 'binding-knot of the two lands'. This may be so, although a doubt lurks. In the Late Period, the term seems to have been a general one for the entire necropolis area of the desert west of Memphis, and particularly the northern sector where lay the shrines of Osorapis, Isis mother of the Apis, Thoth the Ibis, Imḥōtep, Anubis, and Bastet, 'lady of ʿAnkhtawy'. This area as a whole was also commonly termed 'the Serapeum'.

[3] See note *ad locum*, p. 40.

[4] A more genuinely ritual use of this same feature is seen in Text **25**, 6–7: *nꜣ wʿbw nty ʿḳ m-bꜣḥ Ptḥ n tꜣ wsḫyt*.

[5] See notes to Texts **11**, V° 2–3, p. 50; **15**, V° 4 (p. 60); **24B**, 5 (p. 91), and the section on the administration of the ibis-cult above.

other information is forthcoming, and the subject must be left unsolved. It is regrettable that Ḥor tells us little of the great city where he must often have walked, and our attention must turn to its necropolis, on the high desert *gebel* where for three millennia its dead had already rested.

Upon a bluff of the western desert lay the temple of Osorapis, the great god, and the other shrines of 'the gods who rest in the necropolis of the house of Osorapis'.[1] The nature of this temple with its hypogeum, cult, and oracle is well known from early discoveries, archaeological (Mariette) and philological (notably Wilcken), and shall not be repeated here. One feature of the buildings does claim attention, however; the great dromos (*ḫft-ḥr*), a sphinx-lined avenue, ran from the main temple of the bull-god due east towards the cultivation, terminating in the buildings known to Mariette as the 'Greek Serapeum', to the Egyptians as the Anubieion (*Pr-hn-'Inp*).[2] This bold feature, which formed an obvious point of reference for the inhabitants, is mentioned in Text **8**, R° 14, where Ḥor describes himself as going up from the valley to the desert plateau.

The term 'Serapeum' was not confined to the temple of the deified bull, but was extended to cover the entire area enclosed by the dromos and a second 'great street', where the other animal-cults were situated. In this sense, both the ibis- and hawk-cults and several others could all be said to lie within the Serapeum, and an employee of the ibis-cult in *UPZ* 119, 17 describes himself as 'an ibis-feeder from those of the Serapeum'. It is probably in this extended sense that the ibis reform texts refer to 'assembling the people of the Serapeum' (*thm pꜣ mšꜥ n Pr-Wsir-Ḥp*) for a procession.[3]

Another detail of the Serapeum should also be considered in this light. In Text **8**, R° 23–4; V° 6 Ḥor dreams that he shall be buried in 'the house of rest of the Serapeum'. This is probably the same as 'the house of rest of the House of Apis' of Text **9**, V° 9. This would normally be taken as a description of the underground bull-sepulchre, but it seems an unlikely wish to be buried in the vaults of the Apis. The phrase perhaps refers to a human cemetery near by, similar to the group of priestly graves found 'north of the Serapeum' by Mariette.[4] The location of this cemetery (if we assume that Ḥor had a definite site in mind, which he may not) is unknown.

In our texts, the title 'Serapeum' (*Pr-Wsir-Ḥp*) is sometimes linked with a 'sister' locality, with the name of Ḥepnēbes (*Ḥp-nb·s*).[5] This link is well expressed in the prooemium of Text **13** (4–6), 'Come to me my great lord Osorapis, the great god, and the gods who rest in the necropolis of the Serapeum, and the necropolis of Ḥepnēbes, together with those who rest upon the sleeping-place of the House of Thoth'. The name Ḥepnēbes has long been known as the description of part of the Memphite necropolis, but it was impossible to define it more closely. Early references are collected by Gauthier, *Dictionnaire géographique*, iv. 10, and a notable example is found in the autobiographical inscription of Pshenptaḥ, son of Petubasti, high priest of Memphis (Brugsch, *Thesaurus*, 941), who held priestly offices of nearly all the Serapeum deities. Pap. BM. 10299, a document of the Later New Kingdom,[6] has a mention (l. 3) of 'Sokar-Ḥenu in

[1] Text **13**, 4. For a rough description of this site in the Ptolemaic period see Ray in Ucko, Tringham, and Dimbleby (eds.), *Man, Settlement and Urbanism* (London, 1972), 699 ff. and literature cited.

[2] For the dromos, among the literature mentioned in the previous note, see especially Guilmot, *Cd'É* 37 (1962), 362 ff., and the observations of F. de Cenival, *Associations*, i. 41–2; for the Anubieion, Wilcken, *UPZ* i. 577; De Meulenaere, *Cd'É* 35 (1960), 94, 103–4; and the cautious remarks of Pierce, *Three Demotic Papyri in the Brooklyn Museum* (Oslo, 1972), 40. See further de Cenival, *BIFAO* 71 (1972), 11 ff.

[3] Text **19**, V° 10; **21**, V° 12. For the wider use of the term, cf. Guilmot, op. cit. 364, n. 7.

[4] *Mémoire sur la mère d'Apis*, 14.

[5] See index for detailed references.

[6] Caminos, *MDAIK* 16 (1958), 20 ascribes it to Dynasty XXI.

the midst of the *šṯ3yt* of *Ḥ3p(t)-nb·s*', an earlier form of our name.[1] Now the evidence of the stelae from the galleries of the Mothers of the Apis[2] leaves little doubt that, at least in the Late Period, *Ḥp-nb·s* was the site of the funerary temple and burial-place of these animals. As such the name will have covered the area of the galleries, as well as the great temple platform with its shrines, dedicated perhaps to Osorapis and the Mother of the Apis (under the form of Isis), with side-chapels devoted to 'Osiris the baboon' and other manifestations of the god Thoth.[3] Evidence will be given below to show that it also covered the galleries of the Ibis and the Hawk. A list of the gods of the place, the 'great souls of Ḥepnēbes', is given in Text **19,** R° 5–9, and includes most of the major gods of Egypt.

Several buildings of Ḥepnēbes are named in our texts. Text **22,** R° 10–11 refers to the 'embalming-place' (*wʿbt*) of Ḥepnēbes, in a context which is clearly describing the cult of the Ibis. This would be natural, for the greater animals, such as Apis and his mother, were probably embalmed at Memphis, by the temples in which they had spent their lives.[4] The same may well have applied to the baboons, which were kept in the temple of Ptaḥ 'under his moringa-tree'. The hawks and ibises, on the contrary, were probably maintained near, and embalmed by, the galleries in which they were destined to rest.

In Text **22,** R° 3–4 Ḥor describes how he 'stood with the magician at the gate of the *wmtt* of Ḥepnēbes'. The word *wmtt* seems to have been used indiscriminately to refer to a tower, or to a high walled enclosure.[5] This seems an excellent description of the large compound, surrounded by brick walls, which formed the forecourt to the temple platform (*JEA* 55 (1969), pl. XI); immediately to the north of this, however, lay the pedestals for another large gateway, directly to the west of the entrance of the so-called Iseum, the burial-place of the Mothers of the Apis. Either this gateway, or the great western entrance to the compound, may be the gate by which Ḥor stood with the magician in June 165. Gateways were regular meeting-places, sites of dispensing justice, or of swearing oaths.[6] Another gateway, a 'corner gate' (*r3 ḳḥy*), occurs in Text **30,** 4 as the place where Ḥor the secretary receives documents. The context is not certain, but if correctly read, the term may be a fit description for the northern gate, leading to the Iseum, which stood outside the north-west corner of the great compound. In this case, the site of Ḥor's interview in Text **22** would be the gate of the great brick compound. Further evidence is required to test these identifications.

In addition to these buildings above ground, it is possible that the subterranean galleries of the Iseum are recalled in the title of Isis given in Text **10,** R °2 as *nbt knḥy*, 'lady of the vault'.[7]

We have already seen from Text **22,** R° 4 and other passages that the shrine of the Ibis was thought to be situated in Ḥepnēbes, and indeed this is not surprising to anyone who, studying the excavation plans, sees the complex of ibis-galleries which lie immediately to the south of the brick compound and the vaults of the Mothers of the Apis. It is clear, however, that the area covered by the ibis-cult also had a second name of its own. This is the *Pr-wʿb-nb·s*, 'Abaton-of-her-lord' of Text **21,** R° 7, 13; V° 12–13. Here the burial of the ibises is said to

[1] The name 'concealer-of-her-lord' is thus an example of a common type, as is the Theban toponym *ḫftt-ḥr-nb·s*, 'opposite-her-lord', or possibly 'dromos-of-her-lord'.

[2] In the process of publication by Smith and others.

[3] Preliminary report in *JEA* 55 (1969), 31 ff.

[4] El-Amir, *JEA* 34 (1948), 51 ff.

[5] See note *ad locum*, p. 86.

[6] Cf. Kaplony-Heckel, *Die demotischen Tempeleide*, 21 ff.

[7] The term is of course also known in the meaning 'naos, shrine' (Erichsen, *Glossar*, 541), but the use to describe the burial vaults of the Apis (cf. *ZÄS* 50 (1912), 32) and his mothers is so common in the Serapeum that one would expect the word to convey this meaning to a local scribe.

take place, here the inspectors to come at the time of the burial, and here the 'people of the Serapeum' to be assembled for the funeral procession. The name Pi-waʿb-nēbes is not known from any other text, where it is always replaced by Ḥepnēbes, and it seems that the word was a local identification only, used perhaps to differentiate the ibis-cult from that of the adjoining 'Iseum'. In rough parlance it was probably included in the more conspicuous area, just as Ḥepnēbes itself was loosely said to fall within the 'House of Osorapis'.

The sanctuary of the Ibis was known as *Pr-Ḏḥwty*, the 'House of Thoth'.[1] The fullest description of this shrine and its setting comes in the opening lines of Text **23** (R° 2–6): 'the house of Thoth, which is upon the southern mountain of the Serapeum which is in Memphis, (from Ḥor) who serves his days in Ḥepnēbes, in the desert of the House of Osiris (*Pr-Wsỉr*) which is upon the mountain of the north of the necropolis of ʿAnkhtawy'. This important description may be explained as follows (see map which concludes this section): the 'north of the necropolis of ʿAnkhtawy' is little more than the equivalent of the modern North Saqqâra. The 'mountain' (which corresponds to the modern *gebel*) is presumably the low plateau containing both the archaic cemetery of Dynasties I and II, and the later *mastabas* of the Old Kingdom. The galleries of the various animal-cults, ranging from north to south through ibises to cows, baboons, hawks, and ibises again, are cut into the western face of this plateau. It is true that a passage such as Text **21,** R° 7–8 refers to 'the houses of rest which are *upon* the mountain', but this is perhaps a legitimate extension of what is, even for the Egyptian language, a very vague preposition. The expression 'desert of the House of Osiris' (*ḫ3st n Pr-Wsỉr*) is more difficult to place. One would expect a group such as *Pr-Wsỉr* to refer to a temple complex of Osiris, but none is known, in spite of the large number of bronzes of this god found during the excavations. Another explanation is therefore needed, and one turns to the near-by village of Abusîr. It is true that hardly anything is known of this settlement before the tenth century A.D., although a Byzantine text found during the excavations does mention a village of Βουσῖρις, but it is *a priori* likely that the modern name conceals an original *Pr-Wsỉr*. It is possible that the known toponym *Pr-Wsỉr-rwḏ-ỉswt*, which will recur below in connection with the feature known as 'the Peak', may have given its name to the village. The phrase 'desert of Pi-osīri' would then be merely a further attempt to specify the exact locality. Textual support for this assumption is lacking,[2] but it would be an excellent description of the known site of Ḥepnēbes. More problematic is the description of the House of Thoth as lying 'upon the southern mountain of the Memphite Serapeum'. There is nothing at first sight particularly southerly about the ibis-galleries, all of which lie well to the north of the Serapeum proper. There are, however, two sets of galleries, one to the south of the great brick compound, another, partially cleared in the season of 1970/1, to the north of it and set into a spur of the *gebel* (see map, Fig. 4). It may be that Ḥor is trying to distinguish the southern group of galleries and buildings from the northern. This would provide very useful evidence for the relative dates of the two complexes, but the passage is unfortunately not conclusive.

Other buildings of the ibis-cult, notably the courtyard (*ỉnḥy*) of the Ibis and the Hawk, have been discussed in § 4 above. There remain two features of the Serapeum which are mentioned occasionally in our texts: the lake and the peak.

[1] Detailed references in the index; see also the account of its administration in the section above, and Smither, *JEA* 34 (1948), 35–7.

[2] The phrase *p3 tš n Pr-Wsỉr* in **58,** 12 is too isolated to be of help. See however *OGIS* ii. 761, l. 8 (Athribis, 95 B.C.), and n. 5 on p. 150 below.

Of the lake (*pꜣ šỉ*) there is little to be said. Isis in Text **10,** 3–4 is called 'the great goddess of the *wady* (a rough translation of the demotic *ḳꜣn*) of the lake'. Reasons have already been given in the previous section for identifying this lake with the 'Pool of Abusîr', a feature of older maps, whose dried-up bed may still be seen at the entrance to the desert *wady* which leads south to the Serapeum. It may also correspond to the λίμνη of several Greek texts from the site. In Text **33,** 2 this lake is qualified as 'the lake of Pharaoh' (*pꜣ šỉ n Pr-ꜥꜣ*). This grandiose epithet probably means little more than that it was put to public use.[1] In the same text we are told that the lake was the site for a 'chapel of birth' of the ibis, and it is very likely that large pens and other buildings for housing the birds stood on its banks. The interesting inscription of Pshenptaḥ son of Petubasti (Brugsch, *Thesaurus*, 941, l. 3) adds that, in addition to many other offices, this important official held a priesthood of the Ram, lord of Mendes (*Bꜣ-nb-Ḏdt*) 'at the head of the lake of Pharaoh' (*ḫnty šỉ n Pr-ꜥꜣ*). The same deity is named in the headings of several stelae from the 'Iseum', and fragments of ram-mummies have been discovered by the mud-brick buildings which lay to the north of the southernmost ibis-galleries. The exact position of the shrine (and no doubt galleries) of this sacred ram is still unknown, and the words *ḫnty šỉ n Pr-ꜥꜣ* may apply to any point along the Serapeum *wady*; further excavation is required to locate the Lord of Mendes.

More controversial is the second feature, the peak. The word used (*thn(y)t*, in its older form *dhnt*)[2] is a common one for a crag or bluff overlooking the valley, and survives in place-names to this day.[3] At Memphis, the particular connotations of 'the Peak' have been well summarized by De Meulenaere.[4] The name corresponded to an area containing a temple, and devoted to several cults, prominent among which was that of Imḥōtep. This link is brought out in Text **18,** V° 2–3, where this same god is characterized as 'offspring(?) of south-of-his-wall (i.e. Ptaḥ), [lord] of the Peak (*thn*), lord of ꜥAnkhtawy in Memphis'. The researches of De Meulenaere and others have shown that this 'Peak', at least in the Ptolemaic period, was surrounded by walls and contained its own temple (*ḥt-ntr*); furthermore there is some evidence to suggest that the area which bore this name contained several smaller cult-sanctuaries, notably that of Anubis (which is well attested) and of Osiris *rwḏ-ỉswt* (a site almost unknown).[5] It would also seem that the great temple of Imḥōtep stood on this Peak, or at least close enough to it to be linked with it in ordinary speech. It is in this light that we should view the description of our Text **23,** V° 21–3, 'the men, the pastophoroi, and those who are over the windows of the forecourt of the temple of the Peak'. These officials are urged to exercise care in their dealings with the Ibis. From this description several points are clear; the temple (again the word *ḥt-ntr* is used) of the Peak contained pastophoroi. This is confirmed by the inscription of another High Priest of Memphis, Petineftēm,[6] who in addition to his Memphite offices, was 'overseer of mysteries in the lake' (quite possibly the feature discussed above; the hieroglyphic version gives *ꜥnḫ-tꜣwy*, rather more drily), 'scribe of the treasury of the temple of the Peak', and 'scribe [.....] of the pastophoroi of Imḥōtep, son of Ptaḥ, the great god.[7] Wilcken

[1] As in the common *ḫyr n Pr-ꜥꜣ* 'public street', and *ꜥ(y)š n Pr-ꜥꜣ* 'public auction', Zauzich, *Enchoria*, 1 (1971), 79.

[2] See philological note to Text **23,** V° 23, p. 88.

[3] Gardiner, *AEO*, ii. 93*; Spiegelberg, *ZÄS* 53 (1917), 1–2.

[4] *Cd'É* 35 (1960), 104 ff.

[5] Unfortunately there is no good evidence to link this name with that of the village *Pr-Wsỉr* (Abusîr), although the equation is tempting; Yoyotte, *GLECS* 8 (1959), 59.

[6] Brugsch, *Thesaurus*, 887–8; this and other biographical inscriptions most recently rediscussed by Otto, *MDAIK* 15 (1957), 203 ff.

[7] Another interesting inscription in this series is that of Esḳite (Brugsch, 907), who in addition to holding a rather

(*UPZ* i. 45–6) has collected the Greek evidence for pastophoroi and for their shrines (*pastophoria*) at the Serapeum, and it is quite possible that some at least of these should be located in the area of the Peak.

In addition to the pastophoroi, we are also told that the forecourt of the temple of the Peak possessed windows (*sštw* for the older *ssdw*). These are in all probability windows of appearance, a common enough feature of Egyptian temples and palaces. ʿAnemḥo was 'prophet of Horus of the window of appearance' (*ḥm-ntr n sšd n ḫʿ*) and Horus is also known as a deity of a window of appearance in another biographical inscription from the Serapeum.[1] Whether this implies that a falcon or falcons was exhibited in the forecourt of the temple of the Peak, as happened on festival occasions at Edfu, is uncertain, and such questions must await the excavation of the site.

Let us attempt to combine this evidence. The temple of 'the Peak' included, or was closely connected with, the cults of Bastet, Anubis, Osiris *rwḏ iswt*, and Imḥōtep. It was therefore located in part, or possibly the whole, of the complex at the end of the dromos termed by the early excavators 'the Greek Serapeum'. The evidence of Pap. Louvre 2412, 4, suggests that the cult of Imḥōtep also possessed a vault or cavern (*ṯpḥt*) of the god.[2] In the forecourt (*wsḫyt*) of the temple were windows, probably of appearance; and attached to this forecourt were pastophoroi (*wnw*) whose authority extended at least in part over the cult of the Ibis and the Hawk.[3] We may reasonably conclude that Ḥor was no stranger to the temple of the Peak, for either he or his secretary must have spoken with the magician of Imḥōtep when seeking an interpretation for the oracle of Thoth (Texts **16, 17**). Thus the irony that the search for the temple of Imḥōtep, which was one of the motives for the excavation of Ḥepnēbes and its shrines, has produced more evidence to lead us to its source.

Postscript

Of some relevance here may be a small wooden plaque excavated at Saqqâra during the season of 1967/8. It bears the excavator's number H6-161 [1957], and will be published by the excavators in due course.[4] It was discovered in the loose fill (*radîm*) outside the western wall of the great temple enclosure, and bears a short inscription incised in demotic.

1. *tꜣ sbt(t) n Ḏḥwty nb Ḫmnw*
2. *rꜣ inḥy rs*
3. *Pr-Wsir-Ḥp.*

1. The compound of Thoth, lord of Hermopolis:
2. the gate (of) the southern courtyard
3. (of) the Serapeum.

The word 'compound' (*sbtt*) has a respectable history of learned discussion; Reich (*Mizraim*, i (1933), 58 ff.) discoursed upon the meaning of similar features in the Serapeum dedicated to Horus, Isis, and Sakhmis, and concluded that they were 'hill-compounds'. Guilmot (*CdE* 35 (1962), 367 ff.) seems to have agreed with this interpretation, and sought to locate these sanctuaries within the precinct of the temple of Osorapis himself. This is possible, although the resultant map is very crowded, and the shrines pictured are rather small to occupy the prominent

obscure priesthood in the Peak, was also 'scribe of the rations (*ḫrt*) of the Cow in the temple of Memphis'. This cow is almost certainly the Mother of the Apis; the date is Year 38 of Philadelphus.

[1] Brugsch, *Thesaurus*, 904, 9–10 and 914, 5.

[2] See notes to Text **2**, R° 2, p. 15. The nature of this 'cavern' is uncertain, although the possibility arises that it represented the burial chamber of the sage's tomb. Note too the legend of 'Joseph's prison' discussed by Stricker, *Acta Orientalia*, 19, i (1941), 101 ff.

[3] Note again, in the light of the explanation of pastophoroi given at the end of § 3 above, that these priests are attached to the forecourt, the public part of the temple.

[4] Now in the British Museum, no. 67225.

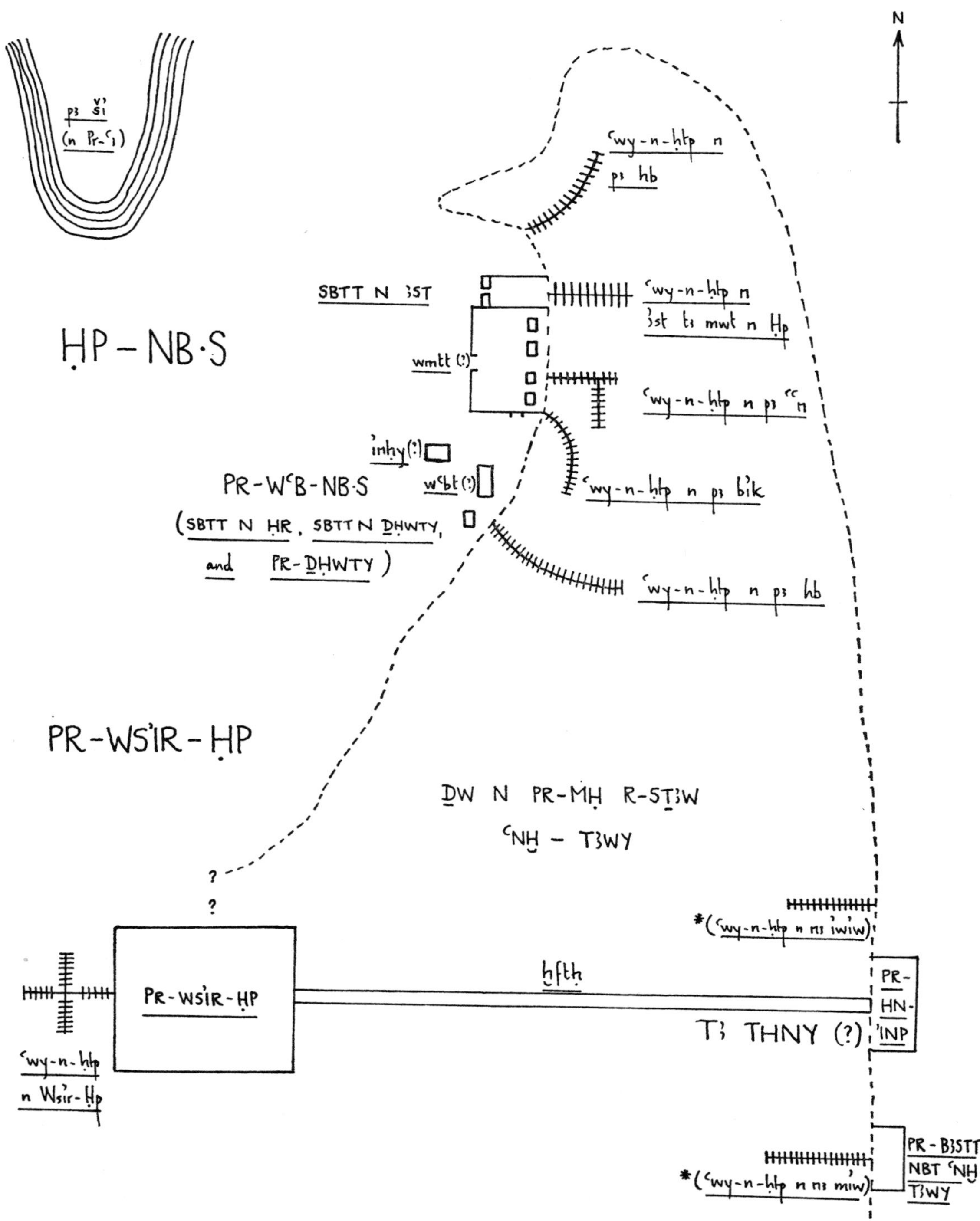

FIG. 3. Sketch map of the Memphite Serapeum, with ancient names.

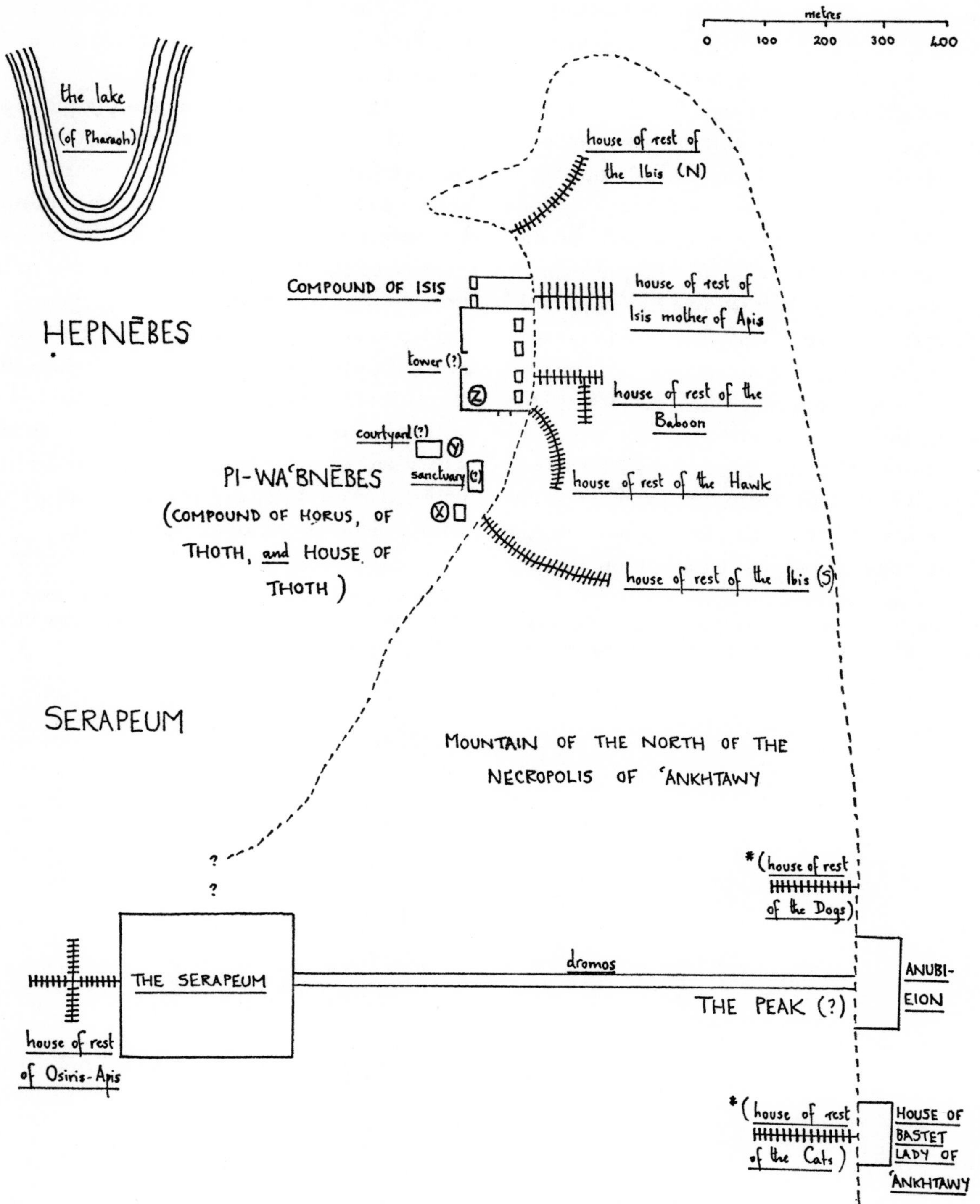

Fig. 4. Translation of fig. 3.

X = Findspot of the main archive; Y = Findspot of Texts **6**, **10** and **21**; Z = Findspot of Text **33**.

place given to them in the papyri, where individual houses are confidently located by reference to them. If we take the designation 'Serapeum' in the wider sense, as referring to the entire settlement which covered the northern mountain of ʿAnkhtawy, it then becomes possible to relieve the congestion of Guilmot's map. It is unlikely that a plaque describing a minor chapel of the Serapeum precinct should be discovered far to the north of the temple proper, but not implausible that its inscription should refer to one or more of the ibis-buildings near by. On this same argument the 'compound (*sbtt*) of Horus' would be the precinct of the hawk-cult, and the 'compound of Isis' would be a part of the sacred buildings of the Mothers of the Apis.[1] The fourth compound, that of Sakhmis, is unknown, and the descriptions of the papyri are vague. Perhaps it too lay on the line running north from the Serapeum towards the 'lake of Pharaoh'. If so, the tantalizing prospect of a lioness-gallery may lie before future excavators; but this is unproven.[2]

The third line of our wooden plaque is something of a mystery; the 'southern courtyard of the Serapeum' seems a bad description of a feature so far to the north. We are reminded of the similar problem in Text **23**, R° 2–4, where the area of the 'house of Thoth' is said to lie 'on the southern mountain of the Serapeum'. This strange description was explained tentatively as an attempt to distinguish the two groups of ibis-galleries, south and north of the 'Iseum'. A similar explanation may lie behind the 'southern courtyard' of our plaque; but certainty in such matters, as in so many others, must await the hand and notebook of the excavator.

[1] See maps, pp. 152–3.

[2] A fragmentary Greek papyrus discovered in the *sondage* of El-Khouli at Saqqâra by the Serapeum proper (see note to Text **1**, 2, p. 9 above) bears the phrase ταφὴ καὶ τροφὴ τῶν λεόντων 'burial and nourishment of the lions'; but the context is still too vague for any bouts of theory.

IV. APPENDICES

§ 1 : The titles of Isis

THE paramount importance assumed by Isis during the Hellenistic period in the religion not only of her native Egypt, but of the entire Graeco-Roman world, is of course well known, and literature upon this subject is now legion. Primary sources from our period are, however, rare; hieroglyphic texts, beside the information contained in the opening sections of the Metternich Stela and the Bremner–Rhind papyrus,[1] are confined to the difficult and disparate inscriptions of the Graeco-Roman temples. Litanies to the goddess are preserved in Pap. Dem. Heidelberg 736 (Spiegelberg, *ZÄS* 53 (1917), 33–4 and pl. 8), and in Greek in Pap. Oxyrhynchus 1380 (*Oxyrhynchus Papyri*, ix. 301 ff.). The various Greek aretalogies, which are expressly said in some cases to derive from Memphite originals, are also of great value. The most recent studies are now summarized in the *Répertoire analytique des travaux relatifs à la diffusion des cultes isiaques, 1940–1969* (*IBIS*), edited by J. Leclant, while much epigraphical material is grouped in L. Vidman, *Sylloge inscriptionum religionis Isiacae et Sarapiacae* (Berlin, 1969). Recent publications include the latter's *Isis und Sarapis bei den Griechen und Römern* (Berlin, 1970), as well as D. Müller's *Ägypten und die griechischen Isis-Aretalogien* (Berlin, 1961); M. Münster, *Untersuchungen zur Göttin Isis vom alten Reich bis zum Ende des neuen Reiches* (Berlin, 1968); J. Bergman, *Ich bin Isis* (Uppsala, 1968), and R. E. Witt, *Isis in the Graeco-Roman World* (London, 1971); these latter are quoted extensively below and are abbreviated to the names of their authors. In addition to these works, unpublished dissertations by Fr. Dunand and A. Forgeau are signalled in *Annuaire de l'É.P.H.É.* (*Sect. Sci.-Relig.*), 79 (1971–2), 199, 205. It is therefore clear that the material of our present ostraca will provoke much discussion. The titles of the goddess have been divided arbitrarily and are numbered consecutively.

(*a*) *Titles emphasizing her greatness*

1. *ḥnwt* 'mistress': Text **8**, V° 3 (in *ỉmt n·ỉ tꜣy·ỉ ḥnwt ꜣst*; **9**, R° 11; **28**, 15 (*tꜣy·s ḥnwt*).
   A very common epithet of goddesses, cf. *Wb*. iii. 107.
2. *tꜣ ntrt ꜥꜣt* 'the great goddess': Text **1**, 12 (*tꜣ ntrt ꜥꜣt n pꜣy Kmy pꜣ tꜣ Ḫr*); **2**, V° 14; **10**, R° 8; **47**, 1(?)
   Again common. The association with Egypt in **1**, 12 is natural, but the reference to Syria is interesting. Pap. Oxyrh. 1380 locates her cult in various towns of the coast, notably Gaza, Ascalon, and Berytus (cf. Witt, 109). Such insistence may have added weight to the Ptolemaic claim to Coele-Syria; intermittent though this was, the reign of Philometor was characterized by a strong desire to recover this territory. Ḥor's reference may therefore have been intentional, designed to secure the king's good will. Isis as guardian of home affairs is recalled in Text **3**, R° 7 *nts* (*tꜣ*) *nty ḥrḥ pꜣ ḳḥy n Kmy*.
3. (*tꜣ*) *wryt* 'the great one': with article, Text **24A**, 5; without, as *ꜣst wry*(*t*), **10**, R° 3, 7.
   The Greek equivalent (Θ)ουῆρις is common, as is the composite Ἐσουῆρις (Preisigke, 109), cf. Bergman, 156, n. 3, 270, n. 8.
4. *tꜣ wꜥt wꜥt·s* 'the one alone': Text **3**, R° 24, preceded by *ỉw·s rḫ wꜥt·s*. A natural expression for the uniqueness of the goddess. A Greek transcription θιουῖν is attested in the Isis hymn from Medînet Mâdi (Bergman, 225 and esp. n. 1).[2] This fact alone suggests a strong Egyptian influence upon these texts.
5. *nbt pt ḥnꜥ tꜣ* 'lady of heaven and earth': Text **10**, R° 10.
   The epithet *nbt pt* is dealt with in Bergman, 162–3. Isis οὐρανία is well known, and even the speech put into her mouth beginning ἐγώ εἰμι μήτηρ θεῶν

[1] Conveniently published in the editions of Sander-Hansen, *Die Texte der Metternichstele* (= *Analecta Aegyptiaca*, 7, Copenhagen, 1956) and Faulkner, *The Papyrus Bremner-Rhind* (*British Museum No. 10188*) (= *Bibliotheca Aegyptiaca*, 3, Brussels, 1933).

[2] The Coptic equivalent ⲧⲟⲩⲓ (Fayyûmic), in which the -ⲟⲩ- is a consonant, shows that the accentuation of the Greek should be revised from the θιουιν of the publications.

ἡ καλουμένη Οὐρανός (Brugsch, *Thesaurus*, 753). Lucius in Apuleius, *Metamorphoses*, xi. 2 opens his address to the goddess with the words *regina caeli*. One is reminded of the claim in Text **9**, R° 10, *di·i wꜣḥ tꜣ pt*,[1] and such words recur in the Aretalogy of Cyme 12, ἐγὼ ἐχώρισα γῆν ἀπ' οὐρανοῦ (Bergman, 301), a phrase which introduces the earth (*ḥnꜥ tꜣ*) of our present example. The phrase in Text **10** concludes with the additional *nbt bꜥy* 'lady of the sepulchre', thus making of the goddess a universal deity, an aspect well brought out by Apuleius (xi. 4), where she introduces herself as ***rerum naturae parens, elementorum omnium domina*** (nbt tm nb), ***saeculorum progenies initialis, summa numinum*** (nbt nṯrw), ***regina manium*** (nbt bꜥy?), ***prima caelitum*** (nbt pt), ***deorum dearumque facies uniformis, quae caeli luminosa culmina, maris salubria flamina, inferum deplorata silentia nutibus meis dispenso***. Again the resemblance is marked.

6. *iw·s mšꜥ rdwy·s ḥr ḥr pꜣ mw (n) pꜣ ym (n) Ḫr* 'walking upon the face of the water(s) of the Syrian sea': Text **1**, 12–13; cf. **47**, 1–2.
   Although a description rather than a title, the connotations are those of a common role of Isis, one which may well have influenced the form of a dream. She was regularly a goddess of harbours, λιμενῖτις, especially at Alexandria (Text **1**, 14 *pḥ·s pꜣ ꜥwy-n-mr n Rꜥ-ḳd*), cf. also Cyme 43 ἐγὼ πραΰνω καὶ κυμαίνω θάλασσαν (reminiscent of the *maris salubria flamina* of Apuleius) and 49 ἐγὼ ναυτιλίας εἰμὶ κυρία (Bergman, 302); for Ἶσις Φαρία cf. Witt, 126. Nevertheless it remains true that the land-bound Ḥor makes little of this aspect of the goddess.
7. Two attributes of the goddess are listed in Text **10**, R° 12–13: *ḥst* 'praise', which is said to be among men, and *šfyt* 'prestige', which is located among the gods. For the latter cf. Bergman, 182, 190 and the remarks of Gardiner, *JEA* 27 (1941), 45–6.

(b) Isis as a royal goddess

8. *tꜣ Pr-ꜥꜣt tm nb (nty wꜣḥ-sḫn n pꜣ tꜣ dr·f)* 'the Queen of all entirety, who holds sway in the entire land': Text **3**, V° 6; **10**, R° 16; without the second epithet, Text **6**, V° x+9.
   The merits of the alternative reading *iwꜥ nb* are discussed in the note to Text **10**, R° 16. For *tm(m)* cf. *Wb.* v, 305; the whole title probably corresponds to the παντοκράτειρα of Witt, 145. With the addition of *pꜣ tꜣ dr·f* the phrase begins to look like the original of the common ἡ βασίλισσα (Bergman, 29, 161)/τύραννος (op. cit. 149, 301) πάσης χώρας; for the alternation between the translations 'whole earth' and 'every land' see note 4 to 149–50. The expression is yet another tribute to the universal role of the goddess. The words *(n) pꜣ tꜣ dr·f* are also added to *tꜣ nṯrt ꜥꜣt* in Text **10**, R° 7.
9. *tꜣ nbt tꜣwy* 'the lady of the two lands': Text **1**, 10; **10**, R° 3.
   This queenly title needs little more by way of credentials than *Wb.* v. 218, 2; Bergman, 153.
10. *tꜣ nbt tꜣ grpyt* 'the lady of the diadem': Text **3**, R° 5–6; cf. Text **6** (?).
    Perhaps a description rather than a standard title: see notes *ad loca*.
11. *tꜣ nbt ꜣrꜥy* 'the lady of (the) uraeus': Text **10**, R° 2–3.
    For the associations, cf. Witt, 34.
    For the entire subject, cf. Bergman, 146–71. The role of Isis as a goddess of the throne is well brought out in the opening of the verso to Text **3**, where she is pictured as bringing the royal diadem to Pharaoh's descendants in the temple of Memphis, traditional and (since the crowning of Ptolemy V) actual site of the royal coronation. The special protection of the goddess is invoked for the earthly queen in the sadly damaged lines of Text **28**.

(c) Isis as mother and lover

12. *mwt-nṯr* 'god's mother': Text **10**, R° 3, 7, 8(?), in each case preceded by *ꜣst wryt*.
    This title seems originally to have meant 'mother of the god' (i.e. Horus, *Wb.* ii. 54), in conformity with the principle of the direct genitive that both nouns are essentially definite (Bakir, *JEA* 52 (1966), 35), but the Greek equivalent μήτηρ θεῶν (Bergman, 274) implies that the idea was understood in a more general sense. That the specific notion of the motherhood of Horus was not forgotten, however, is shown by Cyme 8 (Bergman, 301) ἐγώ εἰμι μήτηρ Ὥρου βασιλέως. The ex-

[1] See note *ad locum*.

tension of this relationship to cover all children, or the sick seen as helpless infants, is familiar from the magical texts.[1] The power of Isis over birth and the newly-born is expressed in such Greek texts as Cyme 18.

13. *nbt mrt* 'lady of love': Text **10**, R° 8.
Another Egyptian concept amply grasped by the Greeks, cf. Cyme, 27 ἐγὼ στέργεσθαι γυναῖκας ὑπὸ ἀνδρῶν ἠνάγκασα. For the rich identification of Isis with Aphrodite cf. Vandebeek, *De Interpretatio graeca van de Isisfigur* (Louvain, 1946).

(*d*) *Isis and the worshipper*

14. *šꜣy* 'fate' and *špšy* 'uraeus-goddess'. These two concepts are associated with the goddess in Text **3**, R° 4, and identified with her in Text **10**, R° 8–9. For iconographic and other parallels see note to Text **3**, R° 4, and Dunand, 'Les représentations de l'Agathodaemon à propos de quelques bas-reliefs du Musée d'Alexandrie' in *BIFAO* 67 (1969), 9 ff. The place of Isis as a goddess of fate is recognized by her identification at Alexandria with the concept of Tyche, and a very close parallel to the themes of Text **3** is shown by a representation (Dunand, op. cit. 37) of an amuletic ibis holding a caduceus and inscribed ΘΑΥΤ ϤΑΕ (*Ḏḥwty pꜣ šꜣy*); the second female serpent will then correspond to *špšy* and Isis-Thermouthis. Here too we have a close association of Isis and Thoth which in all probability springs from the same source as the statement of Text **3**, R° 16 that the god was the father of the goddess. Such a belief may possibly have arisen at North Saqqâra itself, see note *ad locum* above.
Closely linked with the idea of Isis as fate is the notion of her as inaugurator of time: in Text **3**, R° 5–6 she 'opens' a new year. This is more than a passing conceit, for Isis is regularly identified with the dog-star Sothis (*Spdt*), whose heliacal rising coincided with the Nile flood. This idea too passes into Greek, cf. Cyme, 9 ἐγώ εἰμι ἡ ἐν τῷ τοῦ κυνὸς ἄστρῳ ἐπιτέλλουσα, and the litany Pap. Oxyrh. 1380, 203 ff.

15. In *incubation*. Text **9** of the present archive makes clear this function of the goddess; see Commentary § 3 above. Such an important role as the defender of the suppliant (Ἶσις ἐπήκοος) is also clear from passages such as Diodorus I, 25.

16. *wrt ḥkꜣ* 'great of magic': Text **18**, R° 14. A function familiar from the magic- and healing-texts described above; cf. also Sbordone, *Iside maga*, in *Aegyptus* 26 (1946), 130; Bergman, 285–9.

17. The *mdt-nfrt*.
The fullest description of the benefits which Isis confers upon the faithful worshipper occurs in Text **10**, R° 13–14, 'for thou givest sustenance to a man throughout his days of life, and when he dies, thou art the one that suppliest (his) burial'. In the following lines these boons are prescribed for Ḥor himself. In Text **9**, and possibly **11**, burial is also at the bestowal of the goddess. The matter is discussed in the Commentary, § 3; here the most important feature is the similarity to the denouement of Apuleius, where the same goddess claims the devotion of the worshipper Lucius for the rest of his life, and promises (XI, 6): *vives in mea tutela gloriosus; et cum spatium saeculi tui permensus ad inferos demearis, ibi quoque in ipso subterraneo semirotundo me, quam vides . . . tibi propitiam frequens adorabis*. The whole relationship is summed up in the descriptive line of Text **8**, 18: *ꜣst ḏd mꜣꜥt n nꜣ nty mꜣꜥ* 'Isis speaks truth to those who are true'.

18. *nbt pꜣ nwḥ nty snḥ* 'lady of the bundle which is bound': Text **10**, R° 18.
For this enigmatic phrase see note *ad locum*; the underlying idea may be funerary, possibly agricultural, or perhaps a reference to the power of fate. It is equally likely that its meaning has escaped me.[2]

[1] A full example occurs in the Metternich Stela (v. Sander-Hansen, op. cit. *supra*; a translation in Brunner-Traut, *Altägyptische Märchen* (second edn., Düsseldorf-Köln, 1965), 109–15).

[2] Various sources may be cited to support these guesses, but none is anything like conclusive. Diodorus I, 14 refers to sheaves of corn carried in Isiac processions, ἀπομνημόνευμα τῶν ἐξ ἀρχῆς τῇ θεῷ φιλοτέχνως εὑρηθέντων. Tertullian, *De Corona*, 7 describes how the goddess wore on her head a crown of the corn which she discovered; in such a guise ancient authors (Herodotus II, 59 and others) identify her with Demeter. Another possibility is that the phrase is funerary, and refers to mummy bandages; the sacred cows, Mothers of the Apis, come to mind here. A third explanation, that of fate, evokes the common metaphor of loosing and binding (e.g. Ikhernofret, 24). A further intriguing possibility emerges on

(e) Isis and other gods

19. *Osiris*
Associated with Isis in invocations: Texts **8**, V° 9; R° 11; **18**, R°; and probably in Text **10**, R° 6–7. In Text **25**, 3 the Hawk is said to be the soul (*by*) of Osiris, Horus, and Isis conjointly.

20. *Horus/Harpocrates*
Occurs with his mother in the dreams of Text **9**, although the exact relationship is unclear. Associated in evocation of Text **18**, R°, while in Text **20**, 5 is named specifically as *Ḥr pꜣ ẖrd* (*n*) *ꜣst* 'Horus the child of Isis'. See also the end of the previous section.

21. *Nephthys*
Appears only in combination with her sister. In Text **18**, V° 17 reference is made to 'the power of Isis with Nephthys the great' (*ʿw ꜣst ḥnʿ Nbt-ḥt ʿꜣt*). In Text **19**, R° she appears in a compendium of gods, in Text **20**, 6 she is 'Nephthys the sister of Isis', and in Text **15**, R° 7 we are told that 'the two sisters (mentioned in an oracle of some sort) are Isis together with Nephthys'.

22. *Thoth*
In the verso of Text **8** this god appears with Isis and Osiris; in Text **3**, R° 13 he is said to be her father. See no. 14 above, and the note *ad locum*. In the dream of Text **1**, Thoth 'takes the hand' of the goddess as she gives her prophetic announcement.

23. *'All the gods of Egypt'*
Are associated under the presidency of Isis in the V° of Text **11**; a similar phenomenon occurs at the beginning of the *Somnium Nectanebi* (*UPZ*, 270–1), itself almost certainly a Greek translation or adaptation from a native source.

(f) Cult-places of Isis

24. *Alexandria*
In Text **1** Isis appears as guaranteeing the protection of the capital (Text **1**, 14 *Rʿ-ḳd smn wbꜣ pꜣ hf*); here she is clearly Ἶσις πολιοῦχος.

25. *Temenēsi* (*Isios polis*)
The full name of this locality is given in Text **2**, R° 2–3; V° 1–2 as 'the town of Isis, lady of the cavern, the great goddess, in the nome of Sebennytos'. The 'cavern' (*tpḥ*, if this is the correct reading) is an unknown feature of her cult. For the location of Temenēsi see the note to Text **2**, R° 2, p. 19 above.

26. *Memphis*
In Text **10**, R° 2, 6, 10, 16, 18 occurs the name *Tꜣnꜣ*, in three cases qualified by a possessive *tꜣy·i*; this is clearly a name of the goddess. If a connection with the Memphite cult-place *Ṯnnt* (*Wb.* v. 382; Bergman, 247–50) is admissible, the name would be a Memphite sobriquet of Isis. It is otherwise unknown.
In the same text (**10**, R° 3–4) Isis is described as 'the great goddess of the *wady* of the lake', a description very appropriate to the site. The geographical terms of this passage are discussed in § 5 of the Commentary above.
Finally, the opening of Text **10** qualifies the goddess as *nbt knḥy*. Although the word *knḥy* may well be used of a naos, it is also common, especially in the Memphite necropolis, as a designation of the vaults in which animals such as the Apis or his Mother were laid to rest. This explanation is also discussed in § 5 of the Commentary.

(g) Conclusion

The wealth of information given by the Ḥor archive is far from being exhausted by these brief and tentative remarks. In a preliminary publication of this kind it is impossible to investigate matters in the detail which they deserve, and a preliminary observation must suffice; this is simply that it is impossible to read the epithets of Isis contained in our ostraca without realizing how naturally they fall into the traditional imagery and vocabulary of Egyptian religion. It would be absurd to deny that the Hellenistic period saw considerable development and elaboration of the cult of Isis, but equally absurd to ignore the true origin of the images and conceptions which surround the goddess. This is not a surprising conclusion, for it is merely the truth which the Greek aretalogies never cease to proclaim: χαῖρε Αἴγυπτε θρέψασά με.

§ 2 : The titles of Thoth

The titles and functions allotted to the god Thoth in our texts do not exhibit quite the variety of the names

a reading of Pap. Leiden I, 348 (Borghouts, op. cit. 161), where the bull deity *Ṯꜣ-sp·f* is said to be the 'bearer of cords' (*ḥry nwḥ*); these are explained by the editor as ropes for land measurement (cf. *ẖt-nwḥ*, schoenus). The context is a child-birth spell, and it may be that Isis has taken over this function from the obscurer deity. But there is little to distinguish any one of these explanations from the rest.

of Isis, but they achieve some importance in confirming attributes known to us from other sources, and above all in supplying clues to the origins of that important figure, Hermes Trismegistos.

Two items of circumstantial value are given to us in the texts: Text **3**, R° 13 names a 'great festival' (*ḥb ꜥꜣ*) of Thoth, celebrated at North Saqqâra on the twelfth day of the month which bore his name. This is partially confirmed by Text **8**, R° 1; the event is not known from other sources. The second item is the tradition, already discussed above, that Thoth was the father of Isis.[1] This idea, although by no means incompatible with Egyptian religious thought, nevertheless seems to be unparalleled in native texts. Even the Cyme aretalogy 3b can muster only the information that the god had been Isis' tutor, καὶ ἐπαιδεύθην ὑπὸ 'Ερμοῦ; yet the tradition was grasped by the ever-watchful Plutarch (*De Iside et Osiride*, 3, 352 A; 12, 355F). In the later Hermetic corpus its future was to be assured; it is therefore welcome to have confirmation of the belief from the mid-second century B.C.

The arrangement of the following titles is arbitrary.

1. *pꜣ nṯr ꜥꜣ* 'the great god': Texts **1**, 10; **16**, R° 1–2; **17**, 2; **22**, R° 2; **23**, R° 7, V° 8–9, 16; **25**, 11; **32**, R° 6.
   This epithet of gods in the late period is too common to require much comment. An interesting feature is that in all cases the epithet precedes the name of the god, the order always being *pꜣ nṯr ꜥꜣ Ḏḥwty*. The reasons for this change in the standard order, whether euphonic or religious, are not clear. A similar phrase *pꜣy·i nb ꜥꜣ Ḏḥwty* 'my great lord Thoth' occurs in the evocation of Text **8**, V° 1.
2. *pꜣ ꜥꜣ* 'the great': Texts **22**, V° 2*; **47**, 6(?).
   Doubtless a variant of the preceding or of the following.
3. *ꜥꜣ* 'great': Text **23**, R° 2.
   The shortest possible form, squeezed between the name of the god and a cult-title.
4. *ꜥꜣ ꜥꜣ* 'twice great': Text **25**, 4(?).
   A reduplicated form of the preceding, perhaps used for emphasis; but the context is not one of the clearest.
5. *ꜥꜣ ꜥꜣ nb Ḫmnw* 'twice great, lord of Hermopolis': Text **28**, 12.
   The reduplicated form, followed by the major cult-place of the god.[2] This version is obviously the first step towards the triplicate forms discussed below; a further step, *ꜥꜣ ꜥꜣ ꜥꜣ nb Ḫmnw* 'thrice great, lord of Hermopolis', is found transliterated into Greek letters in an inscription of the late second century B.C. (Girgis in *MDAIK*, 20 (1965), 121). The examples given below are designed to show that the all-important expansion of the title had already taken place by the middle of this second century.
6. *pꜣ ꜥꜣ pꜣ ꜥꜣ nty ꜥꜣy n ms* 'the twice great, who is the elder born': Text **12**, 9 = **12A**, 2.
   Used in a description of Thoth as the introduction to a prophetic dream. The word for 'great', duplicated, is now preceded by the definite article; the following *nty ꜥꜣy n ms*, which seems to have been grafted on to the original expression, may refer to a Hermopolite theory of creation in which Thoth acted as demiurge (Morenz, *Ägyptische Religion*, 187 ff.). It may also be a reflection of the belief which made the god the father of Isis, and possibly of other gods besides,[3] or it may be that the phrase is used in a less specific way, to portray the god as possessor of hoary wisdom. A Greek version of *Ḏḥwty pꜣ ꜥꜣ pꜣ ꜥꜣ*, namely μεγίστου καὶ μεγίστου 'Ερμοῦ, is to be found in the Raphia decree of Ptolemy IV (Gauthier and Sottas, *Décret trilingue*, 72, ll. 3–4). An early version of the demotic *ꜥꜣ ꜥꜣ nb Ḫmnw* is discussed by Hughes, *JNES* 17 (1958), 8; even Saite versions are known, clearly demonstrating that the expansion of the god's title took place before the Hellenistic period.
7. *pꜣ ꜥꜣ pꜣ ꜥꜣ pꜣ ꜥꜣ* 'the thrice great': Text **2**, V° 15; **19**, R° 5; **26**, V° 10.
   The triplicate form with the definite article marks the culmination of the god's development, and there can be little doubt that it is a title of this sort, natural to Egyptian religious vocabulary, which lies behind the Greek equivalent τρισμέγιστος. The early history of this important identification was discussed by Skeat and Turner in their edition of the Greek ostraca from our archive (*JEA* 54 (1968), 208); the conclusion of these editors is that it is to the Ḥor ostraca

[1] See notes to Text **3**, R° 13, p. 27 above; also Commentary, §§ 3, 5 and Appendix 1, no. 22; Griffith, *ZÄS* 38, 87.

[2] For a discussion of all the place-names in Egypt known to the Greeks as Hermopolis, see § 1 of the Commentary above.

[3] For this notion, see the introduction to this Appendix and the passages quoted.

(Greek Texts **A**, **B**, and **D**) that we must look for the earliest unequivocal use of the Greek adaptation. The later form τρισμέγιστος is of course not used in these ostraca, for Ḥor restricts himself to the double superlative followed by a positive (μεγίστου καὶ μεγίστου θεοῦ μεγάλου Ἑρμοῦ). Now it is surely of significance that when the article of Skeat and Turner was written, the demotic equivalent *pꜣ ꜥꜣ pꜣ ꜥꜣ pꜣ ꜥꜣ* had not yet come to light in the rest of the archive; the present references can therefore serve only to strengthen their conclusions.

It is not the point of least interest in our documents that they should provide the earliest clue to the origins of a most remarkable figure in the history of thought, a philosopher, whose reputation as the sage 'Trismegistus' was transmitted through the Middle Ages and Renaissance to influence even such forerunners of modern thinking as Bruno and Copernicus.

A similar threefold title, *ꜥꜣ ꜥꜣ wr*, is applied to Thoth in the hieroglyphic inscriptions from Dendera (Chassinat, *Dendara*, i. 30); this may well be an adaptation from *pꜣ ꜥꜣ pꜣ ꜥꜣ pꜣ ꜥꜣ*, although the contrast between the first two elements and the final *wr* reminds one slightly of Hor's μεγίστου . . . μεγίστου . . . μεγάλου. A second, and perhaps more likely possibility is that the hieroglyphic phrase is a parallel to *pꜣ ꜥꜣ pꜣ ꜥꜣ nty ꜥꜣy n ms* quoted above, for *wr* in the meaning 'elder' is attested (*Wb.* i. 327). Unfortunately, the answer to such a question lies outside the scope of this volume.

8. *pꜣ wr-di͗w* 'the great of five': Text **3**, R° 16; **16**, R° 12; **17**, 11. (The last two examples are followed directly by the name of the god.)
For the title, also applied at an earlier stage to the high priest of the god cf. *Wb.* v. 420; a Greek transcription πόρτις is known. Further references are to be found in Boylan, *Thoth*, and Bonnet, *Reallexikon*.

9. *pꜣ rḫ* 'the knowing': Text **3**, R° 16(?).
An obvious reference to the magical and other learning of the god, but the context is faint and obscure.

10. *pꜣ nb rḫ* 'the knowing lord': Text **17**, 22; **18**, V° 11 (in form *pꜣ nb i͗r-rḫ*).
An extension of the preceding. For the notion, cf. Text **17**, 11 ff. (*r pꜣ wr-di͗w Ḏḥwty i͗r-rḫ r pꜣ nty i͗r mdt-nfrt n pꜣ hb*) and similar sentiments.

11. *ꜥꜣ wpyt* 'great of judgment': Text **32**, R° 1.
Although some doubt concerns the place of Text **32** in our archive, there can be little suspicion of the title, which is paralleled by the obvious role of Thoth as recorder of judgements in the *Book of the Dead* and similar writings. The notion of Thoth as a giver of verdicts pervades the whole archive (see, for example, § 3 of the Commentary for the role of the god in oracles). In Text **31B**, 5 there is mention of *tꜣ mdt wpy Ḏḥwty* 'the matter of the judgement of Thoth'; in Text **32**, R° 6 we have a matter *wpy-s pꜣ ntr ꜥꜣ Ḏḥwty* 'adjudicated by the great god Thoth', and Text **7** records 'the law of the verdict (*wpyt*) of the ibises of Egypt'.

12. *pꜣ i͗·i͗r ḏlꜥ-mdt* 'the one who records': Text **1**, 10–11 (cf. Text **17A**, 11–12).
Although properly a description of the god rather than a title, it is included here because it aptly summarizes one of his major functions, that of scribe of the gods. This activity of the deity is equally shown in Text **12**, R° 9–10 (= **12A**, 1–2), where the gods who are in the *Sktt*-barque are said to revere him *r-dbꜣ pꜣy·f i͗r sẖ nfr* 'because of his making a beneficent writing'.[1] In this image there may be an echo of Thoth as vizir, standing in the prow of the sun god's bark (cf. Roeder, *Mythen und Legenden*, 312, Abb. 60).

13. *nb ꜥḥꜥ* 'lord of lifetime': Text **17**, 7–8.
A clear evocation of Thoth as recorder of time, as he appears in numerous temple scenes, sometimes notching tallies upon a palm branch (Roeder, *Die Ägyptische Götterwelt*, 330, Abb. 56).

14. *nb mꜣꜥt* 'lord of truth': Text **18**, V° 11.
This epithet, used only in the dream-invocation of Text **18**, is qualified with phrases such as *nty i͗w mꜣꜥ rn·f* 'whose name is true', and repeated references to Thoth as magician. The association of Thoth with Maꜥat (personified as a goddess) is also common.

15. *i͗ꜥḥ* 'moon': Text **3**, R° 16.
An identification of Thoth with his celestial

[1] The phrase is oddly reminiscent of the praise of Imḥōtep in Texts **16**, R° 7; **17A**, 8–10 *nty i͗w·w ꜥš n·f n nꜣ tꜣwy dr·w r-dbꜣ pꜣy·f i͗r-spy*(?). For the image see Schott, *ZÄS* 99 (1972), 20–5.

counterpart. That this identification is more than a literary allusion is shown by the creation of a composite Late-Period divinity, *Wsir-iꜥḥ-Ḏḥwty* or 'Osiris Lunus' (Roeder, *Ägyptische Bronzewerke*, pl. 3; *JEA* 56 (1970), pl. VIII, 6); the lunar disc worn by ibis and baboon is also well attested.

16. *hb* 'ibis': Text **3**, R° 16.
§ 4 of the Commentary deals with the affairs of this avatar of the god, who in Text **19**, R° 5 is said to be *pꜣ by* (*n*) *Ḏḥwty*. It is notable that the other emanation of Thoth, the baboon, in spite of being worshipped at Ḥepnēbes, is nowhere mentioned in our texts.

17. *nb ꜥnḫ* 'lord of life': Text **23**, V° 15.
This epithet is reminiscent of no. 13 above. In Text **3**, R° 16 the god seems also to be addressed as *pꜣ ꜥnḫ* 'the living one', but the passage is too obscure for any certainty.

18. *pꜣ ḥry* 'the superior': Text **26**, V° 10.
This stark epithet (which may have celestial connotations) follows *pꜣ ꜥꜣ pꜣ ꜥꜣ pꜣ ꜥꜣ* in the strongest description in our archive of the power of the god. Other references to the might of the thrice-great are to be seen in our texts; Text **16**, R° 2 (= **17**, 2) acquaints us with the god 'whose power is known in every matter which concerns the Ibis in his heart', while Text **16**, R° 12 (= **17**, 7–8) calls upon the god *irm pꜣy·f nꜥš* 'together with his might' to crush the writer's enemies.

19. *pꜣ nb n pꜣ ḥꜣty* 'the lord of the heart': Text **26**, V° 10.
This enigmatic title, which follows the praise of Thoth mentioned in the previous section, is capable of several interpretations. One possibility would be a connection with the psychostasis, in which the heart is weighed against the feather of *mꜣꜥt*, but this does not seem convincing; a more likely explanation would be a reference to the heart as seat of emotion and intellect, over the latter of which Thoth was particularly thought to be the master. The epithet would then picture him as director and inspiration of rational thought.
In conclusion two epithets must be mentioned which link the god with his cult-centres. The topographical questions, and the relations between the various cults of the Serapeum and the main temple of Ptaḥ in Memphis have already been discussed in § 4 of the Commentary above; the significance of the phrase itself is discussed in the notes to Text **19**, R° 2–3.

20. *pꜣ ntr rn·f i·ir-sḫy n ḥt-ntr Mn-nfr* 'the god in person who holds sway in the temple of Memphis': Text **19**, R° 2–3.

21. *nb Pr-Ḏḥwty* 'lord of the House of Thoth': Text **23**, R° 2.
For the House of Thoth, the sanctuary of the ibis-cult at North Saqqâra, see § 4 of the Commentary.

At the end of this *exposé* of the god Thoth some reference should again be made to the interesting metaphor of 'the path' (*pꜣ myt*/*tꜣ mit*). This idea, which appears commonly in the writing of the Memphite Ḥor, has been discussed in the notes to Texts **16** and **17**, where it first appears, in Text **23** (R° 7–8), where the metaphor is extended by the secretary's assertion that he has 'not abandoned his path for ever', and in § 3 of the Commentary.[1] Whatever the stricter meaning of the phrase, it is clear that the Memphite Ḥor (and perhaps also Ḥor of Sebennytos, on whose behalf the secretary may be writing) felt himself bound in some way to observe the god's injunctions. A close parallel may be seen in the ethical inscriptions of the high priest Petosiris in his tomb at Tûna el-Gebel, in which he too declares his devotion to the ibis-god.[2] That the god could demand such close observance from his followers is confirmed by two sources, and must be taken into any account of the growth of religion in Egypt.

§ 3: Was Ḥor a *katochos*?

We have seen from the first section of the Commentary that, at some time about the middle of the 160s, Ḥor of Sebennytos seems to have taken up permanent residence in Memphis; indeed from his familiarity with the affairs of the ibis-shrine and the other cults of North Saqqâra, it seems natural to assume that it was in the Serapeum that he made his new home. Much more difficult to determine is the status which he acquired in his adopted setting. He refers to himself, on the few occasions in which he describes himself fully, as a citizen of the Sebennytic nome, whether of Temenēsi or of Pi(?)-Thoth; only occasionally does he add the

[1] Detailed references will be found in the index.

[2] Cf. Suys, *Vie de Petosiris* (Brussels, 1927), 129; Lefebvre, *Petosiris*, ii. 36, Inscr. 61, 28, and E. Otto, *Die biographischen Inschriften der ägyptischen Spätzeit*, 177–8.

information 'who is in Memphis'.[1] His former position, that of pastophoros of Isis, is not mentioned in the demotic texts and would be unknown to us were it not for the Greek ostraca. The one title which he retains is that of scribe (*pꜣ sẖ*), and texts such as the ibis-memoranda (Texts **19–23**) make it likely that he acted in some way as a recorder at meetings of the temple council. Nevertheless he seems to have been a man of some influence, judging from his behaviour in Text **22**, and it is likely that he possessed a considerable reputation as a soothsayer. At various points in our notes and commentaries the idea has raised itself that Ḥor of Sebennytos, like his notable contemporary (even acquaintance?) Ptolemaios, was one of those known to the Greek texts of the Serapeum as κάτοχοι, 'people under a restraint'.

The literature on this topic is long and difficult.[2] It had begun already in 1830 with Reuvens' third *Lettre à M. Letronne*, and its history was to prove eventful even before it came under the pen of Sethe (*Sarapis*, 94 ff.; cf. *ZÄS* 53 (1917), 42). The conclusion of the latter was that the persons described in Greek as 'detained within the temple' (ἱεροῦ ἐγκάτοχοι or a similar phrase) correspond to those who appear in Pap. Lille 29, a set of rules for the formation of a priestly guild, as *ḏdḥ n ỉrpy* (*r-pr*) 'confined to (the) shrine', and furthermore that these 'detainees' were restricted to the temple for legal and administrative reasons, as in a form of asylum. This view was followed by Sottas in his publication of the Lille papyri, and by others.[3] The arguments of Sethe and his predecessors were subjected to magnificent scrutiny by Wilcken (*UPZ* i. 52–72), and his conclusion is well known: that the restraint was self-imposed, and was caused by an omen of the god in which he laid a claim to the man's services. Since Wilcken's study some scholars have adhered to the 'secular' view of Sethe (so Woess, *Das Asylwesen Ägyptens*, 240 ff.; 'dont l'interprétation semble à peu près sûre', according to F. de Cenival, *Les Associations religieuses*, i. 33; the latter quotes Pap. Lille 29, 15, which seems only marginally relevant. The passage in question refers to members of a cult-guild who chance to be thrown into prison unjustly; whatever the merits of the 'secular theory', and they are considerable, it is not helped by such a quotation. A temple prison seems to be described in our present archive,[4] and the existence of such institutions is confirmed elsewhere, but nowhere in a context which suggests anything to do with the κατοχή. It is difficult to imagine that Ptolemaios was languishing in the Serapeum gaol; harder still to imagine his volatile brother, who himself became a *katochos* for a short period in the middle of 158, omitting to raise an outcry if he had been incarcerated).

Other scholars, notably Delekat and Erichsen,[5] have chosen to follow the 'religious' theory of Wilcken. It is not easy to decide between two such divergent opinions as those of Wilcken and Sethe, the more so as a suspicion must linger that the matter has sometimes been decided by the personality and inclinations of the writer. The two theories are of course not irreconcilable; it is quite possible that a man escaping from litigation or the police may have been susceptible to divine premonitions, particularly if they seemed to offer him safety, and it is of course known that Ptolemaios, whatever the nature of his κατοχή, had experienced difficulties in his early life. The same seems to be true of Ḥor of Sebennytos, who had become involved in a dispute of some kind while at Temenēsi. Nevertheless if this compromise solution is admitted, we must still decide upon the criterion of a *katochos*: was a man accepted into the Serapeum merely because of past troubles, or would his claim need to be based on proof of divine will? Here the present writer must confess his inclination towards the Wilcken interpretation, together with his belief that the dream of Text **8** provides confirmation of this view; but he must also confess his inability to prove his suspicions.

If the 'secular' theory of the κατοχή is followed, then there can be little or no evidence, apart from our knowledge of a dispute in Temenēsi, to call Ḥor a κάτοχος. The 'religious' theory, however, provides more interesting lines of thought:

(*a*) Text **8**, R° 1–12 records a dream, almost certainly experienced by Ḥor, in which the foreman of a labour-gang who has befriended him reveals himself to be the god Thoth, and commands him not to worship any other deity; Ḥor agrees to this, and his fate is revealed to him. The god then pledges maintenance for him in life and in death.

Qualification: the text of this ostracon is not clear, and the subject-matter is obscure in the extreme.

[1] Text **25**, 1 is the only clear example; **23**, R° 1 is doubtful, and **48**, 1 incomplete.

[2] See the summary and discussion by Wilcken, *UPZ* i. 53–4.

[3] *Les papyrus démotiques de Lille* (Paris, 1921), 57 ff.

[4] Text **19**, R° 22–3.

[5] Delekat, *Katoche, Hierodulie und Adoptionsfreilassung*, *Münch. Beitr.* 47 (1964); Erichsen, *Kultgenossenschaft*, 53 ff.

(*b*) Text **11**, V° 10, in the midst of a dream account, describes a dealing of Ḥor *r-db3 ḫpr irm p3 ntr* 'concerning dwelling with the god'.

Qualification: Text **11** is even more obscure than Text **8**, and the phrase 'dwelling with the god' is susceptible to other interpretations and need not carry the idea of a κατοχή.

(*c*) Text **14**, V° 11 may read *ḫpr p3 wḏ3 irm p3 ntr(?)* 'salvation has occurred together with the god(?)'.

Qualification: Text **14** is the most obscure of the entire archive.

It must be admitted that this evidence, even seen in combination, is weak. The most that can fairly be obtained from (*a*) is that Ḥor in some way felt a strong attachment to the god, and that this manifested itself, as well it might, in his dreams. There is no proof that Ḥor was a *katochos*, or that he became one as a result of the dream in Text **8**, or even that he acted upon this dream at all. To this negative conclusion we must add the argument from silence; Ḥor never refers to himself as a *katochos*, is never referred to as such by others, and his name is not included in the list of *katochoi* given in *Prosopographia Ptolemaica*.[1] We must also count the testimony of Text **1**, 1–2 that at least in the early 150s Ḥor seems to have been free to travel between Memphis and Heliopolis, a situation which is difficult to reconcile with his supposed status of κατοχή.[2] The last resort would then be to claim that Ḥor must have been a *katochos* only for a short period in the late 160s; but there is nothing else to support this explanation.

In spite of this poor conclusion, a kernel of interest remains. The 'religious' theory of Wilcken has much to recommend it, and the notion that it was as a result of inspired dreams that men took up confined residence in the Memphite Serapeum is eminently in keeping with what we know of Egyptian religion. Now it is difficult to resist the belief that it is precisely the sort of experience described in the beginning of Text **8** that Wilcken had in mind. The coincidence is striking; but it is here that we must leave it. Proof may one day appear for this most intriguing of possibilities.[3]

§ 4: Timechart

NOTE: This chart is intended only as a summary of the first two sections of the Commentary, and as a simple guide to the history of Philometor's reign. All arguments are omitted.

c. 200(?)	Birth of Ḥor at Pi(?)-Thoth in the nome of Sebennytos. Much of early life spent at nearby Temenēsi (Isios polis), as pastophoros of Isis.
184 (or, less likely, 186)	19 October: birth of Ptolemy, later Ptolemy VI Philometor.
180	after 20 May: accession of Philometor (Skeat, *Reigns* 32–3).

[1] *PP.* nos. 7324–35.

[2] See the evidence collected in *UPZ* i. 62 ff. on the inability of a *katochos* to leave the shrine to which he was attached.

[3] I have deliberately omitted two minor questions from this discussion: the first is whether the metaphor of 'the path' discussed above can be connected in any way with the institution of κατοχή. For this there is no proof whatsoever. The second is the nature of the Memphite Ḥor's journey to *Pr-p3y·f-iry* recounted in Texts **12** and **25**. Here the Memphite secretary seems to be relating his own experiences. The account is therefore not relevant to our question; in the less likely event of the journey's belonging to Ḥor of Sebennytos, it will prove only that from *c.* 173 to 168 the latter had been in the Delta on the god's business, and will tell us nothing about his later activities. It is of course true that in Text **25** the writer clearly feels a need to justify his journey by quoting from an oracle. This would have been necessary had he been a *katochos*, it is true, but it is not evidence that he was one.

176	8 April: Philometor's mother, Cleopatra I, still alive (BM 10518). 17 May: Cleopatra I apparently dead (Pestman, 46).
175	Spring: Philometor's marriage to Cleopatra II. Reorganization of earlier cult titles. (Antiochus IV Epiphanes succeeds in Syria.)
174	October: the reforms of Text **21**(?)
173/2	Roman embassy to Alexandria (Livy, 42, 6). Ḥor the secretary's journey to *Pr-pꜣy·f-ỉry* begins (Text **12**). Thirty-two years of abuse in the ibis-cult at Saqqâra come to an end (Text **19**).
172	31 January: Ḥor the secretary(?) communicates the oracle justifying his journey to the priests of the ibis-cult (Text **25**). 31 May: session of council under ꜥAḥmosi (Text **19**). 1 June: servants of Ibis arraigned before council (Text **19**). Rules for reform drawn up, to take effect from new year on 5 October. *c.* October: Ptolemy becomes κάτοχος in Serapeum (*UPZ* 15).
171	10 July: Ḥor invokes dream (Text **18**).
170	Between 5 October and 12 November: joint reign proclaimed (Skeat, *JEA* 47 (1961), 108). Second half of November: Egyptian defeat by Antiochus; disgrace of Eulaeus and Lenaeus. Joint reign abrogated; capture of Philometor. 12 December: Ḥor the secretary consults Pshennesōw on the future of Pḥentamūn (Text **12**).
169	18 May: Ḥor writes encomium to Isis (Text **10**); about this time he visits Buto and Pi(?)-Thoth. End: Antiochus retires from Egypt. Garrison left in Pelusium.
168	Beginning: reinstitution of joint reign (Bevan, 285–6); possible date of encouraging verso of Text **12**(?) Early Spring: Antiochus reinvades. Cyprus seized. 1–11 July: *Gry(n)ꜣ* still in Memphis as governor for Antiochus, who has declared himself Pharaoh (Texts **2, 3**). 11 July: Ḥor reports his dream to *Hrynys* (Texts **2, 3**). Late July: embassy of G. Popillius Laenas and Roman ultimatum. (Polybius, 29, 27). 30 July: Antiochus sails from Pelusium (Texts **2, 3**); Cyprus then evacuated. 29 August: Ḥor reports to Pharaohs in Alexandrian Serapeum; he reads out 'the salvation of Alexandria' (Texts **2, 3**). *ꜣmnys* and *ꜣrkhrts* write their account of the Seleucid retreat,

	Pharaoh goes to Memphis. *Nwmnys* goes to Rome to give thanks. *Tynys* goes to reclaim Pelusium. (Text **3**, verso). Events recorded by *Hrynys* (Text **4**) now begin. Egypt still in difficulties (*UPZ* 59, 60).
167	18 September: new regulations enforced in ibis-cult (Text **23**).
167/6	Ḥor's dream to settle in Memphis forever (Text **9**). Possible date of Text **8**(?)
165	16 April: oracle of Thoth interpreted by magician of Imḥōtep (Texts **16, 17**). 13 June(?): this interpretation reported to authorities (Text **22**). More reforms introduced.
164	6 April: death of Apis (*UPZ* 21, 23). 15 June: burial of Apis (*UPZ* 54). October: both kings in Memphis(?) (*UPZ* 42). Unrest in land (*UPZ* 14). End October: Philometor leaves for Rome and Cyprus (Bevan, 291).
164/3	Petitions of Ptolemy the κάτοχος.
168–3 (exact dates unknown)	Revolts of Dionysios Petosorapis (Diodorus 31, 15); ἄμεικτοι καιροί attested *c.* 165 (*UPZ* 19); ἄλλη κίνησις in Thebaid and Greek Texts of Ḥor archive (cf. *JEA* 54 (1968), 207). Remedy proposed for Queen, perhaps after December 165(?) (Text **28**).
163	May: return of Philometor. End of joint reign. July/August: Ptolemy 'the Brother' assigned to Cyrenaica. 17 August: amnesty (φιλάνθρωπα) of Philometor (*UPZ*, 111). Cleopatra II embodied in official protocols. October: Philometor visits Serapeum, to thank god for his safe homecoming. Possible date of his donations to ibis-shrine(?) (Text **3**, recto).
162	Ptolemy 'the Brother' in Rome. Revolt of Ptolemy Sympetēsis (Polybius 31, 10).
161	(from 163): petitions of Ptolemy the κάτοχος on behalf of the Twins.
160	January: Ḥor goes to Heliopolis, having left Memphis to seek instruction (Text **1**). 31 May: he is also in Heliopolis, and consults the priest of Imḥōtep (Text **1**).
159	December: Ḥor reports his findings to *[Sw?]tryn* in Memphis (Text **1**).

158	Summer: public acknowledgement of Eupator as heir to throne and appointment to eponymous priesthood of Alexander (Pestman, 52). Apollonios also briefly κάτοχος in Serapeum; his quarrel with the sons of Djeḥebēs (Reich, *Mizraim*, i (1933), 147 ff.). October: Philometor again visits Serapeum on his way to Upper Egypt. Possible date of Text **3.**
157	19 October: the three resolutions of Text **33** recorded.
156	
155	8–10 March: Ḥor petitions the Ibis, culminating in the dream of Text **13.** March: Imḥōtep dreams of Add. Text **59.** (Archias, governor of Cyprus, convicted of intrigue with Seleucids (Polybius 33, 3).)
154	Unsuccessful attempt of Ptolemy 'the Brother' to seize Cyprus (Bevan, 300–1).
153/2	Between 15 June 153 (Louvre 2416, 2417) and 28 March 152 (Rylands 16): elevation of Eupator to throne (Pestman, 50–2).
152	20 September: last known reference to Ptolemy the κάτοχος (*UPZ* 71).
152/1	Writing of Text **29,** which quotes a document of the joint reign.
151/0	Before 31 January 150: death of Eupator.
147	May/September: date of Text **34** and *terminus ad quem* for petition of Ḥor.
145	*c.* July: death of Philometor in Syria (Skeat, *Reigns*, 34–5). Ptolemy 'the Brother' murders Neos Philopator the rightful heir and succeeds (*c.* September) as Ptolemy VIII Euergetes II.

ADDENDUM

THE following additional ostraca were identified and copied during clearance work at Saqqâra in the winter of 1973–4. The first three texts and **65** certainly belong to the Archive of Ḥor, **62–64** possibly so. References to these new texts have been incorporated into the index.

Additional Text 59

Height	14·9 cm.
Width	11·8 cm.
Thickness	0·6 cm.
Munsell	2·5 YR 5/4
Photograph	Plate XXXVIII
Facsimile	Plate XXXVIIIA
Excavator's no.	H5–(779+787) [2526+2534]

A sizeable ostracon of light reddish ware, joined from five pieces. The bottom sixth piece is lost. The recto bears at least twenty-three lines in a hand which may be that of the Sebennyte Ḥor. The writing is very tightly packed, and is badly faded. The verso bears traces, but these have been erased in antiquity. The fragments were discovered by Emery on 25 November 1968, on the main temple terrace (the point marked Z in the map at the end of Commentary, § 5).

Text

1. (traces)[a] [*tw·ỉ*][b] *wꜣḥ ḥn*
2. *ḥt-nṯr tꜣ ṯhny nb ꜥnḫ*[*-tꜣwy*][c]
3. *ḏd·w n·ỉ rswt ỉw·ỉ šms ḫftḥ*
4. *ḥꜣt-sp 26 ꜣbd-2 prt grḥ nꜣ* [ ]*w*[d] *ḫpr·f*
5. *ỉw·w ḏd wꜥ wꜥb ỉw* (*r*-)*ḫn nꜣ nty-wꜥb*[e]
6. *ḫw wꜥbw ḏd·w 'Iy-m-ḥtp sꜣ Ptḥ pꜣ* [ ][f] ⟨*nṯr*⟩
7. *ỉr·k dỉt n-ỉm·f* [*ḥr*]*-ḏꜣḏꜣ·n*[g] *sẖ. tꜣ mḥ-2t: ỉw·w ḏd*
8. *ỉw·f* (*n*) *wꜥt sntyt wꜥ sḳ ꜥꜣ ḫpr wn nṯr 2 ỉrm*[*·f*]
9. *ḥms·f ḏd·f n·ỉ ḏd pꜣy·k ꜥḳ* [ ][h] *ḥrt*[i]
10. *ḥr* [ ] *ḳyt* [ ][j] *ꜥḳ* [ ] *Ḏḥwty wpy*
11. *bn-ỉw tš mn* [ ][k] *n gy* (*n*) *pꜣ tꜣ bn-ỉw·w ꜥḥꜥ*
12. *bw-ỉr rmt* [[*nb*]] *sḏm m-sꜣ pꜣy·k rmt ꜥꜣ pꜣ nty ỉw·w* [[*sḏm*]]
13. *ḏd-s ỉw·f ḫpr pꜣ nṯr ꜥꜣ* [ ][l] *my ỉn·f*[m] *ḥn*
14. *sty tꜣ* [*ḥꜥ*(*t*)] *mn sp-sn mtw·w ḏtḥ* [ ][n]
15. *pꜣ gy* (*n*) *ỉr nꜣy my ḥn-s Ḏḥwty* [[*bn-ỉw*]]
16. *wn mdt nbt* (*n*) *ꜥwy-drt·f*[o] *bn-ỉw ḥs·k mdt*
17. (*n*) *dỉt mn·s stp dmỉ* (*n*) *Kmy wn*
18. *Pꜣ-ꜣḫ-Ḏḥwty*[p] *'Imn-Rꜥ*[q] *nb Smꜣ-Bḥdt*[r] *n-ỉm·f* (traces)[s]
19. *n-ỉm·f ḏd·ỉ n·f ỉn-nꜣ bn-ỉw gꜣ dmỉ* [*m-sꜣ*][t]
20. *Pr-Ḏḥwty ꜣst ḥtp n-ỉm*[*·f*
21. *ḥꜣty·ỉ m-šs r-dbꜣ* [
22. *tꜣ nṯrt ꜥꜣt nbt m*[*rt*[u]
23. [*ḏd nꜣy* .....

Notes

a. There is no sign of any of the conventional openings to our texts; perhaps the beginning is lost.

b. Restored from the general sense, and difficult to reconcile with the traces.

c. Restored from Text **18**, V° 3.

d. The traces are almost entirely lost, although the plural determinative seems clear. The whole clearly refers to a festival or suchlike in the cult of Imḥōtep at Saqqâra; this makes the loss of the word more regrettable.

e. Cf. the notes to Text **12**, R° 7, p. 52 above.

f. The traces may suit *sẖ*. The following word seems to have stood well below the level of the line, perhaps as an insertion.

g. Extremely faint.

h. The traces suggest *tꜣ mdt Ḏḥwty*, but other readings (*nꜣ hbw*?) are possible.

i. The following line is a space-filler.

j. The whole of this line is too obscure to allow more than the occasional guess at the meaning.

k. *n-ỉm·w* may have stood here.

l. *mr-s* is possible.

m. The syntax of this group is not clear, especially in view of the *mtw·w* in the following line. The translation is approximate.

n. The object pronoun which doubtless stood here is lost.

o. Cf. the similar sentiment in Text **17,** 20–1.

p. The place-name determinative is clear.

q. Not *Wsỉr-Ḥp*, which it resembles.

r. For the absence of place-determinative in this name cf. the writings in Text **16,** R° 6; **17,** 13.

s. Possibly *ntr*. The remaining space is limited; perhaps *ntr nb*(?)

t. Restored entirely from the sense.

u. Restored from Text **10,** R° 8; the group in Text **2,** R° 2 is less likely.

Translation

1. (traces) [I was] situated in
2. the temple of the Peak (of the) Lord of ʿAnkh[-tawy].[a]
3. I was told a dream while I was serving (in the) dromos
4. (in) Year 26, Mekhir,[b] the night of the [.....]. It happened (that)
5. I dreamt (that) a priest came into the sanctuaries.[c]
6. Priests offered incense. They said 'Imḥōtep son of Ptaḥ, the ⟨divine⟩ [scribe],
7. thou shalt place him at our head(?)' It is written. The second (dream): I dreamt (that)
8. he[d] was (in) a panic. A great destruction (had) occurred. There were two gods with [him].
9. He sat down. He said to me, saying 'Your bread [the business of Thoth(?)] food
10. (is) upon [(the) high land ....(?)] bread [.....] Thoth judges:
11. no province shall remain [among them] in any way (on) earth. They shall not stand.
12. No man hears except your great man, the one whom they
13. name. If it happens (that) the great god [wishes it], bring him(?) within
14. (the) flame (of) the furnace(?), lasting, lasting, and may they imprison [him(?)].
15. The act (of) doing this, may Thoth command it,
16. (for) every matter is within his power.[e] You shall not be slack (in any) matter
17. (of) effecting it. Choose a town (of) Egypt.
18. Piaḥthoth and Amen-Rēʿ lord of Sambeḥdet[f] are in it and [every god(?)]
19. is in it.' I said to him, 'Will it be another town [but]
20. Pi(?)-Thoth? Isis rests in [it .....
21. my heart exceedingly concerning [
22. the great goddess, lady of [love[g]
23. [saying this .....'].

Notes

a. For this description of the site of the temple of Imḥōtep (the Asklepieion) see Commentary § 5 above.

b. The date corresponds to March 155. For a festival of Imḥōtep in the Memphite necropolis on 11 Mekhir, cf. Brugsch, *Thesaurus*, 981. The date would then be 10 March, 155.

c. Doubtless of the Asklepieion.

d. It is unprecedented in our texts for a dream, described as 'the second', to follow directly from the first, but no other explanation seems possible. Usually a change of characters or of locale is implied by the new numbering; see § 3 of the Commentary above.

e. For the sentiment see Appendix 2.

f. For Amen-Rēʿ as lord of this city, cf. Montet, *Géographie*, i. 115.

g. See Appendix 1.

Remarks

This text records two connected dreams experienced by Ḥor in March 155. In the first dream the priests of the sanctuary of Imḥōtep beg the god to elect a certain priest to lead them. In the second a being, possibly Imḥōtep, is seized with fear: a cataclysm of some sort has occurred, and Ḥor is asked to choose a town of Egypt. The reason for this is not clear, but it may be that the chosen town would be singled out for survival. Ḥor, not surprisingly, names his home city, Pi(?)-Thoth. The leader of the first dream is mentioned again: he is apparently to be subjected to an ordeal by fire, if the god Thoth so desires.

In spite of the rather late date, the new text falls clearly into the pattern of dream-texts **8–11** above: the same anxiety is present, indeed it reaches a new peak in the apparent destruction of Egypt, and Ḥor's *idée fixe* about bread rations, which was perhaps derived from his experiences in Text **26**, recurs in the badly damaged ll. 9 and 10. Familiar too is the figure of authority who makes demands of the dreamer (Texts **8, 9, 11**), although the reply is now more confident.

Particularly interesting is the information given about the town of Pi(?)-Thoth. It is difficult to know how far to trust a dream-text, but there seems little reason why Ḥor should wish to deceive in such a matter. A place-name Piaḥthoth, 'the field of Thoth', is associated with the town, and a cult of Amen-Rēᶜ, lord of Sambeḥdet, is also located there. If our theory that Pi(?)-Thoth lay in the northern Delta, near Buto, is correct, then the presence of a god of Sambeḥdet, the most northerly town of Egypt, would be easily explained.

More intriguing is Ḥor's reply: he makes no reference to these cults, but lays emphasis on the fact that Isis rests in the town (l. 20). We know that in his early years Ḥor had been a pastophoros of this goddess in Temenēsi, a town which it is difficult to place far from Pi(?)-Thoth. The new information makes one wonder whether Temenēsi and Pi(?)-Thoth are not essentially the same. A similar association of cult places, those of Thoth and Horus, seems to have occurred at nearby Damanhûr, and the conurbation of Pe and Dep at Buto is of course well known. The fact that Ḥor calls himself a citizen sometimes of Temenēsi, at other times of Pi(?)-Thoth, would then be explained; but this theory remains unproven.

The dreamer of this text is, of course, never named, but the hand, the general subject-matter, and above all the reference to Pi(?)-Thoth allow us to ascribe the ostracon to the main archive.

Additional Text 60

Height	8·5 cm.
Width	8·1 cm.
Thickness	0·8 cm.
Munsell	5 YR 6/3
Photograph	Plate XXXVIII
Facsimile	Plate XXXVIIIA
Excavator's no.	H5–780 [2527]

Fragment of fine brownish ware with red slip, joined from two pieces. The recto bears nine lines in the same hand as that of Text **7.** Much of the upper portion of the text is missing. The verso is blank. The sherd was found by Emery on 24 November 1968 in the same area as Add. Text **59.**

Text

x+1. *ỉ·ỉr Tbny*
2. *smn pꜣ mšᶜ*
3. *ẖr w[ḏꜣ pꜣ ᶜḥᶜ] Pr-ᶜꜣ*
4. *mtw·w dỉt [nꜣy·f sꜣbw]*[a] *ẖr*
5. *rdwy·f Ḏḥwty pꜣ ᶜꜣ pꜣ ᶜꜣ pꜣ ᶜꜣ*
6. *pꜣ ḥry pꜣ [nb n pꜣ ḥꜣ]ty*[b] *dỉt-s*
7. *ḥꜣty[·f wḏꜣ*] *ṯꜣy·w nꜣy·ỉ*[c]
8. *Pt(r)wmys*[d] *nty ẖn*
9. *tꜣ ẖnt*[e] *sḏm ḫrw·ỉ*[f] *ẖr nꜣy.*

Notes

a. The determinative of *sꜣbw* is visible. The restorations are made from Text **7,** 8–9. *n·f* may also have stood here, as in Text **7,** but there is barely room for it.

b. Epithets restored from Text **26,** V° 10.

c. Possibly for the pronoun ⲛⲟⲩⲓ?

d. The absence of *r* is disturbing, and the name is very indistinct. Perhaps *ꜣtw*[ ] would be a better reading.

e. Possibly a noun formation from *ẖn* (ϩⲓⲛⲉ), but other readings are possible, notably *snt* 'guild'. The final sign is uncertain: it is hardly *mḥ-1*.

f. Altered from *ẖrw·f*.

Translation

x+1. Daphnae[a]
2. secures the army[b]
3. (for) ever [safeguarded is the lifetime (of)] Pharaoh
4. and [his enemies] are placed beneath
5. his feet. Thoth the thrice great,
6. the master, the [lord of the hea]rt gives it[c]
7. his heart [being prosperous(?) ...]. They have taken my [possessions(?)].
8. Ptolemy(?)[d] who is within
9. the fleet(?) hear my voice in this.

Notes

a. For reading and translation see notes to Text **7**, 6.

b. See notes to the translation of Text **2**, V° 12. The group *pꜣ mšꜥ* 'the army' is perhaps to be restored at the beginning of Text **7**, 8 above.

c. Hardly a reference to the enemies, but otherwise obscure.

d. This word in particular, and the last three lines in general, very uncertain; see notes to the text.

Remarks

The first part of this text bears a close resemblance to Text **7**; indeed it probably marks a stage in its drafting. The second part is more obscure, but seems to contain a plea to a person in authority to right the author's wrongs. It is unfortunate that the concluding lines are too uncertain to allow a more precise dating of Text **7** and the revolt of *Tmpn*; the reference to 'the fleet(?)' is too vague to be of help.

Additional Text 61

Height	11·5 cm.
Width	8·6 cm.
Thickness	0·9 cm.
Munsell	10 YR 7/3
Photograph	Plate XXXVIII
Facsimile	Plate XXXVIIIA
Excavator's no.	H5–999 [2751]

An ostracon of fine pinkish-buff ware. The recto bears some seventeen lines in a hand close to, if not the same as, that of Text **33.** The verso is heavily incrusted and blank. Fading and stains have not made the recto easier to decipher. The text was found by Emery in December 1968 in the same area as Add. Texts **59** and **60.**

Text

1. *wn nꜣ gm[ꜥw ỉrm nꜣ tm-hp]*[a]
2. *nty ỉw·w ỉr [n-ỉm·]w (n) tꜣ ꜥẖyt r-dbꜣ*
3. *tꜣ šnt (n) [tꜣ ꜥẖyt]*[b]
4. *r-dbꜣ [pꜣ tr] wn-nꜣ·w*
5. *pꜣ [ ] ẖr [·f] st ṯꜣy tꜣ ẖrt (n)*
6. *nꜣ [ ]*[c] *mdt nbt st [ ] tꜣ ḳrst*
7. *[dỉt] ḥtp [nꜣ rmtw] ḏryw ỉ·ỉr*
8. *ỉr tꜣ šnt [ ]*[d] *ỉr·s ḥtr*[e]
9. *r·ḥr·ỉ (n) smy n·k Pr-ꜥꜣ ḏd*
10. *my [ ]-s*[f] *tꜣ šnt r tꜣ ꜥẖyt*
11. *pꜣ [ ] ẖt pꜣ snt wn-nꜣ·w smn*
12. *ỉ·ỉr·ḥr nꜣy·k ỉtyw [r-hn] ḥꜣt-sp 19*[g]
13. *[ ]*[h] *ḏd [tꜣ] ẖrt (n) nꜣ [ ]*[c] *ỉrm tꜣ ḳrst*
14. *[ ] rn·k [ ] tw·ỉ tbḥ n-ỉm·s*
15. *ḥn-s [nꜣ sẖw gmꜥw]*
16. *[Ḏḥwty] pꜣ ꜥꜣ pꜣ ꜥꜣ pꜣ ꜥꜣ*
17. *ỉw·f dỉt [ ].*

Notes

a. Restored from Text **26**, R° 19–20.

b. The final traces suggest *ỉꜣwt* 'office', but they are far from clear.

c. Restore *hbw*?

d. The initial traces of this difficult group suit *Ḏḥwty*, but the whole is obscure.

e. Restored from Text **26**, R° 18–19.

f. Restore *ḥn-s*, etc., *ad sensum*.

g. So rather than 39, but the latter is not entirely

excluded. I am grateful to Dr. W. J. Tait for examining this passage and confirming this observation.

h. Apparently not *nꜣ Pr-ꜥꜣw*, as against Text **19**, R° 15. There is just room for **pꜣ it (n) Pr-ꜥꜣ*, but this is scarcely possible: see below.

Translation

1. Account of the cal[amities and illegalities][a]
2. which are being performed (in) the chapel concerning
3. the investigation[b] (of) [the chapel . . . .]
4. concerning [. . . . . the time] when
5. the [. . . . .] beneath [. . . . . . . it(?)]. They steal the food (of)
6. the [ibises] (in) every respect. They [. . . . .] the burial
7. [causing to] rest [. . . . .] the mighty [men] who
8. perform the investigation [. . . . .]. It has placed the compulsion[a]
9. upon me (of) appealing to you, Pharaoh, saying
10. 'Pray [restore] the investigation to the chapel
11. the [. . . . .] namely, the custom which was established
12. before your fathers [until] year 19[c]
13. [. . . . .] for the food (of) the [ibises] and the burial
14. [. . . . . .] your name [. . . . .]. I beg it.
15. Order [the writings . . . . calamities]
16. [. . . . . Thoth] the thrice great
17. who gives [. . . . .'].

Notes

a. Note the parallels with the recto of Text **26** mentioned in the textual notes above.

b. For this investigation see Texts **19–24** and the Commentary, § 4.

c. The king is not certain; it cannot be Philopator, who died at the beginning of his eighteenth regnal year (Skeat, *Reigns of the Ptolemies*, 32), while a date under Epiphanes (187/6) would make nonsense of the implication in Text **19**, R° 13–15 that the affairs of the ibis-cult were languishing throughout the latter's reign. We are left with Philometor himself (whose nineteenth year fell in 163/2), and the purpose of Ḥor's remark remains doubtful; see the remarks which follow.

Remarks

The general drift of this text is clearer than its details. Abuses and maladministration are rampant in the [ibis]-cult, as usual with regard to the feeding and the burial of the birds, and also in connection with the investigation (*šnt*) of the shrine. The writer feels obliged to appeal to Pharaoh to restore the former efficiency of the cult. The similarity of this appeal to the other ibis-texts (**19–24** above) is great enough to enable us to ascribe it to the main archive, in spite of its anonymity.

The date 'Year 19' mentioned in the text remains a problem; if the arguments for a dating to Philometor are correct, it would seem that Ḥor is angry at a temporary recrudescence of the old disorder which took place in 163/2, but unfortunately the context itself is not clear. There are obvious parallels with the idiom of Text **26** above. While the two texts seem to refer to different periods in the life of Ḥor, it is always possible that they were drafted at the same time.

Additional Text 62

Height	5·2 cm.
Width	4·5 cm.
Thickness	0·9 cm.
Munsell	5 YR 5/4
Photograph	Plate XXXIX
Facsimile	Plate XXXIXA
Excavator's no.	H6–393 [2469]

A small fragment of reddish-brown ware. The recto bears parts of six lines, the verso is blank. Found by Emery in the same area as Add. Texts **59–61** above.

Text

x+1.] *Ptrwm*[

2. *s*]*mt Ḏḥwty pꜣ ꜥꜣ* [

3.] *n-drt wpy* [
4.] ·*gs*[a] *pꜣ* [
5. *Mn-*]*nfr m-bꜣḥ* [
6.] (trace)[b] [.

Notes

a. Foreign determinative.
b. Suits *ḏd*(?).

Translation

x+1.] Ptolem[y
2.] likewise Thoth the great [
3.] when [ ] gave judgment [
4.] ·*gs*[a] the [
5. Mem]phis before [
6.] (trace) [.

Note

a. A foreign name, perhaps Greek.

Remarks

Little idea of the contents of this text is possible; some sort of historical narrative seems intended.

Additional Text 63

Height	8·1 cm.
Width	6·5 cm.
Thickness	0·75 cm. (ave.)
Munsell	5 YR 5/2
Photograph	Plate XXXIX
Facsimile	Plate XXXIXA
Excavator's no.	H6–317 i [2165]

A small fragment of brownish ware. The recto bears four lines in a very neat hand, with an insertion and traces of a fifth. The verso is dark and uninscribed. The sherd was found by Emery in March 1968 in the same area as Add. Texts **1–4** above.

Text

1.] *ἰw pꜣ mw bn-ἰw rmt*
2.] *hb* [[*pꜣ*]][a] *ḫpr ḳrst nfr*(*t*) ⟨*tꜣy pꜣ hrw*⟩
3.] *hn Pr-Wsἰr*[b]
4.] *nꜣ tšw* (*n*) *pꜣ tꜣ mḥ*
5.] (trace).

Notes

a. Possibly altered to a space-filler.
b. The clear determinative rules out *Pr-Wsἰr-Ḥp*.

Translation

1.] come the water[a] no man shall
2.] ibis. Good burial (shall) occur ⟨from this day⟩
3.] stretching to[b] Pi-Osīri[c]
4.] the nomes of the north land
5.] (trace).

Notes

a. Perhaps in the sense of 'inundation', and used temporally; cf. also Text **33**, 13.
b. Erichsen, *Glossar*, 276.
c. Possibly the village (modern Abusîr) discussed in the Commentary § 5 above.

Remarks

This fragment seems to be part of a prediction that the burial of the ibises shall henceforth be in good order. The name of the toponym Pi-Osīri is of interest.

Additional Text 64

Height	6·1 cm.
Width	13·3 cm.
Thickness	0·75 cm.
Munsell	(Slip) 2·5 Y 7/4 (Ware) 2·5 YR 5/6
Photograph	Plate XXXIX
Facsimile	Plate XXXIXA
Excavator's no.	71/2–(211+212) [5479+5480]

A fragment of fine red ware with a buff slip, joined from two pieces. The recto bears traces of some six lines on the right-hand piece, but the left hand is entirely faded. The verso, which was written upside down in comparison with the recto, bears traces of seven lines (one being an insertion) on the left hand; signs of erasures and palimpsest are clear. On this side it is the right-hand piece which has faded. The text which follows is far from certain. The sherds were found by Martin in February 1972 in the South Ibis courtyard, the findspot of the main archive, and the area which is marked X on the map at the end of § 5 of the Commentary above.

Text: recto

1. *ỉw·w dỉt mnt ẖr* [[a]]
2. [ ] *n-ỉm·w ỉw·w ḏd* [ ]
3. [ ] *ḫpr* [ ]
4. [ ] *mdt ẖr* [ ]
5. (traces)
6. (traces)

Text: verso

1.] *dỉ·w m*[*nt*
2.] *mn ꜥḳ* .. [
3.] ⟨*r dỉt ỉw·s* ...⟩ [
4.] .. *ms*[b] *nty ẖn smn*
5.] (traces) ÷ *s*
6.] ... *st ḥnk m-bꜣḥ ꜣst*
7.] ... *pꜣ ḥm-ntr Ḥp.*

Notes

a. Restore *pꜣ hb pꜣ bỉk* etc.

b. *ꜥḥyt* may have preceded *ms*, but the traces are not conclusive.

Translation: recto

1. They shall impart regularity into [the Ibis (etc.) .....]
2. [.......] them, they saying [.........................]
3. [.....................] happen [.........................]
4. [..........................] matter concerning [........]
5. (traces)
6. (traces)

Translation: verso

1.] they have imparted re[gularity
2.] bread[a] remains ... [
3.] ⟨to cause it to be ...⟩ [
4.] ..... birth which is in establishment[b] [
5.] ...... it
6.] .... they offer before Isis
7.] .... the prophet of Apis.

Notes

a. Doubtless in the sense of 'rations, income'.

b. Perhaps 'the chapel of birth which is under construction' (?), cf. Text **33** above.

Remarks

This sadly damaged text may record the construction and dedication of a chapel attached to the ibis-cult at Saqqâra, but the details are lost.

Additional Text 65

Height	8·3 cm.
Width	6·4 cm.
Thickness	0·65 cm.
Munsell	7·5 YR 6/4
Photograph	Plate XXXIX
Facsimile	Plate XXXIXA
Excavator's no.	72/3–16 [6002]

A small ostracon of fine brownish ware. The recto contains seven lines in the squat hand of Ḥor of Sebennytos; the verso contains a further seven lines in the same hand, written upside down in comparison with the recto. The bottom left-hand corner of the recto and most of the upper left half of the verso have suffered from fading. Otherwise the text seems to be complete.

The sherd was found by Martin at a spot slightly to the north of the findspot of Texts **6**, **10**, and **21**, a place where it may have been discarded by looters.

Text: recto

1. *ỉm*(*t*) *n·ỉ tꜣy·ỉ* [[a]
2. *ḫr ḏd·s n·ỉ snt*[(*n*)
3. *ỉr ẖt tꜣ mdt* (*ỉ·*)*sẖ·s*[b] (*n*) *nꜣ rmtw*
4. *r-dbꜣ Wsỉr*[c] *ẖn* . [

5. *nꜣ twtw* (*n*) *Wsir* (*i·*)*gm·i*
6. *ir·i tym* (*n*) *pꜣ nty* ˹*ḳ*˺[d]
7. *ir·i ḥrḥ pꜣ nty* [

Text: verso

1. (traces)
2. (traces)[e]
3. *wn* . [
4. *bn-iw·w* . . [
5. *tw·i irm·k* [
6. *ms* . . [
7. *-s in-iw*[f] [.

Notes

a. sc. Tꜣnꜣ (?) cf. Text **10,** R° 2, 6, 10, 16, 18. The confusion of *im* and *imt* is unparalleled in our texts.

b. i·ḏd·s possible, but unlikely.

c. The scribe first wrote a divine sign; possibly *ḥt-ntr*?

d. Almost certainly not ˁ*ḏ*. For *tym*, cf. notes to Text **3,** R° 17.

e. May suit *dit*.

f. Other readings possible, as the syntax is lost.

Translation: recto

1. Come to me my [[a]
2. for she speaks to me (the) custom [(of)[b]
3. acting according to the word (which) she wrote (for) men
4. concerning Osiris within . [
5. the statues (of) Osiris (which) I found.[b]
6. I protect[c] him who enters.
7. I watch over him who [

Translation: verso

1. (traces)
2. (traces)
3. . . [
4. they shall not . . [
5. I am with you [
6. birth . . [
7. she has come (?) [.

Notes

a. Some epithet of the goddess Isis to be restored; cf. textual note above.

b. These restorations are forced if we assume that the sherd is complete. Lines 3–4 make this assumption likely. The change of person in lines 1–2 is paralleled in Text **10,** R° 18–19.

c. tym is regularly construed with *ir* in our texts. The use of *ir* before *ḥrḥ* in the following line is stranger, but two explanations are possible: that *ḥrḥ* is nominal, in which case we must supply (*n*) before *pꜣ*, or that the writer has remembered the origin of *ḥrḥ* as a compound *ḥry-iḥ* (Fecht, *Wortakzent und Silbenstruktur*, 69–70). *ir·i ḥrḥ* would then be for **ḥrḥ·i*. The second explanation is very likely.

Remarks

Although the name is missing, there is little doubt that this short text concerns the goddess Isis. The recto opens with an invocation to the goddess similar to those contained in Text **10.** She is described as delivering an address of some sort, and a reference is made to some statues of Osiris. These may be the same as those mentioned in Text **20,** 6 above, but the whole is rather obscure. The first person pronouns in lines 6–7 are reminiscent of the Isis-aretalogies with their repeated ἐγώ; cf. Appendix 1 above. The speech of the goddess seems to continue on the verso; the change to the third person in the final line may mark its end.

Postscript

At the end of this volume, it is tempting to wonder how much of the original archive of Ḥor is contained within its pages. It is obvious that many of the ostraca are small fragments, whose continuations are missing. It is equally clear that, although we have learnt much of the life of Ḥor, the surviving texts are far from giving a complete picture. This may have been deliberate policy by Ḥor and his secretary, but it is difficult not to believe that further pieces are lost. Some no doubt perished; one or two may even come to light in museum collections where they have gone unrecognized; the rest perhaps still lie scattered along the road that led southwards from Ḥepnēbes to the Serapeum.

February, 1974 J. D. RAY

INDEXES

NOTE: References are given by text, the numbers of which are set in **bold** type.

§ 1. PROSOPOGRAPHY

29. *Tꜣnꜣ*

10, R° 2, 6, 10, 16, 18.

Probably an epithet of Isis; see notes, p. 47, and Appendix 1.

30. *Tyt* Tayit

18, V° 19	*Skr-Wsỉr m sḥ(?)·f Tyt*

Possibly a personification of the idea of weaving: see note, p. 70.

31. *Tfn(t)* Tefēni (Tefnut)

19, R° 7	*pꜣ by n Tfn(t)*

32. *Ḏḥwty* Thoth

1, 10	*pꜣ ntr ꜥꜣ Ḏḥwty*
13	*Ḏḥwty ꜥḥꜥ ḥꜣ·s*
2, V° 15	*Ḏḥwty pꜣ ꜥꜣ pꜣ ꜥꜣ pꜣ ꜥꜣ*
3, R° 8	*Ḏḥwty ỉrm·k*
13	*pꜣ ḥb ꜥꜣ n Ḏḥwty pꜣy·s ỉt*
16	*Ḏḥwty pꜣ rḫ(?) ỉꜥḥ pꜣ ꜥnḫ pꜣ wr-dỉw hb(?)*
5, 5	*(n)-ṯꜣy Ḏḥwty*
7, 10	*mdt Ḏḥwty ḏd*
12	*nꜣ ẖrdw n Ḏḥwty*
8, R° 1	*ḥb Ḏḥwty*
5	*ink pꜣy·k ṯs Ḏḥwty*
V° 1	*m-šm m-bꜣḥ Ḏḥwty ỉ·ḏd-s ỉm n·ỉ pꜣy·ỉ nb ꜥꜣ Ḏḥwty*
12, 2	*Ḏḥwty hb n-ỉm·ỉ*
9	*Ḏḥwty pꜣ ꜥꜣ pꜣ ꜥꜣ nty ꜥꜣy n ms*
12A, 2	id.
16, R° 1–2	*pꜣ ntr ꜥꜣ Ḏḥwty*
12	*pꜣ wr-dỉw Ḏḥwty*
17, 2	*pꜣ ntr ꜥꜣ Ḏḥwty*
7–8	*Ḏḥwty nb ꜥḥꜥ*
11–12	*r pꜣ wr-dỉw Ḏḥwty ỉr-rḫ*
21–2	*n ꜥwy-drt Ḏḥwty pꜣ nb rḫ*
18, R° 6	*Ḏḥwty tpy wtn n Rꜥ*
V° 9	*mdt ỉ·ỉr·ḥr·k Ḏḥwty ḥḥ(?)*
11	id. . . . . . *mdt ỉ·ỉr·ḥr·k Ḏḥwty pꜣ nb ỉr-rḫ*
19, R° 2–3	*Ḏḥwty pꜣ ntr rn·f ỉ·ỉr-sḫy n ḥt-ntr Mn-nfr*
5	*pꜣ by n Ḏḥwty pꜣ ꜥꜣ pꜣ ꜥꜣ pꜣ ꜥꜣ*
9	*r-pr Ḏḥwty*
10	*dỉ Ḏḥwty ḫpr·f n·w snt*
21, R° 1	*nꜣ wꜥbw n Ḏḥwty*
3–4	*ḥt-mdt(?) Ḏḥwty*
8	*smn-s Ḏḥwty n Mn-nfr*
22, R° 2	*pꜣ ntr ꜥꜣ Ḏḥwty*
V° 2*	*Ḏḥwty pꜣ ꜥꜣ*
23, R° 2	*Ḏḥwty ꜥꜣ nb Pr-Ḏḥwty*
7	*nꜣ (ỉ·)ḏd-w pꜣ ntr ꜥꜣ Ḏḥwty*
V° 8–9	id.
16	id. (followed by *ḥt rswt*)
24A, 3	*Ḏḥwty r ḥtp r-ḥn [*
25, 4	*pꜣ by n Ḏḥwty ꜥꜣ(?) ꜥꜣ*
11	*nꜣ (ỉ·)ḏd-w pꜣ ntr ꜥꜣ Ḏḥwty*
26, R° 17	*gm n·ỉ Ḏḥwty lwḥ*
V° 10	*ḥt-mdt Ḏḥwty pꜣ ꜥꜣ pꜣ ꜥꜣ pꜣ ꜥꜣ*
27, V° 8	*Ḏḥwty ỉw·f ỉn sgny*
28, 12	*Ḏḥwty ꜥꜣ ꜥꜣ nb Ḫmnw*
30, 2	*nꜣ sḏyw n Ḏḥwty*
6	*Ḏḥwty hb n-ỉm·ỉ*
31B, 5	*tꜣ mdt wpy Ḏḥwty*
32, R° 1	*m-bꜣḥ Ḏḥwty ꜥꜣ wpyt*
6	*wpy-s pꜣ ntr ꜥꜣ Ḏḥwty*
47, 6	*[Ḏḥwty] pꜣ ꜥꜣ(?)*
59, 10	*Ḏḥwty wpy*
15	*my ḥn-s Ḏḥwty*
60, 5–6	*Ḏḥwty pꜣ ꜥꜣ pꜣ ꜥꜣ pꜣ ꜥꜣ pꜣ ḥry pꜣ nb n pꜣ ḥꜣty*
61, 16	*Ḏḥwty] pꜣ ꜥꜣ pꜣ ꜥꜣ pꜣ ꜥꜣ*
62, 2	*Ḏḥwty pꜣ ꜥꜣ [*

See also *Pr-Ḏḥwty* and *Ḥr* (II) below, and Ἑρμῆς in the Greek Index.

B. 'DEMONS'

1. *ms-rdwy* fashioner of feet(?)

18, R° 2*	*ms-rdwy nty ẖn ḥt-ntr·f*

2. *rḫ-rn·k* knower of thy name

18, V° 12	*ꜣy rḫ-rn·k m wtyt*

C. DIVINE BARKS

1. *Sktt* the *(M)sktt*-bark

12, 9	*nꜣ ntrw nty n tꜣ ḥꜣt tꜣ Sktt*
12A, 3	id.
18, R° 7	*Skty Mtꜣ(?) pꜣ wtn n Rꜥ*

2. *Mtꜣ(?)* the *Mꜥnḏt*-bark

Doubtful: see notes to **18,** R° 7, p. 68.

D. RULERS

1. *ꜣtyk(y)s* (Antiochus IV Epiphanes)

1, 7	(restored)
2, R° 5	*nꜣ mšꜥw n ꜣtyks ꜥws.*
9	*pꜣ rd n ꜣtyks*
V° 8	id.
11	*nꜣ mšꜥw n ꜣtyks ꜥws.*
3, V° 10	*ḥnn ꜣtyks ꜥws.*
14	*r-ḥn r šm . . . ỉ·ỉr ꜣtyks*
4, R° 8	*nꜣ mšꜥw n ꜣtykys*

2. *Pr-ꜥꜣ ꜣrgsntrs* (Alexander the Great)

31A, 2	*pꜣ wꜥb ꜥꜣ n Pr-ꜥꜣ ꜣrgsntrs*

3. *Pr-ꜥꜣ Ptrwmys* (Ptolemy VI Philometor)

1, 8–9	*pꜣ rd n Pr-ꜥꜣ Ptrwmys pꜣy·n ḥry*
2, R° 1	(addressee)
7, 1	id.
27, R° 1	id.
28, 1	id.
29, 1	id.
9	id.
37, 2	id. (restored)

The βασιλεὺς Πτολεμαῖος of the Greek Index.

4. *Pr-ꜥꜣ Ptrwmys pꜣ sn* (Ptolemy 'the Brother', later Ptolemy VIII Euergetes II)

28, 1–2	*Pr-ꜥꜣ Ptrwmys ỉrm Pr-ꜥꜣ Ptrwmys pꜣy·f sn*

Cf. **40**, 4 *ỉrm pꜣy·f sn*(?)
The βασιλεὺς Πτολεμαῖος ὁ ἀδελφός of the Greek Index, and the same personage as 6 below.

5. *tꜣ Pr-ꜥꜣt Ḳrwptrꜣ* (Queen Cleopatra II)

3, R° 2	addressee (name inserted)
7, R° 1	id.
28, 2–3	id. (name inserted)
29, 1	id. (title and name inserted)
9	id.

The βασίλισσα Κλεοπάτρα of the Greek Index.
In **3** and **29** the royal pair are qualified as *nꜣ nṯrw ꜥꜣy* 'the great gods', an epithet which in **3** seems to have been altered to *nꜣ nṯrw mr-mwt·w* = θεοὶ φιλομήτορες.

6. *Ptrwmys* Ptolemy

3, V° 19	*Ptrwmys ỉrm·f*

Apparently a retrospective and neutral reference to Ptolemy 'the Brother'; see notes, p. 29, and 4 above.

7. *Pr-ꜥꜣ* Pharaoh (unqualified)

1, 6	*pꜣ sẖ Pr-ꜥꜣ n Mn-nfr*
10	*pꜣ ꜥš-sḥn n Pr-ꜥꜣ*
14	*Pr-ꜥꜣ ḏlꜥ-mdt ẖn·f*
15	*pꜣ šr ꜥꜣ n Pr-ꜥꜣ*
3, V° 18	*dỉ·w šꜥt rn·s n Pr-ꜥꜣ*
20	*mšꜥ Pr-ꜥꜣ r Mn-nfr*
4, R° 2	*sꜣtrks ḥtr n Pr-ꜥꜣ ỉrm tꜣ Pr-ꜥꜣt*
5	*pꜣ šr ꜥꜣ n Pr-ꜥꜣ*
9	*nꜣ skrw n Pr-ꜥꜣ*
6, V° x+7	*[grpyt] nty n ḏꜣḏꜣ·k Pr-ꜥꜣ*
7, 8	*wḏꜣ pꜣ ꜥḥꜥ Pr-ꜥꜣ*
9, R° 6	*Pr-ꜥꜣ mdt ỉrm·ỉ*
12, V° 2	*pꜣ ꜥš-sḥn n Pr-ꜥꜣ*
18, V° 8	*ḥms Pr-ꜥꜣ*
10	*dỉ·k Pr-ꜥꜣ tym*
14	*mtw·k smꜣꜥ Pr-ꜥꜣ šꜣꜥ ḏt*
19, R° 17	*pꜣ rd n Pr-ꜥꜣ*
23, R° 10–11	id.
V° 13	id.
26, R° 6	*nꜣ ỉtyw n Pr-ꜥꜣ*
V° 13	*nꜣ ḥst n Pr-ꜥꜣ*
29, 10–11	*Pr-ꜥꜣ* [ ] *Pr-ꜥꜣ*
30, 3	*nꜣ sẖw n Pr-ꜥꜣ*
33, 2	*pꜣ šỉ n Pr-ꜥꜣ*
3	*tꜣ ẖrt n Pr-ꜥꜣ*
9	*ỉr ꜥnḫ n Pr-ꜥꜣ*
11	*n rn Pr-ꜥꜣ*
12	as l. 9.
36, 16	(?) (see note *ad locum*, p. 108).
60, 2	*ḥr wḏꜣ pꜣ ꜥḥꜥ Pr-ꜥꜣ*
61, 9	*smy n·k Pr-ꜥꜣ*

In all cases except those of purely official meaning (*ỉr ꜥnḫ n Pr-ꜥꜣ* etc.) the title seems to refer to Philometor.

8. *tꜣ Pr-ꜥꜣt* the Queen (unqualified)

1, 18	*tꜣ Pr-ꜥꜣt ms šr ḥwty*
3, V° 18	(inserted after *Pr-ꜥꜣ*)
4, R° 2	*Pr-ꜥꜣ ỉrm tꜣ Pr-ꜥꜣt*
27, R° 3	*tꜣ Pr-ꜥꜣt*
13	id.
16	*wꜥt pẖrt n tꜣ Pr-ꜥꜣt* [ ] *Pr-ꜥꜣt*
18	id. (traces)
20	*Pr-ꜥꜣt wn* (traces)
37, 3	*[tꜣ] Pr-ꜥꜣt*

Note the article. In all cases the reference seems to be to Cleopatra II. For *Pr-ꜥꜣt n tm nb* as an epithet of Isis see index to gods above and Appendix 1.

9. *nꜣ Pr-ꜥꜣw* the Pharaohs (unqualified).

2, R° 12	*dỉ·ỉ-s n nꜣ Pr-ꜥꜣw*
V° 4	id.
19, R° 15	*nꜣ Pr-ꜥꜣw šꜣꜥ ḏt*
22, R° 3	*hb nꜣ Pr-ꜥꜣw ḥty*(?) *n-ỉm·s*

All cases except **19**, R° 15 refer to Philometor and his brother in the joint reign; the exception clearly implies the monarchs currently ruling, i.e. Philometor and his wife Cleopatra II.

10. *pꜣ ỉt (n) pꜣ ỉt* the father of the father

19, R° 13–14	*ḥꜣt -sp 16 n pꜣ ỉt n pꜣ ỉt*

Apparently a reference to Ptolemy IV Philopator as grandfather of the reigning king; see notes p. 78. A plural, *nꜣ ỉtyw n Pr-ꜥꜣ* 'the (fore)-fathers of Pharaoh' occurs in **26**, R° 6; cf. also **61**, 12.

11. *pꜣ šr (n) Pr-ꜥꜣ* the son of Pharaoh

1, 15	*pꜣ šr ꜥꜣ n Pr-ꜥꜣ grp*
3, V° 1	*ꜣst ỉn nꜣ sḥn(w) n pꜣy·k šr*
4, R° 5	*tꜣ nty ṯꜣy pꜣ šr ꜥꜣ n Pr-ꜥꜣ ḏd ỉw·w ms-f*

In all cases probably the crown prince Ptolemy Eupator; see also notes to **5**, 2, p. 33.

E. PRIVATE PERSONS

1. *ꜣwrys* Eulaeus(?)

Only in the locality *Pr-ꜣwrys* below.

2. *ꜣmnys* Ammonios

3, V° 16	*ꜣmnys nty ẖn tꜣ hyty*(?)

3. *ꜣrstn* Ariston

4, R° 15	*ꜥḥꜥ·ỉ ỉrm ꜣrstn nty ẖn* [
26, R° 1	[*wꜥ mḳmḳ n*] *ꜣrstn n Tbny*

Possibly two different characters. The latter was an important personage, cf. **26**, V° 12–14.

4. *ꜣrkhrts* Archelaidas(?)

3, V° 16–17	*ꜣrkhrts nty ḥr Mn-nfr*

Reading of name uncertain.

5. *ꜣḳtryn*(?)

7, 7	*ꜣḳtryn ỉ·ỉr Tbny smn*

See notes *ad locum*, p. 37.

F. TITLES AND FUNCTIONS

19, V° 1 — *pꜣ ḥm-ntr ḥms ꜥn*(?)
26, R° 12 — *pꜣ ḥm-ntr ꜣst pꜣ wꜥb nty ỉr mnḫ n ꜣst*
27, R° 5 — *ꜣst pꜣ ḥm-ntr* .....(?)
31A, 1 — *Srpyn pꜣ ḥm-ntr Ḥr*
3 — *Ḥr-ḥb ḥm-ntr ꜣst*
64, V° 7 — *pꜣ ḥm-ntr Ḥp*

17. *ḥr-tb* magician

12, R° 3–4 — *Pꜣ-šr-n-nꜣ-ỉsw* ... *ỉw·f n ḥr-tb ẖn nꜣ rmtw*
16, R° 8 — *smy·ỉ ḥr-tb 4*
17A, 3 — id.
8 — *pꜣ ḥr-tb ’Iy-m-ḥtp sꜣ Ptḥ*
22, R° 3 — *ꜥḥꜥ·ỉ ỉrm pꜣ ḥr-tb*
23, R° 9 — *Ḥtp-’In-ḥrt pꜣ ḥr-tb*
V° 19 — *tm dỉt ꜣsk pꜣ ḥr-tb*
45, 5 — *na*(?) *pꜣ ḥr-tb ’Irt·w-r·w*
See the Commentary, § 3.

18. *pꜣ ẖn 20* the twenty administrators(?)

See notes to **33,** 4, p. 105. Reading doubtful.

19. *ẖr-ḥb* lector-priest

15, R° 5 — *pꜣ ẖr-ḥb ’Ibt*
7 — id.

20. *sꜣtrks* strategos

2, R° 8 — *Hrynys ỉ·wn-nꜣ sꜣtrks*
16 — *Tytts pꜣ sꜣtrks*
4, R° 1 — *Hrynys ỉ·wn-nꜣ sꜣtrks ḥtr n Pr-ꜥꜣ ỉrm tꜣ Pr-ꜥꜣt*
5, 4 — [*Hrynys*] *ỉ·wn-nꜣ sꜣtrks ḥtr*

21. *nꜣ sḥnw* the administrators

8, V° 4 — *nꜣ sḥnw n Mn-nfr*
See note, p. 41.

22. *sẖ* scribe

1, 1 — *Ḥr pꜣ sẖ*
2, R° 1 — id.
19, R° 1 — *sẖ tš Ṯb-ntr*
17 — *nꜣ sẖw n Ptḥ*
21, R° 2 — *sẖ tš Ṯb-ntr*
25, 1 — id.
27, R° 2 — *pꜣ sẖ*
28, 2 — id.
48, 1 — *sẖ tš*

23. *sẖ Pr-ꜥꜣ* ‘royal scribe’

1, 6 —]*tryn*(?) *pꜣ ḥm-ntr Ḫnsw pꜣ sẖ Pr-ꜥꜣ n Mn-nfr*
30, 3 — *nꜣ sẖw n Pr-ꜥꜣ*
See notes to **1,** 6, p. 13. The second example may well have another meaning.

24. *sdm-ꜥš* servant

19, R° 12 — *nꜣ sdm-ꜥš n nꜣ hbw ỉrm nꜣ sdm-ꜥš n pꜣ bỉk*
19–20 — id.
21, V° 1–2 — *nꜣ sdm-ꜥš n nꜣ hbw nꜣ sdm-ꜥš n pꜣ bỉk*
22, V° 4–5 — *nꜣ sdm-ꜥš n nꜣ hbw ỉrm nꜣ sdm-ꜥš n pꜣ bỉk*
23, R° 21 — (see notes).
24B, 1 — (restored?)
33, 9 — *Ḏ-ḥr-pꜣ-hb pꜣ sdm-ꜥš n nꜣ hbw*

25. *šn n ḥt-ntr* controller of (the) temple

19, R° 17 — (*’Iꜥḥ-ms*) *pꜣ rd n Pr-ꜥꜣ ỉ·wn-nꜣ šn n ḥt-ntr*
22, R° 6–7 — *Pꜣ-šr-n-tꜣ-ỉḥt nty šn ḥt-ntr*
Cf. also **23,** R° 11 and **31A,** 3–4. See notes, p. 79 above and the Commentary, § 4.

26. *nꜣ nty ḥr nꜣ šštw*

23, V° 22–3 — *nꜣ nty ḥr nꜣ šštw ḥr tꜣ wsẖyt n ḥt-ntr tꜣ thnyt*
See note, p. 90, and the Commentary, §§ 4, 5.

27. *ṯs* foreman, officer

8, R° 1 — *wꜥ ṯs ẖl*
2–3 — *pꜣ mꜣꜥ wn-nꜣ pꜣy·ỉ ṯs n-ỉm·f*
3 — *pꜣy·ỉ ṯs gm ḥt-ntr*(?)
5 — *ỉnk pꜣy·k ṯs Ḏḥwty*
See notes to this text, p. 42.

28. ..... watchman(?)

33, 7–8 — *smn* ..... *rmt-rḫ wbꜣ pꜣ hb tꜣ mst n-s pꜣ hb šꜣꜥ-mtw pꜣ Rꜥ ḥtp ỉw·f ḥrḥ pꜣ hb dỉt wḏꜣ·f*
Reading uncertain; perhaps *mn-nỉwt*. See notes, p. 106, and the Commentary, § 4.

§ 2. TOPOGRAPHY

A. COUNTRIES

1. *tꜣ mꜣy n pꜣ ym* the isle of the sea

4, R° 9–10 — *ỉw·f šm* (*r*) *tꜣ mꜣy n pꜣ ym*
Probably a description of Cyprus: see note, p. 32, and the Commentary, § 2.

2. *Hrmꜣ* Rome

3, V° 21–2 — *mšꜥ Nwmnys* (*r*) *Hrmꜣ*
See note, p. 25, and the Commentary, § 2.

3. (*pꜣ tꜣ*) *Ḫr* (the land of) Syria

1, 12 — *pꜣy Kmy pꜣ tꜣ Ḫr*
13 — *pꜣ ym n Ḫr*

4. *Kmy*(*t*) Egypt

Dem. Text
B, 3 — *mdt rmt-n-Kmy*
1, 7 — *Kmy pnḳ n-ỉm·f*
12 — *ꜣst tꜣ ntrt ꜥꜣt n pꜣy Kmy*

2, R° 6 *ỉw·f šm n·f n sgr r-bl Kmy*
V° 12 id.
3, R° 1 *pꜣ nb n Kmy*
7–8 *pꜣ ḳhy n Kmy*
V° 9–10 *wn-nꜣ Kmy pnḳ n-ỉm·f n Rꜥ-ḳd*
4, R° 4 id. (restored)
8–9 *ỉ·ỉr·f šm r-bl Kmy*
6, V° x+6 *pꜣ hp Kmy*
7, 4 *nꜣ hbw n Kmy*
11–12 *nꜣ ꜥẖyt n Kmy*
11, V° 6 *nꜣ ntrw n Kmy*
16, R° 1 *nꜣ ꜥẖyt n Kmy*
17, 1 id.
22, R° 2 *tꜣ mdt pḥ Kmy*
V° 6* (?)
27, V° 6 *nꜣ ꜥẖyt n Kmy*
29, 2 *] Kmy ẖr·w*
38, 3 *ỉy (r) K[my*
40, 2 *šm·f r-bl Kmy*
46, 5 *dỉ·ỉ-s n·f n sẖ rmt-n-Kmy*
51, 2 (?)
59, 17 *stp dmỉ (n) Kmy*

5. *pꜣ tꜣ mḥ* the north land

11, V° 1 *ꜣst ỉrm nꜣ ntrw n pꜣ tꜣ mḥ*
63, 4 *nꜣ tšw n pꜣ tꜣ mḥ*

6. *pꜣ tꜣ rs* the south land

11, V° 4 *nꜣ ntrw n pꜣ tꜣ rs*

B. TOWNS AND CITIES

1. *ʾIwnw* Heliopolis

1, 1–2 *tꜣ wꜥbt Wsỉr Mr-wr n ʾIwnw*
1, 2 *tw·ỉ ḥr(?) ʾIwnw*
4 *pꜣ r-pr ʾIy-m-ḥtp nty ỉw ẖn ʾIwnw*
5 *ỉw·ỉ ỉy ʾIwnw*
5, 3 *ḥt-ntr ʾIwnw*
13, 7 *tꜣ ḫꜣst ỉꜣbtt n ʾIwnw*
18, R° 4 *Rꜥ-Ḥr-ḥḳ(ꜣ) n ʾIwnw*
8 *nꜣ sštw ꜥꜣy n ʾIwnw*
by ʾIwnw (twice)
32, R° 7 *ḥt-ntr ʾIwnw*

2. *ʾIbt* Abydos

15, R° 1 (restored)
5 *[pꜣ ḥm-]ntr ʾIbt pꜣ ḥr-ḥb ʾIbt*
7 *[pꜣ ḥr-]ḥb ʾIbt*
9 *ḥt-ntr ʾIbt*

3. *Yb* Elephantine

16, R° 6 *Yb r nꜣ wꜥbt Smꜣ-bḥdt*
17, 13 id.

4. *ꜥnḫ-tꜣwy* ꜥAnkhtawy

18, V° 3 *nb ꜥnḫ-tꜣwy n Mn-nfr*
7 *pr m ꜥnḫ-tꜣwy* pꜣ wny ỉ·ỉr wḏꜥ pꜣ kk*
V° 7 (cont.) *ꜥnḫ-tꜣwy**
R° 1* *hh nty ẖn ꜥnḫ-tꜣwy**
23, R° 6 *R-stꜣw ꜥnḫ-tꜣwy**
59, 2 *nb ꜥnḫ[-tꜣwy*
See the Commentary, § 5. The examples asterisked are written in hieratic.

5. *ꜥrḳ-ḥḥ* ꜥAleḳḥaḥ

18, V° 16 *ỉr·k ḥs ꜥrḳ-ḥḥ*
See note, pp. 72–3.

6. *Pꜣ-ꜣḥ-Ḏḥwty* Piaḥthoth

59, 18 *Pꜣ-ꜣḥ-Ḏḥwty*

7. *Pr-Ꜣwrys* Pi-Eulaeus(?)

1, 7 *wn-nꜣ ꜣtyks ḥr pr-mḥ Pr-Ꜣwrys*
3, V° 10–11 *ḫnn ꜣtyks n pr-mḥ Pr-Ꜣwrys*
Identification doubtful: see notes, p. 28 and the Commentary, § 2.

8. *Pr-ỉr-ʾImn* Pelusium

3, V° 13–14 *r-hn r šm r-bl Pr-ỉr-ʾImn ỉ·ỉr ꜣtyks*
22–3 *mšꜥ Tynys (r) Pr-ỉr-ʾImn*
37, 4 *Pr-ỉr[-ʾImn](?)*
See notes, p. 28, and the Commentary, § 2.

9. *Pr-Wꜣḏyt* Buto

10, R° 11 *sẖ Ḥr Pr-Wꜣḏyt*

10. *Pr-wꜥb-nb·s* Pi-waꜥb-nēbes

21, R° 6–7 *dỉt mnt ẖr·f n Pr-wꜥb-nb·s ỉw·w ỉr ḳrs·f*
13 *tn šꜣꜥ-mtw·f ỉy (r) Pr-wꜥb-nb·s*
V° 12–13 *thm pꜣ mšꜥ n Pr-Wsỉr-Ḥp (r) Pr-wꜥb-nb·s*
See the Commentary, §§ 4, 5.

11. *Pr-Wsỉr* Pi-Osīri (House-of-Osiris)

23, R° 4–6 *tꜣ ḫꜣst Pr-Wsỉr ḥr pꜣ ḏw pr-mḥ n R-stꜣw ꜥnḫ-tꜣwy*
58, 12 *pꜣ tš n Pr-Wsỉr*
63, 3 *] hn Pr-Wsỉr*
See the Commentary, § 5, pp. 149 f.

12. *Pr-Wsỉr-Ḥp* the (Memphite) Serapeum

8, R° 14 *ỉn·ỉ-s r-ḥry Pr-Wsỉr-Ḥp*
23–4 *ꜥwy-n-ḥtp Pr-Wsỉr-Ḥp*
V° 6 *pꜣ ꜥwy-n-ḥtp n Pr-Wsỉr-Ḥp*
13, 4 *nꜣ ntrw nty ḥtp n R-stꜣw Pr-Wsỉr-Ḥp*
8 *ỉw·ỉ šms n Pr-Wsỉr-Ḥp*
12 *šms n-ỉm·f n Pr-Wsỉr-Ḥp*
19, V° 10 *pꜣ mšꜥ n Pr-Wsỉr-Ḥp*
14–15 *tꜣ wsḫyt Pr-Wsỉr-Ḥp*
20, 1 (?)
21, V° 12 *pꜣ mšꜥ n Pr-Wsỉr-Ḥp*
18–19 *nꜣ wnw n Pr-Wsỉr-Ḥp*
23, R° 3 *pꜣ ḏw rs n Pr-Wsỉr-Ḥp pꜣ nty n Mn-nfr*

2, V° 5 *Pr-Wsir-Ḥp pꜣ ꜥꜣ nty n Rꜥ-ḳd*
3, R° 2 *nty wꜣḥ-sḥn n Rꜥ-ḳd*
V° 10 *Kmy pnḳ n-im·f n Rꜥ-ḳd*
20 *Pr-Wsir-Ḥp pꜣ ꜥꜣ nty n Rꜥ-ḳd*
4, R° 4 *[Kmy pnḳ n-im·f n] Rꜥ-ḳd*
6 *pꜣ wḏꜣ n Rꜥ-ḳd*
10 *iw·f ꜣrꜥ n Rꜥ-ḳd*
12, 3 *ꜥḥꜥ·i irm Pꜣ-šr-n-nꜣ-isw n Rꜥ-ḳd*
19, R° 18 *hb·w ḥty(?) n Rꜥ-ḳd*
29, 10 *Rꜥ-ḳd [*
30, 8 *]·i ḫrw·i n Rꜥ-ḳd*
41, 2 *] Rꜥ-ḳd ḏd [*

26. *Ḥp-nb·s* Ḥepnēbes

Dem. Text **B,** 4 *] ... Ḥp-nb·s n rn pꜣ ntr ꜥꜣ*
5A, x+4 *] ... Ḥp-nb·s rnpt(?) 25(?)*
13, 4–5 *R-stꜣw Pr-Wsir-Ḥp irm R-stꜣw Ḥp-nb·s*
19, R° 9 *nꜣ byw ꜥꜣy n Ḥp-nb·s*
V° 6 *mtw·w iy r Ḥp-nb·s*
10 *thm pꜣ mšꜥ Pr-Wsir-Ḥp r Ḥp-nb·s*
22, R° 4 *tꜣ wmtt n Ḥp-nb·s*
10–11 *tꜣ wꜥbt n Ḥp-nb·s*
V° 1 *wbꜣ rꜣ Ḥp-nb·s*
23, R° 4 *iw·i šms nꜣ hrw n Ḥp-nb·s*
13 *[dit] mnt ḫr pꜣ hb pꜣ bik n Ḥp-nb·s*
V° 20 *smn pꜣ hp n pꜣ hb pꜣ bik n Ḥp-nb·s*
30, 10 *Ḥp-]nb·s iwty šb*
See the Commentary, §§ 4, 5.

27. *Ḫmnw* Hermopolis

28, 12 *Ḏḥwty ꜥꜣ ꜥꜣ nb Ḫmnw(?)*

Cf. Appendix 2. For a discussion of the various cities known to the Greeks as Hermopolis see the Commentary, § 1.

28. *Sywt* Siut

10, R° 4–5 *drt Ḥr i·di(?) n·f Wsir n Sywt*

29. *Smꜣ-bḥdt* Sambeḥdet

16, R° 6 *Yb n nꜣ wꜥbt Smꜣ-bḥdt*
17, 13 id.
59, 18 *'Imn-Rꜥ nb Smꜣ-Bḥdt*
See notes, p. 63.

30. *pꜣ ši* the lake

10, R° 3–4 *tꜣ ntrt ꜥꜣt n pꜣ ḳꜣn(?) pꜣ ši*
33, 2 *pꜣ ši n Pr-ꜥꜣ*
See notes, p. 48, and the Commentary, § 5.

31. *Tbny* Daphnae(?)

7, 6–7 *pꜣ htm nty iw Tmpn Tbny ḥms ḥr ꜣt·f 3ktryn i·ir (T)bny smn [*
26, R° 1 *3rstn Tbny*
60, 1–2 *i·ir Tbny smn pꜣ mšꜥ*
See notes, p. 36.

32. *tꜣ thn(yt)* the Peak

18, V° 2–3 *'Iy-m-ḥtp kmꜣ(?) rsnfy tꜣ thn nb ꜥnḫ-tꜣwy n Mn-nfr*
23, V° 23 *ḥt-ntr tꜣ thnyt*
59, 2 *ḥt-ntr tꜣ thny nb ꜥnḫ[-tꜣwy*
See notes, p. 90, and the Commentary, § 5.

33. *Ṯb-ntr* Sebennytos

1, 1 *pꜣ tš [Ṯb-ntr]*
2, R° 3 *pꜣ tš Ṯb-ntr*
V° 2 *pꜣ tš Ṯb* (sic)
7, 3 *pꜣ tš Ṯb-ntr*
8, R° 2 *di·w ꜥḥꜥ·i n Ṯb-ntr*
19, R° 1 *n-drt sḫ tš Ṯb-ntr*
21, R° 2 id.
25, 1 id.
26, 2 *pꜣ tš Ṯb-ntr*
28, 3 id.
29, 2 id.
9 id.
31A, 4 id.
See also Σεβέννυτος in the Greek Index.

34. *Dmi-n-3st* Temenēsi

2, R° 2–3 *Dmi-n-3st tꜣ ntrt ꜥꜣt nbt tpḥ(?) n pꜣ tš Ṯb-ntr*
V° 1 id.
7, 3 *Dmi-n-3st tꜣ ntrt ꜥꜣt nbt tpḥ(?) nty iw n pꜣ tš Ṯb-ntr*
26, R° 2 *Dmi-n-3st n pꜣ tš Ṯb-ntr*
27, R° 2–3 (?)
29, 2 *Dmi-n-3st n pꜣ tš Ṯb-ntr*
9 id.
58, 2 (?)
See also Ἴσιος πόλις in the Greek Index.

35. *Ḏdit* Djedit

13, 6–7 *nꜣ ntrw nty ḥtp n R-stꜣw Ḏdit irm nꜣ ntrw n tꜣ ḫꜣst iꜣbtt n 'Iwnw*
18, R° 1* *tꜣy·k st nfrt Ḏdit*
Name of the necropolis of Heliopolis: see notes, p. 55.

C. COSMOLOGY

1. *pt* heaven

9, R° 10 *di·i wꜣḥ tꜣ pt*
10, R° 10 *nbt pt ḥnꜥ tꜣ*
18, R° 1 *Rꜥ-Ḥr nb pt*
2 *hy Ḥr ḥrby(?) pt*
9 *Skr-Wsir n pt Skr-Wsir n tꜣ*
For the link with the goddess Isis see Appendix 1.

2. *Dwꜣt* Netherworld

18, R° 5 *irt·f n-drt·f m Dwꜣt*
7 *Ḫnsw tpy wtn nb Dwꜣt*
14 *wḏꜣ Dwꜣt(?)*
V° 15 *ntr pr m Dwꜣt*
18 *ḥt·k n tꜣ Dwꜣt*

§ 3. CHRONOLOGY AND NUMBERS

A. REGNAL YEARS

B. MONTHS

C. DAYS

D. NUMERALS

E. ORDINALS

F. FRACTIONS

§ 4. IMPORTANT WORDS AND PHRASES

A. ORACULAR AND PROPHETIC

1. *ꜥš-sḥn* fortune

2. *wꜣḥ* oracle, interpretation

3. *tꜣ mit* / *pꜣ myt* the path

4. *mdt-nfrt* benefit

9	id.
13–14	*ṯꜣy-ꜥḳ pꜣ hb pꜣ bỉk*
22, R° 5	*pꜣ hb pꜣ bỉk*
10	id.
V° 5	*nꜣ sḏm-ꜥš n pꜣ bỉk*
23, R° 13	*dỉt mnt ẖr pꜣ hb pꜣ bỉk*
22	*pꜣ bỉk*
V° 10	*pꜣ hb pꜣ bỉk*
20	id.
24–5	id.
24B, 5	(restored)
25, 3	*pꜣ ꜥš-sḥn n pꜣ bỉk pꜣ by n Wsỉr Ḥr Ꜣst*

See the Commentary, § 4.

5. *pꜣ hb* the Ibis

11, R° 12	*pꜣ hb*(?)
12, R° 3	*pꜣ ꜥš-sḥn n pꜣ hb*
13, 1	*pꜣ ꜥwy-n-ḥtp n pꜣ hb*
15, V° 3–4	*ḥrt n pꜣ hb*
16, R° 2	*mdt nbt nty ṯꜣy pꜣ hb n ḥꜣty·f*
5–6	*ỉw·w ỉr mdt-nfrt n pꜣ hb*
17, 2–3	*mdt nbt nty ṯꜣy pꜣ hb n ḥꜣty·f*
12–13	*pꜣ nty ỉr mdt-nfrt n pꜣ hb*
17A, 1–2	*bw-ỉr ꜣbḫ mdt ỉw·s ṯꜣy pꜣ hb*
19, R° 5	*pꜣ hb pꜣ by n Ḏḥwty*
8	*pꜣ hb pꜣ bỉk*
10	id.
12	*nꜣ sḏm-ꜥš n nꜣ hbw*
19	id.
24	*nꜣ ꜥwyw-n-ḥtp n pꜣ hb*
V° 5–6	*tꜣ ḥrt ỉrm pꜣ ꜥš-sḥn n pꜣ hb*
9	*dỉt ḥtp pꜣ hb*
11	*ṯꜣy-ꜥḳ pꜣ hb pꜣ bỉk r pꜣy·f ꜥwy-n-ḥtp*
12	*nꜣ ꜥwyw-n-ḥtp n pꜣ hb*
20, 4	*dỉt mnt ẖr pꜣ hb pꜣ bỉk*
9	*ḥt-nṯr pꜣ hb nb ḥtp*
13	] *nꜣ hbw*
21, R° 6	*tꜣ mdt pḥ pꜣ hb n ḥꜣty·f*
12	*šn pꜣ ꜥš-sḥn n pꜣ hb pꜣ bỉk*
14	*tꜣ wꜥbt n pꜣ hb*
17	*mnt ẖr pꜣ hb*
V° 1	*nꜣ sḏm-ꜥš n nꜣ hbw*
4–5	*dỉt ḳrs pꜣ hb pꜣ bỉk*
9	*pꜣ ỉnḥy ẖr pꜣ hb pꜣ bỉk*
10	*dỉt ḥtp pꜣ hb*
13	*ṯꜣy-ꜥḳ pꜣ hb*
22, R° 1	*di·w mnt ẖr pꜣ hb ỉwty šb*
5	*pꜣ ꜥš-sḥn n pꜣ hb pꜣ bỉk*
10	id.
V° 4–5	*nꜣ sḏm-ꜥš n nꜣ hbw*
23, R° 10	*dỉt mnt ẖr pꜣ hb pꜣ bỉk*
15	*pꜣ rmt nty ỉr n pꜣ hb*
21	⟨*pꜣ hb*⟩ *pꜣ bỉk*
V° 10	*pꜣ hb pꜣ bỉk pꜣ nṯr*[
20	*smn pꜣ hp n pꜣ hb pꜣ bỉk*
24	*dỉt wḏꜣ pꜣ hb pꜣ bỉk*
24A, 2	*wḏꜣ pꜣ hb*
24B, 4	*pꜣ hb*
5	*tꜣ ḳrst n pꜣ hb*
25, 4	*ḥt-mdt pḥ n pꜣ hb pꜣ by n Ḏḥwty ꜥꜣ ꜥꜣ*
26, R° 7	(restored)
8	*ḥrt n nꜣ hbw*
11	*tꜣ nty ỉw pꜣ hb* [. . .] *r·s*
17	*tꜣ ḥrt n nꜣ hbw*
V° 6–7	id.
27, V° 9	*tꜣ ḥrt n pꜣ hb*
30, 4–5	*tꜣ ḥrt* [*ỉrm*] *tꜣ ḳrst n pꜣ hb*
33, 2	*ỉw pꜣ hb lwḥ*
4	*ḥr pꜣ sḥn ỉ·ỉr·ḥr pꜣ hb*
6	id.
7	*smn* . . . (?) *rmt-rḫ wbꜣ pꜣ hb tꜣ mst n-s pꜣ hb*
8	*ỉw·f ḥrḥ pꜣ hb dỉt wḏꜣ·f*
9	*pꜣ sḏm-ꜥš n nꜣ hbw*
12	*wbꜣ pꜣ ꜥš-sḥn n pꜣ hb*
14	*wꜥt sꜥnḫt ẖr pꜣ hb*
45, 2	*pꜣ ꜥš-sḥn n pꜣ hb*
48, 2	id.
63, 2	] *hb ḫpr ḳrst nfr*(*t*)

See the Commentary, § 4.

6. *tꜣ ḥrt n nꜣ hbw* the food of the ibises

7, 4	*pꜣ hp wpyt tꜣ ḥrt n nꜣ hbw n Kmy*
8, R° 18	*pꜣy·k ꜥtrm tꜣy ḥrt n nꜣ hbw 60,000*(?)
15, V° 3	*ḥrt n pꜣ hb* [*nty ḫn*] *Mn-nfr*
4	*dỉt tꜣy·k ḥrt n pꜣ hb ḥr pꜣ tny*
16, R° 4	*tꜣy·f ḥrt ỉrm tꜣy·f ḳrst*
19, V° 5–6	*šn tꜣ ḥrt ỉrm pꜣ ꜥš-sḥn n pꜣ hb*
22, R° 6	*tꜣ nty ṯꜣy tꜣy·f ḥrt ỉrm tꜣy·f ḳrst*
9	*šn tꜣ ḥrt*
24B, 4	(restored?)
26, R° 7	*tꜣ ḥrt n nꜣ* [*hbw*]
8	] *ḥrt n nꜣ hbw*
9	(erased)
13	] *ḥrt rn·s*
17	*tꜣ ḥrt n nꜣ hbw*
V° 6–7	*ỉp tꜣ ḥrt n nꜣ hbw*
27, V° 9	*st ṯꜣy tꜣ ḥrt n pꜣ hb*
28, 2	(?)
12	*ṯꜣy tꜣ ḥrt n nꜣ nṯrw*
30, 4	*wbꜣ tꜣ ḥrt* [*ỉrm*] *tꜣ ḳrst n pꜣ hb*
33, 3	*tꜣ ḥrt n Pr-ꜥꜣ* [*ḥt*(?)] *wꜥ ꜥḳ n ḥrt*
49, 3	*tꜣ nty ṯꜣy tꜣ ḥrt* [
61, 5–6	*tꜣ ḥrt* (*n*) *nꜣ* [*hbw . . . tꜣ*] *ḥrt* (*n*) *nꜣ* [*hbw*] *ỉrm tꜣ ḳrst*

The same word is applied to a human being in **10,** 13, 15, *tꜣy·k ḥrt smn wbꜣ·k nꜣy·k ssw n ꜥnḫ* and in **14,** V° 10 *pꜣ wḏꜣ ỉrm* [*tꜣ*] *ḥrt*. See the Commentary, § 3 and Appendix 1.

7. *ṯꜣy-ꜥḳ* lead in procession

19, V° 11	*ṯꜣy-ꜥḳ pꜣ hb pꜣ bỉk r pꜣy·f ꜥwy-n-ḥtp*
21, V° 13–14	*ṯꜣy-ꜥḳ pꜣ hb pꜣ bỉk* (*r*) *nꜣy·f ꜥwyw-n-ḥtp*

Used of the funeral procession held annually; see the Commentary, § 4.

See further *Pr-Ḏḥwty* (i), Index § 2, B, 20.

C. OTHER WORDS DISCUSSED

1. *mḳmḳ* memorandum

1, 1	*wꜥ mḳmḳ ỉ·ḥr nꜣ wꜥbw*
21, R° 1	*wꜥ mḳmḳ ỉ·ỉr·ḥr nꜣ wꜥbw*(?)
26, R° 1	*wꜥ mḳmḳ n Ꜣrstn n Tbny*
31, 1	*wꜥ mḳmḳ n Srpyn*

See notes, p. 12, and the Commentary, § 1.

2. *tꜣ dnỉt ḥry* the supreme inheritance

3, R° 6–7	*bn-ỉw gꜣ nṯr bl·s ỉ·ỉr-sḫy n tꜣy·k dnỉt ḥry*

§ 5. INDEX TO THE GREEK TEXTS

CONCORDANCE OF NUMBERS

Text no.	Excavator's no.	Antiquities Service Register no.	Plate or fig.
Greek frag.	G7–45	474	fig. 1, pl. VI
Dem. A, B	G7–42	471	fig. 2
1	G7–25	454	pl. II, IIA
2	71/2–131	5399	pl. III
3	G7–26	455	pl. IV, IVA
4	G7–37	466	pl. V, VA
5	G7–27	456	pl. VI, VIA
5A	G7–28	457	pl. VI, VIA
5B	G7–29	458	
6	H6–509	4132	pl. VII, VIIA
7	71/2–120	5388	pl. VII
7A	71/2–220	5488	pl. VII
8	G7–31	460	pl. VIII, VIIIA, IX, IXA
9	71/2–130	5398	pl. X, XA
10	H6–510	4133	pl. XI
11A	71/2–191	5459	pl. XII, XIIA
11B	71/2–113	5381	pl. XII, XIIA
12	71/2–129	5397	pl. XIII
12A	71/2–230	5498	pl. XIV
13	71/2–121	5389	pl. XV
14	G7–32	461	pl. XIV, XIVA
15	G7–(1+2)	432+433	pl. XVI, XVIA
15A	71/2–197	5465	pl. XVI
16	71/2–114	5382	pl. XVII
17+17A	71/2–115	5383	pl. XVIII
18	71/2–112	5380	pl. XIX, XX
19	71/2–116	5384	pl. XXI
20	G7–40	469	pl. XXII, XXIIA
21	H6–511	4134	pl. XXIII, XXIIIA
22	71/2–122	5390	pl. XXIV, XXV
23	71/2–128	5396	pl. XXVI, XXVIA
24A	G7–41	470	pl. XXII, XXIIA
24B	G7–38	467	pl. XXII, XXIIA
25	71/2–124	5392	pl. XXVII
26	G7–24	453	pl. XXVIII, XXVIIIA
27	G7–35	464	pl. XXVII, XXVIIA
28	G7–36	465	pl. XXIX, XXIXA
29	G7–39	468	pl. XXX, XXXA
30	71/2–231	5499	pl. XXIX
31A	G7–4	435	pl. XXXI, XXXIA
31B	G7–3	434	pl. XXXI, XXXIA
32	G7–5	436	pl. XXXI
33	H5–778	2525	pl. XXXII
34	71/2–123	5391	pl. XXXII
35	G7–46	475	pl. XXXIII
36	71/2–160	5428	pl. XXXIII
37	71/2–185	5453	pl. XXXIV
38	71/2–186	5454	pl. XXXIV
39	71/2–183	5451	pl. XXXIV
40	71/2–184	5452	pl. XXXIV
41	71/2–187	5455	pl. XXXIV
42	71/2–188	5456	pl. XXXIV
43	71/2–189	5457	pl. XXXIV
44	71/2–190	5458	pl. XXXV
45	71/2–192	5460	pl. XXXV

46	71/2–193	5461	pl. XXXV
47	71/2–194	5462	pl. XXXV
48	71/2–195	5463	pl. XXXV
49	G7–30	459	pl. XXXV
50	71/2–196	5464	pl. XXXVI
51	71/2–221	5489	pl. XXXVI
52	71/2–222	5490	pl. XXXVI
53	71/2–223	5491	pl. XXXVI
54	71/2–224	5492	pl. XXXVI
55	71/2–225	5493	pl. XXXVI
56	G7–33	462	pl. XXXVI
57	G7–34	463	pl. XXXVI
58	H6–62	1388	pl. XXXVII
59	H5–(779+787)	2526+2534	pl. XXXVIII, XXXVIIIA
60	H5–780	2527	pl. XXXVIII, XXXVIIIA
61	H5–999	2751	pl. XXXVIII, XXXVIIIA
62	H6–393	2469	pl. XXXIX, XXXIXA
63	H6–317 i	2165	pl. XXXIX, XXXIXA
64	71/2–(211+212)	5479+5480	pl. XXXIX, XXXIXA
65	72/3–16	6002	pl. XXXIX, XXXIXA

PLATES

PLATE IIa

Text **1** (pp. 7 ff.)

Text **1** (pp. 7 ff.)

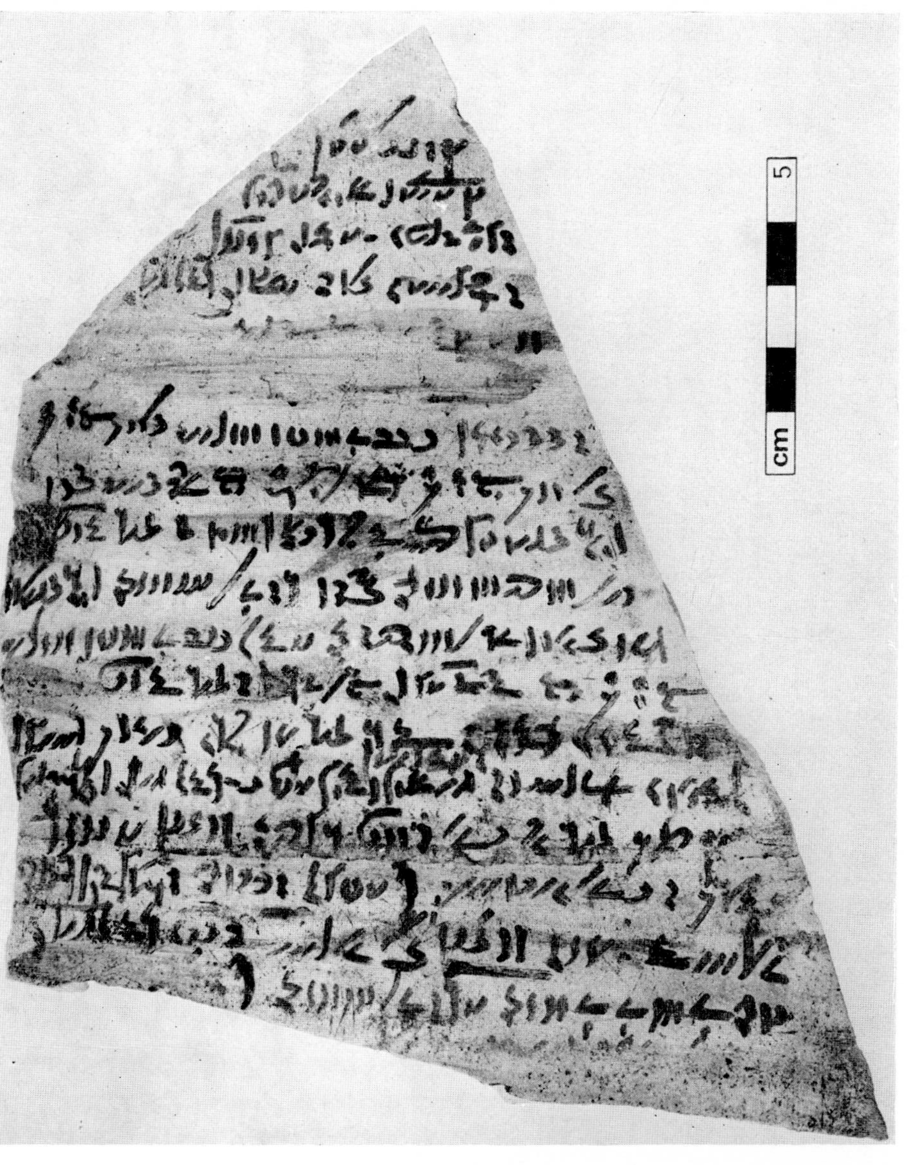

Text 2 R° (pp. 14 ff.)

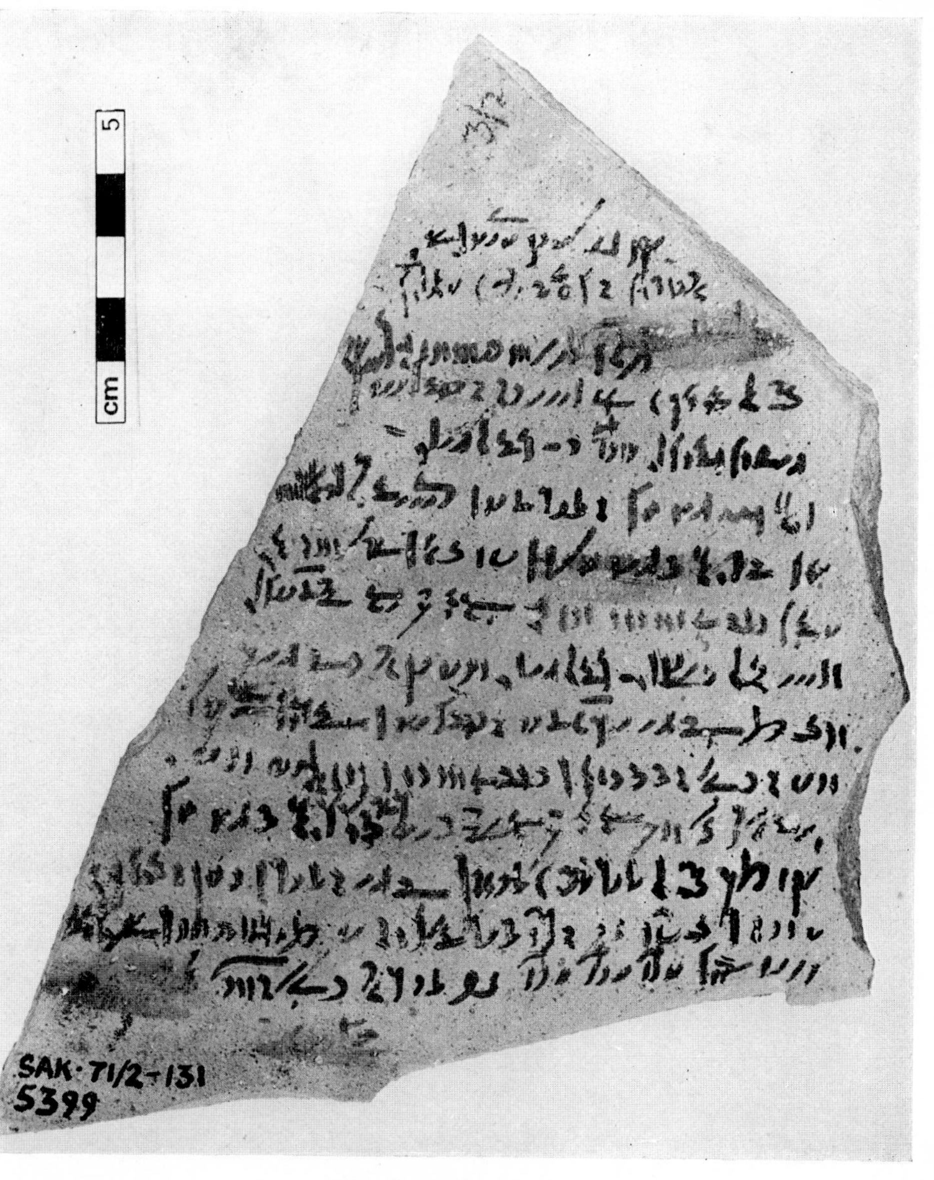

Text 2 V° (pp. 14 ff.)

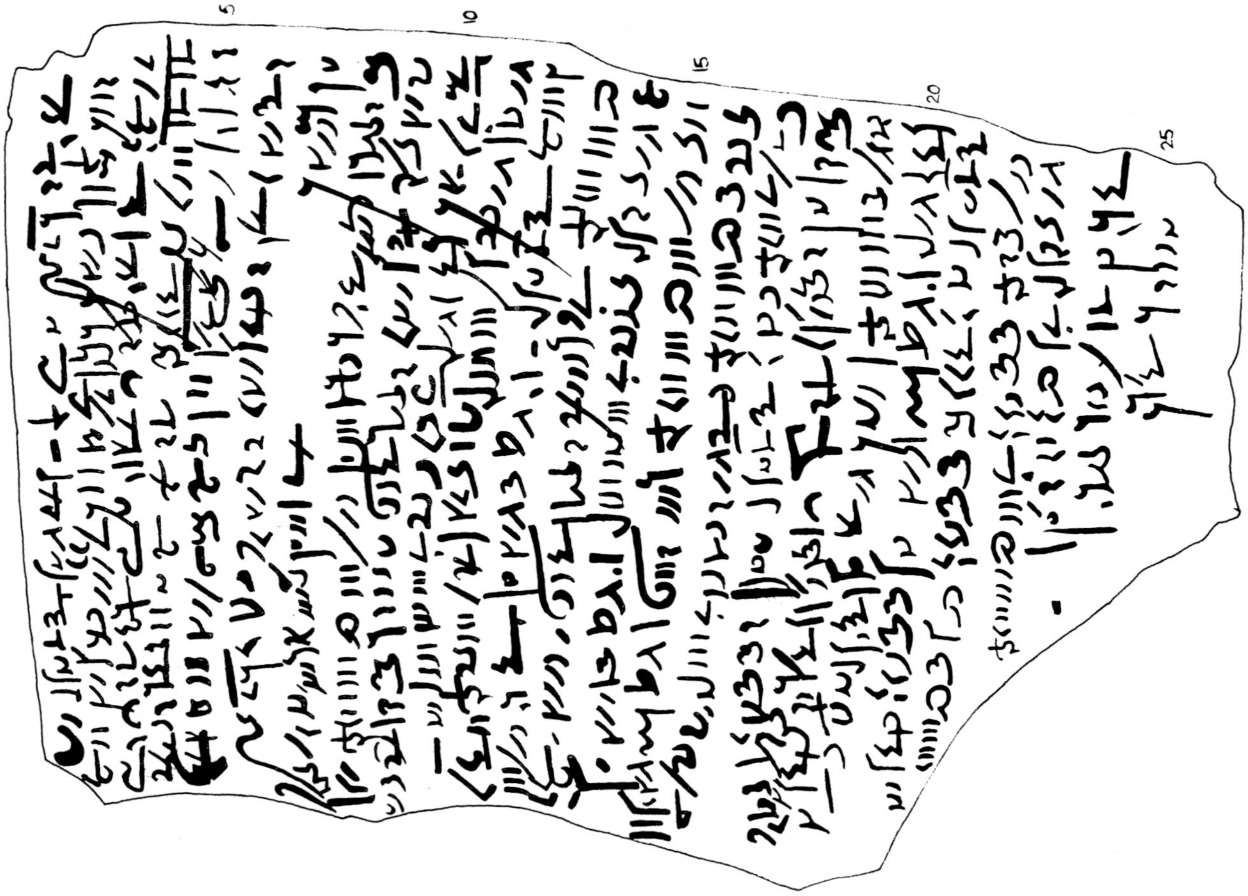

Text 3 V° (pp. 20 ff.)

Text 3 R° (pp. 20 ff.)

PLATE IV

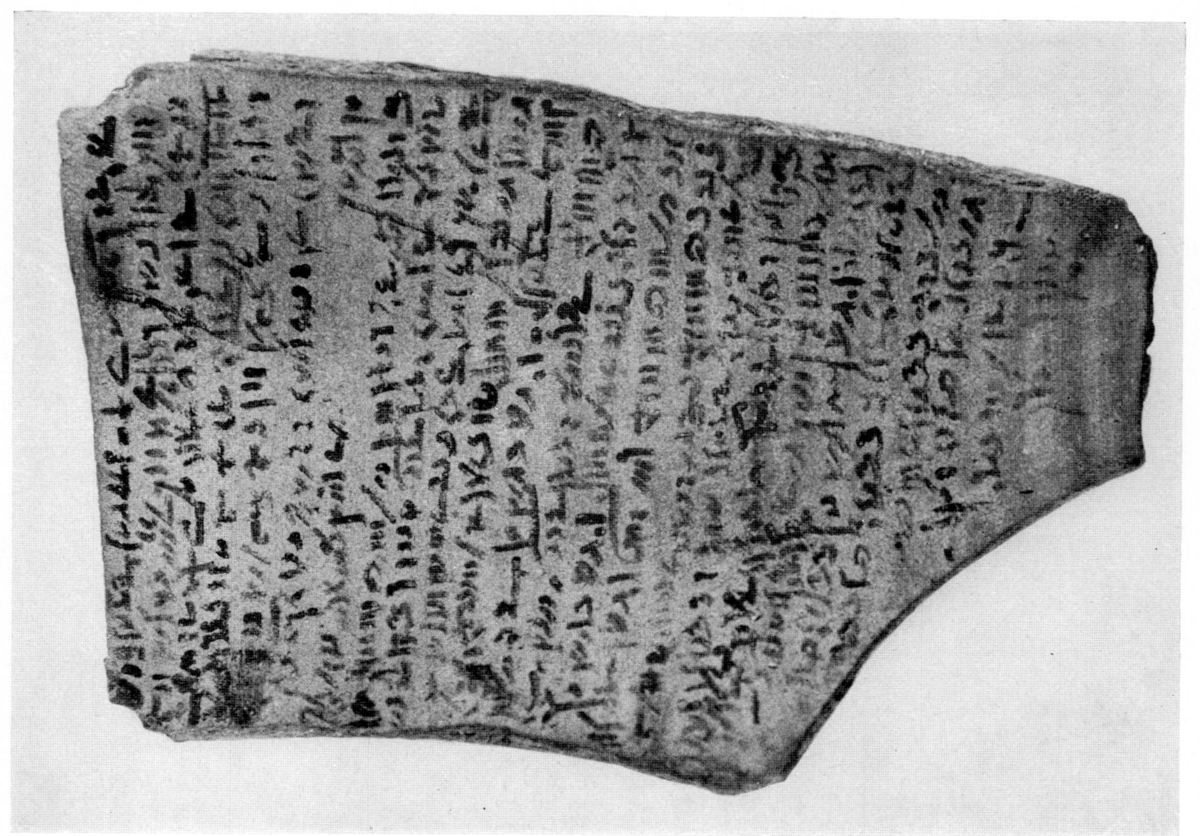

Text 3 V° (pp. 20 ff.)

Text 3 R° (pp. 20 ff.)

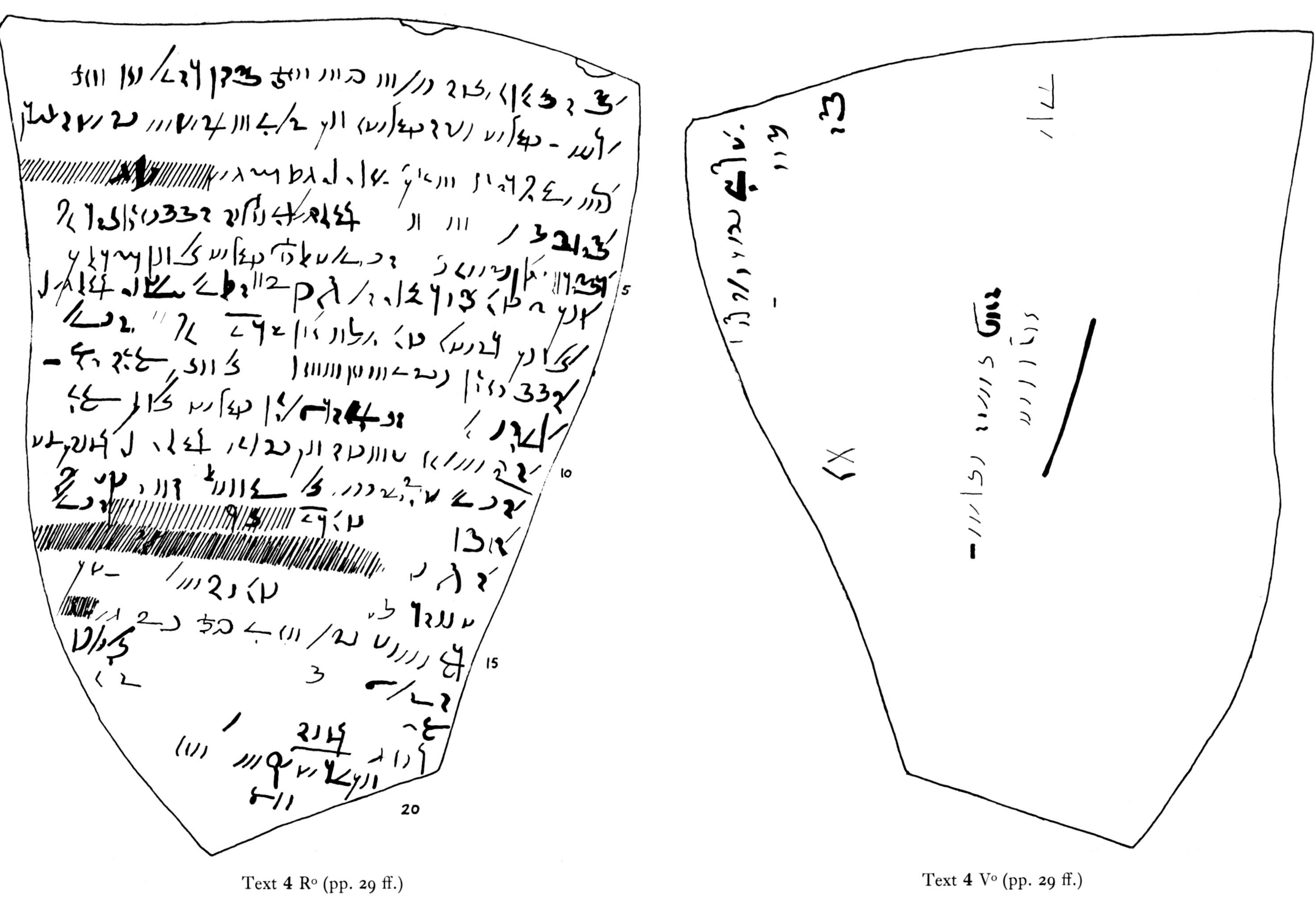

Text 4 R° (pp. 29 ff.)

Text 4 V° (pp. 29 ff.)

PLATE V

Text **4** V° (pp. 29 ff.)

Text **4** R° (pp. 29 ff.)

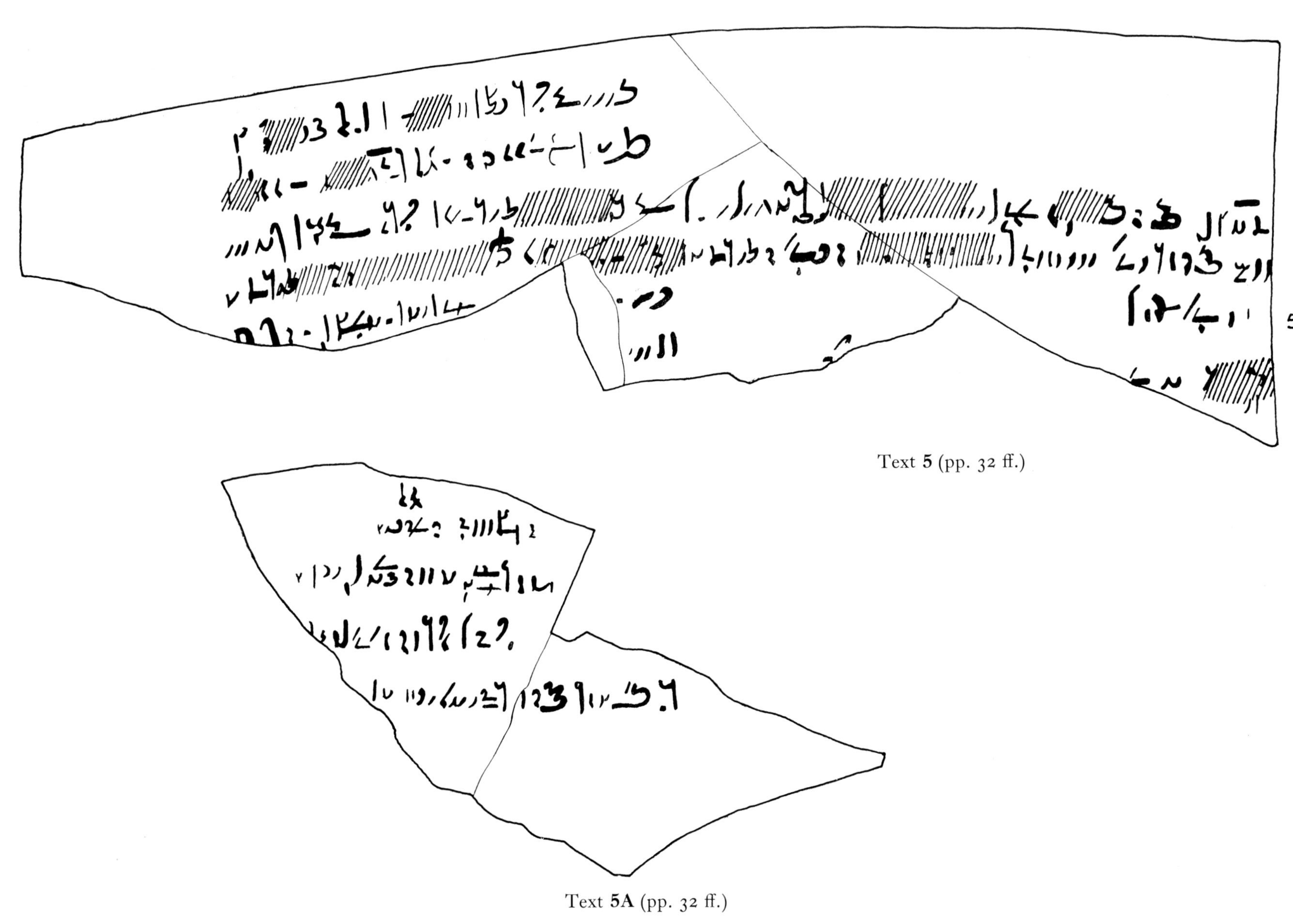

Text **5** (pp. 32 ff.)

Text **5A** (pp. 32 ff.)

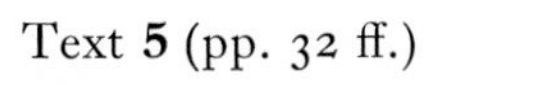

Text **5** (pp. 32 ff.)

Text **5** (pp. 32 ff.)

Text **5A** (pp. 32 ff.)

Greek Fragment (p. 1)

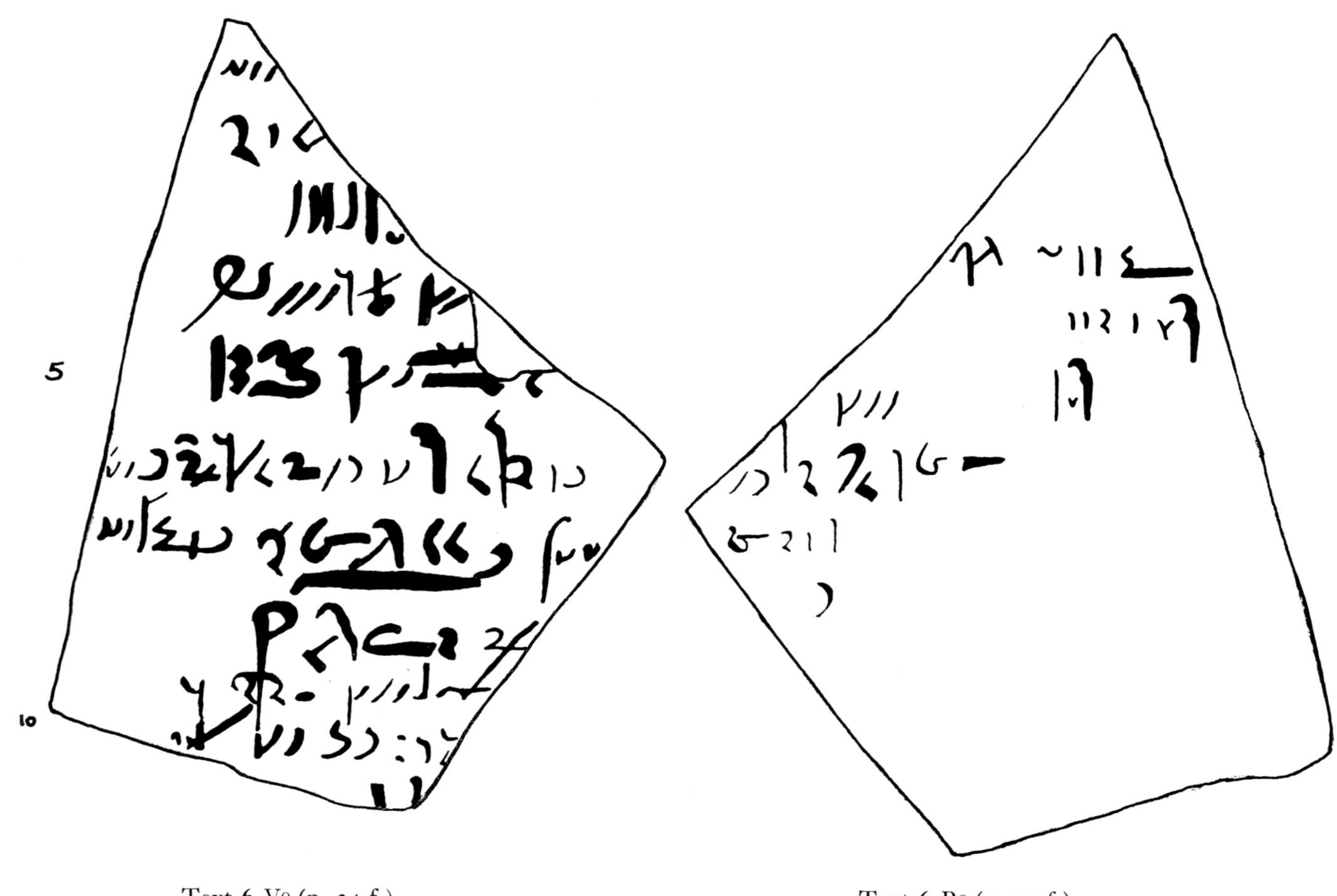

Text **6** V° (p. 34 f.)

Text **6** R° (p. 34 f.)

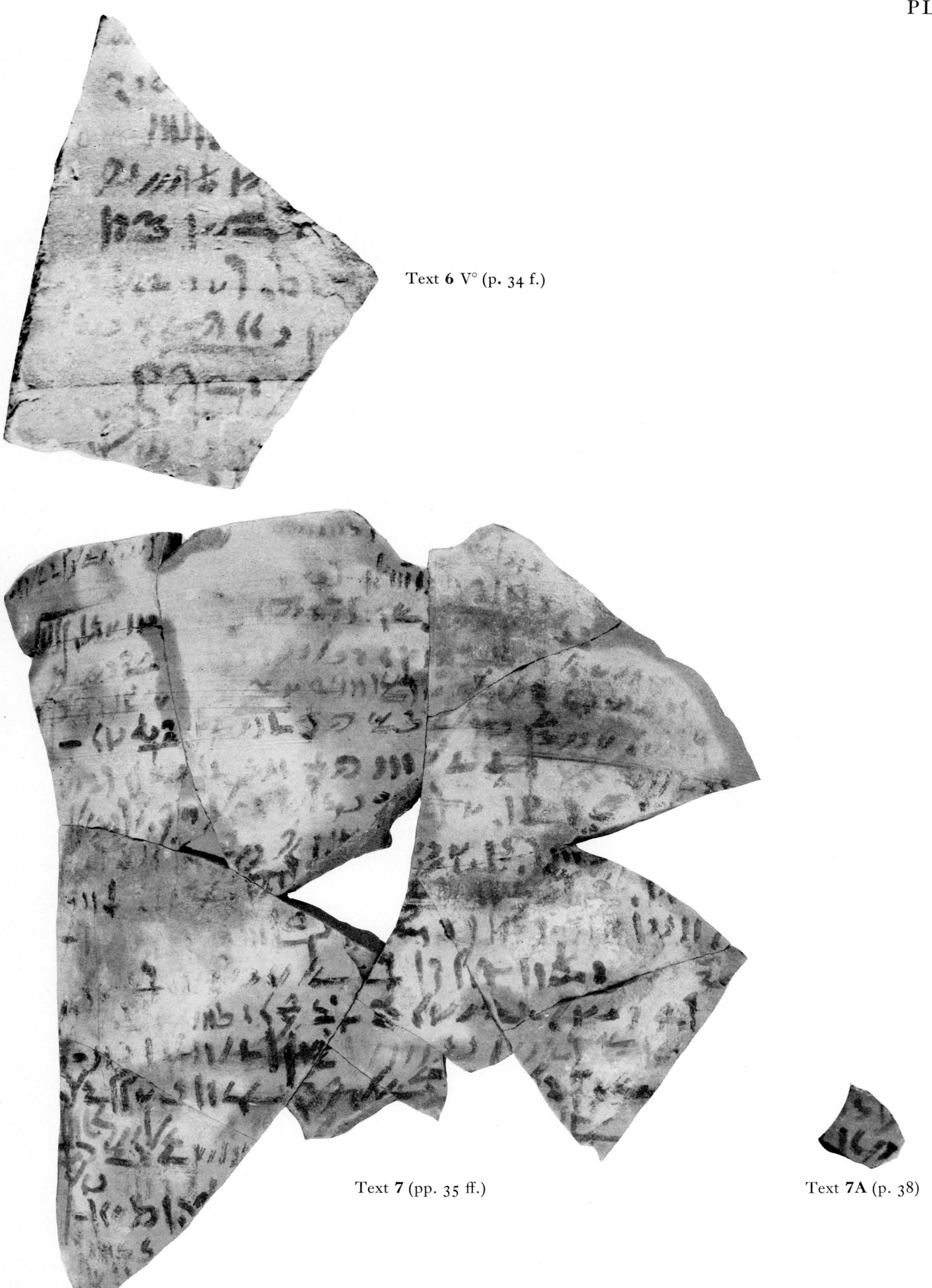

Text **6** V° (p. 34 f.)

Text **7** (pp. 35 ff.)

Text **7A** (p. 38)

Text 8 R° (pp. 38 ff.)

Text **8** R° (pp. 38 ff.)

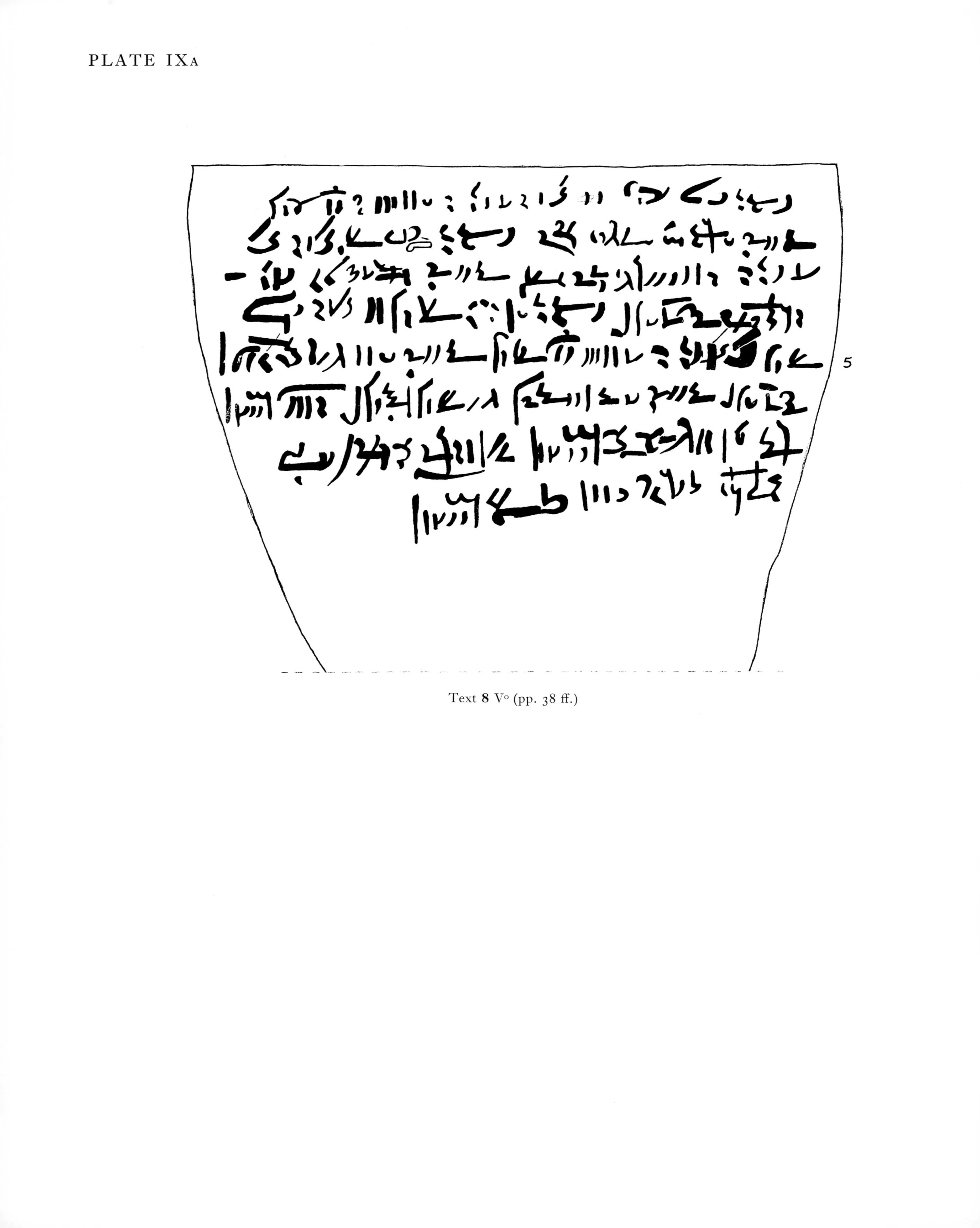

Text **8** V° (pp. 38 ff.)

Text **8** V° (pp. 38 ff.)

PLATE Xa

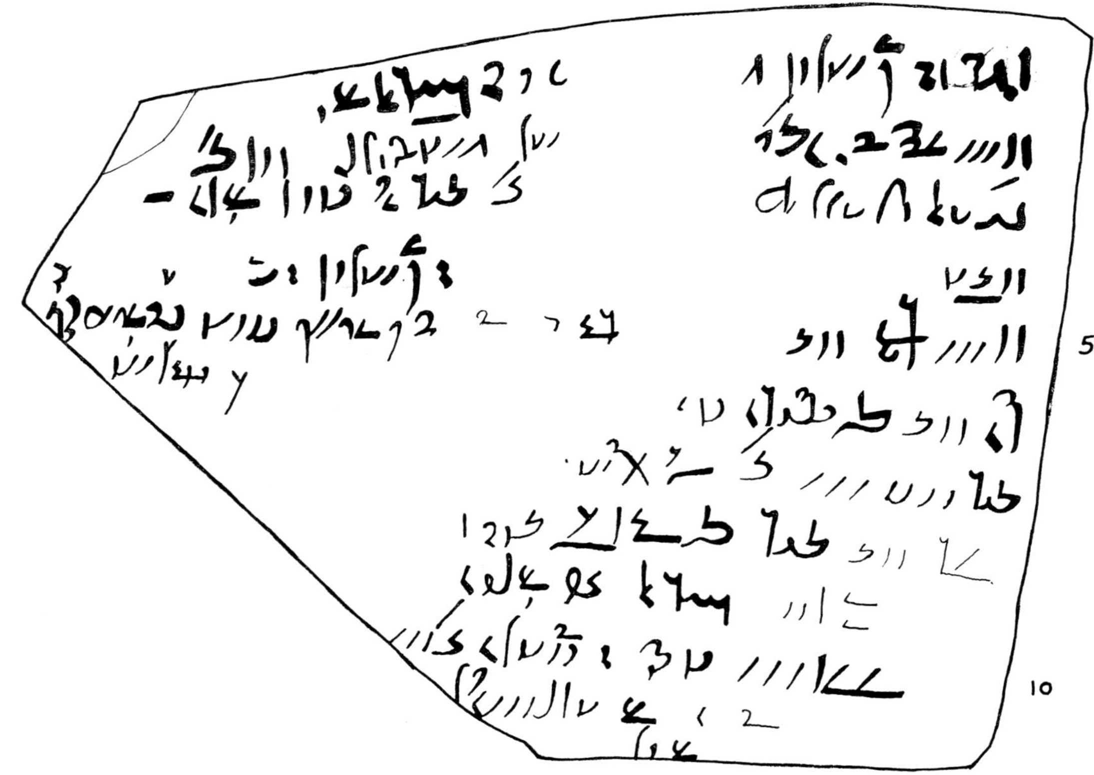

Text **9** R° (pp. 44 ff.)

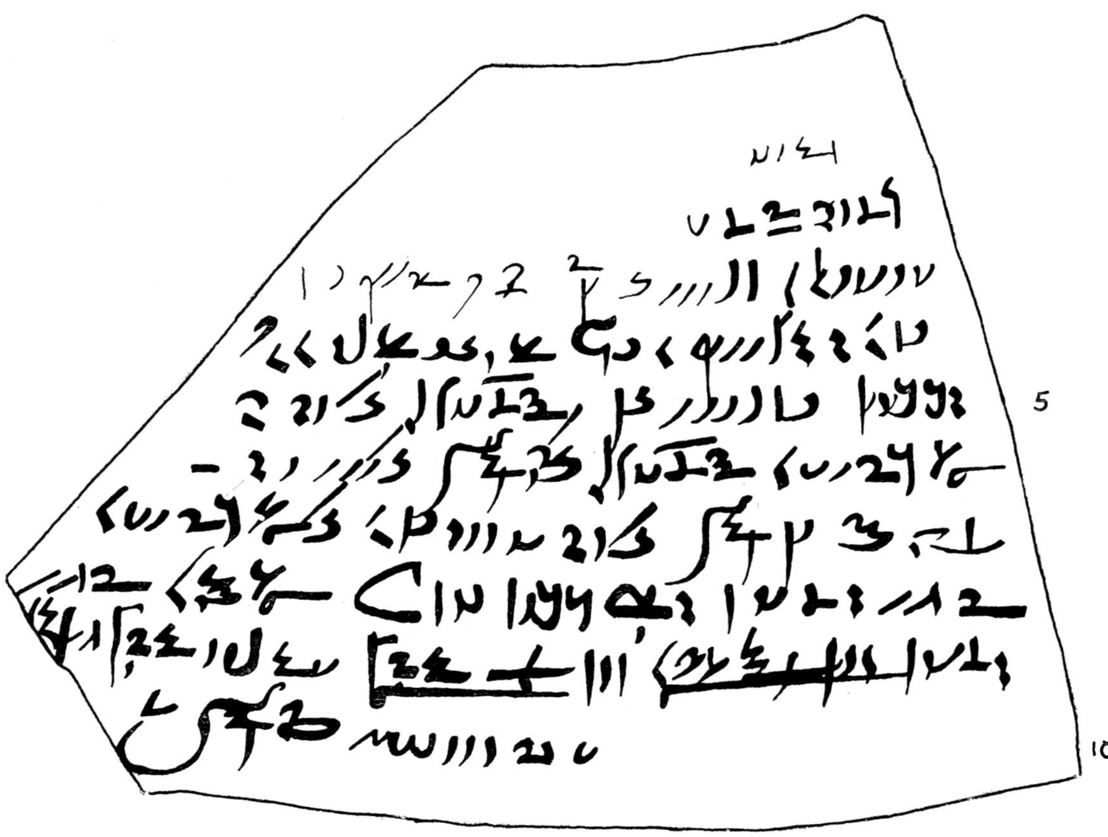

Text **9** V° (pp. 44 ff.)

Text **9** R° (pp. 44 ff.)

Text **9** V° (pp. 44 ff.)

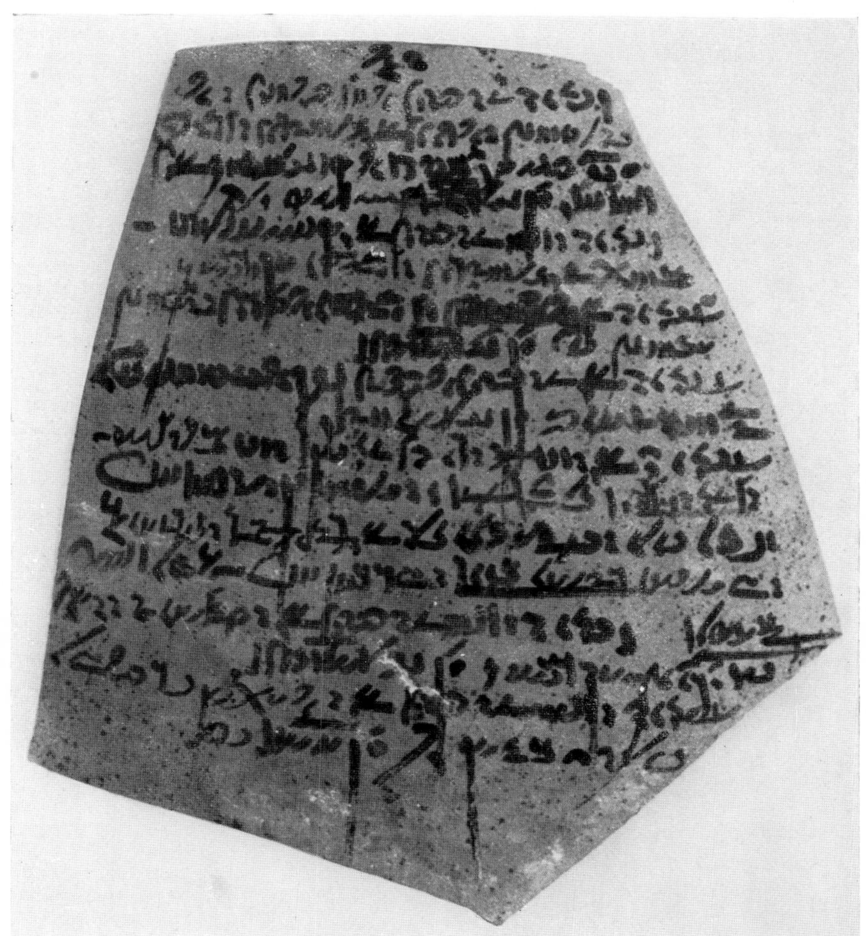

Text **10** R° (pp. 46 ff.)

Text **10** V° (pp. 46 ff.)

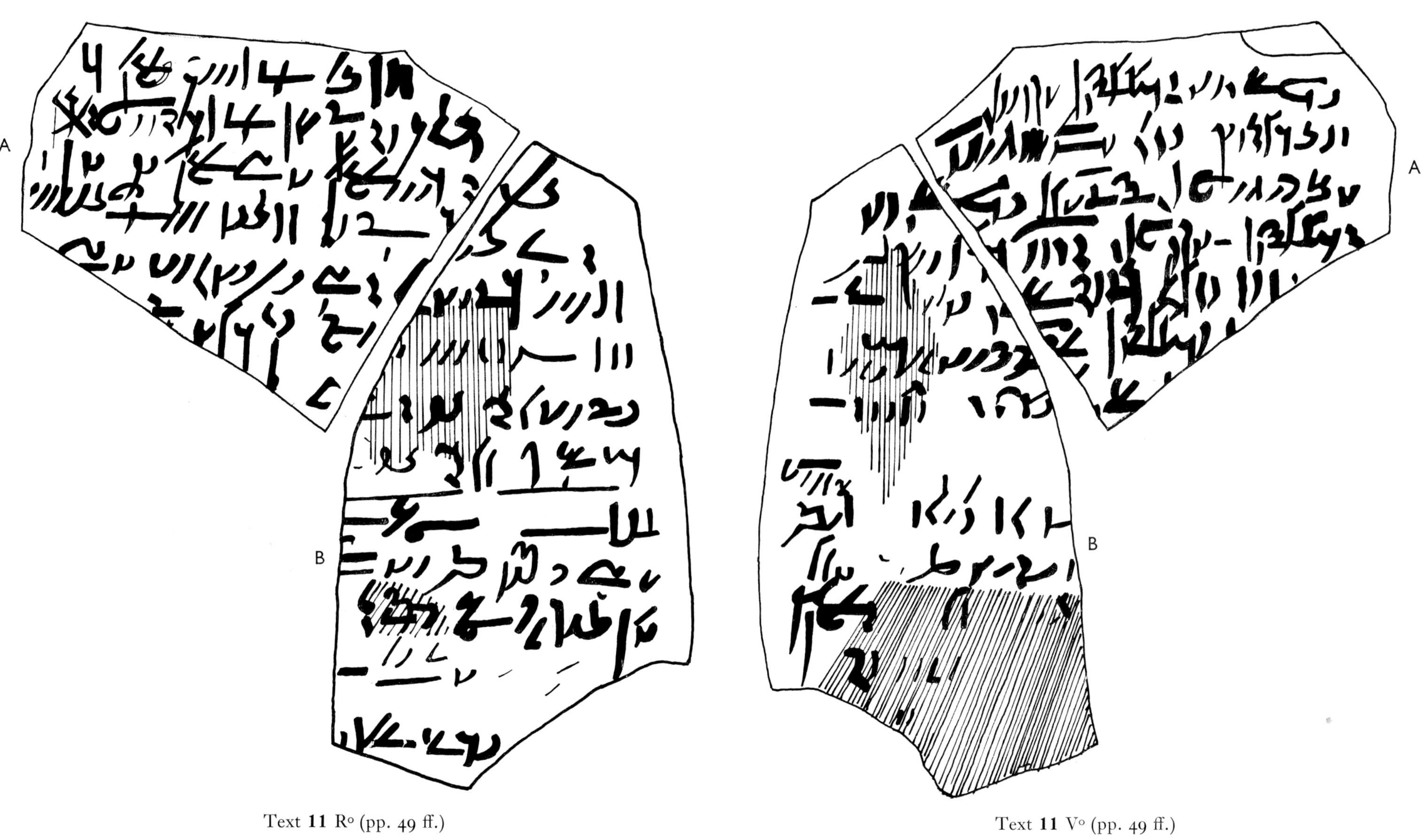

Text **11** R° (pp. 49 ff.)

Text **11** V° (pp. 49 ff.)

PLATE XII

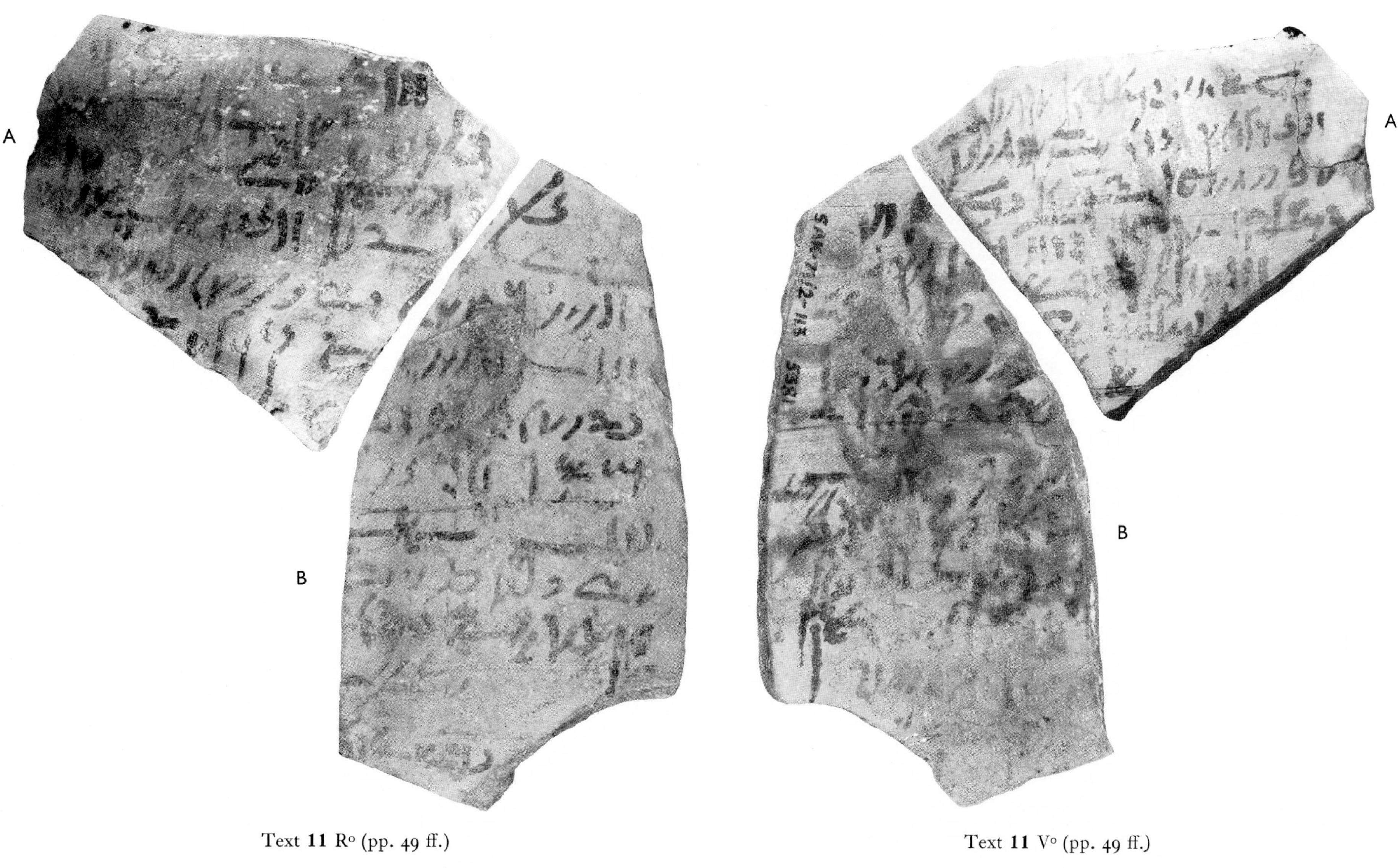

Text **11** R° (pp. 49 ff.)

Text **11** V° (pp. 49 ff.)

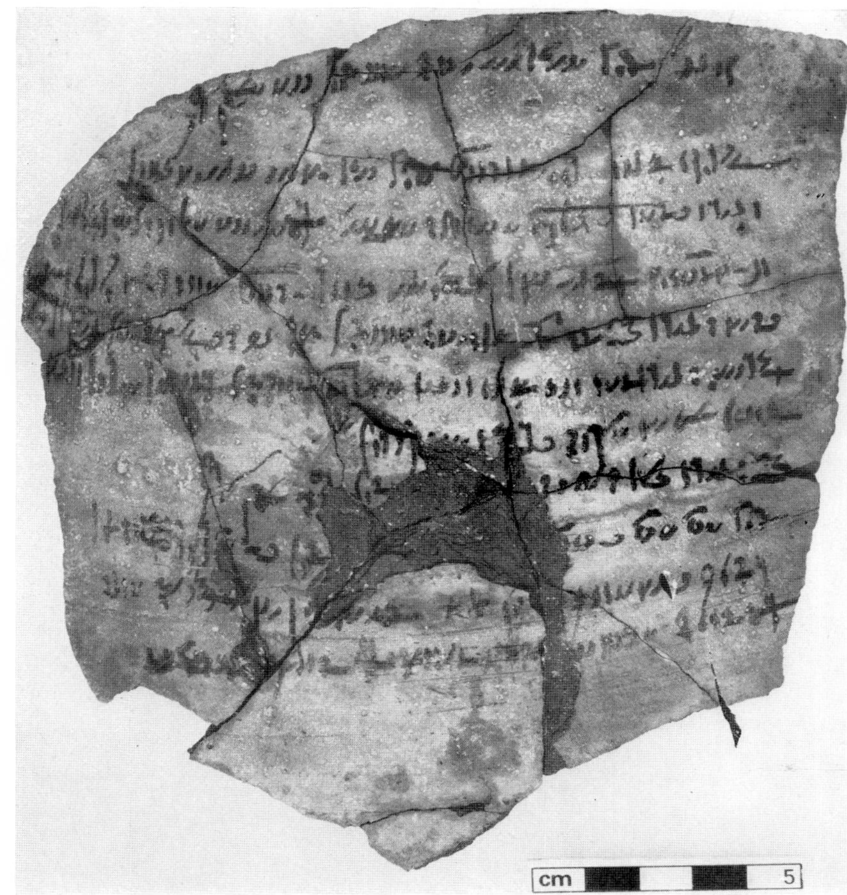

Text **12** R° (pp. 51 ff.)

Text **12** V° (pp. 51 ff.)

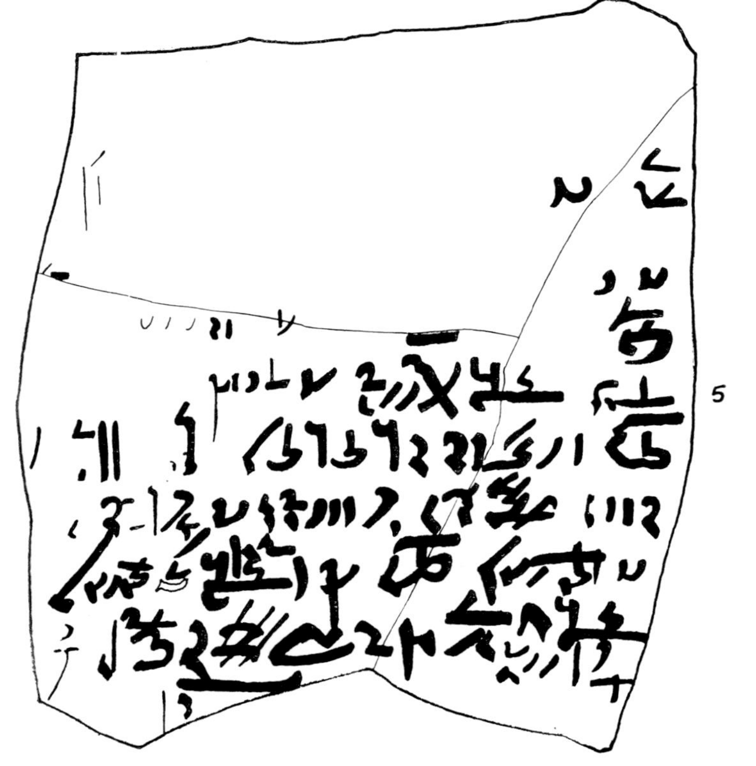

Text **14** R° (pp. 57 ff.)

Text **14** V° (pp. 57 ff.)

Text **12A** (pp. 54 f.)

Text **14** R° (pp. 57 ff.)

Text **14** V° (pp. 57 ff.)

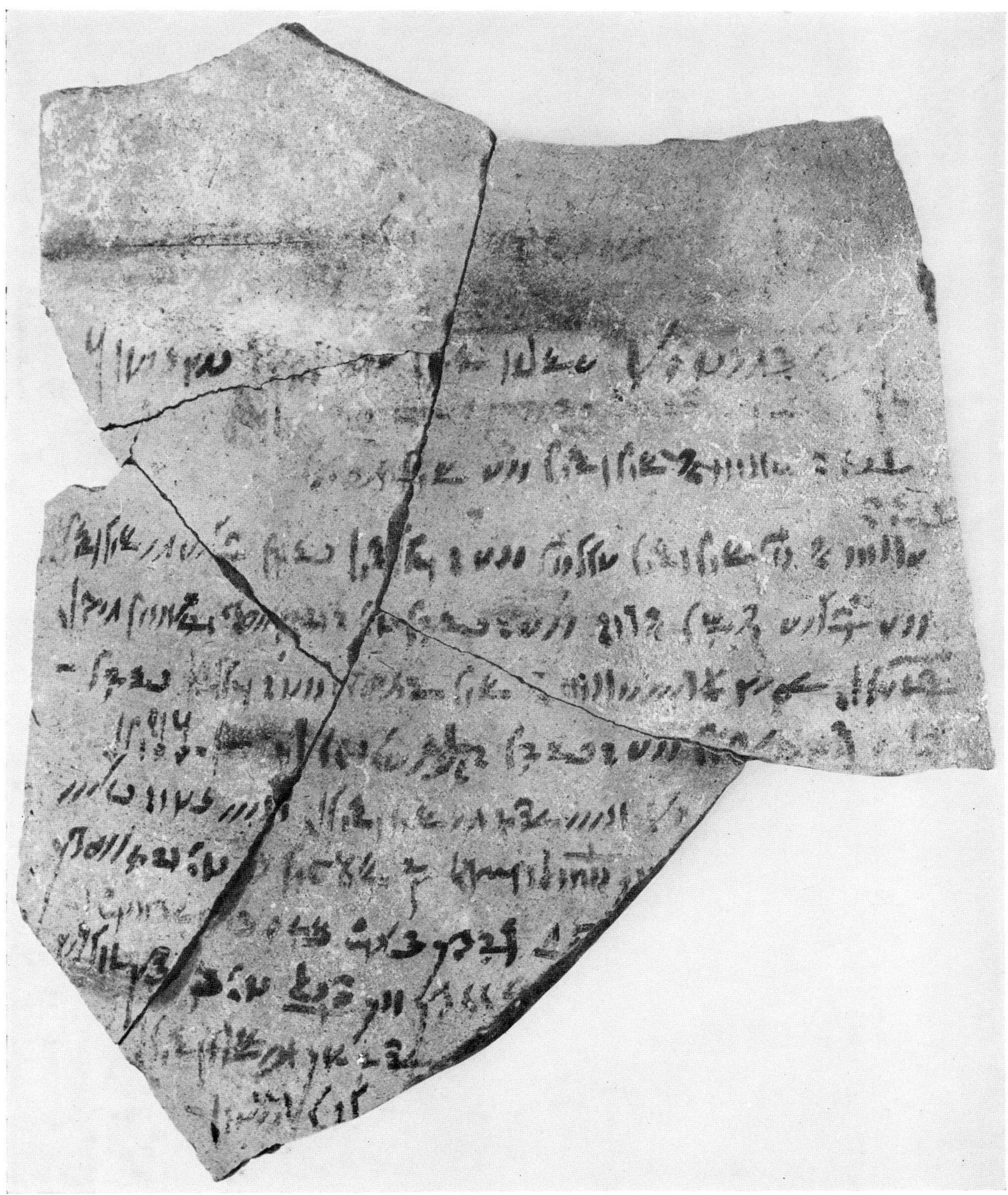

Text **13** (pp. 55 ff.)

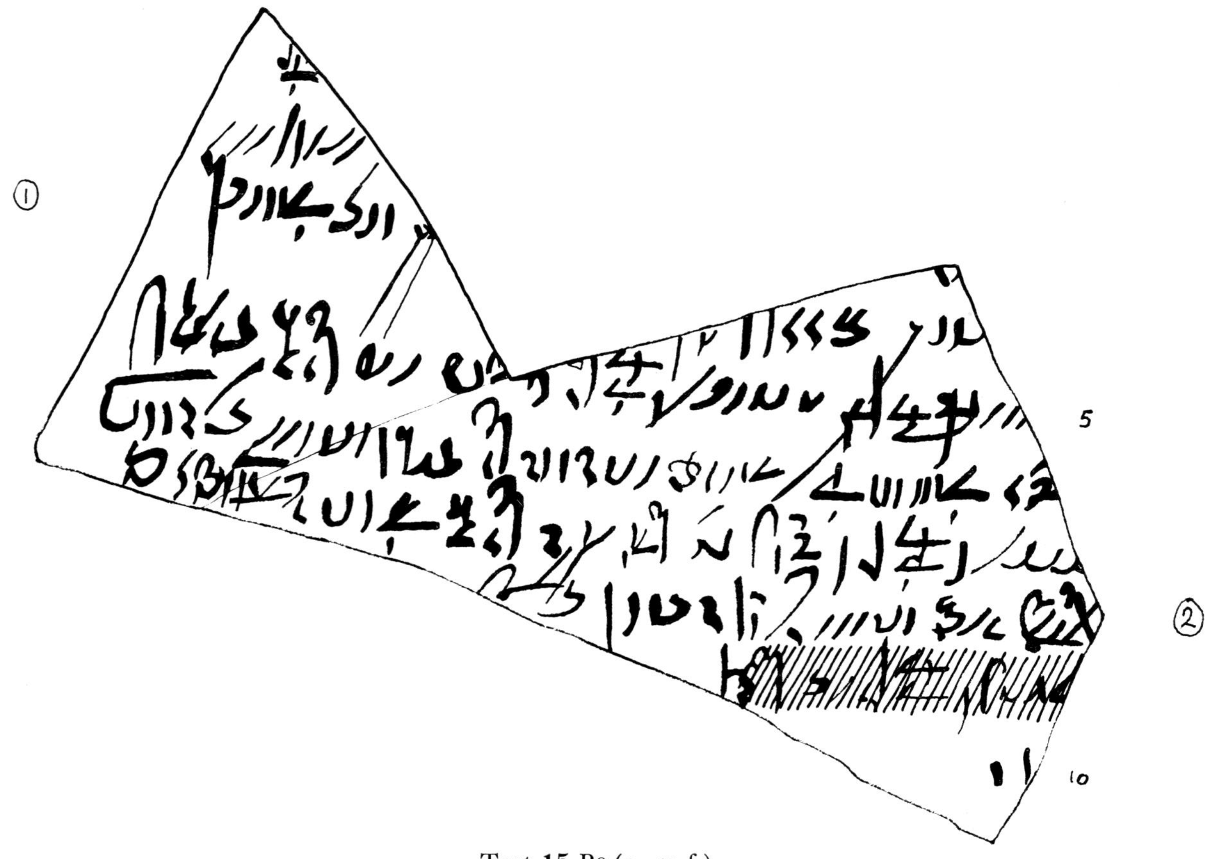

Text **15** R° (p. 59 f.)

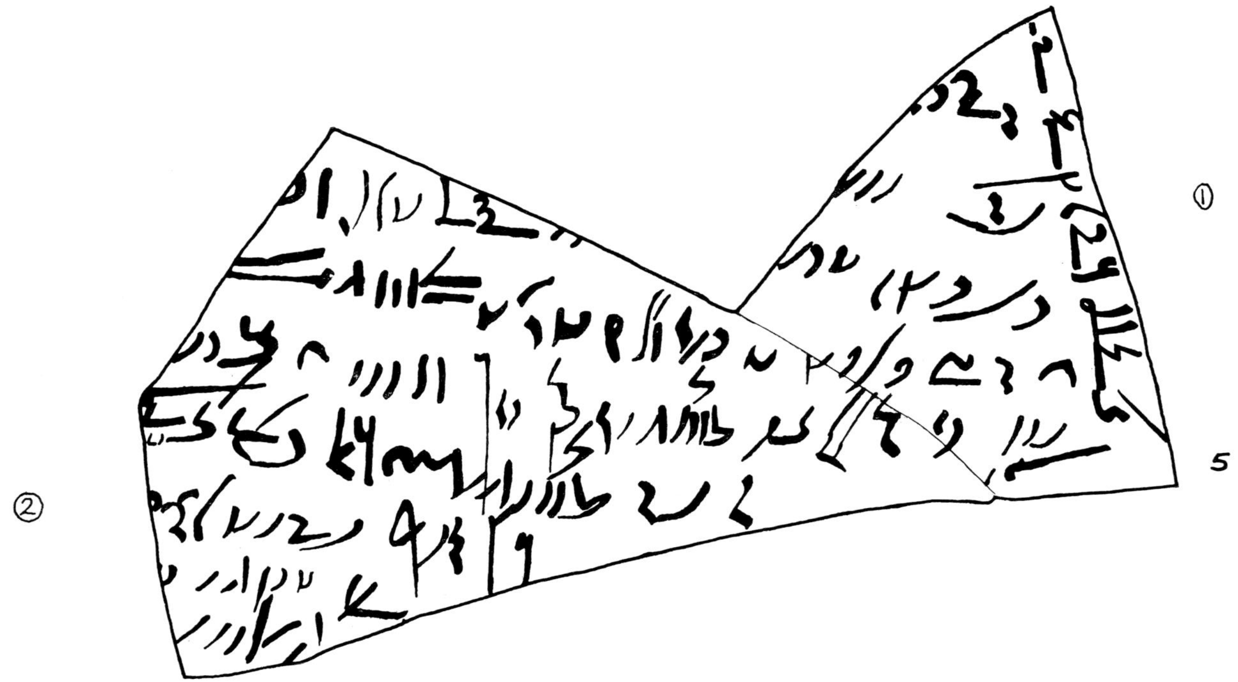

Text **15** V° (p. 59 f.)

Text **15** R° (p. 59 f.)

Text **15** V° (p. 59 f.)

Text **15A** (p. 60 f.)

Text **16** R° (pp. 61 ff.)

Text **16** V° (pp. 61 ff.)

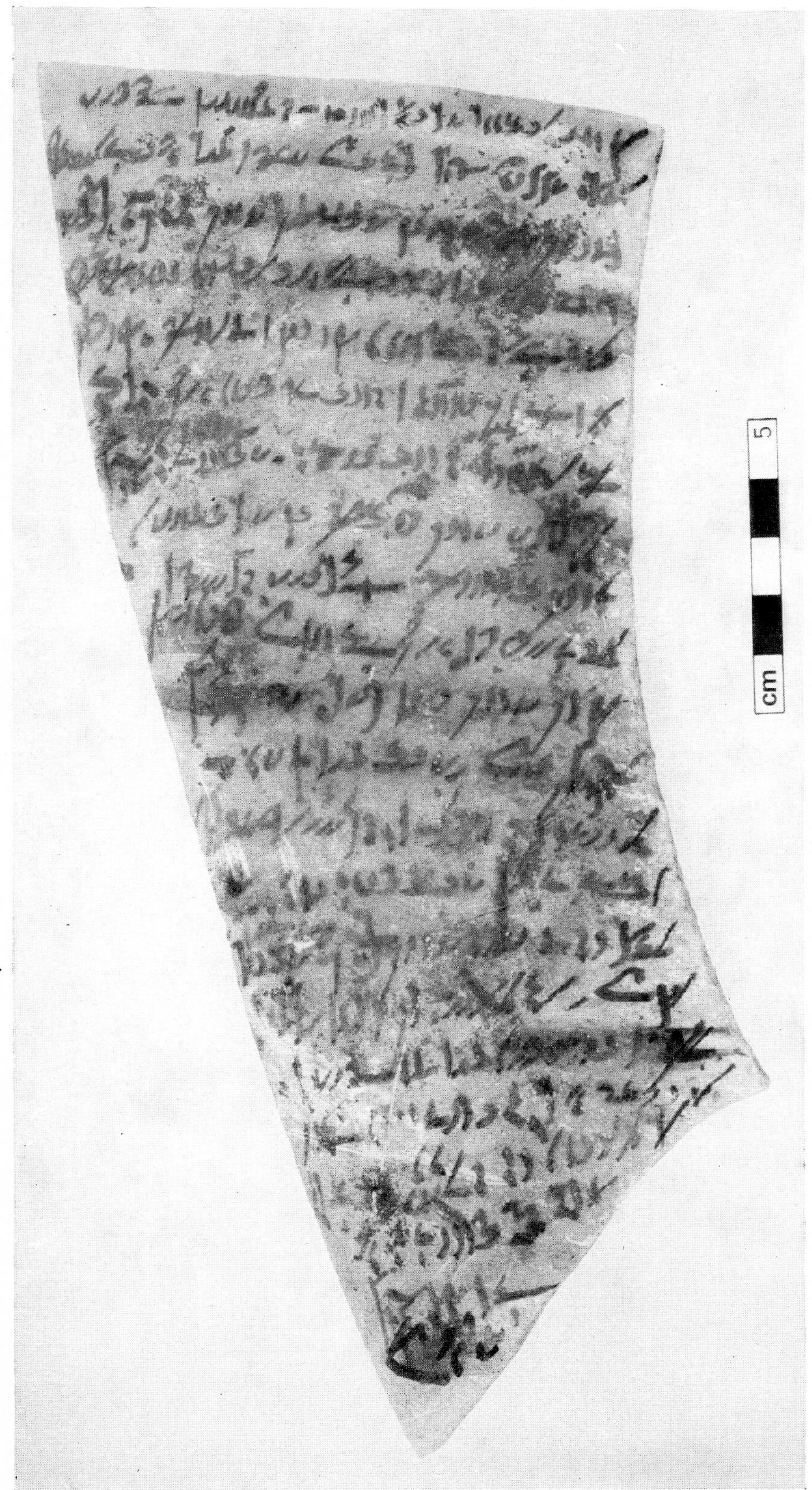

Text **17** (pp. 63 ff.)
(The arrows indicate the join described on p. 63)

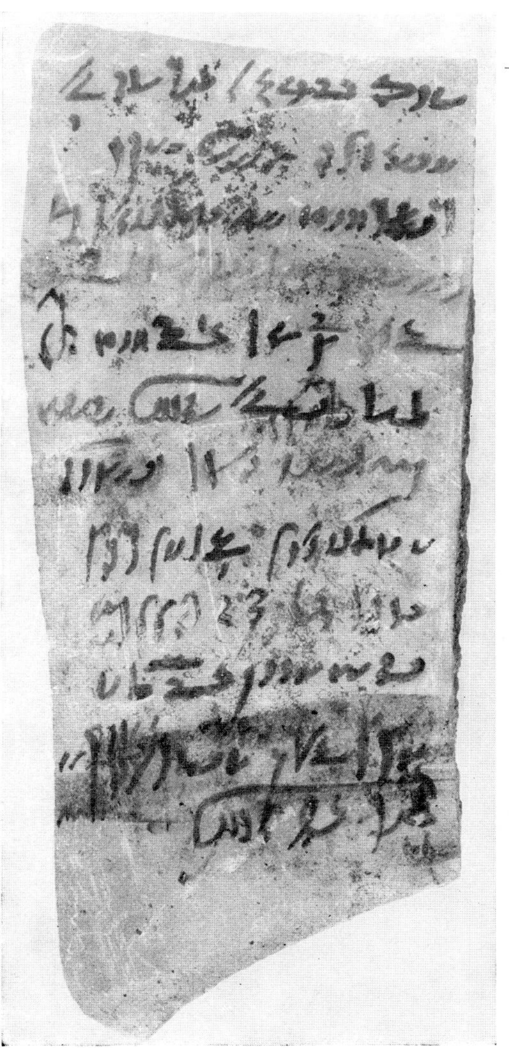

Text **17A** (pp. 63 ff.)

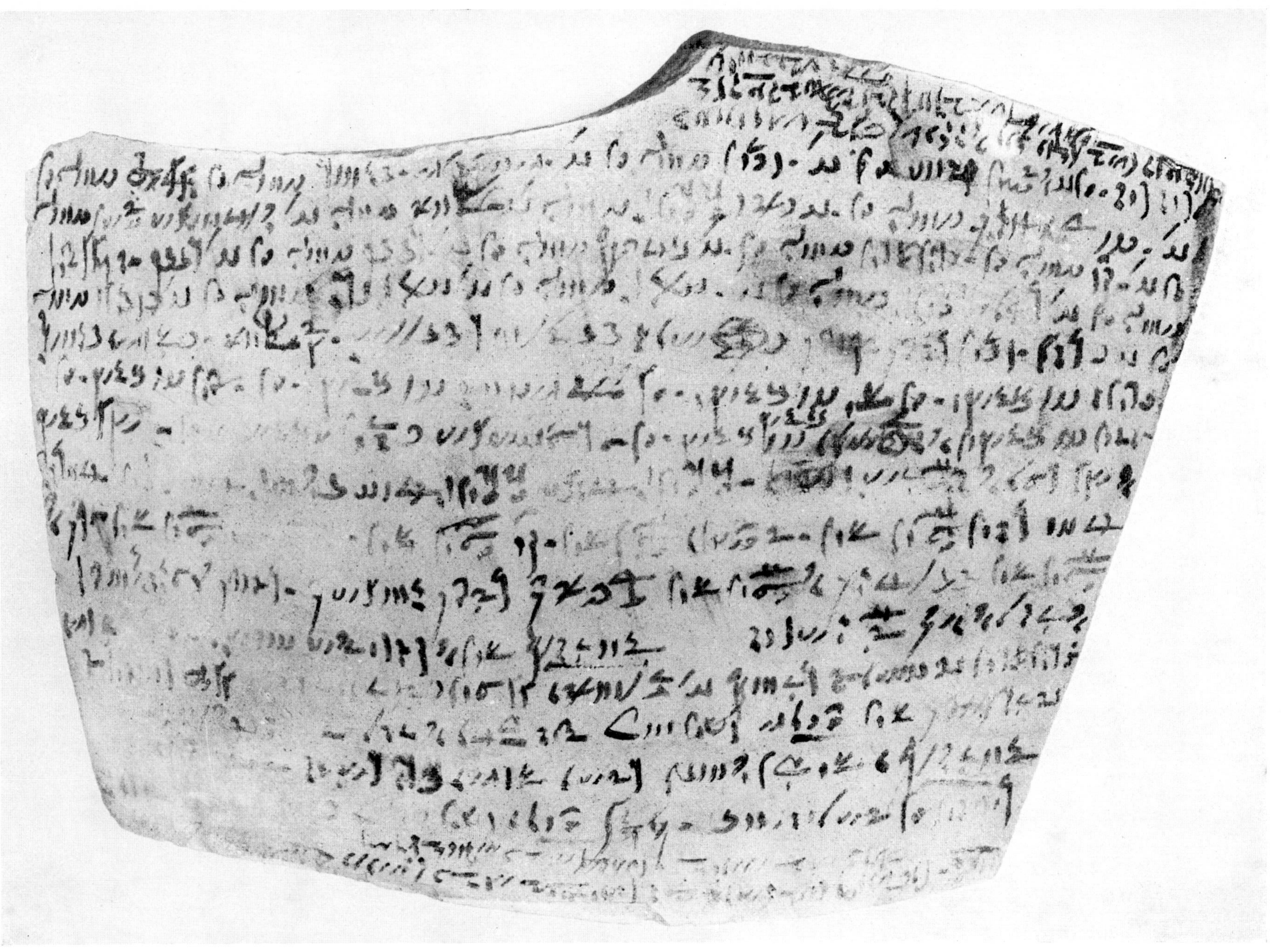

Text **18** R° (pp. 66 ff.)

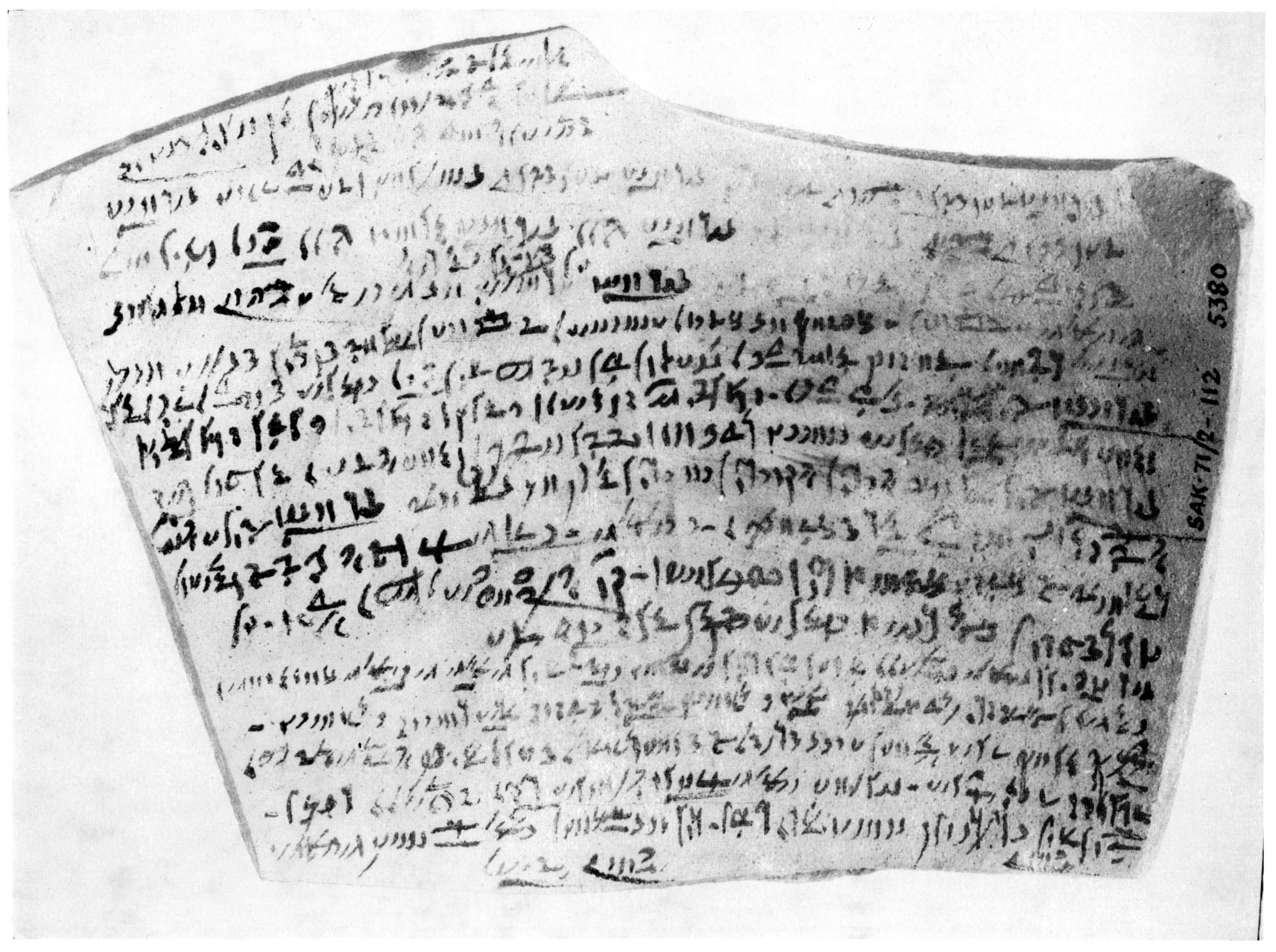

Text **18** V° (pp. 66 ff.)

Text **19** R° (pp. 73 ff.)

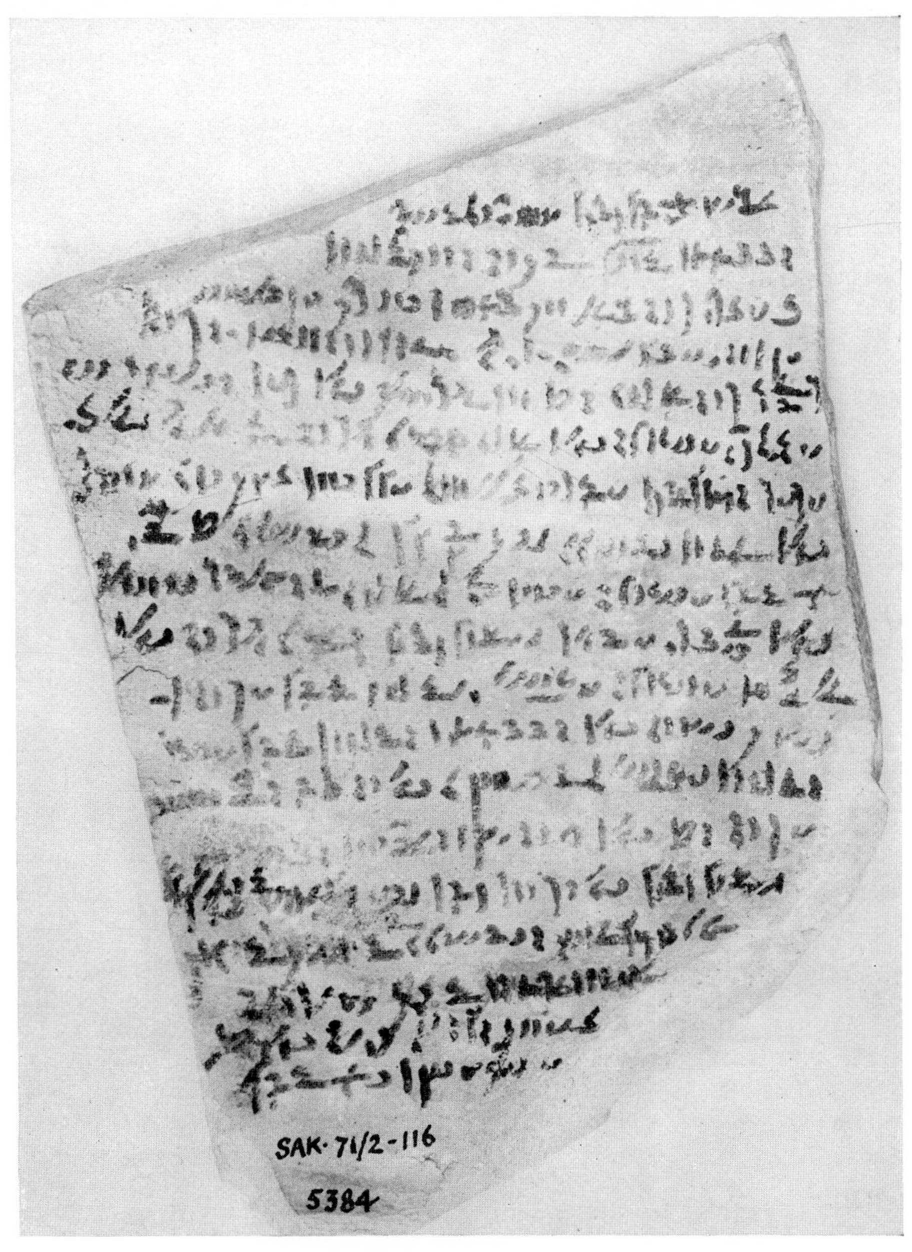

Text **19** V° (pp. 73 ff.)

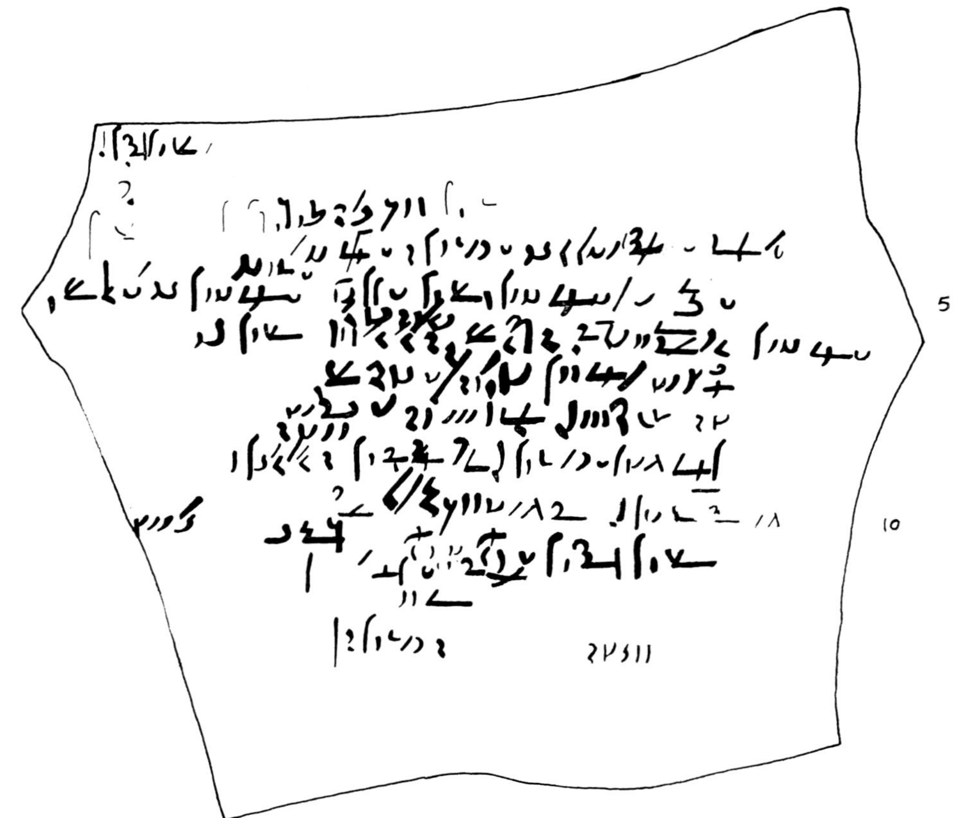

Text **20** (p. 80 f.)

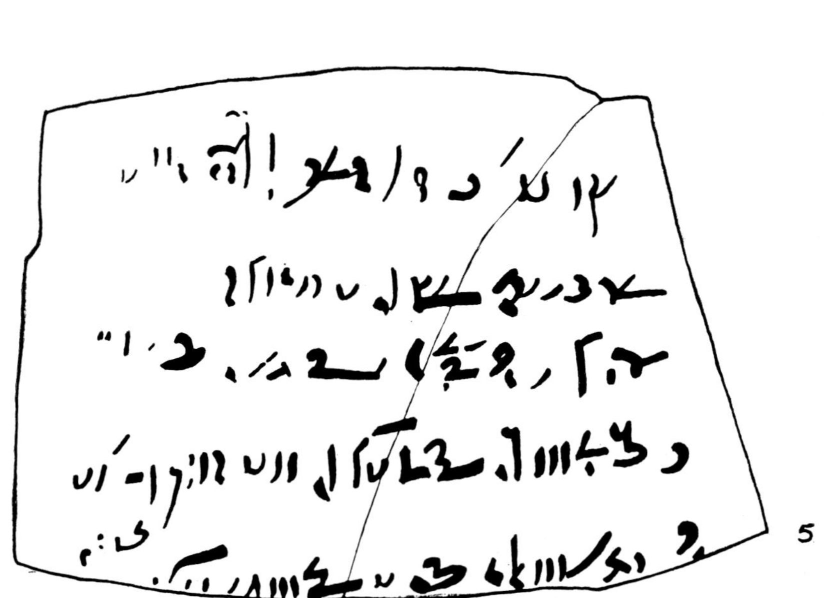

Text **24A** (p. 90 f.)

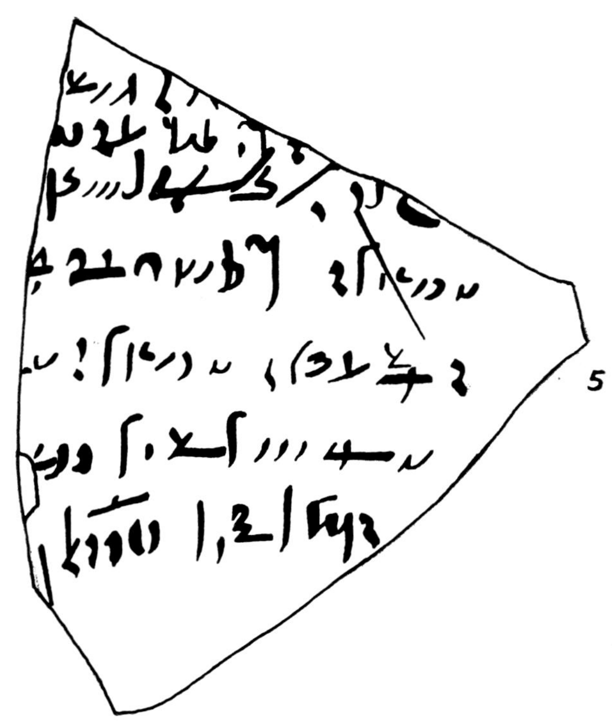

Text **24B** (p. 90 f.)

Text **20** (p. 80 f.)

Text **24A** (p. 90 f.)

Text **24B** (p. 90 f.)

Text **21** R° (pp. 81 ff.)

Text **21** V° (pp. 81 ff.)

Text **21** R° (pp. 81 ff.)

Text **21** V° (pp. 81 ff.)

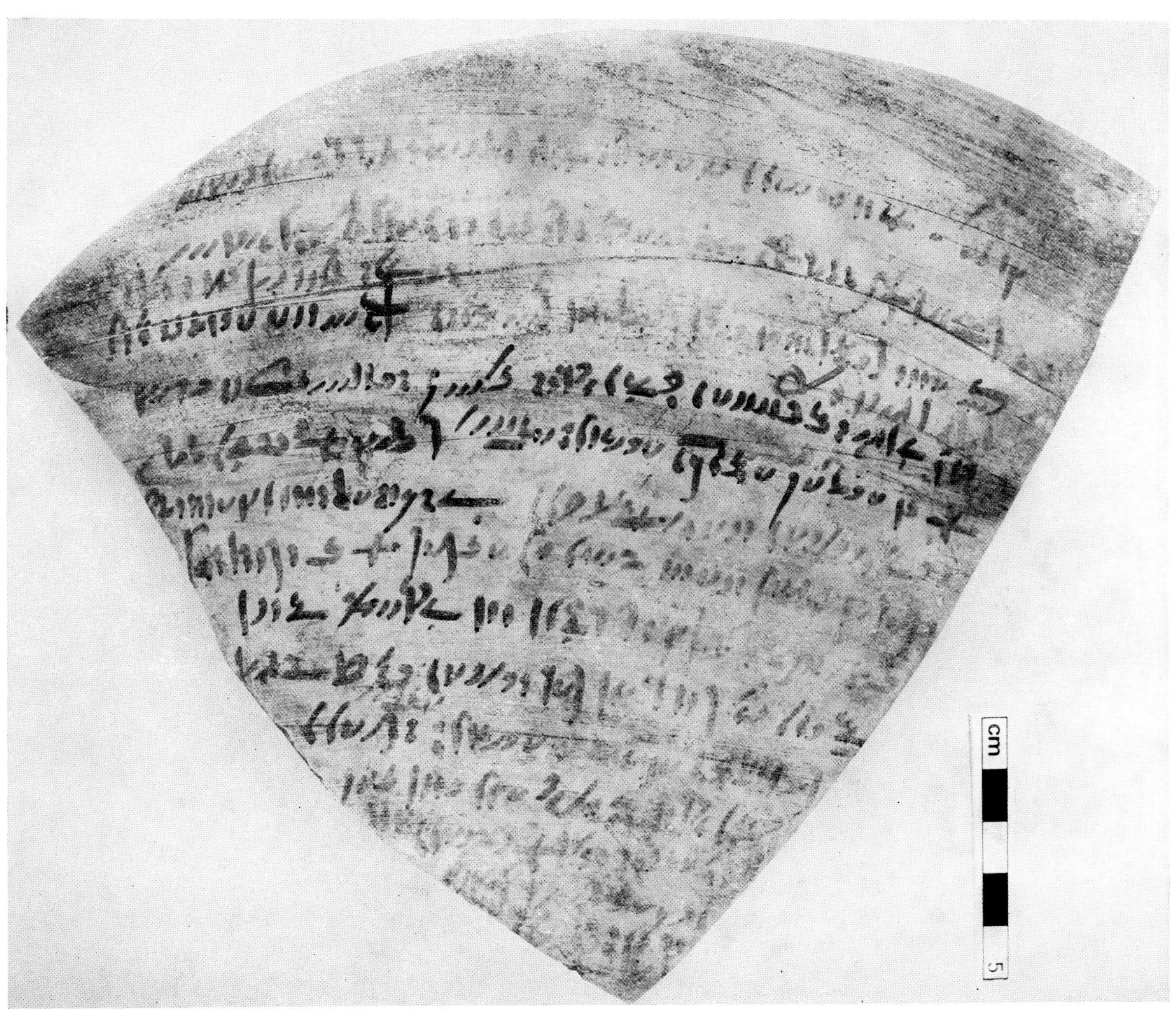

Text **22** R° (pp. 84 ff.)

Text **22** V° (pp. 84 ff.)

PLATE XXVIa

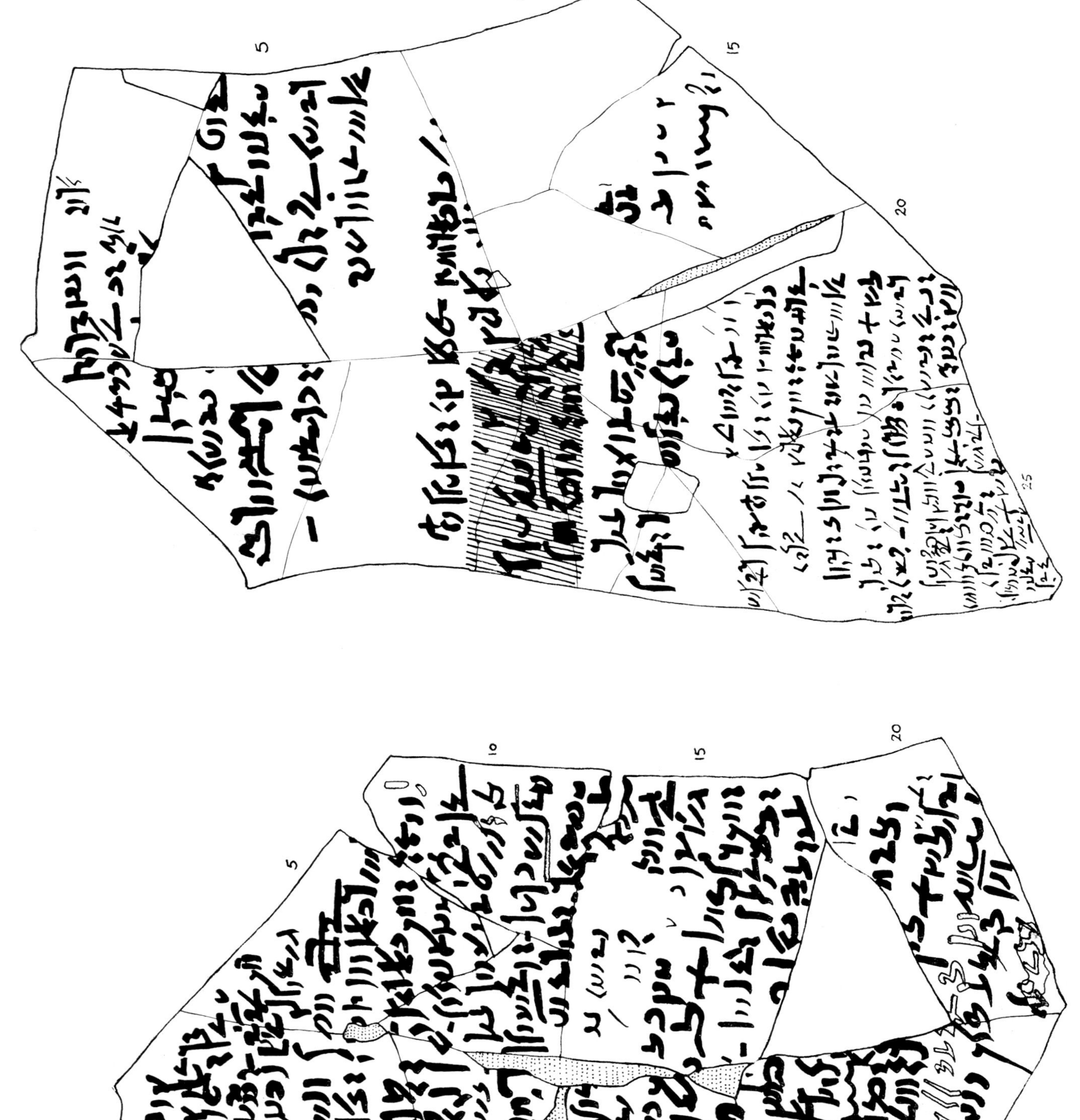

Text 23 Rº (pp. 86 ff.)

Text 23 Vº (pp. 86 ff.)

Text **23** R° (pp. 86 ff.)

Text **23** V° (pp. 86 ff.)

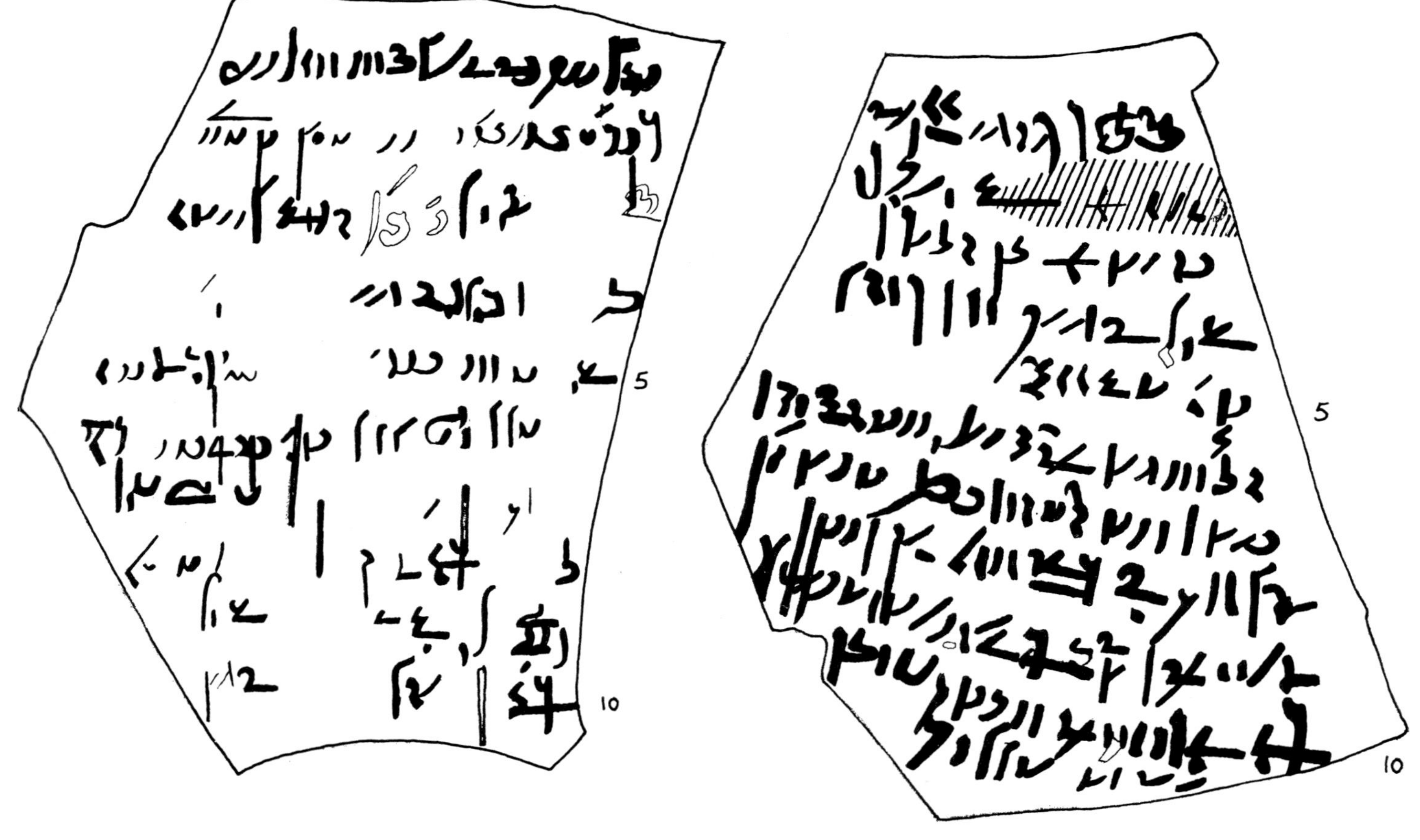

Text **27** R° (p. 96 f.)

Text **27** V° (p. 96 f.)

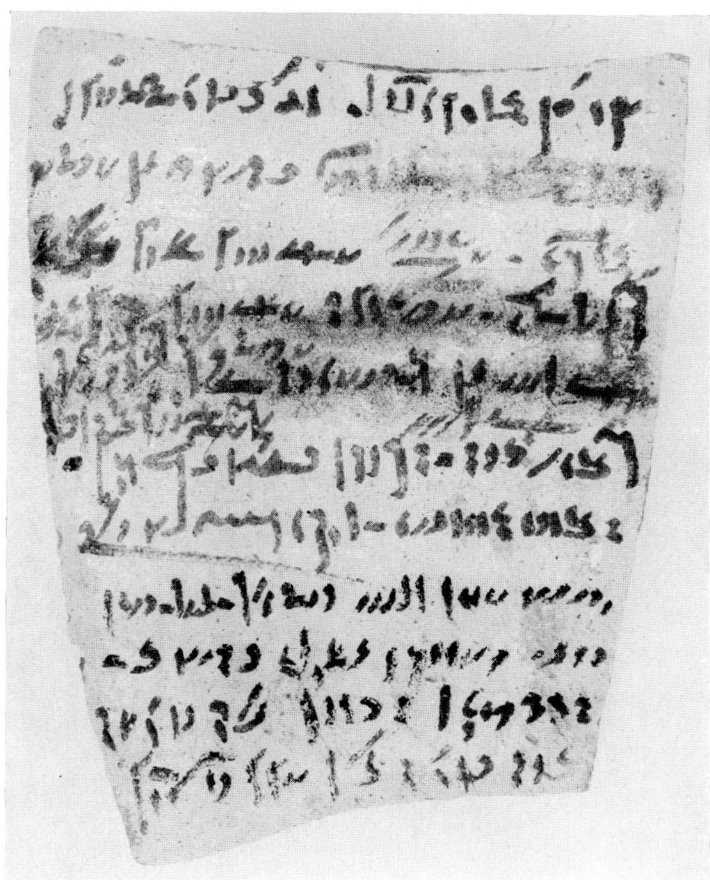

Text **25** (p. 92 f.)

Text **27** R° (p. 96 f.)

Text **27** V° (p. 96 f.)

PLATE XXVIIIa

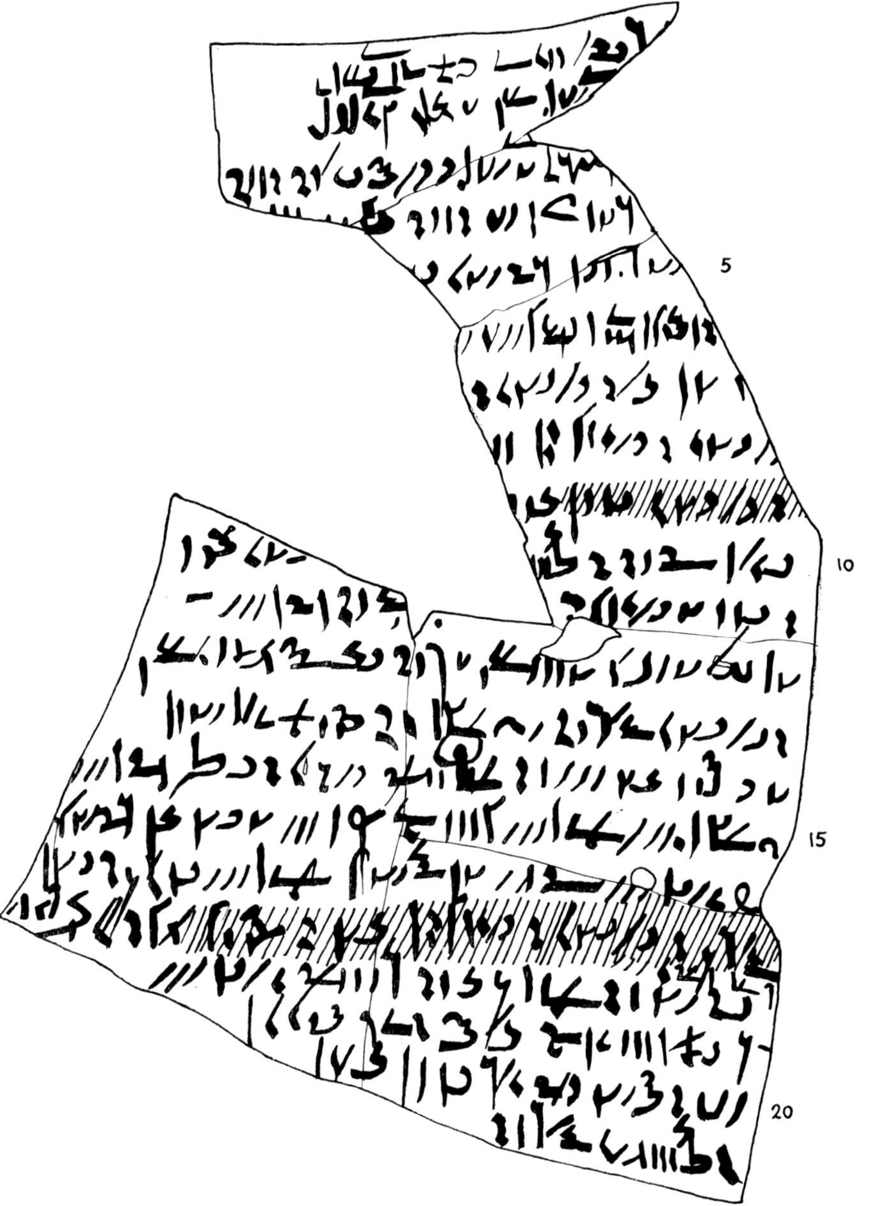

Text **26** R° (pp. 93 ff.)

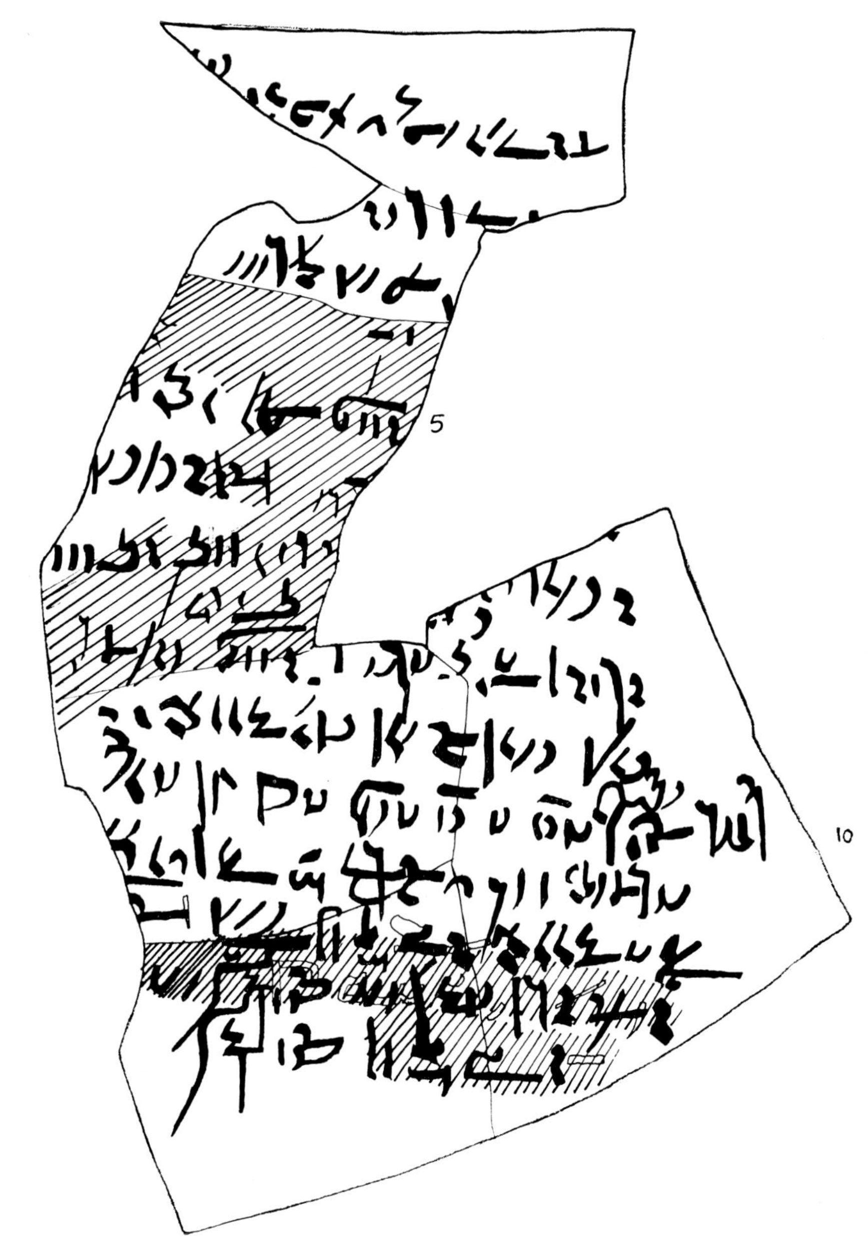

Text **26** V° (pp. 93 ff.)

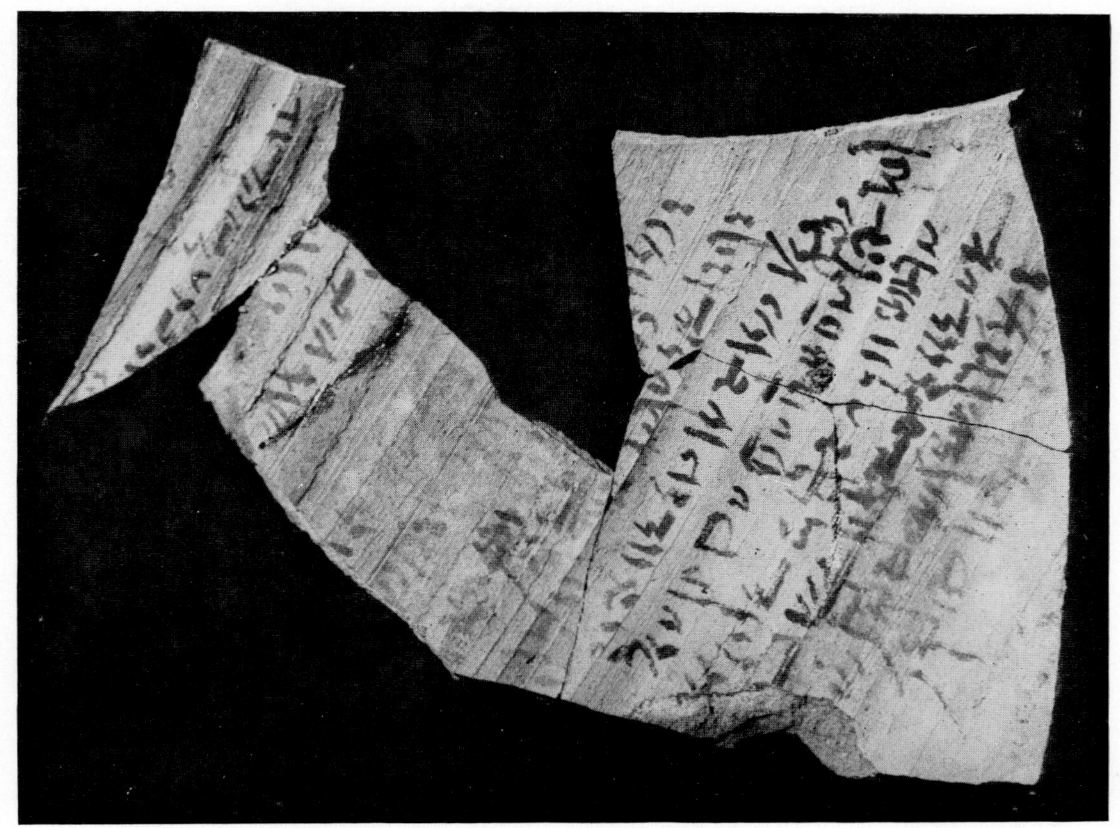

Text **26** V° (pp. 93 ff.)

Text **26** R° (pp. 93 ff.)

PLATE XXIXa

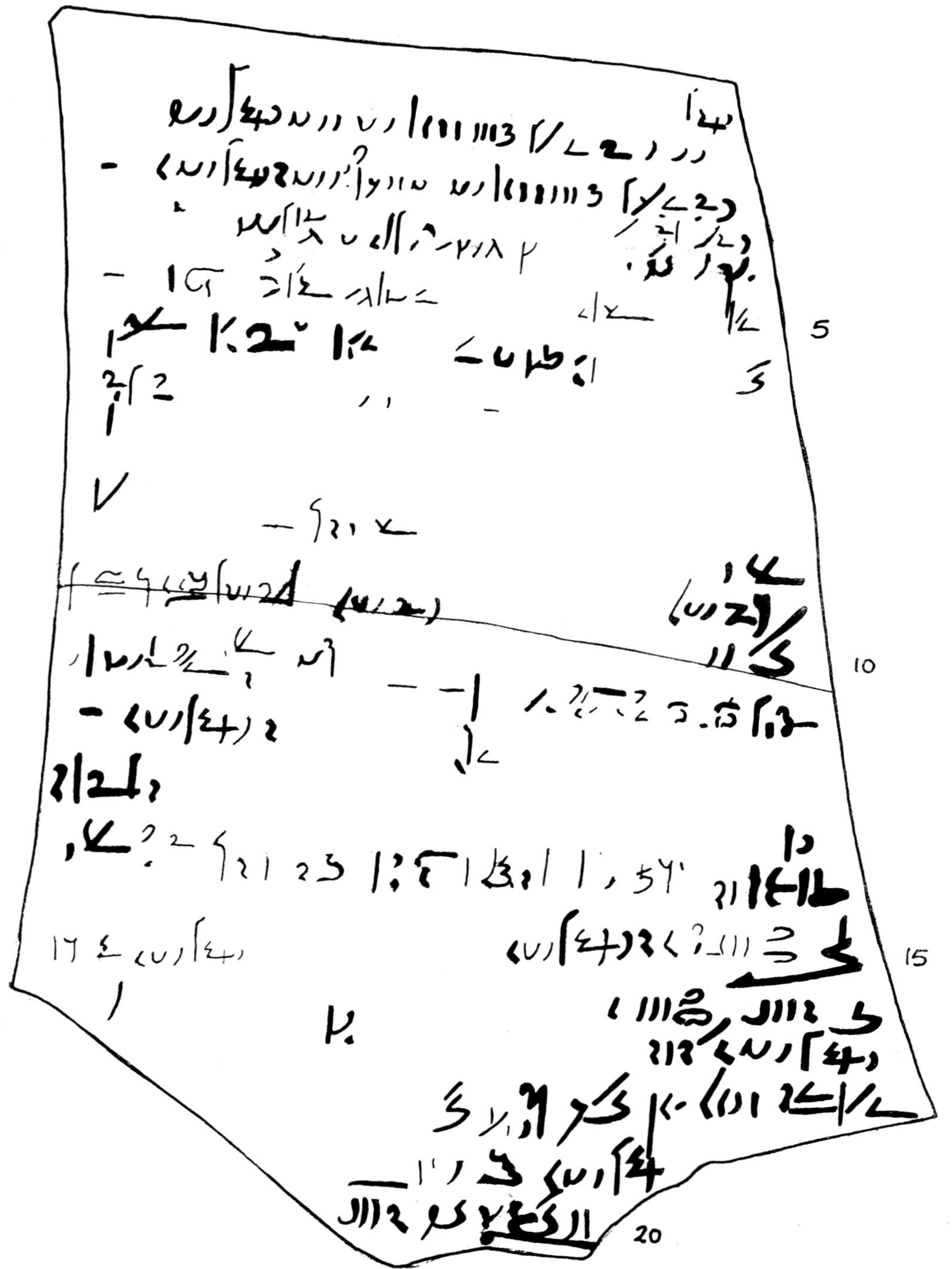

Text **28** (p. 97 f.)

Text **28** (p. 97 f.)

Text **30** (p. 100 f.)

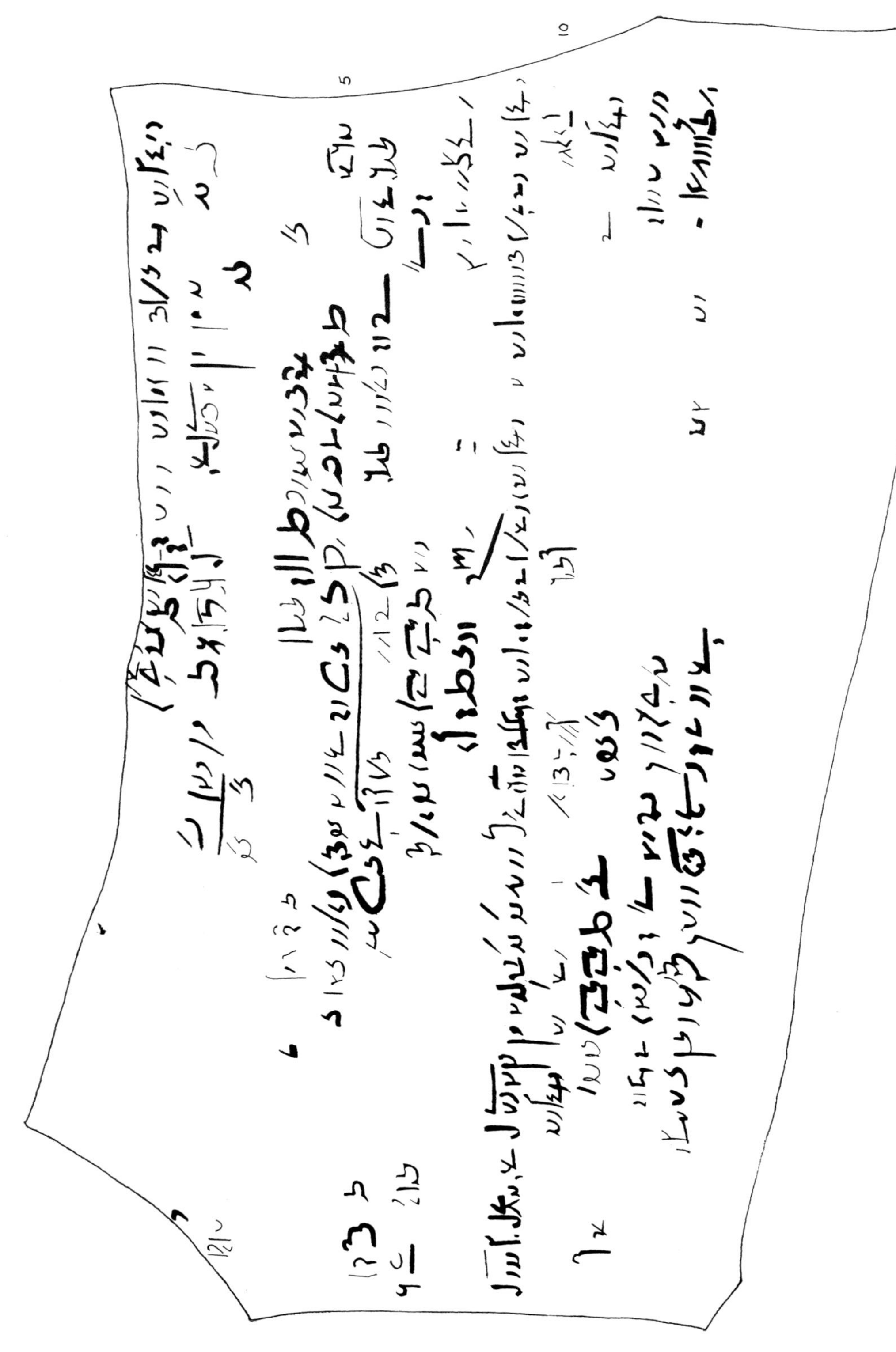

Text **29** (pp. 98 ff.)

Text **29** (pp. 98 ff.)

PLATE XXXIa

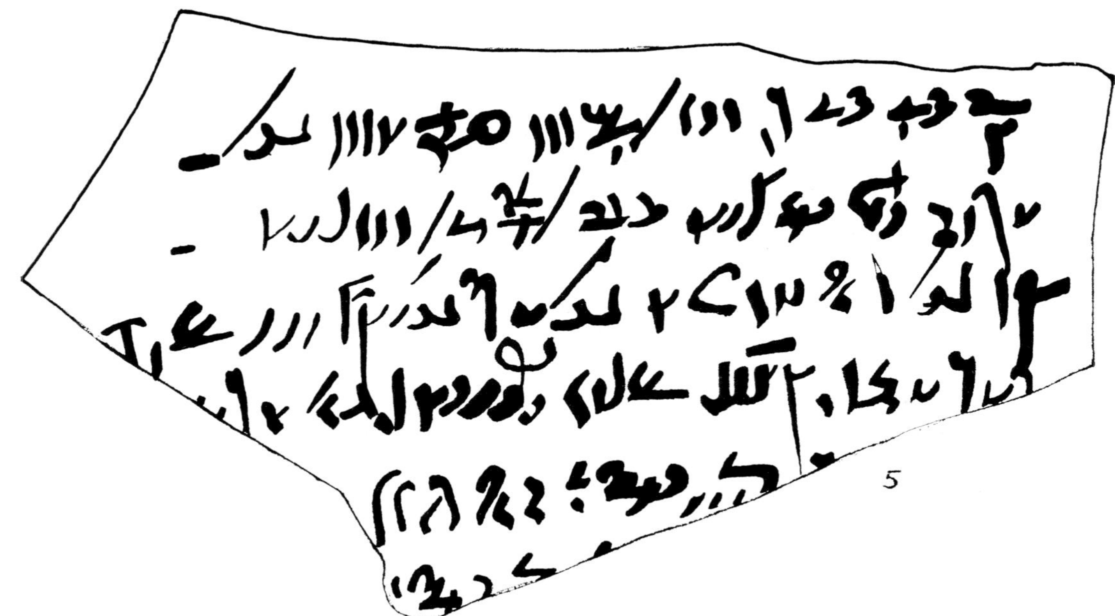

Text **31A** (p. 102 f.)

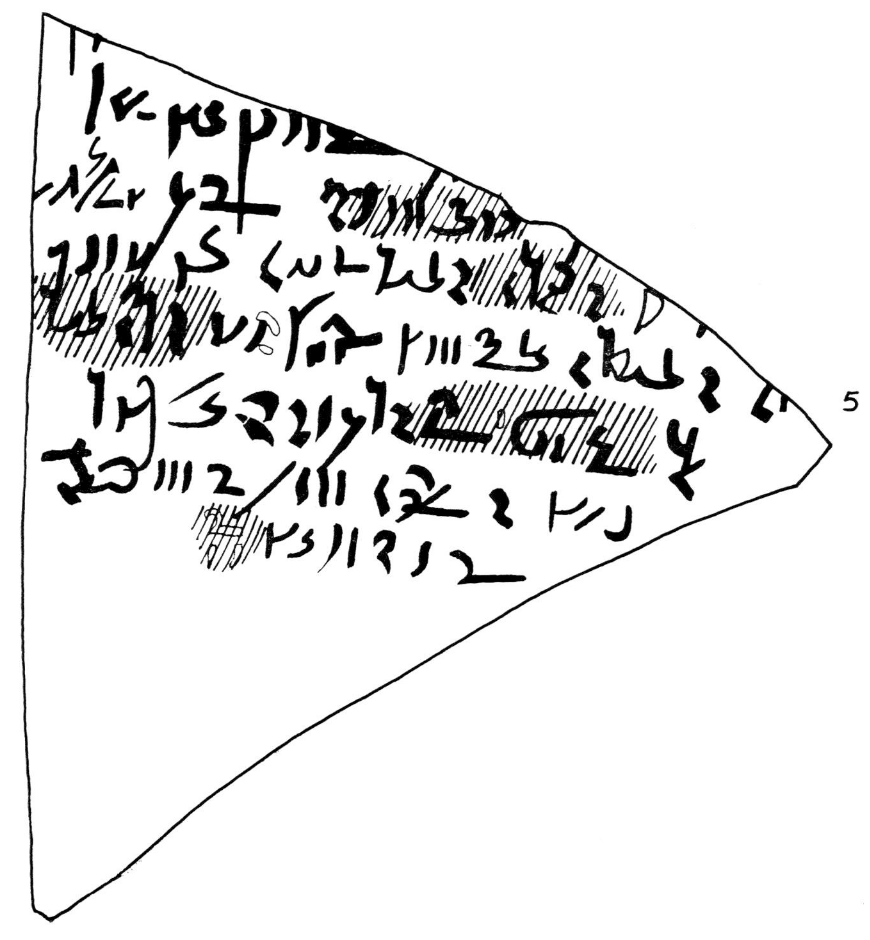

Text **31B** (p. 102 f.)

Text **31A** (p. 102 f.)

Text **31B** (p. 102 f.)

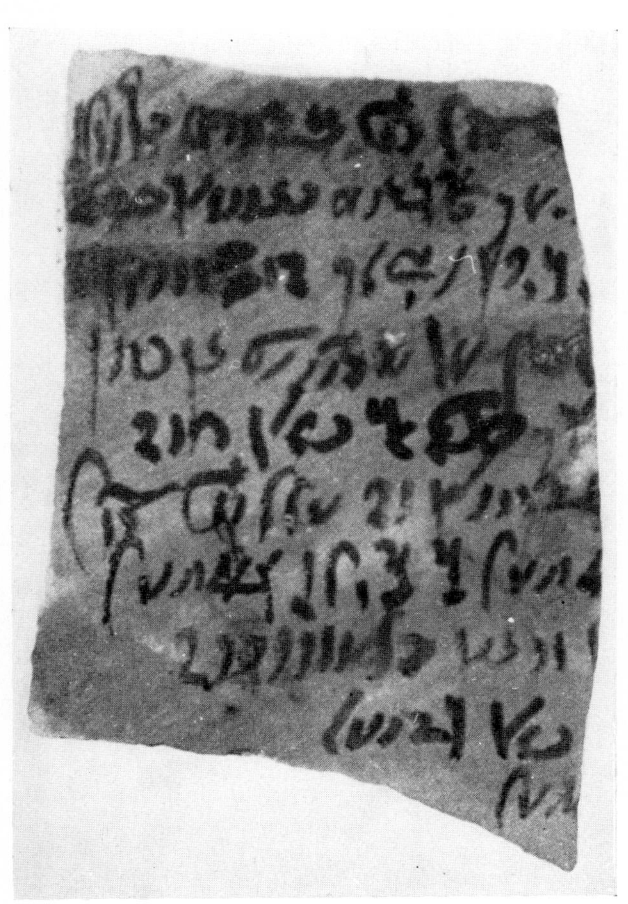
Text **32** R° (p. 103 f.)

Text **32** V° (p. 103 f.)

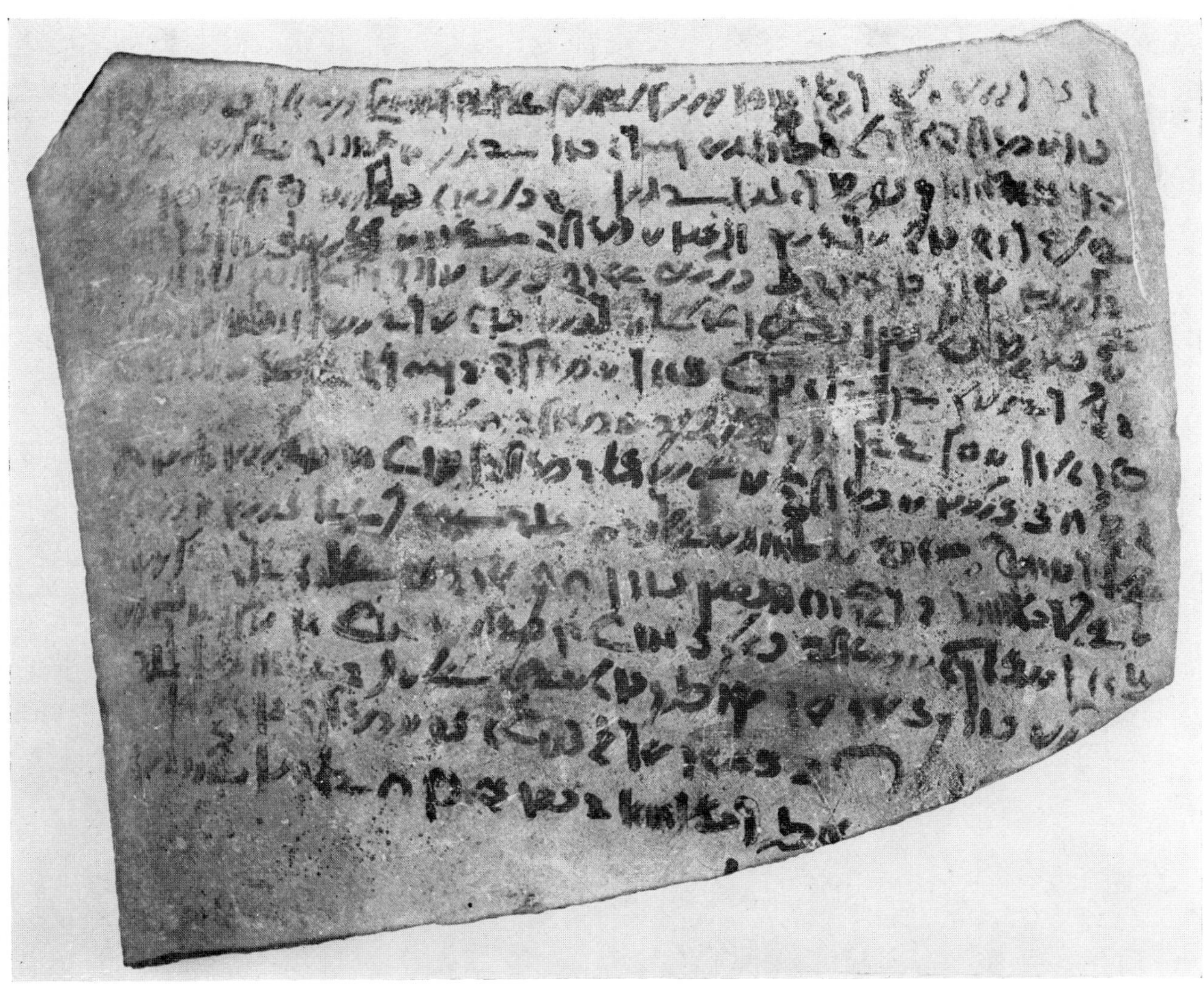

Text **33** (pp. 104 ff.)

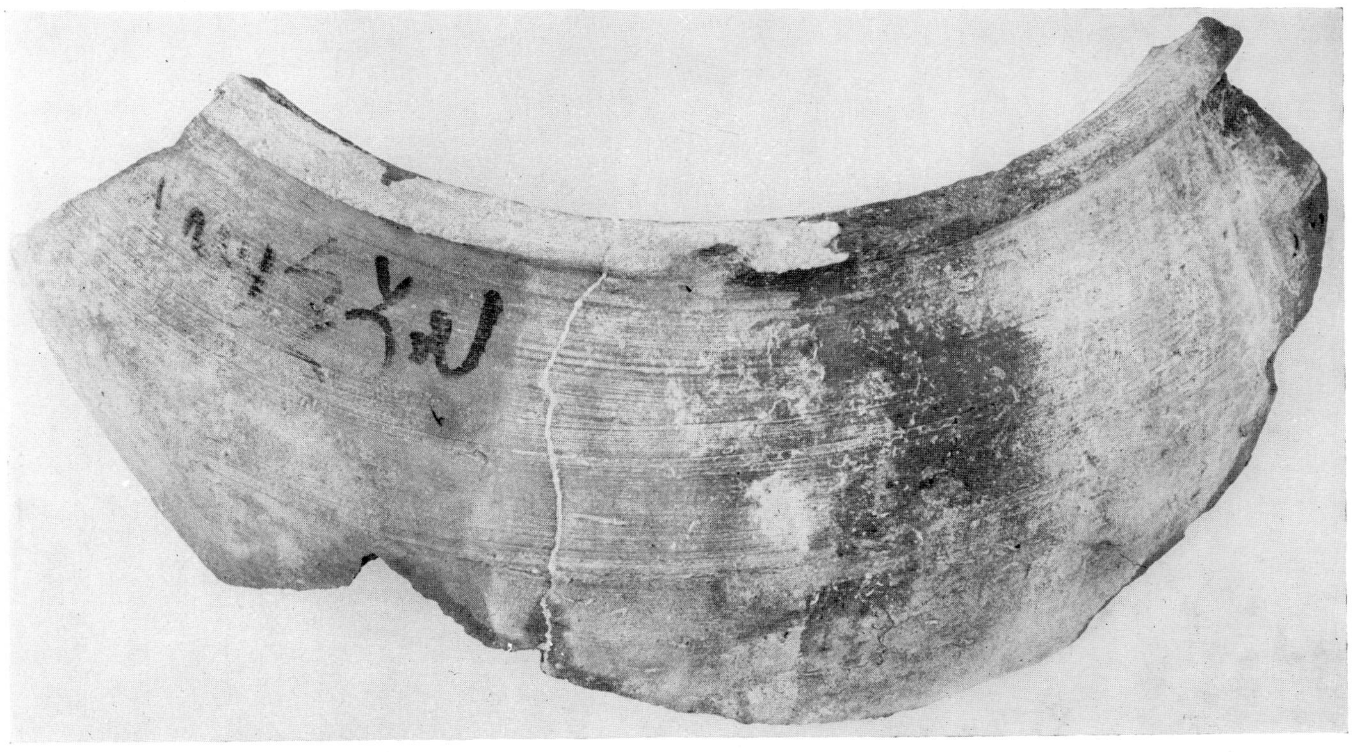

Text **34** (p. 107)

Text **36** (p. 108)

Text **35** (p. 107 f.)

Text **37** (p. 108)

Text **38** (p. 108 f.)

Text **39** (p. 109)

Text **40** (p. 109 f.)

Text **41** (p. 110)

Text **42** (p. 110)

Text **43** (p. 110)

Text **44** (p. 111)

Text **45** (p. 111)

Text **46** (p. 111 f.)

Text **48** (p. 113)

Text **47** (p. 112)

Text **49** (p. 113)

Text **50** (p. 113 f.)

Text **51** (p. 114)

Text **52** (p. 114)

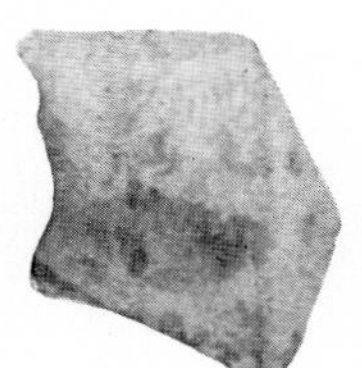

Text **53** (p. 114)

Text **54** (p. 114 f.)

Text **55** (p. 115)

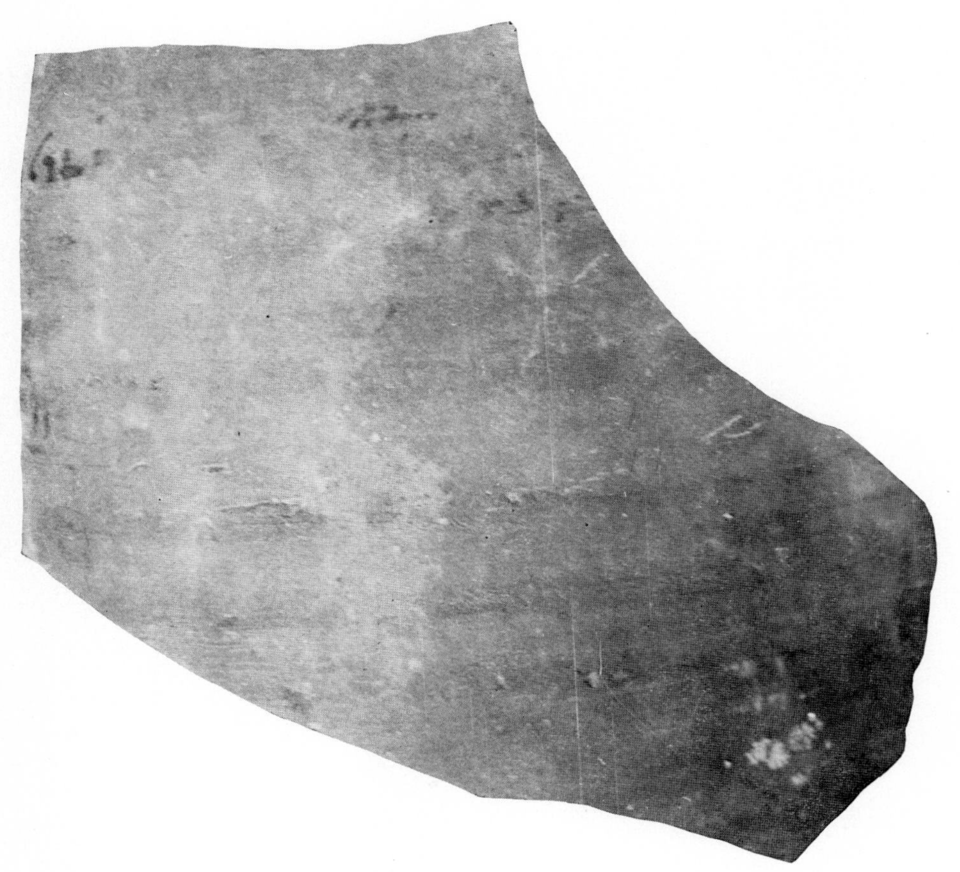

Text **56** (p. 115)

Text **57** (p. 115)

Text **58** (p. 116)

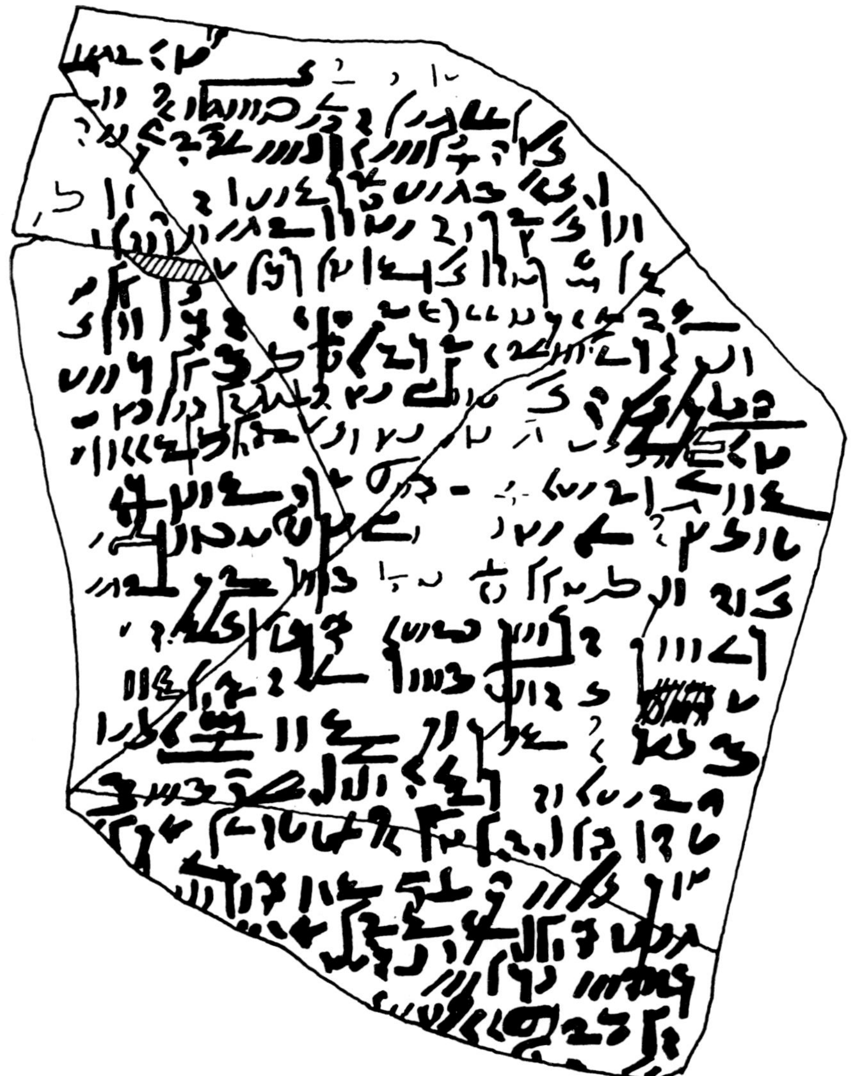

Text **59** (pp. 167 ff.)

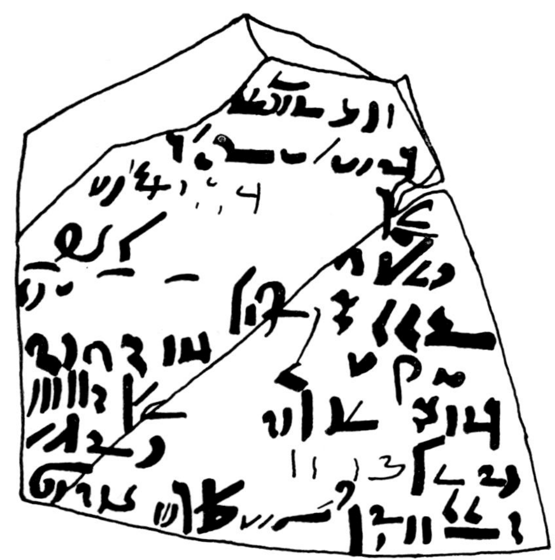

Text **60** (p. 169 f.)

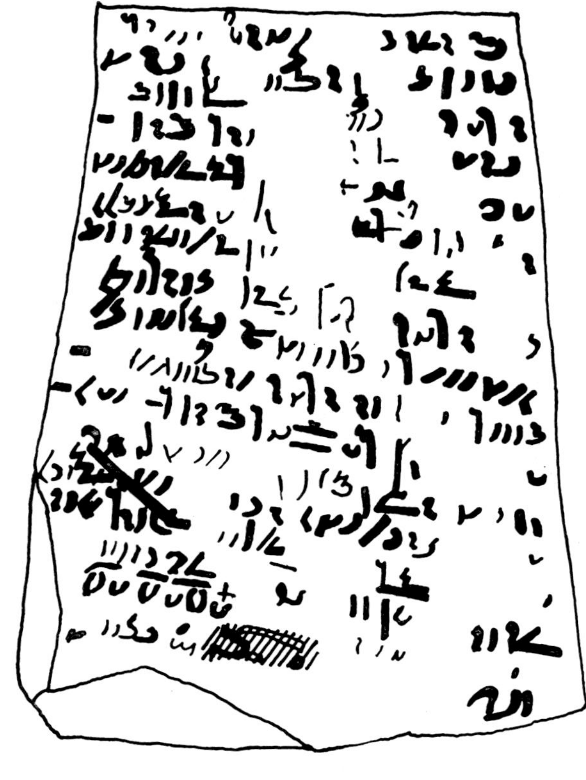

Text **61** (p. 170 f.)

Text **59** (pp. 167 ff.)

Text **60** (p. 169 f.)

Text **61** (p. 170 f.)

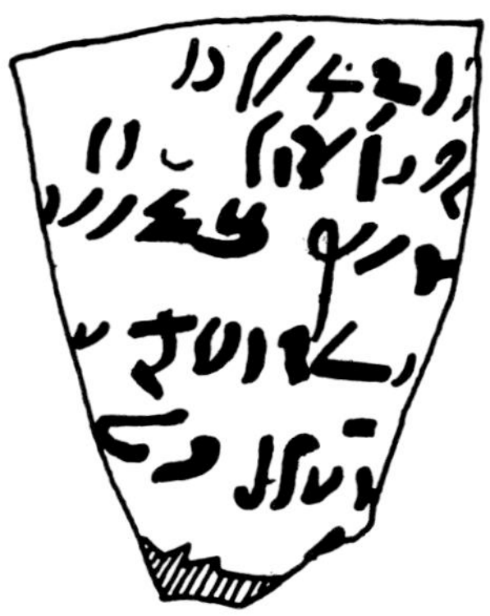

Text **62** (p. 171 f.)

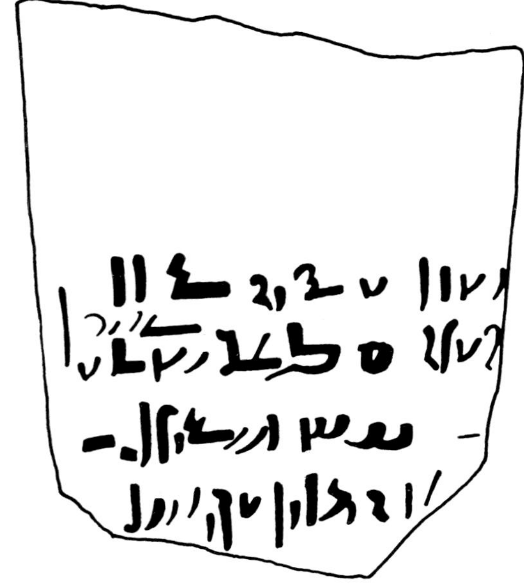

Text **63** (p. 172)

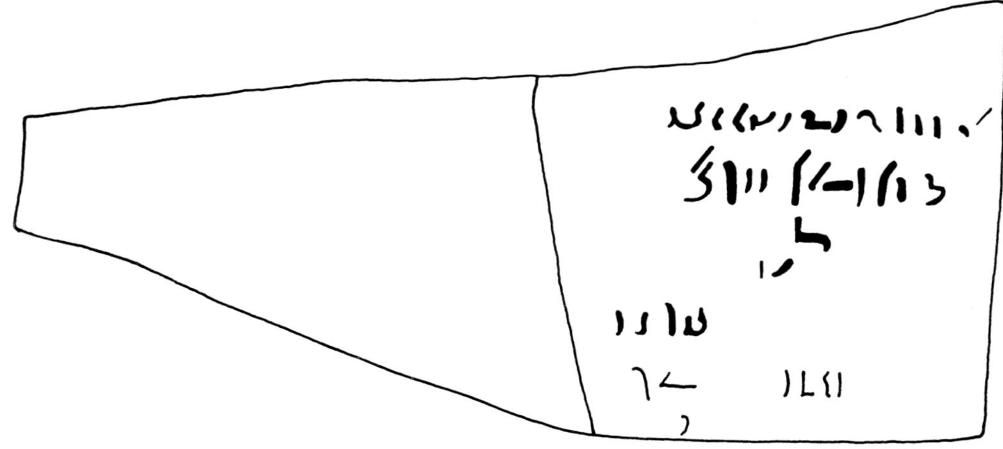

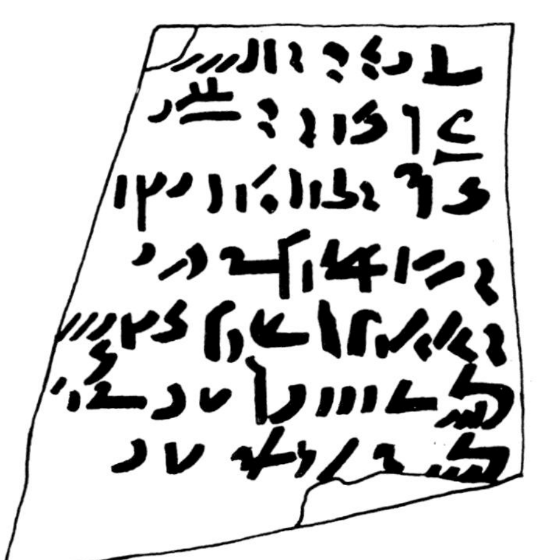

RECTO

RECTO

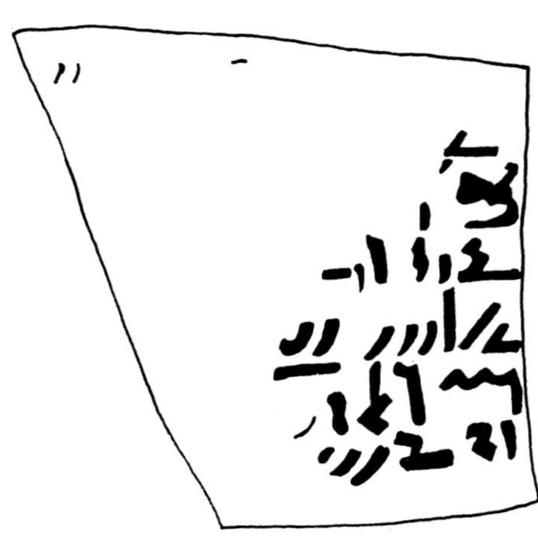

VERSO

Text **64** (p. 172 f.)

VERSO

Text **65** (p. 173 f.)

Text **62** (p. 171 f.)

Text **63** (p. 172)

Text **64** R° (p. 172 f.)

Text **65** R° (p. 173 f.)

Text **64** V° (p. 172 f.)

Text **65** V° (p. 173 f.)